CAMBRIDGE LATIN AMERICAN STUDIES

GENERAL EDITOR
MALCOLM DEAS

ADVISORY COMMITTEE
WERNER BAER   MARVIN BERNSTEIN
AL STEPAN   BRYAN ROBERTS

37

ODIOUS COMMERCE
BRITAIN, SPAIN AND THE ABOLITION OF
THE CUBAN SLAVE TRADE

Odious commerce

Britain, Spain and the abolition of the Cuban slave trade

DAVID R. MURRAY

Associate Professor, Department of History
University of Guelph, Guelph, Ontario

CAMBRIDGE UNIVERSITY PRESS

CAMBRIDGE
LONDON NEW YORK NEW ROCHELLE
MELBOURNE SYDNEY

PUBLISHED BY THE PRESS SYNDICATE OF THE UNIVERSITY OF CAMBRIDGE
The Pitt Building, Trumpington Street, Cambridge, United Kingdom

CAMBRIDGE UNIVERSITY PRESS
The Edinburgh Building, Cambridge CB2 2RU, UK
40 West 20th Street, New York NY 10011–4211, USA
477 Williamstown Road, Port Melbourne, VIC 3207, Australia
Ruiz de Alarcón 13, 28014 Madrid, Spain
Dock House, The Waterfront, Cape Town 8001, South Africa

http://www.cambridge.org

First published 1980
First paperback edition 2002

A catalogue record for this book is available from the British Library

ISBN 0 521 22867 0 hardback
ISBN 0 521 52469 5 paperback

TO ANN

CONTENTS

TABLES

PREFACE

Spain's colonial empire saw the beginning and the end of the trans-atlantic slave trade. In one of the ironies of history, the abolition of the commerce in African slaves preceded the loss of Spain's last American possessions, reversing the process begun nearly four hundred years before when Spain's conquest of the Indies led to the beginning of the Atlantic slave trade. Even before the majority of Spain's American colonies received their political independence in the period 1810–25, the question of the African slave trade in Spain's overseas dominions involved mainly the plantation colonies, and particularly Cuba. Of Spain's once vast American empire only Cuba and Puerto Rico remained after 1825. Essentially then, the story of the abolition of the slave trade within the Spanish colonial empire is the story of the abolition of the slave trade to Cuba.

Cuba was an ideal colony for Spain as long as she could hold it. As the wealth of her largest plantation colony grew, Spain was able to cover the cost of Cuba's administration and the expenses of Spanish military forces stationed there from Cuban revenues. Throughout the nineteenth century Cuba was a very important market for Spanish exports and the carrying trade between Spain and Cuba fostered the growth of a Spanish merchant marine. But Cuba's importance to Spain was much more than that of a self-supporting colony and trading partner for the metropolis. Cuba's revenue was an invaluable source of funds for a beleaguered Spanish government during the Carlist civil wars of the 1830s and the administrative posts in the island were useful stepping stones for ambitious peninsular military officers. The possession of Cuba and, to a lesser extent, Puerto Rico allowed Spain to retain a significant toehold in the Americas. From Cuba Spain tried to reconquer Mexico in 1829, and thirty years later Cuba again provided essential support as Spain prepared to embark on military adventures in Santo Domingo. With perhaps pardonable exaggeration, the instructions to the incoming Captain-

General in 1859 stated: 'The island of Cuba today represents much more for modern Spain than that which all our possessions in the American continent represented for our ancestors ... today the Captain-General of the island of Cuba is not only the governor of a possession as important as were New Spain, Peru or Buenos Ayres, he is even more than that; he is the forward sentinel of our interests in the new world ...'

Threats to Cuba were seen as threats to the vital interests of Spain herself, a Spain determined at all costs to preserve the remnants of her American empire. Captains-General of Cuba saw themselves as surrounded by a bewildering variety of dangers and their paranoia had a certain justification. The United States had fixed her acquisitive eyes on the island, the creoles within seemed to be perpetually plotting independence and the insidious machinations of the British threatened to strike at the foundation of the island's prosperity. If Britain succeeded in fusing the time-bomb of slave liberation, Cuba would turn into another Haiti, or so many white Cubans and Spaniards believed. The Captains-General were kept busy keeping Cuba safe from these ever-present perils and a grateful metropolis bestowed a succession of titles on her sentinels as a small measure of thanks. Many of the Captains-General who served in the island during the 1840s, 1850s and 1860s returned to high political office in Spain no less determined to maintain Spain's Caribbean possessions.

Nineteenth-century Cuba was a Caribbean anomaly; a thriving, expanding plantation colony built on the twin foundations of the slave trade and slavery at a time when the other West Indian plantation colonies were declining in economic and political importance and slavery was disappearing. That Cuba should follow the path of these other West Indian colonies was really the greatest danger in Spanish eyes and the one her Captains-General feared most. They believed the plantation economy would be doomed without slave labour and they were sure that the presence of a large enslaved African population acted as a check on the creole desire for political independence. In the minds of the colony's rulers, including the planter class, the security of Cuba and the continuance and expansion of an adequate labour force were tied to slavery and the slave trade.

Britain's abolitionist campaign against the Spanish slave trade thus challenged the basic assumptions of Spanish colonial policy. British pressure was powerful enough to force Spain to sign a treaty in 1817, prohibiting the slave trade in Spain's empire from 1820. A subsequent treaty was signed in 1835, strengthening the provisions of the earlier agreement. Yet it took more than thirty years after the second treaty to abolish the slave trade to Cuba. Britain's campaign to abolish the Cuban slave trade is the subject of this book and in it I attempt to explain why it was that Britain was able to force Spain into signing two treaties against the slave trade as well as why they failed to achieve their purpose. British abolitionism and British abolitionists caused a tremendous reaction in Cuba during the 1830s and 1840s, and none more so than David Turnbull to whom a chapter is devoted. Britain's attempt to suppress the foreign slave trade became a controversial issue in Britain during the era of free trade and I try to show how this controversy affected British policy towards the Cuban slave trade as well as how Britain had to tailor her Cuban policy so as not to assist American annexationists in their ambition of acquiring Cuba. I have also described the fate of the slaves released at Havana from captured slave ships, because the history of these *emancipados* reveals much about Cuban slavery in the nineteenth century. Finally, I discuss the reasons for the abolition of the Cuban slave trade in the 1860s.

Part of this book originated as a doctoral thesis and I owe a great debt to Dr John Street who supervised my work at a time of deep personal tragedy for him and who has assisted me in many ways since. I am grateful to the Master and Fellows of Churchill College, Cambridge, for granting me a Fellow Commonership which enabled me to complete the writing of the book. Both the Canada Council and the British Council provided financial assistance to defray research costs which I gratefully acknowledge. I am indebted to the Trustees of the Broadlands Archives Trust and the Commissioners of the Royal Commission on Historical Documents for permission to consult the Palmerston (Broadlands) Papers in the National Register of Archives, London, England, and to the Earl of Clarendon for permission to quote from the Clarendon Papers in the Bodleian Library, Oxford. I thank Dr Simon Collier for many kindnesses and Dr J.C.M. Ogelsby for his helpful comments on part of the manuscript. Pat Law and Donna Pollard typed a difficult manuscript with great care.

I could not have written this book without the unstinting support of all members of my family, one of whom assisted without even knowing it. My wife above all others gave constant encouragement when it was most needed and as a small gesture of thanks for so much I dedicate the book to her. I remain solely responsible for the content of the book and for any errors or omissions it might contain.

Guelph, Ontario   D.R.M.
March 1979

CHAPTER 1

The 'opening' of a legal trade

From the middle of the eighteenth century Cuba began to experience the remarkable economic growth which was to transform the island from a relative backwater of Spain's colonial empire into the world's richest colony and leading sugar producer by the late 1820s.[1] Cuba's importance to Spain hitherto had arisen chiefly from the strategic geographical location of its main port and capital, Havana, the traditional rendezvous for Spanish treasure ships on their way back to the peninsula. Prior to 1763 Cuba's economy was a mixed agricultural one based on tobacco, sugar and cattle grazing. Cuba was not yet dependent on sugar as were the other major Caribbean islands, Jamaica, Barbados and St Domingue. Even in the 1750s, however, the seeds of the later sugar latifundia were germinating; in spite of a tobacco boom the number of sugar plantations was growing. Cuba's sugar revolution occurred in the years after 1763. The official export figures of sugar from Havana offer dramatic evidence of sugar's conquest of Cuba. A yearly average of 13,000 boxes of sugar left Havana in 1760–3, rising to 50,000 boxes in 1770–8 and to over 80,000 in 1778–96. Yearly averages from 1796 to 1800, amounting to nearly 135,000 boxes a year, illustrate how well Cuba capitalized on the vacuum created by the devastation of St Domingue.[2]

The French colony of St Domingue had been the leading sugar producer in the Caribbean prior to the French Revolution, but the Revolution in 1789 set off a series of slave rebellions in the island which escalated into civil and race war, destroying the island's economy but leading eventually to the creation of Haiti, the first independent, black republic in the Caribbean. Cuba was the greatest beneficiary of the economic collapse of her neighbour, yet the export figures for Cuban sugar in the late 1790s pale into insignificance beside the yearly totals of the 1840s; over 700,000 boxes were exported from Matanzas and Havana in 1840, rising to nearly 850,000 boxes by 1844.[3] At the end of the Napoleonic Wars Cuba's sugar production was only slightly more than half of that of Jamaica, by then her leading Caribbean rival. Twenty-five years later, by 1840, Cuba's sugar production was 60% greater than all the British West Indian colonies combined and twice as large as Brazil's. The enormous rise in the export figures of Cuban sugar reflected an increasing economic prosperity but a prosperity that by 1850 was almost wholly dependent on the sugar industry.

Cuba's transformation came during a period when her leading Caribbean competitors either were declining economically like Jamaica and Barbados or, like St Domingue, being consumed by revolution. Cuba's sugar revolution was solely economic and it did not affect her status as a Spanish colony. Cuba remained 'the ever faithful island' during the Wars of Independence which saw all of Spain's mainland American possessions win their political independence. There were many reasons for Cuba's rapid economic development as a plantation colony, both internal and external, but none was more important than the assurance of a slave labour force continually replenished by new arrivals from Africa.[4] Without the African slave trade Cuba's economic transformation could not have occurred. As one Cuban historian has stated, 'the number of slaves determined the volume of production'.[5]

The African slave trade to the Spanish Indies began before the conquest of Cuba in 1511 and African slaves either arrived in the island accompanying Diego Velásquez and his *conquistadores* or very shortly afterwards.[6] The division of the world into Spanish and Portuguese spheres of influence first by a Papal Bull of 1493 and then by the Treaty of Tordesillas in 1494 meant that Spain was denied direct access to the coast of Africa and thus deprived of owning slave factories herself. She was forced to rely on foreigners to supply slaves to meet the great demand for servile labour in her American colonies. By 1517 the *asiento* or contract system had evolved whereby the Crown sold licences to individuals or to companies for the export of slaves to Spanish America. The *asientos* were designed to provide revenue for the Crown, slaves for the colonists and royal control over the number and religion of African slaves arriving in the Indies. Ideally, the *asiento* system offered a number of advantages to the Crown, the greatest of which was a guaranteed revenue. As the slave trade grew so did the royal share of the proceeds. The Spanish monarchy in the sixteenth century, becoming more desperate for money, soon developed the practice of selling slave licences in larger and larger blocks, and the licences themselves became objects of speculation.[7]

These licences or *asientos* which were attempts by the Crown to regulate the supply of slaves through monopoly contracts never developed into a true monopoly system.[8] But they retained all the defects of monopolies and both the holders of the contracts and the colonists had every incentive to resort to contraband trading to avoid the restrictions of royal regulations. From the very beginning the African slave trade to Cuba, as to other areas of Spanish America, had certain distinct and lasting characteristics. It was controlled by foreigners, starting with the Flemish, Portuguese and Dutch, and then the English after 1713. They supplied slaves under the provision of contracts whose conditions were negotiated in Spain, but at the same time both *asentistas* and purchasers connived in a lucrative and expanding contraband trade. A clandestine African slave trade existed alongside the legal and much more restrictive *asiento* system from the outset of the Atlantic slave trade to Spanish America, certainly not on the scale of the nineteenth century but sufficient to imprint a lasting tradition.

A memorial drawn up by the *Consulado* of Havana in 1811 suggests the War of the Spanish Succession, when the French came to Havana to trade slaves for tobacco, stimulated a demand for slaves and gave Havana merchants the means of paying for them.[9] The number of slaves brought to Cuba legally increased after Britain's acquisition of the *asiento* through the Treaty of Utrecht and continued to rise during the years 1740–60 when the *Real Compañía Mercantil de la Habana* held the monopoly. Because of the high prices charged by the *asentistas* and royal taxes, the demand for slaves was never satisfied and a contraband trade with the other West Indian islands flourished. The British South Sea Company, holder of the *asiento*, wrote to its factors in Panama in 1724:

We are Concerned to hear of the Illicit Trade you Advise, is Carryed on to the Havana from the South Kays of Cuba, And have too great Reasons to Complain of the Remissness of our Factorys both at Havana and St. Iago on this Head: Notwithstanding they have so Little to do: this may well be a cause of their vending so few Negroes.[10]

Yet, both the *Consulado* of Havana and the Cuban historian of the slave trade, José Antonio Saco, agree that prior to 1763 comparatively few slaves were brought to Cuba. The *Consulado* estimated that 25,000 slaves had been brought to Havana and 35,000 into the eastern part of the island through Santiago where clandestine trade with the English and French colonies was much easier.[11]

The British conquest of Havana in 1762 threw open the commercial gates of Cuba which until then had been shut against foreigners by Spain's mercantilistic commercial policies. British and British colonial merchants descended on Havana to sell merchandise and slaves. Britain held Havana for eleven months before returning it to Spain and in this period reputedly over 700 vessels entered Havana to trade, glutting the market with British goods.[12] An English merchant, John Kennion, received a monopoly to bring in 2,000 slaves a year and, even though he could not preserve it, he apparently managed to import 1,700. The total number of African slaves brought in during the short British occupation probably exceeded 4,000, adding significantly to Cuba's slave population and providing additional slave labour for the expansion of Cuba's sugar industry.[13]

The British occupation also awakened the metropolitan authorities to the commercial and agricultural potential of Cuba. Reforms in 1764 and 1765 eased the restrictive commercial regulations and tried to instil more administrative efficiency in the island's government. Spain introduced the intendancy system into Cuba where this administrative innovation for the Spanish colonies was tested before being adopted for the rest of the Spanish American empire. The political head of the island remained the Captain-General but the intendant was put in charge of royal revenues, fortifications and trade with the aim of rooting out corruption and strengthening royal control.[14] Besides greater administrative efficiency, another object of the reforms was the expansion of Cuban commerce. Cuban trade with Spain was no longer confined to the peninsular ports of Cadiz and Seville, and direct commerce was permitted now between Havana and Spanish Caribbean ports such as Vera Cruz, Portobello and Cartagena.[15] Other royal orders continued to widen Cuban facilities for trade within the bounds of the Spanish empire until the *Reglamento* of October 1778 ratified the West Indian concessions by extending them to the rest of Spain's American empire except Venezuela and New Spain.[16] Cuba, in company with other parts of Spain's colonial empire, profited from the theory of expansion of trade implicit in these decrees.

When Spanish forces arrived to repossess Cuba in 1763, along with them came General O'Reilly as *visitador* to examine the state of the island. His reports prepared the way for the administrative and commercial reforms. O'Reilly's conclusions on the island's agriculture reflected the interests of the planters and merchants. One of the principal causes of the backwardness of the island was the scarcity and high price of African slaves. 'It can be stated as an absolute principle that the prosperity of this Island depends mainly on the importation of African slaves.'[17] He advocated the removal of taxes on the importation of slaves and the adoption of a less restrictive policy on the slave trade to permit direct contacts with the foreigners who controlled it. 'The King will derive much more revenue from the taxes on sugar produced by slaves than he will obtain from the import duties on the slaves themselves.'[18] O'Reilly's recommendations for a more 'open' slave trade were ignored in Spain; the *asiento* granted to Uriarte in 1765 marked a return to the old system of monopoly.[19]

The terms of the *asiento* stipulated that slaves could be brought to Puerto Rico, designated as the deposit area, by slave traders of any nationality; in fact, most were English. After reaching Puerto Rico the slaves were then sent off in smaller Spanish ships to their destinations. All operations, including the transport of slaves from Africa to Puerto Rico, were supposedly under the direct control of the company holding the *asiento*.

The Uriarte contract was not exclusive – the *Compañía de la Habana* imported an estimated 4,957 slaves in the three years after the peace of 1763[20] – yet its restrictions were doubly irksome to the planters at a time when restrictions on other forms of commerce were being loosened. The grievances of the Cubans went to the Spanish government in a *representación* of the Havana *Ayuntamiento*, dated 8 January 1767.[21] Because of the *asiento*, the planters claimed they were forced to pay exorbitant prices for their imported slaves, prices fixed in the terms of the contract. They also protested at having to pay cash. They argued that the Cuban allotment of 1,000 slaves a year was inadequate and proposed, as an alternative, that at least 3,400 slaves should be introduced per year in each of several, specified Cuban ports. What the Cuban planters really wanted was permission to trade directly with the British West Indies instead of being forced to purchase slaves through the agents of the monopoly holders. The *Contador General de Indias* who examined the Cuban complaints recoiled in horror from their proposal: 'the proposition is scandalous'.[22] Havana was censured for its temerity. Even the Captain-General was not exempt from the tongue-lashing because he had supported the planters.

The Spanish authorities were not yet prepared to adopt a system of 'free trade' for the slave trade in spite of the pressures from Havana. Undeterred, the Havana planters continued to petition against the high prices charged by the *asentistas*. Not all the petitions were in vain. The Council of the Indies, in a report of 8 January 1768, recommended the resumption of the original tax, the *derecho de marca*, at a lower rate and the abandonment of the *capitación* which had replaced it in 1765. The King agreed and a royal order, based on this advice, was sent out to Havana.[23] This measure was designed to reduce the price of slaves to the buyers by 15 pesos. The thinking behind it was in line with the earlier recommendations of General O'Reilly that a decrease in the price of imported slaves would increase agricultural production and thereby add to the royal coffers.

Official policy was headed in the right direction as far as the Cuban planters were concerned, but it had a long way to go. A reduction of 15 pesos still left the price far higher than that quoted by British slave traders. Even worse, events proved the difficulty of speedy implementation of royal directives. Two slave ships, belonging to the *asiento* company, arrived at Havana early in May 1768, carrying 310 Africans. The price for *Negros Piezos*, or prime male slaves, was 260 pesos, 10 pesos higher than the previous year instead of 15 pesos lower as ordered by Madrid. The Cubans were astounded and enraged by this apparent exploitation, but their representation to the Council of the Indies was regarded with suspicion in view of the Cubans' known desire for unrestricted trade with the British slave traders, and the Council of the Indies took no action against the *asentistas*.[24]

Complaints continued to flow into Spain from Cuban planters about the high prices they were forced to pay for slaves sold under the *asiento*. Even if the peninsular officials had wanted to accede to the planters' wishes, their hands were tied by the financial losses of the company holding the *asiento*. A royal *cédula* of 1 May 1773, modifying the original terms of the Uriarte contract which had been taken over subsequently by Lorenzo de Arístegui and Francisco Aguirre, two Cadiz merchants, revealed that the company had lost 1,200,000 pesos in 8 years.[25] Thus any suggestions that the company lower its prices were countered with statements of its losses. Alternative proposals from Cuba that payments be made in crops, at prices fixed by the planters, were also rejected in Spain.[26] Spanish attitudes were, however, slowly changing. 'Henceforth, not revenue, but the provision of ample labor at the lowest possible cost was to guide the crown's attitude toward the slave trade.'[27]

Some relief did come to the Cuban planters from the financial straits of Aguirre, Arístegui and Company. In the revised contract of 1773, even though the prices established in the original *asiento* were to remain approximately the same – Cuban planters would still have to pay 250 pesos apiece for the slaves – the *hacendados* no longer had to rely on the entrepôt of Puerto Rico. The company received the right to send Spanish ships from Havana or Santiago de Cuba to foreign colonies to buy slaves and such was the importance of Havana by then that it became the chief factory of the company.[28]

Cuba's slave supply, which for a long time had been indirectly dependent on Jamaica and British slave traders, was now directly so. A contemporary account makes clear the extent of this dependence:

For some time previous to the Year 1769 untill 1779 the Spanish West India Islands and the Continent of South America were supply'd with Slaves by means of a Royal Asiento, or Company of Merchants in Spain who had an exclusive privilege from H.C.M. for that purpose – This Asiento was under the direction of an Agent General established in the Havana, from whence he despatched Spanish Vessels in Search of Slaves to the different Foreign Islands, but particularly to Jamaica from whence at least three fourths of all the Negroes were supply'd . . .[29]

The British Free Port Act of 1766, renewed in 1774, enabled Jamaica to take full advantage of the lucrative re-export trade in slaves. Aguirre, Arístegui and Company, the supposed beneficiaries of the modifications of 1773, now became 'unnecessary middlemen', for all that lay between Jamaica and Cuba was their monopoly.[30] The slave trade in this mercantilist period managed to overcome the economic barriers to trade between rival empires, whether by legal or illegal means, and was one of the forces responsible for the collapse of mercantilist trade walls.[31]

Clear evidence that colonial, including Cuban, planters managed to circumvent the Aguirre, Arístegui *asiento* came in a royal *cédula* of 18 July 1775, which reaffirmed the monopolistic character of the *asiento* and castigated the clandestine importation of slaves from foreign colonies.[32] The existence of a contraband trade in slaves to Cuba had been tacitly recognized through a tax, known as the *indulto de negros*. This levy, equal in value to the regular import charges on slaves, was paid by slaveowners to secure legal possession of illegally imported slaves.[33]

Aguirre and Arístegui did not have an exclusive right to the Cuban slave trade from 1773 to 1779. Another *asiento* held by the Marquis of Casa Enrile resulted in the introduction of 14,132 slaves during those same years.[34] If the supply still did not match the growing demand of expanding agricultural production in Cuba, the number of imported slaves was increasing rapidly. The metropolitan authorities in Spain were preoccupied equally with developing their agricultural colonies and reducing the dominance of foreigners in the slave trade to Spanish America. It was with these ends in view that the rights to the islands of Annobon and Fernando Po, located in the Gulf of Guinea off the West African coast, were acquired from Portugal in 1778. But Spain's inability to take effective possession of the islands left the slave trade still in the hands of foreigners.[35] More radical proposals also existed. A paper presented to one of the Councillors of the Indies, Bernardo de Yriarte, in 1781, advocated government support for an all Spanish slave trade, even to the point of stationing Spanish frigates off the coast of Africa to protect slavers. 'Our past experience has taught us not to rely on companies or assientos.'[36]

War with Britain from 1779 to 1783 illustrated Spain's difficulties in providing her colonies with slaves. The Aguirre, Arístegui *asiento* was not renewed in 1779, no doubt due to the loss of the English contacts as well as to the continued unprofitability of the contract in spite of the revisions of 1773. War did not reduce the demand for slaves and to meet this demand a royal order of 25 January 1780 gave permission to the colonial authorities of Spanish America, except those of Chile, Peru and La Plata, to buy slaves from the French colonies during the war on condition that they were imported in Spanish ships.[37] An Englishman familiar with the slave trade to Cuba reported, though, that when war broke out between Britain and Spain, 'a general Licence was granted to all Spanish Subjects to Introduce Slaves into the Havana, either in National or Neutral Bottoms'. When the war ended neutral flags were prohibited.[38] Saco includes a table in his *Historia de la esclavitud de la raza africana en el Nuevo Mundo* which shows that the tax yield on slave importations was greater in the war years of 1780 to 1784 than in the two years following the war.[39] The planters took full advantage of the relaxation of restrictions made necessary by the war.

There was a close link between measures to expand commerce and the increased importation of slaves since much of the slave trade to Cuba was, in fact, part of a much larger intra-Caribbean commerce. In 1779 Spain authorized a limited trade with friendly powers, principally the thirteen Anglo-American colonies, to ensure a sufficient supply of food for Cuba.[40] This chink in the Spanish mercantilist armour enabled Cuban merchants to take advantage of the wider markets for their goods offered by neutral ships and increased the likelihood of neutral vessels, many of which also carried slaves, visiting Cuban ports. This pattern, not a new one, was to continue throughout the Napoleonic Wars. When maritime communication between Spain and Cuba was interrupted as a result of war, Havana was permitted to trade with neutrals, the permission being withdrawn as soon as peninsular or colonial monopolists persuaded the government that relaxation of restrictions on trade with foreigners was no longer needed.[41] The Congress of the United States Confederation in 1781 appointed an agent to reside in Havana to assist American traders, an indication of the rapid growth of this commerce. Even after the permission to trade with neutrals was withdrawn, United States vessels continued for a brief time to trade with Havana. In 1783, after the end of the war, 22 ships cleared the port of Philadelphia for Cuba while 18 returned to Philadelphia from Havana.[42] A bank in New York reportedly was saved from bankruptcy by the arrival of ships with specie from Cuba. The contrast was evident in 1785 when only one United States vessel cleared Philadelphia for Havana and none entered from Havana. Between 1785 and 1789 United States trade with Cuba died away almost completely.[43]

The growth of commerce with the new republic of the United States was not the only external stimulant to the Cuban economy in the 1780s. Cuba received a substantial number of slaves as a result of the slave-trading activities of several European colonial powers. The French slave trade experienced a remarkable resurgence after the end of the American War of Independence. The peak of that trade occurred in the year of the French Revolution in which an estimated 130 slaving voyages were launched from French ports. The decline in the French slave trade did not really begin until 1792 after the revolution in St Domingue and the last French slaving vessels left at the beginning of 1793.[44] The nine years from 1783 to 1792 were the most prosperous in the history of the leading French slave-trading port of Nantes, surpassing the previous peak period from 1748 to 1754. At least 350 slavers were outfitted in Nantes alone between 1783 and 1792, an average of 35 per year.[45] French slave traders had always practised a lucrative contraband trade with Cuba and the other Spanish colonies and undoubtedly the 'boom' in the French slave trade had a spillover effect in Cuba, reflected in the number of French slavers arriving at Havana after 1789 and in additional clandestine landings of African slaves in other parts of the island. Even after 1792, the French slave trade resurfaced during the years of peace in 1802–3 and again in an illegal form after 1815. Nantes continued to dominate in the years 1814–33 when it was responsible for nearly half of the French illegal slave trade, with Cuba as the major destination.[46] The Danish West Indian islands also were the centre of a brisk re-export trade in slaves to the Spanish colonies during and after the American War of Independence. This transit trade flourished during periods of war with the greatest volume occurring during the years 1799–1805. Danish subjects were prohibited from participating in the slave trade from Africa in 1803, but Cuban planters received African slaves via the Danish West Indies at least until 1805 after which the Danish involvement rapidly declined.[47]

The trend to free the Spanish slave trade from restrictions, discernible at various points in the reign of Charles III, accelerated at the end of the 1780s, just in time, as it turned out, for the Cuban planters to capitalize on the agricultural shortages caused by the ruin of St Domingue. It is generally agreed that Cuban pressure was responsible for the experiment which changed the nature of the slave trade to Spanish America from a closed commerce operated by monopolies to a trade open to Spaniards and foreigners alike. After the American War of Independence the Spanish Crown reverted again to the *asiento* system. In 1786 the firm of Baker and Dawson of Liverpool received a contract to supply between 5,000 and 6,000 slaves to Cuba and Caracas on the same terms as a previous contract to supply Trinidad and Caracas.[48] Two other *asientos* ran concurrently involving smaller numbers of slaves.[49] When the Baker and Dawson contract came up for renewal in 1788, their new proposal was sent out to Havana for examination. It called for no fewer than 3,000 slaves to be supplied annually to Caracas and Havana but the terms were ambiguous especially those concerning prices.[50] To many of the planters they were unacceptable and their opposition was made known in Madrid through their representative, Arango y Parreño. He presented a memorandum to the *Junta Suprema de Estado* on 6 February 1789, the arguments of which tallied with the provisions of the royal *cédula* issued on 28 February.[51]

Philip Allwood, the agent of Baker and Dawson in Havana, had been convicted on charges of contraband trading and the Spanish authorities were opposed to encouraging additional contraband trade by renewing the Baker and Dawson *asiento*. This is evident in a letter from the British Minister in Madrid to Allwood:

It is sufficient to say that there lies against you a sentence, as yet unreversed, for contraband trade; that the Minister of Indies, through whose hands this affair must pass, is by no means persuaded of your innocence;- and that there exists a prejudice (perhaps but too well founded) that one great view in the proposal of negro contracts is the fraudulent introduction of uncustomed goods.[52]

The terms of the renewal of the Baker–Dawson contract and fears of contraband trade were not the only reasons for the change in policy marked by this *cédula*. News had reached Madrid of the proposal to abolish the slave trade which was then before the British Parliament.[53] This illustrated again the dilemma of the Spanish position. Should Britain abolish the slave trade, Cuba and the other Spanish Caribbean possessions would be affected since they had no sources of supply apart from the British or other foreigners. Realizing their awkward situation, the Cuban planters took steps to improve it. The colonists' desire to take the slave trade into their own hands found a sympathetic hearing in Spain where more liberal views of commerce had been gaining ground. The *Reglamento* of 12 October 1778 which completed the process of opening Spanish colonial trade to all Spanish and colonial seaports and to all Spanish subjects, although not to foreigners, also has been credited with influencing the abolition of the slave trade monopoly.[54]

From its opening statement the *cédula* emphasized the great importance of the slave trade to the agricultural development of the Spanish Caribbean colonies which it was designed to stimulate.[55] All Spanish subjects, whether from the peninsula or the colonies, were free to go to any foreign colony in order to buy slaves whom they could bring into designated ports free of duty. Foreigners were also permitted to import slaves into the *puertos habilitados* free of duty, but they were limited to twenty-four hours in port and their ships had to be under 300 tons. One third of the slaves brought in were to be female, and Spaniards and foreigners alike were forbidden to engage in any other foreign trade. At Havana either foreigners or Spaniards could import slaves, while at Santiago de Cuba, the only other Cuban port included, only Spaniards could engage in the slave trade. Unlike the former *asientos*, this *cédula* ruled out any price-fixing, stating that prices were to be agreed on by buyer and seller without any outside interference. As a further incentive to Spanish subjects to engage in the slave trade, a subsidy of 4 pesos was offered for each slave imported by a Spaniard in a Spanish ship. The owners of domestic slaves were to pay for this by contributing an annual *capitación* of 2 pesos for each slave in domestic labour.

The *cédula* of 28 February 1789 was to run for a trial period of two years which ended none too soon. For the confusion it caused among colonial officials who had to administer it necessitated a complete rewriting of its provisions.[56] Protests about the *capitación* resulted in a reduction by half even before the new *cédula* was published.[57] The royal *cédula* of 24 November 1791, while continuing the liberalizing trend of its predecessor, also cleared up the remaining ambiguities.[58] Having proved unworkable, both the subsidy to Spanish slave traders and the *capitación* were abandoned. Similarly, the clause stating that one third of the slaves imported must be female was removed, and the tax on products exported to pay for slaves was standardized at 6%. Apparently not all the defects were removed. The Marquis of Yranda wrote to one of the Councillors of the Indies: 'I have carefully checked the second *cédula* on the slave trade. It has fewer defects than the first and I hope that when its successor emerges in due time it will be a *chef d'oeuvre.*'[59]

Foreign and Spanish slave traders benefited anew from the provisions of the second *cédula*. The permission granted to foreigners to introduce slaves into the *puertos habilitados* was prolonged for a further six years under less stringent conditions. The tonnage limit on foreign ships was raised from 300 to 500, and they were now permitted to remain in port for eight days instead of the previous twenty-four hours. Spanish slave traders were given up to four months to visit foreign colonies in search of slaves and unlimited time if they were going to Africa. Three Cuban ports, Nuevitas, Batabano and Trinidad de Cuba, were added to the list of those at which Spaniards could carry on the slave trade. A fourth, Manzanillo near Bayamo, was later included by a royal order of 23 March 1794.[60] The ideas underlining the *cédula* of November 1791 appear again to coincide with the requirements of those Cuban planters represented by the *Apoderado General* of Havana in Madrid, Arango y Parreño. Havana still found itself dependent on foreign, especially British, slave traders and, recognizing the situation, Arango petitioned both for an extension of the privileges of the 1789 *cédula* and for greater latitude to the foreign slave traders who furnished Cuba's labour needs.[61]

These two *cédulas* marked the beginning of a decade of legislation intended to augment the number of African slaves in the Indies through the slave trade. The French, who were excluded from the provisions of the 1791 *cédula* as far as Havana was concerned, were included by a royal order of 9 June 1792.[62] This may have been simply a recognition of an already large French participation since, according to Herbert Klein's calculations, 32 French slavers arrived in Havana from 1790 to 1792.[63] A royal order of November 1792 lengthened from eight to forty days the time in port permitted to foreign slave traders.[64] Cuban authorities had shown considerable ingenuity in getting around the eight-day restriction by forming a company which bought the slaves from the foreign slave traders and then sold them to the planters.[65] Later decrees enlarged the list of articles which could be imported by Spaniards employed in the slave trade. Barrel hoops and staves were included in a royal order of 14 December 1794, while earlier permission to import machinery and tools for *ingenios* was repeated in a royal order of 19 March 1794.[66] Efforts of the Cuban authorities to promote Spanish slaving expeditions to Africa received peninsular encouragement in a royal order of 24 January 1793. This relieved Spanish expeditions on their way to Africa from paying any taxes on the goods they exported, provided that half the crew and the captain were Spanish.[67] The order also stated that foreign vessels purchased by Spaniards for African expeditions no longer had to pay a registry tax. The first direct Spanish slaving voyage to Africa under these new provisions occurred in the summer of 1792 when the *Cometa* arrived in Havana from the Guinea coast with 227 slaves.[68] There were altogether 11 royal decrees between 1789 and 1804 aimed at expanding the Cuban slave trade.

The increase in the supply of slave labour through the 'open' slave trade enabled Cuban planters to take advantage of the devastation of St Domingue. A modern Cuban historian has described the last decade of the eighteenth century as 'the dance of the millions', a reference to the extraordinary boom experienced by Cuba in the aftermath of the revolution in the French island.[69] Sugar and coffee prices skyrocketed after the downfall of St Domingue. Cuban planters quickly realized their good fortune and figures of the sugar exports from Havana in the 1790s show how they capitalized on this opportunity.[70] The fact that Cuban planters were able to seize the chance which the collapse of St Domingue presented was due also to a reforming mood among the planters themselves. With the inspiration of the Captain-General, Las Casas, a *Sociedad Económica de Amigos del País* and a *Real Consulado de Agricultura y Comercio* were founded in Havana in the 1790s, both dedicated to improving agriculture.[71] It was with this spirit and under the auspices of one or both societies that men like the economist Arango y Parreño worked to make Cuban agriculture competitive with that of the other West Indian islands.[72]

The royal decrees on the slave trade removed the hindering obstacles which formerly had faced the Spanish colonists in their search for an adequate supply of slave labour. Yet the basic pattern of the slave trade to Cuba was not materially changed. However great the desire of the Spanish authorities to diminish the colonists' dependence on foreign slave traders, the effect of the *cédulas* was to increase it.

From the publication of the royal *cédula* of 28 February 1789 to the end of June 1790, 2,507 slaves were brought to Havana by 17 slavers, half of them, carrying the majority of slaves, having come direct from Africa. In the same period 10 Spanish vessels carried 367 slaves back to Havana from foreign colonies.[73] A substantial number of slaves came to Havana from foreign colonies in the 1790s; an account drawn up by the *Administrador de Rentas* in Havana on 2 January 1795 showed a total of 5,279 imported from foreign colonies since September 1789.[74] The total number of slaves brought to Havana in this five year span has been given as over 35,500.[75] The majority of them came in foreign vessels either sailing direct from Africa or coming to Havana from foreign colonies. In asking for more privileges to be given to foreign slave traders, Arango y Parreño was trying to put Havana in a better position to compete with the other West Indian islands for the favour of the mainly foreign slave traders. As part of this effort to expand the Cuban slave trade, Arango y Parreño, accompanied by another Cuban planter, visited Portugal, Britain, Barbados and Jamaica in 1794 to learn how to apply the industrial revolution to sugar production and to pick up what direct knowledge he could about the slave trade.[76]

Arango y Parreño made the point in his *representación* of 10 May 1791 that the slave trade to Havana was still largely run by the company which had held the *asiento* before 1789.[77] The Baker-Dawson partnership apparently dissolved in 1788–9 after the failure to renew their contract, but John Dawson, the largest slave trader in Liverpool in 1790 with a capital investment in ships, outfitting and cargo of over £150,000, continued in business with Philip Allwood as his Havana agent. Allwood reputedly imported or financed the importation of more slaves in the period 1790–95 than all other slave traders put together. He was so important to the island's economy that the Captain-General defied orders from Madrid to expel him as an undesirable foreigner.[78] Liverpool, and especially Dawson, thus dominated the slave trade to Cuba in the first half of the 1790s as they had in the 1780s. Indeed, as Professor Anstey has shown, British slave traders exported more slaves and earned higher profits in the decade 1791–1800 than in any other decade between 1760 and 1807.[79]

The British were not the only foreigners to take advantage of Spain's new laws on the slave trade. The French, Americans and Danes all quickly moved into this new market for Caribbean trade, although, as has been seen, French participation declined rapidly after 1792. A recent analysis indicates that United States merchants, using the trade permission granted by the slave trade *cédulas* as a cover for a wider commerce, soon emerged as serious rivals to the British for the lion's share of the Cuban slave trade in spite of the fact that very few United States vessels brought slaves direct from Africa; most American slave-trading in the 1790s was part of a broader intra-Caribbean commerce.[80] The growing American role in the Cuban slave trade by the middle of the 1790s increased the supply of slaves so quickly some United States merchants feared a glut. The Havana representative of a New England firm complained in 1796 that 'the Negro business is overdone here' because his firm had sold 1,800 African slaves since 1794.[81]

Fears about the unprecedented growth of the slave population may have been aroused by events in St Domingue but they remained hidden below the surface in Cuba. The planters and merchants were interested solely in maintaining the inflow and in securing a continuation of the privileges granted by the *cédulas* of 1789 and 1791. They were even willing to put up with the astonishingly high interest rates which Humboldt credited to the slave trade.[82]

The 'open' slave trade was the buttress of the prosperous plantation system being built in Cuba. There was certainly no desire to return to the old *asiento* system. When rumours reached Havana in 1802 that an *asiento* had been granted to the Marquis of Colonilla to bring 6,000 slaves from the Guinea coast to Havana in foreign ships. the protests from the *habaneros* were quick and vigorous.[83] On the basis of these protests and some reports from the rest of the American colonies, the Spanish government reviewed its policy on the slave trade in 1803. Havana, through the Intendant, already had petitioned for a four-year extension of the existing regulations on 13 February 1802.[84] An official *memoria* sent from the palace at Aranjuez to the Council of the Indies on 15 April 1803 made it clear that the question before the Council was not whether the slave trade should be prolonged, but for how long and on what basis. The opening statement of the *memoria* set out the need for the slave trade: 'American agriculture, which because of its impact on the commerce and navigation of European nations and on the prosperity of the colonies themselves is so important, cannot exist without the slave trade.'[85] The benefits to Cuban agriculture were noted as proof of the need to continue it. There was even hope of Spanish colonies rivalling those of other European powers in agricultural produce, provided protection and favour were shown to the slave trade.

With this forceful document before it, as well as the emphatic petitions of the Cuban colonial officials and planters, the decision of the Council of the Indies to renew the slave trade concessions was predictable. A royal *cédula* based on the opinion of the Council was promulgated on 22 April 1804.[86] This granted permission to Spaniards and foreigners to continue the slave trade, the former for a further twelve years and the latter for six more years, according to the regulations laid down in the *cédula* of 24 November 1791. The right of remaining forty days in port to sell their slaves, granted to foreign slave traders in 1792, was maintained. One alteration in these rules was that all slaves imported had to be *bozales* brought directly from Africa. In an accompanying but unpublished *cédula* of the same date, the governors of Cuba and the other islands were ordered to facilitate the importation of female slaves and to promote marriages among the existing slave population.[87]

For the Cubans even this extension was not sufficient. The *Consulado* of Havana petitioned the King to approve a project to set up an African company in Havana with the object of beginning a direct trade in slaves from Africa.[88] A period of apprenticeship under one of the established slave-trading nations was required since, as the *Consulado* admitted, 'we do not have experienced men, acquired knowledge nor the equipment which the slave trade demands'. They therefore proposed to establish a commercial house in London or Liverpool which would outfit slavers and send them to Africa. Nothing came of the project, which in any case would have been impossible to implement.

This proposal, like attempts to increase the female slave population, was an expression of the deep concern among Cuban planters at the dependence of their labour supply on the slave trade and foreign slave traders. If Cuban prosperity hinged on the provision of slave labour through the slave trade, better that it be in the hands of Spaniards or Spanish colonists than those of foreigners. Better still if the continuation of adequate numbers of plantation slaves was insulated from the vicissitudes of the international slave trade and relied solely on domestic reproduction. But successive royal orders to ensure a specific proportion of females in slavers' cargoes reflected not a success in augmenting the number of female slaves but a failure to do so. Schemes to free the slave trade to Cuba from foreign control up to this time had not been feasible plans but mirages. In the end it was the decision of Cuba's chief suppliers, the British and the Americans, to abandon the slave trade which finally led the Cubans to take over control of the Cuban slave trade themselves.

The *cédula* of 1789 sanctioned the 'open' slave trade to Cuba and from 1790 to 1820 the African slave trade to Cuba remained legal according to Spanish law. The number of slaves officially imported into Cuba through Havana was recorded by customs officials at Havana. The figures were gathered together in monthly returns by the Intendant of Havana and forwarded to Spain.[89] A succession of historians have accepted (and published) these figures as accurate numbers for the Cuban slave trade from 1790 to 1820. Baron von Humboldt used them in his account of Cuba published in 1826.[90] H.H.S. Aimes later published the same figures in an appendix to his book, *The History of Slavery in Cuba, 1511–1868*.[91] Professor Philip B. Curtin in his recent study of the Atlantic slave trade argues that these figures can be accepted as reasonable for the period they cover, and rejects a viewpoint advanced in 1842 by James Bandinel, an official at the British Foreign Office, that the Havana customs house figures ought to be doubled on account of illicit trade.[92] Curtin states in a footnote, 'illicit trade may have existed but no evidence is available to show its level'.[93]

The figures of slave imports into Havana for the years 1790–1821, taken originally from the customs house records of Havana and reproduced in Table 1, represent only the numbers of slaves brought in legally through Havana in this period and cannot be taken as the total slave imports for the island of Cuba. These figures do not include the number of slaves legally introduced into Cuban ports such as Santiago de Cuba and Trinidad, nor do they make any allowance for the contraband trade which continued throughout the period of the 'open' slave trade.

There is no question but that this illicit slave trade existed throughout the 'open' period from 1791 to 1820. Havana was the only port listed in the 1789 *cédula* where foreigners could introduce imported African slaves into Cuba; Spaniards living in Santiago de Cuba were permitted to go to foreign colonies and purchase African slaves, but foreigners themselves were not allowed to sell African slaves at Santiago. The *cédula* of 1791 increased the number of Cuban ports through which Spaniards could import African slaves in Spanish-owned vessels, but Havana remained the only port on the island which foreign slave ships could enter legally. Since the bulk of the slave trade from Africa to Cuba was in foreign hands at least until 1808, there were obvious reasons for merchants and planters in the outlying areas to connive at an illicit trade in slaves.

There are clear indications that the Spanish government was aware

Table 1. *African slaves imported through Havana, 1790–1821*

Years	Numbers	Years	Numbers
1790	2,534	1806	4,395
1791	8,498	1807	2,565
1792	8,528	1808	1,607
1793	3,777	1809	1,162
1794	4,164	1810	6,672
1795	5,832	1811	6,349
1796	5,711	1812	6,081
1797	4,552	1813	4,770
1798	2,001	1814	4,321
1799	4,949	1815	9,111
1800	4,145	1816	17,733
1801	1,659	1817	25,841
1802	13,832	1818	19,902
1803	9,671	1819	15,147
1804	8,923	1820	17,194
1805	4,999	1821	4,122
		Total	240,747

Source: José Antonio Saco, 'Análisis de una obra sobre el Brasil', *Revista bimestre cubana* (1832), reprinted in *Colección de papeles científicos, históricos, políticos y de otros ramos sobre la isla de Cuba*, 3 vols. (Havana, 1960), vol. II, p. 74. I have relied on Saco's figures. Both Saco and Humboldt used the same original statistics, but there are minor differences for the years 1797, 1799 and 1816, and a major discrepancy for 1819 and 1820. Humboldt's table can be found in *Ensayo. político sobre la isla de Cuba* (Havana, 1960), p. 191. For a comparison of Humboldt's table with the surviving original figures, see Herbert S. Klein, 'The Cuban Slave Trade in a Period of Transition, 1790–1843', *Revue française d'histoire d'Outre-Mer*, vol. LXII, n°s 226–7 (1975), Table 1, p. 70.

of this illicit commerce and of its extent. As early as 1791 the Intendant of Havana was told to make sure that certain coastguards were on the lookout for the clandestine entry of African slaves. The following year the Governor of Santiago was warned by the Madrid authorities of their suspicions that a large contraband slave trade was being carried on between Jamaica and Santiago.[94] It would appear, then, that the permission granted to Spaniards in Santiago de Cuba in the *cédula* of 1789 to conduct the slave trade in Spanish ships merely gave an impetus to a long-standing clandestine trade between Santiago and Jamaica.

Cuban historians have been more aware of the inadequacy of these figures. In the hope of awakening his countrymen to the dangers of the slave trade, José Antonio Saco, in 1832, published an article analysing the statistics of the African slave trade to Cuba, using the Havana customs house records as the basic guide for the years 1790–1821.[95] Saco added 60,000, or approximately one-quarter of the total, to his total of 240,747 for the years 1790–1821 to cover legal entries through other Cuban ports, customs omissions and contraband trade. To accept Saco's calculations would mean a total of 300,747 slaves imported into Cuba during the years 1790–1821, in addition to his estimate of 98,684 as the number of slaves brought to Cuba before 1789. Confirmation of the reliability of the original customs house records of Havana can be found in a memorial sent by the *Consulado* of Havana to the Spanish Cortes in February 1811, warning against any precipitate action to abolish the slave trade. The *Consulado* calculated that since 1789, 110,000 slaves had been imported into Havana at a cost of 33 million pesos.[96] This figure roughly coincides with the totals from the Havana customs house records. A later Cuban historian, Fernando Ortiz, also basing his calculations upon the Havana customs records, agreed with Saco that an addition of one-quarter should be made to cover clandestine trade, etc.[97] In round numbers, then, the years of the 'open' slave trade saw 300,000 African slaves brought into Cuba, in contrast to the estimated 100,000 imported during the more than two and a half centuries of Spanish colonial rule over Cuba prior to 1789.

Britain's decision in 1807 to prohibit the British slave trade, coupled with the American and Danish prohibitions, accelerated the structural changes which the Napoleonic Wars had forced on the Cuban slave trade. During the 1790s there had been two or three variants of the Cuban slave trade, as Klein has established: a direct trade from Africa to Cuba carried on almost exclusively by foreign slave traders, a direct trade from Africa to a number of Caribbean islands or to an entrepôt like Jamaica from which slaves were then transhipped to Cuba, and the shipment of slaves from one part of the Caribbean to another as part of a complex intra-Caribbean commerce.[98] The withdrawal of the British, Americans and Danes meant that from 1809 to 1815 the Cuban slave trade became an almost exclusively Iberian trade, although after 1815 it became more international with French participation becoming more evident. With Iberian domination two of the three variant forms of the Cuban slave trade disappeared. Cuba's slaves were now brought directly from Africa to Cuba. Table 2, also based on the Havana customs records, demonstrates the official value of the slaves brought to Havana during the years 1803–16 and the surprising fact that Spanish officials did not begin recording the value of produce shipped to Africa to purchase slaves until 1811 even though Cuban slave trade expeditions certainly had begun on a large scale as early as 1809.

The number of slaves brought to Cuba rose and fell according to the international factors governing the Atlantic slave trade. While the Haitian revolution cast a long shadow over Cuba, it affected the slave trade only incidentally. Events further away in Britain were to have a greater impact. The tenuous fabric of growing Cuban prosperity was far more vulnerable to the insistent pressures of British abolitionist sentiment seeking to wipe out the slave trade wherever it was to be found. After 1806 British governments would adopt the abolitionist crusade as their own. The trade to Cuba became a focal point of this crusade because of the Cuban planters' continual demand for slave labour. The royal *cédula* of 1804 was the Spanish Crown's last clear-cut permission for the slave trade to Spanish

Table 2. *African trade through Havana, 1803–16*

Years	Imports	Exports (in Spanish dollars)
1803	2,683,800	—
1804	769,120	—
1805	1,400,000	—
1806	1,582,200	—
1807	960,665	—
1808	594,590	—
1809	406,700	—
1810	2,335,200	—
1811	2,032,304	169,016
1812	2,189,747	198,159
1813	1,621,800	102,332
1814	1,512,950	58,481
1816	2,659,950	643,852

Source: Ramón de la Sagra, *Historia económico-política y estadística de la Isla de Cuba* ... (Havana, 1831), p. 156; 1815 was omitted from La Sagra's table. The figures for imports represent the official value placed on the slaves brought into Havana.

America. Before its provisions expired the independence movements of mainland Spanish America had overtaken it. Apart from Brazil, the Atlantic slave trade would continue only to the Spanish Caribbean islands and primarily to Cuba. The conflict was thus joined between Cuban labour needs and British pressure, first to prohibit and then to enforce the prohibition of the slave trade to Cuba.

CHAPTER 2

Parliament versus Cortes

Early in the struggle to abolish the British slave trade, the leading abolitionists realized that to make any abolition effective it would have to be universal. Another reason for seeking foreign co-operation was to undermine the domestic opposition argument that Britain's maritime rivals would be the chief beneficiaries of a British abolition.[1] In December 1787 the Prime Minister, William Pitt, himself an advocate of abolition, wrote to William Eden, then Minister in Paris and Minister-designate to Madrid, referring to the abolitionist crusade, 'if you see any chance of success in France, I hope you will lay your ground as soon as possible with a view to Spain also'.[2]

The Parliamentary leader of the abolitionists, William Wilberforce, initiated several other attempts to obtain international agreement on the prohibition of the slave trade during the next twenty years, but the French Revolution, the revolution in St Domingue and the Napoleonic Wars dashed any hopes of success just as they acted to frustrate the abolitionist campaign within Britain.[3] Wilberforce never lost an opportunity to press for international action, especially prior to the peace negotiations leading to the Treaty of Amiens in 1802, but the failure of these tentative overtures accentuated the importance of the struggle in Britain. British abolitionists were morally certain other nations would follow Britain's lead if only Britain would set the example. Henry Brougham confessed:

We have been the chief traders, I mean, the ringleaders in the crime. Let us be the first to repent, and set an example of reformation. It becomes the dignity of Great Britain to take the lead, and to trust that her example will be followed. No great reform has ever taken place in one part of the international and intercolonial systems, without a similar change being soon effected in all the other parts; and the measure which is adopted in order to prevent the ruin of the British colonies, will surely be imitated by the other states, whose colonies are exposed to still more imminent dangers from the same quarter.[4]

For seventeen years, from 1787 to 1804, the British abolitionists doggedly worked without noticeable success to get Parliament to abolish the British slave trade. Measures were passed to regulate the slave trade, but no abolitionist could be satisfied with these. Yet, after these long years of failure, victory was achieved in three short years in the midst of the Napoleonic Wars when circumstances did not seem propitious for the abolitionist cause. Why should the British Parliament in 1807 have been willing to adopt what many members previously had seen as a radical measure, linked to the detested doctrines of French Jacobinism, after obstinately holding out against abolitionist pressure for so long?[5]

The abolitionists, many of whom were at the forefront of the contemporary Evangelical revival within the Church of England, saw the hand of God at work. Indeed, God had punished Europe severely for not abolishing the slave trade earlier. James Stephen, a leading abolitionist and Evangelical, early in 1807 but before the abolition bill had passed, catalogued a gloomy list of the sufferings Britain had undergone because of her refusal to abolish the slave trade:

As we multiplied and aggravated the impious crime, God multiplied and aggravated the punishment. Treason, famine, mutiny, civil war, the loss of our specie, the sale of our land tax, the enormous growth of our national debt, the intolerable pressure of taxation, the discomfiture of our military enterprises, the destruction of our armies by disease, the deplorable ruin of our allies, the stupendous exaltation of our enemies; these, and other plagues, followed like those of Egypt, in a rapid succession, upon every iteration of our refusals to obey the voice of God by renouncing the execrable Slave Trade.[6]

Although there was an obvious danger of raising the expectations of the benefits to follow from the abolition of the slave trade to an unrealistic level – would taxes and the national debt decline and Britain's military fortunes change immediately? – Stephen's powerful message of Britain's desperate need for the spiritual regeneration which only could come from throwing off the awful sin of the slave trade was calculated to appeal to the genuine religious consciousness of British abolitionists and their supporters. God had not singled out Britain alone. France, Spain, Holland and Portugal, 'the great commercial nations of Europe, all at the same era, resolve[d] to extend the desolation, the miseries and crimes of Africa, to the utmost of their power . . . But the eye of the Almighty was over them, and to avenge devoted Africa at least, if not to save her, he dropped down among them the French Revolution.'[7]

Such a providential explanation of the British Parliament's conversion to abolition in 1807, to redeem Britain from the sin of the slave trade and the mounting punishments for that sin, disguised a number of important changes that had occurred since 1800 and which the abolitionists themselves made shrewd use of to attain their long-looked-for victory.[8] Abolitionism no longer carried the same unsavoury taint of French democratic and revolutionary ideas now that Napoleon had succeeded to absolute power in France. Under Napoleon the French again had become advocates of the slave trade which enabled British abolitionists to clothe their appeal in patriotic language. The Union of Britain and Ireland in 1800 brought Irish Members to the Westminster Parliament, most of whom were prepared to support the abolitionist cause, thus adding significantly to the core of abolitionist support. After the failure of a general abolition bill to pass in two successive years, 1804 and 1805, the Parliamentary abolitionists, led by Wilberforce and ably advised by James Stephen, decided to alter their tactics. For the moment they ceased trying to storm the Parliamentary ramparts with a general abolition bill. Temporarily turning away from arguments based on morality, humanitarianism and religion, they began to push for specific, but limited, measures of abolition which could be justified on grounds of the national interest.

In 1805, they persuaded the Prime Minister, Pitt, to ban by order-in-council the importation of slaves into the newly acquired Caribbean territory of Guiana. This at least prevented an expansion of the British slave trade due to wartime conquests. The abolitionists then supplemented this minor victory with an attack on the supply of slaves to foreign colonies and the use of neutral flags by Britain's enemies to fill their colonies with slaves. James Stephen exposed the way neutral flags were being used in his influential book, *War in Disguise*, and he did it so well that both British planters and the British government were persuaded that these abuses had to be stopped. Cuba was one of the major enemy colonies to benefit as Stephen took pains to point out: 'The gigantic infancy of agriculture in Cuba, far from being checked, is greatly aided in its portentous growth during the war, by the boundless liberty of trade, and the perfect security of carriage. Even slaves from Africa are copiously imported there . . .'[9] For the first time, the abolitionists were able to make common cause with their traditional enemies, the British West Indian planters. Stephen was so convincing, he sounded like an agent of planter interests: 'I protest, in every event, on behalf of the British planter, against the further settlement of Cuba, by a relaxation in any mode, of the rules of maritime war. During the last war, the produce of that vast island was at least doubled; and if the present system continues, it will soon be doubled again, to the destruction of our own sugar colonies.'[10]

This new abolitionist strategy coincided with the death of William Pitt early in 1806 and the coming to power of a new coalition government, headed by Grenville and Fox, both of whom would outdo Pitt in the support they gave to the abolitionists. Wilberforce and his colleagues received the full co-operation of the new government in their effort to eliminate the British slave trade to foreign colonies. By the middle of May 1806, legislation prohibiting British subjects from supplying foreign colonies with slaves had passed and, such was the size of this commerce, greater even than the abolitionists themselves suspected, that this act alone abolished approximately three-quarters of the British slave trade.[11]

Hard on the heels of this measure, the abolitionists succeeded in having both the Commons and the Lords pass a joint address which was presented to the King on 25 June 1806, asking him to negotiate with foreign powers to achieve the international abolition of the slave trade. Domestic and international action now would complement each other and with this two-pronged offensive the abolitionists were optimistic of success. They envisaged the joint address as a weapon which would enable the British government to work towards a universal abolition at the peace negotiations once the war was over. In the meantime, Britain held talks on the slave trade with France as part of an attempt to conclude peace. Since peace was not concluded, nothing was done about the slave trade. Treaty negotiations with the United States also were in progress in 1806, leading to the signing of the Monroe–Pickney Treaty in December. As a result of the joint address, a vague article on the slave trade was included, but in the end the treaty never was ratified. British statesmen and abolitionists were aware of the likelihood of the abolition of the American slave trade from the beginning of 1808 and, therefore, Britain took no further action except to welcome the United States abolition when it finally came.[12]

The passage of the Foreign Slave Trade Bill and the Resolution for Abolishing the Slave Trade in the 1806 Parliamentary session noticeably weakened the opposition to complete abolition. Both the government and the abolitionists were determined to capitalize on their initial success. James Stephen's tone typified that of his fellow abolitionists:

The foreign slave trade indeed is at last abolished by law; a reformation the value of which I am by no means inclined to disparage; but with many supporters of that great measure, its principle was purely political: and its effect in permanently reducing the extent of the slave trade, as well as in diminishing the guilt of that commerce will be very equivocal, unless we now proceed to a radical and well-principled reformation.[13]

This 'radical and well-principled reformation' came at the beginning of 1807 when the government, strengthened by additional seats won in the 1806 autumn election, brought forward a bill for the complete abolition of the slave trade at the opening of Parliament. The total co-operation between the government leaders, especially Lord Grenville the Prime Minister, and the abolitionists aided its speedy passage. There was less opposition than anticipated and the bill ending the British slave trade received royal assent on 25 March 1807.

To the abolitionists the reformation within Britain had come at last. It remained to convince other slave-trading nations to follow Britain's example. The British abolitionists now set out on what was for them a new missionary journey, full of the zeal of the righteous, triumphant in Britain and confident that with government support they would soon succeed abroad. But the struggle to achieve international abolition turned out to be far longer and full of greater frustrations than the twenty-year movement to abolish the British slave trade. Nowhere was this illustrated more vividly than in the Spanish empire.

The Cuban slave trade had been struck a seemingly mortal blow by the passage of the Foreign Slave Trade Bill of 1806. Cuba had been completely dependent on the foreign slave trade, and the British slave trade had been responsible for supplying a large percentage of Cuba's slaves, albeit indirectly. Cuban planters were now forced to find alternative suppliers or to enter the African slave trade themselves to maintain the flow of slaves for their steadily expanding plantations. The total prohibition of the British slave trade in 1807 made British West Indian planters just as eager as the abolitionists to prevent the slave trade from benefiting their Cuban competitors, but both planters and abolitionists knew that only a well-enforced Spanish prohibition would eliminate the Cuban slave trade.

Since Britain's goal after 1807, and that of the abolitionists, was universal abolition, to look at Britain's negotiations with Spain in isolation is, in a sense, unrealistic. They were one part of an extensive diplomacy carried on by successive British governments with each of the slave-trading powers. Within this wide framework there were, though, many similarities between Britain's endeavours with Portugal and her efforts to persuade Spain to abolish the slave trade. Britain concentrated initially on Portugal, for Portugal 'was the traditional sinner and on account of the peculiar relations existing between the two governments offered special opportunities for action by Britain'.[14] Her first attempts to obtain an agreement from Portugal were frustrated by the uncompromising opposition of the Portuguese Foreign Minister.[15] When the Portuguese Court had to move from Lisbon to Rio de Janeiro in 1808 because of the French invasion of Portugal, George Canning, the British Foreign Secretary, instructed the British Ambassador, Strangford, to renew his representations. 'If these considerations were pressed upon the attention of the Portuguese Government at a time when its South American possessions were only secondary objects of its solicitude their importance is increased tenfold, now that Brazil is become the Seat of the Monarchy.'[16] Since the contents of Canning's despatch applied just as well to Spanish America as they did to Portuguese America, he sent a copy to the British Minister at Madrid, Frere, in October 1808.[17]

The instructions to Strangford stated that he was

to renew his representations to the Portuguese Government not to continue to maintain a traffic as unjustifiable as impolitic; and productive of so much misery to the Country from which the supply of slaves was drawn – as well as insecurity to that into which they were imported . . . that a continued importation of negroes, neither capable of being incorporated into the class of the community nor of imbibing any sentiment of attachment for the Prince, must contribute to weaken the general capacity of resistance against an enemy; multiply the sources of internal danger, and check the growth of native population.[18]

While Strangford was instructed to include an article on the slave trade in any treaty between Britain and Portugal, Canning's instructions to the British Minister at Madrid were not as forceful. Frere was instructed simply to take any opportunity to expound the British reasons for abolishing the slave trade without proposing any specific measure.

In the summer of 1809, Canning again wrote to the British Ambassador in Spain, now the Marquis of Wellesley, urging him to persuade the Spanish government of the desirability of a gradual abolition of the slave trade throughout the Spanish Empire.[19] This initiative arose directly from the receipt of Strangford's draft treaty with Portugal, including an article on the slave trade which remained in the Treaty of Alliance with Portugal, signed in 1810. Canning enclosed a copy of this article in the despatch to Wellesley in the hope of inspiring Spain, but Portugal's example had no effect on her.

Behind the diplomats were the abolitionists, constantly looking for new ways to achieve their desired object. Wilberforce saw in the Spanish revolts against Napoleon in 1808 the hope of extending the crusade against the slave trade to Spain. He wrote to his brother-in-law, James Stephen, in the summer of 1808, stating his intention to write to Canning and ask him to mention the abolition of the slave trade to the Spanish deputies from Galicia, Asturias and Andalusia who were then in England. Perceval, Holland and Brougham were also to be enlisted.[20] Canning's co-operation is evident from his diplomatic activity. Wilberforce later recognized this while, characteristically, taking all the credit for initiatives himself. 'Canning is, and to do him justice has always been, as earnest as we could desire in looking out for openings for making the attempts I have had in view.'[21]

Wilberforce added his voice again to the diplomatic effort in 1809 in a personal letter to the Marquis of Wellesley before the latter left on his mission to Spain. After pointing out how important it was that other nations should follow the British example in abolishing the trade, Wilberforce outlined what he foresaw as the primary task: 'The great object should be to communicate as generally as possible, and especially among their leading men both in Letters and in Politics the Knowledge of the Nature and Effects of the Slave trade, and of the Abomination in which it was held almost without Exception by every Man of Note in this Kingdom.'[22] An entry in Wilberforce's diary, probably in the summer of 1810, reveals the extent of the co-operation between the then Foreign Secretary and the abolitionists: 'Marquis Wellesley called, and sat with me, and walked in the verandah three-quarters of an hour talking about the Abolition cause in Spain.'[23]

Up to 1810 Britain was unsuccessful in trying to persuade Spain to move toward an abolition of the slave trade. The British government did not press very hard, nor did the abolitionists demand that it should. For the abolitionists, the enforcement of Britain's own laws against the slave trade needed their overseeing vigilance. Their hopes for Spanish abolition rested with the Spanish liberals fighting Napoleon. To the British government, Spain was not the culprit in the slave trade that Portugal was. More important, Britain's political influence in Spain from 1808 to 1810 was preoccupied with the primary aim of winning the war. Spain's domestic political situation encouraged Britain to handle her delicately. On 13 March 1810, Canning, speaking in Parliament after Henry Brougham had moved for papers on the efforts Britain had made to persuade foreign states to abolish the slave trade, pointed out that 'good management' was necessary with Spain. 'There was hardly time to enter into any stipulation with that government with respect to its colonial policy.'[24]

The Cortes debate of 1811

Neither tentative overtures by the government nor the persuasive efforts of the English abolitionists had succeeded in firing the abolitionist cause in Spain. Both the British government and the leaders of the English abolitionist movement, however, remained optimistic and persistent. A list of the subjects of action and deliberation for the abolitionists, drawn up by Wilberforce and dated 3 December 1810, had as point three: 'to consider whether any thing and what can be done to engage the Spanish Cortes and other governing powers in Spain and Spanish America in the cause of Abolition'.[25]

Just after writing this, he went to see Wellesley both about the interpretation of Article 10 of the Portuguese Treaty and about 'the cause of Abolition in Spain'.[26] On 8 December 1810, the Marquis of Wellesley sent new instructions to his brother, Henry, British Ambassador to Spain. Again the precedent of Portugal was quoted. This, along with the liberal flavour of the Cortes, seemed to make it an auspicious moment to request Spain to act herself.

The liberal principles on which the Cortes have acted with regard to the Spanish Colonies in America, lead to an expectation, that the same assembly might be disposed at an early period of time to declare an intention of abolishing the slave trade, in concert with the opinions of the representatives of America, as soon as those opinions can legally be collected.[27]

Wellesley was ordered to use his 'utmost endeavours to inculcate the wisdom and justice' of passing an act against the slave trade. His instructions, though, did not authorize him to bring any pressure to bear either on the government or on the Cortes: 'You will freely offer your counsel and advice, provided you shall have reason to think they will be thankfully received.'[28]

These instructions did not go as far as some abolitionists in Parliament would have desired. Their growing resentment against the foreign slave trade had been revealed the previous summer. After Brougham in the Commons and Holland in the Lords moved in March for papers on the government's efforts to induce foreign countries to follow Britain's abolition of the slave trade, a full debate was held on 15 June 1810 in the Commons and echoed in the Lords on the 18th.[29]

Brougham revealed the extent of the Spanish slave trade, mainly to Cuba, by statistics and advocated the use of British influence to press for abolition. He felt that Spain, in particular, should be only too willing to come to an agreement with Britain in return for Britain's help against Napoleon. Though he realized Cuba would suffer, it would be the only Spanish colony to suffer materially, 'and it was reasonable to expect that the Spanish Government would not refuse this inconsiderable sacrifice'.[30] More vigorous support for this idea came from Joseph Marryat, Colonial Agent for Trinidad and an eminent West Indian planter: 'We should tell those Slave Traders who come to ask for our assistance, that we would not fight for liberty with one hand and for slavery with the other.'[31] Slightly incongruous words from the mouth of a West Indian planter, but they illustrate the deep-felt belief among the British planters that the Spanish slave trade was ruinous to the British West Indian colonies. Writing later, in 1816, Marryat felt the opportunity of persuading Spain to abolish the slave trade during the war had been lost. It could have been demanded then as the price of the alliance. 'We have now reason to regret that we acted with more delicacy to them [Spain] than justice to the inhabitants of Africa.'[32]

Not all abolitionists would go this far. James Stephen, for one, could not agree that Britain could 'warrantably compel' foreign states, even allies to relinquish the slave trade.[33] Even for this expert on international law it was a tricky point. Allies prosecuting the slave trade hindered British efforts to prohibit it and frustrated attempts to civilize Africa. These were strong grounds upon which to negotiate. 'And we had an unquestionable right to make their renouncing the Slave Trade the condition of our further support; though he was not prepared to say that it would be right under the circumstances of the case to do so.'[34] Canning, although not in the government, defended it. He believed the difficulties in abolishing the foreign slave trade had been underrated; the situation of the Spanish government, preoccupied with self-defence and constantly shifting its seat, had to be taken into account.[35]

Impatience with the government's inability to convert other countries to abolition came from the British West Indian planters, jealous of Cuba's prosperity and fearful of their own, and from British abolitionists, frustrated in their attempt to wipe out British participation in the slave trade. The abolitionists were also angry at Americans, whom they accused of using foreign flags to cover slavers operating between Africa and South America.[36] Some foreign slaving expeditions had even originated in London and Liverpool.[37]

But government and abolitionist alike were governed by the priorities of war and the instability of the Spanish government. In broaching the subject of abolition to the Spanish, the British Ambassador was authorized to do nothing more than discreetly persuade. His execution of the instructions was a model of tact, at least as far as the British government was concerned.[38] Before making a representation to the Council of Regency, he sounded the feeling of the Cortes to find out whether an abolition measure could be passed without government interference. The deputies he talked to were all in favour of abolition, but suggested deferring the discussion until the arrival of deputies from Cuba and Puerto Rico.[39]

Abolition of the slave trade and the campaign by Britain to export her humanitarianism were not ignored by the Spanish colony most likely to be affected by a Spanish prohibition of the slave trade. On 24 February 1811 the *Consulado* of Havana, guardian of the economic interests of Cuban merchants and planters, sent a *representación* on the slave trade to Spain.[40] Wellesley's efforts to persuade Spain to abolish the slave trade and the slave trade article in the treaty of 1810 between Britain and Portugal had been duly noted by the Cubans. In the *Consulado*'s memorial they revealed their belief that England was acting from self-interest as well as humanitarianism: 'The British cut off the slave trade so resolutely because they recognized that the proportion of blacks to whites in their islands had, in reality, reached the danger level.'[41] Turning the argument to their own advantage, the *Consulado* then illustrated how Cuba did not face such a serious problem. Slaves in Havana and other big cities of Cuba constituted less than one-third of the population, while the number of free coloured equalled two-thirds the number of whites. Only in areas of *ingenios* and *cafetales* did the number of slaves exceed the other classes of population. But even these *haciendas* were surrounded by populous centres of whites and free coloureds.

After contrasting the composition of Cuba's population with that of the British West Indies, in order to show that Cuba could go on importing slaves for many years without any risk, the memorial pointed out the value of slaves in bald economic facts. Since 1789, 110,000 slaves had been imported at a cost of 33 million pesos. These had helped produce nearly 3 million boxes of sugar which, exported, yielded over 73 million pesos, 'without taking into account the other branches of agricultural production and an infinite variety of smaller industries etc. which slave labour had been instrumental in assisting to grow and prosper'.[42]

Although these were the main justifications for continuing the slave trade to Cuba, the *Consulado* also advanced the spurious argument of the civilizing influence on the Africans and attempted to prove that the more liberal slave code in force in Spanish colonies accounted for Cuba's success in avoiding racial troubles. Fearful of the outcome of British pressure on the Spanish government, the *Consulado* pleaded to be heard before any action by the Cortes.

This plea was in vain. According to Wellesley, the subject was brought forward for consideration in the Cortes shortly after the arrival of the deputies from Puerto Rico and Cuba.[43] The British Ambassador summed up his own role as follows:

I was of the opinion that it would be more suitable to the character of Independence, which the Representatives of the People are so anxious to maintain, to leave this important and interesting question to be discussed in their own way, and at their own time, than to press it upon their consideration at a period, when they might perhaps be occupied in discussions, which might appear to them to be of greater moment.[44]

A deputy from New Spain, Miguel Guridi y Alcócer, introduced a resolution against the slave trade into the Cortes on 26 March 1811, but the actual debate on 2 April took place on resolutions submitted by the Spanish liberal, Agustín Argüelles. His resolutions provided for the immediate abolition of the slave trade by Spain and co-operation with Britain to secure a complete prohibition of the trade.[45] Argüelles' resolutions dealt only with the slave trade, but those of Alcócer, introduced again at the end of this debate, brought in the question of slavery itself. An account of the debate by a United States historian, H.H.S. Aimes, implies the Cortes were debating the abolition of slavery, which was not the case, as Argüelles underlined.[46] Confusion about the nature of the debate was bound to aid the cause of the Cuban planters. As it was, the Cortes did not formally pass the resolutions. A commission of five was appointed to examine them, one of whom was a Cuban deputy and prominent planter.[47] The British Ambassador reported a strong tendency in the Cortes to concur in Argüelles' resolutions, no doubt believing that the commission examining them would reflect the opinions of the Cortes.[48] But this delaying action gave the Cuban planters and merchants an opportunity to display their adamant opposition.

When news of the debate reached Havana it caused a sensation. The Captain-General immediately wrote to the Cortes, warning of the results of the abolition of the slave trade and describing Havana's reaction to the news of the debate. Before accounts of the debate reached Havana, the topic of conversation was a subscription to help the Spanish armies: 'now no one talks of anything but the Cortes debate'.[49] The Captain-General implied that abolition of the slave trade might cause the loss of the island and, equally frightening, turn it into another Haiti. William Shaler, the United States commercial agent in Havana in 1811, confirmed the hysterical reaction of the Cuban planters to news of the Cortes debate. He reported to Washington that an extraordinary session of the Havana *Cabildo* met for two evenings and among the proposals discussed was one calling for immediate separation from Spain. Some of the Cuban planters then began making overtures to Shaler about joining the United States which he was not unwilling to receive. The planters, represented in these discussions by José de Arango y Núñez del Castillo, a former treasurer of Havana and a cousin of Arango y Parreño the economist, fearing that Spain in her weakened condition could not protect their interests were prepared to turn to the United States.[50] When nothing more was heard about abolishing the slave trade, both the fear of the planters and their interest in annexation died down, but this was not to be the last time that threats, real or imagined, against Cuban slavery would push Cuban planters in the direction of annexation to the United States.

Cuban anger was not only directed at the Cortes for being in favour of the abolition of the slave trade; the Cubans denied the authority of the Cortes to debate such a major colonial question because its representation was heavily balanced in favour of Peninsular Spaniards and, therefore, unsatisfactory to the Cubans as well as to other Spanish Americans. Nor did the opposition of the Cortes to the right of the Spanish Americans to unrestricted trade with foreigners help to make its attitude on the slave trade any more palatable to the Cuban merchants who had enjoyed unrestricted trade through extended periods of the American revolutionary wars and the Napoleonic wars.[51]

Against this threat to the livelihood and even the existence of

Cuba, the Havana *Ayuntamiento, Consulado* and the *Sociedad Económica* united in protest. Their memorial, which Arango y Parreño edited and presented, opposed both the resolutions introduced into the Cortes and the public debate on such an explosive subject.[52] Basically, the memorial was a plea for the continuance of the slave trade, a trade permitted to Cuba almost from its beginnings as a Spanish colony and, therefore, hallowed by prescription as well as by royal consent. As might be expected from the three bodies that presented the memorial, its main arguments were economic. 'There is not one plantation on this Island with a full complement of slaves.'[53] Not only did plantations lack slaves, none had an equal proportion of females and, thus, ending the slave trade would cause the rapid decline of the slave population on the plantations.[54] The planters argued with a warped humanitarianism that only by continuing the slave trade would there be any chance of avoiding a condition óf perpetual celibacy for the majority of male plantation slaves. A modern Cuban historian has characterized this memorial as 'the first of the great ideological documents of the sugarocracy and perhaps the most important because it was the most sincere. And perhaps also the most tragic and the most cynical.'[55]

The Cuban planters pointed to the English precedent of appointing a Committee of the Privy Council to investigate the whole problem and claimed they were being condemned unheard.[56] While the Spanish liberals who supported the motion looked to England's example in abolishing the slave trade, the Cuban planters had learned the methods of those opposed to the English abolition, an opposition that delayed the abolition for twenty years. Nothing more was heard of Argüelles' resolutions. Contemporaries and historians alike agree that colonial pressure forced them to be dropped.[57] Some Cuban historians have also pointed out that a slave rebellion in Cuba in 1812, known as the conspiracy of Aponte, was a direct result of the controversy in Spain over the abolition of the slave trade.[58] This causation, certainly believed at the time, was not likely to make Cubans more amenable to abolition the next time it was brought up.

One of the first Spanish liberals to speak out against the slave trade in the nineteenth century, Isidoro de Antillón y Marzo, who had read a dissertation against slavery to the *Real Academia Matritense de Derecho Español* in 1802, tried to bring up the question of colonial slavery in the Cortes in 1813.[59] Once again the efforts of Arango y Parreño were successful in persuading the Cortes to bury the issue.

The slave trade and Spanish bureaucracy, 1809–13

Away from the public clamour of the Cortes the slave trade was also being considered in the labyrinthine passages of a Spanish bureaucracy hampered by its confinement in Cadiz. As had happened before, the issue was raised by a despatch from the Intendant of Havana. He wrote to the Minister of Finance on 17 October 1809 to draw to the latter's attention the fact that the permission to introduce slaves into Cuba, given to foreigners by the royal *cédula* of 22 April 1804, would expire in April 1810.[60]

The shortage of African slaves for plantation labour was as chronic as ever and, because of this scarcity, the sugar and coffee estates in the area surrounding Havana were not producing to capacity. The Intendant advocated the continuation of the privileges extended to foreign slave traders in 1804, with some additional concessions in order that Spaniards could be drawn in to participate in the slave trade themselves. Now that Britain and the United States had prohibited slave-trading by their nationals only clandestine expeditions would come to Cuba. Necessity demanded that Spaniards and Spanish colonists enter the slave trade on a scale large enough to supply the needs of Spanish colonies.

His principal new proposal was therefore designed to stimulate Spanish slaving expeditions. It amounted to a modified form of free commerce. Any Spaniard would be allowed to export in Spanish ships 'merchandise, produce and assets' to any foreign country or colony and there exchange these for supplies needed in the slave trade. The Spanish ships would then return to their home ports and the supplies they brought would be used in outfitting slaving expeditions direct to Africa. All the articles or goods involved in this three-way process of export, import and re-export would be free of any duties, but former restrictions prohibiting the importation from foreign colonies of goods not destined for the slave trade would still apply. The Intendant's other proposed additions were mainly repetitions of hitherto ineffective suggestions such as orders that a third of all slave cargoes be female so as to improve domestic reproduction.

The Intendant's despatch was referred to the Council of the Indies for a report on 8 July 1810.[61] After nearly a year without a reply, the Minister of Finance reminded the Council of the problem on 5 April 1811.[62] Upon investigation, the Council discovered that the Intendant's despatch had been added to an *expediente* on the problem of *comercio libre*.[63] Since all the documents relating to the slave trade had also gone into the *expediente*, another set had to be copied before the normal process of consultation could begin. This was authorized on 19 April and, as was the practice, the question was then referred to the *Contaduría General* for an opinion.[64]

The *Contaduría* noted in its report of 19 August 1811 that the question of the slave trade had been taken up by the Cortes.[65] All recommendations had to bear in mind the possibility of a definite pronouncement on the slave trade by the Cortes in the proposed Constitution or earlier. Nevertheless, the *Contaduría* was not afraid to expose the many dangers inherent in the Intendant's proposed additions to the 1804 *cédula*. The greatest was the danger of contraband by Spanish merchants who would take advantage of the Intendant's plan to stimulate direct Spanish slave-trading to Africa. In many ways this idea was impractical and the modifications suggested by the *Contaduría* amounted to a veto. But the *Contaduría* saw no harm in extending the privileges granted to foreigners by the 1804 *cédula* for a further eight or ten, or even more years.

With the recommendation of the *Contaduría* before him, the *Fiscal* of the Council of the Indies thought that the *Consulado* of Cadiz ought to be asked for its opinion, since the Intendant's proposals had included the free export of Peninsular goods to be exchanged in foreign countries or colonies for articles needed in the slave trade.[66] The Council agreed[67] and, accordingly, on 28 September 1811 the *Consulado* of Cadiz was asked to report on the suggestions of the Intendant of Havana for stimulating and enlarging Spanish participation in the slave trade.[68]

The *Consulado* did not reply and here the matter rested. With no permission for foreigners to continue the slave trade under the conditions of the 1804 *cédula*, their right to do so had legally expired in April 1810. This apparently did not bother anyone in Havana; a fact to which the monthly figures of slaves imported into Havana give ample testimony. For example, the figures for the nine months, March – November 1811, reveal that of 27 slavers disembarking 5,327 slaves, 4 were Portuguese and 2 were Swedish.[69] The real nationality of the remainder is almost impossible to determine, but it is certain that not all were Spanish.

The tremendous influx of African slaves into Cuba and the resulting disproportion between Africans and Europeans (a factor very much in the minds of Cuban and Peninsular colonial officials) was called to the attention of the Minister of Finance in May 1812 by the despatches of the Havana Intendant. These detailed the number of African slaves landed at Havana from December 1811 to March, 1812.[70] Over 2,000 had entered in these months alone.

Once again the issue of the slave trade was turned over to the Council of the Indies, even though the Council had not yet replied to the previous request. This time the Council was asked to look at the question of the introduction of slaves into all parts of Spanish America with a view to 'reconciling the security of all the provinces and Islands which the nation has confided to you with the prosperity of their agriculture and commerce'.[71] The question was promptly referred to the *Contaduría* and to the Council's *Fiscal*.[72] Back came the reply that all the papers on the slave trade were still with the *Consulado* of Cadiz which apparently had not bothered to report on the slave trade query which had been sent to it in September 1811.[73] The Council, now in some consternation, ordered on 6 June that the *Consulado* send its report with the documents in four to six days, or return the documents alone.[74] The *informe* of the *Consulado* arrived with the documents on 19 June 1812.[75]

Although not strictly relevant to the problem of the slave trade in its new context, the *Consulado's informe* is worth looking at since it advocated a gradual prohibition of the slave trade. The *Consulado's* opinion, quite opposed to that of all the Cuban planters and officials, was that the slave trade was not responsible for Cuban prosperity; on the contrary, it could be the agent of Cuba's downfall. The solution was not the importation of more slaves, but a policy to persuade the Europeans to work in the plantation fields and lessen the island's dependence on African slave labour. The humanitarianism of the *Consulado* is at first sight surprising. One plausible explanation for this is that the original proposals of the Intendant of Havana smelt too much of free trade with foreigners to be to the *Consulado's* liking.

The *Consulado's* delay in complying with the orders of the Council of the Indies had a greater significance in June 1812 than its previous dilatoriness. By the time the *Consulado's informe* with the vital slave trade documents reached the Council of the Indies, the latter was no longer in being. It was abolished by the Constitution of 1812 and its functions were transferred to an enlarged Ministry of Finance. So the accumulation of papers on the slave trade passed from the now defunct Council of the Indies to the Ministry of Finance in the summer of 1812.[76]

Here the slave trade *expediente* was united to one on the question of Spanish emigrants from Louisiana. What did these two subjects have in common? The issue of the slave trade was really whether to prohi-

bit it or not. If it was prohibited the Spanish authorities faced the
difficulty of increasing the labour force of Cuba without the constant
accretions from the slave trade. Whether the slave trade was prohibited or not, it was very desirable 'that the number of proprietors be
much greater than the number of slaves'.[77] One possible solution lay
in the immigration of Spanish colonists from Louisiana. Permission
had been given to Spaniards living in Louisiana to settle in any
Spanish-American province by a royal order of 24 September 1803,
but it had been suspended by a royal order of 12 November 1811.[78]

The now connected subjects of the slave trade and Louisiana emigration were referred to a *Comisión de Hacienda* which, after some delay
due to the need to locate the relevant documents, reported on
13 November 1812.[79] The *Comisión's* report was incorporated in a report of the Council of State dated 18 November 1812.[80] Both bodies
clearly perceived the dilemma. 'The Commission views the slave trade
with the same horror which all sensible men have always felt.' But to
prohibit the slave trade and, in particular, the introduction of African
slaves into Cuba 'would have an overwhelming impact on Cuban agriculture and commerce by depriving the island of the needed labour
which the slave trade supplies'.[81]

Both equally shied away from a solution. Banning the importation
of slaves into Cuba would be such a radical innovation that it needed
not only more consideration but more information before a decision
could be taken. The recommendations of the *Comisión de Hacienda* and
the Council of State were that the *Diputaciones Provinciales* from the
colonies concerned be asked for reports on the composition of the
population and the means of overcoming the shortage of labour
should the slave trade be abolished. Most important, the *Diputaciones
Provinciales* were to be asked whether the slave trade ought to be
prohibited or continued. In a similar manner the question of emigrants
from Louisiana was referred to the *Diputaciones Provinciales* of New
Spain and Cuba. An anonymous *Nota* summed up the attitude of the
Council of State in a paragraph: 'The Council does not dare to give
orders to prohibit the slave trade because of the effect on agriculture,
nor can it sanction the traffic for political reasons, nor can it authorize
the replacement of slaves by emigrants from Louisiana for similar
reasons and, thus, it has asked for reports from overseas.'[82] A royal
order, embodying the recommendations of the report of the Council
of State, was sent out to all the provinces of Spanish America on 1 May
1813.[83] Acknowledgements of the receipt of this order were received,
but there is no evidence of compliance with its provisions.[84]

The last chance had gone to treat the complex issues created by Cuba's dependence on the slave trade for her labour supply as a strictly Spanish colonial problem. Abolitionism, clothed mainly in foreign garb, was bringing a highly charged, emotional content to a question which formerly had been imperial and economic. While the meandering slowness of a bureaucracy confined in Cadiz masked the inability of overworked colonial officials to come to grips with the complex enigma presented by the slave trade, the strident reactions of the Cuban planters to the Cortes debate of 1811 had revealed the strength of the opposition to any proposal implying alterations to the status quo of the slave trade. Henceforward, the Spanish government, motivated only by its desire to retain the ever more profitable colony of Cuba, would be squeezed by the conflicting forces of Cuban desires and British abolitionist pressures. The mainland revolutions quickly narrowed the scope of the slave trade to the confines of Spain's Caribbean islands, but it was no less intractable for this. Spain had thrown away the initiative and the British government, forced by British public opinion, was about to take it up.

CHAPTER 3

Legality and illegality

Force was not one of the weapons in Britain's diplomatic bag of pressures to secure Spain's prohibition of the slave trade.[1] At the same time the British government was not prepared to tolerate the evasion of British laws against slave-trading, either by British subjects engaging in the foreign slave trade or by foreigners smuggling slaves into British possessions.

Two cases, one before the Privy Council and one before the High Court of Admiralty in 1811, showed how far courts would support officers enforcing British laws. In the first, the case of the *Amedie*, a United States ship believed to be engaged in the slave trade to Cuba, it was stated that since the slave trade had been totally prohibited by Parliament, and pronounced contrary to the principles of justice and humanity, *prima facie* the trade was illegal. It was then up to the claimants to prove by their own laws, assuming they were not British, the trade was not prohibited.[2]

This principle was used as a weapon against United States participation in the Atlantic slave trade. In a later case the *Amedie* judgement was interpreted as saying: 'that the slave trade carried on by a vessel belonging to a subject of the United States is a trade which, being unprotected by the domestic regulations of their Legislature and Government, subjects the vessels engaged in it to a sentence of condemnation.'[3] Yet it was also laid down in the *Amedie* decision that: 'This country has no right to control any foreign legislature that may think fit to dissent from this doctrine, and to permit to its own subjects the prosecution of this trade.'[4] The judgement in the case of the *Diana* confirmed this. 'The courts of this country will respect the property of foreigners in the slave trade, under the sanctions of the laws of their own country.'[5]

With the almost universal view in Britain that the Spanish slave trade was carried on by non-Spaniards, chiefly American and British, using the Spanish flag as a cover, legal recognition of a Spanish slave trade existed only in theory. In practice, any slaver flying the Spanish flag might be seized and taken in to a Vice-Admiralty court for trial. There the onus would be on the captain and crew to prove they were really Spanish and not American or British operating under false colours. The Vice-Admiralty courts were not liable to quibble over fine points of law. In one decision at the Vice-Admiralty court in Sierra Leone in 1810, the sentence declared: 'that the slave trade, from motives of humanity, hath been abolished by most civilized nations and is not at present time legally authorized by any'.[6] This statement was quite an exaggeration in 1810 since three countries, which had been and still were sizeable participants in the Atlantic slave trade – Portugal, Spain and France – legally authorized it.

It soon became clear that the enforcement of British laws would bring Cuban objections, for who could tell the difference between a fraudulent use of the Spanish flag and a legal Spanish voyage? Orders issued to a British officer by the Governor of Sierra Leone in June 1810 illustrate how wide the net of capture was spread.[7] He was to detain all American vessels with slaves on board, any vessel with slaves belonging wholly or in part to British subjects and all Spanish and Portuguese vessels really the property of Englishmen or Americans; any foreign vessels which had fitted out for the slave trade at a British port or which had received provisions from a British ship were also liable to be seized. But, 'all vessels, *bonâ fide* Spaniards or Portuguese, and navigated by and under the direction of Subjects of those nations, are not to be molested'.[8]

The Havana *Consulado*, in a memorial of 24 February 1811, complained to the Spanish government of seizures of Cuban slave ships by British warships.[9] Taking advantage of favourable opportunities, Havana merchants had sent out 70 expeditions from December 1808 to February 1811, but some of these had been detained by the British and taken to the Vice-Admiralty court in Sierra Leone. Condemnations resulting from these seizures, the memorial complained, lacked proof or were founded on the pretext that foreigners were involved in expeditions. What the *Consulado* did not say, of course, was that most of the expeditions had been successful.[10]

Further evidence of the Cubans' dissatisfaction came from the observations of an Englishman in Havana later in the year. After outlining cases of seizures of Spanish slavers by English warships he had heard of, he went on: 'these are their great causes of complaint against England who, they say, instead of acting the part of an ally by protecting their Merchant Vessels when engaged in a Trade permitted by the Laws of Spain treats them as bad as their avowed enemies the

French'.[11] The grievances of the Cubans were laid before the British government by the Duke of Infantado, Spanish Ambassador in London, in December 1811.[12] Both in this, and in an earlier Note,[13] he pointed out the obvious: that since the slave trade was not prohibited by Spanish law no British tribunal had a right to apply British laws to Spanish ships. Little sympathy was shown by the British government to these and other similar complaints in 1812. They were referred to the King's Advocate, whose only advice was that any injustice could be remedied by appealing the decision to a higher court in Britain.[14] Portugal had also protested vigorously against British seizures of Portuguese slavers. The British Foreign Secretary, Castlereagh, gave the same reply to Portugal as he did to Spain. Seizures of Portuguese vessels, however, were based on the British interpretation of the treaty of 1810 between Britain and Portugal, and Britain's assumed right to enforce Portuguese law.[15]

Wilberforce, who was also asked for his opinion, thought that the Spanish Ambassador ought to submit a detailed list of the seizures he complained about. These could then be checked. Sceptical of the genuineness of these complaints, Wilberforce believed that, even though the ships were under 'Spanish Colours', they were really American or British. 'Indeed the Circumstance that hitherto not a single Appeal has taken place, is a strong presumptive argument in favour of the above Supposition.'[16] The British authorities, prodded on by the abolitionists, were far more concerned with stamping out British and American participation in the Atlantic slave trade. Their humanitarian concern with Americans involved in the trade was not appreciated in the United States where maritime grievances with Britain were a large factor in provoking the Americans to declare war in 1812.[17] Complaints by Spanish colonists over apparent high-handed treatment by British naval officers and British Admiralty courts paled beside the enormous criminality of the slave trade these same colonists perpetrated.

Brougham had fulminated against the Spanish slave trade to Havana in June 1810, pointing out the involvement of British and American capital and ships.[18] At an interview with the Foreign Secretary on 5 July 1810, Brougham, accompanied by Wilberforce and two others, presented documents proving that Tenerife was being used as a rendezvous for foreign ships engaged in the slave trade to Havana. Here Spanish colours and documents were obtained from Spanish officials, and slavers set off with two or three nominal captains 'to suit all Circumstances which may occur'.[19] The anonymous informant went on to say that, as the practice was lucrative to Spanish officials in Tenerife as well as facilitating a desirable colonial purpose (the importation of slaves into Havana), action by the British government was urgently needed to stop it.

Apparently nothing was done then but, by the spring of 1811, the abuse was becoming intolerable not only to the abolitionists but to the Cabinet as well. The War Department sent instructions to the Foreign Office on 23 April 1811, on how Spain should regulate her slave trade. These were to be forwarded to the Spanish government.[20] It is doubtful whether these regulations would have been favourably regarded in Spain even if they did seem sensible to the British War Office. They provided that Spanish subjects would only supply slaves to Spanish colonies, no foreign slave traders were to be allowed the protection of the Spanish flag, only certain enumerated ports would be allowed to send out ships on slaving expeditions and these expeditions were to be confined to south of the equator; finally, British officers were to be allowed to enforce these regulations.

The Marquis of Wellesley had already prepared a despatch for his brother in Cadiz when he received the War Department's suggestions. They were not, therefore, sent on to Spain, but they reveal the extent to which one important part of the British government was prepared to go. While not as dictatorial in tone, the Foreign Secretary's instructions left no doubt that Britain would not tolerate what she regarded as evasions of her own laws. Gone was the discreet language of persuasion used earlier to convince Spain that abolition was the right course. 'The Subject of this Despatch admits of no delay, and the object of these Instructions cannot be denied or evaded with any Semblance of Justice.'[21]

The British Ambassador was directed to require Spain to take all necessary action to curb the use of Spanish colours and documents by British and American slavers. Co-operation of British cruisers and diplomats was to be offered in implementing any regulations the Spanish government chose to adopt. But the sting lay in the tail of the despatch. If there was any sign of avoidance of the issue or delay, Wellesley was to state that British Admiralty Courts would administer the law 'in the most effectual manner'.[22] Captures of suspicious vessels with Spanish papers and colours would be lawful unless there was positive proof 'that the whole concern, Vessel, cargo, and capital employed are *bonâ fide* the property of Spanish subjects, and the Vessel is navigated by Spanish Seamen'.[23]

The Spanish reply was conciliatory, but admitted no knowledge of practices said to be going on at Tenerife. Nevertheless, 'the most positive orders' would be sent to the authorities at Teneriffe, to prevent any aid being given to 'such a commerce on the part of the English and Americans'.[24]

With the international character of the slave trade to Cuba and the fact that Spain, herself, possessed no African settlement from which slaves could be procured, the existence of a Spanish slave trade could not be anything but incompatible with British policy on the West African coast. A formerly legitimate trade in the eyes of international law had now become illegitimate in the eyes of the only maritime power capable of enforcing international law. However much the Spaniards and Cubans who indulged in the trade, under whatever auspices, believed it was legal, and according to Spanish law it was, they faced the inescapable fact that only British law was being enforced.

In Havana by 1815 the volume of protests over British seizures of Spanish slavers had swelled considerably. Strong representations were made to the British government by the Spanish Ambassador in London, Count Fernán Núñez.[25] Every representation was referred to the Law Officers of the Crown, but the answer was invariably the same; all complaints ought to be put before the higher courts in Britain.[26] Fernán Núñez summed up the position of the Spanish government in a Note of 20 October 1815.[27] He stated that Ferdinand had agreed in the Treaty of July 1814 to recognize the principle of abolition of the slave trade, but reserved the date and methods of accomplishing the abolition to himself. Pressed by the British government to fix a definite limit, a term of eight years from 1814 had been set. Nothing but the principle of abolition had been recognized at the Congress of Vienna, the enforcement of it being left to individual governments. Yet British warships still captured Spanish slavers, taking it upon themselves to enforce a prohibition not yet in existence. They had done this without any legal basis for searching or detaining Spanish ships.

Even this lengthy attack received little notice. The British reply merely stated that English courts would never sanction captures of *bona fide* Spanish ships and suggested that Fernán Núñez submit a list of ships claimed to have been illegally taken.[28] Fernán Núñez complied. He submitted the names of two ships, belonging to a Barcelona merchant, which had been attacked and captured by four boats of the English frigate *Camus* in Old Calabar river on 28 March 1815.[29] They had been encouraged to carry on the slave trade as a result of a decision in the British Court of Appeal the previous summer. Then it had been stated that Britain did not interfere with slave traders, provided they were subjects of a country which permitted the trade, and provided they were not covering others who were prohibited from carrying it on. Again the Spanish Ambassador received no satisfaction. Castlereagh, after receiving the Law Officer's report, replied that the government had no information about such captures and advised the Spanish merchants to take the matter up in British courts.[30]

The Havana merchants and planters not only sent their complaints in memorials to Madrid which eventually reached London: they also appointed an agent to represent them in London and to appeal cases on their behalf. Page, the man selected, wrote a long memorial to the Foreign Office in June 1815. In this document he stated that, since the establishment of the Vice-Admiralty court at Sierra Leone, upwards of 200 vessels belonging to Spanish subjects resident at or engaged in the slave trade with Cuba had been seized and condemned.[31] Because of the difficulties of communication between Sierra Leone and Havana, as well as the fact that captains of slavers taken to Sierra Leone were imprisoned, the period for entering appeals against decisions in many cases had elapsed.[32] Page was hampered in trying to get appeals because the prize money had been distributed as soon as the period for appeal finished. He also accused the authorities at Sierra Leone of malpractices in selling condemned slave ships.

Page's petition, however, was ignored. Early in 1816 he sent another one, this time endorsed by the Spanish Ambassador.[33] His primary request was that the British government allow owners of captured vessels the right of appeal to higher courts after the expiry of the time limit, if it could be proved they were hindered from filing an appeal in time. The Law Officers did not feel there were grounds for the government to interfere with the appeal court, and their opinion was passed on to Count Fernán Núñez.[34] Page tried again in June 1816.[35] Referring to the British government's payment of an indemnity to Portugal for seizures of Portuguese slavers, Page intimated that Havana shipowners would prefer to have their claims settled this way than go to court. The Law Officers disregarded this hint, advising that the treaty with Portugal was a special case and not a precedent. Britain had signed a Convention with Portugal on 21 January 1815, agreeing to pay £300,000 as settlement for all claims of illegal detention and capture of Portuguese vessels by British warships; in return, the Portuguese declared illegal any slave-trading north of the equator.[36] The Law Officers pointed out that British courts of appeal were willing to include appeals from shipowners even when the time for them had expired if there were extenuating circumstances. But even in cases where a court had refused an appeal because the prize money had already been distributed, the government would not interfere.[37]

In September 1816, Page repeated his claim for compensation to be paid to Spanish owners of seized slave ships, but this time the British government laid down the principle it was to follow until the treaty of 1817 between Britain and Spain settled the matter permanently. Such applications for 'favour' could only come from the Spanish government since they would be an object of negotiation and not of right.[38]

Not put off by this concealed rebuff, Page immediately wrote to the Spanish Foreign Minister, Pizarro, and warned him against including any article in a slave trade treaty which would prejudice the interests of Cuban slave traders who might win their appeals in the British High Court of Admiralty.[39] Their cases were a matter of legal right as far as Page was concerned, while compensation for those slave traders who had forfeited their chance to appeal in a British court would be a matter of 'favour' or negotiation between the two governments. His appeal was not without some result. In the final negotiations on the slave trade treaty between Britain and Spain in 1817, the Spanish Foreign Minister used Page's arguments in an attempt to obtain more money from the British. The British Ambassador rejected these additional claims and held to the original British offer which was ultimately accepted.[40]

There was no question of Page's commitment to his cause or of his belief in its essential justice. His campaign amounted to a vendetta against the African Institution which he held responsible for the plight of his 'constituents' as he called them. The African Institution had been founded by leading British abolitionists, headed by Wilberforce, after the passing of the act prohibiting the slave trade within the British Empire. Its aims were to ensure the implementation of the act and to work for the suppression of the foreign slave trade. Page attributed the capture of Spanish vessels to secret instructions of the African Institution which the Institution had persuaded the Lords of the Admiralty to send out to the cruisers operating off Africa. These cruisers were using all the rights of a belligerent power and taking no account of the independent rights of Spanish or Portuguese subjects.[41]

Page did not confine his counter-attack to court actions. He obtained permission from the Colonial Office in 1816 for a Spanish consul to go to Sierra Leone and act on behalf of captured Spanish slave traders.[42] Page even prepared instructions for the man whom he nominated.[43] The nominee, an individual named Sutherland, was to fill in on a form provided by Page details of each case against a Spanish slave trader in the Sierra Leone Vice-Admiralty court and send these forms back to London along with powers of attorney from the masters and super-cargoes of the Spanish slavers. With these documents Page could obtain an appeal within the time allotted by the Prize Act.

Sutherland's second task was to prevent condemned Spanish slavers from being sold in Sierra Leone at rock-bottom prices to members of the Macaulay family. Zachary Macaulay, the abolitionist and father of the historian, Thomas Babington Macaulay, had been one of the first governors of Sierra Leone. He had then returned to London and gone into business as an African merchant with a nephew, Babington. Their firm, Macaulay and Babington, became the prize agent for many of the British naval officers who captured slave ships off the West African coast. Page believed the Macaulays' practice was to bring these slavers to Britain, procure British registry for them and then sell them at a large profit. Sutherland was not to buy these Spanish slavers himself; he was told just to bid the price up to the approximate value of the ship. Lastly, Sutherland was to help the crews of condemned Spanish slavers and see that they were returned to Havana. There is no evidence of any activity by Sutherland in Sierra Leone and, anyway, his position was soon superseded by the Spanish Commissioners to Sierra Leone appointed under the terms of the treaty of 1817 between Spain and Britain.

Page made one last attempt in 1818 to recover direct compensation from the British government for losses suffered by Spanish slave traders operating out of Havana. He petitioned the House of Commons in February 1818.[44] Disclaiming any opposition to the slave trade treaty between Britain and Spain then before the House, he confined himself to asking that compensation be awarded by the British government to any Cuban slave trader who had obtained a favourable verdict from a British Court of Appeal. A slave trader who had been unable to win an appeal hearing would have recourse only to the Spanish government.

If Page's petition had been granted, he stood to collect £187,000 on behalf of his clients. A sympathetic M.P., Dr Phillimore, put his demands before the Commons in the debate on the treaty. The Commons, however, agreed with the British Foreign Secretary, Castlereagh, that all claims should be referred to the Spanish government, even those in which judgements had already been given by

British appeal courts.[45] Spain could decide how to distribute the indemnity. Page's efforts to obtain compensation for the Cuban slave traders from the British government had failed.

Early in 1816 the Spanish Ambassador tried to open negotiations with the British government on a scheme designed to stop abuses by British cruisers. The essence of the plan was that authorized certificates or passports would be given to Spanish slavers enabling them to carry out their voyages immune from British seizures.[46] Castlereagh consulted the Law Officers whose opinion was that if such a scheme could be used to restrict the Spanish slave trade to south of the equator it could be useful. But, as it implied protection to Spanish slave traders, it was undesirable since it would promote the slave trade by lowering insurance costs, and conceivably it would allow Portuguese traders a further protected entry into the Cuban slave trade.[47] Therefore, Fernán Núñez's proposal was officially turned down.[48] Other Spanish overtures on similar lines were also rejected.[49]

Neither the Spanish Ambassador nor the agent of the Havana merchants and shipowners could achieve anything for their clients, the Spanish slave traders to Cuba. The British government was not prepared to make any concessions to Spain over the slave trade until Spain showed a willingness to meet Britain's conditions on its abolition. If there were abuses by British cruisers they could be corrected in the courts. This attitude of the British government overlooked the fact that abuses were bound to occur if only because of 'the very unsettled State of the public law respecting the right of restraining the Slave Trade of Foreign Nations'.[50]

As far as the Spanish slave trade was concerned there was no law or treaty empowering British ships to seize Spanish slave traders before 1817. In the spring of 1816, however, the British government found out that the Spanish *cédula* of 1804, authorizing Spaniards and Spanish colonists to trade in slaves for twelve years, had expired. The term of the *cédula* having expired, the British government assumed that the slave trade was then illegal by Spanish laws: 'and being unsanctioned by the Law of the particular State, all Spanish Vessels engaged in it are liable to detention by the Ships of War of any other Power as engaged in a traffic *malum in se* to which the municipal Law of their own State gives no Sanction'.[51] Slavers that were seized while flying the Spanish flag were normally taken on the pretext that they were not *bona fide* Spanish. The onus of proof was on the captain and crew of the slaver to prove themselves Spanish to the satisfaction of a British Admiralty court. That they should have to appear at all before a British court angered the Spanish and Cuban slave traders, when by Spanish law the slave trade was legal.

Appeals from decisions of the Vice-Admiralty courts were difficult if not impossible for Havana slave ship owners to obtain as their agent pointed out. In the climate of British public opinion no British government could admit abuses or make concessions to foreign slave traders. There was only one solution. Spain must formally renounce the slave trade. Until then British cruisers and British Admiralty courts would be the arbiters of Spanish slave-trading laws.

CHAPTER 4

The treaty of 1817

The Congress of Vienna and Spanish abolition

After Britain's behind-the-scenes role in the Cortes debate of 1811, the British government took no further diplomatic action to persuade Spain to abolish the slave trade until 1814. By then the war was over and British abolitionists were leading a feverish agitation against the slave trade. Their chief aim in the spring of 1814 was to persuade the European powers to agree on a convention to prohibit the slave trade. In a letter to James Stephen on 18 April, Wilberforce summed up his attitude to the Spanish and Portuguese slave trade: 'It happens quite providentially that the only powers which are interested in carrying the Slave Trade on, are Spain and Portugal, and they may surely be compelled into assent.'[1]

The campaign focussed on the task of preventing the revival of the French slave trade. When the abolitionists discovered that in the treaty of peace with France all France's colonies were returned to her in exchange for a promise to give up the slave trade in five years, they were bitterly disappointed.[2] Redoubling their efforts, they roused public opinion in the country and were the instrumental force behind the overwhelming flow of petitions to the House of Commons which protested against the revival of the French slave trade. In thirty-four days beginning 27 June 1814, the House of Commons received 772 petitions with nearly one million signatures.[3] As Webster says, 'the subject was one in which almost the whole nation had become interested. It could not be ignored'.[4] The public campaign had been heralded by unanimous addresses to the Prince Regent from both Lords and Commons on 2 May 1814, asking the British government to obtain a pledge to prohibit the slave trade from all the Allied sovereigns involved in the peace negotiations.[5] As a result of the addresses, a circular despatch was sent to all British Ministers abroad asking them to do their best to prevail upon the governments where they resided to ban the slave trade.

On 17 June 1814, Henry Wellesley, British Ambassador in Madrid, sent home a *projet* of a treaty of alliance between Britain and Spain.[6] One article of this *projet* committed Spain to a general prohibition of the slave trade. Attacked in the Commons by the abolitionists for the peace treaty with France and pressured by public opinion, the Foreign Office would have been only too happy to present a Spanish abolition of the slave trade to Parliament.[7] Wellesley, however, had no doubts that the Spanish government would refuse the article:

> I cannot, however, flatter myself that this Article will be agreed to, for none of the considerations which have determined other Nations to abandon the Slave Trade have sufficient weight with the Spanish Government to induce them to relinquish a traffic which they consider to be essential to the very existence of their Colonies.[8]

Here Wellesley hit on what was to be the nub of the problem in the long and tedious negotiations to follow. Powerful planter and commercial interests in Cuba had convinced the Spanish government that the slave trade was a vital factor in the island's agricultural prosperity, and the Spanish government was not willing to risk Cuba in order to abolish the slave trade.

Wellesley's strategy, in including an article prohibiting the slave trade, was to force some concessions on a gradual abolition. Britain's primary object in signing a treaty of alliance with Spain was to keep her out of France's hands. Spain's attitude was largely determined by her financial state, for she badly needed not only the continuation of the British subsidy, worth £2,000,000 a year in cash and military stores, but she needed a loan as well.[9] Even with these pressing financial needs, the Spanish government was unwilling to include an article on the slave trade in the treaty.[10] Wellesley then framed a modified version and this, after great difficulty and further alteration, was accepted. It was a separate article to the treaty and provided that the King of Spain would not allow his subjects to engage in the slave trade to supply any other than Spanish possessions, nor allow protection of the Spanish flag to foreigners engaging in the slave trade. The original treaty was signed in Madrid on 5 July 1814, and the additional articles on 28 August 1814.[11] Regardless of the views of the abolitionists, the British government would not refuse to sign the treaty because the article on the slave trade was unsatisfactory. But Spain's financial distress was a lever which the British government determined to use ruthlessly, in spite of the British Ambassador's hopes that Britain would provide both a subsidy and a loan.[12]

Castlereagh pointed out the influence of abolitionist pressures in a private letter to Wellesley:

You must really press the Spanish Government to give us some more facilities on the subject of the Slave Trade, else we can do nothing for them, however well inclined; the nation is bent upon this object, I believe there is hardly a village that has not met and petitioned upon it; both Houses of Parliament are pledged to press it; and the Ministers must make it the basis of their policy.[13]

The Duke of Wellington, about to go to Paris as the British Ambassador, had also noticed the effects of the abolitionist campaign:

I was not aware till I had been some time here [London] of the degree of frenzy existing here about the slave trade. People in general appear to think that it would suit the policy of the nation to go to war to put an end to that *abominable* traffic; and many wish that we should take the field on this new crusade. All agree that no favour can be shown to a slave trading country; and as Spain next to Portugal is supposed to be the country which gives most protection to this trade, the interests and wishes of Spain are but little attended to here.[14]

Feeling against the slave trade and the unpopularity in Britain of the Spanish King, Ferdinand, dictated the government's policy which was set out in a despatch from Castlereagh to Wellesley on 30 July 1814.[15] The despatch stated that, unless Spain agreed to prohibit the slave trade north of the equator immediately and abolish it entirely within five years, the payment of the subsidy to Spain would not continue beyond the first of August. As for Spain's request for a loan of $10,000,000, the government could only ask Parliament for this if Spain agreed to an immediate and entire prohibition of the slave trade. The loan was to be on the joint credit of Britain and Spain, but clearly the British government would provide the security.

Wellesley put the British proposals before the Spanish Foreign Minister, the Duke of San Carlos, in August and also informed him that the Pope, after his re-establishment in Rome, intended to use his influence with the Catholic nations of Europe to try to persuade them to abolish the slave trade.[16] The Duke of San Carlos was indignant about the Pope's intention to work for abolition. It was 'inconsistent with his duty as head of the Catholic Church by which he was bound to use his best endeavours to make converts to the Catholic Faith, and that every Negro became a Catholic from the moment he set his foot in any of the Spanish possessions'.[17] British liberals like Lord Holland were cynical about efforts to enlist the

Pope's help. Holland later wrote to Wilberforce, 'I am afraid you will not find his Holiness as much disposed to anathematise rapine and murder committed under the sanction of the powerful Crown of Spain, as to disdain the extravagances of the Catholicks in Ireland.'[18]

In spite of the tempting British bait, the Spanish government refused to give in. It would promise no more than to abolish the trade within five years and, in the meantime, to confine it to ten degrees north of the equator in return for the remainder of the year's subsidy and a $10,000,000 loan. Wellesley's negotiating position had been undermined by a report from the Spanish Ambassador in London, Fernán Núñez, that Britain would be prepared to grant a subsidy for the rest of the year if Spain would agree to confine her trade to a certain part of the African coast. Britain's offer was contingent on Spain also agreeing to abolish the trade within five years, which Fernán Núñez had not mentioned.[19]

Wellesley, far away from the furore created by the British abolitionist movement, was more inclined to be conciliatory to Spain. He suggested that Britain pay the subsidy for the rest of the year and propose the loan to Parliament in return for Spain's agreement to abolish the trade in five years and to confine it meanwhile to south of the equator. The Foreign Office reply could not have been less encouraging, terming Wellesley's proposal as 'totally inadmissible on our part, and you need not hesitate to give them a positive Declaration to that Effect'.[20] The British Prime Minister, Lord Liverpool, reinforced this opinion in a private letter to his Foreign Secretary: 'it would be obviously impossible to give the least countenance to the proposition for a Spanish loan, without a stipulation for the total and immediate abolition of the slave trade'.[21] As the Prime Minister made clear, this was the view of the British Cabinet.

The British Ambassador to Spain, the British government and the abolitionists all believed that the Spanish slave trade was essentially a smuggling trade carried on in foreign ships, but under a Spanish flag.[22] The enforcement of the additional article to the Anglo-Spanish treaty, therefore, would go a long way towards suppressing it. From Madrid Wellesley confirmed this interpretation. 'This is so much felt here, that attempts have been made to alter the Article, and even to get rid of it altogether.'[23] Nevertheless, in September and October 1814, Wellesley returned to the task of trying to wrest further concessions from Spain. Still using the carrot of British financial aid, on instructions from the Foreign Office he now added the stick of a possible boycott of colonial produce by Britain, Russia, Austria and Prussia.[24]

This new approach brought two small concessions, neither of which was at all satisfactory to the British. In return for British financial support, the Spanish Foreign Minister said he would be willing to abolish the slave trade on the African coast except for the region comprising the Guinea coast and finally abolish it after eight years. This offer was interpreted in London as an indication of the revival of the slave trade on the Guinea coast where it was believed to have ceased for several years during the war. Wellesley was ordered, therefore, not to renew the subsidy.[25]

Wellesley had previously noted with some surprise the existence of a very powerful interest in Spain against abolition:

otherwise such are the pecuniary distresses of the Government that I do not think they could have resisted the liberal offers of the British Government, as the sum offered by Great Britain would have afforded the necessary relief to their finances, and would have enabled them to provide for their expeditions to America which are suspended for want of means to fit them out.[26]

The main reason for the Spanish refusal to concede more was the risk of discontent in Cuba 'where it is so necessary to the Spanish Interests that tranquillity should be maintained'.[27] Had Spain chosen to sacrifice Cuba and accept British aid, the Latin American independence movements might have taken a radically different course. As it was, the British government was saved the embarrassment of appearing before Parliament as Ferdinand's banker. The position of the government was compromised enough in the eyes of the opposition as a debate on the Spanish subsidy revealed. As a result of this debate, Wellesley did not renew the offer of British monetary aid to Spain in subsequent discussions on the slave trade.[28]

With Wellesley's failure to modify Spain's obdurate attitude, the focus of British efforts shifted to Vienna, although Wellesley continued to press the Spanish government at Madrid. Britain's overall strategy on the slave trade was outlined in a letter from Liverpool to Castlereagh on 9 December 1814. Seeing very little chance of obtaining an agreement for general abolition at the Congress of Vienna, British policy was to support France and, at all costs, to prevent her from allying with Spain and Portugal on the slave trade.[29] As far as Spain and Portugal were concerned, while it would be unfair to expect them to concede more than France, 'we ought to insist, with all the earnestness in our power, upon the *general* adoption of the arrangement already agreed upon between Great Britain and France, that is, the total abolition of the slave trade at the end of five years, and the immediate abolition of it north of Cape Formosa'.[30] Castlereagh addressed a Note to Labrador, the Spanish Ambassador to the Congress, embodying Liverpool's proposal of immediate abolition north of the equator. Labrador, however, had no instructions to negotiate on the slave trade.[31] At the Congress, itself, Castlereagh proposed that the question of the slave trade be dealt with in special sessions.[32] His suggestion won the day in spite of an attempt by Spain and Portugal to have the slave trade discussed as a purely colonial question which would have restricted the number of participants. Castlereagh had enlisted Russian, Austrian and Prussian support, all non-colonial powers.

At four conferences the most the British Foreign Secretary could achieve was a declaration against the slave trade and a qualified agreement to set up a permanent commission to effect the abolition.[33] The Spanish Ambassador signed the declaration but he made it clear in a blunt statement that, since the Spanish government regarded abolition as a matter for individual states, its signature would not commit it to any definite action. Spain was bound by a promise given by Ferdinand to deputies from 'His American Provinces' that they could continue the slave trade for eight years. The Spanish Ambassador to the Congress had earlier given Spain's justification for an eight year extension. During the war Spain's colonies had been almost completely prevented from supplying themselves with slaves. Now that the war was over Spain had a duty to her colonies. Labrador then compared the ratio of whites to slaves in Jamaica to that in Cuba, as further evidence that Cuba lagged behind the other West Indian islands in its supply of slaves. When asked to agree to restrict the trade to south of the equator, Labrador informed the Conference he had no instructions on the point. He was more definite on the question of setting up commissions to oversee the abolition of the slave trade. He doubted Spain would even participate and she certainly would not recognize the committee's jurisdiction to dictate conditions of abolition to individual countries.

At the second to last special conference, Castlereagh, frustrated in his efforts to modify Spain's position by negotiation, invited all the powers present to agree publicly that five years was the maximum time the slave trade would be allowed to continue. If after five years any nation still carried it on, the others would boycott its colonial produce. Seeing this for what it was, a thinly veiled threat against Spain, Labrador warned that any country which boycotted Spain's colonial produce would face prohibitive tariffs on its most valuable exports to

Spain. Although Spain signed the declaration against the slave trade at Vienna, in fact she conceded nothing. Castlereagh realized this but he felt little would be gained by prolonging the discussions. He believed more could be achieved by separate negotiation after the publication of the Vienna proceedings and declaration had given moral force to Britain's argument.[34]

Meanwhile the British Ambassador in Spain, Henry Wellesley, continued discussions with Cevallos, successor to the Duke of San Carlos as Spanish Foreign Minister, in an attempt to get further concessions.[35] But Cevallos would not budge. He said the Spanish government was constantly receiving memorials from Havana of the difficulties arising from the scarcity of slaves. Ferdinand dared not cede any more 'without endangering the safety of the Island of Cuba'.[36] Cevallos did use the excuse of the Congress to evade sending replies to Wellesley's Notes of 20 January and 13 February. A further representation in the summer of 1815 was no more successful. Finally on 18 July, Cevallos replied that the King had referred the whole problem of the slave trade to the Council of the Indies.[37] With that Wellesley had to be content and he returned home on leave.

In spite of Spain's obduracy, the British government was satisfied with the slave trade negotiations at Vienna. The abolitionists were also pleased.[38] A treaty with Portugal meant that Spain, alone of the former European slave trading powers, refused to restrict her slave-trading to south of the equator. The British Prime Minister, Lord Liverpool, regarded Spain's attitude as 'mere perverseness'.[39] Only Spain and Portugal held out for an eight year continuation of the slave trade. While Congress diplomacy had failed to shake Spain's attitude, it provided Britain with strong moral support to back her private efforts.

Final negotiations, 1815–17

After the Congress of Vienna Spain was the only substantial European power that still claimed the right of unrestricted slave-trading on the coasts of Africa. This claim was intolerable to British public opinion, unanimous in its denunciation of the slave trade, and to Castlereagh's diplomacy, the avowed aim of which was the international prohibition of the slave trade.

Towards the end of 1815 and the beginning of 1816, everything pointed to an increase rather than a diminution of this trade, an increase in a new and dangerous form. Consuls' reports from Spain in 1816 told of numerous armed slavers fitting out in Spanish ports.[40] A memorial from merchants in Sierra Leone revealed that Spanish slavers, in reprisal for seizures by British cruisers, were coming to Africa armed and determined to resist capture with force. They were also reported to be destroying all trading craft they met. The merchants complained they were being excluded from the trade of a large section of the African coast by these armed Cuban pirates.[41] Not only were the merchants excluded from the African trade by slave traders, they were undersold as well.[42] Piracy by ships flying Spanish colours and armed resistance to British cruisers were also reported by British naval officers.[43] Equally strong reasons for attacking the Spanish slave trade lay on the other side of the ocean. As long as a flourishing trade in slaves to Cuba existed, British officials would be unable to prevent some of these being smuggled into the British West Indian colonies.[44] This combined pressure on the government reflected itself in renewed British diplomatic activity in Madrid.

Napoleon's brief resumption of power in 1815 had helped the cause of abolition, for he prohibited the French slave trade without any qualifications. Castlereagh was able to ensure that Louis XVIII would ratify Napoleon's abolition law when he regained his throne. The British Minister then in charge of the British Embassy in Madrid, Vaughan, was instructed to make a new overture in August 1815, when he announced France's decision to abolish the slave trade to the Spanish government. In a long Note, he reiterated the British desire for a general abolition north of the equator.[45] This argument had little effect upon the Spanish Foreign Minister who countered with the pressure Cuba and Puerto Rico were putting on the Spanish government. Vaughan's Note, along with previous British ones, was sent to the Council of the Indies. Nothing more was achieved in 1815 since Castlereagh was not inclined to press further.[46]

The Council of the Indies did not present its report until February 1816. A majority recommended the immediate abolition of the slave trade, along with a demand to Britain that she restore captured slave ships and indemnify individuals who had suffered from the actions of British cruisers. This majority report emphasized that the Spanish slave trade had been permitted with great reluctance and subject to restrictions. After 1789 Spaniard and foreigner alike were free to engage in it, but for periods of time and under conditions fixed by successive royal *cédulas*. The report observed that the slave trade, in addition to being opposed to the dictates of religion, carried with it serious risks of slave revolts. Possibly for this reason, and because recent import statistics told a different story, the majority of the Councillors were not inclined to take seriously planters' reports of shortages of slaves in Cuba. Labour, however, was recognized as Cuba's great problem, and as a solution this report included a recommendation to encourage white immigration from foreign countries as well as Spain. A minority, including Arango y Parreño, now a member of the Council, dissented. These seven stated that, although they knew Britain possessed sufficient power to force Spain into an immediate abolition, in order not to ruin the planters they believed abolition ought to be gradual. They, therefore, recommended that the slave trade should cease north of the equator immediately, but be permitted to continue south of the equator until 22 April 1821. The signers of the majority report replied, refusing to change their view that abolition of the slave trade ought to be immediate and total.[47] The report of the Council of the Indies then went to the Spanish Council of State which had the choice of accepting either the majority or the minority position.

The British Minister in Madrid, Vaughan, managed to acquire a copy of this report and forwarded it to London. This gave the British government the information that the last *cédula* on the Spanish slave trade had been issued on 22 April 1804 when Spanish subjects were permitted to introduce African slaves into Spanish colonies for a period of twelve years, foreigners for six.[48] The Spanish Ambassador in London soon found out the British government possessed a copy of the report and informed Madrid which caused some embarrassment for the British Minister there who had procured it.[49] It also made things more difficult for the Spanish Ambassador in London, Fernán Núñez, who could not convince the British Foreign Secretary the Spanish Council of State was superior to the Council of the Indies; that even though a majority of the Council of the Indies had recommended immediate abolition of the slave trade, the Council of State was entitled to adopt the minority report calling for abolition south of the equator after five years. The British government now regarded the Spanish slave trade as illegal according to Spanish law since the provisions of the 1804 *cédula* had expired. Vaughan's representation to the Spanish Foreign Minister on 17 February 1816 and later overtures in the same year were based on this belief.[50]

In fact, the Spanish government did not regard the slave trade as legally prohibited even though the *cédula* of 1804 had expired. Fearing this would happen, the *Consulado* of Havana had taken action in time to prevent it. The danger for the Cuban slave traders was that with the ever greater risk of capture by British cruisers no maritime insurance company would insure a slave trader if the royal authorization to continue the slave trade had expired.[51] When the *Consulado* first took up the question they believed the provisions of the 1804 *cédula* would run out on 22 April 1816. An examination of the *cédula*, however, revealed a loophole. The time was to be counted from the day of publication, which in Havana was 31 July 1804. To cover themselves, the *Consulado* asked the Captain-General to authorize a provisional extension of the terms of the 1804 *cédula* until 31 July 1816 and, if no further orders had been received by then, to extend the terms on an *ad hoc* basis. The Captain-General, acting in concert with the Intendant, approved this idea on 29 April 1816 and sent a report of his decision to Spain.[52]

The authorities in Spain felt the decision of the Captain-General ought to be ratified. After the permission granted to foreigners by the 1804 *cédula* to introduce slaves had expired, the Captain-General had allowed a Swedish slaver to introduce 63 slaves into Havana on 12 January 1815. This decision had received royal approval in a royal order of 25 November 1815, amounting to an extension of the provisions in favour of foreigners given in the 1804 *cédula*.[53] It would be unjust not to concede the same privileges to Spaniards. The Spanish Minister of the Indies agreed with his advisers, at the same time warning that this extension must be a temporary measure.[54] Royal orders dated 6 June 1816 and 2 September 1816 were sent out to the Captain-General approving his actions.[55] They also, in effect, prolonged the terms of the 1804 *cédula*.

Further confirmation of the legal continuation of the Spanish slave trade after the expiration of the 1804 *cédula* came in a letter from the Minister of the Indies to the Minister of Finance on 16 September 1815. The latter had written three days previously, saying the customs officers in Spain's American ports were not sure whether the provisions of the 1804 *cédula* still applied. Vallejo, the Minister of the Indies, replied that the privileges conceded by the *cédula* of 22 April 1804 to nationals and foreigners, 'who are employed in the slave trade to our American Dominions remain in force without any change whatever even though no other royal order or *cédula* has extended these privileges and in spite of the fact that the ten year period granted to foreigners has elapsed'.[56] If the slave trade was still legal, it was swaying on shaky foundations. The Cubans knew this. On 26 November 1815, Francisco de Arango y Parreño, the Cuban advocate of an unrestricted slave trade and a member of the Council of the Indies, wrote to the Havana *Consulado*: 'the slave trade is about to fall'.[57] The report of the Council of the Indies was an unwelcome confirmation to the Cubans of just how fast it was falling. The Cuban planters re-doubled their efforts to prevent this from happening and relied upon their powerful allies in Spain to fight a delaying action. They were not disappointed.

No one in the Spanish Council of State held strongly to the slave trade, for when the Spanish Foreign Minister, Cevallos, suggested in a session held on 7 February 1816 that abolition would be the easiest concession to make to Britain at a time when relations between the two countries needed patching up, there was no opposition.[58] After receiving the report of the Council of the Indies, Cevallos drew up a *projet* of a treaty, basing it not on the majority recommendation of immediate and total prohibition but on the minority recommenda-tion of immediate abolition north of the equator and abolition south of the equator after five years. In addition to articles containing the above stipulations, two articles were included to guarantee legitimate Spanish slavers freedom from molestation by British cruisers. The draft treaty also included three conditions for the total abolition by Spain in five years. Britain would pay an indemnity of £500,000 to cover losses resulting from British captures of Spanish slavers. A further indemnity of £1,000,000 would be paid by Britain, ostensibly to enable Spain to finance European immigration to Cuba, and Britain would sign a defensive treaty with Spain against the Barbary States on Spanish terms.

The draft was approved by the Spanish Council of State on 27 March 1816, and submitted to the British Minister in a Note of 31 March. Vaughan replied on 4 April before he sent the draft treaty to London.[59] Repeating what he had said in an earlier conversation with Cevallos, he asserted the terms were 'perfectly inadmissible by the British Government'. The demand for an indemnity of £500,000 as compensation to owners of slave ships was not substantiated by any authentic documents, and the proposal that Britain pay £1,000,000 besides was so extraordinary it could only be seen as a bribe. Vaughan concluded that although a majority of the Council of the Indies had reported immediate abolition to be compatible with Spain's 'Interests and welfare', the Spanish government had chosen to adopt the view-point of the minority.

As soon as Castlereagh had received the report of the Council of the Indies, he sent Vaughan new instructions.[60] They were out-dated before they arrived, although they contained one or two new arguments to use on Spain. For example, Castlereagh drew attention to information he had received that the local governments of all Spain's revolted provinces in South America had prohibited the slave trade. Castlereagh's reaction to Cevallos' *projet* treaty was little different to Vaughan's initial impression. Because of Britain's heavy war expenditures and postwar loss of revenue, only 'a reasonable remuneration' for captured slave ships could be admitted. Britain would not include any other payments to Spain or, as Vaughan later put it, 'purchase in any shape the abolition of the slave trade'.[61] Nor would she consider an alliance against the Barbary Powers until Spain had completely abolished the slave trade. After further sessions with Cevallos, haggling over the terms of a possible agreement, the issue was shelved for the summer. Vaughan wrote:

> It is not a measure in which the people or the Ministers or the King of Spain appear to take any interest – They are ignorant of the horrors of this Traffic or insensible to them, and as the prospect of obtaining money from the British Government for any concession on this subject diminishes, the repeated Representations which have been made have less weight with the Spanish Government than the active and continued opposition with which the Abolition of the Slave Trade meets from the Planters of the Island of Cuba.[62]

The planters, apparently with considerable influence in the Spanish Court, offered large sums to be permitted to continue the trade.

Behind the direct diplomatic negotiations lay a propaganda campaign sponsored both by the abolitionists and by the British government. Vaughan saw his task as awakening feeling against the slave trade in Spain and particularly among the King's ministers. Part of this was an effort to bypass the Spanish Foreign Minister whom both Vaughan and Castlereagh believed to be opposed to abolition.[63] Vaughan lobbied every member of the Council of State in July and in August he was in 'indirect communication' with the Dukes of Aragon and Infantado.[64] He even had a hand in having presented to the King a paper containing arguments favourable to abolition. This apparently impressed the King for he sent it to his Council of State.[65]

To aid his campaign, Vaughan wrote to London for copies of an essay on the slave trade, written in Spanish by Blanco White, the editor of the London liberal periodical, *El Español*. The African Institution supplied 200 copies of White's *Bosquexo del Comercio en Esclavos* on 26 October 1816.[66] In Britain the growing feeling of the abolitionists against the continuation of the Spanish slave trade, especially in an area where Britain was trying to abolish it, was illustrated in a pamphlet written by James Stephen, a leading British abolitionist. Referring to Ferdinand's Ministers, he said: 'It would almost seem that the Slave Trade, like the Inquisition, had positive attractions to the perverted taste of these men.'[67] The main purpose of this pamphlet was to justify the right of suppressing Spain's slave trade by force. While force was advocated as a last resort, there was more than a hint that it was time to use it and the advantages of a war with Spain were set out.[68] In a letter to Stephen informing him about the report of the Council of the Indies, Wilberforce observed, 'it appears that Lord Castlereagh made good use of your pamphlet in impressing the Spaniards, and that they are afraid of our quarrelling with them'.[69] There was, however, no unanimity within Britain over the question of using force to suppress the slave trade. Stephen's pamphlet came out in the midst of the controversy about the Registry Bill and, since he was one of its main proponents, opponents of the Registry Bill attacked this as well as his other pamphlets.[70]

Just when these efforts appeared to be on the verge of bearing fruit in Spain, the British Minister found himself foiled. The slave trade problem was removed from the Council of State in September before the Council had come to a decision and negotiations were again placed in the hands of the Spanish Foreign Minister. At a lengthy interview on 16 September 1816, Cevallos put forward modified proposals which were embodied in a Note presented to the British Minister on 20 September.[71] This Note stated that Spain would abolish the slave trade north of the equator immediately on the same terms and under the same limitations as Portugal and south of the equator five years after ratification. In return, Britain would pay £500,000 compensation for losses as a result of the action of British cruisers and renounce the right of visit south of the equator during the period the trade remained legal. She would also be invited to join the alliance against the Barbary States.

Referring the terms back to London, Vaughan included an analysis of the pressures operating for and against abolition. He felt the King and certainly some of his Ministers favoured it to conciliate Britain, but the pressures from Cuban and Puerto Rican planters were such that without 'a liberal compensation' immediate abolition was out of the question. A rumour existed that the planters of Havana had offered the Spanish government $2,000,000 for permission to continue the trade and $500,000 for every year the permission continued. Vaughan himself believed that no compensation ought to be given

until Spain agreed to immediate abolition. Compensation need not
be entirely in money. Spain would probably accept some in military
stores. Earlier in the summer Vaughan had reported that Spain
might be willing to receive some of Britain's old troop transports.[72]
Clearly the whole problem of compensation was bound up with
Britain's attitude to the Spanish American revolutions. As became
apparent later, Castlereagh was unwilling to appear in Parliament in
the guise of the financier of a Spanish expedition to South America.

Castlereagh used his absence from London and the Parliamentary
recess as an excuse to delay answering the Spanish proposals.[73]
Since the spring he had been trying without success to get Spain to
send a delegate to the conference of Allied Powers in London. This
came into being as a result of the second additional Article of the
Treaty of Paris and one of the aims of the conference was an effective
agreement on the abolition of the slave trade. Like earlier international efforts, it was frustrated by the refusal of Spain and Portugal
to co-operate. Castlereagh, nevertheless, wanted to consult with the
Allied Powers before answering the Spanish proposals, since he had
managed to obtain renewed agreement on total abolition by May 1819
with the threat of a boycott of colonial produce to enforce it.[74]

By the autumn of 1816, the frustrated anger of the abolitionists was
matched by the cynicism of the diplomats. Discussing the recently
concluded conference at London, Castlereagh stated that Spain's
stipulation to limit her slave-trading to within ten degrees north of
the equator could not possibly come within the Vienna principles. He
believed Spain had limited its trade to this area, 'because perhaps
Slaves might be rendered somewhat Cheaper there, by all other
Nations agreeing to Spare that part of the Coast'.[75] Vaughan, on his
part, suggested that if Britain did not find Spain's terms acceptable,
she ought to dictate her own as an ultimatum.[76]

Spain's terms were never formally answered. Frustration, cynicism,
anger – the British mood of the fall did not have time to coalesce into
more severe action before Spain once again presented a different proposal. Gone now was Cevallos, a definite obstacle in British eyes,
replaced by Pizarro as the new Spanish Foreign Minister. The latter
was more conciliatory to Britain, even if, in the respective states of
both countries' finances, money would still be the stumbling block.
On 30 November, Vaughan received Pizarro's Note containing the
new offer, approved by the Spanish Council of State two days previously.[77] Spain now agreed to the total abolition of the slave trade in
1819, with a further term to be agreed on for completing expeditions.

Abolition north of the equator would take place immediately. England was to pay £400,000 at the signing of the treaty, both as compensation to the Spanish colonies giving up the slave trade and as compensation to owners of captured vessels.

In a separate Note of the same date, Pizarro stipulated that the British government grant a loan to Spain of £700,000 on securities to be furnished by Spain.[78] A second separate Note made clear that acceptance of the loan proposal was connected with proposals for the abolition of the slave trade.[79] Commenting on the connection between the loan and the proposals to abolish the slave trade, Vaughan wrote, 'the object however of treating these two questions in separate Notes is evidently to avoid the refusal of one of the proposals, involving absolutely that of the other'.[80] Vaughan reported that General Castaños, Governor of Catalonia, was the man responsible for the moderation of the Spanish attitude. Worried about the state of Spanish foreign relations, Castaños had persuaded the King that Britain's friendship was vitally necessary and the best way to cement it would be the abolition of the slave trade.[81] The British Minister, however, was over-optimistic when he intimated that refusal of the loan would not prejudice the slave trade negotiations. Like the British Ambassador to Spain, Henry Wellesley, who returned to his post in December, Vaughan was anxious to prevent a Russian–Spanish connection which, in the intrigues of the Russian Ambassador at Madrid, Tatistcheff, seemed likely. This concern and desire for a strengthening of the British–Spanish alliance, as an antidote to Russian influence, led Vaughan to overestimate Spanish willingness to forego the loan.

Castlereagh welcomed the Spanish proposals as a 'conciliatory overture', and authorized the British Ambassador to accept Pizarro's offer as a basis for negotiation.[82] He also gave Wellesley definite instructions on the negotiations. Spain's desire for a loan was not to form part of the talks on abolition and the two issues were to be treated separately. Underlying the question of the indemnity as far as the British government was concerned, was Parliament's willingness to pay. Only an indemnity which had a reasonable chance of success in Parliament could be considered. Castlereagh planned to use the payment of the indemnity to ensure Spanish compliance with the terms of the abolition. Half would be paid when abolition north of the equator came into effect and half when total abolition occurred. He was also prepared to trade a British guarantee not to molest legitimate Spanish slavers south of the equator for Spanish acquiescence in regulations to implement the proposed treaty effectively – essentially a right of search.

In a separate despatch Castlereagh informed Wellesley why a British guarantee of a Spanish loan was impossible. A bad harvest in Britain and Britain's difficult financial situation, combined with Parliament's dislike of all foreign loans, created an unfavourable background. (That very month Britain had been forced to refuse her credit to the French government.) The conclusive reason, though, was the unpopularity of the autocratic Spanish government with both the British Parliament and the British public. Any loan submitted to Parliament would arouse a violent party attack:

the Bill in every stage would be opposed and argued as a covert attempt to impose by force of arms, through the means of our Money, on South America a System which the Spanish Government for its own sake should not propose, to which no great Country can be expected permanently to submit itself, which this Government had uniformly refused to countenance as a Basis of Mediation between Spain and her Colonies.[83]

Early in January 1817, Castlereagh sent a sketch of his plans to enforce the abolition of the slave trade as a guide to Wellesley in drawing up the treaty. By the time his despatch arrived the negotiations were stalemated, but it is worth examining Castlereagh's ideas as they formed the basis of the treaty eventually signed.[84] To ensure enforcement, article five of Castlereagh's *projet* was an agreement for a mutual right of search by Spanish or British warships applicable to any merchant ship of either country suspected of trading in slaves. To prevent abuse of this right of search, all detained vessels were to be judged before a mixed tribunal of both nations, one to be stationed in the West Indies and the other to be placed on the coast of Africa. During the period of legal slave-trading south of the equator, Spanish slavers would carry a passport issued by the Spanish government. With the document slave traders could complete their nefarious voyages unhindered.

Knowledge of Britain's refusal to grant Spain a loan arrived at the Spanish Court before Castlereagh's instructions to Wellesley reached Madrid.[85] Angered at this refusal, Pizarro replied to the formal receipt of Castlereagh's views that the Spanish government had always insisted the loan and Spanish abolition were inseparable. The Spanish proposal had been put in separate Notes only 'to afford the Ministry facilities with Parliament'.[86] In a previous conversation, Pizarro had suggested that, if it was impossible for Britain to grant Spain a loan, this difficulty could be overcome by adding to the proposed in-demnity. Wellesley firmly rejected any increase in Britain's original offer and emphasized that a loan was out of the question. Further consultations with the Spanish Finance Minister, Garay, on the possibility of Britain receiving commercial privileges in exchange for a subsidy, raised the price still higher. On 18 January, Pizarro intimated that Spain would accept £600,000 compensation in lieu of a loan.[87] Here the negotiations bogged down. Britain refused to pay more than £400,000 and Spain would not accept less than £600,000. Throughout the spring the sterile exchange of Notes continued, neither side giving an inch.

In his frustration Wellesley ascribed the blame not to Pizarro, whom he regarded as favourable, but to 'some secret influence to which he feels it necessary to bend, in order to retain his situation'. Yet the British Ambassador still felt Ferdinand would agree to abolition in return for £400,000, if only from Spain's great need of money.

> Your Lordship is too well acquainted with H.M.'s character to expect that he will be induced to consent to this measure upon any principle of justice or humanity, or from any sentiment of friendship for Great Britain, or feeling of gratitude for her past services, or from any motive whatever but personal interest.[88]

Wellesley attributed Spain's attitude to two things. One was the obstinacy of the Spanish Finance Minister; the other was that, as a result of the London riot of 2 December 1816, Spain believed Britain to be on the verge of revolution which would diminish the importance of a British alliance.[89] More important, in the background lurked Cuba. Wellesley reported in March that both Pizarro and Garay dwelt upon the discontent which abolition would cause in Cuba 'which both he [Garay] and M. Pizarro declare to be the most valu-able Settlement now belonging to Spain'.[90]

While the slave trade issue hung fire between the two countries, the other main bilateral issues were affected. Britain would not mediate between Spain and her colonies until Spain abolished the slave trade.[91] Castlereagh, however, did not react with the expected imperturbabi-lity to the rupture of negotiations. He worried for fear that the necessity of justifying Britain's policy in Parliament, in the event of an opposi-tion inquiry, would worsen the already bad opinion of the Spanish government in Britain. He summed up his own feelings in a con-fidential letter to Wellesley in April: 'There is nothing I should be less anxious for on the part of Great Britain than Influence at Madrid, if it were not that the System of the Government towards South America, and upon the point of the Slave Trade embarrasses our own political System'.[92] In May, Castlereagh wrote to his Ambassador in Madrid in order to make clear to the Spanish government that the amount Parliament would be prepared to pay in compensation for abolition, was falling in proportion to the diminution of Spain's influence in South America.[93] Even ardent abolitionists like Wilberforce were no longer willing to pay any price for Spanish abolition.[94]

Spain's international situation was certainly becoming critical by the summer of 1817. News of San Martín's entry into Chile arrived in Britain in May, and probably was known in Spain by then. At the same time the United States was demanding not only the Floridas, but a large section of the Viceroyalty of New Spain from Spain.[95] Spain, alone, was in no condition to meet either threat. Her annual deficit, given in Garay's financial report in June, was well over 400,000,000 *Reales*.[96]

Conscious of Spain's difficulties, Pizarro approached Wellesley at the end of May. In a conversation with the British Ambassador on 28 May, he admitted that cordial relations between the two governments were impossible until the slave trade problem was settled. He proposed to lower the Spanish demand for compensation to £400,000 if Britain would consent to postpone the period of final abolition until May 1820. This overture coincided with Pizarro's increasing concern over United States claims and his evident desire to enlist Britain on Spain's side.[97]

Pizarro represented his position as too shaky for him to take the initiative with the King and the Council of Ministers. He, therefore, asked Wellesley to address a Note on the slave trade to him, to enable him to put a new proposal before the Council of Ministers. Wellesley wrote a Note on 8 June regretting the difficulties holding back a settlement on the slave trade, but saying Britain had done all she could.[98] Pizarro replied on 14 June with a proposal to delay final abolition of the slave trade until May 1820, in return for compensation of £400,000.[99] Wellesley believed these were the best terms Britain was likely to obtain and advised acceptance. Castlereagh agreed and authorized Wellesley to conclude a convention on those terms, provided the Spanish government agreed to the British stipulations for enforcing such a treaty. Britain insisted on a mutual right of search with detention authorized only in cases where, in violation of the law and treaty, slaves were actually found on board. Every captured vessel would be taken before a mixed tribunal; no longer would British Admiralty courts judge foreign ships. Agreement to these provisions was demanded as a *sine qua non* to the payment of the indemnity.

As a guide for Wellesley in drawing up the treaty, Castlereagh enclosed an annotated copy of a treaty about to be signed with Portugal, designed to secure the effective abolition of the Portuguese slave trade north of the equator.[100] Article 5 of this treaty embodied the right of search clause. To emphasize its importance, Castlereagh noted: 'this Article is *Indispensable*. It is the basis of the whole without which Treaties to abolish it are mere Waste Papers.'[101] Next in importance was Article 8, setting up Mixed Commissions, 'a most material Provision'. In advocating Mixed Commissions, Castlereagh was going on the experience of the one set up by the Treaty of Paris to adjudicate claims against France by allied subjects. It had worked very well in settling financial claims and the fact that it had been so successful recommended it to Castlereagh as a useful way of checking abuses of the right of search. The other suggested articles merely put flesh on what had been laid down as the essential skeleton of the treaty. Wellesley drew up a *projet* and sent it to Pizarro on 8 August.[102] Included in it was an article designed to force the Spanish King to promulgate a law making the slave trade a criminal offence. Castlereagh thought this was too strong and advised Wellesley to be satisfied with a declaration of intent by Spain. A loose declaration of intent was included in the final treaty, and Ferdinand promulgated a royal *cédula* in accordance with the treaty on 19 December 1817. Illegal slave-trading would be punished with ten years' imprisonment and confiscation of the ship.[103] There were minor difficulties over the date on which the compensation would be paid and the period of grace for slave traders to complete their expeditions, but these presented no serious problems. Negotiations continued through August and into September, ironing out the terms of the agreement. The treaty was finally signed in Madrid on 23 September 1817.

The British Ambassador doubted whether Spain had agreed to prohibit the slave trade on humanitarian grounds, in spite of the public professions of the Spanish government: 'The Spanish Government have been solely guided by motives of interest…although it is probable that at the present moment they may be in some degree influenced by political considerations, yet the money, which they are to receive is the principal motive for acceding to the Abolition.'[104]

Pizarro had said previously that an immediate sum was necessary to enable Spain to meet the ordinary expenses of government. But writing later in his *Memorias*, the Spanish Foreign Minister suggested political reasons were predominant: 'The English Government and the Embassy always presented this subject as an obstacle to all the other pending negotiations.'[105]

The slave trade was certainly uppermost in the minds of the British government. Agreement on it had to precede any British mediation between Spain and her colonies.[106] Pizarro had also been trying to persuade Britain that she had an equal interest with Spain in resisting United States claims against the Spanish Empire. While Wellesley had avoided committing Britain, he intimated to Castlereagh that an offer of 'the good offices' of the British Ambassador in Washington would help the slave trade negotiations. Castlereagh left the door open enough so that hope of British help would push Spain into signing the slave trade treaty.[107]

Documents in the Archivo Histórico Nacional, Madrid, reveal, however, the real reason for Spain's sudden willingness to sign a treaty prohibiting the slave trade.[108] On 11 August 1817 the Spanish Minister of War, Francisco de Eguía, and the Russian Ambassador to Spain, Tatistcheff, signed a treaty providing for the sale of five Russian frigates and three ships of the line to Spain. A separate and secret article of this treaty revealed that Spain planned to use the £400,000 compensation she would receive from Britain in return for signing a slave trade treaty to pay for ships Russia would sell her. The arrangements for the purchase of Russian ships had been initiated some time before the summer of 1817, undoubtedly with the idea of using British money.[109] Ferdinand, himself, directed the 'negocio escandaloso', for such is the name given to the Russian purchase by a Spanish naval historian.[110] Thus, even before a treaty on the slave trade had been signed, Spain had spent the money she hoped to receive from Britain, and not for the purpose designated in that treaty. Had this fact been made public in Britain it is very doubtful the British Parliament would have approved the treaty with Spain. Not that the secret remained hidden for long. The British Ambassador in Spain had learned the real truth by the beginning of December 1817, and hastened to send arguments for Castlereagh to use in case the cat was let out of the bag.[111] But it was not, and the treaty was approved by a Parliament which knew nothing of its sordid background. Motives of expediency were not confined solely to the Spaniards. If Britain was high-minded in trying to bring about an international prohibition of the slave trade, the treaty, as signed with Spain and sanctioned by Parliament, was a cheap way of escaping the obligation of paying compensation for any judgements which had been or might be obtained by Spanish slave traders in British Courts of Appeal.

Even if the treaty were to be fully implemented by both sides, it was not an air-tight guarantee of the prohibition of the Spanish slave trade. Article ten stated that no British or Spanish cruiser could detain a slaver which did not actually have slaves on board.[112] This constituted a large loophole through which the crafty and unscrupulous slave traders could evade seizure, and it was to inhibit greatly the efforts of the British navy. Another cloud on the horizon was the judgement in the *Le Louis* case in 1817, making the right of search in peacetime illegal except when permitted by the country concerned.[113] Zachary Macaulay expressed the fears of the abolitionists about the results of this judgement in a letter to Castlereagh. Slave traders would be able to escape seizure under the 1817 treaty by sailing under the flag of a country which did not permit a mutual right of search. In this way the Spanish slave trade could be carried on even north of the equator, free of any interference.[114]

On the credit side, article one declared that the slave trade from Africa would be abolished completely throughout the Spanish dominions on 30 May 1820, with five months grace to vessels which had cleared before 30 May. The Spanish slave trade north of the equator was banned from the date of the exchange of ratifications with five months grace for ships which had left before that date. The illicit slave trade as far as the two nations, Britain and Spain, were concerned, was defined; a mutual right of search was established; and further measures to execute the treaty's provisions were set down. These provided for the creation of courts of mixed commission, and detailed the conditions under which the warships of each country could operate in searching suspected slave ships.

On 9 February 1818, when Lord Castlereagh moved the adoption of the treaty to abolish the slave trade, signed between Britain and Spain on 23 September 1817, nearly all the House of Commons welcomed it as sounding the death knell of the Atlantic slave trade to Spanish America. Even those who placed little trust in the word of Spain were reassured by Castlereagh's promise that the regulations included in the treaty were sufficient for its implementation. Only two members objected to the payment of £400,000 to Spain in return for her pledge to prohibit the trade north of the equator immediately and south of the line on 30 May 1820.[115] The British abolitionists also had greeted the treaty with relief and optimism.[116]

The applause which met the treaty in Britain soon died away. In Spain and her colonies most affected, Cuba and Puerto Rico, no applause was to be heard. The implementation of the treaty, in spite of Castlereagh's reassuring words, dragged on into a long and expensive impossibility. About the kindest word said of the treaty by Spanish or Cuban historians is the comment in the *Historia de la nación cubana*: 'the 1817 Treaty was always a dead letter'.[117] Nineteenth-century Spanish and Cuban comments on the treaty were more caustic. Pezuela described it as 'that treaty so premature, so impolitic, so prejudicial and so inopportune'.[118] In Cuba a myth grew up about Spain's reasons for signing the treaty. 'In the eyes of the slave trader and the bureaucrat, Spain had been forced against her will to give way on the prohibition of the slave trade by Britain's selfish and forceful pressure.'[119] For those who believed this explanation, and they included most of the planters and slave traders, resistance to British pretensions was seen as a patriotic duty. If the negotiations preceding the treaty had been long and tedious, the attempts to implement it effectively were to prove even more exasperating.

Enforcement and re-enforcement: the attempt to make the slave trade prohibition effective

Conflicting approaches to the implementation of the treaty, 1817–24

Two dilemmas faced the Cuban government when copies of the slave trade treaty arrived in Havana in February 1818. Genuine administrative difficulties were involved if the treaty was to be implemented. Ramírez, the Intendant of Havana, wanted to know which tribunals were to be responsible for judging cases of illegal slave trading not covered by the provisions of the treaty, specifically in connection with slavers arriving in Cuban ports after eluding capture at sea. It was clear that a contraband trade would continue and Ramírez advocated the merits of using the courts under his jurisdiction, suggesting that they be authorized to enforce the royal *cédula* of the previous December.[1] The Council of the Indies ruled against the Intendant in a report to the King of 11 May 1819, in which it assigned overall responsibility for the implementation of the treaty to the Captain-General.[2]

Far more serious were the apprehensions of Cuban planters and merchants who foresaw a catastrophe for Cuba if the treaty was fully implemented. The catastrophe they feared was economic, although there were other dangers as well. Even the publication of the royal *cédula* was resisted on the grounds that it might set off a chain reaction among the slaves. The Captain-General was forced to adopt a compromise formula, publishing the *cédula* only in the newspapers of Havana, and communicating it to the rest of the island through the various lieutenant-governors.[3] At first the merchant and planter groups in Cuba expressed their opposition tentatively. Ramírez forwarded representations from the Havana *Consulado* and the *Compañía de Seguros* in April 1818 asking for modifications to the treaty so that, among other things, slave trading expeditions despatched before the arrival of the treaty in Havana would not be molested. He also raised the question of Cuba's longstanding shortage of female slaves which, as he pointed out, could not be remedied in the two years left for the legal continuation of the slave trade.[4]

The attitude of the Cuban merchants and planters changed when they learned of the terms of the slave trade treaty signed between Britain and Portugal in July 1817. Their tone became more bitter and they began to protest loudly that they were victims of British persecution. Although this additional convention Britain had signed with Portugal to enforce the existing treaties between the two countries provided for a mutual right of search, it still left untouched the Portuguese and Brazilian slave trade south of the equator.[5] Faced with a total prohibition of the slave trade from Africa after 30 May 1820, the Cubans believed they were victims of a Luso-British plot to monopolize the export of tropical fruits to Europe. Their grievances were summarized in a petition from the *Consulado* of Havana to the Spanish Minister of Finance in the autumn of 1818.[6] Charges that English capital was financing new coffee and sugar plantations in Brazil buttressed their case against what they regarded as Britain's underhanded manipulations. They cried out for a repeal of the treaty prohibiting the slave trade so Cuba could compete on equal terms with Brazil; at the very least they wanted the rules for the slave trade made equal for both Spanish and Portuguese colonists. If Brazil insisted on preserving the fiction that bringing slaves from Portuguese African colonies to Brazil was the same as moving them from one place to another within the same country, the Cubans wanted to make use of a similar fiction themselves by using the Spanish islands of Fernando Po and Annobon as African bases for their slave trade.

This petition, supported by accompanying letters from the Intendant of Havana and the Cuban Captain-General, was referred to the Council to procure a Spanish translation of the Anglo-Spanish treaty of 1817, and more delays occurred while the *Contaduría General* and the *Fiscal* of New Spain examined the Cuban complaints. Their respective reports of 30 August and 14 September 1819 contained no new remedies for Cuba's situation, although both were sympathetic to the arguments advanced by the Havana *Consulado*.[7] The *Contaduría General* was convinced the abolition of the slave trade had been too abrupt and undertaken without enough effort to provide alternative supplies of labour for Cuba's agriculture but, as it recognized, 'the fact is that the damage is already done'. It was too late to alter matters. All that could be done was to place the whole problem in the lap of the Ministry of Foreign Affairs, which had been responsible for signing the slave trade treaty, with a recommendation that Britain be approached to see if she would agree to bring the treaty signed with Spain into line with the one signed between Britain and Portugal.

The Council of the Indies in its report of 25 October 1819 merely adopted the recommendations of its two advisers.[8] The Minister of Foreign Affairs apparently decided nothing was to be gained by asking Britain to make conditions equal for Portuguese and Spanish slave traders, for no approach along these lines was made to Castlereagh. Later, the Havana *Consulado* complained of receiving no replies to its representations.[9]

With no hopes of obtaining major alterations in the treaty or of using the British–Portuguese convention as a means of wringing concessions from Britain, the Cubans and Spaniards next attempted to persuade Britain to delay the full implementation of the 1817 treaty. Various overtures were made to Britain claiming that the five-month period of grace given to Cuban slavers which had sailed for Africa before the official prohibition came into force on 30 May 1820 was not long enough to enable them to return safely.[10] The British government rejected these overtures, believing them to be devices for prolonging the slave trade, which they undoubtedly were. British officials were unanimous in believing that the three years' legal continuation of the slave trade provided in the treaty plus the five-month period of grace gave the Havana slave traders more than enough time.

These last-minute efforts by the Spanish and Cuban governments to win a reprieve for their slave traders had no effect whatever on the British police operation against the slave trade along the African coast. The 1817 treaty legalized British seizures of Spanish slavers, provided these were captured with slaves on board and the operation was subsequently ratified by a court of mixed commission which sat in Sierra Leone. Nine Spanish slavers were condemned by this court in the first two years after the total prohibition came into force on 30 October 1820. Yet it remained true that while far more Spanish slavers were captured off Africa and brought to Sierra Leone for trial than was the case on the other side of the ocean, these captures had little or no impact on Havana where the Cuban slave trade was centred. The slave-trading expeditions were planned and financed in Havana and the Spanish policy towards the slave trade was guided if not governed by the views of colonial officials and colonial interests in Cuba.

The campaign to delay the operation of the 1817 treaty originated in Cuba in the form of petitions and representations to the metropolitan government. The Spanish Council of State, in a report of 15 May 1822, observed that ever since the treaty had been signed, an unending flow of representations against it had come from Cuba.[11] The British commission judge in Havana reported a conversation with the Intendant of Havana at the end of August 1820, in which the latter said Spanish officials on the mixed commission court would not condemn any captured slaver brought to Havana by a British cruiser before the end of March 1821.[12] What this amounted to was a determination not to implement the treaty as long as Spanish representations to Britain for a ten-month extension of the slave trade were pending.

Long after the treaty was due to come into operation, the Spanish Council of State gave official backing to the statement of the Havana Intendant. The Council fully supported the petitions of the Havana *Consulado* and Cuban government officials for an extension of the period of grace from five to ten months so that slavers which had sailed before 30 May 1820 would be able to return unmolested.[13] It was clear, said the Council's report, that a return voyage from Cuba to Africa could not be done in less than ten months. Confident that Britain would rectify what the report called a hydrographic error in the treaty, the Council of State approved the *Consulado's* suggestion that in the meantime no slaver would be condemned and the cargoes of all returning slavers could be sold conditionally.

Officially, all the Council of State said was that no slaver which had left Cuba before the end of May 1820 was to be condemned while negotiations were in progress with Britain to extend the term of grace from five to ten months. Thus, the thirty-two slaving expeditions from Cuba which were affected by this ruling could count on a safe return if they managed to escape the preying British cruisers off Africa. So confident were the Cuban slave traders that twenty expeditions left Havana just prior to or on the day the treaty came into force.[14] As it happened, no captured slavers were brought into Havana to be tried by the court there until 1824, saving the British commissioners from adjudicating what could have been, in the words of the British judge, 'a hard and aggravating case'.[15] Unofficially, the Council of State's judgement encouraged the feeling in Cuba that the peninsular government was indifferent to the enforcement of the slave trade prohibition, a view believed by the British commissioners to be widely held in Cuba.[16] The British judge was convinced that the Captain-General's hesitancy in enforcing the treaty could be attributed to the indifference of the Spanish government.[17]

While Spanish diplomacy, inspired by Cuban pressure, aimed first at modifying the treaty and then at delaying its implementation, the British government worked to put the treaty into operation. By

1818, the British government had signed treaties to prohibit the slave trade with Portugal and The Netherlands, as well as with Spain, each treaty conceding a mutual right of search and establishing courts of mixed commission on both sides of the Atlantic. Apart from the British navy, whose task was to capture illegal slaving vessels, the British effort to eliminate the slave trade rested on the mixed commission courts and the officials who manned them. Each country appointed a commissary judge and a commissioner of arbitration to the court. The court had to decide whether or not a captured slaver had violated the treaty provisions and, accordingly, whether the ship was a lawful prize and its slaves illegally taken; if not, the court restored the ship and the slaves to the owner. There was no appeal from the decision of the court.[18]

The British government made its first appointments to the Havana court of mixed commission in 1819. The commissary judge was an Irish lawyer, Henry Theo Kilbee, who had served for nine years as secretary to the British Ambassador in Spain, Henry Wellesley. Kilbee was familiar with all the background to the Anglo-Spanish treaty of 1817 and, because he was the first British official to be appointed to Cuba, he was instructed to report privately on Cuban politics.[19] His successors continued the practice until 1833 when the British government appointed a consul to Cuba. Kilbee's colleague, the British commissioner of arbitration, was an author named Robert Jameson who wrote the first British travel book on Cuba as a result of his brief stay in the island.[20] From the beginning the British officials in Cuba were not as impartial as their positions implied, although they were suspected of far worse by both the Cubans and the Americans.

The mixed commission court in Havana was regarded by the Cubans as an 'inquisitorial tribunal of foreigners' and hated by individuals and institutions alike.[21] Even its very limited powers were too much for the Havana *Consulado*.[22] This unpopularity stemmed from two things: the public belief that the prohibition of the slave trade was a measure which Britain forced on Spain under a cloak of philanthropy, but really as a means of hitting at Cuban prosperity, and the extensive participation in slave-trading ventures by Cubans of all classes. Jameson reported in 1821 that shares in slaving expeditions sold for as little as 100 Spanish dollars, 'and are eagerly sought for by clerks in public and mercantile offices, petty *caballeros* or gentry . . . and shopkeepers, overseers, etc.'.[23] Local government officials owned slave ships and, when the first Spanish slaver captured by a British cruiser was brought into Havana in 1824, it was found that General Morales, the successor to Morillo as Spanish Commander-in-Chief on the mainland, was one of the chief shareholders. Commenting on this revelation Kilbee wrote, 'this fact speaks volumes as to the state of the slave trade in this Country; and indeed I have good reason for saying that with very few exceptions, all the employés under the Government are directly or indirectly engaged in the Traffic'.[24] Despised by the Cubans, unsupported by the British navy, neglected by the British government, yet responsible to Parliament for the prohibition of the slave trade to Cuba, understandably the British judge spoke of his position as an 'odious office'.[25]

Kilbee did not confine his criticisms of the operation of the court to his despatches. He poured out his frustrations to a United States special agent who had been sent to Cuba in 1824. Kilbee complained that in the four years the Anglo-Spanish treaty had been in force it had had no effect whatsoever. For all the good it had done, 'it might as well be in Jerico'. Kilbee particularly lamented the lack of inquisitorial powers. The court was completely reliant on the respective navies and the Spanish authorities. The British commissioner, realizing the impossible limitations imposed on the court, wanted its powers increased. Even though Thomas Randall, the United States special agent, agreed with Kilbee's analysis of the treaty's failure to suppress the slave trade, he did not advocate United States support for Britain's position. The United States was too interested in Cuba's fate to identify itself with what Randall described as a 'Convention so odious to all Spaniards that they make a merit of violating it'.[26]

The court of mixed commission at Havana could operate only if the British and Spanish navies succeeded in capturing slave ships. Neither the British nor the Spanish naval forces in the Caribbean regarded the prohibition of the slave trade as their most important task. Of the two navies the Spanish performance was by far the worst. In the twenty-two years from 1820 to 1842, the Spanish navy captured two slave ships, both of which were Portuguese and, therefore, not subject to the court's jurisdiction under the Anglo-Spanish treaty. From the beginning there was a contrast between the effectiveness of the British navy's policing activities on the African coast and its work in the Caribbean. Eleven Spanish slavers were captured and condemned in the Sierra Leone court of mixed commission under the Anglo-Spanish treaty from 1818 to the end of 1821,[27] but before 1824 the British navy in the Caribbean did not succeed in capturing one Spanish slaver.

This was not due to a lack of slave ships. Jameson, one of the British officials at Havana, revealed that in the first eleven months after the prohibition of the slave trade came into force 26 slave ships had entered Havana carrying nearly 6,500 slaves, and of these ships, 18 had been Spanish and therefore liable for capture and condemnation.[28] There were many excuses offered for the performance of the British West Indian squadron, among them: the vague nature of the slave trade treaty, the extent of Cuba's coastlines and the difficulty of too many tasks in the Caribbean for the available British warships. But the British commissioners in Havana had no doubt what the real reason was. In their view British naval commanders competed vigorously among themselves and with American and French commanders to carry specie leaving Havana and other Caribbean ports, and the officers hesitated to risk unpopularity and loss of lucrative cargoes by capturing Spanish slavers.[29] Kilbee dismissed the argument attributing the difficulty of capturing Spanish slavers to the length of Cuba's coastlines. He pointed out that slavers landed their cargoes at or near towns where the slaves could be sold. The slave-trading coast did not, therefore, extend very far, and the British judge was convinced that if an effective watch could be kept on the two or three main slave-trading ports the slave trade would receive a severe setback.

The inadequacies of the British navy's excuses were made even more glaring by the fact that Colombian privateers had no difficulty in capturing numbers of Spanish slavers. The Haitians, with their warship appropriately named the *Wilberforce*, were also able to capture Spanish slave vessels, liberating the captives on Haitian soil.[30] Not unnaturally the lack of captures by British warships had a profound effect on Cuban public opinion. Kilbee summed this up in a private letter to the Permanent Under-Secretary at the Foreign Office: 'The inactivity and want of success of our Navy, which is here considered to be omnipotent and omnipresent, has very generally given rise to the opinion that England is weary of the subject of the Slave Trade and is grown indifferent about it.'[31] These charges were denied by the Commander of the West Indian station, Admiral Halsted, but it is notable that the West Indian squadron, goaded by Kilbee's accusations, captured 5 Spanish slavers during the remainder of 1825 and 1826.[32]

The nature of the slave trade, too, had been changing. When the first crisis of supply had hit the Cuban planters during the Napoleonic wars just after Britain had prohibited the slave trade within the British empire, the planters had begun to outfit their own slaving expeditions direct to Africa. Their success led to the creation of large slave-trading companies within Cuba. By 1819, Havana had 22 slave-trading *grandes comerciantes* who had almost totally displaced the old foreign slave traders.[33] These slave traders combined with foreigners to flood the island with slaves during the five years from the end of the Napoleonic wars to the prohibition of the slave trade to Cuba in 1820. The figures of legal slave importations through Havana for the years 1816–20 are much higher than those for the preceding years or the estimated figures for the following years. An estimated 95,817 African slaves arrived in Havana during this period, although this figure does not include African slaves brought to other ports in the island or smuggled in.[34]

With the prohibition of the slave trade, accurate statistics are much harder to compile. Those which are available for the first decade of the illegal slave trade, the 1820s, suggest that the prohibition, itself, even though it was not enforced, caused a sharp decline in the number of slaves brought to Cuba. It is possible to piece together a tentative estimate of the arrivals in the Havana area based on the reports of the British commissioners. Robert Jameson reported on 1 September 1821 that since the end of October 1820, 26 slavers carrying 6,415 slaves had entered Havana.[35] The United States historian, Aimes, included this figure as the total number of arrivals for 1821, which it is not, but it corroborates Saco's figure of 4,122 for 1821 (included in Table 1, p. 18).[36] In his annual report dated 1 January 1825, Kilbee enclosed a list of slavers covering the years 1821–4. This list contains his estimate of the number of slave expeditions which landed at or near Havana from 1822 to 1824, respectively 10, 4 and 17.[37] Kilbee thought an average of 250 slaves per ship was a 'low calculation', but on this basis the arrivals in the Havana area would be approximately 2,500 in 1822, 1,000 in 1823 and 4,250 in 1824.

Kilbee's report for 1825 was more specific. Thirty-seven slavers had returned to Cuba, bringing 11,190 African slaves.[38] He calculated that half this number was imported into the rest of Cuba, for a total importation of 17,885 for 1825. The annual report for 1826 stated that 14 expeditions arrived at Havana in 1826, of which 3 were captured, carrying in all 3,738 slaves.[39] Ten expeditions landed in the Havana area in 1827, bringing 3,500 African slaves,[40] but the next year Macleay, the British judge, wrote that 28 expeditions had come to Havana bringing no fewer than 7,000 and this figure did not include slaves on captured slave vessels.[41] There were 1,002 captured slaves

Enforcement and re-enforcement

Table 3. *Number of African slaves landed in the Havana area, 1822–29*

Years	Number of expeditions	Numbers
1822	10	2,500
1823	4	1,000
1824	17	4,250
1825	37	11,910
1826	14	3,738
1827	10	3,500
1828	28	8,002
1829	32	8,250
Total	152	43,150

Source: Annual reports of the Havana commissioners, 1822–9.

A recent calculation of Cuban slave imports, based on a quantitative analysis of the nineteenth-century transatlantic slave trade, suggests that Kilbee's average was too low and that the number of slaves actually landed in Cuba was significantly higher than reported by the British commissioners. David Eltis, in his doctoral thesis, 'The Transatlantic Slave Trade, 1821–43' (University of Rochester, 1978), and in his article based on the thesis, 'The Export of Slaves from Africa, 1821–43', *The Journal of Economic History*, vol. 37, no. 2 (1977), pp. 409–33, calculates a higher import figure for Cuba as a whole than the British commissioners' reports which concentrated on the Havana area. His yearly totals, with which he kindly provided me, are as follows:

1821 –	4,574
1822 –	4,105
1823 –	1,938
1824 –	7,831
1825 –	13,775
1826 –	4,000
1827 –	4,983
1828 –	12,831
1829 –	14,696
Total –	68,733

in 1828, so the total was 8,002. The number of slavers coming to Havana increased to 33 in 1829, and although Macleay did not estimate how many slaves were landed, 8,250 is a possible figure using Kilbee's average of 250 per ship.[42] The total of slaves landed in the Havana area during the period 1822–9 is given in Table 3.

British diplomats in Europe, attempting to persuade Spain to uphold her side of the treaty, faced frustrations similar to those of the British commissioners in Havana. While abolitionists nibbled at the heels of the British Foreign Secretary in London, British diplomats laboured in vain in Madrid.[43] Not until October 1821 could the British Minister in Madrid report that the Spanish Foreign Minister had promised Spain would enforce the treaty of 1817.[44] The promise was easier to give than to uphold, as a case of a slaver in 1821 illustrated. On 6 November 1821 a Spanish privateer brought into Havana a number of African slaves taken from a wrecked Spanish slaver. After the court of mixed commission had decided the case did not fall within its jurisdiction, the commissioners ordered that it be referred to a Spanish tribunal to be heard according to Spanish law as laid down in the royal *cédula* of December 1817. The Spanish Court of Admiralty, the Auditor of War and the Judge of Finance immediately began hearings on the case, but the inevitable result of this competition for jurisdiction was the referral of the case to Madrid. Meanwhile the Captain-General restored the African slaves to the owners of the wrecked vessel on the grounds that the slaves were embarked on the Cape Verde islands, not on the coast of Africa and, therefore, the provisions of the treaty did not apply to them.[45]

Captain-General Mahy, in his report of the affair, underlined the predicament in which he found himself: 'This is an affair which in the current circumstances will place the island in the greatest jeopardy if the prize comes under article 7 of the slave trade treaty and the slaves are freed according to its provisions; or if through some loophole the treaty does not apply in this case, our government will be in trouble with the British.'[46] The Spanish Council of State, when it examined Mahy's despatch, saw it as another in the long series of Cuban protests against the slave trade treaty. The Council itself was no less critical of the treaty. Cuban losses in agriculture and those suffered by the slave traders could not begin to be compensated for by the paltry sum which Britain had paid. After reviewing this incident and other Spanish grievances on the slave trade, notably the preferential treatment which Portugal and Brazil had received from Britain, the Council of State laid down the rule to be followed on the interpretation of the treaty. In cases which came under the provisions of

Article 7 of the treaty, that is, slavers captured and brought to Havana for trial by British or Spanish cruisers, a literal obedience to the treaty was ordered. But no decision was to be taken which might jeopardize the security of the island.[47] A wide loophole for evasion remained which the Cuban authorities were not slow to use.

Attempts to persuade Spain to declare the slave trade piracy and to get the Spanish Cortes to pass more effective laws against the slave trade were no more successful. In February 1821, Wellesley, the British Ambassador in Madrid, in a Note to the Spanish Foreign Minister, enclosed the British Act of Parliament of 1820 which imposed more rigorous penalties on British subjects engaged in the slave trade, hoping this Act would inspire similar Spanish legislation.[48] The Spanish Council of State thought the existing penalties were quite adequate and saw no reason to increase their severity.[49] Again, in 1824, the Spanish government debated the question of declaring the slave trade piracy after a Note from the United States Minister in Madrid suggested the United States Act of 1820 as an example for Spain to follow, but this approach had the same result.[50] The Spanish Ambassadors in Paris and London, and the Council of the Indies, were united in their opposition to making slave-trading an offence of piracy, although their reasons differed slightly from the ones advanced by the Council of State in 1821. The Marquis of Casa Irujo, the Spanish Ambassador in Paris and formerly Minister of Foreign Affairs, advised against any measure the effect of which would be to diminish Cuba's prosperity and endanger the Spanish possession of the island.[51] The implication was plain: if the slave trade was declared piracy, rebellion in Cuba would soon follow. The Council of the Indies thought the existing penalties adequate. It could not support the death penalty for a trade which had been legal for three centuries. The criminality of the slave trade had now been established, but in Spanish eyes it was a crime of contraband and ought to be punished as such.[52]

Henry Wellesley's indirect role in trying to get the Spanish Cortes to pass a more stringent law against the slave trade in 1821 was virtually a re-enactment of the scene in the 1811 Cortes, and it had a similar ending. A conversation the British Ambassador had with the Spanish Minister of Foreign Affairs, Count Torreno, early in March 1821, secured from the latter a promise to attempt to persuade the Cortes to stiffen the penalties for illegal slave-trading.[53] Wellesley supplied Torreno with the necessary information on the slave trade, and the Count fulfilled his promise by moving a resolution in the

Cortes on 23 March for the appointment of a committee which would draft new laws for the prohibition of the slave trade. The motion was carried in a full house with only the two deputies from Havana opposed.[54]

The committee's report was read three times, according to the procedure of the Cortes, without any opposition, but when a day was proposed for the discussion of the report the Minister of the Indies intervened and arranged to have the report discussed in a secret session where it was decided there were no grounds for bringing it to a vote.[55] Torreno was faced in 1821 with the same powerful Cuban opposition which had proved too much for Argüelles in 1811 and, like the proposals of Argüelles, those of Torreno were still-born. Cuban influence had succeeded in instilling the fear in the Spanish government that if Cuba were deprived of her source of labour she would follow the rebellious lead given by Spain's mainland possessions in America. This form of blackmail by the Cuban planters succeeded for the moment in neutralizing British efforts in Spain.

Cuban pressure managed to thwart British manoeuvres to make the slave trade prohibition binding, but the instructions which the leading corporations of Havana gave to the Cuban deputies elected to the Cortes for the 1821–2 session had ordered them to do even more. Specifically, they were instructed to obtain the revocation of the 1817 treaty or modifications to make the abolition of the slave trade a gradual process, spread over six years. Saco states, however, that none of them dared to ask for the revocation of the treaty and, aside from the successful campaign against Torreno's measures, the only other accomplishment was a pamphlet written by one of the deputies, Juan Bernardo O'Gavan, opposing the slave trade treaty.[56] The Cuban deputies elected to the Cortes for the 1822–3 session were given the same instructions on the slave trade, but one of them, Father Félix Varela y Morales, broke ranks and became the first Cuban to publish his opposition to slavery. He wrote a pamphlet, addressed to the Cortes, arguing for the gradual abolition of slavery. His pamphlet had no effect whatever in Spain and made him the enemy of the planter class in Cuba, but it was an inspiration to younger Cuban Creoles like Saco who were later to take up the struggle against the slave trade.[57]

The second period of constitutional rule in Spain did bring two positive steps against the slave trade, but unfortunately, one was temporary and the other was ineffective. In the new Criminal Code approved by the Cortes in 1822, there was an article containing the stiffer penalties against slave-trading for which Britain had been pressing. Hervey, the British Minister in Madrid, was optimistic about its probable effect when he forwarded the article to Castlereagh in March, and in June he was able to inform the Foreign Secretary that the Spanish monarch had approved the Criminal Code including the slave trade article.[58] The British commissioners in Havana criticized the new penal code for not including any incentive to informers. In any case their experience of four years at Havana proved that no matter how imposing on paper the law was, it would be 'a mere dead letter' unless it was enforced by the local government.[59] Whether the commissioners' foreboding would have proved right no one can say for, after the downfall of the constitutional system in Spain in 1823, the new penal code was declared null and void, and the *cédula* of 1817, vague and loosely worded as it was, remained the only Spanish law on the slave trade.

The diplomatic work which went into the signing of additional Articles to the 1817 treaty was also without result. A case in the Sierra Leone court of mixed commission had revealed one weakness of the treaty. Even if there was irrefutable evidence that slaves had been on board a slaver, if the capturing officer did not discover slaves actually on board a suspected vessel he could not seize the ship. Anxious to correct this defect, the British Foreign Secretary, George Canning, sent a draft of additional Articles to the British Minister in Madrid at the end of September 1822. By the end of December the additional Articles had been signed, and in the spring of 1823 Canning forwarded them to the Havana commissioners. At the beginning of 1826, however, the commissioners reported that the Cuban government had still not officially received the Articles, signed over three years before; and the Captain-General's attitude was that Articles which had not been officially received could not be implemented. Canning was informed in 1826 by the British Minister in Madrid that the additional Articles had never been sent because the King had not confirmed them. Early in that year Ferdinand at last confirmed them and they were then sent out to Cuba.[60]

The royal order of 2 January 1826

The real source of opposition to any curtailment or abolition of the slave trade lay in Cuba. The British judge on the court of mixed commission, Henry Kilbee, continually agitated for changes in the Spanish law on the slave trade but, as he put it:

Above all things it will be necessary to correct the public opinion of this Country upon the Subject of the Slave Trade. It is universally believed that the Abolition was a measure which Great Britain, under the cloak of Philanthropy, but really influenced by jealousy of the prosperity of this Island, forced upon Spain by threats or other means: – That, the latter fulfills her engagements, as far as Great Britain is directly concerned, because she fears to do otherwise, but that in reality she is indifferent upon the subject or is even willing to connive at its continuation provided appearances be kept up.[61]

Nothing illustrates this analysis better than a despatch written five days later by the Captain-General of Cuba, then Francisco Vives. After reporting the capture of the Spanish slaver, *El Relámpago*, by the British schooner, *Lion*, about which he could do nothing, Vives stated:

I conceal the existence of the slave trade and the introduction of slaves as much as is possible given the treaty obligations, because I am completely convinced that if the lack of slave labour continues the island's wealth will undoubtedly disappear. within a very few years since the flourishing agriculture is dependent on these labourers and at the moment there is no other means of obtaining them; I must also point out the unfavourable consequences which such a decline would produce on the state and on the inhabitants in particular when they compare their own situation with that of foreign colonies which prosper and grow.[62]

Tacón, one of Vives' successors as Captain-General, some years after his return to Spain wrote that in 1818 a confidential royal order had been sent to the Captains-General of Cuba and Puerto Rico ordering them to overlook the illegal importation of slaves since without them the agriculture of the islands could not progress.[63]

The Cuban view that the slave trade was vital to the island's prosperity benefited from the incomplete nature of the prohibition specified in the 1817 treaty. When the British judge's proposal for a reward to informers was examined by the *Fiscal* of the Council of the Indies in 1824, he rejected it because of the difficulties it would create.[64] Kilbee had wanted to put the onus on the slave-holders to prove they had acquired their slaves legally, a principle which had been recognized by Spain as early as 1542 when Article 27 of the New Laws stipulated that if persons who held Indians as slaves could not prove their title to them, the Indians were to be freed by the *audiencias*.[65] The *Fiscal* did not see how a legal acquisition in the case of African slaves could be defined because the 1817 treaty had not prohibited slave-trading within Cuba or between Cuba and Puerto Rico. All that had been prohibited, as far as he and other Spanish lawyers were concerned, were slaving expeditions to Africa.

By 1825 neither the British commissioners in Havana nor the British government were willing to accept Spanish excuses or to tolerate any longer the open evasion of the treaty. Canning, who was exasperated by the steadily worsening reports from Kilbee in Havana, early in April sent a long and very detailed account of the abuses going on in Havana to the British Minister in Madrid. Lamb was ordered to tell the Spanish government that Britain would do nothing to help Spain preserve Cuba if the slave trade treaty was not fulfilled. Canning relayed more of Kilbee's accounts at the end of May as additional ammunition for Lamb to use. After notifying the Spanish Foreign Minister that British interest in helping Spain to preserve Cuba would cease if the slave trade was not stopped, Lamb forwarded Kilbee's long catalogue of Spanish abuses and evasions in a Note of 13 July 1825.[66]

Britain's threat not to help Spain preserve Cuba was an empty one and the Spanish government knew this. In any case it was soon withdrawn. Canning was anxious to see that neither the United States nor France, Britain's two major maritime rivals in the Caribbean, took advantage of Spain's weakness to occupy Cuba. In May 1824 he had offered Britain's guarantee to help Spain hold Cuba if Spain would recognize the independence of her mainland colonies, an offer which Spain summarily rejected. By 1825 he was proposing a tripartite guarantee by Britain, the United States, and France that none would seize Cuba. Canning clearly described the motivation for this proposal in a letter to the United States Minister to England: 'You cannot allow that *we* should have Cuba; we cannot allow that you should have it; and we can neither of us allow that it should fall into the hands of France.'[67] Canning's projects proved abortive, but Spain could see that the chief maritime powers in the Caribbean, wary of each other's intentions, represented no immediate threat to her possession of Cuba.

The slave trade had not been mentioned in Canning's diplomacy to guarantee Cuba, apart from his threats uttered in the spring of 1825, but, for the first time since the signing of the 1817 treaty, the Spanish government appeared to accept the British complaints about the abuses of the treaty and began to search for remedies. The Spanish Foreign Minister, then Cea Bermúdez, turned the British complaints over to his Ambassador-designate to the United States, José de Heredia, and asked for a report.[68] As a result of the continuous complaints of the British commissioners in Havana, Heredia had before him not only the British Note of 13 July, but an *expediente* drawn up by Francisco de Arango y Parreño now the Intendant of Havana. The British judge, Kilbee, in 1825 described Arango as 'one of the few persons in this Island really friendly to the Abolition of the Slave Trade'.[69] Arango y Parreño's conversion, for it was nothing less than that, was remarkable. He had been largely responsible for persuading Spain to unshackle the slave trade from the monopolistic restrictions of the Spanish mercantilist system in 1789; he had defended the existence of the slave trade to Cuba before the Spanish Cortes in 1811; and, as a member of the Council of the Indies in 1816, he had strongly opposed the immediate abolition of the African slave trade. Now, at last aware of the evils of the slave trade, he tried to get the Spanish government to wipe it out. He reported that stricter customs regulations alone would not be enough to check it and he offered his co-operation to enforce any measures the peninsular government chose to adopt.[70]

Heredia proposed six new steps to stop what he called the scandalous breach of the treaty and the dangerous increase in Cuba's African population. All ships sailing to Africa with merchandise were to return directly to their port of departure and any which did not were to be confiscated; a special tribunal was to be set up in Havana to deal with cases of clandestine importation of slaves not covered by the 1817 treaty; Spanish warships were to be given specific orders to detain all vessels carrying Africans in Cuban waters; a reward of 2,000 pesos was to be given to anyone who denounced an illegal landing of slaves; the captain and crew of a condemned slaver would face sentences of four to six years' imprisonment; and buyers of illegally imported slaves would lose possession of them and, in addition, face a fine of 300 pesos for each slave purchased. Since some of his proposals required new legislation, Heredia recommended that the Council of the Indies examine them.[71]

The Council of the Indies disagreed with Heredia's analysis. It viewed the existing law as generally adequate; the fault, in the eyes of the Council, was that, owing to a conflict of jurisdictions in Havana, none of the Spanish officials was enforcing the law. The Council, however, was prepared to recommend additional measures, not nearly as drastic as Heredia's, but such as would stop any other form of contraband trade. Its report recommended that the log-books of all vessels arriving in Cuban ports from Africa be turned over to the naval authorities who would examine them for any sign that the ships had been on slaving expeditions. Informers were to be encouraged, and any slave who denounced an illegal slave landing was to receive his freedom. The report also advised that the Archbishop of Cuba and the Bishop of Havana be asked to pronounce publicly that the slave trade was prohibited by law and was, therefore, a moral offence.[72]

When the Council of the Indies' report was referred to the Council of State, the latter body suggested that the provision for giving freedom to any slave who denounced an illegal slave landing be extended: 'would it not also be right to free slaves who denounce the slave vessels in which they were brought to Cuba after the Order to this effect has been published?' The Council of the Indies thought this suggestion was not only just but in accordance with the 1817 treaty. Accordingly, it incorporated into its previous proposals the suggestion that any slave who had been brought to Cuba from Africa after the prohibition of the slave trade could claim his freedom by proving his illegal introduction. Ferdinand agreed with the other recommendations of the Council of the Indies, but he wanted the clause giving freedom to slaves who denounced illegal importations to have effect after the publication of the royal order. In other words, no slave brought to Cuba before the order was published could benefit from it. A royal order, based on the modified recommendations of the Council of the Indies, was promulgated on 2 January 1826.[73] Spain informed the British government almost immediately of this new measure and, as soon as the order arrived in Havana, the British commissioners were similarly informed.[74] Lamb, the British Minister in Madrid, was unqualified in his optimism about the success of the royal order, while the Havana commissioners thought it would work if the Cuban tribunal encouraged the protected informers. Their disillusionment was quick and complete.

For, in spite of the apparently well-intentioned work of the Council of the Indies to produce more stringent legislation against the slave trade, not one clause of the royal order had the desired effect. The clause ordering vessels arriving from Africa to turn over their log-books to the Havana naval authorities, far from inhibiting the slave traders, added a cover of legality to their clandestine operations. The Naval Commander complied literally with his orders and examined the log-books of the arrivals from Africa, although at first he confined his examinations to ships accused of slave-trading by the British commissioners. None of the log-books, however, had the slightest indication that the vessel might have been on a slaving expedition. Having been cleared by the Havana naval authorities, captains of slave ships then had proof of their ostensible innocence which they could use against the charges of the British commissioners. The commissioners denounced every vessel suspected of being a slaver to the Captain-General. Each accusation was followed by a ritual examination of the vessel's log-book and occasionally the evidence of the captain and the crew was taken. Every one of these examinations cleared the ship in question.

For example, in 1827 the commissioners protested to the Captain-General that the Spanish brig, *Breves*, which had arrived in ballast at Havana, had previous to its arrival landed 400 slaves on the Cuban coast not far from Havana. The examination of the log-book by the Cuban authorities revealed nothing, which prompted the commissioners to comment: 'The results of this and similar investigations are very soon and generally known, and they are regarded by the Publick as marks of the ingenuity displayed by this Government in thwarting the attempt made by His Majesty's Commissioners to check the illicit slave trade.'[75] It was not difficult for the commissioners to distinguish slavers from other vessels. They informed Canning at the beginning of January 1827 that 111 ships had sailed from Havana for Africa in the previous five years and not one had returned with a cargo of merchandise.[76]

The other provisions of the royal order were equally ineffective. Captain-General Ezpeleta reported in 1839 that there had been no instance of a Spanish or Cuban denunciation of an illegal landing of slaves according to the 1826 royal order, and he attributed this to the universal belief in Cuba that without African slave labour the island's wealth would be destroyed.[77] A scathing indictment of the royal order can be found in a report written for the Spanish Foreign Minister by José Verdaguer, who had been a judge in Havana for nine years.[78] He confirmed all the criticisms of the British commissioners about the apathy of the local authorities when it came to the enforcement of the laws against the slave trade; even the Church was not exempt from his criticism. He accused the Archbishop of Cuba of benefiting from the slave trade by 4 pesos for every slave illegally introduced. Verdaguer asserted that the royal order of 1826 proved two things: the willingness of the Spanish government to co-operate with Britain in the enforcement of the 1817 treaty, and the connivance of the Spanish authorities in Cuba in the illegal slave trade.

Two incidents in 1826 revealed the flagrancy of the abuses. The first case involved the *Mágico*, a slaver which had barely escaped capture by British cruisers in 1825. She was captured and condemned at Havana early in 1826, but the British schooner, *Union*, which captured her, was only able to bring back half the number of Africans originally on board the vessel, the rest having been forced ashore by the slaver's crew when they ran the *Mágico* aground. When the British commissioners pressed the Captain-General to capture the crew and locate the missing Africans, Vives replied that it was not his responsibility; he had turned the investigation over to the naval authorities. The commissioners' denunciation of the Captain-General's conduct reached Madrid by the normal though indirect route via London.[79] Vives had consulted his *Auditor de Guerra*, and on his advice, he defended his conduct by saying that nothing in either the 1817 treaty or the royal *cédula* of 1817 said anything about persecuting the slave trade on land. The prohibition was limited to the sea.[80]

By the time the Council of the Indies examined the case in September 1826, it seemed that the only remaining question was whether the Africans who had been landed from the *Mágico* were entitled to their freedom. The Council's report, based on the advice of its *Fiscal*, ruled that they were so entitled, but it virtually nullified this ruling by stating there was no point after such a long lapse of time in trying to locate them. The Council of the Indies certainly did not want to initiate an enquiry into the legal title of Cuba's slaves.[81]

What the British commissioners feared would happen, did happen. Captain-General Vives sent a despatch in February, 1827, stating that the captain of the *Mágico* had managed to re-embark the Africans by using a false name and pretending he had been run aground by an insurgent privateer. Vives found the local official concerned guilty of negligence for allowing the captain to escape with the remainder of his slave cargo, a judgement which was confirmed in Madrid, but that was the end of the case as far as Spanish officials in Madrid and Cuba were concerned.[82]

An even worse example of the protection given to the slave trade by Spanish officials in Cuba occurred in the summer of 1826. The Spanish schooner, *Minerva*, whose departure for Africa had been reported by the British commissioners early in April,[83] was chased into the harbour of Havana by two British cruisers on 16 August 1826. The senior British officer, convinced that the *Minerva* had a cargo of slaves on board, attempted in vain to obtain permission to search the vessel. He then placed a boat to watch the *Minerva*, and between eleven and twelve that night the British officers observed 6 boatloads of Africans being landed from the *Minerva* at one of Havana's main wharves. The next day when one of the British officers was granted permission to search the *Minerva* he found conclusive evidence that the vessel was a slaver.

Captain-General Vives refused to permit the court of mixed commission to hear the case, holding that the capture did not occur on the high seas. On the basis of reports from Spanish naval officers who visited the *Minerva*, the Captain-General dismissed the accusation of slave-trading put forward by the British officers as an 'idle rumour', even though according to Macleay, one of the British commissioners, the facts were as 'notorious as noon-day'.[84] In his despatch to Madrid, Vives combined his doubt that the *Minerva* could have landed any slaves with an explanation of the difficulty of preventing contraband articles from coming into Cuba. The main part of his despatch was, however, a strong demand for the recall of the British commissioner, Macleay, whom the Captain-General accused of slandering Spanish officials in Cuba and of attempting to extend the powers of the court of mixed commission beyond those laid down in the treaty.[85] A United States historian, who examined some of the documents on this incident, called it 'an extremely perplexing case'.[86] It is one on which the observer must accept either the British or the Spanish evidence, there being no middle course. That said, there can be little doubt that a slave landing occurred and there is strong evidence that subordinate Spanish officials, if not more senior ones, were in collusion with the slave traders.[87] These two cases, among others, provided convincing evidence for the British Foreign Secretary that the 1826 royal order had not changed the attitude of the Spanish authorities in Cuba.

Cuba in 1825 faced external threats of invasion and internal threats of uprisings. To counter these the restored absolutist government of Ferdinand VII invested the Captain-General of Cuba, Francisco Dionisio Vives, with *facultades omnímodas*, in effect, powers of martial law which became the only real constitution the island possessed. The British commissioners and the British government hoped the Captain-General would employ his unlimited authority to root out the slave trade, but the failure of the royal order of 1826 brought home to the British the realization that neither the powers of the Captain-General nor the existing laws were sufficient to eliminate the Cuban slave trade; they were being used to protect the slave trade rather than to prosecute it. This realization set the British government on a nine-year struggle to obtain additional concessions from Spain so that Britain herself could play a more effective role in suppressing the slave trade to Cuba.

CHAPTER 6

The treaty of 1835

When the Duke of Infantado informed the British Minister in Madrid of the royal order of 1826, he asked Lamb if the British government could suggest any other measure which would help to suppress the slave trade. Canning responded to this opening with a proposal that Spain follow Holland's example and sign an equipment article which would then mean that suspected Spanish slavers, equipped to carry on the slave trade, could be seized and condemned even if they did not have slaves on board. This proposal was made official in a Note addressed to the Spanish Foreign Minister on 19 February 1826.[1] The suggestion was then turned over to the Council of the Indies for study. Their report was quite favourable.[2] The Council did not find any objection to the additional article, although it felt more ought to be done to make the existing laws effective. Should the equipment article be approved, the Council recommended a six-month period of grace to date from the publication of the new article, and it believed that the punishment for infractions should be limited to the confiscation of the ship and its cargo.

Ferdinand referred the report to his Council of State which, in turn, asked the Spanish Foreign Minister for his opinion; however, before the Duke of Infantado had a chance to examine the problem he was replaced as Foreign Minister. A Foreign Ministry memorandum succinctly describes what happened next: 'here the affair remained paralysed'.[3] A further Note from Lamb in the summer of 1826, repeating the need for an equipment article, in the light of cases like the *Mágico*, also went to the Council of the Indies which again stated that it had no objections.[4] With the Duke of Infantado and his successor, Salmón, apparently receptive to the British Minister's warnings of the dangers Cuba faced from new importations of slaves, and with the Council of the Indies favourable to stronger measures against the slave trade, the question remains why stronger measures were not immediately adopted.

The second report of the Council of the Indies had to wait four months before the Minister of Foreign Affairs passed it on to the Council of State. Salmón did approve the report and so the suggestion of the equipment article went to the Council of State early in 1827 with the support of both the Foreign Minister and the Council of the Indies. When nothing had been heard from the Council of State by May 1827, the Foreign Minister sent a reminder to the Council, stating he needed a decision to answer the incessant British complaints. Back came the reply that, owing to a bureaucratic mix-up, the Council of State lacked the necessary papers to make such a decision.[5]

The whole issue of the enforcement of the slave trade treaty, for this was the underlying point of the arguments over the equipment article, languished in the hands of the Council of State until 1829 when that body finally made a decision. British diplomats were exasperated by this Spanish procrastination, but could do nothing. One of them, Bosanquet, complained in January 1828 that a British Note on the slave trade, sent the previous June, still had not received an answer.[6] To him it was obvious the Spanish government had no intention of enforcing the slave trade treaty; Spanish rule in Cuba depended on the good will of the proprietors there and the government was unwilling to do anything which might alienate those proprietors and destroy a rich source of revenue for Spain. It might have surprised Bosanquet and his British colleagues to learn that the delaying tactics of the Council of State caused equal difficulties for the Spanish bureaucrats in the Ministry of Foreign Affairs and in the Council of the Indies. Lacking an essential policy decision from the higher authorities, they could not resolve any of the slave trade cases constantly being referred to the Spanish government by the British Minister in Madrid.

Thus the British Note of 12 June 1827, embodying the Havana commissioners' annual report for 1826, was dealt with in the Ministry of Foreign Affairs and then sent to the Council of the Indies. The Council in its report again rejected the idea of declaring the slave trade piracy, but agreed with the British commissioners that in one or two of the cases mentioned a more detailed investigation might have taken place to determine whether slaves had been landed. The report recommended that orders be sent to the Naval Commander at Havana to examine the log-books and other papers of vessels returning from Africa in ballast within twenty-four hours of their arrival. Any vessels suspected of slave-trading were to be reported immediately to the Captain-General. In making this report, the Council of the

Indies emphasized the great difficulty it faced in giving any advice because it did not know whether the recommendations on the slave trade, contained in its previous reports, had been adopted or rejected. The hands of officials in the Ministry of Foreign Affairs were tied in a similar manner. The report of the Council of the Indies, with its accompanying documents, followed its predecessors to the Council of State there to await a decision.[7]

Additional proof of the Council of the Indies' inclination towards stronger measures against the slave trade came in its report arising out of the case of the *Tres Manuelas*. The British commissioners in Havana had obtained sworn statements from four shipwrecked British sailors that the ship which brought them from Africa to Cuba was the slaver, *Tres Manuelas*, carrying a cargo of between 180 and 190 slaves. When the Captain-General refused to act on this evidence, and even refused to admit the British commissioners' power to take statements when not acting with their Spanish colleagues, the commissioners sent their correspondence to London. After being passed along to Madrid, the commissioners' reports were given to the Spanish government in a Note of 31 December 1827. The Council of the Indies in its report was critical of the Captain-General's action and thought his *Auditor de Guerra* deserved a reprimand. Another recommendation called for the Captain-General to send an account of the trade between Cuba and Africa in order to give the Council accurate information on which to base further steps against the slave trade.[8]

Early in 1829 when the Council of State finally released its decision on the equipment article and other pending issues connected with the slave trade to Cuba, the Spanish officials in the Ministry of Foreign Affairs, whose job it was to co-ordinate the various threads of government policy, found themselves in an even worse dilemma. In the clearest statement yet of Spanish policy on the slave trade, the Council of State's report set out the reasons why no new restriction on the slave trade was desirable.

Through force of habit and the lack of any other supply of labour, wrote the Council, the slave trade had become the vital source of Cuba's plantation labourers. 'To forbid the introduction of additional slaves into the island would produce the rapid and inevitable destruction of its agriculture and commerce, because the introduction of European colonists [as a substitute] is a chimera.' Natural reproduction could not supply the deficiencies in the labour force, so that Cuban planters had to rely on the slave trade, 'forced by the need to replace the annual deficit of 10,000 slaves out of the 400,000 in the island . . . without this replacement that rich colony is doomed to decline faster than it has recently developed'.

Once again Britain was the villain. She had filled up her own colonies with labourers and now she sought to strike at the labour supply of foreign colonies in order to improve the competitive position of her own. Referring to the additional convention Britain had signed with Portugal in 1817, the Council of State observed that Britain was willing to give preferential treatment to countries like Brazil where British merchants had considerable financial interests. Humanitarianism was not the motive behind the actions of the British government, it was the tool which the unscrupulous British used as a weapon against their competitors.

Cuba had to be protected from this British offensive. Any new restriction on the slave trade, such as the equipment article, would soon cause a decline in productivity on Cuba's plantations, 'and the way to avoid this and preserve that precious possession is to dissemble without being unfaithful to the treaties'. There were other specific objections to the equipment article itself, notably to the unlimited right of search that would be given to the British navy if Spain agreed to it, but the danger to Cuba stood out as the paramount consideration. Summing up, the report stated, 'since we cannot obtain what is desirable, the suspension of the damaging treaty of 1817, at the very least we will refuse any new restriction or addition to that convention'.[9]

Officials in the Ministry of Foreign Affairs were now caught between the opposing recommendations of the Council of the Indies and the Council of State. The former was in favour of increasing the restrictions on the slave trade while the latter, as its report had underlined, was implacable in its opposition to any new restriction.[10] Meanwhile, more British protests about the ineffectiveness of the existing regulations continued to arrive in Madrid.[11] With contradictory recommendations from the two advisory Councils on the one hand and mounting British pressure for stronger action on the other, Spanish bureaucrats found themselves in the distinctly uncomfortable position of being unable to suggest a solution. The whole issue was turned over to Ferdinand's Council of Ministers in the autumn of 1829.[12]

In a decision ratified by Ferdinand, the Council of Ministers found the arguments advanced by the Council of State compelling, and advised that Spain should not consent to any additions to the slave trade treaty. The Council of Ministers may have hoped that by sending out yet another royal order telling the Captain-General of Cuba to adhere to the slave trade treaty it would coat the pill which was being presented to Britain.[13] If so, there must have been disappointment and even annoyance when another Note arrived from the British Minister in Madrid in December 1830, containing documented evidence of Spanish slave trade practices which were in open violation of Spanish regulations to suppress the slave trade.[14] Spain was urged in the strongest terms to accede to the equipment article because, in the opinion of the British government, nothing less could succeed in finally abolishing the slave trade.

After another Note early in 1831, in which Addington furnished more examples of the many provided by the British commissioners in Havana of the open contempt in which the treaty of 1817 was held in Cuba, the Council of the Indies was asked to re-examine the proposed equipment article. The task of the Council of the Indies was the seemingly impossible one of reconciling the insistent British agitation for the equipment article with the adamant opposition of the Council of State and the Council of Ministers to any new restriction on the slave trade. Not unexpectedly, the Council of the Indies was unable to re-concile the irreconcilable, but it did have one new suggestion. It proposed that a clearance be given by the Cuban government to every vessel sailing from Cuba to Africa. This document would state the vessel's destination and purpose, and those Spanish vessels without it would be liable to confiscation. Even though such a plan would not have begun to meet the British objections, which were aimed not only at the regulations but at the way they were enforced, it was sent to the Council of Ministers for consideration.[15]

Here it was joined during the next two years by a growing pile of British protests, each increasingly vehement and each equally fruit-less. The British commission judge had reported from Havana that the royal order which had been sent to the Captain-General on 4 March 1830, ordering him to adhere to the provisions of the 1817 treaty, had never been published, and this was communicated to the Spanish government in November 1831. The British judge was quite correct. Captain-General Vives had acknowledged the royal order and had stated that it had been sent in the usual manner to all the government authorities, but it had not been published.[16]

Further Notes in 1832 emphasized with tiresome repetition that only with an equipment article could the continual evasions of the slave trade treaty be prevented. Warnings of the eventual loss of Cuba to Spain if nothing was done to stop the huge importation of African slaves alternated with soothing words about Holland's experience with the equipment article. The Council of Ministers refrained, probably deliberately, from touching this contentious issue again, and a succession of Spanish Foreign Ministers either ignored the British Notes or avoided replying to the main point raised in them which was the need for an equipment article. Without a decision from the Council of Ministers, the Spanish Foreign Ministers, Salmón and his immediate successors, Calomarde, Alcudia and Cea Bermúdez, found themselves in a diplomatic strait-jacket. They could not answer the British demands, a fact which further annoyed Palmerston who was now the British Foreign Secretary,[17] nor could they do anything to stop the British protests.

Spanish tactics occasionally varied. Alcudia, who took over as Spanish Foreign Minister in the spring of 1832, decided to let the Captain-General of Cuba bear the responsibility of replying to the British charges. He forwarded a British Note sent in the spring of 1832 to Havana and ordered Captain-General Ricafort to report on the accusations it contained. The Captain-General consulted both the Intendant and the Naval Commander before replying. Their combined view was that the length of Cuba's coastline made it impossible to prevent every illegal landing of slaves, and they pointed out that the efforts of the authorities to prevent the slave trade were frustrated by the eager desire of the plantation owners to obtain African slaves.[18] However effective this gambit was in relieving the pressure on the Spanish Foreign Minister, the Captain-General's reply certainly provided no answer to the British demands for an equipment article.

Early in 1833 a new proposal was added to the long-standing British campaign for an equipment article.[19] Several slavers had been condemned in the mixed commission courts a second time, proof that an initial condemnation had not prevented the refitting of these slave ships. To put an end to this practice the British government wanted all condemned slavers to be broken up immediately after the sentence had been passed.

The extremely complex nature of Spain's dilemma was summarized in a memorandum written by an official in the Ministry of Foreign Affairs in the summer of 1833. On the one side it involved incessant and escalating British pressure and on the other the acute shortage of labour in Cuba which, in addition to the great profits in the slave trade, gave added incentive to the slave traders. There still seemed to be no way of satisfying Britain without causing damage to Cuba. The memorandum suggested that a special committee be appointed with instructions to examine both the equipment article and the problems posed by the accumulation of emancipated Africans in Havana.[20] Cea Bermúdez, the Spanish Foreign Minister, accepted this idea and appointed a commission of three men who presented their report at the end of October 1833.

The commission recognized the intractable nature of the problem it was called on to solve.[21] 'It involves nothing less than reconciling English demands with Spanish necessities, and how can two such contradictory things be reconciled?' But, as previous Spanish inquiries had done, this one exaggerated the difficulties by completely failing to understand the real motives behind Britain's international advocacy of a slave trade prohibition. British public opinion, which wanted the slave trade abolished for humanitarian reasons, remained the *raison d'être* of the Foreign Office's unrelenting drive to uphold existing treaties against the slave trade and to procure new ones. The commission, in its report, reflected a view widely held by Spanish officialdom on both sides of the Atlantic when it stated that behind the public professions of British statesmen lay a desire to gain for India and Brazil a monopoly in the export of sugar to Europe. The obvious way to do this would be to ruin their main competitor, Cuba, by cutting off her labour supply. In fact, Britain was trying to persuade both Portugal and Brazil to agree to an equipment article at the same time as she was negotiating with Spain, but they were even more obdurate than Spain.[22]

The three men who signed this report were not inexperienced. One of them, José de Heredia, had advised Cea Bermúdez before on issues relating to the slave trade. Yet the clear thinking which was so badly needed was prevented by their myopic view on these colonial problems (and none was more serious nor had wider ramifications than the whole issue of the slave trade) coupled with an unjustified suspicion of British motives. Instead, recriminations against the circumstances which had forced Spain to sign the degrading treaty with Britain were mixed with admiration at how well the Cuban planters had managed to avoid its evil consequences. Fearing that Spain's submission to the equipment article or to any other new restriction on the slave trade would lead inevitably to the loss of Cuba, the commission limited itself to suggesting a reply to Britain which amounted to a very diplomatic refusal.

Palmerston was not the sort of man to be deflected from his objective by the negative arguments advanced by Cea Bermúdez and his advisers. He gave strict orders to George Villiers, his new Minister in

Madrid (and destined later, as Lord Clarendon, to be one of Palmerston's successors as British Foreign Secretary), to secure Spain's agreement to the British proposals, particularly to the equipment article.[23] But the delaying policy which had been used to frustrate British diplomacy up to this time plagued Villiers as well. He complained to Palmerston in March 1834 that he could get no action from the liberal government of Martínez de la Rosa. Later he wrote, 'it is only by goading and the exhibition of the whip in a manner which I should be sorry came to the ears of Fowell Buxton [the British abolitionist], that I ever get answers to my various reclamations'.[24]

Palmerston remained emphatic on the importance of the equipment article: 'there is nothing the Spanish Government could do that would be so acceptable to us'.[25] It was British support for the liberal cause in Spain which enabled Villiers to prevail in the end over the opposition of the Cuban interests. Villiers bluntly informed Palmerston in a private letter that Spain would sign 'simply as an *obsequio* as it is called here'. Her signature did not mean her cooperation. Villiers was equally forthright about this: 'There can be no greater mistake than supposing that Spain is sincere in wishing to put down the slave trade.'[26] Later, sending information to his brother to use in preparing an article on the treaty for the *Edinburgh Review*, Villiers urged him to stress how important 'personal negociation' had been in obtaining the slave trade treaty so that the readers of the *Review* would have a proper appreciation of his own vital contribution. He ridiculed any suggestion of Spanish humanitarianism motivating the Spanish government:

for it cannot be sufficiently borne in mind that all those Spaniards who are not absolutely indifferent to the abolition of the slave trade, are positively adverse to it. We think that an appeal to humanity must be conclusive. The word is not *understood* by a Spaniard . . . Appeal then to the humanity of such a nation in favour of a race which they look upon as mere beasts of the field . . . Then Cuba is the pride and hope and joy of Spain. It is cherished as the only fraction of the world which once owned Spain as mistress. Cuba is the place whence revenue comes and whither every bankrupt Spaniard goes in order to rob *ad libitum*.[27]

Even with British support for the Spanish liberals, it was a near thing. Early in September 1834, Villiers announced Martínez de la Rosa's agreement to an equipment article. Villiers had to overcome obstacles every step of the way. He reported that Martínez de la Rosa faced 'endless intrigues' aimed at scuttling this new restriction on the slave trade.[28] Cuban opposition was foremost. One of the more moderate opponents, José Maria Calvo, the *procurador síndico general* of Havana, believed Spain should continue its policy of deception until European colonization had reached the point where the abolition of the slave trade could be undertaken.[29] No one in the Spanish government really supported further concessions to Britain on the slave trade issue except as a price to be paid for British support. This accounts for the Spanish Foreign Minister's reluctance to sign the treaty, a reluctance which exasperated the British government. Villiers blamed Martínez de la Rosa himself for much of the delay. 'But with that extraordinary irresolution which marks the whole of M. Martínez de la Rosa's conduct, he still hesitates to take a definite step.'[30]

The equipment article was the main provision of the treaty which was finally signed on 28 June 1835.[31] It provided for the seizure and condemnation of vessels carrying specific equipment for the slave trade, even though slaves were not on board at the time of the capture. The equipment comprised: hatches with open gratings, more bulkheads than normal, spare planks, shackles, bolts or handcuffs, and suspicious quantities of water, water-casks, mess-tubs, etc. Villiers had earlier described the equipment provisions as 'the only useful articles in the Treaty'.[32] Unlike the 1817 treaty which had not prohibited the slave trade between Spanish colonies and thus had left a legal loophole for slave traders, the 1835 treaty declared the Spanish slave trade 'totally and finally abolished in all parts of the world'. Other articles extended the area of mutual right of search and provided that condemned slave ships were to be immediately broken up. Spain also committed herself to pass stronger legislation against slave trade offenders.

For Britain the 1835 treaty was signed at a time when the slave trade to Cuba was growing into a huge and uncontrollable monster. The British Parliament had abolished slavery in the British West Indian islands in 1833 and British planters and abolitionists alike were unanimous on the need to protect the British islands from the unfair competition of Cuba which relied on a continuing supply of African slaves. Abolition of slavery in the British West Indies alone was a tremendous stimulus to the slave trade to Cuba as Cuban planters sought to take advantage of the new opportunities presented to them, but Cuba had also been ravaged by a cholera epidemic in 1833 which had struck particularly hard at the African population, especially the plantation slaves. At the very time when sugar prices were rising and prospects for Cuban sugar exports improving, Cuba's slave population suffered a drastic decline. Without hope of replacing their slave losses through domestic reproduction, due to the marked inequality of sexes on Cuban plantations, Cuban planters saw themselves as dependent on the slave trade. They also feared time was running out on the slave trade and this fear was a further stimulus to purchase as many African slaves as possible. The British commissioners in Havana reported 33 slave landings during 1834 and a huge increase to 50 during 1835.[33] Could the new treaty check this enormous expansion in the Cuban slave trade?

The treaty was a godsend to the British West African Squadron. From 1830 to 1835 it had captured an average of only 10 slavers a year, all with slaves on board. From 1835 to 1839 this average rose to 35, nearly all destined for Cuba. Thirty-seven slavers flying the Spanish flag were seized in 1836 and taken to the mixed commission court at Sierra Leone. Of these, 28 were captured and 24 were condemned under the equipment article.[34]

The success of the British West African Squadron was in marked contrast to the lack of success in Cuba. This was not the fault of the British navy in the Caribbean, British officials in Havana nor really of the new treaty itself. The reasons for the failure lay in the combination of Spanish determination to give unofficial protection to the slave trade in spite of the treaty and the criminal ingenuity of the slave traders themselves. The Spanish commissioners on the mixed court at Havana refused to act under the new treaty until they had received specific orders to do so and these did not arrive until March 1836.[35] Prior to this, in January 1836, a British naval officer brought a suspected slaver, the *General Laborde*, into Havana. When captured, the vessel had no slaves on board and the capture created a sensation in Havana as the first to occur under the new treaty. Whatever psychological effect the capture might have had on the slave traders was lost because the court could not hear the case under the new treaty and freed the vessel since it could not be condemned under the 1817 treaty. The British commissioners believed the vessel would have been condemned if the 1835 treaty had been in force. The knowledge that the British commissioners possessed the treaty and the capture of the *General Laborde* created a temporary set-back for the slave traders, but the opportunity for a far more effective blow had been missed.[36]

Operating under the 1817 treaty, the court of mixed commission at Havana had acted both effectively and harmoniously in the limited task given to it, that of adjudicating suspected slavers captured by ships of either the British or Spanish navies. The procedures it fol-

lowed were the same as those of other courts of mixed commission
located in Freetown, Sierra Leone or in Rio de Janeiro and, although
the British and Spanish commissioners did not always agree on the
cases before them, captured slavers brought to Havana with slaves on
board regularly were condemned by the court.[37] The new treaty was
designed to make the court's operation more effective by giving it the
power to condemn captured slave ships on which equipment for
carrying on the slave trade was found even if the actual slaves themselves were not on board. At Havana the new treaty had just the
opposite result, threatening for the first time to introduce a divisive
and partisan nature to the court's proceedings.

The case which brought these unforeseen problems to the forefront
involved the very same vessel, the *General Laborde*, which earlier had
escaped conviction because the 1835 treaty was not yet in force. A
British cruiser, the *Pincher*, arrived in Havana harbour on 2 January
1837 with the *General Laborde* which she had captured off the north
coast of Cuba, completely equipped for the slave trade. When the
court of mixed commission heard the case, the British judge voted for
conviction, but the Spanish judge voted to free the vessel on the
grounds that her papers established she was on a legal voyage to a
European port. To resolve the impasse a roll of the dice appointed the
Spanish arbitrator who sided with his colleague. Thus the very ship
whose condemnation had been predicted under the new treaty, was
freed by a vote of the Spanish commissioners.[38] A similar division
along partisan lines over another case later in the same year further
undermined the court's reputation for impartiality.[39] These cases and
the use of the dice box to decide whether the British or Spanish
arbitrator should make the final decision received considerable publicity at the time, but this publicity disguised the real importance of
the Havana court which, in fact, was diminishing rapidly because of
actions taken by the slave traders to circumvent the new treaty.

The British consul at Havana, Charles Tolmé, was in the best position to report on the reactions of the Cuban slave traders to the 1835
treaty. His report of October 1836 disclosed how the slave traders had
evaded the new restrictions.[40] When it was first known in Cuba that
another treaty had been signed, the slave traders were seriously
alarmed. Many expeditions were given up entirely and others were
stopped before the fitting out process began. Insurance companies,
which had previously insured the whole voyage, refused to underwrite anything but the return voyage.

The interval between the signing of the treaty and its promulgation in Cuba raised the hopes of the slave traders that it would never be ratified, or even if ratified, it would not be enforced by the Cuban government. The pause of August and September gave way to renewed activity and before the end of 1835 20 expeditions had been despatched from Cuba. Individual slave traders experimented with various devices to elude British cruisers which were now operating under the equipment article. Then, pooling their experiences, the slave traders agreed on general rules. Factories were to be established on the coast of Africa which would try to keep a constant supply of slaves and equipment for slave ships to facilitate swift departures. Equipment was to be shipped under foreign flags, United States or Portuguese, to Africa. The actual slavers were to be smaller and sent from Havana in ballast. They would congregate in groups of three or more at the African factories so that, if a British cruiser approached, they could scatter and reduce the risk of capture. On the homeward journey to Cuba the Portuguese flag was to be used.

Since Britain had no treaty with Portugal permitting British naval vessels to seize suspected slavers flying the Portuguese flag, British naval officers and British officials of the mixed court at Havana had to look on in helpless frustration as fully equipped slavers left Havana flying the Portuguese flag. Until Palmerston's Act of Parliament of 1839, authorizing British cruisers to capture all Portuguese slavers and to send them to British Vice-Admiralty courts for adjudication, the British government had no way of dealing with slave vessels flying the Portuguese flag.[41] The slave traders knew this and the majority of slaving expeditions to Cuba during this period took advantage of the fact. The dramatic increase in the use of the Portuguese flag can be

Table 4. *Nationality of Cuban slave trade vessels, 1834–40*

Year	Spanish	Portuguese	United States	Other	Total arrivals
1834	29	3	—	1	33
1835	42	8	—	—	50
1836	29	14	—	—	43
1837	3	48	—	—	51
1838	4	44	—	2	50
1839	2	29	6	—	37
1840	7	29	5	—	41

Source: James Bandinel, *Some Account of the Trade in Slaves from Africa . . .* (London, 1969), pp. 232–3.

seen in Table 4, which gives the nationality of the slavers landing
cargoes in Cuba, 1834–40.

The abuse of the Portuguese flag became all the more blatant when
a notorious slave trader became the Portuguese consul in Havana in
1837. He had a brother living at a factory in Whydah on the African
coast and together they assisted slave traders to overcome the obstacles which the 1835 treaty placed in the way of the Cuban slave
trade. Registers of lost or broken up Portuguese ships sold in Havana
for $1,000 to $1,500, a small price for the slave traders to pay compared with the enormous profits to be made.[42]

The Portuguese flag was not the only one the slave traders found
useful to counteract the 1835 treaty. They began to resort to the United
States flag, a practice which steadily increased after 1836. Many of the
slave trade vessels in use after 1835 were actually constructed in United
States ports, often at Baltimore, and then were sold to slave trade
interests in Havana. Construction of schooners for the slave trade
produced a boom in the Baltimore shipyards in 1838 at a time when
other United States shipyards were in the midst of a depression.[43] A
favourite technique of the slave traders was for a vessel to leave
Havana flying a United States flag and carrying United States papers
but before leaving Africa on the return voyage, the United States
papers and flag would be exchanged for Portuguese papers and a
Portuguese flag. In this way the slave traders hoped to evade British
cruisers operating under the 1835 treaty. Table 5 indicates the use of
the United States flag by suspected slave trade vessels leaving Havana
during the years 1834–40. A comparison of Table 5 with Table 4 above
illustrates that more suspected slavers left Havana in any one year than
arrived, the difference being due to a combination of captures,

Table 5. *Nationality of suspected slave trade vessels leaving Havana, 1834–40*

Year	Spanish	Portuguese	United States	Other	Total departures
1834	60	2	—	—	62
1835	78	2	—	—	80
1836	28	5	5	—	38
1837	19	40	11	1	71
1838	8	42	19	2	71
1839	8	26	23	2	59
1840	12	32	9	1	54

Source: British commissioners' annual reports, 1834–40.

faulty information and unaccounted for landings in other parts of the island.

The case of the *Venus*, alias the *Duquesa de la Braganza*, typified the changes in the Cuban slave trade after 1835. The British commission judge reported the arrival at Havana in August 1838 of a 460-ton Baltimore clipper named the *Venus*.[44] It had been built expressly for the slave trade and its speed and size made it ideal for the long voyage to Mozambique. Voyages to Mozambique by Cuban slavers were very rare. The British consul at Havana analysed the papers of 100 slave vessels captured during the period 1834–38 to find out where the African slaves had been purchased and he discovered only one expedition which had gone to Mozambique. Nearly three-quarters of the embarkations had occurred either in the Bight of Benin or the Bight of Biafra and half had taken place in the Bight of Biafra.[45] At Havana the *Venus* was renamed the *Duquesa de la Braganza*, given Portuguese papers and equipped for the slave trade. Four months later, after a remarkably fast voyage during which it outsailed a British cruiser to escape capture, the *Duquesa de la Braganza* arrived back in Havana in ballast, having landed 860 African slaves, to that date the largest number brought in one voyage in the history of the Cuban slave trade. The *Venus* originally had cost 30,000 dollars to build and the costs of the voyage including the purchase of the slaves amounted to 60,000 dollars. The 860 slaves sold for 340 dollars apiece yielding a net profit to the vessel's owners of close to 200,000 dollars.[46] The combination of Baltimore clippers and either United States or Portuguese nationality was more than sufficient to overcome the equipment clause of the 1835 treaty.

The British commissioners also reported that it was the United States consul at Havana, Nicholas Trist, acting for the Portuguese consul, who had authenticated the necessary papers for the notorious voyage of the *Venus*.[47] They accused Trist, who later negotiated the Treaty of Guadalupe–Hidalgo ending the United States war with Mexico, of aiding United States vessels engaged in the Cuban slave trade instead of trying to halt what amounted to an open violation of United States laws against the slave trade. Trist countered the British commissioners' charges with a 260-page polemic which Palmerston termed an 'Extraordinary Production', while one of the British officials, R. R. Madden, saw to it that the accusations were published in the United States.[48] Ten years later Madden wrote a book on Cuba and he had not forgotten Nicholas Trist: 'this wily gentleman . . . the reader will notice the Cuban apprenticeship of this American diplomatist – the preparatory course of intrigue, to fit him for the State-swindling diplomacy in Mexico'.[49]

The British accusations led the United States government to send an investigator to Cuba to examine the British charges. Alexander Everett, the man nominated by President Van Buren to investigate Trist's supposed collusion with the Cuban slave traders, was a former United States Minister to Spain (1825–29) and was therefore familiar with the problem of the Cuban slave trade. He was also a long-standing advocate of the United States annexation of Cuba, although he did not allow his annexationist sympathies to influence his investigation of Trist.[50] The report he submitted to the United States Secretary of State on 21 July 1840 was severely critical of Trist's actions in Havana.[51] Everett stated it was 'a matter of public notoriety' that the United States flag had been used in the Cuban slave trade. He accepted the statistics on its use compiled by the British commissioners and blamed Trist for his complicity in the slave trade by authenticating United States and Portuguese documents for suspected slave-trading vessels. He denounced Trist particularly for not demanding the seizure of the *Venus*, a case which Everett described at some length as the worst example of the illegalities practised by the Cuban slave traders. Trist was dismissed by the new Whig administration in 1841, but the United States government carefully refrained from making any judgement on either the British charges or the Everett report.[52] The real answer of the United States to these charges and to the growing American involvement in the slave trade was the treaty signed with Britain in 1842 in which the United States agreed to station a naval squadron off the west coast of Africa to capture United States slavers and, equally important although obviously not included in the treaty, to prevent the British navy from harassing American ships.

British officials were convinced that Cuban slave traders would not have been successful in combatting the new powers of the 1835 treaty had it not been for the co-operation of the Spanish colonial officials in Cuba. Clearly, the unofficial sanctioning of the slave trade emanated from the Captain-General who had tacit, if not explicit, approval from Spain. The Captain-General during this period was Miguel Tacón y Rosique, like his predecessors a military officer who had risen through the ranks of the Spanish army and who had served successively in Peru during the wars of independence and then in the Peninsula after a brief term as Captain-General of Puerto Rico.[53] Tacón had been identified as a liberal, even a radical, in Spain and both the British officials and the Cuban creoles held out great hopes for reform when Martínez de la Rosa's administration, the first Spanish liberal government after the death of Ferdinand VII, announced his appointment as Captain-General in 1834. These hopes were quickly dashed because Tacón turned out to be as reactionary in Cuba as he had been liberal in Spain.

As an *ayacucho*, a Spanish veteran of the Latin American wars of independence, Tacón shared the views of his fellow officers that Spain had lost her empire because she had conceded political rights to her colonists which made them equal to Spaniards living in the peninsula. The colonists had reacted to these concessions, according to the *ayacuchos*, by seizing their independence. The moral was clear to him. The initial mistake of offering concessions must not be repeated. As Tacón warned the Spanish government in 1835, 'If we wish to preserve what little we still have of America, we must not make any change in the present system of colonial government, whatever innovations may occur in Spain.'[54] He therefore opposed the extension of political reforms to Cuba. Although he was unable to prevent the Spanish Constitution of 1812 from being proclaimed in Cuba in 1836, after it had been re-established in Spain, he was instrumental in preventing the elected Cuban deputies from taking their seats in the Spanish Cortes. When Spain adopted a new constitution in 1837, Tacón successfully petitioned to have Cuba excluded from its provisions. Cuba was promised 'special laws' which never came, and the island continued to be ruled by the harsh dictates of martial law. No Cuban deputies sat in the Spanish Cortes until 1878, as successive Spanish governments followed Tacón's policy of keeping Cuba under rigid control. Freedom of the press, another of the desires of the Cuban creoles, was non-existent. José Antonio Saco, one of the leaders of the Cuban intellectuals, was expelled from Cuba by Tacón for publishing ideas which aroused the anger of Spanish officials. Tacón allied himself with planter interests and his sole aim, apart from constructing public works and enforcing law and order, was to preserve Cuba for Spain as a wealthy and secure plantation colony.

Cuban history records Tacón as the greatest protector the slave traders ever had. He allegedly received half an ounce of gold for every slave brought to Cuba and one of his most influential advisers was the foremost slave trader in Havana, Joaquín Gómez.[55] There was little hope that the new treaty would change the mind of the chief protector of the Cuban slave trade and Tacón later revealed that the Spanish attitude towards the 1835 treaty had been deliberate.[56] The British Minister to Spain, who had negotiated the 1835 treaty, George Villiers, wrote to the British consul in Havana in the autumn of 1835 to find out the effect of the new treaty on the Cuban slave trade, only to receive a reply saying that at the end of November 1835 no official announcement of the treaty had yet been received in Havana. When Villiers then found out that the treaty had been sent to the Cuban Captain-General in July 1835, and therefore had been deliberately suppressed by Tacón, he angrily demanded of Mendizábal, the Spanish Foreign Minister, that Tacón be dismissed.[57] The Captain-General was not dismissed and the slave trade was left to flourish as before.

Tacón believed public opinion in Cuba supported the continuation of the slave trade and Spanish policy of resisting British efforts to wipe it out while ostensibly complying with the terms of the treaty. Certainly the planters and the peninsular merchants of Havana supported this policy and their opinions were the only ones Tacón was likely to hear. Open discussion of the slave trade was discouraged. A correspondent of the Cuban creole, Domingo del Monte, reported a dinner conversation in which a companion admonished him for bringing up the subject and commented, 'only the poor criticize the slave trade'.[58] The British commissioners in their annual report for 1836 noted that a veil of secrecy had come down over the slave trade operations in Havana and blamed Cuban public opinion for the ineffectiveness of the treaty: 'we likewise apprehend that amongst a society where every one, be their station or calling what it may, benefits from the prosperity of the Slave Trade, when once secrecy shall be considered no object towards the prosecution of it, few persons will betray it gratuitously'.[59]

The British government was far from content with a treaty which was not accomplishing its object or with the Spanish government which was not co-operating. Palmerston tried various means in order to break down the apparent Spanish attitude of indifference and make the prohibition of the slave trade effective, but none worked. For example, in 1838 the British Minister to Spain proposed that the court of mixed commission in Havana be authorized to summon and examine those suspected of involvement in the slave trade, a proposal which the Spanish Foreign Minister was advised by his officials to reject out of hand as there was nothing in the 1835 treaty to justify it.[60] After the British commissioners had received a copy of a royal order sent in 1838 to Tacón's successor as Captain-General, Ezpeleta, ordering him to comply with the terms of the 1835 treaty, they asked

Ezpeleta to publish the royal order in the main Havana newspaper, the *Diario*. Ezpeleta refused to do this and defended his position in a despatch to Madrid. He stated that the order had been sent in the normal manner to all the lieutenant-governors of the island, but if it was published it might lead to disturbances among the slaves, and equally dangerous from the Captain-General's point of view, publication would anger the proprietors whose support the Spanish government dared not lose. Ezpeleta also included statistics which eloquently emphasized Cuba's economic value to Sapin. The yield from customs duties at Havana alone in 1838 had amounted to over 4,200,000 pesos. The Captain-General's explanation was a very convincing one as far as Madrid was concerned, and he received the full support of the peninsular government.[61]

When the new slave trade treaty with Spain had been signed in 1835, British statesmen and the British public welcomed it with somewhat qualified enthusiasm, but seven years later the head of the slave trade department of the Foreign Office could still call it 'the most efficient for its purpose of any of the Treaties yet concluded in reference to this subject'.[62] George Villiers, who had negotiated the treaty for Britain, arranged to have his brother praise it in an anonymous article in the *Edinburgh Review* in 1836 because it gave Britain all the powers she needed to eliminate the Spanish slave trade. 'The great and *essential* difference between this treaty and all others concluded with Spain, is that it does not depend for its fulfilment upon Spanish co-operation. All is left to the regulations of the British Government, and the activity of British cruisers.'[63] Other champions of the treaty appeared even after critics in Britain began to condemn it. One of them was David Turnbull, later to play a prominent role in Cuba himself. He devoted a chapter in his book on Cuba, written in 1839, to defending what he termed an 'undervalued' treaty against the increasing attacks of British abolitionists.[64]

The British abolitionists began to take notice of the foreign slave trade in the late 1830s because it appeared to be on the increase rather than declining as a result of Britain's offensive. Brazil was the main culprit, but the Cuban slave trade was not ignored. Within Britain the abolitionists had concentrated their attack upon slavery in the empire until its abolition in 1833 and then they were naturally concerned with the aftermath of abolition especially in the British West Indies. The British House of Commons did not debate the issue of the foreign slave trade from 1835 to 1838 and by then it had increased alarmingly. Lord Brougham told the House of Lords in 1838 that the numbers of victims brought to Havana by the slave trade were as great as ever.[65]

The conversion of one of the leaders of the British abolitionist movement, Sir Thomas Fowell Buxton, brought the subject of the foreign slave trade into the forefront of British politics. Until 1837, Buxton had led the battle against slavery and then against the apprenticeship system which had replaced slavery in the British West Indies. Buxton's defeat in the general election of 1837 prompted him to assess the state of the anti-slavery movement in Britain and he decided as a result of this assessment that the continuing and apparently growing evil of the Atlantic slave trade should be the primary target of the abolitionists. From the 1820s the British abolitionist movement had been largely indifferent to the slave trade, leaving it to the British Foreign Office to enforce the treaties for its suppression. This was now to change as Buxton and fellow abolitionists worked to arouse British public opinion to the horrors of the slave trade. Buxton plunged into research on the subject, channelling all his zeal and ability into it and in 1838 he published *The Slave Trade*, a forceful attack on the system of suppression which Britain had constructed. Two years later he published a second edition which contained his remedy: Britain should concentrate her efforts on civilizing Africa, substituting legitimate commerce for the illegal and inhuman slave trade. Buxton's ideas played a prominent part in Britain's efforts to open up the Niger river.[66] Buxton did not neglect the Cuban slave trade. He included a strong condemnation of the treaty Britain had signed with Spain in 1835, finding ample evidence in the Parliamentary Papers to illustrate his conclusion that the 1835 treaty was mere waste paper and that, as interpreted by the Spanish commissioners in Havana, it was 'an impudent fraud'.[67]

Buxton's campaign against the slave trade had little direct effect on Cuba other than to make British officials there much more conscious of the importance of accurate statistics on the slave trade to Cuba. Buxton's purpose in writing his book was to prove that the Atlantic slave trade was much greater in the 1830s than it had been before 1807. His statistics, far more than those provided by the British Foreign Office, created a public controversy. By taking statements from the British commissioners at Havana out of context, Buxton estimated that 60,000 slaves a year were brought to Cuba.[68] His figures were immediately challenged by other abolitionists as being too high.[69] Buxton stood his ground, but the controversy became a subject of debate at the Anti-Slavery Convention held in London during June 1840.[70]

British officials in Cuba were just as concerned with the inaccuracy of Buxton's statistics as were Buxton's abolitionist allies, especially since Buxton had obtained his statistics from the reports of the British commissioners and the British consul. David Tolmé, British consul in Havana from 1833 to 1840, sent a despatch to Lord Palmerston, dated 17 September 1839, which was essentially a refutation of Buxton's statistics.[71] He enclosed a list 'which is an estimate of the number of Slaves imported in the years 1830 to 1838 inclusive . . . from vessels which afterwards entered this port . . .', based on the lists compiled by the British commissioners. This list is included here as Table 6 with the number of slave-trading expeditions in brackets. Tolmé doubted that very many slaves who had been landed at the outports had been left out of the list, because nearly all slavers eventually came to Havana. He was also convinced that relatively few slavers landed at the outports since the main agricultural area where demand for labour was greatest was in the Havana–Matanzas region. Tolmé believed a 20% addition to his figures would more than cover unknown landings. His figure for 1838 was based on his own information of slavers arriving in Havana as well as on the reports of the British commissioners. Tolmé went to some trouble to justify the accuracy of

Table 6. *British consul Tolmé's estimate of slave landings in Cuba, 1830–38*

Years	Numbers	Number of expeditions according to the reports of the British commissioners
1830	9,808	(36)
1831	10,400	(36)
1832	8,200	(27)
1833	9,000	(27)
1834	11,400	(33)
1835	14,800	(50)
1836	14,200	(43)
1837	15,200	(51)
1838	14,438	(50)
Total	107,446	353

Source: Tolmé to Palmerston, no. 18, 17 Sept. 1839, F.O. 84/280.

the statistics,

because a work recently published, by one [Buxton] whose talents and
philanthropy, (to which the humble tribute of my praise is not wanting)
entitle him to the confidence of the public, may create some misconception,
and I hold it to be essentially important, for many reasons, and among others,
that we may judge of the proportion of the vessels captured to those which
arrive and thereby the probable effect of our naval operations against the
Trade, that correct ideas should prevail on the matter.[72]

In their annual report for 1841, the British commissioners included
a list showing the numbers of slaves landed in the Havana–Matanzas
area from 1835 to 1841. These figures were obtained from the books of
the slave traders in Havana. They provide a check on the numbers in
consul Tolmé's estimate for the years 1835–38, the biggest difference
occurring for the year 1838. This list is reproduced as Table 7, with the
commissioners' estimate of the number of expeditions each year in
brackets. The statistics of the slave trade compiled by British officials
in Cuba were far closer to the truth than the distorted version published by Buxton, but they revealed all too clearly how completely ineffective the new treaty had been in stopping or even curtailing the
Cuban slave trade.

Neither British diplomats nor British abolitionists had so far
succeeded in eliminating the slave trade to Cuba. The main reason of
course was Spain's refusal to co-operate. Spain followed a paradoxi-
cal policy of implementing both the 1817 treaty and its successor of
1835 in such a way that the slave trade to Cuba, bringing slave labour

Table 7. *Numbers of slaves imported into the Havana–Matanzas
area, 1835–41, taken from the books of the Cuban slave traders*

Years	Number of expeditions		Number of slaves
1835	47	(50)	15,242
1836	41	(43)	14,082
1837	29	(51)	12,240
1838	32	(50)	10,495
1839	31	(47)	10,995
1840	28	(44)	10,104
1841	21	(27)	8,893
Total	229	312	82,051

Source: British commissioners to Palmerston, no. 4, 1 Jan. 1842,
F.O. 84/395, and annual reports of the British commissioners,
1836–42.

for Cuba's plantations, was not affected. Initial opposition to each treaty in turn gave way to an ostensible desire to uphold them. The Spanish government even found both treaties useful as defensive weapons to ward off imagined British threats to Cuba in the form of attempts to strike at the slave trade by expanding the powers of the court of mixed commission in Havana. In Britain the frustration developed by so many years of futile striving against the foreign slave trade was largely responsible for the resurrection in the late 1830s of the abolitionist movement aimed at wiping out that trade. Spanish officials in Cuba could not know that out of this new wave of British abolitionist discontent would arise a new and more dangerous threat to Cuba's security and prosperity.

CHAPTER 7

An abolitionist era

The abolition of slavery within the British empire in 1833 had a revolutionary impact on Britain's West Indian colonies, but the Caribbean effects of British humanitarianism were not confined to British colonies.[1] The influence of British abolitionist ideas and subsequently of British abolitionists themselves spread quickly from Jamaica to Cuba, the nearest and largest of the remaining slave plantation colonies of the Caribbean. Cuban planters and Spanish colonial officials knew only too well that it had been British pressure on Spain to abolish the slave trade, after Britain herself had prohibited it, which had led to the Anglo-Spanish treaties of 1817 and 1835, prohibiting the slave trade to Cuba; the abolition of slavery within British colonial possessions portended a similar campaign to eliminate slavery in Cuba. Within Cuba abolitionism was viewed as a foreign import which, in the eyes of the European planter class and Spanish officials, was a foreign menace. In an ironic and unwitting interaction of British colonial and foreign policy, the emancipation of slaves in the British West Indies provoked a greater reaction in Cuba than the long and persistent effort of British officials to stop the Cuban slave trade.

The Cuban government, supported every step of the way from Madrid, took all possible precautions to prevent abolitionist ideas from seeping into the island. Beginning in the late 1820s as the campaign against slavery in the British empire began to gather force, Cuban authorities enacted a series of measures designed to guard the island against this intangible enemy. The measures were similar to those enacted after the St Domingue revolution and they were implemented in a growing atmosphere of emotion and hysteria which also was reminiscent of the 1790s.

One of the measures taken, dating back to the St Domingue revolution, was to prevent any Africans who had been exposed to so-called corrupting influences from entering Cuba. Captain-General Las

Casas had issued a circular in 1796 ordering slave traders to bring in only *bozal* Africans – that is, African slaves brought directly from Africa. Under no title or pretext were Africans who had lived in foreign countries to be introduced into Cuba.[2] Captain-General Vives followed this precedent in an 1829 circular, prohibiting the entry of Africans into Cuba from either mainland America or foreign colonies.[3] Two years later he took extra precautions to ban the entry into Cuba of any Africans from Jamaica because of the slave unrest there that year. The danger came not only from the Africans who, according to the Cuban government, had been seduced by the spirit of liberty, but even more from the British Methodists who were the principal seducers.[4] Vives and his subordinates were not slow to learn from the British planters their hatred of the missionary sects. Another circular in 1832 repeated the prohibition on the entry of Africans from Jamaica. This policy of insulating the island from the effects of revolution on the mainland and emancipation in the British West Indian colonies received the warm approval of the Council of the Indies.[5]

The Cuban planters were now so conscious of the vulnerability of their slave-built prosperity they began to develop a siege mentality. They saw themselves as living in a beleaguered fortress where they had to be always on the alert lest the enemy launch an attack from an unexpected direction or try a new ruse to catch them offguard. The Intendant of Havana, in a despatch reporting the emancipation of slaves in the British West Indies, reflected this attitude: 'Those islands are in such close proximity to our own, and the evil which that blind example can bring here with the other consequences which always follow in the wake of such changes, that even if there is no likelihood of an immediate threat, we have plenty of reason to remain constantly on guard.'[6]

Miguel Tacón's appointment as Captain-General in 1834 opened a new stage in the Spanish struggle to preserve Cuba from the fate of its neighbours, Jamaica and Haiti. His own reactionary ideas did nothing to calm the anxiety of the peninsulars and Cuban creoles. Tacón saw abolitionism as one of the chief dangers besetting the island, closely followed by the Cuban creoles' desire for political rights and the acquisitive designs on Cuba by Britain and the United States. No political concessions could be contemplated in such a dangerous climate and repression was the answer to all threats whether internal or external. Tacón described the abolitionist dangers surrounding Cuba in a despatch dated 31 August 1835 and sent both to the Minister of the Interior, then in charge of overseas colonies, and to the Minister

of Foreign Affairs.[7] It was bad enough that large numbers of freed
African slaves lived in Jamaica and Haiti, 'filled with exaggerated ideas
of liberty and equality', but worse in that they were supported by a
large party in Europe whose aim was the triumph of the Africans over
the Europeans. He enclosed an anonymous letter which he had
received warning of the activities of the Methodists who had translated
the Bible into many languages, changing the text to inspire ideas of
absolute equality in all classes and especially among slaves. Methodist
agents reportedly were in Jamaica and had a huge supply of Bibles
waiting to be introduced into Cuba in whatever way possible. To
Tacón this Methodist activity clearly was aimed at subverting Cuba's
slaves.

Further proof had come with the discovery of a figurine of a kneel-
ing slave in chains with the English inscription: 'Exodus, chapter 21,
verse 16'.[8] The Captain-General had ordered the Military Commission
to investigate the appearance of the figurine, but this body was unable
to discover who had brought it to Cuba. Apart from a conviction
that the figurine had been made in Britain and brought over to Cuba
from Jamaica and a belief that it was not the only example, the Cuban
authorities were totally baffled. When Tacón's description of these
incidents reached Spain, Mendizábal, the head of the Spanish liberal
government, applauded his vigilance, but to both peninsular and
Cuban governments the lesson was evident: no abolitionist emissary
must be allowed into Cuba.[9]

The next wave of abolitionist panic to break over Tacón's administration began early in 1836 with the report by a captain of a Cuban
schooner, the *Nueva Esperanza*, that when he had put into Gran Cayman
island he had found 5,000 free blacks there, some of whom had
robbed him. The captain had obviously exaggerated his tale for
effect but Tacón, instead of investigating the affair thoroughly before
acting, assumed this was part of the anti-slavery campaign being
waged against Cuba from Jamaica and prepared to meet the expected
invasion. When the Governor of Matanzas later repeated this rumour,
Tacón convened a meeting of the leading officials of Cuba which
recommended an immediate increase in the number of naval vessels
patrolling on the south side of the island.[10] The invasion did not
materialize and no one ever located the 5,000 free blacks but the
damage had been done. Each new rumour, whether true or not,
reinforced the spectre of an abolitionist menace threatening Cuba
with violent revolution.

The Gran Cayman incident also prompted Tacón to send a naval officer to Jamaica on a secret mission to report on anti-slavery societies there. His findings supported Tacón's own views and provided useful material for justifying the Captain-General's actions to Madrid. Captain Apodaca, the man chosen to spy on the abolitionists, reflected the bias of his superiors and, obviously anxious to do a good job, was careful not to underestimate anything that might be of importance to Cuba. He might have entitled his report with his first sentence about the Methodists, 'the Methodist churches dominate the whole island'. Apodaca's report confirmed what the Cuban government already believed: the British government was using the Methodists as agents to destroy Cuba by fomenting slave rebellion. Tacón quickly sent off copies of the report to Madrid as additional evidence of the British conspiracy against Cuba.[11]

Although Tacón's worst forebodings did not come to pass, new examples of the ever-present danger kept appearing as if to reinforce the need for a constant look out. Calderón de la Barca, the Spanish Ambassador to the United States, wrote to the Minister of Foreign Affairs in December 1836, reporting a great increase in the number of abolitionist societies in the northern United States, from 200 in 1835 to 526 in 1836. He included a newspaper clipping which mentioned that two abolitionists were about to leave for the British West Indies. From this Calderón concluded that many would likely be sent secretly to Cuba, 'which is for them the land promising the most abundant harvest'.[12]

The Spanish government responded to Calderón's warning by ordering Tacón to expel immediately any abolitionist agent who might arrive in Cuba.[13] Tacón made use of this order to do even more. He found it a convenient pretext for imprisoning all foreign black seamen who arrived at Havana in British or other foreign vessels. Protests, first by the British consul in Havana and then by the British Minister in Madrid, failed to obtain any significant alteration. David Tolmé, the British consul, attempted in vain to prove to Tacón that the British abolitionist societies were not sending agents to Cuba and in any case the black seamen coming to Cuba from British colonies were in no way connected with the abolitionist societies.[14] Fear of abolitionists led to mistrust of the entire free coloured population and accentuated the growing racism within Cuba. The order also coincided with a period of large scale slave importations, illustrating how repression and fear of slave uprisings had little effect on the illegal slave trade.[15]

Even if the suspicions of the Spanish Ambassador to the United

States and Cuban distrust of foreign black seamen were groundless, and the Spanish authorities saw no reason to think they were, by 1837 Tacón could point to other incidents to justify his repressive measures. That year Spanish authorities captured a mulatto in the Matanzas area who had come from the Bahamas and who, on his own admission, had passed out abolitionist literature. Apparently fearful of taking stronger action against a British subject, the Captain-General had him deported, although he argued the need for more severe punishment in his despatch on the case.[16] When the British consul at Havana reported this arrest to the British Foreign Office, Lord Palmerston ordered him to protest strongly against any punishment inflicted on a man 'for merely distributing Tracts in favour of the abolition of Slavery, if there was nothing in those Tracts which was addressed to the Negroes and which could be considered as exciting them to Rebellion'.[17] This Palmerstonian distinction between proper and improper abolitionist activity was unlikely to convince anyone in Cuba of the legitimacy of British abolitionist practices, but the British consul credited his own intervention, following Palmerston's instructions, with obtaining a sentence of banishment instead of the capital punishment specified in Spanish law.[18] Captain-General Tacón had interpreted Tolmé's involvement very differently, viewing it as unusual and therefore proof of how much influence the Methodists exercised on the British government.

It was in this irrational climate of enhanced fear where every foreigner, especially a British subject, who visited Cuba might be an abolitionist, that James Thompson, a member of the British and Foreign Bible Society, came to Cuba in June 1837 as part of a general tour of the Caribbean islands. Completely ignorant of Cuban suspicions of foreign missionaries, he had come well prepared for his work, carrying two cases of Bibles, containing over 300 in all. He advertized his wares in Havana and sold a number of Bibles to local booksellers. Then he proceeded to tour several other leading Cuban towns before he reached Santiago de Cuba where, to his astonishment, he was arrested as an abolitionist agent. Thompson described his plight in a letter to the Secretary of the Bible Society: 'It was conceived, as I understood, that I was travelling through the island with some evil designs in regard to the government of the country, on the slave question ...'[19] Thompson was more explicit in a later letter written from Jamaica after he had been banished from Cuba:

I gathered from the Collector's [of Customs, Santiago] conversation the strong impression made on his mind and on the minds of others, that your society was in truth a part and portion of the Antislavery society, and further, that your main object in circulating the Bible was to lead the people to rebel and destroy the whites and thus to accomplish the object, which they imagine the British Government has, of making an end of Cuba as a Spanish Colony. Hence their suspicions of me and all their investigations.[20]

Nothing in Thompson's letters suggests any connection with British abolitionists either in Britain or in Jamaica, and the open, indeed naive, manner in which he toured Cuba indicates he was there only to distribute Bibles and not to preach abolitionist doctrines. The Cuban authorities who, surprisingly in light of their precautions against the entry of abolitionists, were unaware of his presence until he arrived at Santiago de Cuba, saw Thompson's mission in a much more sinister context. He had been sent to Cuba to promote slave rebellion. Reporting Thompson's arrest to Madrid, Captain-General Tacón summed up the Cuban government's view of the abolitionists: 'The aim of all the fanatics who call themselves friends of the Africans is to light the fires of revolution in our island through the violent emancipation of the slaves.'[21]

Tacón's alarming reports to Madrid were buttressed by a petition from the *Ayuntamiento*, or municipal corporation, of Havana in September 1837. A copy of *The Abolitionist*, published in Britain by the Anti-Slavery Society, had come into its hands and this was enough, when coupled with the recent cases of abolitionists in Cuba, to cause the *Ayuntamiento* to ask the metropolitan government either to act on its own against the abolitionists or to denounce them to the British and United States governments; Cuban officials were equally fearful of abolitionism emanating from the United States.[22] The Spanish government, acting on the *Ayuntamiento*'s request, sent diplomatic Notes to both the British and United States Ministers in Madrid early in 1838, formally protesting against the actions of foreign abolitionist organizations directed at Cuba.[23] The Spanish Foreign Minister did not believe the Notes would have much effect and the replies proved him correct.[24] Their real purpose, however, was to warn the British and United States governments that Spain would not allow anyone to foment rebellion among Cuba's slaves and thus serve to prepare the way for criminal charges to be laid against any more foreign suspects caught in the island.[25]

Since Jamaica appeared to be the headquarters of the British abolitionists in the Caribbean, Spain appointed a consul there in 1836 and gave him specific instructions to gather as much information as possible about the abolitionists. He more than fulfilled his task, faithfully including every rumour, substantiated or not, of abolitionist plots, unrest among the Jamaican black population or anticipated rebellion. In 1838, for example, he reported that Jamaican abolitionists had received a large sum of money from their counterparts in Britain in order to send agents to Cuba equipped with money and propaganda material.[26] The metropolitan government reacted to these frightening tales from Jamaica with still more orders in an effort to insulate the Spanish colonial possessions from foreign infiltration. After the consul in Jamaica wrote that the most enthusiastic of the abolitionist groups were the Methodists and the Anabaptists, he was instructed to refuse passports for any of these people who wanted to go to Cuba or to Puerto Rico and if they should arrive they were not to be permitted to land.[27] The consul's despatches, besides reflecting the unease of British planters and officials in the period preceding the end of the apprenticeship system in the British West Indies, helped to magnify the dimensions of the abolitionist movement in the minds of the Cuban Captain-General and his fellow Spanish officers and added to the reputation which British abolitionists now had in Cuba, that of trained revolutionaries carrying out an organized campaign of sedition and terror.

A series of incidents, and the interpretation placed upon them by Cuban and Spanish officials, had convinced both the colonial and metropolitan governments that British abolitionists, supported by the British government, were intent on destroying Cuban slavery. This conviction aroused an almost hysterical fear among the European population and government officials which grew into near panic when a British official, reputed to be a committed abolitionist, took up his post in Havana. His appearance also added to the credibility of the Cuban belief in a British abolitionist conspiracy. Because of this belief, British representatives trying to obtain Spanish co-operation to fight the illegal slave trade instead ran into a wall of hostility. What the British saw as humanitarianism, the plantocracy and bureaucracy in Cuba interpreted as a revolutionary doctrine calculated to destroy the very basis of their existence.

Britain had included a provision in the supplementary slave trade treaty of 1835 to transfer all slaves freed from ships captured by British cruisers to British colonies. As usual, British motives were mixed. Abolition of slavery had led to labour shortages in the British West Indies and the liberated slaves, or *emancipados* as they were known, might help to fill the gap; but the British government also wanted to remove the freed slaves from the slave society of Cuba where reports of their mistreatment were legion and where freedom was only a name. Early in 1836, after consultation between the Foreign Office and the Colonial Office, the government decided to send someone to Havana to arrange these transfers. He was given the title of Superintendent of Liberated Africans, and unlike the British commissioners who sat on the court of mixed commission, he was accountable to the Colonial Office for his actions.

The first person chosen to fill this position was Dr Richard Robert Madden. Madden was an Irish doctor who was picked for the job because of his medical background and his recent experience in the Caribbean as a stipendiary magistrate in Jamaica. He had given up his medical practice after the passage of the British Emancipation Act and had received an appointment in Jamaica as one of the magistrates who were to enforce the provisions of the Act. His career in Jamaica was short and controversial. He was determined to treat the black population of Jamaica as he would any other British subjects. This soon brought him into conflict with the entrenched planter interests and when one of the cases he dealt with caused such emotion that he was assaulted in the streets of Kingston, he resigned. Madden's diagnosis of the need for change in the plantation system, his strong conviction that the Jamaican economy could survive on free labour, his trenchant criticisms of the apprenticeship system and his analysis of the evils of the Abolition Act all availed little in the period he spent in Jamaica.[28]

After resigning, he returned to Britain and published a book, *A Twelvemonth's Residence*, describing his stay in Jamaica and publicizing his criticism of the apprenticeship system: 'slavery is, indeed, scotched in our colonies, but is not killed. Its name is changed: its character remains to be changed hereafter.'[29] When Parliament established a Select Committee to inquire into the working of the apprenticeship system, Madden was one of the first witnesses called to testify. He also had close ties with the Parliamentary leader of the abolitionists, Sir Thomas Fowell Buxton.[30] From a British viewpoint, Madden was admirably qualified for his new job, combining the attributes of a dedicated humanitarian, a doctor and an abolitionist. There is no indication, however, either in his own writings or in the British archives that his purpose in going to Cuba was to start a slave rebellion, although that is certainly how the Cuban government interpreted his mission.

When the British government informed Spain of Madden's appointment, the Spanish government, not yet aware of his background, expressed no opposition and asked only that every effort be made to prevent large numbers of freed Africans congregating in Havana where they would be a dangerous example to the slave population.[31] It did not take long for the storm clouds to cross the Atlantic. Captain-General Tacón wrote a confidential despatch, shortly after Madden's arrival in Havana, which left the Spanish government in no doubt that it had been duped into allowing an abolitionist agent into Cuba in an official position and one in which he would have the full support of the British government. Tacón had heard of Madden's appointment even before the royal order announcing it had reached Havana and Madden's reputation, based on his controversial stay in Jamaica and on his writings, also had preceded him. To say the least, Madden was unwelcome in Cuba. As the Captain-General wrote, 'Dr Madden is a dangerous man from whatever point of view he is considered, and living in this Island he will have far too many opportunities to disseminate seditious ideas directly or indirectly, which not even my constant vigilance can prevent.'[32]

No sooner had Madden landed in Havana than the clashes between him and the Captain-General began. Madden desired a depot on land where emancipated Africans could be housed before being transferred to one of the British West Indian islands. There were certain necessary sanitary precautions before these transfers could take place, such as the purification of the slave ship before transporting the Africans and the separation of the sick from the healthy to reduce the risk of transmitting cholera to British colonies. In spite of Madden's continual reassurances that he would do everything possible to prevent an accumulation of *emancipados* in Havana, Captain-General Tacón remained adamant in his refusal to permit any *emancipados* to land. They would be forced to remain on the captured slave ship until the British removed them. In his correspondence with Madden, Tacón gave medical reasons as the justification for this harsh policy, but in his despatches to Madrid he identified Madden's abolitionism as the real cause of his fear. The danger was not easy to describe: 'the evil consequences of this affair are easier to understand than to explain'.[33] This did not reduce the implicit threat posed by Madden. If anything, it increased it.

When the Spanish government received Tacón's despatch it acted immediately to try to have Madden recalled. The Foreign Minister, Calatrava, sent a Note to Villiers, reproducing Tacón's language about Madden's abolitionist leanings and asking that Madden be replaced by someone 'whose opinions and conduct will not prove dangerous to the safety of the Island of Cuba'.[34] At the same time the Foreign Minister instructed Spain's Ambassador in London to obtain Madden's removal.[35] Neither overture succeeded in changing Palmerston's mind. His reply to Villiers emphasized that Madden had been chosen because of his humanitarian opinions. The fault lay not in Madden's opinions, but in the fact that these were not shared in Cuba.[36] The Spanish Ambassador informed Captain-General Tacón of Palmerston's refusal and asked for more facts. But the correspondence exchanged between the Spanish Ambassador in London and the Captain-General in Havana during 1837 failed to produce any evidence which could convince Palmerston that Madden ought to be removed.[37] In Madrid, officials had little solace to offer Tacón when they discovered nothing could budge Palmerston; they advised the Captain-General to continue sending evidence to the Spanish Embassy in London so that eventually the British government might be persuaded of Madden's misdeeds. The Cuban Captain-General could not support his assertions of Madden's danger to Cuba with sufficient documentary proof to change Palmerston's mind, and Madden remained in Cuba until 1839 when he returned to Britain and resigned his post as Superintendent of Liberated Africans.

Tacón's refusal to allow any emancipated slaves from captured slave ships to land at Havana created a crisis that was hypothetical only as long as no captured slavers were brought to Havana. The capture of the Spanish brig *Empresa* in October 1836 with more than 400 African slaves on board transformed the dispute. As soon as they heard of the capture, Madden and his fellow commissioner, Schenley, wrote to the Captain-General repeating their request that the Africans be permitted to land temporarily, but Tacón again flatly refused.[38] When the problem was brought to his attention, Palmerston decided the only way to overcome the obstacles put up by Tacón was to station a British ship at Havana to receive the Africans. He instructed the British Minister at Madrid to obtain Spanish approval for this plan which was granted early in 1837.[39]

The arrival of the British hulk, *Romney*, at Havana in August 1837 solved the problem of where to house the liberated Africans until their transfer to a British colony could be arranged, but Tacón saw the *Romney* as another phase of the subtle British abolitionist campaign against Cuba. The British government had given orders that black soldiers of one of the West Indian regiments should man the ship, and the *Romney* arrived with a crew of 15 uniformed, black, British soldiers, later to be supplemented by 15 more. Coming at the same time as the arrests of a British mulatto and a representative of the British and Foreign Bible Society for handing out abolitionist propaganda, Tacón's suspicions were instantly sharpened. Madden loomed larger in the minds of the Cuban authorities as the mastermind of this spreading conspiracy. Acting on the basis of a royal order issued earlier in the spring of 1837 which banned the admission to Cuba of any free blacks from foreign territories, Tacón demanded that the soldiers be replaced by white soldiers and in the meantime he refused to permit them to land on Cuban soil. He also redoubled his efforts to have Madden removed from the island.[40]

The commander of the *Romney* said his instructions would not allow him to remove the troops, but because of Tacón's prohibition and the aroused public feeling caused by the appearance of the black soldiers, he undertook to keep his men from going ashore until the two governments had come to an agreement.[41] Madden, still unaware of the real beliefs of the Cuban government, argued that Tacón's objections could not have been foreseen. The choice of black soldiers had been deliberate. They had been picked because the British government believed they would be more effective in controlling freed slaves and because they could stand the climate and the confined existence better than white soldiers. They were also likely to be more familiar with the language and habits of the emancipated Africans.[42] Palmerston, who could not believe that orders from the Spanish government forbidding the entry of free coloured people into Cuba could be applied to British soldiers, instructed Villiers in Madrid to explain the background to the Spanish government and obtain permission for the troops to go ashore under proper supervision.[43] In addition to the British protest, the Spanish government had a despatch from the Cuban Captain-General emphasizing the additional risks to Cuba's security caused by the *Romney* and its crew. Tacón reviewed the history of the abolitionist menace and defended his action as a necessary, even a minimal, precaution given the island's precarious position.[44] Spain faced the familiar but unwelcome task of trying to reconcile the British demands with Cuban interests as presented by the Captain-General.

It quickly became apparent that there was no solution satisfactory both to the Captain-General and to the British government. While the Spanish government professed itself anxious to yield to Britain, it insisted that only the Captain-General could decide whether, in the light of the abolitionist threat to Cuba, the British soldiers could be allowed to come ashore. The instructions sent to Tacón stated that, if he wished to permit the soldiers to land occasionally, he was to ensure this would not endanger Cuban security.[45] In other words, he was to prevent any contact between the soldiers and Cuban blacks, whether slave or free. Palmerston had seen Tacón's initial refusal to permit the soldiers to land as another attempt 'to frustrate by all indirect Means in his power the fair and full execution of the Treaty [of 1835]'.[46] Spain's unwillingness to countermand Tacón's orders confirmed British suspicions of Spanish intentions, but Britain was now hamstrung by the presence of the *Romney* in Havana. If Palmerston withdrew the *Romney*, the Cuban slave-trading interests would claim a victory over the British; if the ship remained the British soldiers would be subjected to severe hardship and any hope of co-operation from the Cuban authorities against the slave trade would disappear.

The British commissioners in Cuba had refrained from negotiating any further with Tacón because of 'his well known character and opinions', hoping that negotiations in Madrid would settle the matter.[47] Tacón was replaced as Captain-General in 1838 by Joaquín de Ezpeleta who, as the son of a former governor of Havana, had been born in Cuba but, because of his long military experience in the peninsula, was a peninsular at heart. With Tacón gone, the British commission judge tried again to obtain some relief for the soldiers who had been entombed in the *Romney* since they arrived, and 'were suffering greatly'. Ezpeleta refused to make any changes until he had heard from Madrid.[48] His implied neutrality was only a mask since he shared to the full the attitudes of his predecessor.

Ezpeleta was certain the abolitionist societies would use these men 'to instil thoughts of liberty and rebellion in the slaves of Havana'. Basing his fears on the evidence of the abolitionist conspiracy sent to Madrid by Tacón, he advised that, while the present policy appeared sufficient to neutralize the operations of the foreign abolitionists, any relaxation might lead to catastrophe. Black soldiers imbued with abolitionist ideas and dressed in British uniforms, he said, 'will just by their words and dress arouse in those of their race a strong desire for freedom at any cost and in defiance of all danger. The very sight of those soldiers presents serious difficulties which are easier to perceive than to describe.'[49] He stated flatly that Tacón's action in forbidding the landing of the soldiers should be upheld. The Spanish government's delicate juggling act became apparent when it approved Ezpeleta's rejection of the British commissioners' petition on behalf of the *Romney* soldiers.[50] It did not dare to overrule the Captain-General when to do so might mean grave risks for Cuba, nor could it openly reject the British demands. The result was an oscillating policy, bending first to one and then to the other as the situation required.

Unaware of the real explanation for the Cuban government's stubborn refusal to allow the British soldiers to come ashore even for exercise, British officials worked to break down Spanish resistance. A British naval officer arrived in Havana in August 1838 with instructions from the Admiralty and the Colonial Office to negotiate an agreement with the Captain-General on landing privileges for the *Romney* soldiers. Kennedy, the British commission judge, persuaded the officer that further talks in Havana would be hopeless without a decision from Madrid.[51] From the moment the *Romney* had appeared in Havana harbour it had increased the anti-British feeling, a fact which Kennedy had noticed at once. He advocated the removal of the *Romney* in order to improve relations between British officials and the Cuban government but, in spite of the trouble it had caused, Palmerston opposed its withdrawal.[52]

Instead, renewed pressure was put on Madrid to extract tolerable conditions for the soldiers. A series of diplomatic Notes reiterated the British case. Finally, the Spanish government yielded and conceded permission for the soldiers to land under certain conditions which Palmerston accepted.[53] It was one thing, though, to obtain a concession in Madrid and another to have it implemented in Havana. Palmerston wrote to the British commissioners at the end of September 1838, giving instructions to work out the necessary arrangements with the Captain-General. But when the commissioners contacted the Captain-General late in December, they discovered he had never received the necessary royal order from Madrid.[54] The tortuous process had to begin all over again. After complaints by the British Minister in Madrid, Spanish officials were forced to acknowledge that the instructions had not been sent. They attributed this 'involuntary error' to the confusion accompanying the change of government in the peninsula in 1838. The requisite royal order finally was mailed to Havana in April 1839.[55]

It had taken nearly three years to wrest from the Spaniards what the British government regarded as a very minor concession; but far from the easing of tension hoped for by Palmerston, the *Romney*'s presence in Havana harbour remained a source of endless bickering and dispute, fomented by the hostile suspicion with which the soldiers were viewed by the populace and officials. British complaints about the unhealthiness of the place allotted for the soldiers' exercise were followed by a continuous series of incidents in Havana. When the British judge investigated a Spanish officer's complaint about the arrogance of the soldiers, he discovered that local inhabitants had been trying to lure them into their homes with liquor. A detention of four soldiers by the Cuban government was no sooner cleared up than a party of Spaniards visited the *Romney* to check on the number of soldiers on board and their equipment.[56]

By the autumn of 1839 the British commissioners in Havana had decided the *Romney* and its crew were far more nuisance than they were worth. Kennedy believed the *Romney* was 'an unnecessary incurring of dislike' since the Cubans regarded it as 'an exercise of superior power'. The main reason for the indignation, in Kennedy's opinion, was the crew of black soldiers who were quartered on the vessel. He suggested Britain could achieve 'more moral influence' by taking the *Romney* away than by retaining it, an argument which Palmerston now found had 'a good deal of Force'.[57] The *Romney*, however, remained as a British hulk in Havana until 1845 when it was sold to the Spanish government. During this period it was a vivid symbol of the futility of British efforts to stop the slave trade to Cuba. But its symbolic effects varied with the beholder. To British abolitionists the *Romney* offered powerful moral support, symbolizing official British sanction for their humanitarian crusade; to the Cuban government it was a much more sinister presence, conjuring up the image of abolitionist societies who worked, in the words of one Captain-General, 'for the complete abolition of slavery, even at the cost of the white race'.[58] Or, as a modern Cuban historian concluded, 'it was a bulwark of abolitionism in the heart of a slave society'.[59]

The anti-British feeling caused by the *Romney* and its black soldiers lingered on even after the *Romney* had been sold and the soldiers had left. An American annexationist, Richard Kimball, writing in 1850, was able to use the *Romney* episode to bolster his case for United States annexation of the island on the grounds of the British threat to Cuban slavery: 'These soldiers . . . were the first instruments of spreading discontent among the slave population.'[60] As late as the 1870s, a Spanish history of Cuba written by a senior official in the Cuban government referred to the *Romney* as 'not only an armed fortress which offended the national honour and a stimulus to subversion among the coloured people, but also a center of propaganda and even a depository of arms for the rebels'.[61] The passage of time did not diminish the reaction to the *Romney*; it added hyperbole to the myth.

British abolitionists like Madden were more aware than their counterparts in Britain of the need to change public opinion within Cuba as a prerequisite to a real enforcement of the existing slave trade prohibition, let alone a movement in the direction of abolishing slavery itself. For this reason Madden did not confine his role in Cuba to his job as Superintendent of Liberated Africans. He made contacts with Cuban creoles opposed to the slave trade in an effort to stimulate an effective Cuban public opinion as well as to procure information which might be useful in Britain. Although Madden's purpose was to encourage Cubans willing to protest the continuation of the slave trade, the Cuban government interpreted such contacts as an attempt to involve Cubans in a foreign abolitionist conspiracy. Since the Cubans in 1837 had been denied any political representation in the Spanish Cortes, the creole grievances extended well beyond the slave trade. They saw the existence of the slave trade, however, as one of the major obstacles in the way of political advances. To talk of a Cuban abolitionist movement as such in the island in the 1830s and 1840s would be an exaggeration, but there were individual creoles prepared to defy the censorship imposed by the metropolitan government and publish condemnations of the slave trade, though not of slavery.[62]

José Antonio Saco was the first Cuban creole to attack the slave trade publicly within Cuba. In a review of a British travel book on Brazil, published in 1832 in a Cuban periodical which he edited, Saco condemned the continuation of the illegal slave trade to Cuba and called attention to the increasing percentage of Africans and the relative decline of Europeans in Cuba's population.[63] His statistics and his interpretation of them, that the European population which had formed 56% of Cuba's total population in 1775 amounted only to 44% by 1827, while the African population, both slave and free, had increased from 44% to 56% in the same period, played on the deepest racial fears of the Europeans, conjuring up spectres of Haiti and race rebellion in Cuba. Saco asked his countrymen to look at the volcanoes erupting in other parts of the Caribbean, a commonly used metaphor to refer to Haiti and later to Jamaica, and warned that the only way to avoid the perils confronting Cuba was to put an end to 'the horrid traffic in human flesh'.

If Saco showed courage in publicly opposing the illegal slave trade and in forcing his fellow creoles to face the truth of its consequences for Cuba, he did not act from a genuine humanitarian concern with the tragedy of African slavery and the slave trade. He feared the imminent loss of European supremacy because of the rapidly increasing African slave population. In many ways he was the spokesman for his generation of Cuban creoles. Their ancestors had developed Cuba's plantation agriculture with a relatively small African slave population until late in the eighteenth century. By the 1830s, however, the enormous expansion of the slave trade and the sugar plantation economy, besides bringing unheard of prosperity to the planters and merchants, had radically altered the racial mixture of the island, making the younger creoles, especially, conscious of how insecure their heritage was in a colony where they possessed neither political authority nor political influence. By making public the statistics that Europeans were no longer in a majority within Cuba, Saco revealed this insecurity in all its nakedness, but at the same time he was trying to use it as a weapon to force change.

He paid heavily for breaking the Cuban conspiracy of silence on the slave trade. His article created a sensation and when Tacón arrived in Cuba as Captain-General in 1834 he quickly banished Saco from the island. Saco remained one of the acknowledged leaders of the Cuban creoles for over four decades but he spent most of his life in European exile campaigning for political reforms in Cuba and writing his major work on the history of African slavery in Spanish America. The continuation of the slave trade was clearly one of the major issues in the growing rift between the younger creoles and the peninsular interests. W. S. Macleay, the perceptive British commission judge in Havana who in 1834 had been there nearly ten years, reported to London: 'My own opinion, however, is and many others in this agree with me that Tacón dreads the effect of Saco's writings against the Slave Trade and his influence on the opinion of the rising generation.'[64]

The rift widened to become an unbridgeable chasm in 1836 when the Spanish government re-established the liberal constitution of 1812 and then refused to concede any of the political benefits to her colonies. The constitution called for elected representatives from all parts of the Spanish empire to sit in the Cortes. Saco was elected three times in 1836 by the province of Santiago de Cuba but he was never able to take his seat. The first time the government dissolved the Cortes before Saco's election return arrived, the second time a revolution intervened and the third time the Cortes denied representatives from the Spanish colonies permission to sit in the imperial legislature. Spain's withdrawal of political rights from her overseas colonies was due in large measure to a profound uneasiness in the peninsula at the thought of granting political liberties to slave colonies, although the loss of the American mainland colonies had made Spaniards of all political parties wary of any colonial concessions. Thus by 1837 slavery and the slave trade had become major obstacles to any political reforms for Cuba.

After being denied his seat in the Cortes, Saco published a succession of angry pamphlets, rebutting point by point the arguments used by the Spanish legislators to justify expelling him and his fellow colonial deputies.[65] He attempted, in vain, to dispel the fears aroused by Cuba's large number of slaves and accused the Spanish government of enslaving Cuba's European population to protect them from what Saco tried to portray, in these pamphlets at least, as the imaginary dangers presented by Cuba's African slaves. He failed utterly in his pamphlet campaign to reverse Spain's decision and, faced with this failure, he turned his efforts again to persuading his own countrymen to give up the slave trade. The tone of an article he published in 1837, urging the abolition of the slave trade, was very different from his earlier political pamphlets.[66] Ostensibly, he was trying to demonstrate to the Cuban planters that it was in their economic interest to move to free labour and end the constant influx of African slaves, but what he really wanted to do was to change conditions in Cuba as a prerequisite to a new campaign for political reforms from Spain. He obviously hoped that persuasion and logic would be more effective with the Cuban planters than polemics but it was a forlorn hope. His arguments in 1837 stirred up controversy just as his 1832 article had done, but they did nothing to stop the growing illegal slave trade. Spanish censorship interposed an additional barrier for Saco because his writings were now officially banned in Cuba, although some copies penetrated the ban and circulated among the younger creoles.

His 1837 pamphlet began by pointing out the errors in the popular myths that only African slaves could withstand the harsh regime of plantation labour in the tropics and that paid labour was too expensive to be an alternative for the plantation owner. He included statistics to show how the British Caribbean colonies had actually increased their sugar exports after abolishing the slave trade, carefully skirting any assessment of production figures after the abolition of slavery in the British empire by assuring his readers he was only recommending the abolition of the slave trade. After resorting to statistical comparisons with the rest of the Caribbean to demonstrate that ending the slave trade would not result in the diminution of the slave population, Saco went on to arguments based on what he termed Cuba's security.

Should the slave trade continue the risk of slave uprisings would increase, and Britain would be much more likely to intervene directly to ensure compliance of the slave trade treaties. Any outbreak of war in the Caribbean might light the spark of slave revolution. The essence of Saco's message was plain: the abolition of the slave trade was the only way to preserve the existing slave property.

To Saco, African slaves were the enemy and his antipathy to the African was very real. African slaves stood in the way of political liberty for the Cuban creoles. Saco sought to reverse a process which was submerging the creoles in a plantation colony where they still possessed wealth and social status but where they had lost their political rights and where the menace of race revolution seemed to them to be coming closer every day. His solution was really a means to an end, even if the end was nothing more than a mirage: the achievement of political rights for the creoles without the loss of their slave property nor of their slave-built prosperity. To do this would require redressing the racial balance in the direction of what Saco was later to describe as the *blanqueamiento*, or the Europeanization, of Cuba.[67]

Saco in Europe and his fellow creoles in Cuba, notably Domingo del Monte, thus had little in common with British abolitionists like Madden and later David Turnbull except a mutual hatred of the slave trade, albeit for very different reasons. Their co-operation could never be close, certainly there could not be any fusion into a unified abolitionist movement combining Cuban creoles and British abolitionists. Hampered by censorship, persecution and the hostility of Cuban government officials, the abolitionist campaign achieved little within Cuba. British abolitionists made use of the tenuous contacts they had with creole opponents of the slave trade to gather information which would help to reveal the true nature of Cuban slavery to audiences in Britain. In 1839 Madden persuaded Domingo del Monte to answer a questionnaire covering all aspects of slavery and the slave trade which later formed the basis of an address by Madden to the Anti-Slavery Convention of 1840. The Anti-Slavery Society subsequently financed the publication of the address as part of its programme to inform the British public of the horrors of slavery in different parts of the world.[68]

In 1839 the first stage of the abolitionist era in Cuba came to an end with the departure of Richard Madden for England. Cuban officials breathed a sigh of relief, but it was premature. The continuation of the Cuban slave trade in defiance of treaties outlawing it created growing international repercussions. Madden himself, on his way back to

Britain, became involved in one incident which illustrated the spreading ramifications of the slave trade. Shortly before he left Cuba, a report was received in Havana of a mutiny of African slaves aboard the slaver which was taking them to a Cuban plantation. The Africans, unwilling victims of the illegal slave trade, took over the vessel, the *Amistad*, but it, in turn, was captured by an American surveying ship. The slaves were then taken to Hartford, Connecticut, for trial. The British officials at Havana and the British government had a strong interest in the outcome of the case because the Africans had been taken illegally to Cuba as slaves in open violation of the Anglo-Spanish slave trade treaties. Madden resolved to attend the trial and give evidence on behalf of the Africans. The trial itself aroused great interest in both the United States and Britain and the fate of the Africans became an object of concern for the abolitionist movements in the two countries. Madden's testimony, along with information supplied by the British government, was instrumental in obtaining a favourable decision for the Africans. He left a deposition of his evidence to be used in the event of an appeal which did occur. The case ultimately went to the Supreme Court where former United States President, John Adams, defended the Africans and obtained their acquittal and freedom.[69]

The public campaign against the foreign slave trade, led in Britain by the British and Foreign Anti-Slavery Society, had reached its peak at the time Madden arrived back in London. His experience in Jamaica and Cuba made him invaluable to the British abolitionists and he played a leading role in the Anti-Slavery Convention convened in London in June 1840. This renewed British abolitionist activity, signalled by the Anti-Slavery Convention, was to affect Cuba even more dramatically than the spillover from the emancipation of slaves in the British empire. Cuba had not seen the last of the British abolitionists and for the Cuban government worse was yet to come.

CHAPTER 8

The Turnbull affair

The celebration of the end of apprenticeship in the British Caribbean colonies in 1838 was a triumphal acknowledgement by British abolitionist leaders that their long campaign against slavery in the British empire was over. This great success encouraged them to set their sights on much larger targets, the foreign slave trade and foreign slavery. The goal now was to abolish slavery all over the world. The United States, naturally, was the main culprit in the Americas, closely followed by Brazil and Cuba where the slave trade still flourished in spite of treaties outlawing it.

Led by the Quaker businessman, Joseph Sturge, the abolitionists in Britain organized the British and Foreign Anti-Slavery Society in 1839, believing that a new and efficient organization was a necessary prerequisite if the movement was to accomplish its world-wide aim. The international emphasis of the British and Foreign Anti-Slavery Society was only natural since the battle had been won in the British empire, but it implied changed tactics. Pressure on the British Parliament could at best have an indirect effect on the foreign slave trade and on foreign slavery. The focus would have to be on world opinion and, to some extent, away from direct political action. Given the dominance of Quakers in the Society – nearly half the members of the governing committee in the first thirty years of the Society's existence were Quakers – the strong pacifist convictions of this resurgent abolitionist movement should not be surprising.[1] Moral force rather than armed force was the way to combat the international slave trade and foreign slavery.[2] Having reorganized themselves, the British abolitionists next turned to planning the Anti-Slavery Convention of 1840 which brought American and British abolitionist leaders together for the first time. This international co-operation and the publicity of such a large convention were designed to attract international attention and to mobilize abolitionists in other countries for the struggle ahead.

Not all leading British abolitionists took an active part in the formation of the British and Foreign Anti-Slavery Society. Sir Thomas Fowell Buxton, the parliamentary leader of the abolitionists until his defeat in 1837, although a nominal member in fact had very little to do with the Society. He had concentrated instead on attacking the ineffectiveness of the naval blockade system which was Britain's principal weapon in the war on the Atlantic slave trade. Naval force must not be abandoned; Buxton believed it had to be strengthened but, in addition to the naval blockade, Britain must also concentrate on the civilization of Africa through the substitution of legitimate commerce for the slave trade. Only through a combination of force and the civilizing influence of commerce could the foreign slave trade be eliminated.[3]

There were obvious differences between the Quaker abolitionists on the British and Foreign Anti-Slavery Society and Buxton, especially over the use of force, but the arguments of both had a pronounced effect on British government policy. This was largely due to the domestic political situation in Britain between 1838 and 1840. Lord Melbourne's Whig government depended on the support of the humanitarians to help it cling to power. Thus, abolitionist suggestions, whether practical or not, were at least ensured a hearing and a number were implemented. Both Lord Melbourne and Palmerston were very sceptical about Buxton's proposals in 1838, but the Whig government eventually agreed to sponsor an expedition to explore the Niger river in 1841 which, however, proved to be a tragic failure.[4]

Buxton was not alone in proposing new methods to end the foreign slave trade. In 1840, the same year that Buxton published *The African Slave Trade and its Remedy*, David Turnbull published a book entitled *Travels in the West*, containing a very different remedy for the slave trade.[5] Turnbull had been a *Times* correspondent in Europe and had lived in Madrid when Britain and Spain were negotiating the 1835 slave trade treaty. *Travels in the West* was dedicated to George Villiers, Earl of Clarendon, the British Minister at Madrid who had been responsible for the treaty negotiations and who had apparently stirred Turnbull's interest in the problem of the slave trade. Turnbull resigned from *The Times* in 1837 and the next year he travelled to the West Indies, including Cuba.[6] Out of this trip came his book which, apart from being a first-rate travel account of Cuba, received considerable public notice because of his graphic description of slavery in the island and his proposal for combatting the slave trade. Turnbull and his abolitionist ideas were to have a profound impact on Cuban slave society not least because he was later to return to Cuba as the British consul in Havana determined to do everything he could to implement them.

Turnbull's solution, in contrast to Buxton's, was to check the slave trade by hitting at the demand for slaves. His plan was applicable both to Brazil and to the Spanish colonies but, if enacted, it was bound to have the greatest effect on Spain's colonies where the legal prohibition of the slave trade had been in force longer. Because of his familiarity with Cuba, Turnbull thought it would be an ideal testing ground. The essence of the scheme depended upon the courts of mixed commission obtaining more extensive powers, which the British commissioners at Havana had been advocating since the inception of the court.[7]

Turnbull believed that by amending the existing treaty, the court at Havana could be given the power to operate under Spanish law and hear suits brought by or on behalf of individual Africans seeking their freedom on the grounds that they had been imported illegally after the prohibition of the slave trade. One or two successes would strike at the heart of the slaveowner's vested property right in the illegally imported African. As Turnbull put it, 'the first consequence would be to produce a radical and practical change in the legal condition of the imported African'.[8] This, in turn, would undermine the continuing demand for imported African slaves. If a slaveowner's legal right to his slaves could be successfully challenged in court, assuredly he would be reluctant to invest in importing more. 'The first decree of liberation will stagger the men who embark their capital in the slave-trade, and the property being made insecure the objects of the traffic will speedily become unsaleable.'[9] Destroying the money value of the illegally imported slaves would remove the slave traders' incentive to continue their criminal business. Turnbull's plan was far more radical than Buxton's since it would open the door virtually to a social revolution within a slave society such as Cuba's in spite of his specious argument that no danger existed of a chain reaction among the slaves because the court would be empowered only to hear single cases.

David Turnbull was not content just to present his proposal to the British public. He had all the zeal of a convert and certainly saw for himself a key role in the implementation of his ideas. After sending a copy of his book to Lord Palmerston, he followed this up early in February 1840 with a brief outline of his plan. The Foreign Secretary was modestly encouraging in his minute on Turnbull's letter: 'glad to receive any further particulars, but fear it would be difficult of execution'.[10]

Modest encouragement was all Turnbull needed. He proved indefatigable in pressing both himself and his proposal on the Foreign Office. An article in the *Morning Chronicle* early in March 1840 reviewed his book and published details of his plan, and a few days later another newspaper article, in *The Times*, caught the eye of the Secretary of the newly established British and Foreign Anti-Slavery Society. Turnbull carefully made sure the Foreign Office was aware of the newspaper articles and the interest of the leading abolitionist society.[11] Amid this whirlwind of self-publicity, he had even managed to arrange interviews with two leading officials at the Foreign Office, one being the Permanent Under-Secretary, Backhouse. After Palmerston consented to receive further details, Turnbull sent a closely argued, 45-page brief to him.[12]

This paper contained the clearest summary of Turnbull's views. He advocated either that a new convention be signed with Spain or that additional articles be inserted into the existing treaties to give the courts of mixed commission the power of enforcing the laws of the country where they sat, declaring in individual cases whether the applicant was a native-born creole or a *bozal* illegally brought from Africa. The slave's master would have to prove in each case that the slave had not been imported after the prohibition of the slave trade. Placing the onus of proof on the slave's master and not on the slave created, in Turnbull's words, 'a legal presumption in favour of freedom' which he claimed was not new in Spanish law but the established right of every Spanish citizen.

Realistically, Turnbull did not expect Spain's outright agreement to these changes. He anticipated strong opposition both from the slave dealers and from government officials in Cuba for whom the slave trade bribes were lucrative supplements to inadequate salaries. Turnbull believed, as did many Cuban creoles and British officials in Cuba, that Spain used the slave trade as a political weapon to repress creole desires for independence. Because of this belief, he predicted the ostensible grounds of Spanish opposition would be quite removed from the real reasons. To prevent the Spanish delaying tactics he thought likely, Turnbull was prepared to offer a practical concession: that only slaves imported after a specific date be subject to the enlarged powers of the courts of mixed commission. Thus, the property right to slaves imported before 1840 could not be questioned if the date 1840 was chosen as Turnbull suggested. This point was not made public at the time nor was it in his book, but it made his proposal much less radical than the one which appeared in print and was later to shake Cuba. Should the Spaniards prove particularly obstinate and refuse the British demands, Turnbull favoured a British commitment to recognize and guarantee Cuban independence. On the other hand, if Spain accepted, Turnbull recommended that Britain guarantee Spain's possession of Cuba as long as the island remained free of the slave trade.

Palmerston was sufficiently impressed with Turnbull's paper to order the preparation of a draft treaty for presentation to the Spanish government, but he had no illusions about the result:

It is not very likely that we shall persuade the Spanish Government to accede; but if it refuses, the very making of the Proposal will do good – If the Spanish Government consents, such a Convention will do much good; but it would be quite visionary to suppose as Mr Turnbull does that by investing 2 or 3 Mixed Commissions with Power to decree the Liberation of *Bozal* negroes brought before them we could extinguish the Slave-Trade and lay our cruizers up in ordinary – If he could also enact and enforce that every Cargo of *Bozal* Negroes imported into Spanish Islands or into Brazil should be forthwith brought before the Mixed Commission and set free his Plan would be Effectual; but it is evident at a glance that not one negro in a Thousand would be brought up. This Plan can only be considered as Subsidiary – nevertheless if carried into Execution it would be useful both in Principle and in Practice.[13]

The head of the slave trade division in the Foreign Office, James Bandinel, pointed out in a memorandum on Turnbull's brief how difficult it would be to bring slaves and their owners from all over Cuba and Puerto Rico before the court of mixed commission in Havana. Palmerston was fully aware of this, but agreed with Bandinel that the British government should try to have the principle of the proposed convention recognized by Spain and Brazil.[14]

Palmerston's hesitations were echoed in other places. The *Morning Chronicle* wrote: 'We are far from thinking that it will be as readily conceded by the Spaniards as he [Turnbull] seems to conceive, or as easily carried into execution if conceded.'[15] A well-known writer on Africa, MacGregor Laird, was even more critical in a review of both Turnbull's and Buxton's books in the *Westminster Review*. He doubted that anyone in Cuba could be persuaded to testify that a slave had been illegally imported and without such testimony no Spanish judge would be prepared to recognize even the obvious fact of illegal importation. But to think that Spain would ever agree to such a plan was utterly naive. If it was carried out, wrote Laird, 'it would shake to its foundations, if not destroy, the whole social fabric in Cuba. The very attempt would be sufficient to create a complete social revolution in society . . .'[16] But, in spite of reservations both inside and outside the British Foreign Office, Palmerston sent a despatch to the British Minister in Madrid, enclosing a draft treaty based on Turnbull's scheme with instructions to present it to the Spanish government.[17]

While the Foreign Office was considering his plan, Turnbull was exploiting his new-found fame as an abolitionist to obtain the official support of the British and Foreign Anti-Slavery Society. Turnbull's proposal, emphasizing a diplomatic approach and legal means rather than force, appealed to leading members of the new British abolitionist society. He had suggested in the preface to his book that his suggestions could 'lead to an easy, cheap and almost immediate solution' to the foreign slave trade.[18] In the spring of 1840 the abolitionists were preparing for their forthcoming anti-slavery convention. Turnbull's plan was both timely and attractive to British abolitionists frustrated at the long, expensive and so far in-effective campaign to stop the foreign slave trade. Conceivably, it might also interest a frugal Victorian public no longer quite as dedicated to shouldering the immense humanitarian burden of cleansing the world of the slave trade and slavery.

Turnbull himself had not been connected in any way with the British abolitionist movement when he first visited Cuba in 1838, although on his return journey, at the invitation of the Executive Committee of the American Anti-Slavery Society, he reported to them on the findings of his West Indian tour.[19] The first evidence linking Turnbull to the British and Foreign Anti-Slavery Society dates from 1840 after the publication of his book. He attended two meetings of the Society's Executive Committee in April 1840 and at the second his plan to end the Atlantic slave trade was referred for consideration to the Anti-Slavery Convention which was about to convene in June. It was then put on the agenda of the Convention and formally debated.[20]

Turnbull introduced his ideas in a long speech to the Convention and asked the gathering of abolitionists for their support. It was not given immediately. Turnbull and the Executive were initially taken aback by the number of delegates who rose to oppose his plan. Some questioned its practicability and doubted the Spanish government would ever permit Britain to interfere to such a degree in Cuban affairs. More serious to many delegates was the ideological dilemma which Turnbull's plan posed for them. Would they by endorsing it compromise their principles? Was Turnbull trying to tantalize them into adopting a gradualist approach of modifying Cuban slavery from motives of expediency when, as abolitionists, they should be concerned only with the total abolition of slavery? As one delegate said, 'if the Spanish government are disposed to ameliorate the condition of their slaves, let them do it on their own responsibility. We should go for immediate emancipation and that alone; let us not peril our great object.' After considerable discussion, a committee was struck to analyse Turnbull's proposals. When it reported back to the Convention, it endorsed Turnbull's solution but qualified the endorsement with a statement of abolitionist principle: 'the only security for the extinction of the slave-trade is the universal abolition of slavery'. Turnbull added a series of resolutions to clarify his proposal and convince his opponents that his ultimate aim was the freedom of the Cuban slave. With this careful preparation, the Convention passed a general resolution of support.[21] By the summer of 1840 Turnbull had the satisfaction of seeing his proposal endorsed by the Anti-Slavery Society and implemented by the British government.

Having persuaded the British government to adopt his ideas, Turnbull set about, again successfully, to be appointed British consul at Havana. He had never been diffident about advancing his own claims. Now he wrote a series of letters to the Foreign Office applying for the post of consul and making suggestions for expanding the powers and scope of the position. Turnbull believed the British consul at Havana ought to be the chief agent of the British government in Cuba, possessing the rank of consul-general, with overall responsibility for the suppression of the slave trade. He would have under him a number of vice-consuls located in the main outports of the island and a British cruiser, preferably a steamship, at his disposal.[22] Clearly, Turnbull envisaged his role as that of a British proconsul, bringing British humanitarianism to a backward area. He might not have succeeded in obtaining the Havana consulship without the strong backing of the British and Foreign Anti-Slavery Society. When a delegation from the Society met with Palmerston in July 1840, to present to him the resolutions of the Anti-Slavery Convention, they also managed to obtain Turnbull's appointment to Havana.[23]

His predecessor as consul, David Tolmé, had been the first British consul appointed to Havana in 1833.[24] Tolmé had been appointed because he was a merchant and not a slave trade commissioner, but in the late 1830s British commercial interests in Cuba were coming into more open conflict with British humanitarian goals, especially the campaign against the Cuban slave trade. Almost from the beginning of his tenure of office, Tolmé had faced complaints about his involvement with slave-trading interests and he, in turn, criticized Britain's policy of concentrating on abolishing the slave trade even to the extent of harming the promotion of British commerce.

Tolmé's criticisms had little weight but the persistent reports about his behaviour received by the British Foreign Office were bound to influence Palmerston. The British commission judge wrote in 1838, 'It is certainly most trying to have the conduct of the British Consul constantly brought forward against us.'[25] To prevent British moral influence being further undermined, a Foreign Office memorandum the following year recommended that in any future consular appointment at Havana, 'it will be right that the person be forbidden from engaging in trade and commerce'.[26] Palmerston accepted this advice and from 1840 the principle was upheld that at Havana the British consul had to avoid any commercial connections in order to prevent any involvement, direct or indirect, with the slave trade. Tolmé's activities as a merchant were incompatible with British foreign policy towards Cuba and they cost him his job. In the rest of Latin America, British commercial interests were primary; in Cuba they were subordinated to the often opposed humanitarian goal of suppressing the slave trade.[27]

Palmerston went so far as to exclude merchants from consideration for any Cuban posts because of the slave trade: 'With respect to Cuba, considering that all Persons who are Established there in Trade become more or less interested in the Slave-Trade, it seems to me objectionable to appoint to a Consulship in Cuba, any Person who is established as a Merchant.'[28] Turnbull was not a merchant which was to his advantage in obtaining the consular appointment in 1840. He obviously represented British humanitarianism, but this did not make him more acceptable to British merchants in Cuba. The rivalry between British commerce and humanitarianism at Havana festered until 1842 when it contributed to Turnbull's dismissal from his consular post. Even then it was not resolved and Cuba was one area in Latin America where Britain did not achieve commercial preeminence in the nineteenth century. The growing economic influence of the United States was visible already by 1840 and Americans with few qualms about the slave trade or slavery took advantage of Britain's weakness caused by the inherent conflict between the rival aims of her foreign policy to gain an increasing share of the trade and wealth of the world's richest colony.

Turnbull's impact on Cuban society was quite unparalleled, but the Cubans were not the only ones made aware of his presence. Within a month of his arrival he had succeeded in alienating his own colleagues, the British commissioners on the Havana court of mixed commission. Turnbull had commented in his book on the impropriety of British officials being connected in any way with the slave trade or slavery, and at his instigation the Anti-Slavery Convention of 1840 passed a resolution stating that no British representative abroad should have either a direct or an indirect interest in slave property. Palmerston accepted the resolution and adopted it as official policy.[29]

One of Turnbull's first acts when he arrived in Cuba in November 1840 was to alert the British commissioners to the new policy. Their conduct, to say the least, had been incongruous. Kennedy, the British judge who previously had complained so vociferously about the consul, Tolmé, admitted he had hired slaves, although he was strictly opposed to owning them.[30] Worse was the case of the Englishman who had gone out to Havana as clerk to the court of mixed commission. Turnbull's accusations and a subsequent investigation revealed that this man, Jackson, had bought and sold slaves and had punished his *emancipado* servants 'after the manner of the Country'.[31] Personal animosities prevented a quick settlement of such a sensitive issue, but there is little doubt that Turnbull's abrasive approach helped to end the scandalous abuses practised by the British officials. Unfortunately for Turnbull, the charges and counter-charges between him and Kennedy lasted the entire length of Turnbull's stay in Havana and crippled any hope of effective co-operation against the common enemy, the slave trade.[32]

These personal differences spilled over into their official duties and led to wrangles over the functions of the respective offices of commissioner, Superintendent of Liberated Africans and consul. Beneath the acrimony there did lie an honest difference of opinion. Before Turnbull's arrival, the commissioners regarded all issues connected with the prohibition of the slave trade as their legitimate preserve. Even after Palmerston had reaffirmed that one of the consul's principal duties was to watch over the fulfilment of all treaties between Britain and Spain, the commissioners replied that they were better equipped to stand guard over the treaties, leaving the consul to his consular and commercial functions. They distinguished between their work as commissioners representing British interests and their judicial role as members of the court of mixed commission, obviously convinced that the two elements could be separated.[33] The commissioners took this jurisdictional dispute even further. Unwittingly, perhaps, they provided ammunition for what became a Spanish campaign against Turnbull by revealing to the Captain-General their opinion that the consul had no authority to deal directly with him on anything related to the slave trade. The proper channel of communication was through the commissioners. The Captain-General promptly refused to recognize Turnbull's authority to make representations to him on alleged breaches of the slave trade treaties.[34] This marked the first check to Turnbull's activities in Cuba and significantly reduced his effectiveness in his chosen task of securing a permanent prohibition of the slave trade. Turnbull's continuous demands for higher pay and the excessive garrulity of his despatches also got on Palmerston's nerves and weakened the support the consul was soon to need from the Foreign Office.

Turnbull's clashes with his colleagues may have been disruptive to British interests in Cuba, but they were minor compared to the reaction he aroused among Spaniards and Cubans.[35] Had he been given the powers as consul which he desired, an open clash between Britain and Spain over the illegal slave trade would likely have occurred. Even without these powers he had an explosive impact upon Cuban society. Pedro Tellez y Girón, Prince of Anglona, who was the Captain-General of Cuba when Turnbull arrived, wrote to the Spanish government in great alarm, describing the perils facing the island as a result of Turnbull's appointment. Turnbull may be the only British consul ever to have had his recall demanded before arriving at his post. His abolitionist ideas, even more than the man himself, made him unpalatable. These had preceded him in his book, *Travels in the West*, apparently a best seller among Spanish officials. The *Westminster Review* containing MacGregor Laird's review had also come to the Captain-General's attention illustrating how dangerous Turnbull's schemes were. 'His ideas are certainly those of that type of reformer who, in exchange for upholding the principle of protecting the Africans, would be capable of sacrificing the white race.'[36]

The Captain-General's urgent request for Turnbull's recall was supported by the leading corporations of Havana, notably the *Junta de Fomento* which petitioned the Captain-General to expel Turnbull a few days after he had reached Havana. Turnbull personified the hated doctrines of abolitionism which they believed he was about to propagate in Cuba. 'What is the gap between the dissemination of the doctrine and the extermination of the whites by the coloured races?'[37] The *Junta* saw a sinister connection between Turnbull's plan for increasing the powers of the court of mixed commission and his presence in the island. If Spain agreed to the British request, the court of mixed commission would become an inquisitorial weapon in the hands of British abolitionist agents. Should Turnbull be permitted to remain, the nightmare prophesied by the *Junta* members was the desolation of the island and the sight of their children in the hands of the Africans. The attack on Turnbull led by the landowning and commercial interests, especially the peninsulars, was not directed at his efforts to stop the slave trade but at his abolitionism. To them he was the harbinger of Cuba's doom, the agent who would turn the island into another Haiti.

The *Junta* was not satisfied with the Captain-General's assurances that he was well aware of the danger and had taken appropriate action. The corporation petitioned the Spanish government directly and pleaded for Turnbull's removal. Cuba had never been in a more perilous situation. In the midst of a population of 500,000 blacks, both slave and free, there now stood 'an apostle of black freedom'. The Intendant was even blunter in his covering letter. Turnbull's presence in Cuba, with his abolitionist beliefs, 'would be a disaster and would lead inevitably to the loss of this section of the Monarchy'.[38] The Captain-General used a similar argument in another despatch. Attributing the growing concern of the planters to their suspicions that Britain had taken advantage of Spain's weakened circumstances to force concessions which would end in emancipation, he warned against capitulating to British pressure. Cuba could be preserved for Spain only if the system of government remained unaltered. But alter the basic institutions and the door to dissension and independence would open.[39]

To keep Turnbull in check as much as possible, the Cuban authorities refused to recognize any other than his commercial functions until they received the Royal Exequatur from Madrid. Not that there was any hurry about sending it. The Captain-General urged the Spanish government to deny it after failing in his first attempt to have Turnbull recalled. Even without the Exequatur, Turnbull, in fulfilling what he regarded as his legitimate duties, managed to make himself thoroughly hated by the Cuban government. The Captain-General thought his language was offensive and his claims exaggerated. There were ample grounds for suspecting his self-appointed role as protector of the Africans. He made a public spectacle of the release of some black British sailors, and his action in claiming the liberty of an *emancipado* was further proof of his machiavellian con-

duct. Turnbull's fears for his own life, expressed in a letter to the
Captain-General after only two months in Havana, aroused the
latter's suspicions further. Was Turnbull trying to advance the
abolitionist cause through martyrdom?[40]

The allegations against the British consul mounted month by
month, but seemingly nothing could be proved except the disrespect-
ful tone of his language for which he was rebuked by both Palmerston
and Aberdeen, the two Foreign Secretaries under whom he served.[41]
There was no doubt Turnbull's activities were bound up with the
black population, whether trying to free black British sailors imprisoned by the Cuban authorities, working for the full liberty of the
emancipados or protesting at the illegal landings of African slaves.
Gestures like these merited, and received, the full diplomatic support
of the British government. By the latter part of 1841 he was assuming
the role of tribune of Cuba's oppressed blacks in a more open manner. He was in constant contact with numbers of *emancipados*, for
whom he acted as a public advocate, where before he had dealt with
them through agents.[42] Plans to facilitate the emigration of free blacks
and emancipated slaves from Cuba to the British West Indies or to
British Guiana had his enthusiastic support and he reported growing
interest in such schemes. 'Within the last few months scarcely a day
has passed on which applications to this effect have not been addressed to me by some of the most active and intelligent creole people
of colour.'[43]

Cuban attitudes towards British abolitionism were anything but
homogeneous and Turnbull's presence brought out the glaring con-
tradictions. Spanish officials from the Captain-General down stood
in awe of British power even while they raged at Turnbull's acts.
Fearing to deport or imprison him themselves, they bombarded
Madrid with urgent demands that something be done to remove him.
The *emancipados* and free blacks, and possibly some of the slave
population, seized upon Turnbull as a symbol of hope, a physical
manifestation of a far-away but all powerful British abolitionist
society which would soon extend to Cuba the freedom given to
slaves in British colonies. This naturally gave rise to a spate of rumours about British intervention.

The idea of a relentless British abolitionist movement aimed at
Cuba gripped Europeans, peninsular and creole, with a growing
panic, verging at times on hysteria. A report from Matanzas pictured
the planters as 'Caribs or possessed of the devil judging from their
threats of bloodshed or death against abolitionists and even England

herself'. At the end of March 1841, Gaspar Betancourt Cisneros wrote to his creole friend, Domingo del Monte, and mentioned a conversation in which another Cuban had seriously affirmed that 100,000 men in Cuba were prepared to assassinate every Englishman in the island the moment England interfered in the issue of Cuban slavery. In May an Englishman reportedly was arrested in Camaguey after some Catalans charged him with declaring that Cuba would belong to England within six months after which the slaves would be freed. Even those few Cuban creoles who wanted to see the slave trade abolished were ambivalent in their attitude towards Britain and harboured nagging suspicions of British motives. Cisneros who was later to be one of the leaders of the Cuban annexationists expressed his concern to del Monte. Britain had the energy, the force and the knowledge to make Spain comply with the slave trade treaties. Why then did the slave trade continue? Were Turnbull and the government he represented plotting to acquire Cuba, or worse still, to destroy it? Cisneros warned that behind British policy 'there are sinister designs which will be realized by sinister means'.[44]

The vigilance of the slaving interests in Cuba against the wiles of the British abolitionist campaign was not confined to the island. Spain herself presented a greater danger and more possibilities for the infiltration of British influence. In December 1840, two Quaker members of the British and Foreign Anti-Slavery Society visited Madrid and met the distinguished Spanish scientist and historian, Ramón de la Sagra. Shortly thereafter La Sagra published a letter in a Spanish newspaper urging the suppression of the slave trade as a preliminary step to the abolition of slavery and lamented that the Cubans were deluding themselves in the belief that slave labour was superior to free labour. This letter outraged the plantocracy in Cuba, coming as it did just after Turnbull had descended upon them. The ominous combination of these occurrences seemed to presage another debate in the Cortes on Cuban slavery with British abolitionists appearing everywhere. Two of Havana's leading corporations argued vehemently that the Spanish government should ban the discussion of slavery in the peninsular press and warned in the direst terms of Cuba's fate should ideas like La Sagra's gain ground in Spain.[45]

It was into this highly charged and unstable climate of opinion that news of the Turnbull plan hit Cuba in the summer of 1841 sending a ripple of electric shock throughout the island. Turnbull's plan had called for additional powers to be given to the court of mixed commission in Havana to enable it to hear cases brought by or on behalf of slaves seeking their freedom on the grounds that their importation into Cuba had been illegal. Palmerston had sent a draft convention embodying Turnbull's ideas to the British Minister in Spain who, in turn, presented it to the Spanish government.[46] Playing for time and needing ammunition with which to refute this new British demand, the Spanish government eventually referred the question to the Cuban authorities in a royal order of 25 June 1841 which stipulated that leading corporations and certain individuals were to be asked for their opinions of the British proposal.[47]

The publicity thus given to the Turnbull plan and the request for advice from prominent members of the plantocracy added greatly to the wave of hysteria sweeping the island. Another of Domingo del Monte's friends has left a very vivid account of Cuban reaction:

Some, filled with terror, believe they have arrived at the awful day of judgement, which their feverish imaginations have painted in the bloodiest of colours: others consider the affair as a legal dispute and hope that with intrigues and deceits they can make Great Britain's rights as meaningless as those of their own creditors, and with this thought they have calmed themselves a little.[48]

The repercussions quickly spread beyond Cuba to the United States where the Spanish Minister wrote of American alarm over the proposed convention.[49]

A new Captain-General had come to command Cuba and to cope with the complex of difficulties which Turnbull presented. Gerónimo Valdés, a general in the tradition of his predecessors, had been a supporter of Espartero and benefited from the latter's seizure of power in 1840 by receiving the Captaincy-General of Cuba. His military career actually had begun in 1808 when he joined with other students of Oviedo in rebellion against the Napoleonic occupation of Spain. He fought throughout the Napoleonic War and then was posted to Peru in 1816, serving there until Spain's defeat. He was a genuine *ayacucho* having taken part in the actual battle, and he shared to the full the feelings of his fellow peninsular officers on the loss of Spain's American colonies. He came to Cuba in the spring of 1841 pledged to preserve it for Spain.[50]

Valdés complied with his instructions to find out Cuban views on the British proposal, although his sampling of opinion was far from random. He reported to Madrid that the private individuals whom he had approached were those 'noted for their prosperity and social position'. But to give an appearance of impartiality, he had asked two or three 'whose opinions approximate to those of prejudiced foreigners interested in abolition either from pure fanaticism or with other designs which they cloak under veils of humanity or philanthropy'.[51] Turnbull rightly complained: 'The Evidence that will go to Madrid will come from those who have become wealthy from the slave-trade.'[52]

The Captain-General forwarded the accumulated reports to Spain early in November 1841. Turnbull and his British colleagues also acquired copies of the main ones and sent them to London.[53] The reports were unanimous in rejecting the essential part of the British convention, namely, the expansion of the powers of the court of mixed commission, and most had trouble finding enough words to articulate their hatred of British intervention. In requesting the reports, Valdés had specified three general headings: judicial, economic and Cuba's national dignity. From the surplus of objections put forward, he picked two to sum up the Cuban case. The judicial power to be given to the British commissioners was intolerable and the probable results on Cuba's slave system were all too plain. There was nothing in Spanish law to justify such a move and to give a foreign court these extra powers with no right of appeal would make a mockery of Spanish justice. The *Junta de Fomento* in its report feared that some fanatical Methodist 'would be at the same time the judge, the accuser and the instigator of the slaves'. Moreover, as many of the reports underlined, no basis for the proposed additional powers of the court existed in either of the Anglo-Spanish slave trade treaties.

The planters and merchants, even those ostensibly sympathetic to the complete prohibition of the slave trade, saw it as an issue of enormous complexity, full of hidden and dangerous traps. If a female slave were to be freed by the court what would become of her children? There was also the question of compensation. No planter, no matter how well disposed towards his slaves, was willing to face sanguinely the loss of his property without compensation. Since neither treaty nor any royal order had made it illegal for planters to buy slaves, they were able to picture themselves as 'innocent' third parties who would suffer for the sins of the slave traders.

The reports put the worst interpretation on British motives. Whether Britain's aim was to reduce the competition for her own West Indian colonies, struggling in the aftermath of emancipation, or to obtain a better return on British investments in Brazil, seen by the Cuban planters as their main competitor in the increasingly lucrative sugar export market, the Cubans completely discounted humanitarianism. The Cuban picture of British hypocrisy was reinforced by the project, then beginning, of bringing liberated Africans from Sierra Leone to Jamaica as labourers.[54]

General Valdés buttressed the planters' arguments with some of his own. He stressed the unhappy results of emancipation in the British West Indies where the plantation system seemed to be on the verge of collapse as an instructive example of what would happen in Cuba if the British convention was implemented. He also underlined the risk of Cuba seizing its independence, reinforcing the rhetoric of the *Junta de Fomento* members who had said they were prepared to resist such a change by force. The Captain-General ended his long despatch with a warning that if Spain accepted the British convention she might as well surrender Cuba. He, for his part, would resign rather than allow the convention to be enforced in the island.

The Spanish government's exercise in public opinion sampling had produced exactly what had been hoped for, ample evidence with which to justify rejecting Britain's proposal. Only a small, carefully selected, sample of peninsular and creole opinion had been canvassed. But what was remarkable was not the unanimity displayed by the reports in rejecting what the Europeans viewed as a thinly disguised attempt by Britain to force emancipation on them, but the bitter and public debate stirred up by the proposals.[55] To allow even the European elite to debate the pros and cons of the Turnbull plan in a closed and autocratic society with no outlet for dissent and no legislative forum was a considerable risk in itself, but it was one the Spanish government was willing to take to ward off the greater evil of direct British interference with Cuban slavery.

The Captain-General had been very careful to confine the debate to the European population, thus excluding an estimated half of Cuba's population from any say in its outcome. In this context, Turnbull's rather passive role in not attempting to discover what any of the black population thought about his proposals seems strange. He diligently gathered the Spanish reports and solicited statements representing the beliefs of the younger creoles. But his despatches make no mention of any effort to seek support from that section of Cuba's population most likely to endorse his ideas. Having worked so actively to publicize his plan in Britain and to have it adopted, he now had to report to London the negative results of the Spanish government's limited enquiry.

The only dissenting voices to the chorus of rejection came in two

papers written by creoles and given to Turnbull to forward anonymously to the British government.[56] One was written by Domingo del
Monte, the leading literary figure among the Cuban creoles of the
1830s and 1840s and a close friend of the exiled José Antonio Saco.
Born in Venezuela, he had come to Santiago de Cuba in 1810 and then
moved to Havana. Like many others of his generation he had gone to
the United States in the 1820s and returned to Cuba where his literary
talents were frustrated by his growing opposition to the autocracy of
the Spanish colonial regime. He had become a friend of Dr Richard
Madden in 1837 and Madden had introduced him to Turnbull during
the latter's first visit to Cuba in 1838.[57]

Del Monte's cogent presentation of the arguments of the younger
creole intellectuals never reached the Spanish government and did
not even circulate within Cuba. He isolated three causes contributing
to the continuation of the slave trade: Spain's determination to permit
the introduction of African slaves to deter any incipient Cuban revolt
against Spanish rule, the rapacity of the Captains-General and the
local governors who became enormously rich from the bribes given
to them by slave traders and the insatiable cupidity of the slave traders
themselves. Del Monte, like Saco, inveighed against the slave trade
as an instrument of Spanish political oppression. Madrid had de-
creed that Cuba must be Spanish or belong to the Africans. Therefore,
any new British diplomatic measures would fail unless Spain could be
convinced of two things: the presence of a large black population
would not deter an independence movement nor would the end of the
slave trade lead inevitably to independence. Because del Monte saw
the slave trade essentially as a political problem, he believed only
political reforms could bring about its end. He advocated representative institutions 'such as those which the English colonies enjoy' at
the provincial and municipal level and freedom of the press as the
most effective ways to change public opinion in Cuba. Without that
necessary alteration in public opinion, the slave trade would continue
indefinitely. He ridiculed the attempts which had been made to solve
Cuba's labour needs through European immigration. 'It is an axiom
of truth for the Island of Cuba, that as long as Africans enter, Europeans will not.' Yet del Monte and his fellow creoles still looked
ultimately to European immigration to rescue them from their political bondage.

The other anonymous paper given to Turnbull came from the
Cuban 'Native Sons' and was addressed to the London Anti-Slavery
Society. Turnbull admitted that the native sons had an exaggerated

impression of the powers of the English abolitionists, but he thought they were representative of the younger men in the higher classes of creole society in their hatred of the slave trade. The native sons wanted England to extinguish the slave trade while at the same time within Cuba the gradual abolition of slavery would begin. While the British navy systematically destroyed African slave factories and captured any remaining slave ships, local tribunals, each with a British commissioner, would be set up all over the island to create a comprehensive register of Cuba's slave population. The registers would be published and brought up to date annually, and rewards would be given for information on slaves whose names were not in the register. *Coartación*, the system of fixing a maximum price in order for a slave to buy his freedom, would be expanded and children of slaves born after 1842 would be free at age 15 when they would leave Cuba for Africa. Ideally, the native sons wanted to encourage both African emigration and European immigration simultaneously. The latter would be financed by a tax on domestic slaves. They also wanted to see the creation of experimental plantations with free European labour.

Spain could not be trusted to enact any of these radical proposals because her policy of racial equilibrium – African versus European – necessitated the continuance of the slave trade. The native sons relied instead upon Britain assuming a more active role in Cuba, in effect making Cuba a British protectorate to eliminate the slave trade and begin the abolition of slavery. The mixed court at Havana would have a much larger role, consisting of overall jurisdiction in everything related to the freedom of the slaves. All British representatives in Cuba were to be members of the Anti-Slavery Society. The native sons were willing to contemplate such far-reaching reforms as the only way of breaking the chain of the slave trade to gain their political freedom. It was all in vain. Their petition to the London Anti-Slavery Society elicited no response from Britain and would have been anathema to the Spanish government. The voices of dissent went unheard in London and Madrid, and the younger creoles were quickly disillusioned in their naive hope that British abolitionism might be the road to their own political liberty.

The Spanish government wasted no time in rejecting the British convention.[58] Palmerston was no longer in office when the Spanish rejection was made known in London. Sir Robert Peel's Conservative party formed the government and the Earl of Aberdeen had replaced Palmerston as Foreign Secretary. Aberdeen was content to let the issue drop as soon as he discovered the strong Spanish objections. This was an enormous relief to Spain but the British abolitionists saw it as a callous betrayal.[59] The immediate threat of the Turnbull convention passed away as soon as Aberdeen indicated he would not press it, but the shadow of British intervention hanging over Cuba did not disappear. Any time the British government wanted to make a similar demand it had merely to resurrect Turnbull's plan or a variation of it. Neither Spanish officials nor Cuban planters would forget this. The panic engendered in Cuba in 1841 bedevilled future British attempts to suppress the Cuban slave trade.

The Cuban plantocracy had been made aware of the frailty of their slave society and the dangers of replenishing the stock of slave labour through the Atlantic slave trade. Most of the proprietors and corporations presenting reports to the Captain-General had stressed the need to abolish the slave trade and promote European immigration. How serious they were is open to question since the slave trade continued unabated and European immigration projects were no more successful in the 1840s than they had been in the 1830s.[60] Faced with the likelihood of a renewal of the British abolitionist offensive at any time, some planters flirted initially with the idea that independence would be preferable to British abolitionism. But, if independence was the thought of the moment, many were beginning to think of annexation by the United States. Madden had noticed this feeling gaining support among educated Cuban creoles before he left the island in 1839.[61] There would be more security for Cuban slaveholders within the arms of a larger slave society than in confronting Britain alone.

From the moment of Turnbull's arrival, both Spanish colonial and metropolitan authorities had been making frantic efforts to have him removed from the island. After failing in one attempt to persuade Palmerston to recall him, the Spanish government renewed its campaign in the middle of February 1841, this time with greater intensity. Notes demanding Turnbull's prompt recall were presented both in Madrid and in London to no avail.[62] But Aston, the British Minister in Madrid, was sensitive to Spain's growing insecurity over Cuba caused by the flow of despatches and rumours about Turnbull emanating from Cuba. He wrote to Palmerston privately: 'Anything that endangers the prosperity of Cuba becomes a vital question to Spain, as the Government depends entirely, at present, upon the revenues of that Island for the means of meeting the pressing exigencies of the State.'[63] Before the latest accounts had arrived from Cuba, the Spanish government had drawn bills on Havana, amounting to 11,000,000 *Reales*, and was about to realize them at 'a very moderate rate of discount', but after the arrival of the despatches about Turnbull the Spanish Minister of Finance found he could not discount the bills even at 35%, a grave situation for the Spanish government since the money was going to pay the Spanish army.[64]

In this emergency Spain sent a special envoy to London supplied with material from the Intendant and Captain-General of Cuba, the Spanish Embassy in Washington and the Madrid government. It was not enough. No Turnbull bonfires could be lit. The tinder was insufficient and the abolitionist wind still blew too strong. Palmerston said that while he had not the slightest personal wish to maintain Turnbull in his post, without substantiated charges with which to dismiss him he would not risk a public furore by doing so. The British Foreign Secretary countered the vague fears of Turnbull's danger to Cuba advanced by the Spanish envoy with specific accusations of Spanish breaches of the slave trade treaties.[65]

The Spanish case as it stood was not a happy one. A Spanish Ministry of Foreign Affairs memorandum summed it up.[66] Turnbull's appointment had jeopardized the very existence of Cuba. It was true that the reception of this prickly individual might have been handled with more discretion in Havana. Best of all, he should not have been permitted to land. Even so, gossips and rumour-mongers had no doubt whipped up the alarm to an exaggerated degree. Rationalizations, however, would not make Turnbull disappear and everyone in the Spanish government knew that Spain could not yield. Despatches from Captain-General Valdés crying out for Turnbull's dismissal kept arriving during the spring and summer of 1841 and, as they piled up on the desk of the Ministry of Foreign Affairs in Madrid, beleaguered officials vainly searched for a way out. The replies to Cuba and the orders to the Spanish Ambassador in London were peremptory and full of bluster; but underneath the bluster there was fear, fear of what Turnbull might do in Cuba and greater fear of what Britain might do in retaliation if Spain expelled the British consul from Havana.[67]

It was not until July 1841 that the Spanish government believed it had at last found definite proof of Turnbull's seditious work in stirring up the hitherto pacific Cuban slaves. The alarm in Cuba had reached such serious proportions the evil had to be attacked quickly at its point of origin. A letter written from Havana on 1 May 1841 and published in a July number of the *Anti-Slavery Reporter*, the organ of the British and Foreign Anti-Slavery Society, stated in a key paragraph that abolitionist principles had begun to take root in Havana and Matanzas.[68] The Spanish government believed Turnbull had written it. It certainly expressed Turnbull's own views but in actual fact it had been written by a protégé of Turnbull's, F.R. Cocking, who had become the *Anti-Slavery Reporter*'s correspondent in Cuba. The Spaniards took the paragraph to mean that the fuse of slave revolts had been primed in both cities and needed only a match to set the island alight. Cocking's meaning was ambiguous, perhaps deliberately so, but his British readers understood it as an expression of hope in the progress of the abolitionist movement, designed to convince the members of the British and Foreign Anti-Slavery Society that every British official sent to Cuba must be an abolitionist missionary filled with proselytizing zeal. Of course it was every bit as important to keep the people at home aware of the good work being done in Cuba. Both Cocking and Turnbull were prone to exaggerations in their accounts of the progress of abolitionism in the Spanish colony. Abolitionists such as Turnbull saw themselves as missionaries working in a heathen land. Their joy came from conversions but, to keep up their own morale and to maintain the support coming from Britain, they tended to inflate the number of souls won over.

Spanish officials swallowed these reports whole. Three days after the copy of the *Anti-Slavery Reporter* was sent to London for the Spanish Ambassador to show to Palmerston, strict orders along with copies of the offensive publication went out to the Captains-General of Puerto Rico and Cuba, enjoining them to discover the persons who were perverting the black population and remove them from the islands immediately. They were also warned against admitting any foreign consul without a thorough investigation of his background. There must be no repetition of the Turnbull affair.[69]

Not even this new evidence would make Palmerston change his mind. As long as he remained in office, he refused to bring back the troublesome abolitionist from Havana. But when the Whigs were defeated in Parliamentary elections held in the summer of 1841, Palmerston gave up the office of Foreign Secretary to Lord Aberdeen. Having failed completely with Palmerston, the Spanish envoy in London turned to Aberdeen without much hope of success. Aberdeen showed himself to be more conciliatory than his predecessor, but to begin with he was no more willing to recall Turnbull without definite proof of the latter's wrongdoing than Palmerston had been.[70] The situation was now becoming desperate for the Spanish authorities both in Spain and in Cuba. Captain-General Valdés composed a despatch at the end of July setting out all of Turnbull's worst offences, such a formidable list of charges that Valdés was sure it must produce the desired result when presented to the British government.[71] Yet by the autumn of 1841, after nearly a year of unremitting effort by everyone in the hierarchy of the Spanish colonial administration, Turnbull was still in Cuba carrying on his crusade.

In November he visited Matanzas to discover whether some blacks believed to have been kidnapped from Jamaica were living as slaves on a plantation nearby. On the pretext of the alarm which his presence caused the planters, he was forbidden to visit any estates, and the fact that he had interviewed blacks privately in his hotel room was remarked on by all the witnesses whose testimony the Governor of Matanzas assiduously collected. The Captain-General was sufficiently worried by the account of this Turnbull incident to order the district official involved to keep a special lookout for abolitionists or foreigners spreading revolutionary propaganda among the slaves. In Spain news of this latest Turnbull venture prompted another attempt to get Britain to recall him.[72]

But in Cuba more effective forces were working for Turnbull's removal. David Tolmé, Turnbull's predecessor as consul, and his British merchant friends now saw an opportunity to get back at Turnbull. The trouble he had caused was affecting their business and he certainly was not devoting full time to the interests of British commerce. The rivalry between commerce and humanitarianism in British foreign policy which had, in part, been responsible for Turnbull's appointment surfaced again to bring him down. Whether inspired or not by the Captain-General who had orders to do so, the British merchants in Havana joined forces with the shipowners and merchants of London who traded to Cuba and together they petitioned Aberdeen.[73] They did not ask directly for Turnbull's removal. Using the argument that British business interests in Cuba had suffered from the union of the two positions of Superintendent of Liberated Africans and consul, they suggested separating them. Turnbull, as Superintendent of Liberated Africans, could then quarrel as much as he liked on slave trade matters without hindering the progress of British commerce.

These petitions offered a way out for Aberdeen who had grown weary of the endless Spanish protests. He rejected the aggressiveness of Palmerston's policy towards Spain and sought to achieve by conciliation what Palmerston had been unable to gain through confrontation. Having agreed to drop the Turnbull plan in the face of overwhelming Spanish objections, he now effectively dropped Turnbull. He informed Turnbull of the division of the two offices in February 1842, but permitted him to continue as Superintendent of Liberated Africans.[74] David Tolmé's revenge on his successor was only half successful for he was not reinstated as consul.

It was only half a victory for Spain as well and half was not enough for the thoroughly frightened officials in Havana. Turnbull remained in Havana and victory would only be achieved when he had gone. His growing popularity among the blacks of Havana and his image as their protector reinforced the plantocracy's attitude towards him. As Saco later remarked of Cuba, 'To be called a negrophil there is far worse than being labelled a revolutionary; the latter at least implies the support of a party but the former incites the hatred of every European.'[75] The Captain-General pinned both labels on Turnbull. Valdés said his intrigues aimed not only at liberty for the Africans; he also 'works with Europeans, seducing them with thoughts of independence'.[76] Valdés was adamant that Turnbull must go and his despatches were forwarded to the Spanish Ambassador in London who was not inclined to treat them with the same urgency now that Turnbull's wings had been clipped. Nevertheless, the Spanish Ministry of Marine and Colonies ordered the Captain-General to take special precautions to guard the coasts of Cuba against revolutionary agents from Jamaica and Haiti.[77]

Even without his consulship, Turnbull's dramatic flare was evident and his actions increased rather than diminished Spanish fears of him. He had been a victim of a persecution mania from his arrival in Havana and now, deprived of the official protection he had enjoyed as consul, he feared for his life and sought asylum on board the British hulk, *Romney*, moored in the bay of Havana.[78] He attributed his persecution to his views on the slave trade and, in particular, to the Havana authorities' knowledge of his authorship of the plan for the suppression of the slave trade. The misunderstanding of his ideas, he felt, had contributed to the bitterness. The details of his plan had been designed to conciliate 'the present good-will of the landed proprietors of the Island', but these had been completely overlooked in the hysteria after his plan became public knowledge in Cuba.[79]

Turnbull, sitting in the *Romney* and waiting for a new posting, still appeared to the Cubans as the high priest of abolitionism plotting their destruction in his maritime sanctuary. At the very least, Valdés surmised, Turnbull was preparing for his return to England as a martyr to the abolitionist cause, but probably his revolutionary ambitions remained uppermost in his mind. Of all the abolitionists capable of causing an upheaval in Cuba, the Captain-General saw Turnbull as the 'most likely and the most fearsome'. Turnbull was not alone, for in the eyes of the Captain-General foreign abolitionists abounded. Valdés thought the commander of the *Romney* was in league with Turnbull.[80]

Valdés had done everything he could to reduce Turnbull's influence, even going to the extreme of arranging to have his corresponding membership in the Royal Economic Society of Havana cancelled on the grounds that Turnbull was an enemy of Cuba. This was done in a secret session of the Society at a time when the Society's Director was absent. When the Director, a leading creole named José de la Luz y Caballero, heard of these machinations, he sent in a vehement and eloquent protest, forcing the matter to be reconsidered at another meeting. Turnbull's creole friends allied with Luz y Caballero and reinstated him in the Society, a successful, if minor, protest against Spanish autocracy.[81]

Turnbull's wife finally succeeded in doing what the efforts of the Captain-General and the persuasions of the Spanish Ambassador had failed to do. She got him to leave Cuba. Two months of cramped shipboard life and constant worrying about her husband had affected her health, so on 15 August 1842 Turnbull asked for his passport and departed that day for the Bahamas.[82]

Turnbull's association with Cuba did not end with his departure in the summer of 1842. As consul, he had tried to investigate rumours of free Africans who had been kidnapped from the Bahamas and brought to Cuba as slaves. He continued this investigation after he left and, prompted by the hope of freeing British slaves, he returned in October 1842. He chartered a sloop in Nassau and with a crew of free blacks he landed at a small town near Matanzas. An Englishman in the area at the time thought Turnbull's visit was 'strange' and remembered that 'it did a great deal of harm, by unsettling the negroes'.[83] All the Cuban authorities had been warned to be on the lookout for him, and he was immediately arrested. Since he no longer held any official position, he was fortunate that his trial resulted only in his permanent expulsion from the island. The fact that he had a passport issued by the Spanish vice-consul at Nassau saved his life. Captain-General Valdés had been under strong pressure from the European population to execute him.[84] Turnbull's successor as British consul, Joseph Crawford, had no doubt that Turnbull had acted in a questionable manner, but the redoubtable abolitionist had no such qualms and demanded indemnification from the Spanish government for his imprisonment. He received no support from the British Foreign Office which viewed his behaviour as indefensible and even suspicious, although Aberdeen did write to him regretting the inconveniences Turnbull had suffered.[85]

Far from believing Turnbull's reasons for his voyage, Spanish officials detected a more ominous purpose. They believed that Turnbull, relieved of his official posts, had now decided to visit certain areas of Cuba in person to preach his seditious doctrines, and they were sure his plans included violent revolution. The discovery of some Anabaptist literature among the possessions of one of the crew accompanying Turnbull confirmed their suspicions.[86] Sixteen emigrant planters from the United States and the British West Indies, living in the area where Turnbull had landed and fearful of another visitation, petitioned the Captain-General for guarantees against this British menace.[87]

Further proof, if more was needed, came with the arrest of an English mulatto who claimed Turnbull as his protector. The Cuban Military Commission tried this man, Mitchell, later discovered to have been born in Africa and not in the British West Indies. The British consul, Crawford, intervened on his behalf, believing there was no evidence of subversive activities. Nevertheless, Mitchell was sentenced to death, later commuted to life imprisonment, on a charge of inciting insurrection among the slaves. His connections with the English and Turnbull were responsible for this heavy sentence.[88] So great was the danger which Turnbull presented that merely associating with him had become a capital crime in Cuba.

Captain-General Valdés cited the capture of Mitchell in support of his unalterable conviction that somehow Turnbull must be prevented from residing anywhere in the Antilles. Wherever he was in the West Indies, 'he will not give up his plans and in spite of constant vigilance he might succeed sometime in an unforeseen manner'.[89] The Ministry of Marine and Colonies in Madrid agreed with the Captain-General. It was ready to authorize him to try and then to sentence Turnbull according to Spanish law 'with the appropriate penalty, even if it is the ultimate' should the abolitionist ever reappear in Cuba. The Ministry of Foreign Affairs recommended the omission of the words, 'even if it is the ultimate'.[90] Colonial officials would not then be encouraged to execute a former British consul and bring down the united wrath of Britain upon Spanish heads.

In London, the Spanish Ambassador welcomed what he saw as a further British concession when Aberdeen abolished the office of Superintendent of Liberated Africans.[91] But Aberdeen would not go as far as Spain desired and remove Turnbull from the Caribbean. He appointed him as a judge in the Anglo-Portuguese court of mixed commission in Jamaica where Turnbull would remain for seven more years. Renewed Spanish pressure would not make Aberdeen relent and Spanish officials suspected the worst. Captain-General Valdés could see no other motive for Turnbull's move to Jamaica 'than his definite mission to cause insurrection in this island in order to carry forward his abolitionist ideas'.[92] Turnbull in Jamaica was scarcely better than Turnbull in Havana and his transfer did nothing to alleviate the mounting Cuban reaction to British abolitionism.

Dr Eric Williams' characterization of the Turnbull affair as 'amusing' may be questioned, but his assessment of its significance is perceptive:

The whole Turnbull episode is most amusing. And yet, from its very character, and from the fact that it could take place at all, it illuminates the violence of the conflicts, the unstable balance of forces, and the uncertain consciences of all who were taking part in the slave-trade and slavery in the middle of the nineteenth century.[93]

With Turnbull out of the island, only his legacy stayed behind. But the question which preoccupied all Cubans the next year and has been a historical puzzle ever since, is the nature of that legacy. Did it comprise the seeds of a well-laid plot to overthrow Spanish rule and free the slaves which burst forth in a slave uprising known as the Escalera conspiracy? Or was the Escalera conspiracy simply invented by the Spanish authorities as a convenient excuse to purge the island of free blacks, dissident creoles and anyone who had been even remotely connected with the hated doctrines of abolitionism and the chief carrier of the plague germ, David Turnbull?

CHAPTER 9

The Escalera conspiracy

Swirls of historical controversy still surround both Turnbull's role in a mass slave conspiracy in 1844 and the very existence of the conspiracy itself. Duvon C. Corbitt, writing in the 1930s, said: 'There are few incidents in the history of Cuba about which there is more uncertainty than there is about the slave uprising of 1843, and the slave conspiracy supposed to have been discovered the following year.'[1] Historians continue to take diametrically opposed positions in their interpretation of what happened. Franklin Knight has claimed that 'the supposed slave "revolt" of 1844 had absolutely no foundation in fact', while Arthur F. Corwin not only accepts the fact of a slave conspiracy but, following an earlier generation of Cuban historians, sees Turnbull as the cause of the revolt and the one who conceived the idea.[2] Another American historian, Gwendolyn Midlo Hall, has concluded, 'there is little doubt that the conspiracy among the estate slaves was very real and extraordinarily well organized'.[3]

Peninsular historians, anxious to demonstrate the reality of a British abolitionist offensive against Spain's major colony, wrote some of the earliest accounts of the events of the 1844 uprisings. Two semi-official Spanish histories which appeared in the 1870s magnified British abolitionist influence within Britain itself and overseas. British abolitionists dominated successive British governments and their sole purpose was to destroy slavery, regardless of the means used. After succeeding in abolishing slavery within the British empire, they sought to extend their social revolution to other slave states. But in these foreign countries 'they were less interested in persuading public institutions to enact legislative measures in favour of abolition than in inciting in any way possible a slave rebellion oblivious of the consequences to the white race'.[4] The first half of Ahumada y Centurión's history of nineteenth-century Cuba is a chronological indictment of British abolitionist interference in the island. The peak of Britain's subversive campaign came with the massive, British-backed slave conspiracy of 1844.[5]

Justo Zaragoza, who published a history of Cuban uprisings during the ten-year civil war in the island (1868–78) and addressed it to 'good Spaniards', also denounced British abolitionism. Having abolished slavery in their own colonies, British abolitionists then used islands like Jamaica as propaganda centres from which to launch campaigns to destroy slavery in the Spanish Antilles and the southern United States. Abolitionist agents were sent in clandestinely to foment insurrection. Their real purpose was not humanitarian; humanitarianism disguised Britain's economic desire to achieve a world monopoly in sugar.[6] The slave conspiracy of 1844 was an abortive attempt by British abolitionists to fulfil their ambition in Cuba, and, thus, Spanish success in putting down the insurrection was interpreted by both historians as a victory over the insidious forces of British abolitionism.

Zaragoza and Ahumada y Centurión essentially were adding flesh to an explanation which had surfaced at the time of the conspiracy and soon gained pretty universal acceptance within Cuba. Captain-General Leopoldo O'Donnell, Valdés' replacement, entrusted the investigation and suppression of the supposed slave uprising to military commissions which operated with unlimited powers in all the major areas of Cuba. The sentence of the Matanzas Military Commission declared there was not the least doubt that Turnbull, 'either alone or with some of his colleagues, if he did not conceive the devastating plan, was at least the prime mover and inspiration from which the current plan and others which also aim to destroy this country have originated'.[7] Notwithstanding the fact that Turnbull had been out of Cuba for a year and a half, the Military Commission named him as the evil genius behind the Escalera conspiracy and, in doing so, provided the basis for a theory of British conspiracy which has persisted to the present.

It is a flexible theory which can be applied in different ways as two recent explanations illustrate. Mario Hernández y Sánchez-Barba, a Spanish historian, using the evidence amassed by the Matanzas Military Commission, argues that Turnbull carefully planned the slave rebellion and received the support of British abolitionists and the British government to carry it out.[8] Sánchez-Barba admits that Turnbull resorted to violence only after his schemes to abolish the Cuban slave trade had collapsed and after he had failed utterly to change Cuban slave society through external pressure. But the Escalera conspiracy, seen in this light, was a British-organized attempt to destroy slavery in Cuba by force and create a black republic similar to Haiti. A Cuban historian, Humberto Castañeda, writing after the

Castro revolution, advances a new version of an old thesis: Britain's intervention in Cuba was aimed at staving off United States annexation of the island. Britain would save Cuba from the grasping hands of the United States and take the island under her own wing to the ultimate benefit of British capitalism.[9] To prevent the southern United States, already the bastion of slavery in the United States, from becoming invincible through the acquisition of Cuba, Britain mounted an offensive on two fronts, one diplomatic and the other subversive. The Escalera conspiracy, according to Castañeda, was the culmination of this subversive offensive, a revolutionary blow to prevent the southern states from adding more slave territory to the United States.

Slave uprisings were not uncommon in nineteenth-century Cuba. The Captains-General had a vested interest in playing down the importance of these uprisings in reports to Spain and in finding explanations which would absolve them from blame. One of the regular means they used to do this was foreign influence. With this crutch, even a comparatively liberal governor like Valdés could shift any responsibility from his own shoulders and at the same time justify the repressive measures he had taken to put down the revolt.

Two accounts of a rebellion within Havana itself in 1841 show how easy it was to blame foreigners, especially foreign abolitionists. Captain-General Valdés reported a slave uprising in a despatch he wrote to Madrid early in October.[10] Fifty slaves working on a building site in Havana had become warlike and refused to work. Their owner asked the Captain-General for troops to restore order. These were readily granted and given instructions to subdue the slaves, using force only as a last resort. Valdés' version was that the presence of the troops did not improve the situation and when the Lucumis (who had a reputation for ferocity) attacked the troops with their construction tools, the soldiers opened fire in self-defence, killing 6 and wounding 10, with no losses themselves. The Captain-General was quick to point out the value of this display of force. The slaves were being corrupted by the false doctrines of liberty proclaimed by an agent of English abolitionism, David Turnbull, but this application of force had reassured the security of the white population and implanted a just and 'salutary fear' in the black population. Valdés claimed, no doubt correctly, that the Europeans had applauded this show of strength.

Turnbull's account of the same episode differed in several important respects.[11] He pictured it as a labour dispute on a construction site which had boiled up due to the overreaction of the impassioned owner. The slaves, all African-born, had been discontented for some time, but they had adopted tactics of passive resistance, refusing to obey the orders of the master builder. When the proprietor appeared with troops at his back and still could not force his slaves to return to work, he lost his temper and ordered the soldiers to fire. The slaves resisted by hurling rocks until half of them were dead or seriously wounded, when at last the remainder capitulated. News of this affair immediately set off hysterical rumours in Havana of an organized insurrection backed by the British. Since it occurred just after the news of the Turnbull plan to abolish the Cuban slave trade had been publicized in the island, the European population was very susceptible to scare stories of British abolitionist invasions or revolutions. In mentioning British influence in his despatch, Valdés gave official support to public rumour which, in turn, added to the credibility of a British abolitionist conspiracy in the eyes of peninsular officials both in Cuba and in Spain. Turnbull, on the other hand, denied he had played any part at all in the uprising and professed himself anxious that misleading tales should not find their way to Britain through the United States press.

It might be easy to apply a similar theory of foreign influence, unsupported by any evidence, as the explanation for the charge levied against Turnbull by the Matanzas Military Commission in 1844 and dismiss it entirely. But the convolutions of the Escalera conspiracy are too involved to do that and it would not resolve the problem of whether or not a conspiracy actually existed and whether, if it did, a massive slave revolt resulted from it. Nor can Turnbull's connection be dismissed out of hand because evidence does exist linking him to a conspiracy during his stay in Havana. This evidence is found in an account, or confession, later sent to the British Foreign Office by Turnbull's assistant in Havana, Francis Ross Cocking.[12]

Cocking, a committed abolitionist and a failed revolutionary, apparently was a British subject who came to Havana from New Orleans in 1839.[13] When he found himself the victim of Spanish law, Turnbull aided him, and he, in turn, became Turnbull's assistant and chief agent. He also became the correspondent of the British and Foreign Anti-Slavery Society in Havana from 1841 to 1843. His letters on the slave trade to Cuba were published regularly in the *Anti-Slavery Reporter* for those years. He really became Turnbull's mouthpiece for his reports reflected Turnbull's views in the innumerable disputes with the British commissioners and the Cuban government.

When Turnbull left Cuba in the summer of 1842, he tried to persuade Crawford, his successor as consul, to employ Cocking but

Crawford refused. Crawford, however, made good use of Cocking for nearly a year to keep abreast of the conspiracy in which Cocking had become enmeshed.[14] He also advised Cocking to go to England in the spring of 1843, no doubt to get him out of Cuba. The consul paid Cocking's passage and gave him some extra money and letters of introduction to a variety of people in England. But, as Cocking lamented later, his reception in London had been anything but friendly. His revolutionary attempts in Cuba, known to the British Foreign Office through Crawford's reports, had not been welcomed at all and he was greeted with a cold rebuff.[15]

He did participate in the 1843 general convention of the British and Foreign Anti-Slavery Society and here his reception was a little warmer. The Society awarded him £50 in recognition of his services as a correspondent in Havana.[16] Cocking, as he later related, had been very careful not to mention anything of his revolutionary activities to the Society which he admitted would certainly have disapproved. Bitter at the treatment he had received in London, and impoverished, Cocking took his family and returned to his wife's native Venezuela to eke out a meagre living as a tutor and occasional secretary to the British Ambassador.[17]

He sent his lengthy statement to Palmerston in 1846 as a last effort to vindicate himself and obtain another position, but he met with a more severe rebuff than before.[18] Completely disillusioned, he eventually tried in 1851 to sell the information he had on the conspirators to the Spanish Chargé d'Affaires in Caracas. The Chargé outwitted him and obtained copies of all Cocking's documents without paying for them. Extracts of these subsequently were published in Havana and the evidence contained in them, along with that in the original report of the Matanzas Military Commission, has been used to bolster the theory of a British abolitionist conspiracy directed at Cuba.[19] Cocking, defeated at every turn, faded away into obscurity.

Because of its importance in unravelling the mysteries of the Escalera conspiracy, the Cocking confession demands careful analysis. Cocking wrote that during the period he had been in Havana, 'I was a Member of a self constituted Committee at Havana, to examine into the possibility of giving Independence to the Island of Cuba and thereby insure to the Slave Population their immediate emancipation from bondage.' To begin with the so-called committee consisted mainly of wealthy, intellectual Cuban creoles led by men like Domingo del Monte. If Britain through her agents in Havana was willing to aid them to achieve their political aims, they were willing to promise some steps in the direction of the abolition of slavery. As time went on, it became clearer to Cocking that creole interest in slave emancipation had cooled considerably, replaced by a growing fear of British-backed slave uprisings. Cocking stated that he became the link between two committees at Havana, one of white creoles and the other of free blacks, and his sole purpose was to harmonize their conflicting interests to achieve the ultimate goal of emancipation. Cocking's self-appointed task, in his own words, was 'to endeavour to unite these men . . . and in this I was successful even beyond my own expectations'. In retrospect, he exaggerated his success, but whatever unity there was it was shortlived.

The programme recalled by Cocking called for a unified movement of creoles and free blacks who would proclaim the independence of Cuba and take up arms to enforce it. Any who refused to follow their banner would be branded traitors, but any native-born slave who volunteered for the cause would be free and his owner indemnified once peace was restored, Cuba's independence acknowledged and her treasury capable of making these payments. Immediate measures were to be taken to free the rest of the slaves 'without endangering the safety of their Masters'. Any slaves who took up arms against their masters would be guilty of 'High Treason and dealt with accordingly'. These halfhearted commitments to emancipation surrounded with safeguards for the planters showed how reluctant the creole plotters were to come to grips with the problem of slavery in Cuba. The most essential and last provision of the platform was that details of the plans were to be revealed to the British government by a qualified agent in the hope that Britain 'would be pleased to lend Her all powerful Influence to establish in Cuba the Political and Civil Rights of all classes and all colours of men'.

The naivety of the programme belied the importance of the movement or at least the importance attached to it by Cubans, Spaniards and Americans. Cocking himself admitted that he was not satisfied with the details, but he believed it was the only plan capable of uniting the divergent groups making up the conspirators. Writing four years after the events he was describing and in desperate circumstances, he inflated his own role and the nature of the movement in the mistaken belief that Palmerston would approve of what he had done and give him a job. He also tried to impress on the Foreign Office that he had always acted under the direction of the British consul in Havana, first David Turnbull and then Joseph Crawford.

When Crawford arrived in 1842 as Turnbull's successor, Cocking reported fully on the progress of the conspiracy. In his 1846 statement, Cocking emphasized that Crawford had 'approved, encouraged and advised in the matter'. Crawford, in fact, had done nothing of the kind as officials in the British Foreign Office were relieved to discover when they reviewed his despatches. From his arrival, he reported the ever-widening rift between the Cuban creoles who opposed slave emancipation and were turning to the United States for assistance and the free blacks who wanted emancipation and hoped for British help.[20] In October 1842 he wrote: 'From what I have lately heard the abolitionists are determined to raise the Cry of Freedom – a dreadful business it will be if it does take place.'[21]

Crawford held out no prospect of British help when representatives of Cocking's committee called on him in October to find out what British reaction would be to an armed insurrection against Spanish rule coupled with the abolition of slavery. As a British officer accredited to the authorities of the Queen in Cuba, he said he could not and ought not to listen to such proposals. While he was not able to say how the British government would react to an insurrection directed against Spanish rule, British policy on emancipation was clear. Emancipation without violence would be 'very preferable' to emancipation as a result of armed rebellion, 'which I could safely assure them would never be encouraged by Her Majesty's Government'.[22]

Cocking had been very discouraged by Turnbull's dismissal, thinking it meant that the British government disapproved of the policy to which Cocking had by then fully committed himself. But for whatever reasons, his own naivety or his acute need for continued employment, he drew entirely the wrong conclusions from his meetings with Britain's new consul-general in Havana. He convinced himself that Crawford backed the movement completely which gave him new resolve and he then passed on this dangerously misleading information to his compatriots so that they were sure they could count on British aid. 'This news gave new life to both Committees, particularly to that composed of coloured Men; and in less than eight days Emissaries were despatched to almost every part of the Island, and a train was laid that only required to be lighted by a Master hand to produce the most favourable results.' Cockings's optimism in retrospect was boundless. 'If I had had a 10 Gun Brig under my command; a few thousand stand of Arms; and a mere handful of men to effect a landing . . . I should have been enabled to establish the Independence of the Island, and the consequent freedom of the slaves.'[23]

Cocking next visited Jamaica in an attempt to enlist some practical help. None was forthcoming and he received no encouragement whatever from any of the British officials he contacted. The only person who showed the least inclination to become involved was General Mariño, then in exile from Colombia who, according to Cocking, was willing to lead the movement. Nothing more came of this offer since Cocking was unable to supply arms, men and money. On his way back from Jamaica, Cocking visited a number of Cuban cities seeking more supporters. One of the people he met and believed he had converted was Narciso López, then the governor of a provincial town, Trinidad, and later to be the ill-fated leader of the Cuban annexationist movement.[24] Cocking returned to Havana to face his increasingly divided committees and to discover that the Cuban creoles wanted nothing more to do with British abolitionists. The momentary flirtation was over and slave emancipation now appeared as frightening to the creoles as it did to the peninsular Europeans. Cocking was equally disillusioned with the creoles and moved completely into the camp of the free blacks.

The growing rift between the two committees was apparently widened by American consuls who cultivated creole opinion and, if we are to believe Crawford, by Spanish agents planted among the creoles to draw them apart from the free blacks.[25] This division did not affect the militancy of some of the free blacks, for Crawford reported in late November 1842 that many had wanted to begin operations immediately but their desire was suppressed by a majority who preached caution.[26]

With the delays and divisions, rumours of the conspiracy began to leak out. Crawford was sure that Captain-General Valdés knew of it in November 1842, but if Valdés was unaware of it then he would soon learn the details.[27] Symbolic of the division between the Cuban creoles and the free blacks, it was a creole, whom Cocking four years later still believed was one of his 'coadjutors' and 'his noble friend', who betrayed the existence of the conspiracy. Domingo del Monte had been a close contact of Turnbull and Cocking during the former's residence in Havana. They corresponded and Turnbull wrote of him that he was a lawyer, 'who stands at the very head of the science, literature and intellect of the Island, and who is closely connected by blood and marriage with some of its wealthiest and distinguished inhabitants'.[28] In spite of this friendship, del Monte shared the suspicions of British motives held by his fellow creoles, and Cocking's promotion of emancipation by force after Turnbull's departure coupled with Turnbull's ominous return to the island in November 1842 awakened an inner fear of race revolt in del Monte which overcame his desire to achieve the political emancipation of Cuba's creoles.

Del Monte, so far as is known, did not inform the Cuban government directly of the conspiracy. Instead, he wrote to Alexander
Everett, formerly United States Minister to Spain, whom he had met
when Everett visited Cuba on an American diplomatic mission in
1840. Everett was well placed to act on del Monte's information since
his brother, Edward Everett, was then United States Ambassador to
Britain, and both Everetts had a number of political connections in
Washington. Both were ardent advocates of United States annexation
of Cuba and both distrusted British intentions towards Cuba. Ironically, David Turnbull had harboured equally strong misgivings about
Everett and American ambitions in Cuba when Everett visited Cuba
in 1840 and cut short a trip to the United States to tail Everett on his
Cuban voyage. Turnbull later sent reports on Everett to the British
Minister in Washington and to Palmerston.[29]

Del Monte first wrote to Everett in November 1842, outlining in
general terms the nature of the conspiracy, but providing no names.[30]
Why del Monte picked Everett can only be conjectured, but it is
possible his fear of Britain had grown so much that in his mind the
United States was all that stood between Cuba and a British-supported
racial revolution. A doctor from South Carolina visiting Cuba in 1844
heard this view expressed: 'Both the Spaniard and the Creole are,
however, sensibly alive to the obvious desire of England to ruin the
prosperity of Cuba by the emancipation of its slaves; and they look
forward with hope, and openly express their belief, that the United
States will not permit her great commercial rival to destroy one of
her best customers.'[31] If this was British policy then it struck directly
at other vital American interests as well, menacing the very existence
of the Southern plantation system. 'The present policy of England
is evidently to form around our southern shores a cordon of free
negroes.'[32] Cuban creoles found they had a lot in common with their
American listeners when it came to discussing Britain's role in the
Caribbean.

With his background and convictions on the fate of Cuba, Everett
accepted del Monte's allegations as genuine and took it upon himself
to act as a nineteenth-century Paul Revere. He first passed on the
information to Daniel Webster, the Secretary of State, but Webster's
reply did not satisfy him. Webster told Everett he found it difficult to
believe the British government would support such a project. Everett
had not the slightest doubt about the truth of del Monte's tale, and
Webster's apparent nonchalance made Everett work even harder to
make the United States government aware of the British abolitionist
conspiracy in Cuba. He wrote twice to Cushing, a member of Congress

and a member of the Committee on Foreign Affairs, and alerted the southern Senator, Calhoun, who promised to write to the President. Everett also sent the information to his brother, Edward, in Britain. The latter replied that he did not think Britain was up to anything because she knew France and the United States would unite to resist any British move to possess Cuba.[33]

Webster's reply to Everett, dismissing the idea of a British conspiracy as far-fetched, disguised the real worry which this report had provoked in Washington. Rumours of British plans to emancipate Cuba's slaves by force had circulated in the United States ever since Turnbull's appointment, and American politicians were hypersensitive to the fate of Cuba.[34] United States policy towards any attempt by Britain to seize the island under any pretext whatever had been plainly set down many times and most recently in instructions to the American Chargé d'Affaires at Madrid in 1840: 'The U. States can never permit it.'[35] Webster now sent immediate orders to the American consul in Havana for a complete investigation. The Secretary of State doubted the accuracy of the disclosures of a British plan to create a 'Ethiopico-Cuban Republic' because 'it is quite obvious, that any attempt, on the part of England, to employ force in Cuba, for any purpose, would bring on a war, involving possibly all Europe as well as the United States'.[36] He could not imagine that Britain was unaware of the dangers she would court by interfering in Cuba, but even the remote possibility was something the United States could not ignore. Webster also sent the information to Spain for the United States Minister, Washington Irving, to pass on to a grateful Spanish government.[37]

Investigations by the American consul in Havana turned up nothing more, and he discredited the rumour completely. Yet, discredited or not, the possibility of some British action against Cuba was implanted more firmly in the minds of many American politicians. One person who had an intimate opportunity to observe the reaction in Washington was that shrewd old New Englander and former President, John Quincy Adams, who read the despatches while engaged in historical research at the State Department. His 'gloomy anticipations' after reading them were prophetic for he perceived that Britain's 'supposed design' on Cuba enabled the American consul at Havana 'to urge us to be beforehand with Britain by taking it ourselves'. He found Webster's secret instructions 'full of the most combustible matter, putrid with slavery and the slave-trade'.[38] Britain's alleged revolutionary attempts on Cuba provided a very convenient rationale for a resurgent American annexationism, something which Adams in his old age was trying to combat. The ripples of del Monte's action quickly reached Cuba. Webster, on receiving Alexander Everett's warning, had called in the Spanish Minister, Argaiz, and the latter relayed the rather flimsy details to Captain-General Valdés. Valdés was given little to go on beyond the fact that creoles were joining with free blacks in a conspiracy to make Cuba independent and emancipate the slaves, or in the contemporary phrase, 'Africanize Cuba'. In a second despatch about his interview with Webster, Argaiz had trouble finding words to express his concern over Cuba. He did, however, urge a policy of repression to nip off any conspiracy at the root. Argaiz wrote that it would be better to hang 20 in a day than 300 in a month, for the first hanging would fill the hearts of the conspirators with terror.[39]

Argaiz's gratuitous advice from Washington was not appreciated in Havana. Valdés refused to take seriously the rumours of a plot to make Cuba a black republic under British protection. He thought it ridiculous to suppose the creoles would unite with the blacks, free or slaves, in order to free the slaves. Self-interest precluded it. The Cuban Captain-General associated Argaiz's allegations with efforts by slave trading interests to remove him from office, and therefore, poured scorn on Argaiz for not sending names or proof to back up his allegations. He was grateful, though, for Webster's assurance of United States support in upholding Cuba's imperial connection.[40] Thus, for a variety of reasons del Monte's disclosure had no immediate results other than to increase the alarm in the United States over British actions in Cuba. Fear of British abolitionism had long ago reached a fever pitch among Cuba's white population, and the continuing rumours even after Turnbull's departure did nothing to calm the atmosphere.

Before investigating the connection between the plot in which Cocking had been implicated and the conspiracy of 1844, it is worth examining Turnbull's role. Unlike Crawford's refusal to associate himself or the British government with the plot, Turnbull, it seems, as long as he remained in Cuba was not only prepared to join with the conspirators, but willing to do what he could to gain the support, direct or indirect, of the British government for their cause. Turnbull remarked in May 1841 that the Cuban creoles with whom he was in contact 'are exceedingly anxious to see an English Man of War, on active service, constantly stationed in this harbour, and its immediate neighbourhood, partly for their own protection, in case of need'.[41]

One can imagine what this need was. Cocking defended himself by saying he had been acting under Turnbull's direction in everything he did.

Turnbull certainly had not reported anything about the conspiracy to the Foreign Office, even though Crawford stated his predecessor was fully aware of what was going on.[42] When Cocking left for Jamaica in the summer of 1842 on his mission to procure British aid for the conspiracy, he took with him a letter of introduction to a prominent Jamaican black, Richard Hill, signed by Turnbull. The conspiracy was not actually mentioned in the letter, but there could be little doubt of Turnbull's meaning when he said Cocking 'was more perfectly conversant with the important events now rapidly advancing to maturity than any other Foreigner whatever'.[43]

Further evidence of Turnbull's involvement came in the spring of 1843 when one of the committee of free blacks, José Rodríguez, 'a coloured man of some respectability', called on the British consul-general, Crawford. Rodríguez alleged that as early as March 1842, Turnbull had promised assistance to the black population of Cuba in the form of arms and ammunition. Crawford quickly disillusioned the unfortunate Rodríguez. He did not know how Turnbull could have made such promises, because he had no authority to do so. The Cuban was assured there were no arms forthcoming, and Crawford did his best to dissuade him from a rebellion which the consul believed could only result in a barbaric butchery. Without arms and leaders, the hapless blacks would have no chance against Spanish professional troops and the Cuban white militia.[44]

When Cocking's tale of the conspiracy, misleading at least in its account of Crawford's part, reached the British Foreign Office in 1846, Palmerston ordered an investigation into the affair, making it very clear that the schemes Cocking had been part of 'were Such as the British govt. most entirely disapprove of'. Any actions 'to effect the Separation of Cuba from Spain' would be '. . . adverse to the Policy & so calculated to impeach the Honor & good Faith of the British govt.' that Palmerston could not believe a British public servant would have had anything to do with them.[45] The investigation cleared Crawford of any complicity; his reports to the Foreign Office had been forwarded to the Spanish government, so, if anything, he had helped indirectly to destroy the plot. The Foreign Office was less certain about Turnbull. The consular superintendent, Bidwell, informed Palmerston, 'there is no Evidence to prove that Mr. David Turnbull was not cognisant of and did not encourage Mr. Cocking in his Labours – It is believed that he did encourage the movement: altho' he denies it.'[46] Palmerston took no further action in the matter. Turnbull remained a member of the Anglo-Portuguese mixed commission in Jamaica. He was not asked to comment on Cocking's allegations nor was he dismissed from his post.

Cocking and Turnbull had been clearly implicated in this conspiracy, but whatever they had done did not have the support of the British government or of the British and Foreign Anti-Slavery Society. The government did not learn of their involvement until after Turnbull's departure and the abolitionist society knew nothing about it until Turnbull was branded as responsible by the 1844 investigation in Cuba. Naturally, the Cubans who came in contact with Turnbull and Cocking could not know they were acting on their own, and both men had every interest in representing their actions as official. But British documents provide the evidence to destroy the theory of an abolitionist conspiracy joining the British government and the British and Foreign Anti-Slavery Society in a revolutionary attempt to emancipate Cuba's slaves, even if they suggest that British agents had been making improper use of their positions in Cuba to engage in abolitionist plots without informing their government or obtaining official approval.

Two further questions about Turnbull and Cocking remain. Since Turnbull left the island permanently in August 1842, except for one brief return, and Cocking departed in the spring of 1843, did their association with the movement last beyond their departures? Secondly, was this movement responsible for the slave uprising late in 1843 which led Captain-General O'Donnell to announce he had discovered a mass slave conspiracy?

None of the available evidence in British, Spanish or United States archives gives any hint of either Turnbull or Cocking being associated with Cuban internal movements after their respective departures from the island. Despite the fact that in 1844 a Cuban creole held that Cocking must bear the major responsibility for everything that had happened, Cocking was in no position to do anything once he had left.[47] He was desperately looking for employment and trying to support his family first in London and then in Venezuela. Whatever Turnbull was up to in Jamaica it does not seem to have affected Cuba. The United States consul reported in October 1843 that he had seen a plan for revolution in Cuba drawn up by Turnbull in Jamaica, but the consul did not regard it as important.[48] The plan has never come to light. Since the consul gave no further details, and in the absence of any other corroborating material, his report must be treated with caution, not to say scepticism. The two British abolitionists had inspired a revolutionary movement within the island which was confined to the free blacks by the time Cocking left, but whether from a sense of hopelessness or the inability to do any more, they abandoned the cause after leaving Cuba.

The connection between the committee they had inspired or supported and the conspiracy of 1844 is hidden in the clouds of obscurity masking the latter event. British documents shed some light on this mystery. Before he left Cuba in 1843, Cocking did his best to persuade the committee of free blacks to abandon their revolutionary plans, but events had gone beyond the point where he could control them. Late in March 1843, a slave uprising broke out in the Cárdenas area not far from Matanzas in which 5 Europeans died and 50 to 60 slaves were shot. The British consul, Crawford, estimated that a further 400 blacks, slave and free, died afterwards, either by suicide or as a result of reprisals.[49] Cocking's later account disclosed that the Cárdenas revolt arose from the impatience of a local group unwilling to wait for the continually postponed general uprising.[50]

The pressure of black discontent was expanding with such force that the explosion could have come any time. Crawford's policy was exactly the opposite of his predecessor, Turnbull. He believed everything had to be done to prevent the rebellion because the only outcome would be a ghastly tragedy. In August 1843, he wrote to London that he hoped he had done the right thing in dissuading the more violent leaders from armed revolt, 'urged thereto as I have been by the preference of a lesser Sacrifice of Human Life, to a little longer sufferance of their present yoke – a choice between their miseries'.[51] For Crawford it had been a near thing. Late in April, 20 delegates from all over the island had met in Havana when it was agreed to delay the rising to the end of June, but no longer. Another meeting in Havana in May advanced the date by a month to the end of May.[52] Crawford was thoroughly alarmed and persuaded the Commander of the West Indian station to send a British frigate to Havana. He did not think the Cuban forces were sufficient to contain the rising should it erupt, a marked change from his assessments the previous year.[53]

Late in December 1843, either an insurrection or the plan of an insurrection on a plantation near Matanzas caused some 70 or 80 slaves to be turned over to the Military Commission.[54] Whether the Military Commission really discovered the existence of a revolutionary plan or whether Captain-General O'Donnell decided to order an island-wide investigation because of suspicion of a conspiracy may never be known. But what is clear is that the black discontent building up within Cuba was matched by the growth of a paranoid fear of race revolution among the whites. When the explosion came, the force of repression produced by this paranoia far exceeded the reality of any of the slave uprisings which had occurred.

The rapid growth of the slave population spawned by the steady influx of African slaves heightened the danger of revolution in the minds of Europeans, both Spanish and creole. The 1841 census of the island showed that the slave population alone, for the first time in Cuban history, exceeded the white population.[55] Cuban planters clamoured for greater protection, and the colonial government, anxious above all to conciliate them, responded with a variety of measures. Free blacks came under increasingly restrictive regulations as they were thought to be the most likely agents of foreign abolitionist societies. In 1842 the Cuban authorities published a new decree of colonial government and appended to it a revised slave code, much more repressive than the 1789 code it replaced.[56]

These acts, harsh as they were on the black population, cannot convey accurately the paranoia which lay behind them, a paranoia resulting from nearly a decade of real and imagined British abolitionist activity in Cuba. As David Brion Davis has suggested in his probing lectures on the slave power conspiracy in the United States: 'The truth or falsity of a given perception is often quite relative.'[57] The Cuban plantocracy's image of a British abolitionist conspiracy which had built up to a certainty that a British-backed revolutionary emancipation of Cuba's slaves was imminent, was not true in the sense that it represented British policy or even the policy of British abolitionist societies, but it was true in the sense that it gave 'symbolic expression to the deepest fears and needs' of the white population in Cuba.[58] Or, as Davis expresses it:

The myth that abolitionists were directly responsible for the bloodbath of Santo Domingo became an entrenched part of master class ideology, in Latin America as well as the United States. It gave substance to the argument of clear and present danger, and thus served as an excuse for suppressing even the slightest criticism of slavery. It also gave expression to fears of being infiltrated, of being secretly penetrated, seized and overthrown at one's most vulnerable point.[59]

When the conspiracy was either discovered, or thought to have been discovered, these intense, violent emotions burst out in savage repression of anyone even remotely connected to the instruments of the conspiracy. Nor was the power of the Santo Domingo myth confined to the plantocracy. When he first heard of the uncovering of the Escalera conspiracy, Crawford, the British consul, saw it as a 'verification' of his fears the previous spring. 'Had the least idea of assistance been held out or anything but discouragement been used, this Island would have presented similar scenes to those of St. Domingo.'[60]

Crawford's belief in the existence of the conspiracy did not change, but his revulsion at the methods and excesses of the military tribunals was no less than that of other foreigners. He described the *fiscals* who were sent out as young officers who, under the threat of the lash, forced large sums of money out of the slaveowners. Where no money was forthcoming, scenes of indescribable horror took place. Those responsible were 'Monsters in human shape'.[61] The number who died from torture during interrogation exceeded those who were executed after sentence of death. Estimates vary, but seemingly over 3,000 Cubans, mainly slaves and free blacks but Cuban creoles and foreigners as well, were tried by the military tribunals. A Cuban historian who carefully examined the evidence produced by these trials places no faith whatever in its reliability: 'These proceedings reek of confusion and irregularity, of irrationality and illogicality, of injustice and arbitrariness, of falsehood, crime and pain.'[62]

The British commissioners in Havana, with no knowledge of the movement in which Turnbull and Cocking had been involved, at first accepted the fact of a conspiracy, but later altered their opinions. Early in April 1844 they had no doubt that an extensive intrigue had been revealed; a month later its scope had narrowed in their minds to a local plot in Matanzas probably with local causes.[63] They discounted completely any truth in accusations of the involvement of the two British consuls, Turnbull and Crawford, because the evidence for this had been obtained from confessions extorted after torture or pried out of scared witnesses by leading questions. The commissioners accused Captain-General O'Donnell of using a local slave uprising as an excuse for a wholesale repression. Tribunals had gone about with a 'frantic cruelty', proving to the British officials 'the bewildered state of their minds rather than the facts they would have the world believe'.[64]

The free blacks were one of the foremost groups picked for persecution. Really it amounted to a purge. Some were tried and executed, among them Cuba's famous black poet, Plácido. An unknown number died from torture, hundreds were imprisoned and between 300 and 400 were deported. In the spring of 1844 all free blacks born in foreign countries were given fifteen days to leave Cuba. This rabid hostility on the part of Spanish officials towards the free blacks did

not die down after 1844; as potential collaborators with foreign abolitionist enemies they could not be trusted. Nor did the purge of the
free black population go unnoticed abroad. The *British and Foreign
Anti-Slavery Reporter*, which gave extensive coverage to news of the
brutalities in Cuba as proof of the decadence of its slave regime,
wrote: 'The fierce hatred which had at first been directed almost exclusively against the slaves, has at length poured itself like a flood
upon the free coloured population and the spirit of vengeance is making frightful havoc among them.'[65]

Slaves, however, as was the usual pattern bore the brunt of the
repression. Because it was in the planters' interests to conceal their
losses, the real number of slave victims cannot be determined. The
British consul, analysing Cuba's population in 1847, wrote of the
slaves that in 1844,

the poor wretches were sacrificed in every possible way; crowded into the
most loathsome prisons and other places of confinement, left to die in the
stocks and of the wounds inflicted upon them by direction of merciless
Fiscals and the application of the Lash, under which numbers expired from
whom no sort of confessions could be extorted, whether they were guilty
or had even been accused, they were treated just the same. Vast numbers
were thus destroyed in every district of the Island, besides those who were
executed publicly under sentence of the Military Commissions.[66]

Gradually the dragnet of repression swept in anyone, foreigner or
Cuban, who had the slightest connection with Turnbull or Cocking.
This enabled the colonial government to tar any creole dissident with
the brush of collaboration. The director of the prestigious Royal
Economic Society, José de la Luz y Caballero, was accused of compli-
city for his part in reinstating Turnbull's membership in 1842. Ironi-
cally, Domingo del Monte who had broken with Turnbull and Cock-
ing and then revealed the existence of an abolitionist plot to the
United States government was another victim, as were many of his
friends. Del Monte's friendship with Turnbull led to his exile from
Cuba and he was forced to join another creole and fellow exile, José
Antonio Saco, in Europe.

But the main target of the Cuban government was the man or men
believed to be behind what was universally seen as the abolitionist
conspiracy. Even before the investigation had identified those responsible, Captain-General O'Donnell had a moral conviction that
the authors were agents of British abolitionist societies. He pointed
out that the Spanish government already had proof of Turnbull's misdeeds, and the feeling in Cuba was that the British commission judge,

Kennedy, was also an abolitionist agent working secretly for the emancipation of the slaves.[67] It was the old theory of foreign influence writ large.

When the villain, Turnbull, was unmasked in the sentence of the Matanzas Military Commission at the end of June 1844, later published in the main Havana newspaper, Spanish peninsulars and Cuban creoles joined together in relief that he had not succeeded and in condemnation of him and of the country he had represented. The only person in Cuba to question the verdict at the time was the British judge, Kennedy, who protested at what he saw as a gross injustice. Not only were the accusations against Turnbull baseless since no documents or acceptable evidence had been produced, but the British commissioners had also been implicated, again with no proof or reason. In his outpouring to the British Foreign Secretary, Lord Aberdeen, Kennedy threw doubts on the existence of a conspiracy. Whatever its character had been, he had been 'credibly informed' that no documents, arms or ammunition had been found.[68] Kennedy's assessment received subsequent confirmation in a book published by Captain-General José Gutiérrez de la Concha, who commanded the island in the 1850s. Writing in 1853, Concha condemned the trials of the previous decade:

The findings of the military commission produced the execution, confiscation of property, and expulsion from the island of a great many persons of color, but it did not find arms, munitions, documents, or any other incriminating object which proved that there was such a conspiracy, much less on such a vast scale.[69]

The sentence of the Matanzas Military Commission did reveal that the investigation had uncovered the network of the movement with which Turnbull and Cocking had been connected. Miguel Flores, alias Juan or José Rodríguez, was named as one of Turnbull's emissaries, the same man who had been interviewed several times in 1843 by the British consul, Crawford. Another of those accused as an accomplice of Turnbull was a free black named Luis Guigot who had also given information to Crawford.[70] But there was no evidence of contacts after the two British abolitionists had left the island and, as Concha later admitted, none of the necessary equipment for a revolution had been discovered. Whether or not the agents named in the sentence of the Military Commission had been responsible for the slave uprising at Matanzas; whether a slave uprising had actually occurred; whether, if it did, it disclosed a wider plot; or whether the terrible repression of 1844 was really a response to the imaginary nightmare of an abolitionist conspiracy are questions which cannot be answered by the sentences or the totally unreliable evidence upon which they are based.

Gwendolyn Midlo Hall's conclusion, 'It is probably true. . . that the methods used by the peninsular authorities to crush the Conspiracy of the Ladder were the only means of holding the colony for Spain', begs the question of whether Spain's hold was genuinely threatened.[71] Since Spain's belief in a British government-supported abolitionist conspiracy ultimately proved unfounded, the only real threat to Spain's hold in 1844 came from the remote possibility of a co-ordinated slave uprising. But such excuses, which Captain-General O'Donnell made liberal use of at the time, cannot stand up to historical judgement as justification for the extraordinary barbarity of the torture and punishment carried out mainly on the black population.

Turnbull formally denied all the allegations and charges levied against him. The British Minister in Madrid protested Turnbull's innocence to an unbelieving Spanish government, enclosing Turnbull's formal denial.[72] These documents were forwarded to Havana and four huge files came back to Madrid at the beginning of 1845 full of documents on everything Turnbull had done during his stay in Cuba. Containing nothing new, they were, nevertheless, given to the British government which decided little would be gained in carrying on a sterile controversy and dropped the matter.[73]

Turnbull never returned to Cuba, but such was the furore he had caused during his comparatively short stay that future British efforts to put an effective end to the slave trade, continuing into the next decade and beyond, could not overcome the obstacles of suspicion and fear to which he had contributed. To the Spanish authorities he was the 'arch-fiend Turnbull' appearing as 'a raw head and bloody bones'. There was more than a little truth in the United States consul's opinion of him: 'His true character is briefly this, a Glasgow bankrupt, with some talent, more pretension, a great fanatic and regardless of truth.'[74] The British Foreign Office took a more charitable view in spite of the trouble Turnbull had caused. He was a man 'actuated by an honest zeal in the cause of humanity, however mistaken in his mode of proceeding'.[75]

The British and Foreign Anti-Slavery Society also became embroiled in the Turnbull controversy. Even before the Escalera conspiracy his methods had been debated at the Society's general convention of 1843. Richard Cobden attended to promote his free trade beliefs and, in the midst of a speech attacking the ineffectiveness of all government measures to abolish the slave trade or slavery, said of Turnbull's 'semi-official interference; it has been more calculated to embitter the feelings of Cuba and Spain than anything else that could have been done'.[76] Turnbull was not present to speak for himself, but his friends and fellow abolitionists rallied quickly to his defence. His assistant, Cocking, praised his work in Cuba and the mention of his name by the Secretary of the Society brought cheers from the assembly. To the abolitionists it was Turnbull's 'firmness, activity and zeal, in carrying out what he believed to be the intentions of the British Government, [which] necessarily brought himself into collision with the Spanish authorities'. Another leading member of the Society, the Quaker, G.W. Alexander, was equally complimentary: 'There is no person to whom the negro has been more indebted of late years than to him.'[77] Turnbull's reputation remained unblemished within British abolitionist circles and he was treated almost as a martyred hero of the great struggle.

Yet at the very moment when Spaniards and Cuban creoles most feared the vaunted power of British abolitionism, that power was rapidly waning. The heady days when abolitionists had exercised direct influence on British government policy were at an end. The British and Foreign Anti-Slavery Society was now preoccupied to the point of bitter internecine rivalry with the great debate over free trade. Turnbull was the last committed abolitionist to go to Cuba in an official position. His successors as consuls did their work conscientiously but felt no obligation to report to the British and Foreign Anti-Slavery Society as well as to the British government. The Escalera conspiracy marked the end of a decade in which a few British abolitionists had posed the most serious challenge to Cuba's plantocracy since the independence of Spain's mainland colonies.

In the aftermath of the conspiracy, fear of further uprisings and more British intervention moved the Cuban planters to ask for effective measures to stop the slave trade. The Spanish government responded to this fear because the alternative was unthinkable and the image of British abolitionism was as powerful in Madrid as it was in Havana. All the conflicting tensions of Spanish colonial policy would emerge as Spanish politicians worked to fashion a penal law which would end the Cuban slave trade but preserve Cuban slavery.

The Escalera conspiracy and the climate of paranoia enveloping it also brought out into the open a virulent racism which had long been latent among Cuba's white population. Blacks, whether slave or free, were the enemy who would destroy the white population if given the chance. Cuban creoles had viewed the blacks as barriers to their own political liberty and now began to express racist ideas more openly. Domingo del Monte, even in exile, continued his correspondence with the former American diplomat, Alexander Everett, and Everett arranged for the publication of del Monte's analysis of the state of Cuba in a leading Democratic periodical in 1844. Del Monte's diagnosis undoubtedly sparked a sympathetic response in many readers, especially in the South:

The Island of Cuba is at present in imminent danger of being irrecoverably lost not only to Spain, but to the white race and the civilized world, unless the Spanish government shall adopt immediately some energetic measures to remedy the evil. The blacks, as might have been expected, threaten the political and social existence of the colony.[78]

Del Monte argued the danger was not just an interior one. Evoking the image of a plague of locusts waiting to descend on Cuba's lush tropical vegetation, he described Cuba's neighbouring islands as 'swarming with blacks, who seem to cover, as if with a dark and ominous cloud, the whole horizon'. Backed by Britain, they might strike not only at Cuba but also at the United States.

The programme of reforms he advocated began with the immediate suppression of the slave trade, not from moral conviction, but because this was the only way to remove the menace of England and the English abolitionists and reduce 'the number of the natural enemies of the white race' who, according to del Monte, formed 60% of Cuba's population. Then a strongly supported white immigration policy would have some chance of redressing the racial balance. Del Monte's friend, Saco, echoed these sentiments several years later in a polemic directed at a Spanish official who had published his own programme of colonial reforms for Cuba. Saco urged the need for white colonization to give the white population of Cuba 'a moral and numerical preponderance over the coloured population which is excessive' and to neutralize to a certain degree 'the fearful influence of the three million blacks who surround Cuba'.[79]

The British abolitionists had counted on the support of the Cuban creoles in the fight against the slave trade. Now, they watched helpless as the creoles instead turned on them for aiding the black population and abetting race revolution. Any hope of co-operation had gone. The Cuban creoles rejected Britain and looked to the United States either for aid to restore their political freedom or for help in the slowly burgeoning annexationist movement. British abolitionism and the Escalera conspiracy had brutally exposed the narrowness and racism inherent in the creole definition of political liberty. This racism persisted especially on the plantations, contributing another cruel element to the harshness of the slave regime in Cuba's rural areas. Franklin Knight has attributed 'the diminishing liberality' of Cuba's slave laws in part to the sugar revolution and to the large importation of African slaves, but the changes in the 1840s are no less due to the reaction against British abolitionist threats to Cuban slavery.[80]

United States suspicions of British motives in Cuba, never far below the surface, rose on a wave of annexationist desire, coinciding with the debate on the acquisition of Texas, when news of the Escalera conspiracy and Turnbull's alleged role in it reached the United States. Alexander Everett sent del Monte's letters about the conspiracy to John C. Calhoun, one of the leading Southern defenders of slavery and in 1844 the Secretary of State. Everett warned that events in Cuba are 'a matter of the deepest concern to this country' and 'have also an important bearing upon the question of the re-annexation of Texas'.[81] In other words, Britain was following a similar policy of trying to block United States expansion in both territories under the cover of abolitionism. Calhoun saw an even greater danger. If Britain was prepared to go to these lengths to establish a black republic under her protection in Cuba, might this be the first step in a campaign to destroy slavery in the southern United States?[82]

John L. O'Sullivan, an ardent expansionist and advocate of Cuban annexation, edited *The Democratic Review* which published del Monte's article on the state of Cuba. O'Sullivan introduced the article with a condemnation of British policy in the island:

The appointment of Turnbull as British Consul at the Havana, his efforts to procure emancipation by placing himself at the head of a servile insurrection, and his probable concern in the late conspiracy, are matters of general notoriety. The only parallel case to be found in modern history was the result of frenzied zeal for propagandism of the earlier apostles of the French Revolution.[83]

O'Sullivan may have been more aware than the Cuban whites that the zeal of British abolitionism was diminishing, but he astutely used it as a springboard for the rising zeal of his own annexationist propaganda.

Direct British involvement in Cuban affairs appeared to die down after the Escalera conspiracy. But, as Cuban planters and peninsular politicians wrestled with the dilemmas posed by the continuation of the slave trade, Britain turned again to Spain herself to try and force the metropolis to live up to the letter of the promises contained in two treaties to abolish the slave trade.

CHAPTER 10

The penal law of 1845

In the treaty she signed with Britain in 1835, Spain contracted to pass legislation to end the African slave trade to her Caribbean colonies. Britain, as the other party to the treaty, had a natural interest in ensuring the fulfilment of Spain's contract. When it became clear as early as 1836 that the Havana authorities had succeeded in blunting the impact of the new treaty in Cuba, what had been originally a subsidiary part of the main structure of slave trade suppression now became, in British eyes, at least as important as the treaty itself. Spanish co-operation was imperative if the slave trade to Cuba was to be stopped. The passage of Spanish legislation would be a tangible demonstration of this co-operation and a definite signal to the Cuban planters that the metropolis was determined to stamp out the slave trade. Little did the British government realize when it reminded Spain of her obligation to promulgate a penal law, two months after the ratification of the treaty, that nine more years would pass before the law would finally appear and that its provisions actually would protect instead of prosecute the slave traders of Cuba.[1]

After the British reminder, an investigation, ordered by the Spanish Foreign Minister, discovered that steps had indeed been taken to fulfil Spain's contracted promise. Civil servants had drafted a law which had been laid before the upper chamber of the Spanish Parliament in December 1835. A commission of three distinguished Spanish jurists, headed by Martínez de la Rosa who had negotiated and signed the slave trade treaty for Spain, had gone over the draft proposal before it went to the legislature. But once before the legislative body, the process had halted. Late in May 1836, the chamber was reminded of the need to comply with Spain's treaty obligations.[2] Yet not a word about the pending legislation, the delay in getting it passed or the reasons for the delay was communicated to the British government.

When, by February 1837, Palmerson still had heard nothing more about the penal law, he again ordered his Minister in Madrid, Villiers, to find out whether the Spanish government intended to pass the required legislation.[3] Villiers' inquiry elicited the information that the chamber had been abolished before the bill could be passed into law and, under the Spanish constitution of 1837, the government now had to seek the sanction of the Cortes. Palmerston immediately wrote to Villiers, instructing him to press for the introduction of the draft law in the Cortes before the end of the current session. Villiers continued the pressure throughout 1837 and 1838, but he was unable to persuade the Spanish government to place legislation before the Cortes.[4] Spain was being torn apart in the dynastic struggle of the Carlist Wars, and the last thing the Spanish government wanted was to arouse the anger of the Cuban planters and risk the loss of their last American possessions. The Spanish Foreign Minister in 1838, Count Ofalia, made this quite clear to Villiers, telling him the timing was not propitious because neither the reverberations of General Lorenzo's rebellion in Santiago de Cuba in 1836 nor the effect of the exclusion of the Cuban deputies from the Cortes in 1837 had died down.[5]

By the summer of 1838, Ofalia hinted that he was willing to bend to British pressure and submit the bill to the Cortes, if Villiers insisted, but with little hope of its successful passage. Villiers, who was sympathetic to Spain's problems, did not insist. He knew there were not enough deputies then in the Cortes to pass the law and nothing would be gained by just presenting it. On the contrary, if this had happened, the Cubans would have had enough time to organize an opposition sufficiently powerful to defeat it. Ofalia had also promised to give a copy of the draft law to Villiers who judged correctly that Palmerston might have amendments to suggest.[6]

When Villiers returned to Britain on leave in August 1838, he brought a copy of the draft penal law with him, which he gave to Palmerston. The British Foreign Secretary went over it personally and his amended version bore little resemblance to the Spanish draft. Having been unable to obtain Spain's agreement to declare slave-trading an offence of piracy in the 1835 treaty, Palmerston made it so in his amended draft for the captain, masters, pilot and crew of any Spanish vessel captured with enslaved Africans on board. He increased some of the punishments and inserted another article to ensure the legal freedom of all Africans who were landed as slaves in Spanish possessions.[7] Palmerston had the amended draft translated into Spanish and he then sent it to Villiers with instructions to give it to the Spanish government. Ideally, they would endorse it and speed its passage through the Cortes.[8] For reasons that are not clear, this despatch was never acted upon. Also, uncharacteristically, Palmerston must have then forgotten about the law, because the subject was not raised again until 1843 when Palmerston's successor, Aberdeen, resurrected it in a new campaign to force the Spanish government to support its own Captain-General of Cuba in his endeavour to put an end to the Cuban slave trade.[9]

Gerónimo Valdés received the Captaincy-General of Cuba as a plum for his support of General Espartero when the latter seized power in 1840 and remained in Cuba until Espartero's fall in 1843. Valdés was unique in the pantheon of Spanish generals who commanded in Cuba during the first half of the nineteenth century because he actually won praise in Britain as the only Captain-General who had really tried to suppress the slave trade. The British Prime Minister, Peel, lauded him in the House of Commons in 1844 for what he had done, and Peel's Foreign Secretary, Lord Aberdeen, also had a very high opinion of him.[10] Valdés' achievements were magnified in retrospect, and when Aberdeen was confronted with O'Donnell's brutal repression of the alleged Escalera conspiracy in the summer of 1844, he wrote to the British Minister in Madrid, 'but there are few things in the political world I should so ardently desire as to see Valdés again in Cuba. Is it quite impossible?'[11] The disillusioned Cuban creole, Domingo del Monte, was far more critical in his article on Cuba in 1844 published in the United States. Del Monte agreed that Valdés had refused to accept the bribes of the slave traders, a welcome change from the practice of his predecessors, 'but it is not true that he displayed much vigor in his efforts to suppress the trade. A great many blacks were imported during his administration, at first, with some attempt at secresy [*sic*], but, afterwards, with the usual freedom, and with increased profits to the slave traders.'[12]

Since 1820 every change of Captain-General renewed the faith of the British officials serving in Havana that a new policy towards the slave trade was in the offing. Valdés' arrival was no exception, but to begin with there were strong differences of opinion about his sincerity in wanting to eliminate the slave trade. Not quite two months after Valdés had taken office, David Turnbull, then the British consul, accused him of giving secret orders to his subordinate officers to protect the slave trade. Turnbull was also certain that Valdés did receive a fee for every African slave brought into the island. Turnbull's colleagues, the British commissioners, disagreed and defended the Captain-General to Palmerston. Valdés had reportedly warned the

slave traders he would seize and confiscate any slaver which arrived in
any Cuban port after a six-month period of grace, an alarming sign to
the slave traders that the days of official toleration might be over.
Nor did the British commissioners believe Turnbull's allegation that
Valdés was receiving head money on illegally introduced African
slaves. Palmerston, with his long experience of Spanish deception, was
not going to be convinced solely by professions of good faith. 'No
doubt can be Entertained that he has the Power of putting a stop to it,
if he will. If therefore the Cuban Slave Trade has ceased Genl. Valdés
will have proved himself sincere; if that Trade still continues he
will have demonstrated that his Professions are as hollow and value-
less as those of all his Predecessors.'[13] To Palmerston, performance
was all that mattered, and by the time he left office in the autumn of
1841 the jury was still out on the Cuban Captain-General.

By October 1841, the British commissioners had changed their
minds completely. They reported that their high hopes of Valdés had
been disappointed. A reply by Valdés to one of their protests about
a suspected slave landing was responsible for this rapid change of
heart. Valdés insisted the slave trade treaties were limited to seizures
on the high sea and therefore he was legally powerless to take any
action on land. This was not a new doctrine. Earlier Captains-General
often had hidden behind it, but the British commissioners saw Valdés'
reiteration of this shopworn legality as a move to disclaim all
responsibility for suppressing the slave trade on the grounds that the
1835 treaty did not bind the Spanish government to take any measures
inside Cuba. Neither the commissioners nor the British government
believed for a moment that such a view could be upheld by any
reasonable interpretation of the treaty. So complete was the commissioners' change of opinion about Valdés that at the end of 1841 they
reported the slave traders were paying double the previous fee to the
Captain-General in order to neutralize his suppression of the slave
trade.[14]

Before another month had gone by the commissioners reversed
their opinions again. Valdés wrote to them early in January 1842 and
enclosed four circulars, ordering compliance with the slave trade
treaties, which he had sent out to his subordinate officers throughout
the island. He had sent out more circulars in nine months than any
other Captain-General had done in a complete tenure of office. Could
the apparent sincerity of the circulars and Valdés' openness in providing copies for the British commissioners signify he was really in
earnest?[15] It seemed he was because before the end of January two

groups of newly introduced Africans had been seized, a sure sign that the Captain-General meant business. Even the sceptical Turnbull noted the different atmosphere prevailing in Havana, but he saw Valdés' co-operation as a ruse to lure Britain into abandoning Turnbull's own plan for ending the slave trade.[16] The British Conservative government had thrown out both Turnbull and his plan before Turnbull wrote this, which Turnbull still did not know. Turnbull had no inkling that the real reason for Valdés' action was his realization of the need to placate Britain at a time when either the British government, British abolitionists, or both acting in concert, could jeopardize the whole plantation system and thus Spanish possession of Cuba. Spain, in the person of her Cuban Captain-General, was finally taking the offensive against the slave trade, not out of a strong moral abhorrence or abolitionist commitment, but from the political necessity of preserving Cuba from the terrors of British abolitionists.

Other instances in 1842 showed just how effective an active Captain-General could be. At the beginning of March a Spanish warship brought a captured slaver into Havana, only the second captured by the Spanish navy since the prohibition of the Spanish slave trade in 1820.[17] More newly introduced Africans were seized in August by the suddenly vigilant Cuban subordinate officers.[18] In June, Valdés made it illegal for anyone in Cuba to buy foreign-built vessels and register them as Spanish. This decree struck hard at the slave traders who bought American clipper ships. The British consul, commenting on the effect of Valdés' measure, mentioned that several Baltimore clippers had been forced to return unsold to the United States.[19]

Building fast schooners, the famous Baltimore clippers, ultimately destined for the Cuban slave trade and infamy, produced a boom in Baltimore's shipyards in 1838. Shipbuilding in the rest of the United States was in the depths of a slump caused by the nationwide depression, but Baltimore yards were rescued by the slave trade. Prosecutions against prominent Baltimore shipbuilders in 1839 at least inhibited the construction of vessels built especially for the slave trade. After 1840 American vessels used in the Cuban slave trade were sold second-hand to slave traders after service in legitimate commerce and then refitted as slavers.[20] British seizures of American slavers in 1839, followed by the subsequent conviction of two of these quasi-American vessels in the Sierra Leone court of mixed commission, highlighted the abuse of the American flag. The American government refused to permit British vessels to capture or search ships flying the American flag and carrying American papers. Instead, in 1842 the United States government decided to create its own African Squadron, a decision ratified in the Webster–Ashburton treaty. The Squadron's performance was ineffective and slave traders found the United States flag and American papers a convenient cover until the 1860s. But Valdés' decree of 1842, the establishment of the American Squadron and a less tolerant American attitude to the slave trade at least were temporary checks to a growing abuse. A short revival in the use of American vessels occurred in 1844–5, but not until the 1850s did American ships and the American flag again play a major role in the Cuban slave trade.[21]

The Captain-General's clampdown in 1842 was a shock to the Cuban slave traders. Unable to circumvent Valdés' rigorous enforcement policy through the usual secretive means, they resorted to open retaliation, an indication of how much they had been hurt. Petitions demanding the removal of Valdés circulated in Havana and one from the *Diputación provincial* of Santander came to the Captain-General who promptly published a portion of it in the main Havana newspaper. The petition apparently had been bought by large sums of money raised by the slave traders.[22] Strong peninsular, as well as Cuban, vested interests stood behind the slave trade as this petition from a major Spanish port indicated, and a Captain-General like Valdés, who prosecuted the slave trade, was bound to encounter serious resistance.

Valdés neither minimized nor ignored this threat. He defended himself and attacked the machinations of the slave traders in his despatches to the metropolitan government. He justified what he had done by pointing out that his adherence to the slave trade treaties and his firm handling of British protests had forestalled a very near crisis with Britain. When he had taken over the government of the island, Spanish relations with Britain had been in a precarious state because of the open flouting of the treaties, but a year and a half later Turnbull had been dismissed, his plan had been dropped and the treaties were being upheld. Valdés naturally took the credit himself for this happy turn of events. But the price to be paid for these triumphs and for good relations with Britain was the continuing observance of the slave trade treaties which meant offending the Cuban slave traders and their partners in the peninsula. Surely, as Valdés remarked, 'this was the least of the problems in a matter where the security of the country is at stake'.[23] Having exposed the petition as part of the slave traders' intrigues against his policies and position, the Captain-General asked his government to disregard it completely.

The Santander petition did not succeed in its avowed object, the removal of Valdés, but there were strong rumours in Havana at the time of its appearance that instructions from Spain had ordered him to connive at any treaty infractions.[24] Perhaps the slave traders' manoeuvres had achieved results after all. The rumours were founded in fact and illustrated the public interpretation of orders which the Captain-General actually had received. Valdés had sent copies of his circulars on the slave trade to Madrid early in 1842 and, in reply, he was warned that, while he was to adhere to the treaties, he was not to exceed the limits imposed by them. Not sure of exactly what this meant in practice, Valdés requested more detailed instructions.[25] Neither his subordinates nor the general public in Havana shared his doubts. The rumours, fully reported by the British officials, indicate the general belief that the Spanish government had insisted on a relaxation of the persecution of the slave trade.

To a certain extent this was wishful thinking by the slave trade interests, but there was enough truth in the rumours to prevent Valdés from gaining the solid backing of his subordinates. Yet even this partial enforcement had a noticeable impact. The British commissioners calculated that the slave trade to Cuba fell off considerably in 1842. In their annual report, written at the beginning of 1843, they concluded that, for the first time in the 23-year history of the Havana court of mixed commission, the Cuban government had complied with the provisions of the slave trade treaties.[26] The compliance was by no means absolute. Crawford, the British consul, was disgusted with a gross example of fraud practised by slave traders to obtain the return of over 250 Africans originally seized near Havana, but, as usual, Britain could do nothing except protest through diplomatic channels.[27] No one in the British government, however, perceived the real reason for Spain's apparent change of heart or the irony inherent in it. The ostensible diplomatic co-operation embodied in two treaties and the courts of mixed commissions at Havana and Sierra Leone had failed to end the slave trade, but Spanish fear of British abolitionism had, in a year, transformed the Cuban slave trade from a thriving business to a persecuted criminal activity, greatly reduced in volume and subject to losses as great as the profits formerly had been.

With Valdés, the real difficulty was not his intentions but the instructions under which he operated. He received nothing more detailed during 1842 than general orders telling him to obey the

treaties but to do nothing more. His request for clarification had gone
unanswered. At the end of March 1843 he wrote again, outlining the
problem facing him.[28] From the moment he took over the Captaincy-
General of Cuba he had seen the necessity of ending the slave trade,
but in a country where African slaves were the main labour force he
understood that the persecution of the slave trade could not be
absolute. The British protests demonstrated that British demands
went far beyond what Valdés judged was politically safe or legally
justified. How far should he go to meet these demands?

He framed his dilemma in a series of questions. Should seizures of
newly introduced Africans be limited to those captured in slave ships
or just landed on shore and still in the hands of the slave traders, or did
the law permit seizures of *bozal* Africans once they had been purchased
by a buyer in Cuba? If it did, should all people involved in the transaction, slave trader, seller and buyer alike, be prosecuted as criminals?
Was he authorized to seize vessels denounced as slavers by the British
commissioners or suspected of embarking on a slave-trading voyage?
The real issue devolved into what the Cuban authorities were
empowered to do once African slaves had been landed in Cuba. Were
the property rights of the slaveholders sacrosanct or could estates be
searched for suspected *bozal* Africans? Could slaveowners be made to
surrender newly purchased Africans if they were found to have been
brought illegally into the island? These questions raised the most
profound legal and political complexities for the Spanish government and its colonial officials because they dealt with the boundary
between the illegal slave trade and the legal institution of slavery.
Spain was unquestioningly committed to defending the latter and all
the property rights implied by it. How far would she go, and in
political terms could she go, in her prosecution of the Atlantic slave
trade? Would she accept the British interpretation that the slaveowner
with his newly purchased African slaves was a receiver of stolen goods
and therefore guilty of a crime? Or would she confirm the Cuban
plantocracy's rationalization that the legality of the purchase of
African slaves could not be challenged even if the slaves themselves
had been introduced illegally into Cuba? The answer was really
not in doubt, although it would not be made public for two more
years.

Before Valdés' despatch reached Madrid, renewed British demands
for penal legislation faced the Spanish government. Admitting
Spain's obligation to pass such a law, an official in the Ministry of
Foreign Affairs noted that many things could delay or impede its

passage and the first was the need for more information. Taking the hint, General Espartero, the Regent of Spain, appointed a commission to examine penal legislation for the slave trade.[29] The commission obeyed its brief to the letter and, reporting at the end of May 1843, it recommended that still further examination was essential. This could be done by referring the penal law proposal to the governments and proprietors of Cuba and Puerto Rico, in the same way the Turnbull proposal had been sent out for scrutiny. The colonists should indicate what the basis of the penal law should be, bearing in mind the overall interests of the islands, whether ordinary Spanish courts should apply the law and what the jurisdictional limits of apprehending cruisers 'who arbitrarily harass our trade' ought to be.[30]

Valdés' despatch arrived in Madrid in May, but his questions posed such fundamental problems that nobody would answer them. Instead, his despatch was referred to the commission appointed to examine the penal law, but this was not done until a day after the commission had presented its report.[31] This bureaucratic bungling may not have been deliberate, but it was one way of avoiding a direct reply to Valdés. The answer he received was a royal order embodying the recommendations of the commission, prefaced with a summary of Spain's Cuban conundrum; although the 1835 treaty prohibited the slave trade, without slaves Cuban agriculture could not be sustained. He never received a detailed response to his provocative queries on how far he should prosecute the slave trade, and the royal order was so obviously an evasive tactic that he refused either to publish it or to act on it.[32]

Earlier Valdés had admitted to the British consul in Havana how powerless he was to suppress the slave trade without the whole-hearted support of the Spanish government. He pledged to Crawford that he would wipe it out if he was backed up from Madrid.[33] Aberdeen had Crawford's despatch reporting this conversation sent to Aston, the British Minister in Madrid, in an attempt to rouse the required support for the Captain-General. Then the British commissioners in Havana suggested to Aberdeen that the British government challenge Espartero's sincerity by calling on him to fulfil the provisions of the 1835 treaty and pass a penal law. Kennedy, the commission judge, reiterated this idea following another discussion with Valdés.[34] A steady stream of instructions flowed from London to Madrid in the summer of 1843 aimed at obtaining a Spanish commitment to legislation on the slave trade. British officials were only too happy to be called on to exert pressure on the Spanish government and, by enlisting British aid, Valdés was trying to force his own government to confront the Cuban slave trade.

In the immediate aftermath of the Turnbull affair and before the Escalera conspiracy gripped Cuba, British officials and the Cuban Captain-General joined in an unprecedented co-operation, each wanting the slave trade to be stopped for very different reasons and each realizing that the key to its ultimate suppression lay in Madrid. This co-operation did not last nor did it succeed immediately in its object. The disordered state of Spanish politics in the summer of 1843 meant that colonial issues and the desires of foreign governments had to take second place to the struggle for power between two rival generals, Espartero and Narváez.[35] Valdés' chief, Espartero, lost and Valdés resigned as Captain-General of Cuba soon after Narváez had established himself in power. He left Cuba, praised for his intentions by the British commissioners who regretted his going.[36] The British government, especially Peel and Aberdeen, shared this regret because Valdés seemed their sole hope for any progress in the unremitting battle against the Cuban slave trade.

Perhaps the best testament both of Valdés' work in suppressing the slave trade and of the limit of his powers to stop it is an account he sent to Spain at the beginning of June 1843, containing statistics of the numbers of African slaves brought to Cuba from 1841 and of the numbers captured during the same period by the Cuban authorities. Nearly 5,000 Africans had been introduced illegally in 1841 and another 413 captured; in 1842 the respective figures were 1,555 and 737; and in the first five months of 1843, 2,275 Africans had arrived and none had been captured.[37] British estimates for these years differed from those of Valdés. The British commissioners reported 27 expeditions in 1841, carrying 9,776 slaves. Valdés' figures were lower than those of the slave traders themselves whose Havana account books recorded 21 expeditions bringing 8,893 slaves.[38] Whatever the correct total was, it appears to have been lower than any year since 1829. British and Spanish figures are closer to agreement for 1842, a year in which the British commissioners reported the arrival of only 9 expeditions with 3,000 slaves. Valdés' incomplete statistics for 1843 confirm later British estimates that the slave trade was on the increase again in 1843 and 1844. From 1843 the British commissioners added one-third to their total to account for unknown landings. In 1843 they counted 19 expeditions with not more than 8,000 slaves, including the one-third addition. In 1844 25 expeditions arrived, but only 18 definitely brought slaves. Adding one-third to the 7,280 slaves known to have been landed resulted in the British estimate of 10,000 for 1844.[39] These statistics, by their very nature, cannot be conclusive, but British and Spanish estimates proved one thing; the slave trade was so entrenched in the Cuban fabric that more than a well-intentioned Captain-General was needed to uproot it.

Valdés' successor, Leopoldo O'Donnell, was a man with a very different approach to the Cuban slave trade. Still in his early thirties when he was rewarded by Narváez with the command of Cuba, O'Donnell was destined to play an influential part in mid-nineteenth-century Spanish politics as one of a generation of military politicians. He would preside over 'the most stable ministry constitutional Spain had seen' from 1858 to 1863.[40] He had been born in Tenerife during the Napoleonic Wars and his family, as the name implies, had originated in Ireland. O'Donnell rode to military prominence during the Carlist Wars of the 1830s and joined Narváez to overthrow Espartero. The coup in Spain in 1843 opened a new opportunity for him and he lost no time in benefiting from it. Like Tacón before him, he left his liberalism in Spain and went to Cuba to make his fortune. His comparatively long stay as Captain-General, five years (1843–8), gave him ample scope. He made no secret of his belief that the slave trade was vital; without it Cuban agricultural prosperity would decline, slowly, perhaps, but inevitably. Shortly before O'Donnell's appointment, another known supporter of the slave trade, the long-serving Intendant of Havana, the Count of Villanueva, was reinstated. He had lost his job in 1841 after holding it since 1825, and his reinstatement in 1843 meant the two chief Spanish officers in the island now defended the slave trade.

With appointments favourable to their cause and the complete absence of British cruisers from the coast of Cuba due to other demands on the overstretched British West Indian squadron, the Cuban slave traders exhibited a new optimism, reflected in the number of expeditions despatched to Africa. At least 6 set out in October 1843, and the British commissioners observed an increasing demand for articles used in the slave trade.[41] Their annual report at the beginning of 1844 concluded that since O'Donnell's appointment the slave trade nearly had regained its former level; only the low sugar prices and a consequent lack of desire by the plantation owners to expand cultivation acted as restraints. But even with these supposed restraints, close to 3,000 African slaves came into Cuba in February and March 1844.[42]

O'Donnell was not simply the inspiration behind this renewed activity, he was an active beneficiary. The British consul commented in August 1844, 'I must confess that I have not the least confidence in any act of General O'Donnell's which will affect his desire to enrich himself by any means', and his colleagues shared his pessimism.[43] Their personal animosity towards the new Captain-General was heightened by his own contempt for the British representatives. He made no secret of his belief that the British were responsible for the Escalera conspiracy and he applauded a royal order of January 1844, which announced the Spanish government's wish to transfer the court of mixed commission from Havana to Puerto Rico. Such a move would ease the dangers to Cuba's security and restore Spain's prestige in the eyes of Cuba's youth by showing that Spain would not be dictated to by Britain.[44] The mixed commission court remained in Havana and O'Donnell's dream of rebuilding Spanish prestige in Cuba by standing up to Britain proved illusory.

The Captain-General stood in the forefront of those interests anxious to protect the slave trade, but arrayed against them was a growing body, composed mainly of creoles, opposed to the slave trade. Within Cuba hostility to the slave trade had taken a long time to develop. In 1837 the British commissioners reported scarcely anyone in Cuba opposed the slave trade, but from 1841 onwards opposition appeared to be increasing.[45] One common element was fear and by 1844 it had become a potent force in Cuba. It was not just a slaveholders' fear of slave uprisings. The continuation of the slave trade was fraught with risk, and a cross-section of white Cubans, creoles and peninsulars, planters and merchants alike, had to admit that Cuba was all too vulnerable. The close proximity of large populations of free blacks in Haiti and Jamaica kept the memory of St Domingue alive, a memory which evoked radically different images among the different groups of Cuba's population. To the slaves it promised the hope of ultimate liberation, but it added enormously to the white population's dread of race revolution. The insurrections of 1843 and the Escalera conspiracy of 1844 demonstrated to Cuban planters the ease with which a slave rebellion could begin. Britain had many ways of enforcing treaty obligations and Cuban proprietors were certain these included the use of abolitionist agents.[46] Some Cubans, on the other hand, realized the cessation of the slave trade might bring economic benefits. A Havana merchant house predicted that Cuban sugar would not be admitted into the British market unless the slave trade was abolished, and without new markets the price of sugar would not rise.[47]

In the aftermath of the Escalera conspiracy O'Donnell no longer could ignore what had become a public clamour to stop the importation of African slaves. He responded in February 1844 by publishing the royal order which had been sent out to his predecessor the previous summer calling for hearings on the penal law proposals. If it was impossible to prevent legislation against the slave trade, a carefully selected planter opinion might be able to influence the content of the legislation in their own interests, or so O'Donnell obviously thought. O'Donnell created a commission in order to examine proposals for a penal law and he asked for reports from various municipal authorities and private individuals, steps that were viewed with unconcealed suspicion by the British officials.[48]

The reports presented to the Captain-General unanimously agreed the slave trade should be stopped, but as Kennedy, the British judge, rightly observed, none of the reports condemned it on principle; opposition was on grounds of expediency, the implication being that as soon as the current dangers faded away the slave traders could continue where they had left off.[49] What occupied the minds of the men who wrote these reports was not the need to find ways to prohibit the slave trade effectively, but the necessity of limiting British interference in Cuba's plantation system. The reports, in the words of the British consul, were all 'clogged ... with pretended conditions to be exacted from Great Britain in case the Penal Laws are formally enacted'.[50]

Cuban officialdom shared these views and in some cases went further in proposing methods to hobble British officials, British cruisers and the Havana court of mixed commission. The *fiscal* of the *Real Hacienda*, Vicente Vásquez Queipo, thought the slave trade should be punished as contraband trade. This would not require legislation since the existing law in force against contraband could be applied to the slave trade simply by substituting the words 'slave trade' for 'contraband'. Vásquez Queipo also wanted the jurisdiction of the court of mixed commission confined to declaring captured ships legal prizes and then turning them over to Cuban courts.[51] Vásquez Queipo's superior, the Intendant, reiterated these arguments. Spanish contraband laws were sufficient to suppress the slave trade. He could not countenance wider powers for the court of mixed commission and special courts were unnecessary.[52]

The implication of these recommendations laid bare the vast gulf separating Spanish officials' real feelings about the slave trade and those of the British representatives with whom they negotiated. The latter branded the slave trade one of the worst crimes mankind could commit, a brutal human piracy meriting capital punishment for those condemned of it. But any moral condemnation was totally absent in the Cuban discussions about penal legislation. Slaves were property and an illegal trade in slaves was just another form of contraband commerce, to be punished accordingly. Besides, Spanish officers in Cuba knew well that no law had ever eliminated contraband. By assimilating the slave trade under Spanish contraband legislation it might continue in a less visible and therefore less provocative manner.

O'Donnell's carefully chosen commission read all these reports and met in August 1844, under the chairmanship of the Captain-General himself, to formulate resolutions on the proposed penal law for transmission to Madrid.[53] The commission recommended prison sentences for Spaniards or Cubans convicted of slave-trading, but added two qualifications; no vessel with fewer than ten slaves on board could be detained without proof of its being a slaver, nor could slave-trading between Spanish colonial possessions be counted an offence. Both of these qualifications, if implemented, would have violated the 1835 treaty. The other resolutions had a similar tenor. They were designed to protect those engaged in the illegal slave trade. The protection could take various forms; either loopholes in the law, or, alternatively, a court or courts which could be subverted. The commission opposed the idea of special courts to hear slave trade cases. All judicial powers should rest solely with the Captain-General, a suggestion which, if the British commissioners had learned of it, they would have criticized as the very antithesis of justice. Lastly, the commission warned the Spanish government of the dangers of public discussion on such an explosive topic. To avoid this, the commission recommended enacting the draft penal law by royal decree, which would obviate the need to submit it to the Cortes.

Had it not been for the combination of intense, behind-the-scenes, British pressure in Madrid and the Spanish government's belated realization of the great risk to Cuba and to Spain's possession of it if the slave trade went on uninterruptedly, O'Donnell's strategy might have succeeded in blocking any legislation on the slave trade. The fears of the Cuban planters, fanned by the Escalera conspiracy, and news of the conspiracy itself had been instrumental in awakening public opinion in Madrid. Ninety planters from the Matanzas area signed a petition asking for an immediate end to the slave trade only to have it torn up by the Governor of Matanzas. O'Donnell wrote a threatening letter to them when the petition reached him. The Captain-General later denied receiving the petition when the British commissioners confronted him with it, but it arrived eventually in Madrid and was published in *El Corresponsal*, one of the city's main newspapers, in February 1844.[54] An article condemning the continuance of the slave trade to Cuba had appeared a few days earlier in *El Heraldo*, the leading journal of the *Moderados*.[55]

These indications of planter unrest, surfacing in Spain after evading O'Donnell's censorship blanket, coincided with an increase in British diplomatic activity. What had begun in 1843 as a British effort to help Valdés win legislative support from his metropolitan government, a year later turned into an open attempt to force the removal of O'Donnell from Cuba. In 1843 quiet British persistence on the subject of penal legislation had met Spanish procrastination. Three British diplomatic notes urging the passage of a penal law all had gone unanswered.[56] This total disregard of British representations, plus the depressing accounts from Havana of O'Donnell's behaviour, prompted Aberdeen to write a long despatch to his Minister in Madrid at the end of 1843. In it he detailed the history of the neglect of the slave trade treaties for Bulwer to use to convince the Spanish government to fulfil its promise and pass legislation outlawing the slave trade.[57] Bulwer sent two Notes early in February 1844, emphasizing that the state of Cuba, to say nothing of Spain's treaty obligations, made a penal law imperative. When no answer had been received by April, he sent another reminder, and, at length, González Bravo, the Spanish Foreign Minister, assured him the penal law would be published immediately.[58]

It was not as empty a promise as the long history of futile slave trade negotiations might have implied. The day before the Spanish promise was made, a commission, appointed by the Spanish government and headed by former Captain-General Valdés, presented its report which included a draft penal law. Both the tone of the document and the articles of the draft penal law contrasted sharply with the recommendations of O'Donnell's Cuban commission and the reports from which they were drawn.[59] Valdés' draft law specified prison sentences for different categories of slave trade offences, provided for ordinary Spanish tribunals to hear cases brought against auxiliaries including those who received or concealed illegally imported Africans and gave the Captain-General power to suspend any subordinate officer implicated in a slave expedition. A convincing series of arguments accompanied the draft law to support the conclusion that the time had come for Spain to proscribe the slave trade through legislation of her own. The report, however, was never made public and two months passed before the British Minister knew of the draft law's existence.

While Bulwer waited in vain throughout the spring of 1844 for some tangible evidence of the long-promised legislation, knowledge of the Escalera conspiracy and the subsequent purges worked in different ways in Madrid and London to hasten it. The Spanish Foreign and Colonial Ministers both agreed on the necessity of maintaining slavery in the Spanish Antilles, but Valdés' report, reinforced by rumours of the involvement of British abolitionists in the Escalera conspiracy, pointed to the urgency of a cessation of the slave trade.[60] Aberdeen, the British Foreign Secretary, heard with mounting anger the stories of O'Donnell's brutal suppression of the conspiracy in Cuba and the blatant violations of the slave trade treaties carried on by Cuban slave traders. The language of his private letters to Bulwer in Madrid took on a new and menacing ring: 'The conduct of the Captain-General is infamous, & shall be fully exposed. The Government at Madrid had better mind what they are about.' Such a state of affairs in Cuba 'must lead before long to very serious consequences'.[61] By the summer of 1844, the Cuban mess had become so bad in the eyes of the British government that O'Donnell's removal headed the list of British demands. Aberdeen told Bulwer:

In fact, it is indispensable; & in urging it in every proper manner, you will also continue to insinuate that should you fail, it would not surprize you if you were to receive orders to quit Spain. I do not wish at present to make a specific threat of this kind; but I really can see no other result if they should persevere in maintaining O'Donnell at the Havana. Let them make him Captain-General of Madrid or anything they please; but let them only send a man who is determined to execute the Treaty, & who is able to resist the Bribes of the Slave Dealers.[62]

Bulwer knew that obtaining O'Donnell's recall would be no easy matter, especially since he was a close friend of General Narváez, the head of the Spanish government, and was firmly backed by the Queen Mother whose private slave-trading interests O'Donnell allegedly protected.[63] But after conversations with the Queen Mother and discussions with the Spanish Foreign Minister, Bulwer was able to report partial success. The Spanish government had ordered O'Donnell to stop the slave trade in order to protect Cuba from the intrigues of British abolitionist societies and the menace of slave revolts.[64] If the reasons given were not those which the British government would have advanced, the instructions themselves were a sign of good intentions. The Spanish Minister of Foreign Affairs then informed his colleagues in the war and colonial ministries that a penal law would be passed. It was the Royal Will that the slave trade be stopped. Another royal order, based on his letter, went out to Cuba the following day.[65] Bulwer believed he had achieved even more. He forwarded Valdés' draft penal law to Aberdeen at the end of June with the firm assurance that when it was published the decree would have the force of law in Cuba without the formal sanction of the Cortes. He wrote again a day later to relay the promise of the Spanish Foreign Minister, Viluma, that his resignation would not affect the law's passage. The law, however, was not sent to Cuba, as Bulwer was to discover, but was dropped after Viluma's resignation.[66]

Some progress had been made in spite of this setback. The royal orders promulgated in June had a greater impact than any previous ones, as indicated in the reaction of the Captain-General. His despatches acknowledging them and his performance in Cuba demonstrated he had not lost his military ability to fight a rearguard action. He was adamant that any change in the methods used to fight the slave trade or any increase in the severity of persecution would endanger the institution of slavery in the island. O'Donnell then interpreted the opinions held by the Cuban planters. There was, he wrote, a contradiction between their words and their acts. A majority of Cuban planters, if asked for their views either orally or in writing, would oppose the introduction of African slaves and the consequent increase of Cuba's black population. But those very men encouraged the slave trade because not one would hesitate to buy an illegally introduced African slave either directly or indirectly through a third party. British officials and the British government would have been surprised to hear O'Donnell claim he had suggested a plan to put down the slave trade. It consisted of advice to the proprietors that they form an association in which each voluntarily would obligate himself not to purchase slaves brought directly from Africa. What O'Donnell, in August 1844, implied was a serious proposal for ending the slave trade, he had thrown out as a taunt the previous January to stifle the genuine expression of creole views.[67] Yet O'Donnell's beliefs had a brutal logic of their own. He was convinced that slave labour was essential for Cuban sugar to remain competitive in foreign markets. If free white labour replaced black slave labour, the costs of sugar production would exceed the revenue from sales. Even if white immigration was subsidized, and O'Donnell vetoed this on political grounds – he had enough subversive elements to contend with – black slave labour was the bedrock of Cuban prosperity.[68]

O'Donnell's logic carried him further. If the slave trade ended, Cuba's sugar plantations would not be affected immediately, but gradually they would decline for lack of labour. Natural reproduction could not maintain the slave population 'because the number of females is infinitely less than the number of males', and labour-saving devices were still too expensive to be considered as a practical alternative.[69] But in 1844 no new cultivation was being undertaken which meant the slave trade was diminishing of its own accord due to a fall in demand. O'Donnell was content to let this natural diminution continue without imposing and implementing more official prohibitions. He was careful not to mention what he would do if demand picked up again.

The Captain-General, whatever his own opinions, did not dare to disregard the royal orders. He reportedly called the slave dealers together and told them the slave trade had to stop, although the dealers obtained from him the usual concession that all slavers already at sea would be allowed to land their cargoes. O'Donnell himself was quoted as saying that as the Captain-General he would obey the orders he had received on the slave trade, but as a Spaniard he opposed them.[70]

Martínez de la Rosa, who had signed the 1835 treaty for Spain, returned as Spanish Foreign Minister in the autumn of 1844. His return saw British-Spanish relations once more at the point of crisis over the failure to end the Cuban slave trade. Tales from Cuba of torture to the black population, imprisonment of British subjects and official confirmation of an increase in the illegal slave trade made the British public and the British government more militant. The British and Foreign Anti-Slavery Society in its annual report, issued in the spring of 1844, had sadly told British abolitionists, 'the British Government has begun to relax in its demands, and to yield to the wrong-doers . . . The people of this country have a right to expect that no demand founded in righteousness, should be relinquished by their Government.'[71] Peel's government had not pressed Spain on the Turnbull plan and now it was coming under abolitionist attack because of the stories from Cuba reaching Britain. O'Donnell's ruthless purge of all abolitionists, real or imagined, stiffened British condemnation of Spain and of him. Palmerston, in opposition, smelled a political issue and charged the Conservative government with allowing the slave trade to increase. Peel defended his government's record, but he, too, was profoundly shocked by the reports from Cuba. He bluntly and publicly warned Spain 'of the condition of Cuba, where the tenure of power over slaves is more than precarious'.[72] British politicians long ago had given up appealing to Spain on humanitarian grounds, but the lesson of the Escalera conspiracy was the same in both Britain and Spain. Unless something was done to check the slave trade, Spain might lose Cuba.

The slave trade debate in Britain renewed the pressure on the British Minister in Madrid. Aberdeen wrote privately to Bulwer, 'You must not forget Cuba, or O'Donnell. Palmerston made an attack yesterday on our Slave Trade Policy . . . It gave Peel an opportunity to enlarge upon the state of Cuba, and the conduct of the Captain-General whom he certainly did not spare.'[73] Because the slave trade was the only sore point of disagreement with Spain in the autumn of 1844, Aberdeen had no intention of pushing matters to an open break, but he was prepared to threaten this in private. In October he wrote to Bulwer again: 'But O'Donnell is really quite intolerable, and unless they remove him, I do not see what we can do but recall you. I have not yet desired you to announce this officially, but you will do well to let it be understood privately. Unless too they make reparation for his monstrous cruelties and acts of gross injustice towards our Countrymen, we shall be obliged to order reprisals.'[74]

Bulwer in Madrid was confident the issue could be settled amicably, but he also knew it was one 'on which the state of our relations with Spain entirely depends'.[75] Aberdeen still wanted O'Donnell removed, but when he found out that Narváez and Martínez de la Rosa would not knuckle under, he was willing to accept a penal law instead. This was to be the face-saving compromise for both countries. Early in November 1844, Martínez de la Rosa informed Bulwer the law would be introduced in the Cortes rather than promulgated as a royal decree, a decision which seemed to be a defeat for O'Donnell and the Cuban slave-trading interests.[76] It took nearly two more months to fulfil his promise, but at last, on 22 December, Martínez de la Rosa presented the penal law to the Cortes with essentially the same provisions as the one drawn up by the Valdés commission earlier that year.

The draft bill had three parts to it. The first part, comprising five articles, set down the penalties for the captains and crew condemned of participating in the illegal slave trade. Senior officers were liable to a maximum of six years' imprisonment, raised to eight for resisting arrest, plus fines and exile from their homes although not from Cuba;

but the penalties varied depending on whether the slaver was captured on the high seas with slaves on board or in port before the voyage began. Owners or backers of slave voyages were liable to the same punishments, but the rest of the slavers' crew were subject to half the punishment of senior officers. Three other articles included provision for the destruction of condemned slave vessels, special punishment if the slaves on board had been tortured or beaten and more severe punishment for repeated offences. Another article gave Spanish officials power to act whenever a suspected slave landing occurred or a suspected expedition was fitting out.

Martínez de la Rosa sent the draft penal law out to Cuba before it had been passed by the Cortes, along with a confidential royal order which emphasized that the Spanish government had drafted the law to comply with its obligations under the 1835 treaty.[77] The order reiterated Spain's determination to end the slave trade once and for all, but it also guaranteed the Cuban plantocracy that their existing property in slaves was not to be disturbed on any account. Recognizing the difficulty of distinguishing between two subjects so interwoven as the introduction of slaves from Africa and the institution of slavery within Cuba, the order nevertheless made this distinction in order to reassure Cuban slaveowners. Their slave property would be respected and this would be written into Spanish law. The Captain-General was told to stress the fact that the cessation of the slave trade would bring greater security to Cuba's plantation owners. No longer would abolitionist agents hiding behind humanitarian cloaks have any excuse to sow seeds of disorder and rebellion in Cuba, and the worries of white Cubans about excessive numbers of blacks in the island could vanish since these numbers would not be increased any more by the slave trade. The problem of agricultural labour which had preoccupied every Captain-General was glossed over with the suggestion that O'Donnell propose substitutes in the form of colonization schemes or increased use of machinery. The two halves of the Cuban slave equation were both present in this royal order: the protection of existing slavery and the prohibition of the slave trade, but the equation did not balance as Martínez de la Rosa believed it would. The protection of existing slavery far outweighed the commitment to the prohibition of the slave trade which became apparent when debate in the Spanish Cortes began.

The passage through the Cortes was not nearly as smooth as the Spanish government and the British Minister had anticipated. First, the bill was referred to a commission of the Senate whose report revealed the latent hostility to Britain and the slave trade treaties. Instead of an objective examination of the draft penal law, the report was a diatribe against those unnamed Spaniards who, in a near traitorous act, had signed the 1817 treaty, jeopardizing the prosperity and existence of Spain's Caribbean possessions and giving Britain a foothold for interference in Spanish colonial matters.[78] The *Times* correspondent in Madrid, in a special despatch to the *Anti-Slavery Reporter*, could not contain his own feelings as he described the 'most vigorous opposition' building up to threaten the penal law. Although there were rumours afoot of the French Ambassador working secretly to block the bill, the main opposition was led by 'those who call themselves Liberals . . . But it is intolerable, I could even say disgusting, to hear men who talk so glibly and so fluently of the oppression under which they themselves groan, attempt to resist the effort now made to put a stop to the abominable traffic in human beings.'[79]

The tactics of the Cuban slave-trading interests and their allies were to emasculate the bill through amendments. Their main target was the powers to be given to local authorities in Cuba to investigate suspected cases of slave-trading and to punish offenders. These powers constituted the ninth article of the draft law, but two amendments passed over government opposition put a definite limit on the action which the Cuban government could take against slave traders. The first one declared the authorities could proceed against participants in a slaving expedition only when the slaver had come direct from Africa, and the second prohibited Cuban officials from entering plantations or conducting any search to investigate the origin of slaves found in the possession of a Cuban proprietor.[80]

This second amendment extended the Spanish government's reassurance to Cuban planters that existing slave property would be protected into a protection of all slave property, no matter whether the slaves were illegally introduced Africans, emancipated Africans illegally sold into slavery or the offspring of slaves born in Cuba. Its worst aspect was the security it gave to Cuban plantation owners who in future would obtain illegally introduced African slaves. Once the slaves were actually on an estate the manner of their entry into the island became immaterial. This amendment transformed the penal law from a weapon aimed at the illegal slave trade into a slaveholder's law where the very fact of possession meant legal possession. It represented a viewpoint long held in Cuba, but had it not been for Turnbull's plan, proposed to Spain in 1840, and the Escalera conspiracy, which showed Cuban planters and Spanish officials how far

Britain would go to enforce her demands, the amendment might never have been conceived. British pressure played a key role in the passage of the penal law, but Spanish reaction to British abolitionism was responsible for the one amendment which nullified its effect.

Bulwer, who followed the Cortes debate very closely, recognized the real meaning of the amendment and protested its inclusion in the law. Martínez de la Rosa replied for the Spanish government, explaining that the amendment was not contrary to the treaties, but his answer did not still the British fears.[81] British diplomacy failed to prevent the amendment or to alter the law once it was before the Cortes. The bill passed into law with the amendments intact.

Far from rejoicing at the passage of the law after nine years of waiting, the British reaction was one of cynicism. Aberdeen wrote to Bulwer, 'I have no great confidence in the efficacy of the new law, otherwise the first person whom they ought to shut up in prison is the Captain-General himself.' Later, after assessing British public opinion, he was even more pessimistic: 'I am sorry to say that the adoption of the Penal Law has produced very little effect in this country. There is a fixed and universal belief that the law is only made to be broken and that there is not the slightest chance of its being honestly carried into effect.'[82] Palmerston expressed this cynicism publicly in a House of Commons debate, using almost the same language: 'But I am sorry to say that I attach no value whatever to any law that the Spanish Government may pass on the subject of [the] Slave Trade.' Peel had to agree that the situation in Cuba had deteriorated since O'Donnell's arrival, but he refrained from attacking the penal law openly.[83] British abolitionists thought Spain had duped Britain by passing the law. The 1845 annual report of the British and Foreign Anti-Slavery Society recorded their condemnation: 'The Committee attach little importance to the enactment. They believe it is intended to silence the just demands of this country for a time and in no ways [sic] intended to lessen the slave traffic.'[84]

Aberdeen's acceptance of the Spanish penal law, knowing it would not accomplish its avowed purpose, is in marked contrast to his much more aggressive approach to Brazil at the same time. Brazil refused to continue the Anglo-Brazilian slave trade treaty, originally signed between Britain and Portugal in 1817 and incorporated into a new treaty between Britain and Brazil in 1826, beyond 1845. When the treaty lapsed, Britain no longer had any legal basis to seize and search suspected Brazilian slavers. Brazil would not sign another treaty and Aberdeen, fully conscious of the unsatisfactory results of Spain's penal law, adopted Palmerston's tactics of placing the powers in British hands. He had Parliament pass an act giving British naval vessels a unilateral right to seize suspected Brazilian slavers and bring them before British Vice-Admiralty courts for trial.[85]

The Aberdeen Act of 1845 was a far harsher measure against Brazil than any Britain took or contemplated taking against Spain, even though the slave trade to Cuba persisted in open violation of the Anglo-Spanish treaties. His failure to persuade Spain to pass a law with teeth may have made Aberdeen more determined to succeed with Brazil even if the unilateral exercise of force was the only way open to him. But Spain, unlike Brazil, was very careful not to let her treaties with Britain lapse and to defend both her conduct and the penal law in the context of those treaties. The legal justification which Aberdeen had for the passage of his 1845 law, directed against Brazil, did not exist in Spain's case. For Spain the treaties with Britain served as a protection, shielding her from the overt exercise of British military power. Brazil's fate was an instructive lesson. Spain's politicians pointed to the penal law as an indication of Spanish fulfilment of the treaties, but, in reality, it was another stone in the wall of Spanish colonial defences around Cuba's slave system.

The debate preceding the passage of the law had forced Cuban planters and Spanish politicians to confront the intimately related questions of Spanish colonial policy in Cuba and the slave trade which buttressed Cuban prosperity. Cuban slavery had been a closed subject in both Spain and Cuba until 1845. It was debated only once, briefly, in the Cortes of 1811, and within Cuba a rigid censorship prevented public discussion. The 1845 debate was remarkable for the public airing of long suppressed viewpoints. Saco, the exiled Cuban creole, congratulated the Spanish government 'because for the first time, in an issue as vital as the slave trade, the Spanish government, cognisant of the real needs of Cuba, has openly condemned the slave trade'.[86] The penal law was the first law passed by a Spanish legislative body against the slave trade, which alone would have made it an historic act.[87]

The agitation prior to the debate and the debate itself sparked the publication of several pamphlets on the slave trade, two of which circulated freely within Cuba. It would take a long time, but slowly public opinion in Spain and in Cuba was being led to oppose the continuation of a commerce almost as old as Spain's colonial rule. The pamphlets, one by Saco, and two by peninsular Spaniards, were unanimous on the need to end the slave trade, but this superficial unity disguised subtle but profound differences over Spanish colonial policy.

Saco's analysis of the agricultural and security reasons for stopping the slave trade was an expanded version of his 1837 work, 'Mi primera pregunta', which had attempted to persuade Cuban planters that it was in their own interests to give up the slave trade. At the urging of his friend and fellow exile, Domingo del Monte, Saco rewrote 'Mi primera pregunta' in 1844 and del Monte sent it to the Spanish government to use as a commentary and defence of the penal law against the slave-trading interests.[88]

Saco noted the change in Cuban opinion in the twelve years since he had first spoken out against the slave trade only to suffer exile to Europe. Now, he observed, with rare exceptions white inhabitants of Cuba, whether Cuban or European, agreed with him. He reiterated his earlier argument that ending the slave trade would not cause Cuban agriculture to suffer and would aid European colonization. 'Close the ports forever to all blacks; open them freely to all whites; and Cuba will be repaid with enduring prosperity while Spain will have the glory of possessing one of the most lustrous colonies to which any European metropolis could aspire.' Carefully disclaiming any intention of advocating the abolition of slavery itself, he concentrated on what he termed the security reasons for abolishing the slave trade. Here he played on the frayed nerve ends of Cuba's white population, whose horror of race revolution had been sharpened by the Escalera conspiracy and constant rumours of British abolitionist subversion. The sheer numbers of blacks in the island made race revolt more likely. In Cuba, Saco wrote, 'two races live, no less divided by their colour than by their state; with no common interest they are irreconcilable enemies'. Warning white Cuba that if the slave trade continued there would be no peace or security, he conjured up the image of Britain as an avenging judge exacting a savage retribution from people who flouted sacred treaty obligations. Since Spain could not stand up to Britain in battle nor resist her diplomacy, it was in her national interest to comply with Britain's demands.

Very different in tone was the soothing message of one of Spain's leading civil servants in Cuba, the *fiscal*, Vicente Vásquez Queipo.[89] Vásquez Queipo had argued strongly for tackling the slave trade by adapting Spanish contraband laws, but after the scare of the Escalera conspiracy he wrote a memorandum on colonial policy, subsequently published in 1845, whose main purpose was to reassure white Cuba that neither the increase of the African population nor the ratio of whites to blacks in the island was as bad as had been alleged. Like Saco, he now believed the absolute suppression of the slave trade was essential along with an increase in labourers and the long term substitution of the white race for the black. The Escalera conspiracy had uncovered the crater on which Cuba had been precariously resting. If it was not to erupt, the slave trade had to be suppressed, slavery had to be extinguished but in a gradual and measured way and white colonization had to be stimulated. Slowly, white supremacy would be restored, although it might take as long as a century to achieve this.

The most radical approach to Cuba's problems came from the distinguished Spanish scientist and reformer, Ramón de la Sagra, in a pamphlet published to coincide with the passage of the penal law.[90] La Sagra, in common with Vásquez Queipo and Saco, believed it was vital for Cuba to end the slave trade. The debate on the penal law convinced him that this long overdue reform was an accomplished fact and, thus encouraged, he challenged what he labelled the great error of previous generations: erecting the complete edifice of colonial agriculture in Cuba on slavery which, sooner or later, would collapse. He wanted slavery abolished because 'the political and economic fate of the Antilles must not rest on the slavery of one race, nor on the coerced application of its strength'. Slavery in Cuba not only had been damaging to agriculture by inhibiting the development of scientific agriculture, it also had planted corrosive germs of immorality 'in the hearts of institutions and in the vital organs of society itself'.

Rooting out slavery would cause tremendous agricultural growth and lead to what La Sagra desired, a reorganization of Cuban agriculture on scientific principles. The value of agricultural property then would be based on land values not on the labour cultivating it, a greater variety of plants could be grown, capital investment would increase and the costs of production would fall. At the same time moral sentiments would be inculcated into the slaves. They would be educated and civilized and taught to regard work not as a penalty but as an integral part of man's social condition. La Sagra saw and favoured, as no other Spaniard of his time, the real meaning of emancipation in the British West Indies: 'the desire for personal independence and the decline of the large plantation'. He thus championed abolition for Cuba, although he, too, saw the future of Cuba as a European colony with property founded on 'solid European cement'. He suggested that the only place where Africans could enjoy real liberty was in Africa, a suggestion which perhaps cloaked a racial myopia akin to that of Saco and Vásquez Queipo. La Sagra's idealistic vision of a reformed Cuba awakened little response either in Spain or in Cuba where his pamphlet was banned. His certainty in the imminent victory over the slave trade also showed a misplaced faith in his countrymen.

Two former Captains-General of Cuba had told their government that if the slave trade was to be stopped, the government had to ensure above all that subordinate authorities loyally carried out government orders.[91] Captain-General O'Donnell already had shown he was not the man who would inspire this needed change of attitude. He insisted he would suppress the slave trade more thoroughly than any of his predecessors had done, but even in the despatch in which he said this he left a suspicion that his chief concern was to moderate any adverse effects the law might have on Cuban proprietors. O'Donnell predicted that Cuba would decline and face ruin within ten years if the slave trade were stopped completely.[92] In the name of security all previous treaties and royal orders on the slave trade had received the minimum of publicity within the island, if they were published at all, and O'Donnell treated the penal law the same way. Some Madrid papers with accounts of it arrived in Cuba, but these were suppressed at Santiago de Cuba and at Havana the local paper made no mention of the law.[93]

The penal law of 1845 was a lost opportunity for Spain to come to grips with the basic element in a colonial problem becoming daily more complex. Pressured by an insistent Britain and responding belatedly to the scared cries from Cuban planters, the Spanish government had the penal law passed. The law made public Spain's ostensible desire to stop the slave trade and by doing so to fulfil her treaty obligations to Britain; Article 9 of the law as amended during the Cortes debate overrode the impulse to prosecute the slave trade and rendered the law impotent. Because it was the first act against the slave trade passed by a Spanish legislature, the penal law soon took on the sacrosanct aura of a colonial constitution, especially when attempts were made to amend it or remove Article 9. Successive Captains-General after 1845 fought the slave trade with one administrative hand tied behind their backs. These men, many sincere in their efforts, were frustrated with their total failure either to suppress the trade or to obtain additional powers against it from a metropolitan government which hid behind the penal law. Twenty-one more years would pass before the corpus of acts, treaties and laws against the Spanish slave trade was capped by a new Spanish slave trade law reforming the penal law of 1845. Until then, the dilemma which Spanish officials recognized throughout the long history of the slave trade negotiations, that of satisfying British demands without prejudicing Cuban planter interests, was not resolved.

CHAPTER 11

Free trade and annexationism

The apparent success of British pressure against the foreign slave trade in 1845, with the passage of the Aberdeen Act (giving Britain unilateral powers to attack the slave trade to Brazil) and the Spanish penal law, masked the crisis over British abolitionist policy which was coming rapidly to a head. The campaign for free trade in Britain had divided the abolitionists among themselves, with the majority joining in an uncomfortable alliance with West Indian merchants and planters and protectionists in Britain in a vain effort to keep out slave-grown sugar. Even before the victory of free trade, abolitionists and some free traders had challenged the naval blockade system off West Africa, the cornerstone of British slave trade suppression. With free trade triumphant, the movement to do away with the cruisers gathered public momentum and by 1848 the defenders of the use of force feared their policy would be swept away just as protection had been. Where in 1840 the British abolitionist movement exercised a powerful influence on government policy, by 1850 the divisions over free trade and the use of naval force noticeably reduced the effectiveness of British abolitionist pressure.

During the same period the British government, facing the growing militancy of American expansionism and with the United States acquisition of Cuba an ever present danger, discovered that its freedom to act against the Cuban slave trade had narrowed considerably. Britain had to be much more circumspect towards Cuba than she had been before and more so than she was towards Brazil. Any British moves which might be interpreted as direct British intervention in Cuba could lead to what no British government wanted – the American annexation of the island. Britain's free trade policy stimulated the expansion of Cuba's sugar plantations which, in turn, increased the demand in Cuba for slave labour. The enduring strength of American annexationism, until the American Civil War killed it, forced Britain to help Spain preserve Cuba. The era of free trade and annexationism saw a change in the climate surrounding the struggle to abolish the slave trade to Cuba, a change which helped to postpone its extinction to another decade.

The free trade movement in Britain, steadily growing in popularity during the early 1840s, posed an acute dilemma for British abolitionists. Sympathetic as most of them were to free trade in principle, if protectionist tariffs on sugar were abolished and slave-grown sugar allowed to compete equally with free-grown sugar for the British market would this not be a tremendous stimulus to slave-grown sugar and a powerful incentive for the continuation and even the expansion of the slave trade? Free trade meant lowering the price of basic foodstuffs for industrial workers in Britain but at the cost of reinforcing slavery in Brazil and Cuba. The majority of British abolitionists were not prepared to pay that price. As Duncan Rice has noted, 'When it came to a choice between encouraging slavery and encouraging monopoly, many of them took the second alternative and jettisoned their free trade principles.'[1]

What has been viewed generally as the victory of free trade was interpreted by the abolitionists as a defeat for humanitarianism, and they were very bitter about it. After the passage of the Sugar Duty Act of 1846, the *Anti-Slavery Reporter*, the organ of the British and Foreign Anti-Slavery Society, accused the House of Commons of voting to admit 'the blood-stained sugars of Brazil and Cuba' into Britain.[2] Not only abolitionists remarked on the contrast between British commercial policy in 1846 and Britain's abolition of slavery in 1833. Stephen Cave, a London barrister connected with West Indian interests who candidly admitted that his pamphlet condemning the Sugar Duty Act of 1846 for encouraging slavery and the slave trade was 'little more than a declaration of adherence to a defeated and unpopular party', nevertheless did not spare his countrymen; '. . . the people of England in 1846 consented to give the greatest encouragement in their power to the same, but a more atrocious form of the same, system which they rose, as one man, to crush in 1833 . . . '. No one could be certain how much free trade would encourage these twin scourges, but Cave's despondency also reflected the prevailing mood among the abolitionists and their supporters; 'Are Slavery and the Slave Trade to continue for so long as the world may endure?'[3]

John Taylor, an Englishman who had lived for some time in Cuba, was another who found it difficult to reconcile Britain's apparently contradictory policies. The 'world's annals do not present a greater practical paradox' than the British abolition of slavery in 1834 followed twelve years later by a measure which ruined her own colonies and doubled or trebled the system of slavery in foreign colonies. When the elimination of the slave trade to Cuba was within her grasp, she instead gave it new life; 'Well convinced am I, that a few sharply-uttered demands for the strict fulfillment of treaties and bonds, a few dark hints quietly thrown out, would have actually turned the scale, that the first steps would have been taken, and that one point only having been gained, we should have had no more to fear from Cuba, our greatest enemy.'[4]

British abolitionists refused to accept the finality of the free trade victory. Even after the two Sugar Duty Acts of 1846 and 1848 provided for the gradual equalization of duties on all sugar entering Britain, irrespective of origin, until by 1854 slave-grown and free-grown sugar would compete equally in the British market, the abolitionists kept after the government to adopt a system of tariffs which would dis-criminate in favour of free-grown sugar. Sir Edward Noel Buxton, the son of the abolitionist leader, Thomas Fowell Buxton, introduced motions annually in Parliament to reinstate the protective duties on sugar. Anti-slavery petitions from 1848 regularly asked for the exclusion of slave-grown produce from the British market.[5] As the economic decline of Britain's own West Indian colonies worsened, the abolitionists linked their demands for the exclusion of slave-grown sugar to the fate of the British West Indies. In 1852 the Secretary of the British and Foreign Anti-Slavery Society wrote to the Prime Minister prior to another reduction in the tariff on foreign sugar tak-ing effect. He urged to no avail that the duties to be levied against Brazilian and Cuban sugar from 5 July 1853 be kept in force and those on sugar from British possessions gradually reduced to a nominal level until the slave trade treaties were fulfilled in every respect and the trade itself abolished.[6] Abolitionists were not just bitter about the triumph of free trade; they could not understand how unlimited access to the British market was freely given away to Spain and Brazil without demanding any concessions in return.

By the 1850s, the British and Foreign Anti-Slavery Society, as the official organ of British abolitionists, ceased to have any real impact on British government policy. Certainly, it had no success whatever in reversing the verdict on free trade. Officials in the Foreign Office grew tired of what they regarded as repetitious representations from the abolitionists and paid little attention to them. T. L. Ward, the head of the Slave Trade Department of the Foreign Office, characterized the British and Foreign Anti-Slavery Society in 1854 as ' . . . a Society which has ceased, since the abolition of Slavery in the British Colonies, to be of any public importance or Utility . . . '.[7] The struggle to overturn free trade was a lost cause and by associating themselves with it the abolitionists were discredited in the eyes of the government.

It was not only their advocacy of protectionism against slave-grown produce which made the British and Foreign Anti-Slavery Society unpopular with government. Opposition to the use of armed force had been an essential part of the original philosophy of the Society when it was founded in 1839. In keeping with this philosophy, the Society decided in 1845 to oppose force as a means of suppressing the foreign slave trade. Maintaining that the cruiser system was a waste of money since, far from suppressing the slave trade, it spurred the slave trader, William Hutt, the M.P. for Gateshead. After a premature and the Middle Passage, the Society wanted the withdrawal of British cruisers from the African coast. Instead of using force, the British government should promote free labour in West Africa and demand the liberation of all slaves illegally introduced into Brazil and Cuba.[8] Thus, from 1845 the leading British abolitionist society actively opposed the key element of British slave trade suppression policy.

The attack on the cruisers likely would have had little impact if the British and Foreign Anti-Slavery Society alone had mounted it. But the campaign was taken up and given new force by a leading free trader, William Hutt, the M.P. for Gateshead. After a premature and somewhat ineffective foray in 1845, he was successful early in 1848 in getting a Select Committee of the House of Commons established to examine the method of slave trade repression being carried out by Britain. His own remedy was in keeping with his *laisser-faire* beliefs. 'It was our own blundering and ignorant humanity which alone sustained the slave trade. To extinguish it, we should leave it alone.'[9] The abolitionists were unable to separate themselves from Hutt's position, with which they had only a superficial connection, but to outsiders it seemed that abolitionists and free traders had now joined together to eliminate the cruisers and thus take away Britain's self-appointed role as prosecutor of the Atlantic slave trade.[10]

Hutt's anti-blockade crusade led to a succession of parliamentary committees over a three-year period carrying out an extensive probe of all aspects of Britain's struggle to stop the Atlantic slave trade. Behind Hutt were a variety of interests, not all solid supporters but, like the abolitionists, at least united in opposition to the African Squadron. One contemporary analyst of the debate found four groups pressing for the withdrawal of the cruisers: the free traders and *laisser-faire* advocates, a small minority of merchants trading to Africa, some West Indian representatives hoping to solve the labour problems of Britain's West Indian colonies by promoting the emigration of large numbers of African labourers and the British and Foreign Anti-Slavery Society with its supporters.[11] But what held these seemingly disparate interests together was not at all clear to contemporaries. As an anonymous barrister, who took it upon himself to analyse the mountain of evidence amassed by the parliamentary committees, commented: 'There has been a strange coincidence of circumstances about the whole of this Anti-Blockade agitation . . . Whigs and Conservatives, West Indians and Abolitionists, Free-Traders and Protectionists, have all become jumbled and jolted together, as if they had been threading the mazes of a country dance blindfolded, and were looking round in vain for the partners with whom they commenced it.'[12]

For the defenders of the cruisers, or, to use W.L. Mathieson's label, the 'coercionists', Hutt's attack was a logical outcome of the victory of free trade and represented the first serious challenge to Britain's anti-slave trade policies since she had embarked upon the international war against the Atlantic slave trade.[13] No group realized this more acutely than the old guard abolitionists led by Denman, the Lord Chief Justice, Lord Brougham and William Wilberforce's son, Samuel, the Bishop of Oxford. For them the crisis was deeply personal, threatening to undo their life's work. The split among the abolitionists between these men and the British and Foreign Anti-Slavery Society added further to the confusion in the minds of contemporaries. The older abolitionists stoutly defended the use of force to put down the slave trade. Each of the men mentioned above sat in the House of Lords, as did the former Foreign Secretary, Lord Aberdeen, another 'coercionist', and under their leadership the House of Lords came to the side of the 'coercionists' when it appeared in the summer of 1848 that Hutt and his 'anti-coercionists' might win over the Commons Select Committee.

The Lord Chief Justice, especially, in speeches to the House of Lords in 1848 and in two pamphlets, tried to rouse his countrymen's flagging spirits and impressed upon them their moral duty to see the fight through to the finish: 'My object is to defend my country for her long perseverance in those righteous efforts; to convince her and the world that no end presented to the mind of man was ever equally important with the extinction of the Slave-trade; that the attempt is perfectly lawful and praiseworthy and that she is bound, by her position still to employ those means, unless they are proved to be ineffectual, or she loses the capacity to do so.'[14] As the title of his pamphlets stressed, Britain's object must be nothing less than the final extinction of the slave trade. Denman remained confident the goal was attainable: 'With a few exceptions . . . the Slave-trade of England fell unresisting before the law, and notwithstanding the enormous profit, has hitherto made no effort to recover. That of Brazil and Cuba will follow its fate if the coercion is adequate, and resolutely proclaimed, and applied in good earnest.'[15]

The national honour of Victorian Britain was at stake as the 'coercionists' reiterated. Henry Yule, a veteran of the African Squadron, asked: 'Shall we retrace the steps of thirty years, and recant all that we have for that time been dinning into the ears of Europe?'[16] A resolution in the final report of the Select Committee of the House of Lords in 1850 warned, 'that to abandon the suppression of the Trade, to which in the face of the whole civilized world, Great Britain is solemnly and repeatedly pledged, would be a fatal blow to her national honour'.[17] These patriotic appeals, ultimately successful, were a measure of how serious the opposition to Britain's slave trade suppression policies had become. Professor Bethell rightly has emphasized the importance of the solid defence of the suppression policy, laboriously constructed over many years by successive British governments, by Palmerston, Russell, Peel and Aberdeen, the leaders of the main political parties, Whigs and Peelites. They preserved the policy intact when without their support it might easily have fallen.[18] Hutt's Select Committee sat both in 1848 and 1849, examining a long list of witnesses, and a House of Lords Select Committee also sat in 1849 and 1850. The massive evidence resulting from these investigations did not point clearly in any one direction, either for or against the continuation of the cruiser system. The 'anti-coercionists' had argued that the cost of the African Squadron was excessive, that it had succeeded only in adding to the horrors of the Middle Passage and that Britain's foreign trade had suffered because of it. Their opponents had countered with statistics on the effectiveness of the Squadron, Britain's moral obligation and the fate of both Africa and Britain's own West Indian colonies if the slave trade was allowed to go on unchecked. The Lords Select Committee in its reports of 1849 and 1850 solidly endorsed the cruiser system, but the Commons Select Committee in 1849, on Hutt's casting vote, recommended the withdrawal of the African Squadron. These reports, far from ending the debate, instead whetted the appetite of the 'anti-coercionists' who prepared to launch what would be their most effective assault yet in the spring of 1850.

By then large sections of the press were critical of the government's policy. Hutt's Commons motion of 19 March 1850, which, if passed, would have required the government to abandon the cruisers and the use of force, seemed to have a good chance of success. It failed only because the government leaders, Russell, the Prime Minister, and Palmerston, the Foreign Secretary, made it an issue of confidence, threatening to resign if the Commons did not stand behind their slave trade policy. At the end of the debate in which the arguments of the two sides were repeated once more, a significant total of 154 MPs voted against the government, but the Squadron was salvaged with the support of 232 Members. How long could the government continue to hold out against these Parliamentary onslaughts if the slave trade continued unabated? What was needed was some tangible manifestation of success to convince Parliament and the country that the end of the foreign slave trade was in sight. It came with unexpected suddenness in Brazil where aggressive action by the British navy, including seizures of suspected Brazilian slavers within Brazilian territorial waters, pressured the Brazilian government into passing effective legislation to suppress the slave trade. Brazil's forced co-operation with Britain very soon eliminated the slave trade to Brazil, the largest component of the remaining Atlantic slave trade.[19]

Britain's intolerant mood on the subject of the continuing foreign slave trade had been evident as well in 1848 in the West Indian campaign to obtain at a minimum some relief for the economic distress of the plantations in the aftermath of free trade. Lord George Bentinck, who had led the protectionist forces in 1846, was successful in having a Commons Select Committee appointed to investigate conditions in Britain's sugar and coffee plantations in the East and West Indies. In the course of his speech asking for the creation of the Committee, he threw out a much more radical suggestion for ending the Cuban slave trade than any which would be heard in the course of the debate over the suppression policy. 'If the people of this country have thought it right to spend £115,000,000 in putting down slave-trading, at the cost of the ruin of the British colonies, will it not be a far cheaper policy to put an end to slavery forever by seizing Cuba, and paying ourselves thereby, at the same time a just debt?'[20] Bentinck was the sole Parliamentarian to advocate the use of force in this way to suppress the slave trade and the government had no intention whatever of adopting his suggestion, but his tone of bitter cynicism accurately reflected the rising anger of the West Indian interests as they contrasted their own ruin with Cuba's obvious prosperity.

The troubles of the British West Indian planters after the Sugar Duties Acts of 1846 and 1848 were so interwoven with the foreign slave trade that Palmerston, as Foreign Secretary, was the first witness to be called before Bentinck's Select Committee. Palmerston explained the slave trade suppression system at some length and, although he assured the Committee that in the two years, 1846 and 1847, 'the Cuban slave trade has been next to nothing', he made clear to them as he did to the Select Committees hearing evidence on the slave trade that he still strongly favoured the employment of British cruisers on both sides of the Atlantic.[21]

Palmerston's testimony about the decline of the Cuban slave trade was correct and it highlighted one of the anomalies of the foreign slave trade, the great disparity in size between the slave trade to Brazil and that to Cuba. The trade to Cuba was about 10% of the Brazilian slave trade in the late 1840s. The British Foreign Office estimated the number of slaves landed in Cuba during 1848–50 at 13,700 compared with a total of 137,000 brought to Brazil during the same period.[22] Commander Matson, testifying before the House of Commons Select Committee on the slave trade in 1848, recounted that on the receipt of the news of the 1846 Sugar Act in Havana, prices of slaves, land and sugar all rose immediately by 15%.[23] Yet, the immediate increase in demand for slaves had been met by the transfer of slaves from coffee to sugar plantations. When considering the British government's future policy towards the foreign slave trade in the spring of 1850, Lord John Russell, the Prime Minister, claimed Spain had done much by her laws and regulations to suppress it and 'that but little further action is required to put an entire stop to the trade'.[24] What British observers saw as a welcome fall in the Cuban slave trade turned out to be a momentary and deceptive lull. At a time when the foreign slave trade occupied British parliamentary attention, Brazil was much the bigger culprit and British anger accordingly was directed at her. Spain figured much less prominently then than she would later.

Bentinck's intemperate outburst against Cuba typified the attitude of many West Indian planters and merchants who resented the assured supply of slave labour possessed by Cuba and Brazil. They claimed that if Britain's plantation colonies could compete equally, by improving their own labour supply and reducing that of their competitors, they would not fear the consequences of free trade. Some West Indian interests had joined in the attack on the African Squadron, but as time went on more and more West Indians began to clamour for the effective enforcement of the slave trade treaties. West Indian agitation was a major force in keeping the subject of the Cuban slave trade before the House of Commons during the 1850s and 1860s.[25]

By 1849 the West Indians had almost abandoned their hopes of reviving protectionism, but David Turnbull certainly spoke for them when he complained that free trade 'has, beyond a doubt, greatly increased the African slave-trade, and has imparted a still greater impetus to slavery in Cuba and Brazil'.[26] Stopping the slave trade to Cuba and Brazil might not restore West Indian prosperity, but it would enable the free labour plantations in Britain's Caribbean colonies to compete on a more equal basis with their slave plantation rivals. Hall Pringle, who had served for ten years as a stipendiary magistrate in Jamaica, told the Lords Select Committee on the slave trade, and later wrote directly to Palmerston, that the British West Indian islands could not compete as long as the slave trade reinforced the slave populations of Cuba and Brazil.[27] Turnbull, in his own testimony to the same Committee, sounded like a West Indian planter in his boast: 'We believe there is nothing formidable in Cuba but the Slave Trade; and that if the Slave Trade could be extirpated there, we believe they could not compete with us at all.'[28]

West Indian associations in Britain goaded the government about the continuing Cuban slave trade as a means of keeping the economic difficulties of the British Caribbean in the public eye. The Glasgow West Indian Association in the spring of 1853 asked for more stringent measures to end the Cuban slave trade. Britain should increase the number of her cruisers on the coast of Cuba and compel Spain to fulfil the slave trade treaties.[29] At the beginning of 1854, on the eve of the equalization of the sugar duties coming into force, the West India Committee sent a much stronger representation to the government.[30] They reminded Lord Clarendon, the Foreign Secretary, of his confident assertion in 1846 that free trade would not encourage the slave trade. Yet, the Cuban slave trade was larger and Cuban sugar production had expanded by 50% in nine years. 'To encourage the beneficial sale of Slave Sugar is to encourage its production – and as the cultivation cannot be increased, or even maintained in Cuba without a continual accession of new slaves – so it is evident that the resolution then adopted by Parliament has stimulated the introduction of multitudes of slaves into that island.' The Committee pointedly told Clarendon that he had a special obligation to enforce the slave trade treaties because he had been such a strong supporter of free trade and therefore bore some responsibility for the increase in the Cuban slave trade.

Clarendon's Parliamentary Under-Secretary, Lord Wodehouse, replied on his behalf.[31] Wodehouse admitted the recent increase in the Cuban slave trade, but he blamed it on the Cuban Captain-General and suggested that some of the largest importations had occurred before Cuban sugar had begun to enter the British market. The worsening Cuban slave trade, however, was more than counterbalanced by the virtual disappearance of the Brazilian slave trade. The amount of sugar imported into Britain from her own colonies also had increased since 1846. 'Ld Clarendon cannot therefore admit that a policy which has been productive of such results can have been so questionable in its nature or so injurious to West India Interests as the Committee apprehend.'

The 1853 Select Committee of the House of Commons on the slave trade produced evidence to demonstrate that neither the price of Cuban sugar nor the quantity of sugar exported from Cuba had risen as a result of free trade, but this did not end the debate.[32] At a public meeting in Kingston, Jamaica, in 1857, the Bishop of Kingston moved a resolution which gained overwhelming endorsement, that free trade had been 'a powerful impulse' in the expansion of the Cuban slave trade. His colleague, the Mayor, speaking to the same gathering, 'could not understand why Brazil should have been called upon by England to abolish the traffic and forced to do it, and Cuba allowed to continue the practice in the face of the world without molestation'.[33] The proponents of free trade were completely unrepentant and insisted there was no connection between free trade and the growth of the Cuban slave trade, but neither the West Indians nor the British abolitionists were ever convinced. They found British policy towards Cuba incomprehensible.

The lengthy British debate on the suppression of the foreign slave trade had been copied in Jamaica where, at a series of public meetings in 1849, speakers inveighed against the slave trade to Cuba and Brazil. In this atmosphere people looked for new remedies. David Turnbull, who now sat on the Anglo-Portuguese court of mixed commission in Jamaica, seized his opportunity and resurrected his 1840 plan of strengthening the existing courts of mixed commission with additional powers. He successfully sold his idea in Jamaica as the panacea everyone desired. Jamaican petitions supporting it flooded into the

Foreign Office in 1849 and 1850.[34] Subsequently, both the Commons and Lords Select Committees on the slave trade endorsed it, but in different contexts.

The Commons Committee of 1848–9, under its chairman, William Hutt, had recommended the abandonment of the use of force against the foreign slave trade, but the Committee went to some lengths to dispel any idea of Britain becoming 'neutral' or 'indifferent' to the slave trade. 'It would still be the duty of the British Government to avow its unabated hostility to the African Slave Trade.'[35] Hutt was particularly interested in any non-violent means to suppress it and he sought details of Turnbull's proposal from the Foreign Office.[36] The Foreign Office provided them and the Commons Select Committee included the plan in its final report, lauding it as 'one of the most important movements ever made by the British Government for securing the fulfilment of her treaties for the suppression of the Slave Trade by Spain and Brazil'.[37] The Lords Select Committee, in contrast to the Commons Committee, had backed the use of force and strongly supported the African Squadron, but they, too, recommended Turnbull's plan as a possible ancillary weapon. Turnbull's testimony before the Lords Committee had skated over all the difficulties of getting Spain to accept it and implied wrongly that Cubans would welcome it.[38]

With such strong public and parliamentary pressure upon him, Palmerston had little choice but to try to persuade Spain to sign a third Anglo-Spanish slave trade treaty along the lines of Turnbull's plan. Shortly after Britain and Spain resumed diplomatic relations in 1850 after a two-year hiatus, Palmerston instructed Lord Howden, Britain's envoy in Madrid, to propose the Turnbull Convention to Spain once more.[39] After Spain's previous experience with Turnbull and his abolitionist ideas, she wanted nothing more to do with either and the proposal was summarily rejected. However much the Spanish government wanted British assistance in 1850 to counter the menace of American annexationism, it was not willing to concede more powers to what it saw as a foreign court sitting in Havana and it certainly would not countenance further interference by British agents in Cuban affairs.[40] Twice Turnbull had succeeded in having his ideas accepted by influential pressure groups and as a result the British government had tried twice without success to obtain Spanish agreement. After this second rejection Palmerston quietly dropped the Turnbull Convention and it was never heard of again.

Far from falling into disfavour, Turnbull received another diplomatic assignment. Palmerston sent him to France to recruit French West Indian planters and merchants, beet sugar growers and French abolitionists to assist Britain in the extinction of the Spanish and Brazilian slave trades. Turnbull, however, died early in 1851 without being able to create this grand abolitionist alliance and even before he could present a paper which he had prepared on the slave trade to the French Academy of Sciences. On hearing of Turnbull's death, Palmerston commented: 'I am extremely sorry. He is a great Loss to the Slave Trade Suppression Cause.'[41]

The angry disillusionment of West Indian interests at Britain's failure to stop the Cuban slave trade expressed itself in other ways. As the annexationist movement to attach Cuba to the United States gathered strength, some of the West Indians began to have second thoughts about the possibility of Cuba in American hands. If it would end the slave trade to the island and force a more equal competition on the Cuban planters, the British West Indian proprietors might support it, or so Turnbull had reported to Palmerston in the summer of 1850.[42] A Scot who was sympathetic to the plight of Britain's West Indies in the aftermath of free trade wrote that the loss of Cuba to the United States would be just retribution for Spanish faithlessness over the slave trade treaties. There might be other advantages for Britain, too: 'I am inclined to believe that Cuba would be a much better customer of England in the hands of our enterprising brethren of the New World than she is at present in the hands of Spain.'[43]

The willingness of West Indian interests to welcome an American annexation of Cuba spread over time to other sections of the British public. Tired of the futile attempts to end the Cuban slave trade and hearing nothing but stories of venality and cruelty connected with it, many gradually came to accept Cuba's annexation as the only solution. Travellers' tales did nothing to counteract these views. One Englishman who believed American annexation was in the offing, thought annexation would be 'more advantageous for the permanent welfare of the negroes than if they were at once unconditionally liberated to-morrow under the sway of Great Britain'.[44] Amelia Murray visited Cuba briefly in 1855 just after the suppression of a creole conspiracy linked to the annexationist movement in the United States. She accused Britain of crusading against the interests of the sugar planters and worsening the lot of the blacks, while at the same time 'abetting murder and tyranny over the whites'.[45] The British novelist, Anthony Trollope, touring the Caribbean in 1859, saw positive benefits for Britain in an American takeover of Cuba. British trade with Cuba would expand, the slave trade would end and Britain's Caribbean colonies would be able to compete again in sugar production. His parting benediction on leaving Cuba showed his enthusiasm: 'My best wish for the island is that it may speedily be reckoned among the annexations of the United States.'[46] Even as late as the 1870s, with the Cuban civil war raging, a British journalist, Antonio Gallenga, went to Cuba believing a majority of his countrymen implicitly accepted the idea that 'an American annexation of Cuba is an event as desirable as it is unavoidable'.[47]

No English traveller, however, experienced the 'vision' which an American visitor, W. H. Hurlbert, claimed he had seen during an Easter Sunday service in the Havana Cathedral: 'As I stood in the Cathedral, and saw this representative of the ancient crown of Spain advance . . . I seemed to be gazing on a "dissolving view", the next mutation of which would present to the eye "lean and hungry" Yankees in black satin waistcoats; for the Captain-General and the Bishop, the "Governor of the State" and the "reverend clergy" and for a grand mass in honor of the Queen a "Fourth of July oration" in the Tacón theatre.'[48]

British governments in the 1850s and 1860s refused to bow to West Indian demands to discriminate against Cuban sugar if the Cuban slave trade did not end, nor were they resigned to the American annexation of Cuba as the only way to stop the slave trade. Official British policy remained unchanged: extinguish the Atlantic slave trade and if possible prevent Cuba from falling into American hands. Though these aims were not incompatible, reconciling them proved difficult especially in the early 1850s. But after 1850, British Ministers no longer had to fight a rearguard action to defend their slave trade suppression policies. Official concern over the fate of the British West Indies, coupled with success in the abolition of the Brazilian slave trade, overcame the divisions on how to suppress the foreign slave trade which had come so close to forcing the withdrawal of the African Squadron in 1850.

Three years later another Commons Select Committee again examined Britain's campaign to suppress the Atlantic slave trade. In marked contrast to the Commons Committee which had sat in 1848 and 1849, the 1853 Committee came to unanimous conclusions which offered solid encouragement to the government. Joseph Hume, the Committee's chairman, had been a convinced opponent of the African Squadron in 1848 and 1849; now he was content to leave the suppression of the slave trade to the government Ministers who, he told Parliament, 'had done everything . . . in their power' to extinguish the foreign slave trade.[49]

The Committee's report began with a brief review of Britain's many attempts to stop the foreign slave trade and then went on: 'These efforts in the cause of humanity continued through so many years, must be considered as honourable to the nation, and the results afford a strong inducement to persevere until this iniquitous trade shall be abolished.'[50] All that was needed was to eliminate Cuba as a market for African slaves and the Atlantic slave trade would be over. The Committee believed the time was propitious for a renewal of the united efforts of Britain, France and the United States. Spain had refused to declare the slave trade piracy and the Committee's report did admit that 'there is little hope that reason or justice will prevail with the Spanish government to abolish the trade'. Yet, surely Spain's self-interest dictated the need to do away with the Cuban slave trade? Britain and France had offered diplomatic support to Spain to block filibustering expeditions aimed at wresting Cuba from Spanish possession, but the United States had declined to join in a tripartite renunciation of any desire to possess Cuba, justifying their refusal in part by the continuance of the slave trade. If Spain wanted to preserve Cuba, the report implied, she had better sacrifice the Cuban slave trade.

The report was carefully written to put the maximum pressure of British public opinion on Spain. Not a word appeared about the economic troubles of Britain's Caribbean colonies. The omission was deliberate even though British West Indian difficulties were the main reason for the establishment of the Select Committee. Joseph Hume revealed this in the covering letter he wrote to Lord John Russell, transmitting a copy of the report:

I hope the accompanying Report of the Select Committee, unanimously agreed to, may be useful to the British Government and assist them in urging the abolition of the Slave Trade upon Spain.

The Time is favourable, the cause is good and I hope that success may speedily attend the representation that the Government will now repeat.

The situation of the British West Indies requires the termination of the slave-trade to Cuba; and then there may be some chance of their being able to continue the Supplies of Sugar and to exist.[51]

The time appeared favourable, but appearances here deceived British statesmen. They saw the annexationist threat to the Spanish possession of Cuba as a powerful incentive for Spain to abolish the slave trade, whereas the truth was more complex. The annexationist move-ment was another complicating element in the Cuban equation, blunting the effect of British pressure on the Cuban slave trade and preoccupying Spain to the point of obsession with the preservation of Cuba rather than the abolition of the slave trade.

Ironically, alleged British ambitions to take the island herself played a major part in the growth of annexationist sentiment both in the United States and in Cuba. Buchanan, the American Secretary of State, made use of them in 1848 to rationalize the desire of the United States to purchase Cuba from Spain.[52] Lord George Bentinck's threat in the House of Commons in 1848 that Britain should seize Cuba was taken more seriously in Cuba and in the United States than it was in Britain. The Cuban annexationist periodical, *La Verdad*, published in New York, ran Bentinck's speech as a lead article, asking: 'What can Cuba hope to do, menaced with this fatal blow and with no expectation of any aid from Spain?'[53] Kennedy, the British judge on the mixed court in Havana, reported that Bentinck's speech had led to the creation in Cuba of an annexationist committee of creole and peninsular planters. These men were prepared to petition to join the United States if anything happened in Spain or in Cuba to suggest emancipation. Kennedy warned Palmerston that 'a very slight pre-text . . . would be sufficient for their taking this step' and urged the British government to issue a public statement repudiating Bentinck and denying any intention to interfere with Cuban slavery or to seize the island.[54]

The 1848 revolution in France with its consequent emancipation of slavery in the French colonies really precipitated the annexationist unrest in Cuba. The Cuban plantocracy had visions of the revolution and republicanism spreading to Spain and Spain then acceding to the combined wishes of British and French abolitionists by emancipating the slaves in Cuba and Puerto Rico. In Cuba annexationism fed on the fear of emancipation being forced on Cuban slaveowners by the wave of revolution in Europe.

Within the United States annexationism and Manifest Destiny fused together to grow into a militant expansionism which, flushed with victory in the Mexican War and the resulting territorial acquisi-tions, now directed itself primarily at the Caribbean and Cuba. Cuban annexationists at first were not confined to one region of the United States; in the 1840s annexationism grew into a national movement. Basil Rauch has pointed out that the movement 'expressed the economic community of interests between northern business and southern slavery'.[55] New York and New Orleans formed the northern and southern poles, each attracting groups of Cuban exiles who were prepared to join with Americans to add Cuba to the United States. The southern pole became steadily more dominant and the northern pole less influential as the United States government's failure to purchase Cuba from Spain was followed by a series of abortive filibustering expeditions organized in New Orleans, the filibustering capital of the United States.

By the 1850s, the American South saw the annexation of Cuba as the key to the expansion of slavery and the beginning of a Caribbean empire. Because it could not be divorced from the ever-widening rifts over slavery within the United States, Cuban annexation was also the focus of fierce political rivalry. The paradisical and erotic imagery of expansionist rhetoric hid the explosiveness of the Cuban question and ignored potential European reaction. One Southern advocate of Cuban annexation pictured Uncle Sam as an ardent suitor: 'Who can object if he throws his arms around the Queen of the Antilles, as she sits, like Cleopatra's burning throne, upon the silver waves, breathing her spicy, tropic breath and pouting her rosy, sugared lips? Who can object? None. She is of age – take her, Uncle Sam'.[56] But Southern anticipations of promised pleasure from seducing another slave state were seen in Europe as threatened rape by a licentious libertine who already had shown an ungovernable lust for new conquests.

Spain refused the United States offer to buy Cuba in 1848 and annexationists with their headquarters in New Orleans began to organize an invasion of Cuba under Narciso López, a Venezuelan who had risen to be a Spanish general and who had held a senior administrative position in the colonial government of Cuba. López's small army was composed largely of Southern veterans of the Mexican War. He launched three filibustering expeditions against Cuba in the three years, 1848–51, before he was finally captured by the Spanish authorities and executed along with some of his American compatriots.[57]

The American government, wishing to acquire Cuba peacefully by purchase from Spain, officially disapproved of the López expeditions and tried without much success to stop them. Europeans remained dubious of American intentions. They connected filibustering with American expansionism and many foresaw an imminent American takeover of Cuba. British officials in Cuba had similar reactions. Kennedy, the acting consul-general in Havana, asked the British navy to patrol around Cuba when rumours of a López expedition reached Cuba in 1849. He wrote to the British naval commander at Jamaica 'that the period is very near at hand of this island being annexed to the United States'.[58]

The following spring, with reports of a further attempt by López rife throughout the Caribbean, the British Chargé d'Affaires in Guatemala stopped off in Havana on his way back to his post. There he found the Captain-General in a high state of alarm and desirous of British assistance to fend off the impending filibuster.[59] Spanish troops, however, foiled López's attack in May 1850, without any British help, but his landing caused a serious reassessment of British attitudes to the possibility of the United States owning Cuba. The most cogent analysis of British policy towards Cuba came from John Gregory, the Governor of the Bahamas. He thought it very likely that López and his soldiers would return for another try and therefore it was imperative for Britain to decide what she would do:

H.M.'s Ministers must be conscious of the vast importance to our interests in a maritime point of view, that Cuba should not fall into the hands of America. It is quite bad enough, that already she occupies the Shores of Florida and extends her dominions over the whole of the Northern Shores of the Gulf of Mexico, but if through the fatal policy of Spain she should acquire possession of Cuba also, and thus become Mistress of Havana, one of the most splendid harbours in the world, she would in time of war obtain the complete control over the navigation of this vast gulf. Havana would be to America, what Gibraltar is to England, and if *we* could shut the Americans out of the Mediterranean they could shut *us* from the Gulf of Mexico.[60]

Gregory advocated all-out British support for Spain to prevent the American acquisition of Cuba. Britain also had to work to reverse the effects of American propaganda on the Cuban creoles. 'These people are taught to believe that England exercises unbounded sway over the Court of Madrid – that Spain is not powerful enough to oppose the designs of the Great "Abolitionist Nation" – that the United States are alone the power that can defy the Machinations of England – and consequently that it would be [in] their interest to shake off the yoke of Spain and to become an integral portion of the United States.'

Gregory realized that Britain's dedication to the cause of suppressing the Cuban slave trade had made her thoroughly hated by the slaveowners of Cuba and accounted, in large measure, for the popularity of the Americans. 'Our wish must be to see England exercising a fair share of influence in the destinies of this valuable Island, but unhappily the fatal institution of Slavery meets us as a stumbling block at every turn, and sets a large portion of the very colony against us, whose interests we are striving to serve for her own sake, as well as for that of the world at large.' Gregory did not suggest any change in Britain's slave trade policies and he knew the problems of Cuba ultimately had to be resolved in Spain, but his was an influential plea for a greater British commitment to preserve the island for Spain.

The British government had no desire to encourage American filibustering attempts against Cuba, but how much was Britain willing to do, or could she do, to prevent them? British naval vessels visited Havana to protect the interests of British citizens and as a gesture of moral support for Spain. British naval patrols also ensured that no part of the Bahama cays could be used as a depot for the filibustering expeditions.[61] In the United States, Bulwer, the British Minister, offered 'any friendly assistance in my power' to the Spanish Ambassador in his negotiations with the American government and obtained Palmerston's permission to use 'his Good Offices' whenever an opportunity arose.[62] British diplomacy worked informally to prevent the filibusters from blowing up into a real crisis between the United States and Spain, thereby giving the Americans a pretext for seizing Cuba. In Parliament some of the strongest critics of the Cuban slave trade condemned the López expedition as open piracy and urged that Britain give naval assistance to Spain to repel any further attacks.[63]

The British government, however, was unwilling to go any further during 1850, and certainly the assistance Britain gave fell far short of what Spain requested. Xavier de Istúriz, Spain's Minister in London, asked Britain to join in a combined European protest in Washington against American tolerance of the filibustering expeditions and later Spain wanted Britain and France together to guarantee her ownership of Cuba. Palmerston sidestepped the first request and refused the second.[64] Spain's non-compliance with the slave trade treaties stood squarely in the way of additional British aid. Palmerston told the Spanish Minister quite bluntly that the British government could not contemplate, and Parliament would reject, any treaty to guarantee Cuba for Spain because the slave trade treaties had been 'systematically and continually disregarded'.[65] In the words of Professor Ettinger, Britain's insistence on complete compliance with the treaties as the minimum price for British help 'stood forth as the rock on which recurrent Spanish requests for aid broke and spent themselves in vain'.[66]

When Spain discovered that the slave trade was the major obstacle to a British guarantee, she belatedly tried to fashion a new policy. A Spanish commission, headed by Count Mirasol, had gone to Cuba in the summer of 1850 to investigate what measures were necessary to defend the island from American annexationists. The Spanish government frantically asked Mirasol to add the suppression of the slave trade to his terms of reference, but, as had happened so often before, Spanish bureaucracy was its own worst enemy when rapid action was imperative. By the time the royal order with these instructions reached Cuba, the Count had left for Spain.[67]

Spain sent out a new Captain-General to Cuba in September 1850, to protect the island from the filibuster peril. José de la Concha received the command of the island and his instructions stressed that he was to comply with the slave trade treaties and he was not to tolerate the introduction of African slaves. Cuba's most immediate danger came from the likelihood of more filibustering expeditions, but Concha was warned explicitly not to forget that two races, blacks and whites, lived there. Each represented a potential risk to Spanish possession. If the Americans planned to undermine Spanish domination through the whites, British abolitionist societies were just as ready to exploit the blacks for the same purpose.[68] Seeking British aid, Spain felt that she, too, had to be very circumspect. British motives were at best questionable and possibly even sinister. Spain, nevertheless, persisted in her entreaties to Britain and France. If they would commit themselves on paper to a formal guarantee, further manifestations of American annexationism would encounter a united front of Spain and the two major European powers. Spain was unable to make any headway at all with these proposals before the last López expedition landed in Cuba in the summer of 1851.

Both Britain and Spain had plenty of advance warning of the 1851 López filibuster, which was preceded by an extensive creole rising in Cuba's interior.[69] Crawford, Britain's consul-general in Havana, had no doubt of the ultimate purpose of the rising and of López's expedition. Both aimed at perpetuating slavery in Cuba.[70] By making Cuba an outlet for the surplus slaves of the American South, Cuban planters would free themselves from dependence on the Atlantic slave trade and Cuban slavery would be secure from British abolitionist machinations. Crawford looked on as López and his American followers were defeated, a defeat followed by López's capture and subsequent execution. Palmerston had no special instructions for his officials in Cuba, regardless of the outcome, but the capture and death of López were greeted with great relief in London. Notwithstanding the result, the last of the López filibusters caused a distinct change in British policy towards Cuba. The possibility that the United States actually might succeed in detaching Cuba from Spain swept aside Britain's previous reluctance to assist Spain on the grounds of the continuing slave trade to Cuba.

Bulwer had recommended from Washington that Britain and France should combine to stop American annexationism without antagonizing the Americans.[71] Palmerston agreed. Acting in unison with the French, Britain issued orders to the Admiral commanding British naval forces in the West Indies to give Spain any assistance she required to defeat any future American filibustering expeditions directed at Cuba.[72] These orders were in force until January 1852, when the British government learned that there was no immediate danger of further expeditions and that the instructions issued to the British Admiral were more stringent than those given to his French counterpart. The orders were then cancelled. Spain naturally welcomed this military help which, ironically, had been facilitated by the increase in the Cuban slave trade reported by British officials at Havana. On receiving these reports in July before the López expedition had left the United States, Palmerston promptly had ordered British naval reinforcements for the British West Indian Squadron. He also had warned Spain that if the slave trade was not suppressed by Spanish actions, Britain would step in and do whatever she believed was necessary, a threat which implied a repetition of the British tactics used against Brazil the year before.[73] But when the naval reinforcements reached the Caribbean they were assigned to protect rather than to blockade Cuba.

Palmerston's language on the Cuban slave trade grew more menacing than ever at the very time he was authorizing British naval help for Spain. He delivered a blistering rebuttal to his own Minister at Madrid who had been defending Spanish conduct:

The real and well-known Fact is, that the Govt. at Madrid has systematically and intentionally encouraged the Cuba Slave Trade for two Purposes; First, in order to afford Income to a number of ill paid Public Officers or to appointed Favourites, by means of the Bribes given by Slave Traders upon the Importation of Negroes; and Secondly, for the Purpose of retaining a Hold upon the Island because it is thought at Madrid that as long as there is in Cuba a large number of Negroes the white population will cling to the Mother Country for protection against the Black Race.[74]

Palmerston rejected both of these reasons. It could never be right for a government to encourage corruption among its officials nor could a colony be retained by fear alone. Spain should enforce the suppression of the slave trade and remove the cause of the fear or face the alternative of Cuba being annexed by the United States. The same day that Palmerston sent this dissertation to Madrid, he enclosed a copy of a law passed by Colombia to abolish slavery and recommended that Spain follow Colombia's example.[75] When the Spanish Foreign Minister recoiled in horror from this suggestion, Palmerston defended the idea of emancipation in Cuba as a means of creating 'a most powerful Element of Resistance to any Scheme for annexing Cuba to the United States where Slavery still exists'.[76] Through emancipation Spain could ensure the loyalty of her black subjects. It was not an option which had the slightest attraction for the Spanish government. Palmerston, for his part, had no intention of trying to force emancipation upon a resisting Spain, and neither he nor his successors as Foreign Secretary returned to the subject until the slave trade was long dead.

Palmerston's Janus-like approach to the Cuban problem, offering Spain naval assistance while simultaneously threatening her over the slave trade, was confusing to the Spanish government if not to his own diplomats. Gradually, however, the protection of the island from American annexation took precedence over the suppression of the slave trade. During the latter part of 1851 and in 1852, Britain and France again co-operated to thwart an American takeover of Cuba. Before Palmerston left office in December 1851, he had contemplated the idea of a tripartite guarantee of Spain's ownership of Cuba by Britain, France and the United States. Palmerston's immediate successor as Foreign Secretary, Lord Granville, was won over by the persuasive arguments of Count Walewski, the French Ambassador in London, and by the fears of his own Minister at Madrid, Lord Howden, that if Britain did not participate she would lose her influence at Madrid to France.[77]

Before these Anglo-French negotiations came to fruition, another change of government occurred in Britain, bringing the Conservatives under Lord Derby to power and Lord Malmesbury to the Foreign Office. Party differences played little part in British policy towards Cuba and Malmesbury simply carried on where his predecessors had left off. On 22 April 1852 the British and French Ministers in Washington presented identical notes to Daniel Webster, the United States Secretary of State, asking the United States to join in a tripartite guarantee of Spain's sovereignty over Cuba. Britain publicly had committed herself to preserve Cuba for Spain without any corresponding Spanish concessions on the Cuban slave trade. The American reply to this Anglo-French overture did nothing to calm European anxiety about American annexationism. Webster contented himself with reiterating American opposition to the cession of Cuba to any other European nation which left open the possibility of cession to the United States.[78]

Edward Everett, Webster's successor as Secretary of State, later composed a more elaborate rejection of the Anglo-French proposal after the American presidential election of 1852 had been won by the Democrat, Franklin Pierce. Everett presented this reply to the British and French Ministers at the beginning of December 1852. In it he set out clearly the reasons for the United States' desire to possess the island. Included among these was the continuation of the slave trade for which there was 'no hope of a complete remedy, while Cuba remains a Spanish colony'.[79] The advocates as well as opponents of annexationism did not hesitate to use the slave trade to serve their cause. Crampton, who succeeded Bulwer as British Minister in Washington, interpreted Everett's reply as 'a declaration that they will and *must* take it [Cuba] whenever they can'.[80] American refusal to participate in the tripartite declaration effectively killed it, but American suspicions of British motives had been aroused and these would contribute to fan the fires of annexationism even higher. For Britain, the dilemma of how to prevent an American acquisition of Cuba while suppressing the Cuban slave trade remained unresolved.

At the end of 1852 Britain confronted a mounting crisis over reports of an alarming increase in the slave trade and the open refusal of the Cuban Captain-General to do anything to check it. American annexationism seemed headed towards a new peak with Everett's rejection of the tripartite declaration and the election of Franklin Pierce as President. Would Britain opt for trying to save Cuba at any cost, or was she prepared to sacrifice Cuba, if necessary, in order to suppress the last remaining element of the Atlantic slave trade? This bleak choice facing British policymakers concealed beneath it the reluctance of any British politician to contemplate war with the United States. Lord Stanley, the Parliamentary Under-Secretary at the Foreign Office and the son of Lord Derby, the Prime Minister, weighed the arguments in a memorandum he wrote in November 1852 for his chief, Lord Malmesbury: 'The Spanish Colonial Govt., backed by that of the mother country, is using its utmost efforts to force on a collision with both of the two nations in whose hands its fate mainly rests – the U.S. and England. In all probability it will soon be called upon to solicit the protection of the latter against the former.'[81] Heedless of the American threat to Cuba, the Cuban planters had expanded their slave-trading. Stanley acknowledged the futility of diplomatic protests when the Cubans were so obstinate in their determination to carry on the trade. 'Still, the alternative of giving in the case of Cuba, orders similar to those which have been given by Palmerston and recalled by us in that of Brazil, is one approaching so nearly to the declaration of War, as to be justifiable only in the last extremity.' He advocated instead that Britain demand the recall of Captain-General Cañedo and if Spain refused, Britain would no longer be bound to aid Cuba against American filibusters. 'At the same time our naval force should be increased on the Cuban coast ostensibly as a means of S.T. repression, really for that object, and also, in case of necessity to repress piratical attempts.'

Malmesbury was aghast at the thought of applying Palmerston's Brazilian tactics to Cuba. 'To revert *anywhere* to such illegal measures as those adopted against Brazil is impossible – It is committing Acts of Piracy to prevent a worse crime.' But he agreed that the Cuban slave trade abuses had reached an intolerable level. Malmesbury gave orders to inform the Spanish government that British naval support for Cuba would be withdrawn and Cuba left 'to her fate if means are not immediately taken by the Captain-General to prevent the S.T.'.[82] Whatever effect this threat might have had was nullified by Howden in Madrid who decided to leave it out of the protest note he sent to the Spanish government.[83] With the fall of the Derby government in Britain, Howden could count on support for his more flexible approach from the Foreign Secretaries who replaced Malmesbury – Lord John Russell temporarily and then Lord Clarendon, who had served himself for an extended period as British envoy to Spain and had negotiated the 1835 Anglo-Spanish slave trade treaty. Yet the Cuban slave trade refused to vanish as a barrier impeding British aid to Spain. Russell, during his short tenure as Foreign Secretary at the beginning of 1853, reiterated the importance of its abolition to Howden: 'Your Lordship may be assured that however friendly the Councils of Her Majesty may be to Spain; whatever may be the interest of this Country not to see Cuba in the hands of any other Power than Spain; yet in the eyes of the People of this Country the Destruction of a Trade which conveys the Natives of Africa to become Slaves in Cuba, will furnish a large compensation for such a Transfer.'[84]

The policies pursued by the different British Ministries and Foreign Secretaries in 1852 and 1853 did not vary significantly in part because room to manoeuvre was so narrow. Shortly before the Conservatives left office in December 1852, Stanley outlined the baffling nature of the Cuban slave trade and his assessment was one with which no Foreign Secretary of the period would have disagreed:

Nothing can be worse than the conduct of the Spanish Govt. and nothing more desirable than to check it, whether by remonstrance or other means. But the difficulty is, how to do this without exciting the jealousy, or encouraging the aggression of the U.S. If you remove the few vessels that occasionally touch at the Havana, you make known your difference to the Americans, and they are thus encouraged in their designs. If on the other hand, you establish a Blockade or anything approaching to one, you excite in America a cry of 'British interference' and instantly it is believed you are going to seize upon Cuba. . .

It is idle to suppose that the Northern States would throw any serious obstacle in the way of an attempt on the island, if it were likely to prove successful. National aggrandisement is popular with all parties.

On the whole – though the case is one of great difficulty and perplexity – I would try the effect of renewed and more urgent remonstrances with the new Spanish Govt. before any more decisive steps are taken.[85]

Annexationism clearly constrained British attempts to suppress the Cuban slave trade and the existence of the slave trade blocked effective British assistance to Spain against annexationist plots. As the slave trade increased still further during 1853 and American annexationists became more militant, British frustrations over Cuba deepened.

The *Anti-Slavery Reporter* in a New Year's editorial at the beginning of 1853 alerted its readers to the significance of President Pierce's election in the United States: 'The annexation of Cuba has passed out of the region of fiction, and almost entered that of fact.'[86] Across the Atlantic, American abolitionists joined in the criticism of the expansionist policies of the Pierce administration, but they also pointed the finger at Britain for not fulfilling her commitments. Lewis Tappan, a prominent American abolitionist, wrote a letter to the editor of the *Anti-Slavery Reporter* asking: 'Why does not your Government enforce the observance of her treaties with Spain? . . . The world expects, in this matter, that England will do her duty.'[87]

But what was Britain's duty toward Cuba? For British politicians and diplomats in 1853, primarily it was to find some way to prevent the realization of American annexationist ambitions. From Madrid, Howden described the Spanish government as 'in a state of fever' over the looming American menace to Cuba. His own analysis of American intentions was unlikely to allay the fever. He wrote to Clarendon

that the Annexation of Cuba is a *fundamental* principle in the Government of General Pierce and of himself individually as President and is as fully determined on as anything human can be, and that he means, thinks & intends his Reign to be as much distinguished by *that* Event, as that of Polk's was by the conquest of Mexico and subsequent & consequent annexation of California. That such is *fully resolved on*, is a fixed fact on which you might bet your life – that it will be accomplished I think – that it will be attempted I know . . .[88]

From Washington Crampton wrote a long private letter to Clarendon just as the latter was about to take over the Foreign Office in February 1853, elaborating how grave a matter the Cuban question had become for Britain, involving her in the risk of war with the United States. Should Britain stand by as the Americans gobbled up Cuba? Crampton thought not. The time had come for Britain to call a halt to American expansionism.

There is another point of view, however, in which I think the question of Cuba is to be looked upon: – this is as a part of the more general question of aggression and domination of the United States in every part of this Continent; and in this regard it may be worth while to consider whether in case the attempt to check this is to be made at all, whether the point of Cuba is not as good a point to make a stand upon as any other.[89]

Perhaps fortunately for a Britain about to ensnare herself in the tangles of a Middle East crisis leading to the Crimean War, she never had to confront Crampton's question directly. The United States did not attack Cuba and American diplomatic manoeuvring did not succeed in detaching Spain's colony. Britain and France assisted Spain to foil the ham-fisted attempts of Pierre Soulé, President Pierce's envoy to Spain, to acquire Cuba for the United States.[90] But British politicians, try as they might, were unable to dispel the rising chorus of rumours during 1853 and 1854 that Britain was behind a Spanish decision to 'Africanize' Cuba, defined by the American historian, C. Stanley Urban, as 'the adoption of any system of labor which had for its ultimate aim the extinction of slavery'.[91]

The 'Africanization' rumours arose directly from the pressure Britain exerted on Spain to abolish the slave trade and they injected an emotional element of racism into an already highly inflammable annexationist atmosphere. Crawford's despatches from Havana in 1853 pictured the slave trade as a growing cancer, tolerated if not encouraged by a corrupt Captain-General. The British consul-general's accusations were echoed in Parliament and his own relations with Cañedo, the Captain-General, reached such a level of acrimony they led to a series of angry charges and countercharges between London and Madrid, culminating in a Spanish demand for Crawford's recall.[92] Britain reacted by pressing for Cañedo's dismissal and threatening Spain with a repetition of the strong arm methods used against Brazil. Clarendon wrote privately to the British Chargé d'Affaires at Madrid that if Crawford was expelled from Cuba 'we would be compelled to take the law into our own hands at Sea, and as in the case of the Brazils commit the fulfilment of the Treaty to our Cruizers, for doing which we should have public opinion here unanimous in our favour'.[93]

Cañedo's equally vigorous counter-attack included sending a personal representative to London to rebut the charges made against him in Parliament. Through his mouthpiece, Mariano Torrente, Cañedo claimed Spain was doing all she could to uphold the slave trade treaties. It would be madness, wrote Torrente, to divert troops and ships from their principal task of defending the island 'to put an end to an illegal traffic, which, so far from injuring, benefits us in a high degree'.[94] Such an attitude was intolerable to the British government in the face of a united public opinion against the foreign slave trade and strong pressure from the House of Commons for its immediate and total abolition. Spain desperately needed British support to counter the overt annexationism manifested by Pierre Soulé's mission to Madrid and she had to give way. Crawford stayed in Havana and Cañedo left for Madrid. His replacement as Captain-General was Juan de la Pezuela who arrived in Cuba in December 1853, with strict instructions to root out the slave trade, instructions which matched his own feelings.

No evidence has been produced to show that Pezuela's appointment and his instructions were proof of Spain's 'determination to Africanize the island as a last measure of defense' against American annexation, as Professor Rauch has alleged, but Pezuela's appointment signalled to the annexationists that Africanization was at hand.[95] Cristobal Madan, a Cuban leader, wrote to President Pierce to ask the United States to save Cuba from a British-inspired emancipation.[96] Clarendon flatly denied to Buchanan, the American Ambassador in London, that Britain wanted 'a Black Government established in Cuba' or that she had 'the most remote idea . . . of ever attempting to acquire Cuba for ourselves. We have, already, too many Colonies, –

far more than are profitable to us.'[97] Clarendon obviously believed he had laid the bogey to rest, because at the beginning of January 1854 he agreed completely with the judgement of Sir James Graham, First Lord of the Admiralty, that for the moment Britain could trust the United States: 'I am not aware that any filibustering expedn. is meditated, the absurd report of our making a black republic of Cuba has died away – The President's speech was moderate – So we may take our chance for the present. '[98]

Far from dying away, the 'absurd report' was gaining new credibility across the Atlantic from the interpretation placed on Pezuela's actions to comply with the slave trade treaties. Pezuela had issued a proclamation in December, declaring that all the *emancipados* in Cuba were to be freed, although their freedom was purely nominal.[99] Whether Pezuela's disguised apprenticeship plan for the *emancipados*, the Africans released from captured slave ships, as well as his forceful circular to his subordinates ordering the absolute prevention of slave landings, 'lent an air of truth to rumors of emancipation', as one historian of these events concludes, or whether they gave annexationists in Cuba and in the United States the excuse they were looking for to circulate propaganda about Africanization, the stories, backed by official American accounts from Cuba, spread rapidly through the southern United States, becoming magnified and distorted with travel and repetition.[100] Crampton reported the rising cry of Africanization in the United States to his government and received a quick denial of any such British plan to help him to counter the rumour mongering.[101]

The American government of Franklin Pierce saw these Africanization rumours as a tool to be used in accomplishing a major goal of the administration, the annexation of Cuba. William Marcy, Pierce's Secretary of State, sent a special agent to Cuba in March 1854 to find out all he could about the Africanization schemes and Marcy wrote to Pierre Soulé in Madrid that the disturbed state of Cuba might 'open the way' for the purchase of the island from Spain.[102] The instructions given to these American diplomats reveal the depth of misunderstanding within the American government of British policy towards Cuba and of Spanish actions within the island. Marcy believed that the Turnbull plan, which Britain had proposed twice only to have it firmly rejected by Spain each time, had been signed secretly and Pezuela had come out to Cuba to implement it. According to this American version, Spain had capitulated completely to Britain to the point of agreeing to the emancipation of all the slaves in her colonies by 1890. Even though this interpretation had no basis in fact, it became an article of faith among southern annexationists.

Diplomacy was not the sole weapon in the American annexationist arsenal. Another filibustering expedition was being readied in New Orleans, headed by General John Quitman who, after serving briefly as the governor of Mississippi in 1835, had risen to prominence in the South through his military achievements in the annexation of Texas and in the Mexican War. Plans had been underway for some time, but Quitman had experienced considerable difficulties organizing his followers. The Africanization rumour galvanized the filibuster preparations with new life. Quitman assumed formal command of the expedition on 30 April 1854 and immediately began to recruit an army from Mexican war veterans, young graduates of southern military academies and a flood of applicants from all over the South. Quitman's movement had a pronounced sectional character. He envisaged it as a southern mission to gather in another slave state while slavery still existed in Cuba. Here lay the unique conjunction of Cuban and American events. Professor Urban has concluded that 'the primary concern of Quitman and his American colleagues was to prevent the Africanization of Cuba'.[103] If emancipation succeeded in Cuba, the southern dream of a Caribbean slave empire would vanish and with it would go all hopes for additional slave states within the American Union. Spain's desire to placate Britain by enforcing the suppression of the slave trade in order to maintain British help against American annexationism had unleashed a new and more terrifying strain of the same annexationist germ the European nations had been trying to wipe out.

British and French involvement in the Crimean War seemed to favour the success of American annexationism in 1854. Crampton in Washington perceived an American determination to seize Cuba while the war distracted European attention.[104] But their preoccupation with the war in the Crimea did not stop British politicians from keeping a wary eye on American schemes to take Cuba. Clarendon privately intimated to the British Ambassador in France that he did not want to see the United States grab Cuba.[105] Graham, the First Lord of the Admiralty, was even more alarmed. Writing to Clarendon in May, he confessed: 'I am more afraid of Cuba than of any other question now pending. I do not like the presence of the Naval American Squadron within the Harbour of Havana; and I shall try to send Fanshawe an additional Man of War if I can possibly spare one.'[106]

Their fear was justified because the Africanization crisis peaked in May 1854 before its rapid denouement. Spain's determination to stop the slave trade had led to the decision to register all the slaves in Cuba so that African slaves illegally brought to the island could be readily identified. The decision was a response to Britain's demands the previous autumn for a series of amendments to the 1845 Spanish penal law including the registration of all slaves in the island. Britain's original proposal suggested registration as a protection for planters in any disputes over the legality of slaves. When Captain-General Pezuela considered the British proposals, he advised his government that Spain had no choice but to agree with what he admitted were extreme measures. The only alternative was to denounce the slave trade treaties. His government reluctantly accepted Pezuela's advice, knowing registration would cause great alarm among the Cuban planters and provide another weapon for American annexationists. But these were risks Spain decided to take because she was unwilling to court British wrath by openly renouncing her slave trade obligations.[107]

The decree containing this news was published in Havana on 3 May 1854. It also authorized Cuban authorities to enter any estate suspected of harbouring African slaves from a slave trade expedition. Pezuela denied the existence of any treaty between Britain and Spain to emancipate Cuba's slaves in the decree itself, but his denial was ignored. To the Cuban planters and their American sympathizers, the decree confirmed their worst suspicions. The Africanization of the island almost had reached the point of no return. William Robertson, the acting American consul in Havana, condemned the document: 'it contains all the poison of a scheme against the white race in Cuba'. Three days later, assessing the reaction of the Havana plantocracy, he reported, 'the consternation here is indescribable'.[108]

Annexationist sentiment welled up in Havana, equalled by the evident enthusiasm of Quitman and his supporters in the southern United States to launch their filibuster. Charles Davis, Marcy's special agent who had gone to Cuba to gather information on the Africanization measures, found exactly what he was looking for, substantial evidence that emancipation had started and strong suspicion that Britain had dictated new slave trade treaties to Spain, requiring liberty for all slaves brought to Cuba since 1820. 'It follows that the new policy must be the result of a Treaty whose only object must be the realization of the Emancipation of the Negroes – for on any other ground the conduct of both Nations [Britain and Spain] would be inexplicable.'[109] Quitman's supporters carried the Africanization propaganda to Congress where Senator Slidell from Louisiana attempted to have the neutrality laws repealed so that Quitman's expedition could proceed under a cover of legality. Crampton explained Slidell's move to Clarendon as an attempt 'to outjockey' Soulé, Slidell's Louisiana rival 'in the race for popular favour among the Fillibusters [*sic*] of Louisiana', but that if it succeeded it would 'let loose all the ruffians of this country upon Cuba' to enlarge the Union and prevent 'the area of Slavery from being diminished by the supposed imminent Africanization of Cuba'.[110]

Slidell received support in Congress from Senator Mallory of Florida who tried to whip up public feeling in a speech brimming with virulent racism: 'For to Africanize Cuba, Sir, is to arm the beastly and brutal African, fresh from the jungle, thirsting for blood, knowing no law, ignorant of all restraints, and to hurry him on to slaughter of the white. To Africanize, Sir, is to sum up, in one word, those horrors of which the world was ignorant until St. Domingo's fiends in liberty's name devised them.'[111] This was the path which Britain allegedly had forced Spain to tread, but annexation, according to its adherents, would liberate white Cuba from such an apocalyptic fate.

Domestic political strife within the United States snatched the Cuban prize from the outstretched hands of the annexationists just as revolution in Spain removed Pezuela from his post as Captain-General. Pierce's administration came under fierce attack from northerners for the Kansas–Nebraska bill, opening these territories to slavery. The bill did not pass until the latter part of May, just after the announcement of Pezuela's registration decree in Cuba, and the United States government found that its hands were tied. It dared not risk further sectional conflict by openly sanctioning a Cuban filibuster. Instead, Pierce issued a proclamation at the end of May that his government would prosecute any illegal filibusters, thus removing any veneer of legality from the Quitman enterprise and forcing its postponement. Pierce turned back to the old idea of purchasing Cuba, but not even Congress was willing to offer financial support.[112]

American annexationism was beginning to crumble from within when revolution in Spain in the summer of 1854 brought a new government to power. One of its first acts was to replace Pezuela. He had vigorously defended his policy of rigorous suppression of the slave trade as the only possible course for Spain to pursue and he pointed to its benefits. British pressure on Spain had ceased, world opinion now looked favourably on Cuba, and Pezuela argued that with these external improvements it would be easier to protect the institution of slavery within the island. But if Britain believed it was impossible to obtain from Spain the total extinction of the slave trade, she would be the first to want to see Spain lose Cuba.[113] José de la Concha returned to command the island a second time, as Pezuela's replacement, and his first priority was to restore the planters' confidence in Spanish administration. He began by repealing Pezuela's most controversial decrees and within Cuba the Africanization fears dissipated quickly.

They were still current in the United States and in Europe. Clarendon took the unusual step of making a formal statement in Parliament that August, denying any British intention to Africanize Cuba.[114] But Africanization was not to be buried so easily. It reappeared in October 1854 in all its malignancy in the Ostend Manifesto, the product of three American annexationist diplomats, Buchanan, Mason and Soulé. When Clarendon asked Buchanan two weeks later why the United States wanted Cuba, Buchanan trotted it out once more. 'I told him the constant danger that Cuba might be "Africanized", and become a second St. Domingo, thus threatening our domestic security, was one principal cause of our anxiety.'[115] Clarendon again tried to correct the American misconceptions of British intentions, and finally he ordered Crampton in Washington to present a formal note to the American government, disclaiming any intention to establish 'an African Empire in the West Indies'.[116]

Heavy electoral defeats in the Congressional mid-term elections in November 1854 over the Kansas–Nebraska Act debilitated the Cuban annexationist drive further and the repression of the Pinto conspiracy within Cuba early in 1855 followed by the collapse of Quitman's filibuster plans and the dissolution of the Cuban Junta in the United States ended the crisis. In Britain, Foreign Office officials did not forget the gravity of the Africanization affair and they were very careful to go out of their way to avoid giving the Americans another opportunity to raise the cry again. Clarendon in 1856 refused to let the British and Foreign Anti-Slavery Society use the diplomatic bag to send an abolitionist pamphlet entitled 'The Slave Trade to Cuba', which the Society had translated into Spanish, to all members of the Spanish Cortes. Lord Wodehouse, Clarendon's Parliamentary Under-Secretary who recommended this refusal, wrote, 'for though we have nothing to do with it, it would give Ground for the Americans to say we were seeking to Africanize Cuba'.[117]

The Africanization scare in Cuba bore similarities to the Escalera panic ten years before. Indeed, memories of the Escalera conspiracy among white planters may have contributed to the venom of the Africanization accusations. Rumours of alleged British emancipationist plots were used to foment racism and racism, in turn, became a potent annexationist weapon. If the annexationists had failed in their attempts, Britain also had suffered casualties. Cuba had been preserved for Spain, but the loss of Pezuela was a sad blow to British hopes of ending the Cuban slave trade. Crawford, the British consul-general at Havana, did not exaggerate when he wrote at the end of June 1854, 'the present is a most critical epoch and the course of the Spanish Government may decide the great question of the extinction of the Slave Trade, or otherways'.[118] The damage to Britain's reputation among Cuban planters made any co-operation to stamp out the slave trade more unlikely and Spain would be even more careful in future not to alienate the Cuban plantocracy.

British statesmen remained unalterably opposed to the American annexation of Cuba even if they acquiesced in the eventual prospect of American Manifest Destiny in the Americas. Lord John Russell was no exception, but by the end of 1854 he was thoroughly fed up with the Cuban question. He suggested Britain should agree on a joint Anglo-French policy towards Cuba: 'If Spain sells it, let her. If Cuba revolts, let it. But if Pierce attempts to take Cuba by force I should not allow it.'[119] When the new British Minister in Washington, Lord Napier, unwisely recommended the benefits of an American Cuba in 1857, his views were rejected in London. Palmerston, the Prime Minister, dismissed Napier's despatch as a 'Tissue of Fallacies and Sophistries', and later warned Clarendon, 'as to propitiating the Yankees by countenancing their schemes of annexation, it would be like propitiating an animal of Prey by giving him one of one's travelling Companions. It would increase his Desire for similar Food and spur him on to obtain it.' At the end of the year, Palmerston again expatiated on the dangers of Britain yielding to American expansionism, even if, as he recognized, Britain might have little choice but to do so in the long run. 'I have long felt inwardly convinced that the Anglo-Saxon Race will in process of Time become Masters of the whole American Continent, North and South, by Reason of their superior Qualities as compared with the degenerate Spanish and Portuguese Americans; But whatever may be the Effects of such a Result upon the Interests of England, it is not for us to assist such a Consummation, but on the Contrary to delay it as long as possible.'[120] British policy during the 1850s helped to delay the consummation of American designs on Cuba, but the threat of annexationism had been a severe setback to the campaign to eliminate the Cuban slave trade. During the era of free trade and annexationism, Britain doggedly carried on trying to persuade Spain to enforce the law and treaties against the slave trade, but in this new international climate the struggle was more difficult than ever. The level of official British concern about the possible American annexation of Cuba contrasted sharply with that over the Cuban slave trade. To prevent the former, Britain mobilized influential diplomatic support and naval force; to stop the latter she placed her faith in existing suppression policies, known to be inadequate, and in repeated Spanish promises which were not kept. Britain, it seemed, could not eradicate the Atlantic slave trade on her own, nor could Spain's commitment to fulfil the treaties and enforce her own legislation overcome the enormous vested interests in Cuba which were prepared to defy both Spain and Britain to procure the African slave labour they believed was essential for Cuba's expanding plantation economy.

CHAPTER 12

The failure of the penal law

Spain enacted the penal law of 2 March 1845 to fulfil her treaty obligations with Britain. For over twenty years it remained the only law under which Spanish officials in Cuba worked to suppress the slave trade. Not until February 1866 did a more extensive law, designed to replace the 1845 legislation, first appear in the Spanish Senate and another year passed before it received legislative sanction. The preamble of the 1866 bill admitted the inadequacies of its predecessor, a long overdue public acknowledgement of the obvious. For years, successive Captains-General had been saying the same thing in stronger terms contained in confidential despatches and letters to the peninsular government; even Spanish legal officials in Cuba, who earlier had defended the law, by the late 1850s and 1860s recognized its shortcomings. The British commissioners in Cuba and through them the British government had been the first to see what was later apparent to all; the 1845 penal law was a failure. Far from aiding in the suppression of the Cuban slave trade, the law actually encouraged what it was meant to stop.

Captain-General O'Donnell acknowledged receipt of the royal orders accompanying the penal law in a confidential despatch dated 15 February 1845. He warned of the grim prospects for Cuba if the enforcement of the law succeeded in cutting off the flow of slaves to the island. With the ratio of female to male slaves at 1 : 5, there was no possibility that natural reproduction would make up for the estimated 5% annual mortality among the plantation slaves. If slave numbers declined, so inevitably, would sugar production; economic decline would give rise to political unrest and within a short time Spain would lose her treasured possession.[1] O'Donnell insisted he would enforce the law, but he left his government in no doubt as to what he thought the consequences would be.

Colonial officials in Madrid took his warning very seriously and prepared a lengthy report on the likely impact on Cuba of the abolition of the slave trade. It made dismal reading for Spanish politicians. Without urgent remedies, Cuba would decline economically within five years and this could have disastrous political consequences. Britain's machiavellian humanitarian policies would destroy Cuba in the same way that St Domingue had been ruined. Britain had chosen to strike at Cuba where she was most vulnerable, in her labour force. If the law succeeded in ending the slave trade, Spanish officials calculated a minimum 5% annual mortality among Cuba's plantation slaves. White immigrants could not replace them and, in any case, none of the schemes to promote white emigration really had worked. There were also political risks for Spain in allowing unlimited European immigration. Apart from advising O'Donnell to maintain the existing equilibrium of the races, because experience had shown that the ratio of 4:6 between whites and blacks in the island did not endanger the security of the island, the officials' only solace came from their cynical forecast of the effect of the penal law: 'Will a traffic carried on for so many years and with ever increasing returns, completely disappear because it cannot overcome the obstacles placed in its way by Spain and England?'[2] Neither in Spain nor in Cuba was there any real desire to enforce the penal law to the point of a complete abolition of the slave trade. The outer forms would be respected, but the intention of the law would be quietly set aside.

O'Donnell could claim with some accuracy, however, that he enforced the penal law during his tenure as Captain-General. From 1845 to 1848 the slave trade to Cuba reached its lowest level until its abolition twenty years later. In the mid 1840s the demand for slaves within Cuba was met by their transfer from the declining coffee plantations to the growing sugar plantations. The combination of available slaves from coffee plantations, the panic engendered by the Escalera crisis and the penal law reduced Cuban participation in the Atlantic slave trade to a minimum level for a three-year period. Paradoxically, this occurred just as Britain converted to free trade which British abolitionists feared would cause the slave trade to grow even more rapidly. The explanation is that the British Sugar Duties Acts of 1846 and 1848 had a delayed effect in stimulating Cuban sugar production. Cuba's plantation economy expanded with a consequent increase in both the size and number of the island's sugar plantations which, in turn, added to the acute demand for plantation labour. This process was not immediately apparent, but by 1856 the British commissioners at Havana saw the relatively high price of sugar as a definite inducement to expand sugar cultivation. The increased demand for labour had meant a rise of 50–75% in the price of slaves over a three year period. Slave prices in Havana in 1856 ranged from $800–$1,000, up from $300–$400 in 1853.[3]Cuban sugar production rose from 220,000 tons in 1849 to over 359,000 tons in 1856, from 21% of world production in the former year to 25% in the latter.[4]Table 8 demonstrates the marked increase in Cuban sugar exports to Britain in 1846 and again in 1854 after the British sugar duties had been removed. After a slight decline in 1855 and 1856, Cuban sugar exports to Britain continued to rise in the latter 1850s when the Cuban slave trade was at record levels.

Statistics for the last twenty-five years of the Cuban slave trade have been the subject of continuing controversy, which is not surprising since they were weapons in the war to abolish it. British officials stationed in Havana compiled the only continuous series of figures on the number of African slaves brought to Cuba. Each year they sent to London their best estimate of the number of slave arrivals during the previous year, and until 1865 they generally followed the practice of adding one-third to their totals to cover unknown landings. The addition of one-third did not occur for 1848, presumably

Table 8. *British imports of Cuban sugar,*
1845–60

Years	Sugar imports in cwts.
1845	197,460
1846	499,906
1847	875,420
1848	694,203
1849	664,264
1850	489,502
1851	811,081
1852	432,364
1853	946,826
1854	1,598,993
1855	711,832
1856	736,166
1857	999,310
1858	1,593,655
1859	1,644,933
1860	1,382,398

Source: *Parliamentary Papers* (1861), vol.
LVIII, pp. 560–1.

Table 9. *Havana commissioners' estimate of the number of slaves imported into Cuba, 1840–67* *

Year	Number of expeditions	Number of slaves landed	
1840	44	14,470	(14,470)
1841	27	9,776	(9,776)
1842	9	2,292	(3,000)
1843	19	6,000	(8,000)
1844	25	7,280	(10,000)
1845	6	950	(1,300)
1846	4	—	(1,500)
1847	4	—	(1,000)
1848	5	1,500	(1,500)
1849	20	6,575	(8,700)
1850	7	2,325	(3,100)
1851	7	3,687	(5,000)
1852	12	5,943	(7,924)
1853	17	9,383	(12,500)
1854	19	8,654	(11,400)
1855	13	4,806	(6,408)
1856	14	5,478	(7,304)
1857	23	7,827	(10,436)
1858	19	12,744	(16,992)
1859	39	22,855	(30,473)
1860	21	13,857 / 17,877	(24,895)
1861	34	17,973	(23,964)
1862	14	8,441	(11,254)
1863	not reported	5,630	(7,507)
1864	not reported	5,105	(6,807)
1865	1	145	(145)
1866	3	1,443	(1,443)
1867	1	—	—
Total	407	185,139 / 189,159	246,798

*The totals in parentheses are the estimates published by the Foreign Office, except for 1841 when no actual figure was published. For most years the published figures incorporate the addition of one-third to cover unknown landings. Three figures are shown for 1860. In that year the commissioners began sending their annual reports at the end of September instead of in January. J. V. Crawford reported that 12,060 slaves were landed in Cuba during the first nine months of the year. He included the numbers because the British judge believed that no unknown landings had occurred.[5] Their figures were estimates, albeit made by men on the spot who were experts in the intricacies of the Cuban slave trade and whose information on clandestine slave landings was acknowledged even by Cuban Captains-General to be superior in many cases to official Spanish sources. The commissioners knew also that their calculations would be published every year in the Blue Books of slave trade papers presented for Parliament's scrutiny and available to be challenged by the Spanish government. In 1865, the totals for the years 1849–65 were presented to the Parliamentary Committee on West Africa.[6] The figures gathered by the Havana commissioners are reproduced in Table 9.

The estimates from the commissioners in Cuba were not always accepted unquestioningly by Foreign Office officials in London, although their doubts and resulting revisions seldom became public knowledge. Thomas Ward, the Superintendent of the Slave Trade Department of the Foreign Office, questioned the accuracy of the figures submitted by the British commission judge at Havana for 1854. Backhouse had estimated a total of 8,654 which, with the one-third addition, came to 11,400, the figure actually published by the Foreign Office. Ward preferred the lower total of 7,673, gathered from the reports of the British consul-general at Havana, and by adding one-third Ward arrived at an estimate of 10,230 for 1854.[7] William Wylde, Ward's successor as Superintendent of the Slave Trade Department, also was sceptical of the figures submitted from Havana for 1859. Instead of the published estimate of 30,473, he thought that no more than 25,000 African slaves had been introduced into Cuba during 1859. Wylde wrote: 'We know nearly every vessel that is engaged in the Slave Trade and the number that are known [to] have escaped with Slaves will hardly bear out Mr. Crawford's calculations, even making a large allowance for vessels of which we may have heard nothing.'[8]

Footnote for Table 9 continued

of slaves captured by British and United States cruisers to arrive at a figure of 13,857, but he sent home a total estimate of 17,877, the original 12,060 with the usual addition of one-third. The Foreign Office later did its own calculations, and arrived at a figure of 24,895.

Source: Havana commissioners' annual reports, 1841–68.

These British estimates do not warrant the attacks made on them as being completely unreliable, nor, on the other hand, can they stand without qualification as the record of the number of slaves imported into Cuba during the last years of the Cuban slave trade.[9] They do, nevertheless, constitute a very useful guide to the extent of the Cuban slave trade, the only such guide available, and they convincingly demonstrate the failure of the penal law to stop it, let alone to check its expansion. After declining in the mid 1840s, the trade to Cuba rose again momentarily during 1849, dropped back in 1850 and 1851 to increase even more by 1853 and 1854. After declining slightly in 1855–6, it reached record heights from 1858–61 before gradually dying out. Until 1851 British attentions focussed on the much larger Brazilian trade, but the dramatic jump of the Cuban trade in 1853, beyond the levels of the preceding decade, made the British government aware that the Cuban slave trade was not going to die of its own accord. That the rise of the Cuban slave trade coincided with a new wave of American annexationism added still another complication.

The annual report of the British judge on the Havana mixed court for 1853 calculated that, at a minimum, nearly 9,400 African slaves had been landed illegally in Cuba that year, and with the addition of one-third to account for unknown landings the figure was 12,500, higher than in any year since 1840.[10] This increase coincided with the large-scale importation of Chinese labourers, 4,000 arriving over the course of the same year, as well as the arrival of some Indians from Yucatan, victims of kidnapping plots arranged by Cuban slave traders with the connivance of Santa Anna, the President of Mexico.[11] Cholera had ravaged the island and, as usual, the slaves had suffered most, so part of the reason for the growth of the trade had been to replace slaves who had died in the cholera epidemic. Backhouse later estimated that 16,000 slaves had died of cholera over the period of a year beginning in June 1853, and during the same time an approximately equal number of African slaves and Chinese labourers had arrived in Cuba.[12] But Cuba's expanding plantation economy and the resulting insatiable demand for slave labour which could only be supplied by the slave trade meant a ready market for all African slaves landed in Cuba. Crawford lamented that 'British interference, and that only, keeps the Slave Trade within the bounds even of its present extensive Scale of operations.'[13]

Under Captains-General who, according to the British consul-general, saw the slave trade as 'indispensable to the safety and prosperity of the island', the penal law had been rendered totally ineffective.[14] There was no record of a slaver reaching Cuba and then being forced to turn back because the inhabitants would not permit it to land or for fear of being seized by the Cuban authorities. Any slaver which eluded British cruisers on either side of the Atlantic successfully landed its cargo in Cuba. The British commissioners calculated there were some 30 men in Havana's jail for slave trade offences in December 1854, but none was serving a lengthy sentence and all were minor offenders.[15] From the passage of the penal law in 1845, no case of outfitters, backers or even the master of a slave ship being tried and convicted in Cuba had occurred. The law was used to prosecute sailors from captured or abandoned vessels, but the masters and the owners who were often notorious in Havana for their exploits always escaped. The only successful prosecutions against masters of slave trade vessels took place in the United States and these were rare occurrences. In November 1854, James Smith, the master of the *Julia Moulton*, was convicted in the United States district court at New York for violating American slave-trading laws. He had landed 645 African slaves on the south coast of Cuba earlier that year and for his offence which really was gross piracy and murder he received a very light two-year sentence and a $1,000 fine.[16]

Two slave landings in 1853 illustrated how the application of the emasculated penal law in Cuba protected the slave trade. After the *Jasper*, an American vessel outfitted in New York, landed her cargo of slaves at a remote Cuban cay in April 1853, all that remained was the burnt hulk of the slaver. No fewer than four special commissions went out from Havana to investigate the affair after three American sailors from the *Jasper* inadvertently fell into the hands of the Cuban authorities. The commissions found no evidence of a landing, let alone the ship's remains, even though Crawford assured his government, 'the circumstances are known to all the inhabitants and were as public and open to be seen as the Sun at noon day'.[17] In a subsequent landing at exactly the same place, the crew of the slaver was captured and brought to trial before the Royal Audiencia court, but the slaves were secreted in nearby plantations and the master and owner were not even charged. Crawford wrote in complete exasperation:

The Slave Trade flourishes; every Slave that is brought to the Coasts of Cuba is landed; the Spanish Officers are bribed; the Slave Traders interested commit their offences and repeat them with the most complete impunity; Commissions sent by the Chief Authority of the Island to investigate such offences are baffled, or corrupted, the Masters and Crews are not punished, the Vessels are allowed to escape, or are destroyed by the Slavers in the face of the Authorities who never capture the Slaves, nor seize the vessels, and when any of the men fall into the hands of Justice (the masters and officers always escape) there is never any evidence to convict them upon their Trial.[18]

Some former Portuguese and Brazilian slave traders now shifted their operations to Cuba. From the summer of 1851 when the trade to Brazil had been shut off, a few slavers from Brazilian ports like Bahia or Montevideo in neighbouring Uruguay had sailed for Africa and landed slave cargoes in Cuba. A Brazilian–Portuguese Slave Trade Association was formed to carry on the trade to Cuba and reportedly succeeded in landing several cargoes, although the Association's activities received an unexpected setback when its agents were ordered out of Havana by the vigilant Captain-General Pezuela in February 1854.[19] But the suppression of the Brazilian slave trade made the Cuban trade even more international in scope and thus more difficult to check.

The Cuban slave traders also had begun to systematize their methods to take maximum advantage of weaknesses in the suppression system and the mockery of the enforcement of the penal law within Cuba. Because there was no right of search between Britain and the United States and because of the superiority and availability of American ships, Cuban slave traders added the slave trade to the developing commercial ties between Cuba and the United States. One convicted slave trader boasted of New York as being 'our headquarters'.[20] The slave ships, either bought or built for the trade, fitted out in New York, or occasionally in Charleston or New Orleans, and set out ostensibly on a legitimate commercial voyage under American colours and usually with an American captain and crew. But each vessel had on board a Spanish passenger who, when the ship reached Africa, would supervize its transformation to a slaver and then command on the return voyage to Cuba. The vessel either was or appeared to be American property, making it immune from capture under the Anglo-Spanish slave trade treaties. In one instance in 1854 where a British cruiser came across an abandoned slaver on the coast of Cuba, the British Law Officers could not uphold the legality of its seizure because it was both an American vessel, manned by Americans and fitted out in the United States, and because it had been captured within Spanish territorial waters.[21] When the slavers arrived at the pre-arranged rendezvous, the slaves were transferred to coasting vessels to avoid suspicion and in small groups the slaves were conducted to plantations. Once inside the plantations, the owners could rely on the protection of the penal law.

Within Cuba, as both Cuban planters and British officials knew, the extent of the slave trade depended to a great degree on the Captain-General. A determined Captain-General could reduce it very markedly within a short period of time, but under a lax or corrupt Captain-General the trade would revive and spread like a tropical weed. All Captains-General came under tremendous and unrelenting British pressure to stop the slave trade, pressure which was exercised directly and indirectly both at Madrid and in Havana. It could not be ignored especially when Spain needed allies to help her preserve the island from American annexationist schemes. Valentín Cañedo, who served as Captain-General in Cuba during 1852 and 1853 when annexationism was rife, writhed under the constant British denunciations of his conduct and eventually succumbed. To prove to the British that he was sincere in his enforcement of the treaties, he decided to override the penal law.[22] He authorized district governors or their subordinate officers to enter any plantations where newly imported or *bozal* African slaves might be concealed and to seize them. His order was in direct violation of Article 9 of the penal law which forbade investigations within estates to discover the origin of slaves and, in informing the British government of this action, the Spanish government carefully did not approve it. Under immense British pressure and relying on British support against American annexationism but equally unwilling to anger Cuban planters, Spain was prepared to condone the violation of her own law rather than to strengthen it through amendments. This way the potentially explosive Cuban issue could be kept away from public debate in the Cortes and any blame for arbitrary or illegal acts would fall on the head of the Captain-General who would then be recalled.

When Cañedo's officers seized slaves on several estates from an illegal expedition, there was a predictable outcry from planters and slave traders who took their case to the Audiencia court. The court ruled that the seizures were illegal and restored the slaves to the planters who claimed them. Cañedo also had arrested Julián Zulueta, Cuba's most prominent slave trader, in June 1853 for his part in the landing of a large number of slaves from the *Lady Suffolk*, but the Captain-General was unable to obtain legal evidence to support his charges. They had to be dropped and Zulueta was released, another damaging blow to Cañedo's own prestige and to the credibility of his efforts to suppress the trade.[23]

Crawford witnessed the total inadequacy of Cañedo's attempts to beat down the slave trade and concluded that Britain must press for amendments to the Spanish penal law as the only effective way to strengthen the powers of the Cuban authorities. His own suggestions were incorporated into the recommendations which Clarendon sent to Spain in October 1853.[24] Article 9 of the penal law had made the whole law 'inoperative', and Clarendon based his demand for amendments on the premise that as long as Article 9 remained unaltered Spain was not fulfilling the treaty she had signed with Britain in 1835. Britain wanted the repeal of Article 9 and specific powers to be given to Spanish officials to capture illegally imported African slaves wherever they were to be found. Property owners who harboured them were to be fined, but as a protection for slaveowners Britain wanted the registration of all slaves in Spain's Caribbean islands. This would prevent contentious legal disputes over the status of slaves and enhance chances for a genuine suppression of the slave trade. Lastly, Britain argued that the punishments to be imposed on convicted offenders under the penal law had to be made much more severe.

Spain had been well aware of the complex difficulties facing her colonial government in Cuba over the implementation of the penal law long before the British demanded its reform. Case after case had been reported to Madrid of slave landings where the facts were notorious but no legal evidence could be found to convict the perpetrators. José de la Concha, in his first term as Captain-General, suspended the governor of Matanzas for suspected complicity in the slave trade only to have him reinstated by the Audiencia court for lack of proof.[25] Cañedo, Concha's successor, defended his conduct to his own government even more vigorously than he did in answering British charges against him. The substance of his defence was that he had done everything possible to suppress the trade, but the hands of Cuba's Captain-General were bound by the restrictions of Spanish law and administrative practice. No matter how well intentioned the Captain-General was, the public opinion of white Cuba which strongly favoured the slave trade was openly hostile to its abolition. Whether they were great planters, rich merchants or rural peasants did not matter, Cañedo informed his government, their attitude towards the slave trade was invariably the same. 'Without exception they all eagerly desire it, protect it and almost sanctify it.'[26] Public opinion backed the private interests of the slave traders and the planters and ignored the public welfare of Cuba.

Cañedo also was frustrated by the lack of unity in the military command of the island. The Spanish navy in Cuba did not come under the direct command of the Captain-General who, therefore, could not utilize Spanish cruisers as effectively as he might. His own sub-ordinate officers were far more likely to be swayed by bribes from slave traders than by any sense of public duty. Yet, Article 9 of the penal law remained the overwhelming obstacle. The majority of estates, especially the new ones, bordered the sea making clandestine landings almost impossible to prevent. Once the slaves were inside an estate, the authorities were forbidden to enter it and the legality of the owner's title to them could not be challenged. Even when Cañedo deliberately violated Article 9, by authorizing searches inside estates, the Audiencia nullified his acts by restoring the slaves and refusing to convict without legal proof which Cañedo could not obtain.

In the aftermath of one seizure of African slaves by Spanish officials, the Audiencia had challenged the legal authority of the Captain-General to act in slave trade matters. According to the court's interpretation of his powers, the Captain-General's authority was limited to being a channel between the mixed commission court and the Audiencia in slave trade cases. Even as President of the Audiencia he had no powers separate from those of the court. Captains-General Concha and Cañedo both refused to accept this narrow interpretation of their functions and the court was duly overruled in Madrid on the grounds that no Captain-General would be able to uphold the treaties with Britain if this interpretation was allowed to stand.[27]

The legal implications from what had begun as a jurisdictional dispute never were cleared up. The court's position, based on its interpretation of the 1845 law, was that it was legal for any person to buy an African slave in Cuba after the slave had been brought to the island, and it was illegal to investigate the origin of any slave on Cuba's plantations. This meant that a successful slave landing, illegally undertaken contrary to Spanish law and the treaties with Britain, almost simultaneously imposed an unchallengeable legality upon the slavery of the imported Africans as soon as they were inside any Cuban plantation. If the Captain-General through his subordinate officers could prevent the landing from occurring or interrupt the process of landing the slaves and seize them, he was to turn them over to the Audiencia court which would adjudicate the case and determine the fate of the Africans. Madrid reaffirmed the powers of the Captain-General to prosecute the slave trade, but warned him at the same time to proceed cautiously. If doubt arose over the status of any Africans seized by Cuban officials, he was either to delay or turn all his evidence over to the courts where the final decision would be made. Throughout all this legal wrangling, the main question both in Cuba and in Madrid was who had the power to declare the Africans to be either slaves or *emancipados*, a legal distinction without real meaning as far as the Africans themselves were concerned. The original purpose of the law to stop the slave trade virtually had faded away.

Confronted by British demands for amendments to the penal law and legal disputes over its interpretation, the Spanish government wrestled with the thistle-like complexities during the early part of 1854 just when it was fending off the clumsy annexationist overtures of Pierre Soulé, the United States Minister to Spain. The easiest decision was to reject the British demands to introduce amendments to Spain's slave trade legislation in the Cortes. With Cuba menaced by American annexationist movements and the planters already uneasy over the future of slavery in the island, no Spanish government contemplated a public debate on any aspect of Cuban slavery. Spain rejected the British amendments with what Howden, the British Minister at Madrid, termed arguments 'of the flimsiest description', but she bowed to the underlying British insistence for stronger measures against the slave trade.[28] Juan de la Pezuela, Cañedo's replacement as Captain-General, who was determined to rid Cuba of the slave trade, had placed an unwanted choice before his government. Spain either would have to repudiate the slave trade treaties and offer appropriate compensation to Britain or she would have to enforce them.[29] With considerable reluctance, the Spanish government accepted Pezuela's recommendation to enforce the treaties with measures bound to be unpopular with the planters and elected to do by royal decree what it earlier had refused to do by legislation.

A comprehensive royal decree on Cuba's most urgent problems went out to Captain-General Pezuela on 22 March 1854, and he published it in the Havana *Gazette* on 3 May 1854.[30] The decree essentially modified the penal law by providing for the registration of slaves in Cuba. In his announcement of the decree, Pezuela delayed its implementation until after the sugar harvest of 1854. Other provisions of the March decree tried to solve the crisis of Cuba's agricultural labour which Spain was sure would worsen rapidly after the abolition of the slave trade. Immigration of other agricultural labourers such as the Chinese and Yucatan Indians was to be promoted, but the centrepiece of the new plan was slave registration.

The British government was happy to accept slave registration as a substitute for the penal law amendments and officials in both London and Havana were optimistic of its success. If all slaves were registered, the Cuban government could then distinguish newly imported African slaves, or *bozales* as they were known, and readily liberate them, depriving the slave traders of a secure market.[31] Apart from the wider repercussions of the registration policy, which have been examined in a previous chapter, it had the initial effect of stimulating the slave trade. Slave traders understood that the existing penal law provisions would remain in effect until 1 August 1854, when the authorities would begin to visit Cuban plantations and inspect slave registers. In the meantime, as Crawford reported, 'cargo upon cargo of slaves continue to arrive'.[32] Pezuela partially countered this by seizing a record number of 2,699 illegally imported slaves during his short tenure of office which lasted from December 1853 to September 1854.

The fall of the Spanish government in the summer of 1854 due to revolution meant Pezuela's recall and his replacement by a former Captain-General, José de la Concha, who was sent out for a second term. Concha was the personal choice of Clarendon, the British Foreign Secretary, and of British diplomats in Madrid. When Howden, the Minister, and Otway, who acted as Chargé d'Affaires in Howden's absence, realized that Pezuela could not be saved, they immediately began canvassing to ensure that their mutual friend, 'Pepe' Concha, went out to Cuba as Pezuela's successor. They were delighted with the success of their backstage manoeuvrings, not realizing how completely their hand-picked choice would disappoint their expectations.[33] The change from Pezuela to Concha was far more than a change of personality at the top of Cuba's government. Concha left for Cuba committed to attacking the slave trade, which was why British diplomats had lobbied so vigorously for his appointment. But he was committed far more deeply to reversing Pezuela's measures in order to restore the confidence of the Cuban planters in Spanish colonial administration. Neither Concha nor his British supporters knew how incompatible these rival goals would be.

Before his departure for Cuba, Concha took care to visit the British Minister in Madrid and reassure him that the suppression of the slave trade would be just as rigorous under his governorship as it had been under Pezuela even if the means employed might be different. Concha told Howden quite frankly of his objections to authorizing searches inside estates. These would have to be abandoned in order to wean the planters away from their annexationist leanings. Howden accepted Concha's argument and placed great faith in his ability to fulfil his promise. Clarendon in London was much less willing to swallow Spanish objections to violating the plantation sanctuaries since Pezuela had proved it could be done, but he was willing to give Concha the benefit of the doubt.[34]

Pezuela, on the verge of leaving Cuba and knowing his registration scheme was in jeopardy, had reached quite different conclusions from those of his successor on the best way to eliminate the slave trade. His own measures by themselves, he now believed, would not suffice to check it. He had learned that five slave trade expeditions were being outfitted to take advantage of his recall. To prevent their success and to deal the long delayed death blow, Pezuela decided Spain must make the slave trade a crime of piracy. He had written a despatch to the Spanish government recommending this, but on hearing from Crawford that it would arrive in Spain faster via the British mails, he entrusted the despatch to Crawford's care, an eloquent gesture of the mutual trust and co-operation between the two men at the end of Pezuela's short career in Cuba. Pezuela suggested that Britain support his recommendation which the British government was only too happy to do.[35] British diplomacy in Madrid now attempted once more to persuade the Spanish government to strengthen Spain's slave-trading laws, while in Havana Crawford watched sceptically as Concha quietly dismantled Pezuela's structure of anti-slave trade measures.

Spain quickly rejected the recommendation to declare the slave trade piracy, using as her excuse the panic created by the Africanization scare in Cuba. Howden advised against pressing the matter further for the moment, because of Spain's real alarm over Cuba and in the hope that Concha would succeed.[36] In Cuba Concha began his term of office by offering to co-operate fully and openly with the British officials to collate all the available information on illegal slave trade operations and to tighten the enforcement net. But Concha placed overriding importance on the need to maintain the support of the planters and the merchants. Without their support he was sure the Cuban slave trade could not be overcome. To gain their backing he cancelled Pezuela's registration decree and promised the planters he would not permit his officials to enter estates to investigate the origin of slaves. The full power of the 1845 penal law had been restored and the underlying fear of the planters, that registration of the slave population would lead to the loss of slaves illegally introduced after 1820 – in fact, most of Cuba's slave population – vanished. But at the same time Concha had ensured a secure market for all new slave arrivals from Africa.[37]

Concha waited two months until the middle of November 1854 before making his slave trade policy public. In a decree published on 17 November, he formally repealed the decrees of his predecessor. He justified this repeal to Madrid by pointing out that Pezuela's policy had infringed Article 9 of the penal law, ignoring the fact that the Spanish government had authorized Pezuela's reforms. Concha claimed he had restored public tranquillity by which he meant that he had calmed the planters, sufficient justification as far as Madrid was concerned for a complete about face. Yet Concha also was confident he could keep the slave trade under control. In place of registration, Concha substituted an elaborate system of rewards for informers and prize money to officers responsible for seizing slave ships or their cargoes. Neither British officials in Havana nor those in London shared Concha's confidence in his new plan. Crawford doubted the decree would do any good and, at the British Foreign Office, Ward, who was in charge of the Slave Trade Department, concluded, 'it will be easily evaded by both Planters and Slave Dealers'.[38] The British consul-general at Havana reiterated how totally inadequate Spanish legislation was and urged his government to push Spain for a declaration of piracy, 'but it must be made to extend to the owners, outfitters, masters and crews of the vessels, to the agents, whether for the embarkation or disembarkation as well as to the owners of the negroes, their agents and Brokers employed in the Sale of the Bozals should they be landed, to all purchasers of such illegally imported negroes and to the Lieut.-Governors and officers of the districts where they may have been landed'.[39]

Clarendon agreed with Crawford on the need for stronger Spanish laws and British diplomats tried again to convince Spain to make the slave trade a crime of piracy. Howden in Madrid was optimistic at the end of 1854 that he had converted Luzuriaga, the Spanish Foreign Minister, and that Spain would at least make the penalties for slave-trading offences equivalent to those for piracy even if she was unwilling to declare the slave trade openly to be piracy. Clarendon said he would be happy to accept this compromise.[40] Howden was still hopeful after the Spanish Cabinet discussed the matter and referred it to the Cuban Captain-General for his opinion, but everything now rested with Concha and Howden doubted whether he would approve.[41] Howden had been unduly optimistic all along. The Spanish government had no intention of altering the penal law in any way and simply referred the piracy question to Concha as a delaying tactic to gain more ammunition with which to reject the British demands.[42]

Concha obliged his government with a long catalogue of reasons why a declaration of piracy would be wrong. More illegal African slaves had been seized by the Cuban authorities in 1853 and 1854 than in any two previous years, but in only two instances had any of the perpetrators been captured. This fact 'talked very loud' for Concha. He assumed the reason was the high level of public support in Cuba for the slave trade. Therefore, he argued, if the penalties for slave-trading were made more severe, either the enormity of the penalties would make it harder still to catch the criminals or, if the government was successful, Concha predicted that this very success would open up 'a lake of blood' between colony and metropolis. Instead, he defended his own approach of educating Cuban public opinion against the slave trade without angering the planters.[43] Concha previously had told Crawford that it was an inopportune time to contemplate a declaration of piracy because of the continuing filibuster rumours from the United States.[44] Spanish politicians refused to accede to British demands because they believed that to do so would risk Spain's hold on Cuba either through planter discontent or through American annexationists taking advantage of harsher measures to exploit Cuban grievances as had occurred in 1854.

The British government would not let Spain off the hook and kept up an unrelenting diplomatic pressure at Madrid, but Spain was equally obstinate in refusing to give way. The subject of Cuba was rarely debated in the Spanish Cortes during the 1850s, but in March 1855 during one of the infrequent debates Luzuriaga pledged Spain's wholehearted support to the Cuban slaveowners. Slavery was a necessity for the island and Spain would uphold it. To do otherwise would endanger Spanish possession of Cuba and the preservation of her richest colony was the guiding principle of Spain's colonial policy. 'The Island of Cuba can only cease from being an integral portion of the Spanish Territory by one of the two following means: – either by emancipation, which would be the thorough extermination of the white race, that is to say, of all Spaniards and Natives of the Island of European origin, or by Annexation.'[45] Since Spaniards believed annexation would succeed only if the Americans offered greater guarantees to Cuban slaveowners than Spain could, Spain was determined not to be outbid in this auction for the affection of Cuban planters. The suppression of the slave trade, while proclaimed as official Spanish policy, would never be pushed to the point where it affected essential planter interests. The line had been drawn by the penal law and successive Spanish governments defended that line with an almost religious fanaticism.

While publicly defending Cuban slavery, privately the Spanish government was exploring ways to strengthen Cuba's slave system through the importation of female slaves from other slave-holding countries, but here Spanish officials ran up against the barrier of the slave trade treaties. At the end of April 1855, the Colonial Ministry in Madrid placed the problem of Cuba's allegedly diminishing slave population before the Ministry of Foreign Affairs, asking whether Spain's treaties with Britain barred her from buying female slaves from slave-holding countries such as the United States or Brazil. The Foreign Affairs Ministry officials assured their colleagues that such a venture would be in accord with the treaties as far as they were concerned, but because Britain certainly would object they advised against it.[46] This problem, too, ended up in the lap of Cuba's Captain-General. In a revealing despatch, the Spanish government admitted to Concha, what he knew only too well, that slavery 'is at the root of many of the difficulties which exist in the province under your command and it explains facts and occurrences which perhaps appear almost incomprehensible to the great majority of people'.[47] It was left to Concha to resolve the paradox of how to conserve Cuba's slave population while suppressing the slave trade and maintaining the confidence of Cuba's planters.

Concha already had proposed a watered down version of Pezuela's registration policy in the form of tickets of security or *cédulas* for every slave in the island. Planters could obtain these tickets for all their slaves from local government officers in return for a small fee per ticket, so instead of an enforced registration of the island's slave population, Concha's scheme amounted to a head tax on the slaves under the disguise of a census, with the aim of forcing more slaves on to the sugar plantations. Concha definitely saw the plan as an aid in the fight against the slave trade, but because the *cédulas* were given out to planters who did not have to present their slaves to receive the tickets, and no investigation took place into the origin of any slave, Concha's naive faith in this very bureaucratic device was badly misplaced.

The *cédulas* were to be renewed every six months and the programme of issuing them was to start in February 1855.[48] Delays in its implementation meant the plan did not really begin until July 1855 and by then it had become so riddled with fraud that it provided more security for slave dealers seeking to land African slaves. The dealers purchased sufficient *cédulas* to cover the estimated number of new arrivals who would then appear before the authorities as legal slaves, immune from any investigation into their origin. Concha quickly became aware of the fraud and imposed a small fine on any slave-owners caught purchasing tickets for non-existent slaves, but fines could not deter what the British consul-general branded a 'scandalous fraud'.[49]

When the Cuban government published the figures derived from what has been seen as the first genuine slave census in Cuba, the British commissioners analysed them with great care because the figures appeared to prove the Spanish case, that the slave trade had stopped and Cuba's slave population was declining. The total number of *cédulas* issued for the first six months of 1855 was 374,806, compared to 366,563 for the second half of the year, indicating a decline of 8,243 slaves in half a year. The commissioners could not accept that Cuba's slave population had diminished at all; they were certain it was still growing because of the slave trade and they estimated the total slave population at over 600,000. They dismissed the Cuban figures as 'absolutely worthless'.[50] Although the commissioners' own estimate of the Cuban slave population was itself biased and undoubtedly exaggerated, their analysis of the frauds inherent in the *cédula* system has not been taken into account by historians who have tended to accept the *cédula* figures as a reasonably accurate census of Cuba's slave population.[51] What was not in doubt was the failure of Concha's plan to end the slave trade.

Clarendon had been reluctant to criticize Concha because the Cuban Captain-General seemed to be sincere in his efforts to combat the trade and the statistics for 1855 indicated a slight diminution in the level of the trade from the previous year. Late in 1855, however, an incident arose which nearly caused the collapse of Clarendon's cautious and pacific approach to Spain over the Cuban slave trade. The British government learned that Spain intended to appoint a notorious slave trader named Mustich as governor of the Spanish island of Fernando Po off the African west coast. Until 1854 the British consul at Fernando Po had governed the island for Spain and the British government wanted to continue the arrangement which, among other advantages for Britain, had facilitated the British West African Squadron's cruising operations. Neither private nor formal British protests succeeded initially in blocking the appointment. Anglo-Spanish relations became more tense when British cruisers seized a Catalan vessel, also named the *Fernando Po*, off West Africa for being equipped as a slaver. The *Fernando Po* was consigned to the infamous Mustich. Alarmed at the prospect of the island becoming an African depot for Cuban slave traders, Clarendon ordered his Minister in Madrid to issue a formal threat to Spain that Britain would reserve the right to take naval action against Fernando Po if Mustich was appointed and tried to make the island into a sanctuary for Spanish slavers.[52]

When he received the despatch, Howden thought Clarendon might wish to reconsider the use of such a strong threat because of the certainty of violent repercussions in Spain. Howden himself was prepared to make the threat 'willingly and joyfully, for I am convinced that none but the strongest measures can bring this Government to a sense of honesty towards Foreign Nations and especially towards England'.[53] Britain still was embroiled in the Crimean War and the risk of further European entanglements was enough to produce sober second thoughts on the wisdom of threatening Spain. Palmerston, the Prime Minister, approved dropping the threat, but he gave vent to his own feelings in blustering language that remained hidden from the British public and from Spain: 'The Spanish Govt. ought to be made clearly to understand that whether they like it or not they will be compelled to fulfil their Treaty engagements for the Suppression of the Slave Trade; That we have the means and the Power to do so & that those means & that Power will be exerted till the End is accomplished. They have trifled with us too long on this matter & their Evasions ought to be brought to an end.'[54]

Palmerston did not say how this was to be done. Spain had rejected every British proposal to strengthen Spanish slave trade legislation and showed no sign whatever of giving the Cuban Captain-General more powers to suppress the slave trade. Short of going to war, which not even Palmerston favoured, Britain was stymied. Howden in Madrid alleged there was a 'systematic opposition' to all his protests which, in any case, 'are practically of no manner of use'. Without new laws, 'everything depends more or less on the good or bad will, personally, of the governor general of the Island' whom Howden still trusted. Spain drew back from appointing a slave dealer as governor of Fernando Po, but she refused to do anything more about the Cuban slave trade which Howden reported in November 1855, on the basis of trustworthy information reaching him from Cuba, 'was never carried on with such activity as at the moment'.[55]

The British government had ample confirmation of the increase in the trade from Crawford in Havana who had written early in October 1855: 'This Island seems to be beset with slavers; they are swarming and what is worse, they appear to succeed in landing their Slaves and eluding the vigilance of the Spanish authorities always.'[56] With

Howden lamenting that his influence in Madrid was 'null, unless vigorously and *ostensibly* backed by the English Government', Palmerston's blustering tone must have seemed to his frustrated subordinates, at least, to lack any underlying substance.[57]

As the British commissioners at Havana watched the slave trade expand in response to the demand for labour created by high sugar prices and the consequent increase both in the number of plantations and in the size of existing ones during 1856 and 1857, they fumed with helpless indignation, powerless to impede the slave traders who easily overcame the obstacles presented by British cruisers and impotent Spanish laws. Concha's apparent sincerity in wanting to suppress the trade had not yielded any material results. If the Cuban slave trade was to be stopped at all, the commissioners' growing conviction was that Britain would have to take the necessary steps herself. Writing privately to the Foreign Secretary in May 1856, shortly after he arrived in Cuba, Francis Lousada, the newly appointed Commissioner of Arbitration at Havana, was horrified at what he saw and thought the time had come for Britain to uphold her honour: 'When I see the impunity existing . . . I ask myself whether it can be right that England with her almost unlimited power does not, discarding all secondary considerations, step in and say "These things *shall* no longer be".'[58]

In October 1856, the commissioners officially recommended that Britain deploy a flotilla of smaller and faster steamers capable of sailing between the reefs and cays of Cuba's coastline, since Spain could not be relied upon to fulfil her treaty obligations.[59] Clarendon agreed with his Havana commissioners that the British 'must rely solely on their own exertions to put down the Slave Trade', and he endorsed their idea of employing a smaller class of fast, steam cruisers around Cuba.[60] The British Admiralty were much harder to convince, and throughout the first half of 1857 the Lords of the Admiralty resisted pressure from the Foreign Office, backed by the Prime Minister, to allocate more vessels, let alone more suitable ones, to the anti-slave trade patrol off Cuba.[61]

The pressure on the Admiralty came from all directions. Crawford wrote directly to the British naval commanders in the West Indies, transmitting his suggestions for an effective naval patrol around Cuba.[62] He felt it was incumbent on him to try every possible method for, as he sadly admitted to Clarendon, 'Never since I have been at this station has the Slave Trade been carried on with such vigour as it is at present and has been for some time past.'[63] His own statistics suggested it had been worse in 1853 and 1854, but there was no doubt the slave trade was on the rise and Crawford's exaggeration doubtless reflected the disillusionment of fifteen years spent at Havana in the same futile task. Clarendon was doing all he could through diplomatic persuasion to get Spain to declare the slave trade piracy, but Howden in Madrid gloomily reported that the Spanish government had not 'the slightest intention' of introducing such a law in the current session of the Cortes.[64]

Outside official government circles in Britain there was a noticeable clamour for stronger measures to be used against Spain. *The Times* in a leading article challenged the government: 'It surely cannot be admitted that a country like England is unable to suppress the African slave trade.' A long-time opponent of the West African Squadron, *The Times* now argued in favour of a blockade of Cuban ports. 'The total suppression of the Slave Trade seems not only possible, but easy, if such means were adopted.'[65] Similar suggestions were raised in a Commons debate on the Cuban slave trade in July 1857 on a motion by Charles Buxton, the son of the English abolitionist leader, Thomas Fowell Buxton. The motion called for an address to be presented to the Queen asking her to employ all the means in her power to eliminate the trade. The House approved it without a vote. During his speech Buxton identified the means he wished to be employed. Britain was to induce Spain to declare the slave trade piracy and to make her own West African Squadron more effective. Britain was also 'to show Spain that, if she could not or would not suppress the Cuban slave trade, we could go into her waters and do it for her'. Palmerston, the defender of similar tactics used with success against Brazil in 1850, deflected this attempt to have them repeated against Cuba by pointing out the differences between the two situations. Brazil had bound herself by treaty, but when the treaty expired she refused to agree to any new arrangements for the suppression of the slave trade. 'But Spain has not refused to enter into treaty engagements . . . Therefore, as long as that treaty remains, unless we can show that there has been a deliberate and positive violation of its stipulations, we have not the same grounds of proceeding in regard to Spain as we had towards Brazil.'[66] The Prime Minister, in effect, told the Commons his government was not going to try and make a case for blockading Cuba.

Captain-General Concha in Cuba also faced criticism from his own government over his slave trade suppression policy, but not on the grounds of its ineffectiveness. Madrid accused him of sending out

a circular to his Lieutenant-Governors throughout the island, authorizing searches within plantations which violated the penal law and
ordered him to rescind it. Concha sent back an impassioned defence
of his policy stating that he had tried to suppress the trade without
alarming the planters or disturbing the stability of slavery. He protested at the acutely embarrassing position in which he was now placed
of being ordered to countermand his own instructions. He even
offered a different interpretation of Article 9 of the penal law he had
been accused of violating. Concha argued that Article 9 had been
inserted into the 1845 law solely to head off a general investigation of
the origin of Cuba's slaves under British pressure. Surely, he insisted,
the words of Spanish legislators could not be used 'to protect the very
crime the law was designed to punish'.[67] He refused to alter his
circulars and he kept on tinkering with his *cédula* system, making it
more cumbersome and unwieldy, in the hope, as he informed his
government, of eliminating the slave trade. Spain was content to place
her faith in Concha's *cédulas*. In the belief that the *cédulas* would
prove to be a 'universal panacea', British suggestions for increased
powers for the Captain-General or new legislative measures were
rejected.[68]

As the Cuban slave trade worsened in 1857 and foreign criticism of
him became more barbed, Concha tried a new tack to get around the
restrictions of the penal law. He asked the Audiencia, the only court
empowered under the penal law to deal with slave trade cases, to rule
on the proper interpretation of Article 9. Concha personally backed
the majority opinion of the court which opposed any alterations to
the law itself, but interpreted Article 9 as permitting searches inside
plantations where the authorities had good reason to believe illegally
imported slaves were hidden. Without this flexible interpretation,
the law became a mockery. 'How can slaves illegally introduced from
Africa against both the provisions of treaties and laws be declared
legal slaves according to the very same law which condemns and
punishes the men who bring them?'[69] While Spanish bureaucrats
wrestled with the tortuous legal complexities posed by Concha, the
Captain-General was taking more practical steps. In July 1857, he
ordered the creation of a special naval force of four small steamers
and schooners to act as a Spanish anti-slave-trade patrol. The British
commissioners who immediately reported this to London were cynical
in their assessment of the force, but they found it hard to criticize
when no British cruisers were to be found off Cuba.[70]

The reports of Concha's creation of a slave trade patrol and the absence of any British cruisers resulted in a change of British policy, in keeping with the demands from the British public and Parliament. On reading the despatches from Cuba, Clarendon admitted: 'We do little or nothing to prevent the S.T. there & now that the Spanish authorities are making a show of activity we ought to assist them but vessels wch draw much water are useless to prevent landings.' Palmerston supported him.[71] The British government decided to send 4 gunboats to operate in Cuban waters and as the gunboats were lighter in draught than other British cruisers they were more suitable for patrols around Cuba's sinuous reefs and cays.[72] To reinforce British naval effectiveness in the Caribbean and on the African coast, the Foreign Office, acting on the legal advice of the Queen's Advocate, authorized British naval officers to capture slavers without colours or papers of nationality and take them to British colonies for trial before Vice-Admiralty courts.[73] The 4 British gunboats allocated to the Cuban slave trade patrol did not reach Cuba until the end of November by which time the Spanish naval patrol had captured 4 slavers, a record for the Spanish navy which was not surpassed during the remaining years of the Cuban slave trade.[74] The Spanish ships, however, were not able to keep up a non-stop patrol and by the beginning of 1858 they were back in port due to mechanical break-downs from constant sea duty.

No one in the British government nor any of the British officials at Havana foresaw how Britain's 'gunboat' patrol of Cuba would back-fire. The Admiralty had agreed to it as a last resort to satisfy the pressure for stronger measures and the British government had to rely solely on naval suppression off both the African and Cuban coasts after the total failure of British diplomacy to obtain concessions from Spain. Even in the spring of 1858 both Clarendon and Malmes-bury, his successor as Foreign Secretary after Lord Derby's Conserva-tive government came to power, still pressed the Admiralty to allocate more vessels to the slave trade patrol around Cuba.[75]

Britain's attitude suddenly changed in May and June 1858, because of strong American protests over British naval searches and seizures of American shipping in Cuban waters. The British gunboats operat-ing around Cuba had obeyed their instructions to capture slave ships, but British naval officers in the Caribbean found it much harder to distinguish slave vessels from legitimate commercial ships in the busy Caribbean sea lanes and harbours than was the case off Africa. The gunboats had captured 2 vessels, fully equipped for the slave trade during March and April, both of which were subsequently condemned in British Vice-Admiralty courts. British officers had boarded 116 suspect vessels up to the end of May, 61 of which were American. American ships and the American flag had a virtual monopoly of the Cuban slave trade, but no treaty authorizing right of search existed between Britain and the United States. The British officer in charge of the slave trade patrol swore his men had taken the utmost care in performing 'this disagreeable duty', but he agreed that in one instance an officer had violated Spanish territorial waters in visiting Sagua la Grande, a small Cuban port, where he boarded 12 vessels, 11 of which were American. Vice-Admiral Sir Houston Stewart, the senior British naval officer on the North American and West Indian Station, ruefully confessed to London that 'indiscriminate boarding' had occurred and accusations of British officers boarding ships at anchor in Cuban ports were 'too true'.[76] Stewart blamed Crawford for the trouble. Even before the Admiral received any reports from the British naval officers concerned, he had convinced himself that Crawford had 'over-stimulated the zeal' of the British commanders because of his ardent abolitionism. This was not the case, but Stewart's conclusion was not challenged in London. The Admiralty and the government in general were very angry that a slave trade patrol very nearly had provoked a conflict with the United States and they were determined it would not happen again. Orders were issued to withdraw the gunboats from Cuban waters and no British naval vessel went on a slave trade patrol off Cuba for the next three years.

In London, Malmesbury learned of the Caribbean incidents through strongly worded American protests. A wave of anti-British hysteria swept the United States whipped up by American newspapers. Malmesbury quickly disavowed the alleged British abuses, mollified the Americans and publicly admitted in Parliament that Britain 'had made a mistake in sending our squadrons to the Cuban waters instead of keeping them on the coast of Africa'.[77] He also slapped down a suggestion from Crawford at Havana that Britain ring Cuba with a cordon of steam ships and gunboats.[78] Britain had no legal right to visit and search American vessels and confronted by American militancy with rumours of war floating across the Atlantic, British politicians backed down. The United States upheld the immunity of vessels flying the American flag from visits or searches by the British navy under any pretext whatever, and Britain bowed to this interpretation to maintain good relations with the United States.[79] From Havana, Crawford offered the best judgement on Britain's dilemma: 'We had to choose between a War with America, or the abandonment of the Searches of Vessels under that Flag . . . We had to choose the least [*sic*] of two evils and [the] Slave Trade will go on and flourish.'⁸⁰

Britain's retreat, for so it seemed to observers in Britain, the United States and Cuba, was an opportunity not to be missed by the enemies of the slave trade suppression policy. The greatest beneficiaries were the Cuban slave traders themselves. With no British cruisers operating off Cuba and the Spanish squadron laid up with mechanical difficulties, they were able to operate freely in Cuban waters. Crawford reported that the news of the withdrawal of the British cruisers had stimulated the slave traders even more than he had feared it would. Within a matter of weeks, 5 slavers were fitting out at Havana, 3 or 4 more at Matanzas and other Cuban ports, to say nothing of the bustle of activity in American ports like New York or New Orleans.⁸¹ The United States reinforced its own African squadron in 1859 and added a Cuban anti-slave-trade patrol, actions which checked slightly the rampant optimism of the slave traders. The number of arrests by American naval vessels rose and in 1860 they seized 18 ships and prosecuted 12 for slave-trading offences. President Buchanan's desire to possess Cuba had not diminished, but his administration did more than it has sometimes been credited with to suppress the slave trade.⁸²

Nevertheless, the captures of slavers by the American navy on the eve of the American Civil War indicate the dimensions of the revived Cuban slave trade rather than any real American success in reducing it. The American cruisers were hampered severely by United States laws. Legally, they were powerless to capture slave ships with equipment for the slave trade but no slaves on board, nor could they arrest vessels whose captains had destroyed all evidence of American nationality by throwing papers and colours overboard. American naval commanders generally made it a practice only to board American vessels, so to avoid being boarded the slave traders hoisted Spanish or other colours. To remedy these obvious gaps the British government proposed first a major conference to develop better methods to halt the slave trade and then a system of joint cruising around Cuba in co-operation with Spain, but the American government refused both overtures. Alone, neither British nor American cruisers could combat the tactics of the Cuban slave traders who exploited every international loophole, and the inability of the British and American governments to agree on joint measures was a major reason for the huge rise in the Cuban slave trade from 1858 to 1861.

Within Britain, the opponents of the costly slave trade suppression policy grabbed the chance offered to them by the Anglo-American dispute over the right to visit to renew their campaign for the abandonment of force to eliminate the Atlantic slave trade. William Hutt, who had almost succeeded eight years before in his crusade to disband the African Squadron, introduced a motion in the House of Commons on 12 July 1858 calling on the British government to discontinue the naval practice of the visit and search of ships flying foreign flags in the suppression of the slave trade. Hutt and his free trade allies aimed their guns at the African Squadron, but his motion was deliberately worded so as not to jeopardize Britain's negotiations with the United States over the Caribbean incidents. Hutt's strategy backfired. Government spokesmen were able to rally their supporters by arguing that no one would want to fetter the hands of British naval officers in the performance of what was universally acknowledged to be a difficult and unwelcome task. Where Hutt claimed that Cuba proved the failure of Britain's suppression methods, Palmerston, now in opposition but still a steadfast defender of the African Squadron, replied that Brazil proved their success and with perseverance Spain, too, would be brought into line. Britain then would have the satisfaction of knowing 'it has accomplished one of the noblest works in which any nation ever engaged'. To Hutt's bitter humiliation, his motion attracted only 24 supporters, while the Tories and Whigs combined to produce 223 votes against, a majority of 199 in favour of retaining the existing slave trade suppression policy.[83] The British government had been quick to withdraw the gunboats from Cuba to avoid a clash with the United States, but there was no thought of surrendering the African Squadron to Hutt's small band of free traders.

The large majority of the House of Commons in favour of the retention of the African Squadron was a firm indication that Britain would persevere, as Palmerston had urged, in her long struggle against the slave trade, but there was little hope that perseverance alone would bring success. All the evidence in 1858 and 1859 pointed to the revival of the Cuban slave trade on an unprecedented scale. Crawford's despatches from Cuba were an endless catalogue of slave landings and blatant infractions of the slave trade treaties. In November 1859, he wrote that 'these waters appear to be teeming with vessels bringing slaves to Cuba', and nearly a year later he referred to the Cuban slave trade as reaching 'gigantic proportions'.[84] He estimated in August 1860 that at least 80 vessels were engaged in the trade and the profits were so great the slave traders could afford to lose 4 vessels for every successful voyage. They were also able to pay enormous bribes to Spanish officials to connive at slave landings. Payments of $25,000 or more to Lieutenant-Governors in the island were not exceptional.[85] Crawford wrote also of the formation of a joint stock company in Havana with a capital of $600,000 to carry on the slave trade. The British Foreign Office had independent confirmation of these reports from other high Spanish sources, including the former naval commander at Havana who recalled a Havana association in which even milliners had shares. The Cubans treated the slave trade as a lottery and people exhibited their newly arrived slaves as prizes.[86]

After withdrawing the British warships from Cuba, Malmesbury set about to convince Spain that she must take stronger action herself. His instructions to Buchanan, his new Minister at Madrid, were 'firm as to facts without being threatening as to consequences', but they had no more impact than those of his predecessors.[87] Malmesbury earlier had told Parliament that if all the British diplomatic notes on the Cuban slave trade 'were woven together [they] would reach from here to Cuba itself'.[88] His own contributions joined the long trail and the slave trade went on oblivious to the flurry of diplomatic paper about it. The British government laboriously compiled statistics on the increase in the Cuban slave trade, based largely on Crawford's despatches, and regularly sent them to Spain, hoping to shock the Spanish government into adopting new initiatives. Thus Malmesbury wrote that British and Spanish cruisers in 1857 together had captured a total of 30 vessels, all engaged in the Cuban slave trade. Six more had been seized in the first half of 1858, but over 50 slavers were known to have sailed from Cuban or American ports.[89] British estimates indicated that 10,436 slaves had been landed in Cuba during 1857 of whom 2,324 had been seized by the Spanish authorities, but in 1858 the number landed rose to 16,992 while the number seized fell to 639.[90] When Lord John Russell took over as Foreign Secretary in 1859 he carried on the practice of sending Crawford's despatches to Spain along with periodic compilations of the extent of the trade. Writing in September 1860, he referred to Anglo-Spanish relations as being in a state 'of embarrassment and uneasiness' because of the slave trade. American newspapers openly published the names of at least 26 vessels which had landed no fewer than 15,000 slaves in 1859, and very probably many more. What was Spain proposing to do about it?[91]

The official Spanish reaction to this deluge of British diplomatic notes was to challenge the credibility of all British statistics on the slave trade and defend the reputation of General Concha. Spain refused to budge, but in Cuba Concha found himself more and more hamstrung by the penal law and the growing American involvement in the slave trade. He dared not apply the penal law provisions to American vessels lest the United States retaliate, and the restrictions imposed by the penal law made it virtually impossible for him to act against the slave traders within Cuba. His pet *cédula* scheme had been an open farce for some time and shortly before he left Cuba for Spain in the autumn of 1859, Concha himself issued a decree abandoning it. He apparently decided to abolish the *cédulas* when he heard that large quantities of forged ones had come from New York to be distributed among Cuban slave traders.[92] Concha later confessed to the British Minister in Madrid that the slave trade had driven him out of the island. But he remained unrepentant about his own suppression policies and would not recommend more repressive measures even after his return to the peninsula for fear of encouraging annexationism among the planters.[93] General Concha left Cuba, having succeeded in preserving it for Spain, but the cost of preservation was the expansion of the slave trade to record levels in flagrant defiance of Spain's own laws. It spread like a cancer enveloping every institution in the island with its corruption.

On the west coast of Africa, British naval officers complained of their impossible task. The French plan for joint cruising and co-operation in the suppression of the trade, signed in 1845, had lapsed and British commanders now received no help from the French or the Americans. Without any reciprocal rights of visit and search, the British cruisers could not cope with the crafty slave traders who showed American or French colours when approached by British vessels. In his report for 1857, Rear-Admiral Grey, the senior officer on the African coast, candidly told the Admiralty that the 'prospect for putting down the Slave Trade has seldom been less encouraging'.[94]

British naval despondency over the spiralling Atlantic slave trade finally reached the point where the Duke of Somerset, as First Lord of the Admiralty, wrote a special memorandum on the Atlantic slave trade for his Cabinet colleagues at the end of 1859.[95] The information reaching Britain from Africa, Cuba and the United States during the latter part of the year 'forces upon us the unwelcome conviction that the slave trade is rapidly increasing and that in the present year it has been carried on more extensively and more successfully than for many years past'. The evidence all pointed to the fact that 'there is now no effective check on the slave trade, and but little risk of capture to those who conduct it. Within six months of this year 37 slavers were known to have visited the [African] coast, capable of containing 24,000 slaves; of these indeed 9 had been captured.' The slave traders could make use of French or American nationality quite freely because neither country would concede any rights of visit or search to British cruisers. The First Lord then confronted his colleagues with the main issue. 'It is now not unreasonable to ask of what use is our African Squadron? Is it necessary to continue sending officers and men to the western coast of Africa with directions to check the slave trade and to capture slavers while laws and treaties exist which incapacitate them from performing the service?' His solution, supported by the Admiralty, was to reduce the size of the Squadron and to give up the attempt to watch the whole West African coast. Instead, he proposed maintaining a small naval force to patrol areas where legitimate trade flourished. Lord John Russell, the Foreign Secretary, agreed that the increase of the slave trade was 'indeed very lamentable', but he successfully argued for a delay in the implementation of Somerset's plan.[96]

By the beginning of 1860, the ramifications of the failure of the Spanish penal law to stop the Cuban slave trade had undermined the whole British suppression policy. Britain first had tried vainly to win more concessions from Spain and when Spain would not yield for fear of alienating the white planters and losing Cuba, Britain resolved to stop the slave trade herself through the device of a gunboat patrol off Cuba to supplement the West African Squadron's work on the other side of the Atlantic. This, too, collapsed when Lord Derby's administration withdrew the gunboats to avoid a confrontation with the United States. British politicians had to swallow the unpleasant truth that in 1860, after more than fifty years spent in trying to eliminate it, the Cuban slave trade was more virulent than ever with no remedy in sight.

Spain also found herself so shackled by the Cuban slave trade that escape was impossible. First through treaties with Britain and then by her own legislation she had committed herself as a nation to abolish it. But Spain and her politicians believed the preservation of Cuba as a colony to be far more vital than the suppression of the Cuban slave trade. They also were convinced Cuba's preservation could be accomplished only by maintaining slavery, the bedrock of Cuban economic prosperity in Spanish eyes and a barrier to creole aspirations for independence. The passage of the penal law of 1845 was as far as any Spanish government would go to abolish the slave trade until the institution of slavery itself started to teeter after emancipation in the United States. At one level the failure of the penal law was the protection it offered to the Cuban slave traders, making a mockery of the law's original purpose, but there was a deeper failure which few Spaniards perceived. Under relentless pressure from Britain to modify or replace the law, Spanish politicians took to defending it in patriotic terms against what they termed unwarranted foreign interference. The peninsular government was equally obstinate in resisting appeals from harassed Captains-General to allow a more flexible interpretation of the law or to amend it. For twenty years, from 1845 to 1865, the penal law was the outer limit of Spanish action on the most controversial colonial issue in Cuba. By refusing to consider amending the law, Spain really rejected any possibility of colonial reforms. She clung to the status quo with such tenacity that any discussion of change, let alone change itself, was precluded until the American Civil War jolted her out of her rigidity. Spain postponed reforms until it was too late and by postponing them she gave an impetus to the independence movement which in the end was to lead to the loss of the colony she wanted so desperately to retain.

CHAPTER 13

A new class of slaves

The two Anglo-Spanish treaties to abolish the Cuban slave trade established a structure of courts and officials in Cuba and on the African west coast to pronounce sentence on every slave ship captured under the treaties' provisions. The treaties also contained clauses guaranteeing the freedom of Africans found on captured slavers. The courts of mixed commission, located in Sierra Leone and Havana, were to free all Africans from condemned slave ships and guarantee their liberty through the issuance of certificates of emancipation. According to the 1817 treaty, all Africans liberated as a result of decisions in the Sierra Leone court would remain in that colony under British supervision and all Africans freed at Havana were to be the responsibility of the Spanish colonial authorities. In Sierra Leone the British colonial officials accepted their role as guardians of the liberty of these freed Africans, although demands for African labourers in the West Indies after 1833 caused considerable exploitation. On the other side of the ocean the fate of the *emancipados*, as the liberated Africans came to be known, became in Cuba as it did in Brazil a form of slavery in many respects worse than that of legal slavery.[1] Because the *emancipado* class was brought into existence by treaty, their treatment emerged as one of the thorniest issues at stake between the British and Spanish governments, with angry diplomatic exchanges continuing until long after the Cuban slave trade itself finally had ended.

What would happen to these liberated Africans set free in the midst of a slave plantation colony perennially short of slave labour? This was a matter of great concern to the first British officials who went out to Cuba. As early as March 1820, Kilbee, the British judge on the court of mixed commission, requested instructions as to what his position on the *emancipado* question should be.[2] He reported that the Cuban authorities also wanted to learn the British view because 'they are quite at a loss upon the subject'. Ultimately, the fate of the *emancipados* rested in the hands of the Spanish government, but the question remained a theoretical one for four more years since no captured slavers appeared in Havana until 1824.

The case of the Portuguese brig, *Maria ·de la Gloria*, captured by a Spanish cruiser and brought before the Havana court in 1824, revealed only too clearly to Kilbee how the Cubans proposed to treat the liberated Africans. When the court declared itself incompetent to judge the vessel because the case did not come within the provisions of the 1817 treaty, the case was turned over to the Spanish Admiralty court in Havana. This court in turn referred it to Madrid for a final decision and, pending word from Spain, ordered that the Africans from the *Maria de la Gloria* be deposited with planters and inhabitants selected by the court. Because the Cubans who were selected paid to receive the Africans, Kilbee concluded that the transaction was a thinly disguised form of slavery, the only difference being that the labour of these Africans was sold for a much cheaper price than that of slaves on the open market. The Admiralty court in a secret decree also warned the Spanish government of the danger to Cuba should these Africans be given unrestricted liberty. In the climate of opinion prevailing in Cuba there was little likelihood of genuine freedom for the liberated Africans. Kilbee protested to the Captain-General that the conditions for the distribution of the *Maria de la Gloria* Africans offered them no security at all and he pressed on both the Captain-General and his own government the need to ensure that the Captain-General alone should have the responsibility for their distribution and care.[3]

This paradox presented by the *emancipados* in Cuba did not change in essentials as long as the *emancipados* existed as a separate element in a slave society. The Cuban government was terrified of the impact of a large influx of free Africans on Cuba's slave population, a fear whipped up by a gnawing realization of Haiti's proximity. Yet, at the same time, planters and other white Cubans were keenly aware that the *emancipados* offered a new and cheaper form of slave labour. Until the latter part of the 1830s, official fear was more influential than the greed of individual Cubans in determining Spanish policy towards the *emancipados* even if greed played a strong part in denying the *emancipados* the liberty to which legally they were entitled.

The capture and condemnation of the Spanish slaver *Relámpago* late in 1824 marked the actual beginning of the British – Spanish conflict over the *emancipados*. Certificates of emancipation for the 147 Africans released from the *Relámpago* were deposited with the Captain-

General. Kilbee also drew up a list of regulations to govern their treatment and with Captain-General Vives' approval these regulations were adopted provisionally by the Cuban government.[4] They were designed to provide a period of apprenticeship for each African: five years for adults, seven for children or females with children, during which time each would be taught a trade. If at the end of this time an *emancipado* was judged incapable of earning a living for himself, the government could prolong his apprenticeship for a maximum of three years. When the apprenticeship was over, the *emancipado* was to be completely free. During the apprenticeship period each *emancipado* was to be assigned to a master and most of Kilbee's regulations laid down the responsibilities of the masters. Kilbee's chief aim was the well-being of the *emancipados* themselves and in designing his regulations he obviously had drawn on the laws governing apprenticeship in Britain. But he did not give sufficient thought to the difficulty of enforcing these regulations within a slave society. Kilbee's apprenticeship idea was adopted in Cuba but it was then twisted into a device for permanently enslaving the *emancipados* in a cruel perversion of the original purpose. At the end of each assignment period, the *emancipados* were reassigned upon the payment of a new assignment fee. Apprenticeship became slavery for the *emancipados* and since they were Africans they worked alongside other African slaves receiving the same treatment from the slave masters.

The ostensible emancipation of the Africans from the *Relámpago* caused a storm of protest from the Havana plantocracy and the Captain-General was under some pressure to reverse the court's action.[5] Instead, the problem of the *emancipados* was referred to Spain. In the spring of 1825 the Council of the Indies debated the fate of the *emancipados*, with Kilbee's regulations before it. As well, the Council had an opinion from Pinillos, the Spanish judge on the Havana mixed commission court and later Intendant of Havana.[6] He stressed the danger of the existence of a large number of newly emancipated Africans in Cuba. If given special privileges they would set a bad example to slaves on the rural plantations. To prevent this, Pinillos advocated that the *emancipados* be treated as slaves, but if this suggestion was contrary to the treaty, as Pinillos knew it was, he proposed instead the removal of the *emancipados* from Cuba either to Africa or to a British West Indian colony – anything to get them out of Cuba, because 'the presence of large numbers of free Africans, still in a savage state, will be a disaster for the island'.

The *Fiscal* of the Council of the Indies rejected Pinillos' opinion that

the *emancipados* should be treated as slaves and he thought it very unlikely Britain would agree either to receive the liberated Africans in her
West Indian colonies or permit them to be returned to Africa. Pinillos'
third idea, that of distributing the *emancipados* among individuals and
institutions of the island, was a far better one and, if adopted, the
regulations drawn up by Kilbee were acceptable. The Council of the
Indies agreed with its *Fiscal* and recommended that the final disposi-
tion of the Africans and the regulations for their treatment be left
to the Captain-General. It did set down a guide, however, emphasizing 'that the Africans must be handed over to be employed either as
servants or as free labourers'.[7] How compatible this was with another
recommendation, that all the freed Africans fit to be labourers ought
to be transferred to plantation owners for field work, was not stated.
It was inconceivable that the treatment of newly emancipated Africans
and that of slaves would be different when both worked side by side
on a sugar plantation.[8] The evils feared by Kilbee were far more likely
to occur on a plantation away from Havana and official supervision,
but the Council of the Indies saw no such incompatibility between the
progress of Cuban agriculture and the well-being of the *emancipados*.

Captain-General Vives added his voice to those who trembled at the
thought of Cuba being inundated with liberated Africans. They could
spark off in the rest of the slave population 'ardent desires to achieve
their freedom'. He believed it would be much better for Cuba if the
same British cruisers who captured the slavers should then return
their cargoes of Africans to Africa.[9] The Spanish commissioners in
Havana expressed the same feeling in a report to the Minister of
Foreign Affairs in April 1825. They dwelt on the ever-present risk of
slave rebellion, now heightened by the new menace of the *emancipados*.[10] Both of these despatches were a direct consequence of the condemnation of the *Relámpago* and the release of its Africans, and both
were turned over to the Council of the Indies. Early in May, the
Council, after examining Vives' views, again rejected the idea of
repatriating the Africans and upheld its earlier proposals. Later on,
when it received the report of the Spanish commissioners, the Council
began to suspect collusion in Havana and was even less inclined to
reverse its previous decision.[11] One Councillor, Manuel Guazo, dissented. He agreed with the arguments from Cuba that freeing the
Africans from captured slave ships would be an even greater stimulus
to the Cuban slaves' natural desire for freedom. If the newly emancipated Africans co-existed with Cuba's slaves there would always be a
violent contrast between the two groups of Africans, making the

condition of slavery insupportable. His solution was to bring the *emancipados* to Spain where they could be put to work building roads, but he was alone in this recommendation.[12]

Notwithstanding the unsympathetic reception in the Council of the Indies to the petitions from Cuba, the campaign to remove the *emancipados* from the island continued. The year 1826 saw an increase in anti-slave trade activity by the British navy in the Caribbean and a significant rise in the number of slavers captured. Four were condemned by the Havana court and from these 685 Africans received certificates of emancipation.[13] Two weeks after the fourth ship, the *Nuevo Campeador*, had been condemned and its 237 Africans released, the *Ayuntamiento* of Havana petitioned the King for a solution to the *emancipado* question.[14] The dangers had not changed but had become more acute, and the *Ayuntamiento* saw the future of the island at stake. Its solution was to open negotiations with Britain to amend the 1817 treaty so that all captured slave ships would be taken to Sierra Leone for judgement. Not only would Havana be spared the dangerous presence of the liberated Africans, but the hated court of mixed commission with its British inquisitors would disappear. If this solution proved impossible, the *Ayuntamiento* pleaded that the Africans be returned to Africa as soon as the slaver carrying them had been condemned.

After a lengthy bureaucratic interval, the petition was referred to the Council of State where the variety of proffered solutions matched the complexity of the problem as seen from Spain's point of view.[15] They ranged from a suggestion that the *emancipados* be taken in lots of 300 to the Mosquito Coast where they would live in settlements run by clerics to a proposal that all of them be brought to Spain and the Balearic Islands. The Cardinal Archbishop of Toledo, the Bishop of León and the *Infante* were all adamant in their opposition to the admission to Spain of any emancipated Africans. There was fairly general agreement, however, on the need to negotiate with Britain modifications of the slave trade treaty. The final decision lay with the King, and Ferdinand adopted the plan put forward by his Foreign Minister.[16] This provided that all Africans emancipated under the provisions of the 1817 treaty were to be brought to Spain or to one of her European possessions where they would be employed as servants or free labourers. The costs of this operation would be met by Spam's share of the proceeds from the sale of condemned slavers and, if this proved to be insufficient, the Minister had advised that the difference be made up from a tax on the inhabitants of Cuba. Ferdinand did not think the time was ripe for negotiations with Britain. Spain would have to resolve the *emancipado* question herself.

A royal order, based on this decision, went out to Cuba at the end of April 1828.[17] After receiving it, Cuban officials decided they could not obey it. The Captain-General learned that the Spanish share of the money derived from the sale of the captured slavers was inadequate to pay for the transfer of the *emancipados* to the peninsula. He also revealed inadvertently to the British commissioners the Spanish plan for the disposal of the liberated Africans.[18] When word of this was relayed back to Britain, the proposals were examined in London by the King's Advocate. He concluded that Britain could not object if Spain wanted to remove the *emancipados* from Cuba, but Aberdeen, the Foreign Secretary, emphasized in a despatch to Britain's Minister in Madrid that Britain would insist upon a formal guarantee from Spain that the legal freedom of these Africans would be upheld in practice wherever they were taken.[19]

In any case it would have been impossible to carry out the projected transfer of the liberated Africans to Spain. The Havana *Ayuntamiento* had suggested that the Cuban government require merchant vessels to carry 50 *emancipados* each, at a cost of 7 1/2 pesos per *emancipado*. The Captain-General questioned this figure as a result of information supplied to him by Joaquín Gómez, the Sub-Prior of the Havana *Consulado* and one of Cuba's foremost slave traders. According to Gómez, 20 pesos per head would be the minimum cost of transporting the *emancipados* either to Europe or to Africa.[20] By 1831, the number of *emancipados* in Cuba had risen to 2,380 and, at 20 pesos per head, the total cost of removing them would be 47,600 pesos.[21] With the court of mixed commission unable to supply any funds and no other Cuban institution able or willing to underwrite the operation, the plan had to be abandoned. Captain-General Vives had been reluctant anyway to send the liberated Africans to Spain where they would have constituted, in his words, 'a mixture as indecent as they would be dangerous'.[22] Foreseeing the difficulties of carrying out the royal order, the Havana *Ayuntamiento* retracted its earlier opposition to the presence of the *emancipados* in the island and suggested they be employed on Cuban public works projects.[23]

Other Cuban corporations had not abandoned the idea of ridding Cuba of the *emancipados*. In a petition addressed to the Minister of the Indies in 1832, the *Junta de Fomento* called for the fulfilment of the 1828 royal order.[24] The *Junta* also asked for an alteration in the policy of distributing the *emancipados* as an interim measure. These newly emancipated Africans could have a very disruptive effect on Cuba's black population, both slave and free. Most *emancipados* were hired out by their masters and the *Junta* could see that comparisons between their situation and that of free black labourers was likely to cause trouble in both groups while the slaves could not help being affected by the example of emancipated Africans. The *Junta* wanted all *emancipados* to be assigned to corporations or institutions rather than to individuals to insulate them as much as possible from contact with slaves or free blacks and at the same time to provide a labour force for public works projects. In 1831 2,006 *emancipados* had been assigned to private individuals and only 374 to corporations, but this proportion began to change under the pressure of organizations like the *Junta de Fomento*. Captain-General Ricafort reported in 1833 that he had assigned over 400 to work on an aqueduct in Havana and the Madrid government later signified its approval of this use of the *emancipados*.[25]

Not even the obvious benefits of the utility of the *emancipados'* labour on public works projects overcame the authorities' fear of their revolutionary potential, a fear which grew as their numbers increased owing to continued British captures of Spanish slavers off Cuba. Nor did the Spanish officials admit to their own hypocrisy over the importation of Africans. The thousands of African slaves landed illegally in Cuba year after year were seen as a positive benefit to the island, but the hundreds of *emancipados* freed from the few slavers that were captured were a menace even though they were under the absolute control of the Cuban government. The Cuban authorities had such respect for the efficiency of the British navy in the Caribbean that they were able to conjure up a spectre of thousands of liberated Africans being landed in Havana and their shivers of panic were felt in Madrid.

The arrival in Havana on 7 June 1832 of the British cruiser *Speedwell* with her prize, the 300-ton *Águila*, transformed the panic into near hysteria. The *Águila* came with a human cargo of 616 Africans, 604 of whom lived to be declared *emancipados* after the ship had been condemned by the mixed court on 18 June.[26] Macleay, the British commission judge, accepted that there was cause for alarm. The lawlessness of the free black population of Havana was proverbial. 'Just before the arrival of the present Captain-General the negroes had reached such a pitch of audacity as to assault with daggers and rob in the streets at midday.'[27] News of the recent insurrection in Jamaica had added to the consternation.

Villanueva, the Intendant of Havana, approached Macleay in desperation to see if Britain would receive the Africans from the *Águila* at

Sierra Leone. The British judge replied that only an agreement between the British and Spanish governments could change the conditions governing the Africans taken from captured slavers. He did, however, encourage the idea of removing the Africans from Cuba in the account of the interview he sent to Palmerston, the British Foreign Secretary.[28] In Havana, at the urging of the Intendant, an emergency meeting of the three leading officials of the island was held.[29] Yet these men, the Captain-General, the Intendant and the Naval Commander, could not agree on the means to remove the liberated Africans, then totalling 3,800, nor on the destination should they be taken away. The Cuban authorities found themselves with no alternative but to petition the home government again, pleading for a quick solution, and in the meantime to distribute the Africans from the *Águila* among the corporations of the island.

There was little likelihood of a quick decision from Madrid where red tape and indecision entangled the question even more. A flustered official had to admit at the beginning of 1833 that all the information on the *emancipados* had been with the Council of Ministers since May 1831.[30] Not that this really mattered. None of the three state councils which had grappled with the problem had been able to agree on a solution. The Council of the Indies, the Council of State and the Council of Ministers were all hopelessly divided. Such were 'the opposed viewpoints, the conflict of rival interests and the growing number of complicated occurrences', that the only way out appeared to lie in the naming of a special committee to examine the connected problems of the Cuban slave trade and the liberated Africans.[31]

A three-man commission was appointed which presented its report to Francisco de Cea Bermúdez, the Spanish Minister of Foreign Affairs, in October 1833.[32] The commission discounted the Cuban authorities' fears of the dangers likely to arise from the number of *emancipados* in Cuba. After all, they accounted for only 1/80 of the black population of the island. If there were any legitimate apprehensions, these arose from the prospect of continual increases in their numbers due to more captures of Spanish slavers by British cruisers. To remedy this potential threat the commission had two solutions. The first was so obvious the commissioners wondered why no one had thought of it before. Negotiations ought to be begun with the government of Haiti to send all the liberated Africans there. An agreement to do that would offer all the advantages of convenience and cheapness. Secondly, since the accumulation of *emancipados* occurred where the court of mixed commission was located, Spain should move the court to Puerto Rico which did not have the same importance as a colony as did Cuba and where the ratio of whites to blacks was more favourable.

Even before the report had been written, events in Havana had superseded it. After Palmerston had received the despatch of the British commissioners in Havana, recommending British co-operation to facilitate the removal of the *emancipados* from Cuba, he approached the British Colonial Office for their reaction. An exchange of correspondence settled the conditions for the reception of the liberated Africans in Trinidad and these were sent to the British commissioners for transmission to the Cuban government.[33] There were three main conditions. One month's advance notice was to be given, Spain was to pay all the expenses and each shipload would have to contain an equal ratio of males and females so that the existing disproportion between male and female blacks in Trinidad would not be worsened. The conditions were in no way agreeable to the Cuban government, because they meant considerable expense and if Cuba had to send an equal number of male and female *emancipados* to Trinidad she would be left with a large excess of male liberated Africans thanks to the slave traders' practice of bringing over far more males than females.[34]

In spite of the objectionable nature of the conditions imposed by Britain, the appearance of cholera in Havana in the spring of 1833 acted as a catalyst in removing the remaining barriers to the transfer of some of the *emancipados* to Trinidad. Early in April the British schooner *Nimble* brought a captured slaver, the *Negrita*, into Havana with 196 Africans on board.[35] Although the Africans were comparatively healthy, considering their hazardous voyage and the harsh treatment meted out on the middle passage, after the condemnation of the *Negrita* the Captain-General resolved to send them to Trinidad. The Board of Health of Havana was afraid that in their weakened condition, the Africans liberated from the *Negrita* would be an easy prey to cholera and might then become the focus of a new wave of infection.[36] After this first transfer of *emancipados* from Cuba to a British colony, Captain-General Ricafort asked for and received permission to send all future *emancipados* to Trinidad.[37] The decision in Madrid to ratify the Captain-General's action came well before the special commission on the *emancipados* presented its report, so that when the report was presented its recommendations were set aside.

Before the end of 1833, British warships had brought in two more captured Spanish slavers, the *Joaquina* and the *Manuelita*. A considerable amount of haggling took place between the British commis-

sioners and the Captain-General before it was agreed to send all the
females from the two vessels with an equal number of males to
Trinidad. Those not sent to Trinidad were assigned to corporations
or to individuals. By March 1834, the British representatives and the
Cuban government had negotiated the conditions for future transfers
of *emancipados*. The commissioners' chief concern was to avoid
any more expense for the British government, while the Spanish
officials, particularly the Intendant, were so anxious to rid Cuba of
the liberated Africans that they agreed to bear the whole cost of the
transfers.[38] For the Governor of Trinidad it was an ideal arrangement
and it could not have come at a better time. Because of the abolition of
slavery in the British empire the year before, labour was at a premium
in the British West Indies. He wrote to the British commissioners in
February 1834, stating that he was ready to receive 1,000 liberated
Africans consisting of equal numbers of both sexes, provided that all
were healthy and under 30 and that the men had not lived in Cuba for
over two years, and as many 'fresh-captured Africans' as the Captain-
General wanted to send. The Intendant and the Captain-General were
delighted to have an outlet for any future shiploads of emancipated
Africans resulting from British captures, but nothing more was said
about the *emancipados* who had been in Cuba for some time.[39] They
were assigned and reassigned or took the place of dead slaves, the
value of their labour far outweighing whatever danger their presence
caused.

Only one other transfer of Africans to Trinidad occurred in 1834,
due to the reappearance of cholera in Havana. This caused the British
commissioners to call a halt for fear of transmitting cholera to Trinidad,
but in 1835 the removal continued. The female Africans from two captured slavers, the *María* and the *Tulita*, along with an equal number of
males, amounting in all to over 300, sailed for Trinidad in February,
and in August 268 more *emancipados* were sent.[40] The number of
liberated Africans removed from Havana to Trinidad in 1835 by no
means equalled the total freed from captured slavers in that year. Over
2,000 Africans became *emancipados* in Cuba in 1835, 1,631 males and
541 females, but of that number only 564 were transferred to Trinidad.
Another rumour of cholera had meant the cancellation of a proposed
transfer of 376 in May.[41] Altogether, over 1,100 *emancipados* went to
Trinidad in the latter 1830s. Had it not been for the British Colonial
Office's insistence on an equal ratio of males and females more undoubtedly would have gone, although how many it is hard to say.
Macleay, the British judge in Havana, hoped the rule would be waived

and the Governor of Trinidad was prepared to stretch it as far as he could to obtain more labourers.[42]

One real stumbling block, as the British commissioners were to discover later, was the reluctance of Cuba's new Captain-General, Tacón, to part with the liberated Africans.[43] Ironically, this Spanish change of attitude came at a time when other British Caribbean colonies, jealous of Trinidad's windfall, were clamouring for a share of the cheap African labour which the Cuban *emancipados* represented. The Superintendent of Belize wrote to the Havana commissioners that British Honduras could use 1,800 liberated Africans; the Governor of the Bahamas intimated he would accept the *emancipados* on his islands even if there was an excess of males; and the Governor of British Guiana sent his personal secretary to Havana to negotiate an agreement for the transfer of *emancipados*.[44] The squabbling and competition among British colonies over the distribution of the Africans liberated at Havana continued well into the 1840s. It was a worthless argument.

At Spain's insistence a not unwilling Britain agreed to receive into her colonies all Africans emancipated at Havana as a result of British captures under the revised Anglo-Spanish slave trade treaty signed in 1835. After the treaty came into force, however, the number of slavers captured and brought to Havana dropped off sharply because Cuban slave traders switched to using Portuguese and American flags. Between 1836 and 1841 six slavers were condemned at Havana and the Africans liberated as a result were sent off to British Honduras (two groups), the Bahamas (three groups) and Grenada (one group).[45] After 1841 at regular intervals a few *emancipados* were turned over to the British commissioners to be taken to Jamaica. From 1844 to 1849, 605 left Cuba in this manner, although there was a suspicion that not all of them were really *emancipados*. Testifying later before a Select Committee of the House of Lords, David Turnbull claimed that 'half, or more than half of them, are persons of free condition, or negroes who are no longer of value to the proprietors, or who are unwelcome to the authorities because they are troublesome . . .'.[46]

When it looked as if the transfer of liberated Africans from Havana to the British Caribbean colonies was going to grow into a sizeable movement, the British government had attempted to impose a veneer of humanity on this scramble for labourers. In regulations sent out to the Havana commissioners early in 1835, they were told that the Africans were not to be removed from Havana against their will except when 'a very extraordinary necessity' demanded quick action. To prevent any misunderstandings about the nature of the voyage, the Africans were to be told 'the plain truth', that is, what they should expect to find in the British colonies. This amounted, in the Duke of Wellington's words, to 'adequate maintenance and protection from injury, in return for moderate but regular labour'.[47] The criterion by which the commissioners were to operate in allocating the *emancipados* among the competing British colonies was the welfare of the Africans themselves. Where one colony offered better terms than another for the maintenance of the liberated Africans, it was to receive preference.[48]

For some time, however, the British commissioners had been more concerned about the *emancipados* who had remained in Cuba. Palmerston asked for a report at the end of 1831 on the condition of the liberated Africans in Cuba, since the British government had heard nothing about them for six years. The commissioners' report, early the following year, painted a bleak picture.[49] The Cuban officials resented any attempt by the British commissioners to interfere with the handling of the liberated Africans or to investigate their treatment. Naturally, the commissioners suspected that many *emancipados* had fallen victim to unscrupulous slaveowners whose practice it was to substitute liberated Africans for dead slaves, afterwards reporting the *emancipados* as runaways. Those who could be accounted for had been assigned to public institutions such as hospitals or the botanic garden or distributed by lot as domestic servants among officers' widows or government clerks, people who were too poor to buy slaves. Many of these people treated the *emancipados* humanely, and the commissioners favoured the assignment of *emancipados* to people who had never owned slaves. Cuba's black population, both slave and free, in general despised the liberated Africans and vilified them as English. As the commissioners admitted in their report, 'the name of *emancipado* or *Inglés* is among the Negroes of the Havana a term of opprobrium or derision'. The commissioners concluded that on paper the regulations governing the care and maintenance of the liberated Africans were adequate, although they were not permitted to ensure that the regulations actually were carried out in practice. What really surprised them was the fact that they had never heard of an *emancipado* being given his complete freedom at the end of the apprenticeship period. Without the definite hope of freedom, apprenticeship would amount to slavery under a different title.

Confirmation of the real state of the *emancipados* existed in abundance in Spain. If the Spanish government was unaware of the situation it could only have been because the reports of its own officials were left unread. The commission appointed in 1833 to examine the problem created by the liberated Africans confirmed that the majority of those assigned to private individuals promptly were taken to plantations and absorbed into the slave population.[50] A memorandum on the liberated Africans written for the Spanish Foreign Minister in 1835 made no secret of the abuses practised on the *emancipados*.[51] A long memorial on the slave trade by a man who had been a judge in Havana for nine years pointed out how easy it was to obtain forged documents which could transform a liberated African into a slave.[52]

In reality, the British commissioners in Havana, as Palmerston recognized, were powerless to do anything except to protest and refer whatever evidence they could collect back to London.[53] Palmerston had asked Kilbee, the former British judge in Havana, to draw up a new set of regulations to cover the care and distribution of the *emancipados*. In his reply Kilbee emphasized the necessity of empowering the British commissioners to oversee the observance of the regulations.[54] Palmerston tried to obtain such powers in the negotiations with Spain preceding the revised slave trade treaty of 1835, but the provisions he desired were completely unacceptable to Spain.[55]

Although the commissioners at Havana were restricted in their powers, they did probe and publicize the evils suffered by the *emancipados*. Macleay protested strongly to the Captain-General in 1834 about the latter's method of financing current public projects, as in the case of a new prison. The Captain-General had hit upon the idea of charging six ounces of gold for each male *emancipado* hired out and three ounces per female, a practice Macleay condemned as a breach of the slave trade treaty. The British judge also identified the man placed in charge of the assignment of *emancipados* as one of the island's worst slave traders. To the first accusation Captain-General Tacón merely replied that the six ounces of gold was a voluntary donation in aid of public works. When he reported this exchange to Madrid, Tacón white-washed his own conduct and accused Macleay of trying to discredit him in order to aid those who wanted to see Cuba independent, a tactic which earned the Captain-General the full support of the peninsular government.[56]

By 1836 the assignment price of an *emancipado* in Cuba had risen to nine ounces of gold, or a third of the cost of a slave. Reporting this to the British government, the commissioners also stated that when they made enquiries about the fate of recently liberated Africans they found that nearly all had been sent into the interior to work on sugar plantations.[57] Tacón made no secret of either hiring out *emancipados* for gold or employing the majority of them on sugar plantations.[58] He defended both practices openly as being beneficial and even necessary for Cuba. When he had arrived in 1834 as Captain-General, there had been well-founded suspicions that government employees were profiting themselves from the traffic in *emancipados*. He had cut this out and substituted a system of 'voluntary' contributions which went into a fund to finance public works. He saw nothing wrong in this since it did not affect the liberty of the Africans. The slave trade treaties and the regulations instituted by his predecessor, Vives, protected the freedom of the *emancipados* and Tacón promised that if anyone attempted to enslave or to sell an *emancipado* he would be punished with the full force of the law. Nothing in either treaty, said Tacón, prohibited the employment of *emancipados* on sugar plantations. To have them all congregated in Havana would add greatly to the already serious problem of the island's security. The rural areas 'offered more opportunity to care for the liberated Africans and greater facility to make them useful citizens, as well as to avoid any contact with suspicious members of the black population'. Such sophistry would not have deceived the British officials or any other perceptive observer, but it was enough for Tacón's superiors in Spain.

Tacón's successor, Ezpeleta, in 1838 firmly rejected a British proposal that all liberated Africans then in Cuba be taken to British colonies as the only places where decent treatment and liberty could be guaranteed.[59] Ezpeleta claimed that after a number of years in Cuba the *emancipados* had many ties to the island and coercion would be necessary to remove them, a means to which he was opposed. A rumour in 1839 that the Spanish government had ordered the transfer of all liberated Africans to British possessions filled the British commissioners with hope. They had concluded long ago that this would be the only way to alleviate the terrible persecution the *emancipados* were suffering in Cuba. The very name, *emancipado*, had become 'a by-word of scorn among the people of their class'.[60] British efforts to obtain Spanish agreement for the transfer of all the *emancipados* to British colonies doggedly continued but Spain was adamant in her rejections.[61] The impasse could not be broken before the arrival of David Turnbull as British consul in Havana in 1840 brought the *emancipado* issue to the forefront of the Anglo-Spanish conflict over the slave trade to Cuba.

Turnbull was well aware of the state of these unfortunate Africans.

He had exposed the abuses practised on the *emancipados* in his book on Cuba, and he went to Havana as British consul not only with a knowledge of the situation but with a stratagem to overcome it.[62] He had been in Havana scarcely a month before he brought the argument over the *emancipados* to the boil once more. The case of one *emancipado*, Gabino, had come to his attention. Gabino, who was working as a water-carrier, had been reassigned four times for a total of thirty-six ounces of gold since his ostensible liberation from the first captured Spanish slaver brought into Havana in 1824. Turnbull tried to secure the man's liberty by interceding with the Captain-General.[63] When this aroused the anger of the Captain-General to the point where he threatened to expel Turnbull from Cuba, the British consul adopted another tactic. He wrote to his colleagues, the British commissioners on the mixed court, stating that he had decided to bring Gabino's plight before the court as a test case to demonstrate publicly the injustice suffered by the *emancipado* class. Turnbull asked them to call Gabino before the court to determine whether he lived as a free man and whether he wanted to remain in Cuba or move to a British colony. The commissioners, however, heartily disliked Turnbull and disapproved of his methods. They condemned his initial intercession with the Captain-General because it jeopardized the negotiations they believed were underway between Britain and Spain to resolve the problem of the *emancipados*.[64]

The commissioners refused Turnbull's request that the court hear the case of Gabino on the grounds that this was not within the court's power.[65] Turnbull responded by forwarding a petition of Gabino's, addressed to the court, 'by himself and by me, as his proctor, Attorney and nearest friend'. The British consul said plainly that he would not regard the rejection of Gabino's petition as a defeat as long as it was publicly discussed. 'I am ready with another case, and after that, with a third, and a thousand until we, the representatives of the Government, and the mighty mind of England, shall at length have conquered the concession of the principle, that the Treaties for the Suppression of the Slave Trade, are not to be perpetually violated.'[66]

Turnbull was prevented even from having the petition heard. The British commissioners, after consulting their Spanish colleagues, emphasized that the functions of the court ceased as soon as the liberated Africans had been turned over to the Captain-General. It was left to Palmerston to resolve the stalemate between the British officials at Havana and, although he came down on Turnbull's side, he decided to take the matter up directly with Spain.[67] Palmerston instructed

Aston, the British Minister in Madrid, to reiterate the British demand that all the surviving liberated Africans in Cuba be brought before the mixed court and offered the choice of remaining in Cuba or moving to a British colony.[68] The British officials in Cuba were told to co-operate in determining the best way to remove the *emancipados* from the island and when this had been done they were to make preliminary arrangements with the Cuban government.[69] The new Captain-General, Valdés, when confronted with these British demands, played a delaying game in Havana while he attempted to convince his own government to reject the British plan.[70]

Valdés stressed that nothing in the slave trade treaties gave Britain the right to make such demands of Spain, but his real concern was political and it reflected the deep fear of British abolitionism then current in Cuba. To allow British agents under the mask of the mixed court to investigate the conditions of the liberated Africans would reduce the hold of the Cuban government over the African population and give the British commissioners added prestige in the eyes of Cuba's Africans. Given the conduct of past and present British agents, this might lead to the forced emancipation of all the slaves and the consequent loss of Spain's most important colony. Statistics on the *emancipados*, which Valdés had compiled, presented another reason for the Captain-General's uncomfortable position. Of an estimated 9,000 Africans included in this class at the end of June 1841, 3,216 were listed as dead and a further 189 as missing. The large number of deceased *emancipados* was explained to Madrid as the result of the cholera epidemic in 1833 and not the treatment they had received.[71] More than likely, many of those listed as dead were really alive as slaves which an investigation by British commissioners would have revealed, another reason for resisting it.

Valdés suggested that Spain could outflank Britain's demands by giving out certificates of emancipation to the *emancipados* as they finished their periods of apprenticeship. The process of liberation would last five years so that Cuba's free black population would not swell suddenly to an alarming level and by extending it over a number of years the plan could be tested in stages.[72] Designed mainly to keep the British officials at Havana from meddling further in the embarrassing controversy over the *emancipados*, Valdés' plan was approved in Madrid. Aberdeen, who succeeded Palmerston at the British Foreign Office in 1841, welcomed the plan when it was presented to him, although he wanted the five-year period shortened. Valdés refused on the grounds of Cuba's security.[73]

The British commissioners had strong suspicions of the real

reasons behind Valdés' action and were equally critical of the five-year duration of the liberation. In spite of these criticisms the plan was implemented and in the two years 1842–4, over 1,200 liberated Africans received their complete freedom.[74] Abuses occurred because the Africans were often victims of extortion, paying money out in return for false promises of liberty. The *emancipados* did not understand the grounds of selection used by the Cuban government, but hearing that other liberated Africans were obtaining freedom many were willing to try anybody in the hope of securing full liberty. While he remained in Havana, Turnbull pressed the commissioners to allow individual cases to be investigated by the mixed court, but the commissioners were reluctant to jeopardize the fate of the *emancipado* class as a whole by bringing forward individual complaints.[75]. Turnbull told a Select Committee of the House of Lords in 1850 that Britain had 'a clear right to demand the liberation of the emancipados now, and I am surprised that it has not been effectually carried out'.[76] His criticism reflected the collapse of Valdés' scheme in the aftermath of the Escalera conspiracy of 1844 and the failure of subsequent British representations to persuade Spain to free the remaining *emancipados*. Captain-General O'Donnell had stopped giving out certificates of emancipation right after the discovery of the 1844 conspiracy 'because it is an undeniable fact that the free men of colour were compromised en mass in that vast plot'.[77] Later, he modified this policy slightly and freed a few each month as a matter of form and in the vain hope of preventing British protests, but the majority of *emancipados* were not affected.

The *emancipados* remained after 1845, as they had been before, slaves in fact if not in law. Their freedom was a significant omission in the Spanish penal law on the slave trade passed in that year. As the apparently unending controversy over their fate went on between Britain and Spain, the only agreement was on the way the *emancipados* were treated and even this was never admitted publicly by Spanish officials. They were less reticent in private. Roncali, the Count of Alcoy, and a former Captain-General of Cuba (1848–50), wrote in 1853, 'the class of emancipados is simply an addition to the slaves, the only difference being that the emancipados are the property of the government'.[78] The British consul in Havana echoed this judgement sixteen years later: 'These poor wretches are neither more nor less than Government slaves.'[79] Over the years since the first *emancipados* had appeared in Havana they had become part of Cuba's slave population, in spite of Britain's struggle to free them, but unlike the remainder of Cuba's slaves, the *emancipados* were state slaves.

Actually, after 1845 there were three classes of *emancipados*, although within Cuba the distinctions meant little, since each group received the same treatment. Under the treaty of 1817 all slaves from captured slave ships which were condemned at Havana became the responsibility of the Cuban government. The treaty of 1835 laid down new conditions to govern the Africans liberated from captured slave ships. Those captured by British cruisers were to be turned over to the British authorities and freed in British territory, while all Africans found on slavers captured by Spanish cruisers were to remain in Cuba. Both governments guaranteed the liberty of the *emancipados* in their respective colonies. After 1845, all Africans seized from illegal slave landings in Cuba came under the provisions of the 1845 Spanish penal law and were categorized also as *emancipados*. The Cuban government classified all the *emancipados* according to the captured slaver which had brought them and assigned each *emancipado* to a master, whether a private individual or institution, for an apprenticeship period in return for a monetary payment. At the end of one assignment period, all the *emancipados* from a given slave ship were called in by the government and reassigned for a specified payment often to the same masters, to undergo an additional apprenticeship period. Under this system of perpetual reassignment, the *emancipados* had no chance to seek their own freedom under Cuba's *coartación* provisions which enabled slaves to make a down payment on the cost of purchasing their freedom and fixed the total price in what amounted to a contract of liberty between master and slave.[80] The *emancipados* suffered other disabilities as well. The British commissioners claimed in 1846 that they had never heard of a legal marriage among them.[81]

The total number of *emancipados* steadily increased after 1845 from the seizure of illegally introduced Africans by the Spanish authorities in Cuba. Statistics on the *emancipado* population of Cuba, published by the Spanish government in 1854, revealed that of 11,243 Africans liberated from captured slave ships to that date, just over 2,000 had been freed and remained in Cuba, over 1,000 had been sent to British colonies, 2,000 still existed as *emancipados* in Cuba and nearly 6,000 were dismissed, as 'dead, lunatic or disappeared'.[82] The 2,000 who were still classed as *emancipados* in 1854 were joined by a further 14,417 during the next twelve years.

The British government tried to act as guarantor of the rights of all the Cuban *emancipados*, a role which Spain refused to accept. Yet, as the reports of the abuses practised on the *emancipados* multiplied, Spain could not evade the British denunciations. Britain renewed her demand for the immediate liberty of all *emancipados* in 1846 after Palmerston learned that Captain-General O'Donnell had assigned 370 *emancipados* to his wife, giving her a monthly income in excess of £800.[83] The assignment and reassignment of *emancipados* had become a topic of public conversation in Havana which prompted a Palmerstonian comment: 'So much for the good Faith of the Havannah government. I suppose the Emancipados handed over from Time to Time for Exportation to Jamaica, are the halt and the blind, the aged and impotent who cannot light lamps or sweep Streets.'[84] By 1847 the reassignment of *emancipados* had developed into a traffic, so great was the demand for labour in Cuba, and the victims of it had become unwilling objects of speculation.[85] British protests availed little. Spain was determined not to deliver the *emancipados* to the British, not least because of a fear of their being trained as abolitionist agents in order to return to Cuba.[86]

There was no desire in Spain or in Cuba to improve the lot of the *emancipados*. Their labour was ever more valuable; the revenue gained from assigning them could be put to many uses, personal and public; and any change in the direction of greater freedom might cause complications in a slave society dominated by a rich and influential planter class. José de la Concha, who went out to Cuba as Captain-General in 1850, carried with him instructions to examine the *emancipado* problem in order to find a solution which would allay British suspicions without actually giving up possession of the *emancipados*. Acting on the orders he had been given, Concha created a special commission to oversee the education and development of the *emancipados* and to award certificates of freedom to those who had completed their apprenticeship term.[87] British officials in Havana saw Concha's reform simply as a means of reclaiming *emancipados* who had been assigned under previous Captains-General in order to reassign them, thereby producing extra revenue for the Cuban government.[88]

Concha believed the greatest abuse connected with the *emancipados* was the lack of uniform rates for their assignment which led to a speculative traffic. He was determined to reform this, but his instructions to his commission reveal he was no less determined to maintain the benefits. The *emancipados* would continue to be a supplementary labour force to augment slave labour on the sugar plantations, to work on state public works and to act as a form of pension for retired soldiers or their widows. Part of the revenue from the reassignment of *emancipados* went into a fund from which pensions were paid to the children of Spanish officials or soldiers who had served in Spain's American colonies prior to their independence. Having been born in Argentina, Concha showed more sympathy for the plight of Spanish veterans than for that of the *emancipados*. Another of his schemes was to use some of the *emancipado* funds to finance a school of engineering. Nearly all of the 600 engineers working on Cuba's plantations and railways were North Americans and they were suspected of spreading annexationist propaganda. At the end of his first term as Captain-General (1850–2) Concha believed he had reformed the abuses of the *emancipado* system, investing the revenue from the assignment of *emancipados* for the public good, but his concept of the public good did not embrace the welfare either of the *emancipados* or of Cuba's African population in general.[89]

Within Spain, the Ministry of Foreign Affairs and the Colonial Ministry both wrestled with the *emancipado* problem, because the gravity and complexity encompassed both internal and external ramifications. The Colonial Ministry ultimately was responsible for the regulations governing the treatment of the *emancipados* within Cuba, although Britain had an acknowledged treaty right to make enquiries. Because the *emancipados* had become state slaves and Spain had not fulfilled her promise to free them, the Spanish government found itself in an acutely embarrassing situation made worse by the need for British support against American threats to annex Cuba. If the Spanish authorities gave Britain proof of the real condition of the *emancipados*, Britain would have powerful ammunition for stronger measures in the fight against the Cuban slave trade; if Spain did nothing British protests would be unrelenting and there would be no British aid to counter United States designs on Cuba. Thus, for the sake of preserving Cuba, Spain sought a way out of the *emancipado* dilemma which would satisfy Britain's demands without disturbing the delicate equilibrium within Cuba.

The real pressure for the liberation of the *emancipados* came from British officials in Cuba. Frustrated and chagrined in their inability to check the growing slave trade, they fastened on the treatment of the *emancipados* as proof of Spanish duplicity. Crawford, Britain's consul-general at Havana, lamented at the beginning of 1852 that the day of final liberation for the *emancipado* is 'far, far off, if it ever does come' and urged the British government to insist that all the *emancipados* originally captured by British cruisers be freed immediately.[90] By 1852 the reassignment of the *emancipados* had become one of the most lucrative operations in Cuba, bringing in 80,000 dollars during the two years of Concha's government. For Crawford, 'the Emancipado's case is more hopeless than that of the Slave. He has no master whose good nature he may propitiate and so gain his freedom, he is nobody's property, consequently he is beyond price, no one can buy his freedom and still he toils on, dealt with as a Slave of the worst description for no one has any interest in him, so, like a beast of burden, he is made to perform one task after another and has no hope.'[91]

During the short-lived Derby administration in 1852, Malmesbury, who had become Foreign Secretary, took up the question of the *emancipados*. He benefited from the advice of his able Parliamentary Under-Secretary, Lord Stanley, son of the Prime Minister, who had visited Cuba two years before and had acquired first-hand knowledge of the state of the liberated Africans.[92] Together, Malmesbury and Stanley decided to press Spain for the strict fulfilment of the 1835 treaty which stipulated that the Cuban Captain-General must keep a register of *emancipados* and give an account every six months to the mixed court. By trying to force Spain to comply with this provision, the Foreign Office wanted to bring the *emancipado* register into the open so that the British judge could discover the real fate 'of men, women and children with regard to whom it may be said that the designation of Emancipado is more a mockery than a name'.[93] British statistics showed that, of 7,040 Africans liberated at Havana under the 1817 treaty, only 3,040 adults and 506 children, or approximately half of the total number, actually had received their freedom. Of these only 585 adults had been freed between 1844 and 1852, although Spain had promised to free them all by 1846. The resulting flow of diplomatic protests had no effect whatsoever in Cuba where the Captain-General used Cuba's precarious position to defend his refusal to release any information.[94]

With the American annexationist threat stronger than ever at the beginning of 1853, Spain desperately needed British support and now the *emancipado* problem assumed even larger dimensions as an obstacle in the way of that support. In these circumstances the Spanish government decided to reform the *emancipado* system itself, and the Council for Colonial Affairs (*Consejo de Ultramar*) set out guidelines for a new policy early in March. These committed Spain to freeing all the Africans liberated under the 1817 treaty as soon as their term of assignment ended with the whole operation to be completed by the end of 1853. The Council favoured liberalizing the terms of apprenticeship for Africans liberated under the provisions of the 1835 treaty, but did not recommend freeing them. Roncali, then Spanish

Foreign Minister and a former Captain-General of Cuba, overruled
the Council on this point, ordering that Africans liberated under the
1835 treaty should be freed after a five-year apprenticeship. A royal
order embodying these provisions went out to the Captain-General
at the end of March 1853.[95]

Roncali was so anxious to have some proof of Spanish good faith
to win back British confidence that he released the new Spanish policy
to the British even before the details had gone out to Havana. Lord
Howden, the British Ambassador in Madrid, was impressed with the
Spanish government's courage in putting forward a measure which
was bound to be unpopular with the Cuban planters, and he recommended that Britain accept it even though it did not meet her
demand for the immediate freedom of all *emancipados*.[96] The British
Foreign Secretary, now Lord Clarendon, happily accepted the plan
and quickly gave it to the Secretary of the British and Foreign Anti-
Slavery Society as evidence of what British pressure on Spain could
achieve. Clarendon also used the information to quiet the angry
criticisms of Spain's conduct in the British Parliament.[97]

In spite of the frenzied diplomacy in Europe over the Cuban
emancipados, Captain-General Cañedo had no intention of implementing the new policy. To free a large number of Africans would
set a tantalizing example to Cuba's slaves, and Cañedo, too, was convinced that unscrupulous British abolitionists would mobilize the
freed *emancipados* to foment race war in the island. Spain could not
afford to back down from its published policy and new orders were
sent to the Captain-General lengthening the period for freeing the
emancipados but insisting the policy must be carried out.[98] By the time
the orders arrived, Cañedo was no longer in Cuba. He had been
replaced by Juan de la Pezuela, a dedicated reformer who is remembered as one of Cuba's most enlightened Captains-General. Unfortunately for the *emancipados* his enlightenment did not extend to
them. Shortly after Pezuela arrived in the island, he took advantage
of the birthday of the heir-apparent to the Spanish throne to issue a
decree of freedom for the *emancipados*, but in Cuba real freedom for
these Africans was an ever-receding mirage. Pezuela's decree, supplemented by more detailed regulations issued on 1 January 1854,
really announced a revised scheme of government-regulated apprenticeship. The *emancipados* who already had undergone years of
assignment were to be apprenticed to masters for renewable periods
of one year. Their wages were fixed at 8 dollars per month for adult
males and 6 dollars for adult females, of which a quarter was retained

for the government-run *emancipado* fund. The commission originally created by Concha was to oversee Pezuela's plan but under a new name, the 'Commission for the Protection of the Emancipados'. The very word 'protection' implied that the *emancipados* could not look after themselves and needed the services of the state as guardian. Pezuela's reform was a cosmetic one leaving the real state of the *emancipados* unchanged. When his decree was analysed in London, a Foreign Office official minuted, 'this concession is so fettered with restrictions that it will probably turn out a mere illusion' – a sad but correct prophecy.[99]

Britain welcomed Pezuela's severe crackdown on the slave trade and did no more than register a formal protest that the *emancipados* had not received their complete freedom.[100] Pezuela himself served less than a year as Captain-General. He was a casualty of the Spanish revolution in the summer of 1854 and José de la Concha returned to Cuba for a second term as Captain-General (1854–9). He was determined to restore the planters' confidence in Spanish colonial government, badly shaken by Pezuela's liberal reforms, and the *emancipados* were one of the groups to feel his iron grip. Concha believed Pezuela's concept of freedom for them was unworkable in practice and dangerous even to contemplate, but he skilfully used Pezuela's outline as the basis of a much more rigorous apprenticeship programme. Under it, all liberated Africans were to be assigned to masters for a five-year period to begin with, during which all their wages would go into the *emancipado* fund, and then for renewable periods of three years under the same conditions as Pezuela's ordinance had laid down, i.e. fixed wage rates of 8 dollars per month for adult males and 6 dollars for adult females, of which one quarter went into the *emancipado* fund. The *emancipados* were not free at any stage to choose their own masters. They were assigned at the discretion of the Cuban government, the majority still being forced to work on the sugar plantations. The state reserved for itself the right to the services of any *emancipados* needed for public works or other government tasks and the Captain-General kept the *emancipado* fund apart from other government revenues for his own uses. Concha's regulations also enshrined his original idea of assigning *emancipados* to widows of Spanish officers or to charitable institutions both as a form of pension and as slaves in fact if not in name.[101]

British officials viewed Concha's measure as a greater betrayal of Spain's promise to free all the *emancipados* than any of the previous decrees, but British protests could not make him change his mind. He

justified his approach on the grounds that without constant guard-
ianship the Africans quickly would become slaves. His own investigations had revealed that 3–4,000 *emancipados* had been converted into
slaves over the past thirty years in such a fraudulent manner that it
was impossible to trace the victims.[102] Some *emancipados* complained
themselves to Crawford, the British consul-general in Havana, about
their compulsory apprenticeship, the low wages – much lower than
those paid to free blacks – and the tax of one quarter on all their
earnings, but Britain was powerless to help them. The system Concha
had instituted first in 1850 and then revised in a much stricter form in
1855 lasted virtually without alteration for another decade.

The principle that the *emancipados* were entitled to complete freedom at the end of an initial five-year apprenticeship was never
challenged in Spain. It was reaffirmed every time the government
examined the subject, but peninsular orders could not penetrate the
thicket of planter objections in Cuba and successive Captains-
General disregarded the wishes of Madrid to conciliate the Havana
plantocracy. In 1861 Captain-General Serrano asked his government
to approve the reassignment of *emancipados* but when, after nearly a
year and a half, the Council of State finally considered his request it
discovered that some *emancipados* had been reassigned for periods in
excess of twenty years. The Council's report had to admit that 'justice
clamours for total liberty for those who have completed a five year
apprenticeship', and attempted to come up with a solution to reconcile their right to liberty with the arguments advanced by Serrano
stressing the security risk if all of them were freed at once. The Council
proposed to free them in three stages beginning with those who had
served longest. In future all *emancipados* were to be conceded absolute
liberty at the end of a five-year apprenticeship. A royal order went out
to Cuba in December 1862, instructing the Captain-General to implement this policy.[103]

General Dulce, Serrano's successor as Captain-General, had no
intention of changing what had worked so well for his predecessors
and he ignored the royal order. Nor had the treatment accorded to
the *emancipados* improved. Terming them 'the most wretched of
human beings', John Crawford, acting British consul in Havana,
confirmed in 1863 that they were being persecuted in every imaginable
way:

They are cheated out of their wages and are subjected to every species of
punishment. They are sold or rather they are transferred for a consideration

generally amounting to from 170 dollars to 204 dollars and terrible abuses are committed on the friendless 'Emancipado' such as reporting him dead whereas he has been made to fill the place of a defunct Slave.[104]

Crawford's denunciation was sent on to the Spanish government and, although it produced no immediate results, it did set in train a lengthy process of reform.[105] Senior civil servants in the Colonial Ministry in Madrid agreed that Spain was responsible for ensuring that no *emancipado* should be treated as a slave and all were entitled to their complete freedom upon the expiry of their apprenticeship terms. General Dulce was asked at the beginning of 1864 to make his own suggestions for cleaning up the *emancipado* problem.[106]

Almost another year went by with no reply from Havana, but the Spanish civil servants who had initiated the enquiry were determined to draw up a set of new regulations to replace those instituted by Concha. These revised regulations did not receive the Council of State's approval until June 1865. Their main purpose was to ensure the freedom of all the *emancipados* at the end of a five-year apprenticeship. The Council insisted 'there is absolutely no cause or reason whatsoever to deprive the emancipados of their freedom by creating a class half free and half slave and by denying them the complete product of their labour. This class must disappear.'[107] Spain now had the example of Brazil before her in the question of the *emancipados* as in the general subject of the slave trade. Brazil freed her *emancipados* in 1863 and 1864, but Brazil's example does not seem to have made any significant impression on Spain. In so far as Spain was ready to redeem a long-standing pledge, it was done to grant overdue justice to the *emancipados* and to fulfil her treaty obligations.[108]

Once again, the interests of the Cuban plantocracy dictated Spain's colonial policy even to the point of overruling decisions of the Spanish Council of State. General Dulce would not enforce the new regulations. To do so, he argued, might imply a prelude to a general emancipation with all its attendant perils. Dulce revealed what a gulf lay between colonial and peninsular images of the African in his complaint that a five-year apprenticeship for the liberated African was too short: 'By his very nature, the African is indolent and lazy, and to give him liberty, something which he has not known even in his own country, will make him into a vagabond.' Dulce also was very angry that the new regulations referred to Spain's treaty obligations. To admit any right of British interference in the matter of the Cuban *emancipados* would be humiliating to Spanish independence.[109]

The Liberal Union government headed by O'Donnell, also a former Captain-General of Cuba (1844–8), which came to power in Spain in the summer of 1865 committed itself to a policy of cautious reformism and, as a first step it resolved to clear up the *emancipado* imbroglio even if this meant going against the wishes of the Captain-General and the Cuban plantocracy. With slavery and possibly Cuba's very existence as a Spanish colony in the balance, the *emancipado* issue could not be permitted to cause further trouble. As a secret royal order to Captain-General Dulce explained, Spain had to sacrifice something to the clamour of world public opinion, poisoned against her by the slave trade, in order to have time to prepare a natural and gradual solution to the question of slavery, free from conflict of any sort.[110]

At the end of October 1865, Spain made public a further royal decree with even stronger provisions. The power to assign *emancipados* was removed from the Captain-General; all *emancipados* who had been in Cuba for five years were to be freed when their existing assignments terminated; and any Africans liberated from captured slave ships in future were to be transported to Africa to Spain's possession of Fernando Po or to the African mainland.[111] Spain achieved her aim of favourable international publicity over her decision to free the *emancipados*, but it still proved impossible to overcome the entrenched vested interests in Cuba. Before General Dulce knew of his government's decision on the *emancipados*, he had reassigned a large number and called in many more to renew their assignments. He was not prepared to go back on contracts with Cuban planters. He set aside the royal decree, justifying his action by the effects the loss of the *emancipados'* labour would have on the sugar harvest and the alarm the publicity had caused to Cuba's slaveowners.[112]

This time the Spanish government would not bow to Cuban protests. The Captain-General was told to calm the planters' fears about imminent emancipation. Spain had no intention of freeing the slaves. Madrid was not at all sympathetic to planter concerns about the loss of labour from freeing the *emancipados*. There were over 75,000 Cuban slaves in domestic service or other work in which free men could take their place. Since there were only 6,650 *emancipados* eligible to receive their freedom, they could be replaced by 1/10 of the slaves in domestic service. While the debate between Havana and Madrid over the effect of freeing the *emancipados* went on, their actual day of liberation kept being postponed. General Dulce recalled the *emancipados* from 33 captured slave ships in March 1866, but few masters complied with the recall order. Under pressure from the planters, Dulce then adopted the device of renting them out for the sugar harvest.[113] By April 1867, Madrid was horrified to discover that the original decree of October 1865 had not been enforced and angrily ordered full and immediate compliance.[114] Yet not until September 1869 did the Cuban government begin the process of distributing certificates of freedom to the *emancipados*. The British consul in Havana tartly observed that 'tardy justice is certainly better than no justice at all', but these 'government slaves' were not even to receive tardy justice.[115]

The many declarations of freedom for the *emancipados* were crowned by a special clause in Spain's first law to abolish slavery, the Moret Law of July 1870, granting the *emancipados* the immediate and full exercise of the rights of free men.[116] But it was clear to observers in Cuba and especially to British officials there, that the ringing declarations of freedom from the peninsula became mere empty words in Cuba. Once ostensibly freed, the *emancipados* were contracted out, supposedly of their own free will, to their former masters for a six-year period 'and are *in all other respects* to be treated as slaves . . . '.[117]

Backed up by British public opinion, the British government mounted another diplomatic campaign of protest, feeling totally betrayed by Spain's long series of broken promises. Spain remained deaf to these British complaints. In the midst of a ten-year civil war in Cuba, the Spanish government was loath to adopt any stronger measures which might alienate planters loyal to the metropolis.[118] As late as 1876 Britain still protested the treatment suffered by the Cuban *emancipados*. An edict of the Captain-General, published in Havana in February 1876, was seen as proof of Spain's failure to give them genuine freedom, even under her own laws which required it.[119] The 26,000 *emancipados* were the intended beneficiaries of the Anglo-Spanish slave trade treaties of 1817 and 1835. Instead they became victims. Their fate was mocked by their very name and their tragedy certainly approximated that of the Africans who were not liberated from the slave ships landing clandestinely and illegally in Cuba after 1820.

CHAPTER 14

The abolition of the Cuban slave trade

The year 1861 was an unlikely one for optimistic predictions about a quick end to the Cuban slave trade. In 1859, and again two years later in 1861, more slave-trading expeditions set out for Africa than at any time since 1820 when the African slave trade had been declared illegal within the Spanish empire. British estimates of slave importations into Cuba during the three years 1859–61 were the highest in forty years; a total of 79,332 African slaves had been added to the Cuban slave population, thought to number 370,553 in 1861, and there was every expectation that the Cuban slave trade would carry on at the same high level.[1] The open participation of American ships and capital, combined with improvements in maritime technology, had transformed the African slave trade. Large steamships were supplanting smaller sailing vessels as the main carriers of slaves. The number of slaves who could be transported in a single expedition rose dramatically. Two steamships alone accounted for 3,000, or approximately 10% of the slaves introduced into Cuba in 1859; one steam vessel in 1860 brought a cargo of 1,500 African slaves.[2]

Technological improvements also were transforming the Cuban sugar economy, increasing its productive capacity and aggravating the labour shortage which the planters traditionally had resolved through the slave trade. Cuba's sugar estates had expanded rapidly in both number and size during the middle years of the nineteenth century, an expansion which the adaptation of steam power had accelerated. The construction of railroads enabled planters to overcome Cuba's transportation problems and to open up hitherto inaccessible areas to sugar cultivation, but the building of railroads added to the demand for labour. In part, railroad companies met the demand by initiating a system of contract labour, bringing in indentured Asians and using *emancipados* hired out from the government. But the question of labour in all its complexity, including slavery and the slave trade which fed it, hung as a menacing cloud over Cuba, then entering what one Cuban historian has termed the age of latifundia.[3]

The capital costs of starting a sugar estate were so high by 1860 that only rich capitalists or companies could contemplate such a venture. The most efficient and most profitable plantations were the largest ones, founded or reorganized during Cuba's railway age.[4] High costs were slowly driving out the small sugar cultivators. Just as the other costs of running a plantation rose during this period, so did the price of slaves as the demand for them increased and the supply through the slave trade fluctuated. By 1860, the average price of a slave exceeded 1,000 Spanish dollars, double or triple the average price in the first half of the century.[5] Only the very richest Spaniards or Cubans could afford to outfit a slave-trading expedition, but the enormous profits to be made and the unceasing demand for slaves offered tempting incentives for those with the necessary capital.

The nineteenth-century 'sugar revolution' in Cuba, to use Franklin Knight's phrase, did not imply an immediate cessation of the slave trade even if it laid the groundwork for the ultimate replacement of slave labour. If anything, it stimulated the reverse, an expansion of the trade as the only way to procure the slaves. The figures of slave importations on the eve of the American Civil War bear this out. Not even the influx of thousands of Chinese indentured labourers during the 1850s reduced the demand for African slaves. Yet within six years after 1861, the Cuban slave trade was extinct. Technological change within Cuba was not responsible. The slave trade to Cuba had been crushed by a powerful combination of international forces.

The outbreak of the Civil War in the United States created the conditions in which the Cuban slave trade finally could be extinguished, although the remnants lingered on until after the end of the American struggle. The major powers involved in the suppression – Britain, the United States and Spain – each had to adopt new and stronger measures, and even then it took time for these to be effective. Britain was the first country to initiate a more aggressive policy, a change which arose out of the deep frustrations felt by all members of the British government and Parliament at Britain's continued and humiliating failure to end the Atlantic slave trade.

Reports from Cuba at the beginning of 1861 confirmed how solidly entrenched the slave trade was in the fabric of Cuban society. Joseph Crawford, who had served nineteen years as British consul-general at Havana and whose knowledge of the island was unrivalled, wrote in bleak despair: 'There is no intention on the part of the Spanish Government or its Officers to carry out the provisions of the [Slave Trade] Treaty.' He could only advise his government that 'we have therefore now to abandon our efforts of persuasion with Spain to put an end to the traffic . . . and proceed to the immediate adoption of the most energetic measures to compel its observance, or submit to the machinations of these people who have hitherto succeeded in rendering that Treaty a dead letter'.[6]

Palmerston, the British Prime Minister, shared similar feelings. He admitted during a debate on the slave trade in the House of Commons in February 1861 that the number of slaves illegally brought to Cuba had been increasing. There was no doubt in his mind who was to blame: 'When we come to speak of Spain it is impossible to express too strongly one's sense of indignation at the profligate – (cheers) – shameless – (cheers) – and disgraceful bad faith – (cheers) – with which the Spanish nation have acted in regard to those treaties contracted with England on this matter – (renewed cheering) – . . . Well, no doubt Spain has given us good cause for war, if we had thought proper to avail ourselves of it.'[7] This gloves-off denunciation of Spain obviously had widespread, if not unanimous, support in the British House of Commons, but it brought angry rejoinders from the Spanish government. Palmerston was completely unrepentant. He even ordered the Foreign Office to prepare a memorandum 'of the strongest expressions of remonstrance and reproach used in official communications to the Spanish Government since 1835 on the nonfulfilment of their engagements respecting the Slave Trade'. After reading it, the Prime Minister commented: 'These Reproaches and Remonstrances would have been more than enough, if addressed to any Government actuated by the slightest Feeling of national Honor and Good Faith. General O'Donnell's Indignation at what I said in the House of Commons is that of a Housebreaker accused of having plundered a House which he had swept clean.'[8] The message was plain. Reproaches and remonstrances had failed and now Britain would have to see what other means were available to her.

This more aggressive mood was evident in various places, although not all the advice received by the government was practical. A British merchant in Havana, after surveying Cuban corruption, wrote: ' . . . The only remedy is to back the Americans to acquire the island. By that method the trade will be stopped. Spain will not be able to increase her fleet. We shall be able to recall ours from the African coasts, and in the way of commerce we shall be gainers.'[9] Palmerston was not prepared to go that far in the 1860s any more than he had been in the 1850s. In any case, the American Civil War buried American annexationism for the time being.

The most surprising example of militancy came from the British and Foreign Anti-Slavery Society which from its foundation had been dedicated to a pacific approach to the twin evils of the slave trade and slavery. The Society arranged to hold a conference at Lord Brougham's house in the middle of June 1861 to discuss measures which Britain might use to stop the Spanish slave trade. From the resolutions circulated in advance of the conference, it is clear that the Society had come to the point of abandoning its pacifism where Spain was concerned, so great was the crime which Spain continued to commit with impunity. The Society's remedies constituted a radical break with its past traditions. Britain should sever diplomatic relations with Spain until the Cuban slave trade ended, and at the same time Britain should apply the principle of the Aberdeen Act of 1845 to Spain to force the suppression of the slave trade upon her. These proposals were too drastic for some of the organizations the Society was trying to recruit into its common front, notably the African-Aid Society. The Council of the African-Aid Society refused to endorse either the severing of diplomatic relations with Spain or the application of the principle of the Aberdeen Act to her. The former likely would have no positive results and might inconvenience British trade while the latter would be resisted by Spain and thus could be the cause of a general European war. The Council urged moderation: 'Evil as the African Slave-Trade is, and none can hold it in greater abhorrence than they do, the Council would not risk a general European war for its problematical suppression.'[10]

The slave trade conference held on 15 June 1861 and attended by a number of prominent M.P.s and abolitionists, with Lord Brougham in the chair, agreed on a series of resolutions to be presented to the British government.[11] Their tone and substance were considerably more moderate than the draft resolutions circulated in advance, but the hostility to Spain and Cuba was very marked as was the conviction 'that if the Cuban Slave-market were closed, the transatlantic Slave-trade from the African continent would cease'. Spain's excuses could be tolerated no longer. As the third resolution put it: 'remonstrances have been tried to the utmost extent compatible with the national honour and dignity; and . . . the gravity of the case imperatively demands a more energetic course'. On a practical level, the conference suggested that steps be taken to obtain the active co-operation of the United States, and that Britain re-establish consular posts on both the African east and west coasts. Legitimate commerce should be encouraged by every means possible and treaties should be signed with chiefs of African areas where the slave trade still was carried on.

The Executive Committee of the British and Foreign Anti-Slavery Society transmitted the resolutions to Lord John Russell, the Foreign Secretary, at the beginning of July. They admitted the failure of diplomacy to bring about an end to the Cuban slave trade. Stronger measures now had to be taken. Without specifying what these would be, they pointed out that Britain had 'many resources all short of actual hostility, which, if employed with determination and vigour, would probably produce a satisfactory result'.[12] The slave trade conference marked the beginning of a steady, but not notably successful, campaign by the British and Foreign Anti-Slavery Society to bring pressure on the British government to force Spain to comply with the slave trade treaties. The abolitionists at least managed to keep the problem of the continuing slave trade to Cuba before the British public.[13]

The American Civil War was the chief preoccupation of the British abolitionists during the first half of the 1860s, but the Cuban slave trade was not forgotten. Nor did British abolitionist agitation go unnoticed in Spain. Early in 1862, the Spanish consul in Newcastle sent a report to his government of an abolitionist meeting he had attended. Although he played down its importance by remarking on the poor attendance of people he categorized as from the lower classes, he forwarded their resolutions condemning Spain's lax repression policy. The militant mood of northern British abolitionists was summarized in a very strong editorial of the *Northern Daily Express*, which the consul also enclosed: 'We cannot submit to be fooled by an insignificant nation like Spain. Our Government must be roused to decisive action; and if Spain will not fulfil her bargain, let her be excluded from the comity of nations ... Let us treat Spain, if she perseveres in her course of truce-breaking and cruelty, as we would treat any individual who had been guilty of similar crimes.'[14] Petitions for more effective action against the Cuban slave trade also came from the British West Indies.[15]

The British government's own thinking was in tune with the advice it was receiving. Britain would have to suppress the remaining Atlantic slave trade on her own because Spain repeatedly had demonstrated her refusal to co-operate. But how best to do it? What became the basis of the new policy was a suggestion contained in a memorandum sent to the Foreign Secretary in 1861 by Captain Wilmot, a veteran of service with the West African Squadron. He was certain Britain could wipe out the slave trade herself by concentrating her efforts on the west coast of Africa. He advocated a close naval blockade of the coast to prevent the embarkation of slaves, coupled with a mission to the King of Dahomey to persuade him to give up slave-trading. There was no risk of breaking treaties or insulting the flags of friendly nations by stopping the embarkation of slaves. Wilmot planned to put the slave dealers out of business by attacking them where they were most vulnerable, the supply of slaves to the slave traders. Whatever the defects of his proposal, at least it had the merit of being new. As he said himself: 'Let us then try the plan – all others have as yet failed.'[16]

The essence of Wilmot's plan was endorsed at all levels of the Foreign Office, although initially the Admiralty objected strongly to parts of it.[17] Because only about 300 miles of the West African coast-line were now infected by the slave trade, an effective naval blockade of this area did seem possible. The worst region was in the neighbour-hood of Whydah, under the control of the King of Dahomey, and British officials agreed that a combination of force, on land and sea, was the best way to accomplish their objective. Wylde, the head of the Slave Trade Department, admitted: 'Experience has, I think, proved that the only effective means of putting a stop to the Slave Trade is by using a certain amount of coercion.'[18]

Although officials in the Foreign Office and Russell, the Foreign Secretary, favoured Wilmot's idea of a close naval blockade, Pal-merston came down in favour of an attack on Whydah:

I quite concur in the opinion that a Blow judiciously struck at [the] Slave Trade on Land would be more effectual than our efforts by sea, because it would go to the root of the Evil. The present is a good Time for Exertion, because it is likely that the civil war in America will divert from [the] Slave Trade Capital and Ships which would otherwise be employed in it, and that fewer ships will sail from New York or Boston to the Coast of Africa, while none will go thither from the Confederate States. The King of Dahomey & the other Chiefs will therefore have fewer Customers, and will be more likely to listen to Reason.

Our first object ought, I think, to be to stop the slave-trade from Whydah . . . I believe that with the present King [of Dahomey] instead of a word and a Blow, we ought to administer a Blow and a word – we begin by taking Possession of Whydah and either tell him why, or wait until he asks us why, and then tell him it is to prevent the export of Slaves . . . It is only the strong arm that can prevail with these Barbarians.[19]

The Foreign Office and the Prime Minister backed the use of the 'strong arm', as Palmerston put it, to take advantage of the oppor-tunity presented by the American Civil War and finish the Atlantic slave trade once and for all. Yet, in spite of the apparent agreement on an attack against Whydah, it was never carried out. The annexation of Lagos in August 1861 was as far as British expansion in West Africa was to go until the 1880s.[20] Faced with stubborn Admiralty resistance to a conquest of Whydah, Russell settled for a diplomatic mission to the King of Dahomey, as Wilmot originally had proposed, and Wilmot was the man chosen to carry it out. He spent two months in Dahomey at the end of 1862 and the beginning of 1863 in a futile attempt to convince the king to abandon slave-trading. His diplomatic failure reinforced Wilmot's convictions about a naval blockade of the remaining slave coast.

A close blockade which will not entail upon the Government any very great extra expense, nor carry with it all those risks, uncertainties, exposure, and loss of life which must assuredly follow in the wake of an expeditionary force, will most assuredly bring the King of Dahomey to our feet and effectually destroy the Slave Trade in the Bights of Benin ... Less than one year will do the business and we shall save millions of money in the end.[21]

A subsequent mission by the explorer, Sir Richard Burton, also was unsuccessful in obtaining the king's co-operation. Diplomacy had not worked in West Africa and Britain had to rely on naval force. As the senior officer of the West African Squadron until 1865, Wilmot was in charge of implementing the blockade. The close blockade of the few remaining areas of the West African coast where the slave trade still flourished lasted for the remainder of the decade, and British officials were unanimous in according it a large part of the credit for bringing an end to the Atlantic slave trade.

Having decided to adopt a more militant approach on the West African coast, the British government then turned again to the Caribbean to see whether the American Civil War offered new opportunities for action there. Without American co-operation or the right to search suspected American vessels, the British navy had been hamstrung in any attempt to initiate effective patrols off the coast of Cuba. Both the British Foreign Office and the Admiralty decided the danger of naval clashes was too great to risk and no patrols were carried out from 1858 to 1861. Reports of slaves being landed on the Bahama cays for transport to Cuba brought only an Admiralty promise to have British vessels visit the area when other duties permitted. Just one British cruiser went on a slave trade patrol off Cuba in 1861, hardly sufficient to deter the slave traders, let alone to check the growing volume of the trade.[22]

But the Civil War forced Lincoln's administration to think again about the Atlantic slave trade for fear it might reappear on a larger scale, encouraged if not controlled from the Confederate states.[23] The war itself meant the federal navy no longer had ships available to patrol the West African coast or the coast of Cuba. The United States squadron patrolling off the West African coast under the terms of the Webster–Ashburton Treaty of 1842 was withdrawn in the spring of 1861 so the ships could participate in the southern blockade. The Federal government knew this action might precipitate a resurgence of the Cuban slave trade under either the American flag or that of the Confederate States and it was prepared to assist Britain to prevent any such recurrence.

The successful prosecution and execution in 1862 of Nathaniel Gordon, captain of the *Erie*, and one of many Americans engaged in the Cuban slave trade, was a welcome indication to the British that the slave trade would not be tolerated by the Union. Gordon was the first and last person to suffer capital punishment in the United States for slave-trading, and the only Cuban slave trader to be executed since no capital punishments were ever imposed for slave-trading in Spanish or Cuban courts. But even more welcome was an indication that Lincoln's government, as a war measure, would be willing, temporarily, to give up long-standing American objections to a mutual right of search if this would help to stamp out the Atlantic slave trade. This change of heart also was designed to win over the British to the northern cause. Previously, Confederate commissioners visiting Europe had assured Lord John Russell that the Confederacy would not permit any renewal of the Atlantic slave trade. Now, as a consequence of Lincoln's new policy, the way was open for a cooperative approach between the Northern States and Great Britain. Lord Lyons, the British Ambassador in Washington, quickly negotiated the Lyons–Seward Treaty of 1862 with Lincoln's Secretary of State. The treaty provided for a mutual right of search over a ten-year period and the establishment of courts of mixed commission to try cases arising from captures by either navy. The United States Senate, meeting in executive session, ratified it unanimously, another dramatic indication of the change of mood brought on by the Civil War.[24]

The British government and British public opinion, especially the abolitionists, rejoiced over its signing. A major obstacle to British cruisers on anti-slave trade patrols had been removed. The American flag no longer would protect Cuban slave traders. The treaty was thus an important turning point in the battle against the last stronghold of the Atlantic slave trade; Brougham called it the most important occurrence in his sixty years of crusading against the slave trade. While this may have been a pardonable exaggeration by an elder statesman among British abolitionists, W. L. Mathieson's critical assessment of the treaty goes too far in belittling it: 'it served rather to signalize than to complete the collapse of a system which was everywhere crumbling into ruins'.[25] The Cuban slave trade was far from dead in 1862, but the impact of the treaty, both psychological and real, definitely hastened its demise.

It did not take long for the benefits of the new treaty and what it stood for – a combined Anglo-American offensive against the Atlantic slave trade – to make themselves felt. The British commissioners in the newly created Anglo-American court of mixed commission at New York reported at the end of 1863 that New York virtually had ceased to be the outfitting centre for slaving voyages. 'New York has for many years furnished peculiar facilities and advantages for organizing and outfitting Slave Trading Expeditions. A large and populous maritime city, the resort of adventurers from other countries – within a few days sail of, and in constant communication with Havana, here have congregated the Spanish and Portuguese projectors of Slave Trading voyages.'[26] With near-immunity from prosecution and conviction, the slave trade backers had operated openly until the beginning of the Civil War. The commissioners believed that 170 slaving voyages had been organized out of New York in the three years prior to 1862, and, of these, 74 vessels actually had cleared from the port of New York. The American consul-general in Havana from 1861 to 1863, Robert Shufeldt, a veteran of the American West African squadron and quite familiar with the Cuban slave trade, privately conceded in 1861: 'However humiliating may be the confession, the fact nevertheless is beyond question that nine tenths of the vessels engaged in the Slave Trade are American.'[27] But the Civil War, combined with the prosecution of slave traders by federal officials and the treaty of 1862, had struck a mortal blow. Not a single slave-trading voyage was organized in New York during 1863. Deprived of American capital and American ships, the Cuban slave trade now entered its final phase.

With the signing of the Lyons–Seward Treaty of 1862, the way was open for Britain to adopt more aggressive tactics. Russell, the Foreign Secretary, enthusiastically exclaimed to Palmerston in reference to the treaty that Britain 'should endeavour to make the most of it'.[28] The West African Squadron was strengthened, with the Admiralty now willing to help, and new ways of checking the slave trade around,

Cuba were examined. Russell momentarily considered applying Palmerston's tactics of 1850 against Brazil to Spain, but abandoned the idea. Britain's aggressiveness towards Spain was muted by broader European considerations which did not apply in Brazil's case. In another private letter to Palmerston, written in 1863, Russell concluded: 'I think we should be wrong to authorise measures of force to do that which the Spanish laws & Govt. prohibit.'[29]

There was now much more that the British navy might do. Russell set about to persuade the Admiralty to institute an efficient system of cruising off the coast of Cuba to shut off the escape route for any slaver which managed to evade the British blockade on the West African coast. The long-looked-for goal at last seemed to be within reach. 'If the Cuban Slave Trade can be put a stop to, which His Lordship believes it may be if vigorous measures are adopted on the African and Cuban Coasts, the Slave Trade on the West Coast of Africa will become extinct.'[30] Russell wanted virtually a blockade force of four steam cruisers to be employed full time in Cuban waters where they would operate in conjunction with the Spanish navy if an agreement could be reached in Madrid. The British Admiralty balked at blockading Cuba in the midst of the American Civil War, but the Admiral commanding in the West Indies responded to Russell's request by agreeing to renew a system of cruising off Cuba.[31]

The only hitch in this new era of international naval co-operation against the African slave trade was Spain's refusal to allow British naval vessels cruising in Cuban waters to anchor off any port of the Cuban coast. Britain had no intention of violating Cuban territorial waters, but the British government was unable to convince Spain of this and the idea of a joint Anglo-Spanish anti-slave-trade patrol never did become a reality.[32] Spain's obstinate refusal to concede anchoring privileges to British vessels patrolling off Cuba was symptomatic of her deep suspicion of British motives. Before the decision was made, the Spanish Council of State examined the whole question very carefully. The thought of granting Britain's request appalled the Council. Britain's demands now exceeded any of her previous ones and for Spain to yield would be a renunciation of her national sovereignty. Serrano, the Captain-General of Cuba, when confronted with the British request, also vehemently argued for its rejection. To give in to Britain would be equivalent to admitting that Spain had neither the will nor the means to suppress the Cuban slave trade herself. Britain would use the concession to establish a blockade around Cuba, as humiliating to Spain as it would be hateful to the Cubans.[33]

Britain would not withdraw her cruisers from Cuban waters because of Spain's refusal to concede anchoring privileges. The Admiralty was told that British cruisers should go ahead and anchor if the necessity arose and the Foreign Office would justify the action to Spain on the grounds 'that in no other way could the orders to cruize for Slavers be carried into effect'.[34]

The change within two years was dramatic. The Admiralty reported that at the end of March 1863, six British naval vessels were cruising in Cuban waters, the largest number since 1858, and a sufficient number to act as an effective deterrent to prospective slave traders.[35] The tightening British naval net off West Africa and Cuba, coupled with the growing American naval presence in the Caribbean because of the Civil War, soon began to yield results. Although no captures were made by British cruisers off Cuba, Admiral Wilkes of the United States navy captured the notorious *Noc Daqui* early in 1863.[36] This was a large steam vessel formerly owned by Julián Zulueta, the leading Cuban slave trader, which had landed several large cargoes of African slaves in Cuba during 1862, the last a cargo of over 1,000 African slaves at the end of November. The capture was made for running the Union blockade, not for slave-trading, but the effect was the same. The *Noc Daqui* was no longer available to the slave traders. Another large slaver was captured off Angola at the end of 1862 just as she was about to embark 1,000 Africans destined for Cuba.[37] The combination of the American Civil War and British naval pressure was not enough to extinguish the Cuban slave trade, but with the protection of the American flag gone, as well as American capital and ships, the Cuban slave trade was so reduced in size that the *coup de grâce* was at last possible. To achieve this Spanish co-operation was essential. The American Civil War and the emancipation of slavery within the United States at last forced Spain to grapple with the Cuban slave trade herself.

Spanish officials, far from welcoming the Lyons–Seward Treaty of 1862, saw it and its results (especially Britain's more aggressive naval tactics in the Caribbean) as posing new threats to Spain and her control of Cuba. Anglo-American co-operation against the Cuban slave trade placed Spain under additional pressure and worsened her colonial dilemma. Spanish politicians looked for a way of stopping the slave trade to Cuba without endangering slavery or risking the loss of the colony. Having rejected any help either from Britain or from the United States, Spain was on her own. Prosecuting the slave trade at sea seemed to present the least objectionable solution. Experience during the 1850s had demonstrated the impossibility of checking it effectively on land without violating the 1845 penal law, and an all-out attack on the Cuban slave trade from within the island might topple the institution of slavery at the same time.

As early as 1860, Captain-General Serrano proposed the creation of a special naval flotilla of ten shallow draught steamships equipped to catch slavers as the best way of ending the Cuban slave trade.[38] He summarized the benefits to Spain of concentrating her efforts on naval force. The ships would be a tangible sign of Spain's willingness to uphold the slave trade treaties and at the same time they would obviate the need for foreign cruisers to patrol Cuba's coasts. Additionally, Cuba would benefit from the labour of the captured slaves instead of seeing them transported to British colonies or to the United States. Checking the slave trade at sea would help to stamp out administrative corruption within Cuba and the extra naval vessels would strengthen Cuba's navy. Serrano's arguments were accepted in principle in Madrid, but their practical implementation ran into a wall of obstacles.

The Spanish government approved the construction of ten vessels for the Cuban anti-slave trade patrol, to be paid for out of the Cuban treasury, in August 1860.[39] Two years later, however, Serrano still was complaining about the total inadequacy of Spanish naval forces in Cuba.[40] The navy had only four ships and they were in such constant use, with so many demands on them, that they were in very poor condition and could not carry out an effective anti-slave-trade patrol. The outbreak of the American Civil War temporarily hindered Spain's own efforts to eliminate the Cuban slave trade. Contracts for the construction of steamships were to be let in the United States, but the war intervened and they could not be built. Four vessels were then constructed in Spain and sent to the Caribbean, but they were immediately diverted to assist Spain's abortive reconquest of Santo Domingo. It was not until 1865 that Spain's naval forces in Cuba were strengthened and concentrated against the slave trade. Even then it took Captain-General Dulce's alarming rumour that 14,000 Africans were being held on the west coast of Africa for transportation to Cuba to arouse the Spanish government to provide the necessary vessels.[41]

Cuban slavery and the slave trade to Cuba had become so inextricably entwined by the beginning of the 1860s that neither Spanish politicians in the peninsula nor Spanish officials in Cuba could separate them, however much they wanted to isolate the former from

The abolition of the Cuban slave trade

the latter. Both of the men who governed Cuba during the first half of the 1860s, Francisco Serrano y Domínguez (1859–62) and Domingo Dulce y Garay (1862–6), were sincere in their attempts to abolish the slave trade just as they were equally dedicated to the preservation of slavery in the island. Serrano bluntly warned his government in 1861 that both the welfare of Cuba and the very existence of slavery depended on the elimination of the slave trade: 'I, for my part, am absolutely convinced that the only way of preserving the one is to end the other.'[42] The implication of his warning also was evident. If Spain could not succeed in exterminating the Cuban slave traffic, emancipation might be forced upon her with the consequent loss of her richest colony. Serrano believed extreme measures were justifiable to attack the slave trade and thus save slavery. As well as wanting a large naval force to patrol Cuba's coasts, he campaigned vigorously to persuade the Spanish government to declare the slave trade a crime of piracy.

Madrid shared Serrano's worry about the continuing slave trade, but it was not willing to adopt his solution. In a lengthy explanation of Spanish colonial policy sent to the Captain-General in October 1861, the Spanish government again refused outright to declare the slave trade piracy.[43] To do this would just increase the protection given to slave traders and make their capture less likely. The history of contraband in every country proved that it always prospered more when it became a capital crime. The peninsular government shied away from what it regarded as extreme measures against the slave trade, fearing that these might provoke the very crisis over slavery which it was trying desperately to avoid. With the Civil War raging on the mainland and the memory of the Africanization scare of 1854 still fresh in the minds of Cuban planters, the Spanish government would not contemplate any fundamental change in its colonial policy even under strong pressure from the Cuban Captain-General. Spain's commitment to the suppression of the slave trade was carefully guarded. Nothing must be done contrary to the existing laws, nor could any action be taken which in the slightest way affected existing slave property. Thus, an impasse developed between Havana and Madrid during Serrano's governorship, although it had been building for some time. Insistent despatches arguing for more effective slave trade suppression came from Havana; equally strong resistance emanated from Madrid. Serrano failed in his bid to change the mind of his government, and it was left to his successor, Dulce, to take up the struggle.[44]

Dulce decided to adopt different tactics. The very day he took command of Cuba in December 1862, an abandoned slaver was discovered. Those responsible for the expedition were soon identified, although no legal evidence existed to lay formal charges against them. Dulce interviewed the suspected slave traders, warning them against any repetition, but when he heard the following February that his warnings had gone unheeded he expelled the two men, Francisco Duranoña and Antonio Tuero, from Cuba, using his wide powers as Captain-General. They eventually received permission to return to the island two years later, but their expulsion was a vivid public signal of Dulce's determination to take a tougher stand.[45]

His actions received a reluctant approval in Madrid, but the Spanish government showed itself more concerned about not upsetting the slaveowners of Cuba than it was about abolishing the slave trade. In instructions sent to Dulce in April 1863, he was authorized to prosecute the slave trade remorselessly with whatever means were available to him, but always provided he did not step beyond existing Spanish laws.[46] Above all, he must not cause any discontent or alarm among slaveowners over the future of Cuban slavery which, the government reiterated, was sanctioned and protected in Spanish law. Spain was doing all she could to insulate Cuba against the possible spread of emancipation from the United States, and it was in this context that the preservation of Cuban slavery assumed more importance in the eyes of the peninsular government than the abolition of the Cuban slave trade. The slave trade could be prosecuted only as long as this did not put slavery at risk.

Dulce also was asked for his suggestions on how to resolve the Cuban labour shortage. Would it be possible to sustain Cuba's plantation economy without the constant importation of African slaves? His reply in May 1863 highlighted the colonial dilemma now confronting Spain: 'Since all aspects of slavery in this country, especially labour, colonization and domestic service, derive from the slave trade, there is no point in trying to solve these without first suppressing the slave trade . . .'[47] Dulce argued that the continued existence of the slave trade was a serious obstacle preventing any modification or improvement in the system of Cuban slavery and for this reason alone the suppression of the slave trade had to be Spain's first priority. Like his predecessor, Serrano, Dulce had come to the conclusion that wider powers than those contained in the 1845 penal law were required but, unlike Serrano, he believed the trade could be checked most effectively by taking steps to block any slave landings or, in other words, attacking it on land rather than at sea. Yet, how could this be done when the authorities in Cuba were forbidden to enter estates to search for illegally imported African slaves? Dulce conclud-ed: 'I am absolutely sure that without adopting different means, the evil is irremediable.' He told his government that as long as the slave trade persisted, it would be impossible to change the mentality of the slaveowners and convince them to maintain their existing slave popu-lation through better treatment. Without reforming the penal law of 1845, no improvements were possible, since all reforms depended on the abolition of the slave trade. But reforms for Dulce meant strengthening Cuban slavery. He was not yet, as he later became, an advocate of gradual emancipation.

Dulce privately enlisted the aid of the British consul-general in Havana, hoping that British pressure would supplement his own forceful arguments and the two together might sway the Spanish government from its rigid adherence to the status quo. He com-plained to Crawford about his lack of powers under the 1845 penal law and the unreliability of his subordinate officers. British diplomacy immediately went to work on Dulce's behalf to persuade the Spanish government to revise its slave trade legislation. Lord John Russell, the British Foreign Secretary, was most anxious to do everything he could to assist a Cuban Captain-General who would act against the slave trade. Britain had long recognized the glaring weakness of Spanish slave trade legislation: 'There can be no question that the good intentions of the Captain-General are thwarted and trammelled by the Provisions of this Law, and by the corrupt connivance in the Slave Trade of the subordinate Spanish Authorities.'[48]

The lack of additional powers did not prevent Dulce from carrying on his war of repression against slave traders in Cuba. He expelled eight Portuguese slave traders from Havana in the spring of 1863, an act which also received hesitant support from Madrid, although Dulce was cautioned to use discretion when proceeding against foreign nationals.[49] In June 1863, in another dramatic gesture, the Captain-General suspended the political governor of Havana, Pedro Nava-scues, for suspected complicity in a slaving expedition. Crawford feared that Dulce might become a victim of the Cuban slave-trading interests and their powerful allies in the peninsula, as had happened to two other Captains-General, and the British consul-general urged his own government to do everything it could to prevent Dulce's removal from office.[50] For the time being, Britain was prepared to give full backing to Dulce as the best hope in years to defeat the slave traders, and in Havana, hidden though it was from public view, the Captain-General and British officials were co-operating more closely and more effectively than had ever been the case before.

This unprecedented co-operation was bound to be tentative on both sides since it rested on British trust in Dulce's sincerity and on Dulce's own awareness of his lack of powers to wipe out the slave trade. Spain, however, refused to bend either to Dulce's potent arguments or to British diplomatic pressure lest it touch off the spark to blow up the powder keg of Cuban slavery. Madrid did give Dulce the authority to suspend any military official from command for suspicion of complicity in a slave-trading expedition, in effect ratifying his earlier actions, but the Spanish government in November 1863 reaffirmed its stubborn refusal either to declare the slave trade piracy or to reform the 1845 penal law.[51] As long as the American Civil War lasted, Spain's persecution of the Cuban slave trade ran up against the defects of her own legislation and the blatant corruption of all levels of Cuban officialdom.

The public revelation in 1864 of the nature and extent of this corruption and the poisoning influence of the slave trade on Cuban official morality put Spain even more on the defensive as she faced what had become by then a joint Anglo-American diplomatic and public campaign to end the Cuban slave trade. In the spring of 1864, the Lieutenant-Governor of the district of Colon, José Agustín Argüelles, fled to the United States after being accused by Dulce of selling for his own benefit some 250 African slaves out of 1,000 seized the previous November. Argüelles ostensibly had captured all the Africans landed by one of Julián Zulueta's slaving expeditions, but in fact Argüelles had been in collusion with Zulueta, the leading slave trader of the island. When he arrived in New York, Argüelles published a revealing exposé of the Cuban slave trade, designed to damage General Dulce but which confirmed to the American public – and to the British and Spanish, for his tale was widely reprinted in the United States, Britain and Spain – how deeply ingrained the slave trade was in Cuba and how easily slave traders could corrupt Cuban officials through bribery.[52] Seward, the United States Secretary of State, responded to Spanish requests by shipping Argüelles back to Cuba where he was tried, convicted and sentenced to life service in the galleys, but the publicity he had generated forced both the Spanish government and the Cuban Captain-General to be more vigilant. Another case like Argüelles' might have far more dire consequences for plantation slavery in Cuba.

Crawford in Havana put his finger on the real effect of Argüelles' revelations: 'Colonel Argüelles it appears is giving to the world an insight into the machinations of the Slave Trade ... it is, alas, but too true.'[53] Argüelles had provided plenty of ammunition for the growing body of Spanish and colonial reformers who wanted to do away with the slave trade and all it represented. The British Foreign Office published Crawford's confidential despatches on the Argüelles affair, including Argüelles' own writings, in their *Parliamentary Papers* on the slave trade, trying to shame Spain into cleaning up the Cuban mess, but because the *Papers* did not appear until the summer of 1865, the publicity of the year before was repeated just as a change of government occurred in Spain. The Argüelles case had been hotly debated in Spain in 1864, in the Cortes and in the public press, and Dulce's conduct as Captain-General had received a solid endorsement. Crampton, the British Ambassador in Madrid, was more sceptical after reading all the reports from Havana. He concluded that Dulce's behaviour towards the leading Cuban slave traders, particularly Zulueta, had been inconsistent and he wrote that 'a suspicious obscurity' covered the whole proceedings.[54] But not even the Argüelles revelations and the glaring international publicity that ensued from them pushed the Spanish government into immediate action to reform Spanish slave trade legislation.

The Argüelles affair completely disillusioned Crawford. In his view, such laws as existed were flouted openly by those with enough money and he blamed the slave trade for the open and shameful corruption of the Cuban government. He feared that even General Dulce had been bought by the slave-trading interests. In the spring of 1864, after twenty-one years' service at Havana, Crawford still could see no end in sight to the slave trade. He poured out his anguished frustration in one of his last despatches before his death in July. Spain had failed utterly to fulfil the Anglo-Spanish slave trade treaties. Crawford urged that Britain demand of Spain: the re-enactment of the penal law with the slave trade declared piracy, a system of rewards and head money for informers or captors of illegally introduced slaves, severe punishment for buyers of African slaves and genuine freedom for all *emancipados*. If Spain refused to comply, as Crawford was sure she would, he proposed the alternative of a differential duty of 50% on Cuban and Puerto Rican sugar entering Britain: 'Retaliatory measures alone will avail with these people as affecting their interests.'[55] Wylde, the head of the Foreign Office's Slave Trade Department, was prepared to consider Crawford's suggestion seriously, 'but it involves the material Question whether the great and costly object of putting down the Slave Trade is Superior to the maintenance of our present fiscal Regulations; or whether the maintenance of our Tariff Rules regarding the admission generally of Foreign Produce is of superior importance to the attempt to abolish Slavery'. Russell, the Foreign Secretary, was not interested in such philosophical speculation or in retaliatory measures, and he dismissed the whole idea abruptly: 'Retaliatory duties are sure to fail.'[56]

Lord Brougham again raised the question of British retaliatory duties against Spanish colonial sugar early in 1865 as a means of forcing Spain to end the Cuban slave trade, but by then Russell's new optimism about Spanish good faith, based on reports from Madrid, and Brougham's own subsequent change of heart about Spain after he heard of the formation of the Spanish Anti-Slavery Society persuaded him to drop the idea.[57] The final steps would have to come from Spain herself. Britain steadfastly refused to use anything stronger than traditional diplomatic methods to prod Spain, a marked contrast to her earlier and much more aggressive approach to Brazil.

The British government also had to work to maintain Parliamentary support in the last years of the campaign against the Atlantic slave trade. While there was no Parliamentary agitation to abolish the expensive West African Squadron in the 1860s, comparable to the militant protest movement of the late 1840s or the weaker attempt in 1858, how long would this forbearance last? There were signs in 1865 of an understandable impatience with the failure to stop the slave trade. This frustration emerged during a debate in the House of Commons on a motion to create a Select Committee to examine Britain's West African possessions. Replying for the government, Cardwell, the Colonial Secretary, felt obliged to defend the Squadron and to exhort Parliament not to give up the struggle just when it seemed on the verge of success. His rhetoric still suggested the religious fervour of a crusade, but one in which the crusaders had lost their original zeal and had to be spurred on to their goal.

I know no enterprise more noble in which this country has ever engaged, and looking around at what is passing in other nations, I cannot help thinking that this is not the moment to flinch from the task. There are signs of promise in the sky, and there is an earnest desire to abolish this infamous traffic amongst civilized and humane countries such as has never been seen since the day when England herself abolished slavery.[58]

The West African Squadron remained in place and Britain pinned her hopes on Spanish reformism.

By 1865, the spirit of colonial reform was beginning to take hold in Spain.[59] Reformist periodicals like the *Revista Hispano-Americana* were founded to provide outlets for the developing discussion, and Spain's colonies were now the subject of frequent debate in the Cortes after years of imposed silence. Underlining the importance of slavery in any Spanish colonial reforms, a Spanish abolitionist society was founded using the British and Foreign Anti-Slavery Society as its model. The year 1865 was crucial for Spanish reformers because the American Civil War was over and slavery had disappeared from the United States; Spain had abandoned her attempt to reconquer Santo Domingo; Napoleon III's Mexican adventure was proving a disastrous failure; and in the British empire Spaniards had the example of the British North American colonies about to join in a federation which would possess internal autonomy within an imperial framework. The age of imperial adventurism and slavery was ending; the age of imperial reform was about to begin, or so it seemed to the reformers.

The one element of Spanish colonial reform on which the reformers were unanimously agreed was the extinction of the Cuban slave trade as a prerequisite to all other change. The editorial staff of the *Revista Hispano-Americana* which included Julio Vizcarrondo, the Puerto Rican abolitionist, stressed this point in their opening editorial.[60] Neither laws, treaties, Spanish officials nor British cruisers had succeeded in exterminating the slave trade. The demand for labour in Cuba was so great that it enabled the private interests of the slave traders to overcome all other obstacles. As long as the shortage of labour continued, the slave trade would be encouraged, but if the labour shortage could be overcome the slave trade would die. For this reason, the editors welcomed the large influx of indentured Chinese labourers into Cuba. Their presence would make it possible at last to shut off the African slave trade. With an abundance of labour and the end of the slave trade, Spain could then proceed to the abolition of slavery.

Yet Spanish defenders of the slave trade could still be found. One of the most remarkable pro-slavery tracts to appear in the nineteenth century was published by José Ferrer de Couto in 1864. Ferrer de Couto had been subsidized by the Spanish government to edit a pro-Spanish paper, *La Crónica*, in New York and his dedication to Spain, which earned him various Spanish decorations, encompassed the cause of Spanish slavery. His *Enough of War*, apart from being a long diatribe against British abolitionism, contained a draft treaty for nations wishing to legalize slavery and the slave trade. The signatory countries would 'agree also in declaring that the so-called *slave trade* is nothing more nor less than the *redemption* of slaves and prisoners, who, from the moment that they are saved by this merciful and humane measure, enter at once into a state of civilization far superior to their former free condition, before they lost it through the tyranny of their rulers or their conquerors'.[61]

More typical of official Spain in 1865 were the views of two former Captains-General of Cuba who campaigned against the slave trade in the upper house of the Spanish Cortes. General Serrano publicly advocated making the slave trade piracy, after having tried unsuccessfully to convince Madrid to do this during his Cuban command. José de la Concha opposed making the slave trade a crime of piracy, but surely, he said, Spain could copy Brazil's example and terminate the slave trade very quickly with a variety of other means.[62] Crampton, the British Ambassador, welcomed these declarations and others which followed, but he observed somewhat sardonically that the forceful speeches in the Cortes by Spanish politicians 'contrast strangely with their steady refusal while in office to adopt the very measures in question'.[63] Serrano's speech, particularly, made a great impact in Cuba and resulted in a petition signed by large numbers of leading planters being sent to the major Madrid papers in the spring of 1865, calling for reforms in Cuba.[64] Heading the list was the removal of the slave trade, 'that repugnant and dangerous cancer of immorality'. When the Liberal Union government of General O'Donnell returned to power in the summer of 1865, colonial reform, especially the abolition of the slave trade, could be put off no longer.

One of O'Donnell's earliest acts was to commit his government to abolish the slave trade. He promised that if the existing law was inadequate new legislation would be brought in.[65] The first fruits of O'Donnell's policy of conservative reform came in a decree of 27 October 1865. His Minister of the Colonies, Cánovas del Castillo, in what was meant as the first in a series of measures to tackle the slavery problem, began by reforming some of the abuses of the *emancipado* system. He hoped at the same time, as the decree stated, to remove some of the incentive of planters to import African slaves. The decree also announced the government's formal intention to submit a new slave trade law to the Cortes. By moving slowly, step by step, with its reform policy, O'Donnell's government was trying to head off any sudden or revolutionary slave emancipation. Slavery itself had become the main colonial issue and to buy time Spain had decided to deal firmly with the slave trade.

Spanish abolitionists and other reform elements, both peninsular and creole, welcomed the government's commitment to eliminate the slave trade.[66] It was the most pressing colonial problem and, unless the slave trade stopped, emancipation without violence and without the consequent loss of Cuba as a Spanish colony might not be possible. What was most welcome of all was that a Spanish government actually had committed itself to action. Inertia had dominated Spain's approach to her colonies and to the slave trade for so long that, whatever its defects, the government decree appeared as the harbinger of a more flexible and more open Spanish colonialism with other reforms to follow.

In Cuba, opponents of the slave trade, acting with the approval of the Captain-General, had formed an association against the slave trade. Dulce had been inspired by the example of the British temperance societies. The Cuban association was modelled on them with its voluntary membership and pledge by each member to renounce the evil habit. Each member bound himself to refuse to purchase, directly or indirectly, any African slave introduced into the island after 19 November 1865, a date picked because it was the queen of Spain's saint's day. The members also agreed to recruit others and to spread the ideas of the association. Captain-General Dulce forwarded the articles of association to Spain with his recommendation of approval, a recommendation he defended on the grounds that the association would demonstrate to foreigners how Cuban public opinion against the slave trade had grown.

Nothing revealed the dichotomy of this new Spanish policy of colonial reform more glaringly than the government's response to Dulce's despatch. It arrived in Madrid just after Cánovas del Castillo had announced that stronger legislation against the slave trade would be coming before the next session of the Cortes. His civil servants in the Colonial Ministry were favourable to the idea of a Cuban association against the slave trade, although they were angry that General Dulce had not consulted them before approving the scheme. The association seemed to be in line with the current policy of the metropolitan government and it might have a beneficial effect on Cuban public morality. The only danger was that the association might become a centre of political agitation. The Colonial Minister did not agree with his subordinates. He opposed the whole idea of such an association in Cuba. At the very time his slave trade bill was being debated in the Cortes, Cánovas del Castillo ordered General Dulce to postpone indefinitely any approval of the association's constitution and to make sure the project did not succeed.[67] The Spanish government wanted to retain complete control of the suppression of the slave trade. A pliant bureaucracy was to be the sole instrument of repression. If a public association was permitted to form in Cuba, it could grow so quickly that its aims might broaden beyond opposition to the slave trade and government control of its activities would become impossible. Here was the narrow conservatism of Spain's cautious reformism. The slave trade would be stopped, but on Spain's terms, not Cuba's, because if the Cubans took control far more than the slave trade might be at stake.

The promised Spanish slave trade bill, comprising 3 sections and 39 articles and prefaced with an elaborate preamble setting out the history of previous Spanish efforts to abolish the slave trade, was presented to the Spanish Senate on 20 February 1866. The first part of the bill extended the definition of criminality to all acts, direct or indirect, having anything to do with a slave trade expedition; the second part defined the criminals more specifically and increased punishments for slave trade offences; and the third part, as well as providing for the registration of all slaves in Cuba, sought to deter potential slave traders by striking at the profits of slaving expeditions. Heavy fines were now to be imposed on convicted slave traders in addition to prison sentences.

The 1866 bill was far more comprehensive than the 1845 law it was designed to replace, and it represented a serious attempt by Spain to correct the admitted faults of her earlier legislation. One of the major improvements was the abolition of exclusive *audiencia* jurisdiction in slave trade cases. Now, ordinary courts would hear cases in the first instance and normal Spanish criminal procedure would apply. Spain was not, however, even at this late date, prepared to declare the slave trade to be a crime of piracy. The preamble to the bill contained a convoluted defence of this omission. While acknowledging that the ancient laws of Castile had punished the stealing of free men with death, and recognizing that Africans were free men, the government still stopped short of prescribing the death penalty for convicted slave traders. Instead, 'the punishment of pirates' would be imposed only on any slave traders who offered armed resistance to a capturing officer. Latent suspicion and fear of Britain still lurked in Spanish

minds and was probably the main reason for the government's refusal
to make the slave trade piracy. Only a year before, the then Spanish
Colonial Minister, Seijas Lozano, had rejected the idea because to do
so would give an English captain the power 'to hang on the yard-arm
of his Vessel a Spaniard for an act which in other Countries constitutes
no crime'.[68]

Colonial reformers and abolitionists like the Puerto Rican, Vizcarrondo, could not fathom the reasons for the Spanish government's
obstinacy. Why should Spain be different in this from Britain, the
United States and Brazil? For them, this omission was a major flaw in
the bill. Another was the lack of adequate provision for court officials
to enter estates and seize illegally introduced African slaves. The
reformers' glowing welcome of the Spanish government's willingness
to tackle the slave trade in the autumn of 1865 had yielded to despair-
ing criticism of the gaps in the actual bill presented to the Spanish
legislature the following year.[69]

The debate in the Spanish legislature in the spring and summer of
1866, in so far as it concentrated on the bill itself, was really about the
efficacy of the means to do the job.[70] There was almost universal agreement that more rigorous measures were required and a petition presented to the Spanish Senate from a group of prominent Cuban
planters, asking for government action to suppress the Cuban slave
trade and enclosing a draft bill of their own, confirmed this.[71] But
underlying the debate on the bill was a fear that if action was delayed,
a sudden, violent emancipation of slavery might overwhelm Cuba
and Spain could lose her treasured colony. Fear influenced the
passage of Spanish slave trade legislation in 1866 just as it had in 1845,
but in 1866 it was not fear of the machinations of Britain and the
activities of her abolitionist agents in Cuba, although some residual
distrust of Britain surfaced in the speeches of the bill's main opponent
in the Chamber of Deputies, Riquelme, a Cuban proprietor. The
dominant fear in 1866 was that Spain, by not acting, would lose
control of events in her overseas colonies, and the outbreak of civil
war in Cuba two years later, even though the slave trade was not a
cause, indicated that these fears were fully justified.

Britain was more than just a casual observer as the Spanish slave
trade bill was debated in the Cortes. Her treaty rights and her sixty-
year struggle to persuade Spain to follow her example meant that her
diplomats and the British government followed the bill's course with
an obsessive interest. Crampton, the British Ambassador in Madrid,
obtained a copy of the legislation the day it was presented to the Senate

and hurriedly sent it to London where British officials scrutinized it as carefully as the Spanish legislators who had to pass it. The British Foreign Office also sent a copy to the British consul-general in Havana for his opinion, and in Madrid Crampton made copies of British reports on the Cuban slave trade available to José de la Concha, the former Captain-General of Cuba, to assist him in his private efforts to secure passage of the bill. The British Ambassador's own confident assessment was that, if passed, the bill would bring an end to the Cuban slave trade.[72]

Wylde, the British Foreign Office's specialist on slave trade matters, gave the bill his seal of approval: 'I have read this Project of Law attentively, and am of opinion that if its provisions are carried out in good faith the Cuban Slave Trade will henceforward be known only as a matter of history.'[73] Lord Clarendon, the Foreign Secretary and the man who had negotiated the 1835 Anglo-Spanish slave trade treaty, echoed his subordinate's optimism. If implemented, the law would be effective. Clarendon had only one amendment to suggest, to cover a situation which British cruisers had been facing recently. Captured slavers were found to have neither papers nor colours to indicate nationality. Clarendon wanted a provision included for the punishment of Spanish subjects found guilty of slave-trading in vessels without any signs of nationality.[74]

The Spanish Senate approved the bill before the end of April. It acted so quickly that comments from other British officials, including the consul-general in Havana, had not yet been passed on to Spain. Clarendon's suggested amendment had been incorporated into the bill before the Senate had passed it. Crampton, who analysed the debate for the British government, found its tone as satisfactory as the substance of the bill. The former hatred of Britain, which had dominated previous Spanish discussions of the slave trade and had hung over the years of sterile diplomatic exchanges, had now dissipated. A welcome change in public opinion also had taken place both in Spain and in Cuba. Crampton attributed this to the effect of the American Civil War and to a growing realization by Spaniards that if Cuba was to be preserved the slave trade had to be stopped.[75] Shortly after the Spanish Senate approved the bill, officials at Cadiz seized a suspected slaver, the first time they had done so, and therefore an important indication to the British of a genuine Spanish change of heart.[76]

In Havana, the British consul-general went over the Spanish slave trade bill with a fine tooth comb, collating it with the Penal Law of 1845. The new bill was 'a vast improvement over the law now in force', but there was still room for improvement. The consul-general favoured the inclusion of a declaration of piracy because he did not believe the slave trade could ever be suppressed entirely unless it was branded piracy. After the twenty-one-year experience of the frustrating effects of Article 9 of the 1845 law, he also wanted a clause inserted in its replacement, specifically authorizing local authorities to visit plantations and examine the registers of slaves and, where owners were suspected of harbouring unregistered slaves, to make a thorough search of the estate.[77]

The British government forwarded the consul-general's recommendations to Madrid, although Clarendon saw no need to press Spain to declare the slave trade piracy. He differed in this from his predecessors, Russell and Palmerston, an indication of the way in which British views on how best to suppress the foreign slave trade had changed in a decade. Wylde, the head of the Foreign Office's Slave Trade Department, argued that a declaration of piracy would not give Britain any more powers than she had already for prosecuting Spanish subjects or vessels caught slave-trading, and he pointed out that slave-trading had never been defined as piracy in international law. As for Spanish law, Britain wanted to facilitate convictions and did not want to see a possible death penalty deter convictions in Spanish courts. Clarendon, however, strongly supported the consul-general's view of the importance of a provision for the visitation of estates and the official registration of all slaves.[78]

The bill, as approved by the Spanish Senate, satisfied the main points raised by the British government and Crampton confirmed that it gave the Spanish government 'ample means for Suppressing the Slave Trade in Cuba'.[79] But to become law the bill also needed the concurrence of the lower chamber of the Cortes and here it ran into a snag. Just before the formal vote of approval, Riquelme, the bill's major opponent, delayed its passage through the procedural manoeuvre of a quorum count as the Cortes was about to adjourn. A quorum could not be found and before the parliamentary tangle could be sorted out the Cortes was, in fact, dissolved through the resignation of O'Donnell's government. The new Spanish government quickly reassured the British Ambassador that the bill was not lost. Its provisions would be applied immediately and it would be presented as the first item of business when the Cortes next met. The bill actually was promulgated as a royal decree in September 1866, before being formally passed as a law by the Cortes the following May.[80] It was finally proclaimed in Cuba in September 1867, ending the long saga of Spanish legislation on the African slave trade.

British officials and British pressure could at last relax. In contrast to all the previous treaties and laws, British influence played a relatively minor role in the passage of the 1866 legislation. Spain had taken it upon herself to extinguish what little remained of the Cuban slave trade. The dream of British abolitionists since the end of the eighteenth century, the final extinction of the Atlantic slave trade, seemed to be coming true. Once Spain had passed the law, Britain was not inclined to push for any more concessions. The humanitarian impulse, as far as Cuba was concerned, was exhausted. The British and Foreign Anti-Slavery Society discovered this when it petitioned the British government in November 1866 in support of the efforts of Cuban and Puerto Rican delegates on the commission called to examine Spanish colonial legislation. British abolitionists wanted to 'stimulate' Spain to abolish slavery in Cuba and Puerto Rico.[81] Wylde, who examined this request, opposed the idea: 'I would venture to submit that it would be more prudent on our part to limit our exertions for the present to procuring the total suppression of the further introduction of Slaves into Cuba, leaving it to time and the course of events to work out emancipation.' Lord Stanley, now Foreign Secretary, agreed with him and rejected the abolitionists' petition.[82] Having fought so long and at such cost to eradicate the Cuban slave trade, the British government was not about to embark on a new crusade against Cuban slavery.

Not all Spaniards, Cubans and Puerto Ricans were satisfied with the new law. Many reformers thought Spain should have abolished slavery outright, making further legislation against the slave trade unnecessary. Others, who saw the total elimination of the slave trade as a fundamental prerequisite to any slave emancipation, believed the law did not go far enough, a feeling now shared by Domingo Dulce, who served two terms as Captain-General of Cuba during the 1860s. He wrote a report for the Colonial Ministry in 1867, advocating a series of colonial reforms. First on his list was the gradual abolition of slavery, but 'the basis of the gradual extinction of Slavery must be the thorough Suppression of Slave importation'. The 1866 law was not tough enough to succeed. Dulce wanted the Cuban authorities to have absolute powers to search estates for illegally landed slaves and he recommended that all known slave dealers be banished from Cuba.[83] The law was not altered, however, and debate within Spain and her colonies shifted from the slave trade to the timing and nature of slave emancipation.[84]

How effective was the last Spanish law on the slave trade? Since it was never really tested, the answer is unknown. The law was never tested because no confirmed slave landings occurred after its promulgation in Cuba and no slave traders were captured to be tried under its provisions. Its importance was largely symbolic. The Spanish government revealed to Spaniards and colonists alike its determination to wipe out the Cuban slave trade, and Spain demonstrated to the rest of Europe and the Americas that she, too, had effectively outlawed the slave trade. Spain, in whose overseas empire the Atlantic slave trade had begun, at last had moved to end it, and if the 1866 law did not kill the trade it certainly was coincident with its death.

More important even than the new law was the unbending determination of the Captains-General of Cuba to prevent any recurrence of slave-trading. When rumours of slave landings percolated about Havana in the summer of 1867, Captain-General Manzano, acting in conjunction with the Naval Commander and the Regent of the Court of Audiencia, drew up additional regulations against the slave trade. Their underlying philosophy was that since no landing could occur without the complicity of local officials and planters, all would be held responsible for any landing in their district. The Cuban government publicized the regulations extensively throughout the island to impress on everyone in Cuba that the days of clandestine slave-trading were over. Manzano's reports of a suspected Portuguese slave expedition heading towards Cuba and his new regulations prompted the Spanish government to reinforce its legislation with a new code of regulations so the slave trade law could be implemented fully.[85]

No historian can say with any certainty when the last slave landing occurred in Cuba and therefore the exact date of the end of the Atlantic slave trade. In December 1867, the commander of the British cruiser *Speedwell* ran a slaver aground in the Congo river and discovered 96 African slaves on board. He heard rumours of a further 700 Africans in a barracoon on shore with Cuba as their destination.[86] This possible final manifestation of the Atlantic slave trade was an ominous sign for both British and Spanish officials that slave dealers had not abandoned the slave trade, but their fears were unfounded. The last slave importation into Cuba which British officials there believed had occurred took place in the summer of 1867. Apparently there were two landings of approximately 300 and 700 slaves respectively. Captain-General Manzano denied the facts officially, but privately he confirmed that at least one landing had been verified.[87] Other reports reaching London warned of a revival of the slave trade, but the British consul at Cadiz was nearer the truth: 'I presume that the "Trade" – tho' tolerably well "Scotched" is not yet killed outright.'[88] The landing in Cuba in the summer of 1867 received additional confirmation in a British Admiralty report that a slave cargo had been shipped from Africa several months previously, perhaps the last one to cross the Atlantic.[89] The last seizure of slaves landed in Cuba had occurred over a year earlier, at the beginning of March 1866. The British consul-general went to see the 275 Africans brought to Havana by the Spanish warship *Neptuno*. His report was proof, if any more was needed, that the Atlantic slave trade had lost none of its barbarity in its dying stages: '... A more shocking sight than they presented I hope it may never be my lot to see ... they looked literally like living skeletons, the flesh having fallen almost completely away; and the knee bones and joints standing out in horrible relief appeared to be the largest portions of their bodies.'[90]

Clearly, the main reason for the sudden collapse of the Cuban slave trade in the 1860s was the tremendous impact of the American abolition of slavery. But if the contemporary evidence of the man who oversaw Britain's war on the Atlantic slave trade is any guide, it took more than the reverberations of American emancipation to defeat the Cuban slave traders. The price of slaves in Cuba remained high and the demand for slave labour was unabating, strong incentives for the slave trade to flourish. Wylde, writing in 1866, attributed the success of the anti-slave trade struggle to three causes apart from American emancipation: the Anglo-American treaty of 1862 giving British cruisers the right to search suspected American slavers, the West African Squadron's strict blockade of the West African coast and the good faith and energetic action of the recent Captains-General of Cuba. Spain's new law coupled with unstinting vigilance on the part of her Captains-General, he wrote, would soon make the Cuban slave trade 'known only by name'.[91]

Britain was anxious to wind up her expensive operation to end the Atlantic slave trade once there was little danger of its reappearance. The West African Squadron first was reduced in size and then was merged with the Cape Squadron in 1870. Treaties were signed with Portugal and with the United States dissolving the courts of mixed commission which had been responsible for adjudicating seizures of suspected slavers, and in 1871 the mixed court at Freetown, Sierra Leone, was shut down.[92] The British government would have been delighted to do away with the mixed court at Havana as well, but after a review in 1871 decided against it because of the 'unsettled state of the Slavery question in the Spanish West Indies'.[93] The court at Havana never functioned again. The British consul-general there retained the title and office of commission judge until 1892 when both were allowed to lapse.

Rumours of slave-trading expeditions were current long after the slave trade had stopped. As late as 1872, the British consul-general at Havana claimed that the Cuban slave trade was still active, although he could not prove his allegations. Wylde, who by then had headed the Slave Trade Department of the British Foreign Office for thirteen years, conducted an extensive investigation because he was sure it was impossible for a slave cargo to be shipped from West Africa without Britain hearing of it. Enquiries through the Admiralty and the Colonial Office turned up no evidence whatever to support the charges emanating from Cuba. Even before he received these reports, Wylde concluded: 'We have seen the last of the Cuban Slave Traffic.'[94]

ABBREVIATIONS

A.G.I.	Archivo General de Indias, Seville
A.G.S.	Archivo General de Simancas
A.H.N.	Archivo Histórico Nacional, Madrid
B.F.S.P.	*British and Foreign State Papers*
B.M.	British Museum, London
F.O.	Foreign Office Archives, Public Record Office, London
H.A.H.R.	*Hispanic American Historical Review*
P.P.	*Parliamentary Papers*
P.R.O.	Public Record Office, London

NOTES

CHAPTER 1
THE 'OPENING' OF A LEGAL TRADE

[1] Hugh Thomas, *Cuba or The Pursuit of Freedom* (London, 1971), p. 61.

[2] Alexandre de Humboldt, *Tableau statistique de l'île de Cuba pour les années 1825–29* (Paris, 1831), pp. 23–4. Each box contained 16 *arrobas*, or about 400 lb. of sugar since an *arroba* was about 25 lb. For the production figures of Cuban sugar, see Noel Deerr, *The History of Sugar*, vol. 1 (London, 1949), p. 131. A provocative recent interpretation of this revolution can be found in Manuel Moreno Fraginals, *El Ingenio: El complejo económico social cubano del azúcar*, vol. 1 (Havana, 1964).

[3] Kennedy to Aberdeen, no. 4, 1 Jan. 1845, F.O. 84/561.

[4] For a good analysis of Cuba's economic transformation see Roland T. Ely, *Cuando reinaba su majestad el azúcar* (Buenos Aires, 1963), pp. 55–115.

[5] Moreno Fraginals, *El Ingenio*, p. 3.

[6] José Antonio Saco, *Historia de la esclavitud de la raza africana en el Nuevo Mundo y en especial en los países americo-hispanos*, vol. 1 (Havana, 1938), p. 115; Irene A. Wright, *The Early History of Cuba, 1492–1586* (New York, 1970), pp. 196–7.

[7] For descriptions of the *asiento* system see Georges Scelle, *La traite négrière aux Indes de Castille* (Paris, 1906), and 'The Slave Trade in the Spanish Colonies', *American Journal of International Law*, vol. IV, no. 3 (July 1910), pp. 612–61; Saco, *Historia de la esclavitud*; Leslie B. Rout, Jr, *The African Experience in Spanish America* (Cambridge University Press, 1976), pp. 27–68; Frederic P. Bowser, *The African Slave in Colonial Peru, 1524–1650* (California, 1974), pp. 26–51.

[8] Bowser, *The African Slave in Colonial Peru*, p. 31.

[9] 'Nota sobre introducción de Negros vozales en la Ysla de Cuba y el estado y actual distribución de las gentes de color libres y esclavos en ella', Biblioteca Nacional, Madrid, Sección de Manuscritos, Colección de Justo Zaragoza, leg. 752.

[10] Elizabeth Donnan, *Documents Illustrative of the History of the Slave Trade to America*, vol. 2 (Washington, 1931), p. 312, footnote 3.

[11] José Antonio Saco, *Colección de papeles* ... *sobre la isla de Cuba*, vol. 2 (Havana, 1960), pp. 74–5; 'Nota sobre introducción de Negros'.

[12] Thomas, *Cuba*, p. 51; Allan Christelow, 'Contraband Trade between Jamaica and the Spanish Main, and the Free Port Act of 1766', *H.A.H.R.*, vol. XXII (1942), p. 329. For the British capture of Havana see David Syrett, ed., *The Siege and Capture of Havana, 1762* (Navy Records Society, 1970).

[13] The Kennion monopoly can be found in an Act of Albemarle, 23 Oct. 1762, C.O. 117/2, fols. 248–50. Thomas also discusses this, *Cuba*, pp. 49–50, as does Moreno Fraginals, *El Ingenio*, p. 5.

[14] On the *Intendencia* in Cuba see W.W. Pierson, 'The Establishment and Early Functioning of the *Intendencia* of Cuba', *James Sprunt Historical Studies*, vol. 19 (University of North Carolina Press, 1927), and John Lynch, *Spanish Colonial Administration, 1782–1810: the Intendant System in the Viceroyalty of the Río de La Plata* (The Athlone Press, London, 1958), pp. 46–51.

[15] Ely, *Cuando reinaba su majestad el azúcar*, p. 49, and C.H. Haring, *The Spanish Empire in America* (New York, 1947), p. 341.

[16] Haring, *The Spanish Empire*, p. 341.

[17] O'Reilly to Arriaga, 1 Apr. 1764, A.G.S., Secretaría de Hacienda, leg. 2342.

[18] *Ibid.*

[19] The terms of this *asiento* are given in a royal *cédula* dated 14 June 1765, A.G.I., Indiferente General, leg. 2770. They are also discussed in Saco, *Historia de la esclavitud*, vol. 2, pp. 221–2, and in James Ferguson King, 'The Evolution of the Free Slave Trade Principle in Spanish Colonial Administration', *H.A.H.R.*, vol. XXII (1942), pp. 37–9.

[20] Saco, *Historia de la esclavitud*, vol. 2, pp. 221–2.

[21] There were altogether five *representaciones*, three from Havana, one from the Captain-General and one from the Intendant. Their complaints were not abstract ones, but related to a specific incident, the arrival of the first slaver under the new *asiento*, the frigate *Verganza* which arrived at Havana on 16 Nov. 1766. The *Verganza* carried 295 slaves who were to be sold at a maximum price of 250 'pesos fuertes, platos, o oro'. The *representaciones* are summarized in 'Informe sobre la representación de la Ciudad de la Habana por el Contador General', 11 May 1767, A.G.I., Indiferente General, leg. 2770.

[22] *Ibid.*

[23] 'Informe sobre la representación de la Ciudad de la Habana por el Contador General', 5 Oct. 1768, A.G.I., Indiferente General, leg. 2770.

[24] *Ibid.*

[25] Royal *cédula*, 1 May 1773, A.G.I., Indiferente General, leg. 2770.

[26] 'Informe sobre la representación de la Ciudad de la Habana por el Contador General', 10 Feb. 1772, A.G.I., Indiferente General, leg. 2770.

[27] King, 'The Evolution of the Free Slave Trade Principle', p. 42.

[28] Royal *cédula*, 1 May 1773, A.G.I., Indiferente General, leg. 2770, King, 'The Evolution of the Free Slave Trade Principle', p. 43.

[29] Philip Allwood, 'Report on the Spanish Slave Trade', November 1787, B.M. Add. Mss. 34,427, fol. 168.

[30] *Ibid.*, and Christelow, 'Contraband Trade between Jamaica and the Spanish Main', p. 338.

[31] Roger Anstey, *The Atlantic Slave Trade and British Abolition, 1760–1810* (London, 1975), p. 4.

[32] Royal *cédula*, 18 July 1775, A.G.I., Indiferente General, leg. 2770.

[33] The operation of this tax was described in a memorandum on Spanish taxes drawn up for the British Commander-in-Chief at Havana in 1762. Enclosure in Albemarle to William Keppel, 25 Dec. 1762, C.O. 117/2, fol. 262.

[34] Saco, *Papeles sobre Cuba*, vol. 2, p. 73.

[35] Saco, *Historia de la esclavitud*, vol. 2, p. 245, and King, 'The Evolution of the Free Slave Trade Principle', pp. 46–7.

[36] B.M., Egerton Mss. 520, fol. 220.

[37] *Ibid.*, fol. 213, and King, 'The Evolution of the Free Slave Trade Principle', p. 44.

[38] Allwood, 'Report on the Spanish Slave Trade', fol. 168.

[39] Saco, *Historia de la esclavitud*, vol. 2, pp. 268–9.

[40] Ramón de la Sagra, *Historia . . . de la Isla de Cuba . . .* (Havana, 1831), p. 134.

[41] Roy F. Nichols, 'Trade Relations and the Establishment of the United States Consulates in Spanish America, 1779–1809', *H.A.H.R.*, vol. XIII (1933), pp. 289–301.

[42] Harry Bernstein, *Origins of Inter-American Interest, 1700–1812* (University of Pennsylvania Press, 1945), p. 36, n. 10, and Nichols, 'Trade Relations'.

[43] On Cuban commerce with the United States in this period see Bernstein, *Origins*, pp. 35–8; Nichols, 'Trade Relations', pp. 289–301; Maria Encarnación Rodríguez Vicente, 'El comercio cubano y la guerra de emancipación norteamericana', *Anuario de Estudios Americanos*, vol. XI (1954), pp. 61–106; and Herbert S. Klein, 'North American Competition and the Characteristics of the African Slave Trade to Cuba, 1790 to 1794', *The William and Mary Quarterly*, 3rd series, vol. XXVIII, no. 1 (Jan. 1971), pp. 86–102.

[44] Jean Mettas, 'Pour une histoire de la traite des Noirs française: sources et problèmes', *Revue française d'histoire d'Outre-Mer*, vol. LXII, n°s 226–7, (1975), pp. 19–46, and 'Honfleur et la traite des Noirs au XVIII siècle', *Revue française d'histoire d'Outre Mer*, vol. LX, n° 218 (1973), pp. 5–26.

[45] J. Meyer, 'Le commerce négrier nantais (1774–1792)', *Annales: économies, sociétés, civilisations*, vol. XV (1960), p. 122, and *L'armement nantais dans la Deuxième Moitié du XVIII'siècle* (Paris, 1969), p. 88.

[46] Serge Daget, 'Long cours et négriers nantais du trafic illégal (1814–1833)', *Revue française d'histoire d'Outre-Mer*, vol. LXII, n°s 226–7 (1975), pp. 90–134.

[47] Sv. E. Green-Pedersen, 'The Scope and Structure of the Danish Slave Trade', *The Scandinavian Economic History Review*, vol. XIX, no. 2 (1971), pp.

149–97, and 'The History of the Danish Negro Slave Trade, 1733–1807', *Revue française d'histoire d'Outre-Mer*, vol. LXII, n°s 226–7 (1975), pp. 196–220.

[48] Allwood, 'Report on the Spanish Slave Trade', fol. 168; King, 'The Evolution of the Free Slave Trade Principle', p. 46.

[49] Saco, *Historia de la esclavitud*, vol. 2, p. 272.

[50] David MacPherson, *Annals of Commerce, Manufactures, Fisheries and Navigation*, vol. 4 (London, 1805), p. 166.

[51] Arango y Parreño, 'Primer papel sobre el comercio de negros', 6 Feb. 1789, A. Carillo y Arango, ed., *Obras del excmo. Señor D. Francisco de Arango y Parreño*, vol. 1 (Havana, 1888), pp. 7–13.

[52] Liston to Allwood, 23 Apr. 1787, National Library of Scotland, Ms. 5559, fol. 217.

[53] MacPherson, *Annals of Commerce*, vol. 4, p. 166, and Saco, *Historia de la esclavitud*, vol. 3, p. 2.

[54] Saco, *Historia de la esclavitud*, vol. 3, p. 2.

[55] 'Real cédula de su magestad concediendo libertad para el comercio de negros con la isla de Cuba, Santo Domingo, Puerto Rico, y Provincia de Caracas a españoles y extrangeros, baxo las reglas que se expresan', 28 Feb. 1789, A.H.N., estado, leg. 8.038.

[56] A *Junta* met in Havana on 3 June 1789 to discuss the *cédula*, and the many difficulties inherent in the *capitación* on domestic slaves and the subsidy to Spanish slave traders were brought out. Encl. in Intendant of Havana to Minister of Finance, 8 June 1789, A.G.I., Indiferente General, leg. 2826.

[57] *Real decreto* to Intendant of Havana, 26 Jan. 1790, A.G.I., Indiferente General, leg. 2826.

[58] 'Real cédula concediendo libertad para el comercio de negros con los virreinatos de Santa Fe, Buenos Ayres, Capitanía gral. de Caracas, e islas de Santo Domingo, Cuba y Puerto Rico: a españoles y extrangeros baxo las reglas que se expresan', 24 Nov. 1791, A.H.N., estado, leg. 8.038.

[59] Yranda to Yriarte, 9 Dec. 1791, B.M., Egerton Mss. 520, fol. 274.

[60] This royal order is summarized in the prologue to the *cédula* of 22 Apr. 1804, A.G.I., Indiferente General, leg. 2770.

[61] Arango y Parreño, 'Representación manifestando las ventajas de una absoluta libertad en la introducción de negros, y solicitando se amplie a ocho la prorroga concedida por dos años', 10 May 1791, Carillo y Arango, *Obras*, vol. 1, pp. 31–9.

[62] This royal order is acknowledged in a despatch from the Intendant of Havana to the Minister of Finance, Gardoqui, 5 Sept. 1792, 'Expediente sobre el tráfico de negros', A.G.I., Indiferente General, leg. 2827.

[63] Herbert S. Klein, 'The Cuban Slave Trade in a Period of Transition, 1790–1843', *Revue française d'histoire d'Outre-Mer*, vol. LXII, n°s 226–7 (1975), Table 2, pp. 72–3.

[64] Royal order to the Intendant of Havana, 22 Nov. 1792, A.H.N., estado, leg. 8.038.

[65] Ely, *Cuando reinaba su majestad el azúcar*, p. 72.

[66] These royal orders are summarized in the prologue to the *cédula* of 22 Apr. 1804, A.G.I., Indiferente General, leg. 2207.

[67] Royal order to the Intendant of Havana, 24 Jan. 1793. For the Cuban efforts, see Intendant of Havana to Gardoqui, 5 Sept. and 26 Nov. 1792, 'Expediente sobre el tráfico de negros', A.G.I. Indiferente General, leg. 2827. The order applied at the same time to other areas of the Indies; King, 'The Evolution of the Free Slave Trade Principle', p. 54.

[68] Fernando Ortiz, *Hampa afro-cubana: los negros esclavos* (Havana, 1916), p. 86. Moreno Fraginals maintains that the first Cuban slave-trading voyage to Africa did not occur until 1798 and its success was celebrated with a fiesta in Havana, *El Ingenio*, pp. 7–8.

[69] Moreno Fraginals, *El Ingenio*, pp. 34–6. For an analysis of the effect of this revolution on Cuba see Ely, *Cuando reinaba su majestad el azúcar*, pp. 77–86.

[70] Humboldt, *Ensayo político sobre la isla de Cuba*, pp. 205–6 and 214.

[71] For an account of the *Sociedad Económica* in its early years see R. J. Shafer, *The Economic Societies in the Spanish World (1763–1821)* (Syracuse University Press, 1958), pp. 183–98.

[72] Arango's 'Discurso sobre la Agricultura de la Habana y medios de fomentarla', written in 1792, is a penetrating analysis of the state of Cuban agriculture, and many of his recommendations were adopted, Carillo y Arango, *Obras*, vol. 1, pp. 53–100. On Arango y Parreño see W. W. Pierson, 'Francisco de Arango y Parreño', *H.A.H.R.*, vol. XVI (1963), pp. 451–78.

[73] Intendant of Havana to the Minister of Finance, no. 13, 14 July 1790, A.G.I., Audiencia de Santo Domingo, leg. 2207.

[74] A.G.I., Audiencia de Santo Domingo, leg. 2207.

[75] Klein, 'North American Competition and the Characteristics of the African Slave Trade to Cuba', p. 90. This total is somewhat higher than Saco's figures suggest, *Papeles sobre Cuba*, vol. 2, p. 74.

[76] Moreno Fraginals, *El Ingenio*, p. 23.

[77] Carillo y Arango, *Obras*, vol. 1, p. 36.

[78] Anstey, *The Atlantic Slave Trade*, p. 6, n. 13, and Moreno Fraginals, *El Ingenio*, p. 21. For documents on the attempt to expel Allwood see the *consulta* of the Council of the Indies, 19 Apr. 1803, A.H.N., ultramar, leg. 4660.

[79] Anstey, *The Atlantic Slave Trade*, pp. 39 and 47. For his argument on the profitability of the British slave trade see pp. 38–58.

[80] Klein, 'North American Competition and the Characteristics of the African Slave Trade to Cuba', *passim*.

[81] Bernstein, *Origins of Inter-American Interest*, p. 37.

[82] Humboldt, *Ensayo político*, p. 229.

[83] Capt.-Gen. Someruelos to Soler, no. 57, 17 Nov. 1802, with encl., 'Representación de la Ciudad de la Habana', 5 Nov., and 'Acta de una

Junta', 28 Oct.; Intendant of Havana to Soler, no. 162, 29 Oct. 1802, A.G.I., Indiferente General, leg. 2826.

[84] Intendant of Havana to Soler, no. 190, 13 Feb. 1802, A.G.I., Indiferente General, leg. 2826.

[85] 'Memoria sobre la necesidad de restablecer el Comercio de Negros', Aranjuez, 15 Apr. 1803, 'Expediente sobre el tráfico de negros', A.G.I., Indiferente General, leg. 2827.

[86] 'Real cédula sobre continuación del comercio de negros, y prórroga de su introducción, en la forma que se expresa', 22 Apr. 1804, A.G.I., Indiferente General, leg. 2770.

[87] Royal *cédula*, 22 Apr. 1804, encl. in Vaughan to Castlereagh, no. 62, secret and confid., 23 July 1816, F.O. 72/186.

[88] Havana *Consulado* to Soler, no. 182, 8 May 1804, A.G.I., Indiferente General, leg. 2826.

[89] Many, although not all, of these returns still exist and can be found in the A.G.I., Audiencia de Santo Domingo, leg. 2207.

[90] Humboldt, *Ensayo político*, p. 191.

[91] H.H.S. Aimes, *A History of Slavery in Cuba, 1511–1868* (New York, 1907, reprint ed., 1967), p. 269.

[92] Philip D. Curtin, *The Atlantic Slave Trade: A Census* (Madison, University of Wisconsin Press, 1969), p. 36. For Bandinel's views see James Bandinel, *Some Account of the Trade in Slaves from Africa* . . . (London, 1842, reprint ed., 1968), pp. 284–6.

[93] Curtin, *The Atlantic Slave Trade*, p. 36, n. 29.

[94] Summaries of letters to the Intendant of Havana, 24 Nov. 1791 and to the Governor of Santiago de Cuba, 4 Oct. 1792, A.H.N., estado, leg. 8.038.

[95] Saco, 'Análisis de una obra sobre el Brasil', *Papeles sobre Cuba*, vol. 2, p. 74.

[96] Representación del Consulado de la Havana sobre las últimas ocurrencias habidas en el Comercio de Negros', no. 212, 24 Feb. 1811, A.G.S., estado, leg. 8277.

[97] Ortiz, *Hampa afro-cubana*, p. 87.

[98] Klein, 'The Cuban Slave Trade in a Period of Transition, 1790–1843', pp. 67–89.

CHAPTER 2
PARLIAMENT VERSUS CORTES

[1] Roger Anstey, *The Atlantic Slave Trade and British Abolition, 1760–1810* (London, 1975), pp. 323–4.

[2] Pitt to Eden, 7 Dec. 1787, J. Holland Rose, *William Pitt and National Revival* (London, 1911), pp. 459–60. In the summer of 1788, Pitt still hoped for foreign co-operation; Pitt to Wilberforce, 28 June 1788, A. M. Wilberforce, ed., *Private Papers of William Wilberforce* (London, 1897), pp. 19–20.

[3] Anstey discusses Wilberforce's activities during this period in his *The Atlantic Slave Trade*, pp. 324–6.

[4] H. Brougham, *An Inquiry into the Colonial Policy of the European Powers*, vol. 2 (Edinburgh, 1803), pp. 490–1.

[5] Roger Anstey has effectively challenged Dr Eric Williams' interpretation of the British abolition. For a comparison of the two views see Eric Williams, *Capitalism and Slavery* (London, 1964), and Anstey, *The Atlantic Slave Trade*, especially pp. 343–409. For another recent and illuminating reassessment of British abolition see D. B. Davis, *The Problem of Slavery in the Age of Revolution, 1770–1823* (Ithaca, 1975), pp. 343–468.

[6] James Stephen, *The Dangers of the Country* ... (London, 1807), p. 213. Stephen's tendency to see God at work on the abolitionists' side also is evident in an earlier work, *The Opportunity: or Reasons for an Immediate Alliance with St. Domingo* (London, 1804): 'In the wonderful events and coincidences which have planted, fostered and defended the liberty of St Domingo, I seem to see that hand by which the fates of men and nations are directed. I seem to see it, in that strange train of public evils which, since the first blaze of light revealed the full guilt of the Slave Trade, and since we rejected the loud call for reformation, have chastized our national obduracy. I seem to see it, in the dark clouds which now menace the domestic security, the idolised wealth, the happiness, and even the liberty and independency, of my country.' (p. 147) Anstey examines the evangelical world view of the abolitionists and analyses Stephen's *The Dangers of the Country* in his *The Atlantic Slave Trade*, pp. 184–99. He also discusses Stephen's role in the abolition movement, pp. 349–56.

[7] Stephen, *The Dangers of the Country*, p. 222.

[8] Anstey, *The Atlantic Slave Trade*, pp. 343ff.

[9] James Stephen, *War in Disguise, or the Frauds of Neutral Flags* (London, 1805), p. 78.

[10] *Ibid.*, p. 204.

[11] Anstey, *The Atlantic Slave Trade*, pp. 375–6.

[12] *Ibid.*, pp. 383–5.

[13] Stephen, *The Dangers of the Country*, pp. 210–11.

[14] A.K. Manchester, *British Preeminence in Brazil: its rise and decline* (University of North Carolina Press, 1933), p. 162.

[15] Strangford to Canning, no. 31, 4 June 1807, replying to Canning's instructions of 15 Apr. 1807, F.O. 63/54. See also Leslie Bethell, *The Abolition of the Brazilian Slave Trade* (Cambridge University Press, 1970), pp. 6–8.

[16] Canning to Strangford, draft, no. 6, 17 Apr. 1808, F.O. 63/59.

[17] Canning to Frere, draft, no. 11, 7 Oct. 1808, F.O. 72/60.

[18] Canning to Strangford, draft, no. 6, 17 Apr. 1808, F.O. 67/59.

[19] Canning to the Marquis of Wellesley, draft, no. 13, 8 July 1809, F.O. 72/75.

[20] R. I. and S. Wilberforce, *The Life of William Wilberforce*, vol. 3 (London, 1838), pp. 372–3 and 384–5. See also Wilberforce to Holland, 12 and 15 July 1808, B.M. Add. Mss. 51820, fols. 104–5.

[21] Wilberforce to the Marquis of Wellesley, 7 June 1809, B.M. Add. Mss. 37,309, fol. 287.

[22] *Ibid.*

[23] Wilberforce, *Life*, vol. 3, p. 459. See also Wilberforce to the Marquis of Wellesley, 1 Aug. 1810, F.O. 72/104. Wilberforce was at this time preparing a work about the abolition of the slave trade to England for circulation in Spain. In this letter he asks Wellesley to use his influence to have it 'Spanished', i.e. translated.

[24] *Parl. Debates* (1810), vol. XVI, p. 13. See also Canning's speech in the debate on 15 June 1810, *ibid.*, vol. XVII, p. 684.

[25] Wilberforce, *Life*, vol. 3, p. 483.

[26] *Ibid.*, vol. 3, p. 486.

[27] Marquis of Wellesley to Henry Wellesley, draft, no. 35, 8 Dec. 1810, F.O. 72/93.

[28] *Ibid.*

[29] For the debate in the Commons, see *Parl. Debates* (1810), vol. XVII, pp. 658ff. and for the Lords' debate, see *ibid.*, pp. 747–50.

[30] *Parl. Debates* (1810), vol. XVII, p. 664.

[31] *Ibid.*, pp. 676–7.

[32] Joseph Marryat, *Thoughts on the Abolition of the Slave Trade and the Civilization of Africa*, 3rd ed. (London, 1816), p. 42.

[33] Stephen interpreted Marryat as having advocated compulsion to achieve this. Marryat in 1816 denied ever having advocated compulsion. J. Marryat, *More Thoughts still on the . . . West India Colonies, and the Proceedings of the African Institution* (London, 1818), p. 126.

[34] *Parl. Debates* (1810) vol. XVII, pp. 681–2.

[35] *Ibid.*, p. 684.

[36] *4th Report of the Committee of the African Institution* (1810), pp. 1–27.

[37] *Ibid.*, p. 6. See, for example, the case of the *Comercio de Rio*, detained by customs officers at Gravesend and convicted in the Court of Exchequer of embarking on an illegal slaving voyage, Cuba being the eventual destination.

[38] Wellesley's handling of the issue was warmly applauded by his brother the Foreign Secretary, the Prince Regent and by Wilberforce. Marquis of·Wellesley to Henry Wellesley, draft, no. 19, 7 May 1811, F.O. 72/108 and Wilberforce to Hamilton, 2 May 1811, F.O. 72/121.

[39] Henry Wellesley to the Marquis of Wellesley, no. 38, 13 Apr. 1811, F.O. 72/103.

[40] 'Representación del Consulado de la Habana sobre las últimas ocurrencias habidas en el Comercio de Negros', no. 212, 24 Feb. 1811, A.G.S., estado, leg. 8277.

[41] *Ibid.*

[42] *Ibid.*

[43] Henry Wellesley to the Marquis of Wellesley, no. 38, 13 Apr. 1811, F.O. 72/103.

[44] *Ibid.*

[45] For a complete text of Argüelles' resolutions see *Diario de las discusiones y actas de las Cortes* (Cadiz, 1811–13), vol. 4, p. 439, and Arango y Parreño, 'Primer papel sobre el comercio de negros', 6 Feb. 1789, A. Carillo y Arango, ed., *Obras del excmo. Señor D. Francisco Arango y Parreño*, vol. 2, pp. 271–82. Included in the latter is an account of the debate and copies of the letter of Captain-General Someruelos and the remonstrance of the city of Havana as a result of the debate.

[46] Hubert H. S. Aimes, *A History of Slavery in Cuba, 1511–1568*, pp. 63–4. For a more accurate account see Arthur F. Corwin, *Spain and the Abolition of Slavery in Cuba, 1817–1886* (University of Texas Press, Austin, 1967), pp. 22–4, and *Diario . . . de las Cortes*, vol. 4, p. 444.

[47] *Diario . . . de las Cortes*, vol. 5, p. 125.

[48] Henry Wellesley to the Marquis of Wellesley, no. 38, 13 Apr. 1811, F.O. 72/103.

[49] Capt.-Gen. Someruelos to the Cortes, 27 May 1811, cited in Carillo y Arango, *Obras*, vol. 2, pp. 282–4.

[50] Shaler to Smith, 5 and 14 June 1811, Consular Despatches, Havana, 2, U.S. National Archives; Herminio Portell Vilá, *Historia de Cuba en sus relaciones con los Estados Unidos y España*, vol. 1 (Miami, reprint ed., 1969), pp. 166–8.

[51] R. Guerra y Sánchez *et al.*, eds., *Historia de la nación cubana*, vol. 3 (Havana, 1952), p. 31.

[52] The text of the memorial is reproduced in Arango y Parreño, *Obras*, vol. 2, pp. 179–229. Aimes also quotes from it, *History of Slavery in Cuba*, pp. 65–71.

[53] Carillo y Arango, *Obras*, vol. 2, p. 196. The instructions given to the Puerto Rican deputy to the Cortes also emphasized the shortage of slave labour in Puerto Rico. Luis M. Díaz Soler, *Historia de la esclavitud negra en Puerto Rico* (Madrid, 1953), pp. 103–4.

[54] This imbalance had existed in the eighteenth century and remained the case in the nineteenth century. See Ramón de la Sagra, *Historia económico-política y estadística de la Isla de Cuba, ó sea de sus progresos en la población, la agricultura, el comercio, y las rentas* (Havana, 1831), pp. 16–17 and Alexander von Humboldt, *Ensayo político sobre la isla de Cuba* (Havana, 1960), pp. 163–4.

[55] Moreno Fraginals, *El Ingenio*, p. 57.

[56] Carillo y Arango, *Obras*, vol. 2, pp. 196–7.

[57] The Cuban protests prevailed in a secret session of the Cortes, held on 7 July 1811. José Antonio Saco, *Historia de la esclavitud de la raza africana en el Nuevo Mundo y en especial en los países americo-hispanos*, vol. 3 (Havana, 1930–40), p. 89.

[58] Guerra y Sánchez, *Historia de la nación cubana*, vol. 3, pp. 36–7; P. J. Guiteras, *Historia de la isla de Cuba*, vol. 3 (Havana, 1927–8), p. 26. Some foreigners resident in Cuba at the time put more emphasis on Haitian

involvement. Joseph Marryat, *More Thoughts Still* . . . (London, 1818), pp. 17–18.

[59] He subsequently published the dissertation. Isidoro de Antillón y Marzo, *Disertación sobre el origen de la esclavitud de los Negros, motivos que la han perpetuada* (Valencia, 1820). For the 1813 episode see Carillo y Arango, *Obras*, vol. 2, p. 285, and Corwin, *Spain and the Abolition of Slavery in Cuba*, p. 25.

[60] Intendant Aguilar to Saavedra, Minister of Finance, no. 99, 17 Oct. 1809, 'Expediente sobre el tráfico de negros', A.G.I., Indiferente General, leg. 2827. (Unless otherwise indicated the material for this section has all been taken from this *expediente*.)

[61] Varea, Minister of Finance, to Collar, Secretary of the Council of the Indies, 8 July 1810, A.G.I., Indiferente General, leg. 2827.

[62] Varea to the Dean of the Council of the Indies, 5 Apr. 1811, A.G.I., Indiferente General, leg. 2827.

[63] 'Nota del Fiscal del Consejo de Indias', and anon. *Nota*, both dated 18 Apr. 1811, A.G.I., Indif. Gen., leg. 2827.

[64] *Minuta*, 19 Apr. 1811, on Varea to the Dean of the Council of the Indies, 5 Apr. 1811, A.G.I., Indif. Gen., leg. 2827.

[65] 'Informe de la Contaduría General sobre el oficio del Intendente de la Habana, no. 99, 17 de octubre de 1809', 19 Aug. 1811, A.G.I., Indif. Gen., leg. 2827.

[66] 'Minuta del Fiscal del Consejo de Indias', 16 Sept. 1811, on Varea to the Dean of the Council of the Indies, 5 Apr. 1811, A.G.I., Indif. Gen., leg. 2827.

[67] *Minuta*, 25 Sept. 1811, on Varea to the Dean of the Council of the Indies, 5 Apr. 1811, A.G.I., Indif. Gen., leg. 2827.

[68] Josef Aldony to the 'Prior y Consules de Cadiz', 28 Sept. 1811, A.G.I., Indif. Gen., leg. 2827.

[69] The figures were compiled from the following despatches: Intendant Aguilar to Varea, nos. 322, 334, 353, 371, 386, 398 and 426, 1 Apr., 2 May, 1 June, 2 July, 1 Aug., 2 Sept. and 2 Oct. 1811; Aguilar to Bardají, nos. 438 and 456, 2 Nov. and 2 Dec. 1811, A.G.I., Audiencia de Santo Domingo, leg. 2207.

[70] 'Extracto de los oficios del Intendente de la Habana al Ministro de Hacienda, nos. 483 de 1 de febrero de 1812 y 505 de 2 de marzo de 1812', 19 May 1812, A.G.I., Indif. Gen., leg. 2827.

[71] Minister of Finance to the Secretary of the Council of the Indies, 3 June 1812, A.G.I., Indif. Gen., leg. 2827.

[72] *Minuta*, 5 June, on Minister of Finance's communication.

[73] *Minuta* no. 2, 5 June, on *ibid*.

[74] *Minuta*, 6 June, on *ibid*.

[75] 'Informe del Consulado de Cadiz sobre el oficio del Intendente de la Habana, no. 99, 17 de octubre de 1809', 19 June 1812, A.G.I., Indif. Gen., leg. 2827.

[76] *Minuta*, 9 July 1812, on 'Extracto de los oficios del Intendente de la Habana al Ministro de Hacienda, nos. 483 de 1 de febrero de 1812 y 505 de 2 de marzo de 1812', A.G.I., Indif. Gen., leg. 2827.

[77] *Ibid.*

[78] *Ibid.*

[79] 'Dictamen de la Comisión de Hacienda', 13 Nov. 1812, A.G.I., Indif. Gen., leg. 2827.

[80] 'Informe del Consejo de Estado', 18 Nov. 1812, A.G.I., Indif. Gen., leg. 2827.

[81] *Ibid.*

[82] Anon. *nota*, n.d., A.G.I., Indif. Gen., leg. 2827.

[83] 'Real Orden a los Vireyes y Capitanes Generales de la America e Yslas', no. 254, reservada, Cadiz, 1 May 1813, A.G.I., Indif. Gen., leg. 2827.

[84] Capt.-Gen. of Cuba to the Minister of Finance, no. 5, reservado, 5 Aug. 1813 and Capt.-Gen. of the Rio de la Plata to the Minister of Finance, no. 89, reservado, 7 Oct. 1813, A.G.I., Indif. Gen., leg. 2827.

CHAPTER 3
LEGALITY AND ILLEGALITY

[1] See Castlereagh's speeches in *Hansard* (1814), vol. XXVIII, p. 284, and *ibid.*, (1816), vol. XXXIII, pp. 599–600.

[2] For the *Amedie* judgement see the *5th Report of the African Institution* (1811), pp. 12–13; *English Law Reports*, vol. 165, p. 1241, footnote, 1 Dodson 85; and J. B. Moore, *Digest of International Law*, vol. 2 (Washington, 1906), no. 310.

[3] Judgement by Sir William Scott in the case of the *Fortuna*, an American vessel believed to be engaged in the Cuban slave trade, cited in the *5th Report of the African Institution* (1811), pp. 15–26; *English Law Reports*, vol. 165, p. 1240, 1 Dodson 81; and Moore, *Digest*, vol. 2, no. 310.

[4] Judgement by Sir W. Grant in the case of the *Amedie*, cited in the *5th Report of the African Institution* (1811), p. 13.

[5] *English Law Reports*, vol. 165, p. 1245.

[6] Judgement by Sir W. Scott in the case of the *Diana*, 21 May 1813, reversing the decision of the Sierra Leone Vice-Admiralty court, cited in *English Law Reports*, vol. 165, p. 1246.

[7] Orders enclosed in Maxwell to Liverpool, 10 Dec. 1811, F.O. 72/137.

[8] *Ibid.*

[9] 'Representación del Consulado de la Habana sobre las últimas ocurrencias habidas en el Comercio de Negros', no. 212, 24 Feb. 1811, A.G.S. estado, leg. 8277.

[10] Manuel Moreno Fraginals points out that thirty successful slaving expeditions were undertaken by Cuban and Spanish merchants in 1809 and 1810, *El Ingenio: El complejo económico social cubano del azúcar*, vol. 1 (Havana, 1964), p. 143.

[11] James Meeks' observations on Havana, 2–10 December, 1811, F.O. 72/137. See also Shaler to Smith, 19 Apr. 1811, Consular Despatches, Havana, 11, U.S. National Archives.

[12] Duke of Infantado to the Marquis of Wellesley, 19 Dec. 1811, F.O. 72/119.

[13] Duke of Infantado to the Marquis of Wellesley, 2 Nov. 1811, F.O. 72/119.

[14] Robinson to Castlereagh, 10 Apr. 1812, F.O. 83/2364.

[15] Castlereagh to Strangford, draft, September n.d. 1812, F.O. 63/122, and *5th Report of the African Institution* (1811), Appendix Z, pp. 116–18.

[16] Wilberforce to Hamilton, pvt., 23 March 1812, F.O. 72/138. The same argument was used in the *5th Report of the African Institution* (1811), p. 31.

[17] Bradford Perkins, *Prologue to War: England and the United States, 1805–1812* (Berkeley, 1961), chaps. 11 and 12.

[18] *Parl. Debates* (1810), vol. XVII, pp. 660–61.

[19] Minute on an anonymous report from Tenerife, n.d., F.O. 72/103.

[20] Robert Peel to Wm Hamilton, 23 Apr. 1811, F.O. 72/120.

[21] Marquis of Wellesley to Henry Wellesley, draft, no. 19, 7 May 1811, F.O. 72/108.

[22] *Ibid.*

[23] *Ibid.*

[24] Council of Regency to Henry Wellesley, 6 July 1811, encl. in Henry Wellesley to the Marquis of Wellesley, no. 78, 17 July 1811, F.O. 72/112.

[25] Fernán Núñez to Castlereagh, 9 Feb. 1815, F.O. 72/179.

[26] Castlereagh to Fernán Núñez, draft, 17 Feb. 1815, F.O. 72/179.

[27] Fernán Núñez to Castlereagh, 20 Oct. 1815, F.O. 72/180.

[28] Bathurst to Fernán Núñez, draft, 4 Nov. 1815, F.O. 72/180.

[29] Fernán Núñez to Castlereagh, 7 Nov. 1815, F.O. 72/180.

[30] Castlereagh to Fernán Núñez, draft, 2 Dec. 1815, F.O. 72/180 based on Robinson to Castlereagh, 29 Nov. 1815, F.O. 83/2364.

[31] W.H.G. Page to Castlereagh, 24 June 1815, F.O. 72/182.

[32] According to the Prize Act the period was a year and a day.

[33] Fernán Núñez to Castlereagh, 29 Jan. 1816, F.O. 72/190.

[34] Castlereagh to Fernán Núñez, draft, 7 Feb. 1816, F.O. 72/190, based on Robinson to Castlereagh, 7 Feb. 1816, F.O. 83/2364.

[35] Page to Castlereagh, 21 June 1816, F.O. 72/193.

[36] Leslie Bethell, *The Abolition of the Brazilian Slave Trade: Britain, Brazil and the Slave Trade Question, 1807–1869* (Cambridge, 1970), p. 13.

[37] Robinson to Castlereagh, 6 July 1816, F.O. 83/2364.

[38] Minute on Page to Castlereagh, 4 Sept. 1816, F.O. 72/194.

[39] Page to Pizarro, 8 Sept. 1816, A.H.N. estado, leg. 8.029.

[40] Wellesley to Castlereagh, no. 112, 31 Aug. 1817, F.O. 72/200.

[41] Page to the Spanish consul general in London, 15 Oct. 1816, A.H.N. estado, leg. 8.050.

[42] Page to Bathurst, 21 June 1816 and Goulburn to Page, 29 June 1816, A.H.N. estado, leg. 8.050.

[43] Page to Sutherland, 15 July 1816, A.H.N. estado, leg. 8.050.

44 'Petition of W.H.G. Page to the House of Commons, 24 Feb. 1818', A.H.N. estado, leg. 8.029.

45 *Hansard* (1818), vol. XXXVII, pp. 1164–77 and Castlereagh to Wellesley, draft, no. 9, 27 March 1818, F.O. 72/209.

46 Fernán Núñez to Castlereagh, 23 Jan. 1816, F.O. 72/190.

47 Robinson to Castlereagh, 13 Feb. 1816, F.O. 83/2364.

48 Castlereagh to Fernán Núñez, draft, 19 Feb. 1816, F.O. 72/190.

49 Fernán Núñez to Castlereagh, 13 May 1816; Castlereagh to Fernán Núñez, draft, 24 May 1816, F.O. 72/190, the latter based on Robinson to Castlereagh, 22 May 1816, F.O. 83/2364.

50 Robinson to Castlereagh, 22 May 1816, F.O. 83/2364.

51 Castlereagh to Vaughan, draft, no. 23, 7 June 1816, F.O. 72/184. This paragraph was not put into the fair copy, but it reveals the Foreign Office view.

CHAPTER 4
THE TREATY OF 1817

1 R.I. and S. Wilberforce, *The Life of William Wilberforce*, vol. 4 (London, 1838), p. 175.

2 *Ibid.*, vol. 4, pp. 187–9.

3 F. J. Klingberg, *The Anti-Slavery Movement in England: a Study in English Humanitarianism* (New Haven: Yale University Press, 1968), p. 146.

4 Sir C. K. Webster, *The Foreign Policy of Castlereagh, 1815–1822*, 2nd ed. (London, 1934), p. 454.

5 *Hansard* (1814) vol. XXVII, pp. 637–47 and 656–62.

6 Wellesley to Castlereagh, no. 50, 17 June 1814, F.O. 72/160. Bécker says the slave trade was one of the issues in many conferences between the Duke of San Carlos and Wellesley. Britain had enlisted Russian aid on the slave trade question, but the Duke's successor, Cevallos, later parried this by suggesting England really wanted a monopoly of sugar exports to Europe. Jerónimo Bécker, *Historia de las relaciones exteriores de España durante el Siglo XIX*, vol. 1 (Madrid, 1924–6), p. 423.

7 A minute on Wellesley's despatch by a F.O. official, perhaps by Castlereagh, reads, 'Approve Projet particularly Article on Slave Trade'.

8 Wellesley to Castlereagh, no. 50, 17 June 1814, F.O. 72/160.

9 Henry Wellesley to Wellington, 17 June and 22 July 1814, Duke of Wellington, ed., *Supplementary Despatches, Correspondence and Memoranda of Arthur Wellesley, 1st Duke of Wellington* (London, 1858–72), vol. 9, pp. 139–41 and 163; Wellesley to Castlereagh, no. 50, 17 June 1814, F.O. 72/160.

10 Wellesley to Castlereagh, no. 60, 6 July 1814, F.O. 72/160.

11 Both the treaty and the articles can be found in *B.F.S.P.* (1812–14), vol. 1, part 1, pp. 273–6 and 292–3.

[12] Wellesley to Wellington, 22 July 1814, Wellington, *Supplementary Despatches*, vol. 9, p. 163.

[13] Castlereagh to Wellesley, 1 August 1814, Marquess of Londonderry, ed., *Correspondence, Despatches, and Other Papers of Viscount Castlereagh*, 3rd series (London, 1848–53), vol. 2, p. 73.

[14] Wellington to Wellesley, 29 July 1814, Wellington, *Supplementary Despatches*, vol. 9, p. 165.

[15] Castlereagh to Wellesley, no. 27, draft, 30 July 1814, F.O. 72/158.

[16] Castlereagh had written to Wellesley on 15 July 1814 to inform him that Cardinal Consalvi, the Pope's special emissary to Britain, had assured the British government of the Pope's support. Castlereagh to Wellesley, no. 23, draft, 15 July 1814. For another effort to enlist the Pope see Liverpool to Wellington, 9 Dec. 1814, Wellington, *Supplementary Despatches*, vol. 9, p. 471.

[17] Wellesley to Castlereagh, pvt., 26 Aug. 1814, F.O. 72/160.

[18] Holland to Wilberforce, 13 Nov. 1815, A. M. Wilberforce, ed., *Private Papers of William Wilberforce* (London, 1897), p. 152.

[19] Wellesley to Castlereagh, no. 71, 25 Aug. 1814 and pvt., 26 Aug. 1814, F.O. 72/160.

[20] Wellesley to Castlereagh, pvt., 26 Aug. 1814, F.O. 72/160 and Bathurst to Wellesley, no. 40, draft, 9 Sept. 1814, F.O. 72/158.

[21] Liverpool to Castlereagh, 23 Sept. 1814, Wellington, *Supplementary Despatches*, vol. 9, p. 279.

[22] See the speech by Brougham, *Hansard* (1810), vol. XVII, pp. 660–1; *5th Report of the African Institution* (1811), pp. 30–1; *6th Report of the African Institution* (1812), p. 8; Castlereagh to Wellesley, 1 Aug. 1814, Londonderry, *Correspondence . . . of Viscount Castlereagh*, 3rd series, vol. 2, p. 73; Wellesley to Castlereagh, no. 77, 31 Aug. 1814, F.O. 72/161; Liverpool to Canning, 16 Feb. 1815, Wellington, *Supplementary Despatches*, vol. 9, pp. 565–7.

[23] Wellesley to Castlereagh, no. 77, 31 Aug. 1814, F.O. 72/161.

[24] Bathurst to Wellesley, no. 40, draft, 9 Sept. 1814, F.O. 72/158.

[25] Duke of San Carlos to Wellesley, 22 Oct. 1814, encl. in Wellesley to Castlereagh, no. 97, 23 Oct. 1814, F.O. 72/161. The concessions were, in fact, a retreat from what Wellesley reported the Duke of San Carlos to have offered in August. For Wellesley's instructions see Bathurst to Wellesley, no. 55, draft, 11 Nov. 1814, F.O. 72/158.

[26] Wellesley to Castlereagh, pvt., 26 Aug. 1814, F.O. 72/160.

[27] Wellesley to Castlereagh, no. 92, 11 Oct. 1814, F.O. 72/161.

[28] *Hansard* (1815), vol. XXIX, pp. 195–209. Wellesley to Castlereagh, no. 11, 26 Jan. 1815, F.O. 72/173.

[29] The Duke of San Carlos had hinted to Wellesley that there were intentions of uniting the slave-trading interests of Spain, France and Portugal at Vienna. Wellesley to Castlereagh, pvt., 26 Aug. 1814, F.O. 72/160.

[30] North of Cape Formosa meant north of the equator. Liverpool to

Castlereagh, 9 Dec. 1814, Wellington, *Supplementary Despatches*, vol. 9, pp. 469–71.

[31] Castlereagh to Bathurst, 9 Oct. 1814; Castlereagh to Labrador, 27 Dec. 1814; Castlereagh to Wellesley, 2 Jan. 1815, *P. P.* (1814–15), Misc. vol. XIII, pp. 50–4. Wellesley to Castlereagh, pvt., 11 Oct. 1814, F.O. 72/161.

[32] Protocol of Conference on 16 Jan. 1815, *P. P.* (1814–15), Misc. vol. XIII, pp. 58–9.

[33] The Protocols of the four Conferences can be found in *P. P.* (1814–15), Misc. vol. XIII, pp. 67–93.

[34] Castlereagh to Bathurst, 13 Feb. 1815, *P. P.* (1814–15), Misc. vol. XIII, p. 60.

[35] Webster implies negotiations were temporarily suspended at Madrid to await the results of the deliberations in Vienna. Webster, *The Foreign Policy of Castlereagh*, p. 458. It appears, however, from the F.O. records that Britain was exerting pressure both in Vienna and in Madrid to restrict the trade to south of the equator and to limit its duration to five years. Wellesley to Castlereagh, no. 11, 26 Jan., no. 14, 14 Feb. and pvt., 10 Feb. 1815, F.O.72/173.

[36] Wellesley to Castlereagh, no. 11, 26 Jan. 1815, F.O. 72/173.

[37] Wellesley to Cevallos, 12 July, Cevallos to Wellesley, 18 July, Wellesley to Cevallos, 27 July and Cevallos to Wellesley, 28 July, all encl. in Wellesley to Castlereagh, no. 88, 1 Aug. 1815, F.O. 72/175.

[38] R. I. and S. Wilberforce, *Life*, vol. 4, p. 244.

[39] Liverpool to Canning, 16 Feb. 1815, Wellington, *Supplementary Despatches*, vol. 9, p. 566.

[40] Allen to Hamilton, 27 March and Archdekin to Hamilton, 30 July 1816, F.O. 72/189.

[41] Memorial of the Sierra Leone merchants, Aug. 1815, and Governor Mac-Arthy to Bathurst, 15 Sept. 1815, both encl. in Goulburn to Cooke, 9 May 1816, F.O. 72/193.

[42] M. N. Macaulay to Zachary Macaulay, 28 June 1817, F.O. 95/9.

[43] Yeo to Croker, 7 Nov. 1816 and 12 March 1817, *B.F.S.P.* (1816–17), vol. 4, 'Correspondence of Naval Officers with the British Government relative to the African Slave Trade', p. 135; enclosures in Barrow to Hamilton, 14 May 1816, F.O. 72/193.

[44] This was the abolitionists' justification for a Registration Bill. For the interrelationship between the two subjects see L. J. Ragatz, *The Fall of the Planter Class in the British Caribbean, 1763–1833* (New York, 1928), pp. 384–407, esp. the pamphlets cited p. 393, n. 9.

[45] Vaughan to Cevallos, 23 Aug. 1815, encl. in Vaughan to Castlereagh, no. 10, 30 Aug. 1815, F.O. 72/176.

[46] Castlereagh to Liverpool, 16 Oct. 1815, Wellington, *Supplementary Despatches*, vol. 11, p. 201.

47 Report of the Council of the Indies, 19 Feb. 1816, A.G.S., estado, leg. 8310. An official English text of the report can be found in *B.F.S.P.* (1816–17), vol. 4, pp. 516–49.

48 Vaughan to Castlereagh, no. 17, secret and confid., 14 March 1816, F.O. 72/185.

49 Fernán Núñez to Cevallos, no. 1011, 16 Aug. 1816, A.G.S., estado, leg. 8310. Vaughan to Castlereagh, pvt., 11 July 1816, F.O. 72/186.

50 Vaughan to Cevallos, 17 Feb. 1816, encl. in Vaughan to Castlereagh, no. 16, 14 March 1816, F.O. 72/185.

51 Havana *Consulado* to Minister of Finance, 28 March 1816, enclosing 'copia del acuerdo de la Junta consular', 20 March 1816, A.G.I., Indif. Gen., leg. 2827.

52 Capt.-Gen. Apodaca to Araujo, no. 23, May 1816, enclosing 'Acta de una Junta de Gobierno', 29 Apr. 1816, A.G.I., Indif. Gen., leg. 2827.

53 Royal order to Capt.-Gen. Apodaca, 25 Nov. 1815, based on *Contaduría General* to the Minister of the Indies, 4 Sept. 1815, A.G.I., Indif. Gen., leg. 2827.

54 Extract of 'Petición del Consulado de la Habana', 28 March 1816, with *Nota* of 29 May 1816 and *Minuta* of 1 June 1816, A.G.I., Indif. Gen., leg. 2827.

55 Royal orders to Capt.-Gen. Apodaca, 6 June and 2 Sept. 1816, A.G.I., Indif. Gen., leg. 2827.

56 Minister of the Indies to the Minister of Finance, 16 Sept. 1815, Minister of Finance to the Minister of the Indies, 13 Sept. 1815, A.G.I., Indif. Gen., leg. 2827.

57 Arango y Parreño to the Havana *Consulado*, 26 Nov. 1815, A.G.I., Indif. Gen., leg. 2827.

58 'Actas del Supremo Consejo de Estado', 7 Feb. 1816, A.H.N., estado, libro 16D.

59 Cevallos to Vaughan, 31 March 1816, and Vaughan to Cevallos, 4 April 1816, encl. in Vaughan to Castlereagh, no. 26, 9 Apr. 1816, F.O. 72/186; Bécker, *Relaciones exteriores*, vol. 1, p. 426, n. 1.

60 Castlereagh to Vaughan, no. 14, draft, 16 Apr. 1816, F.O. 72/184.

61 Vaughan to Castlereagh, no. 61, 23 July 1816, F.O. 72/186.

62 *Ibid.*

63 Vaughan to Castlereagh, no. 86, 5 Sept. 1816, F.O. 72/187; Castlereagh to Vaughan, no. 38, draft, 27 Sept. 1816, F.O. 72/184.

64 Vaughan to Hamilton, pvt., 27 July 1816, F.O. 72/187.

65 Vaughan to Castlereagh, no. 86, 5 Sept. 1816, F.O. 72/187; Bécker, *Relaciones exteriores*, vol. 1, p. 425, n. 2.

66 Harrison to Hamilton, 26 Oct. 1816, F.O. 72/195. A manuscript note by Blanco White in the front of the Cambridge University Library copy outlines how he came to write the book.

[67] James Stephen, *Slave Trade of Spain in Northern Africa* (London, 1816), p. 8.

[68] This was also the policy of the African Institution. See the *10th Report of the African Institution* (1816), p. 16.

[69] Wilberforce to Stephen, 29 March 1816, R. I. and S. Wilberforce, *Life*, vol. 4, p. 285. Webster rightly observes that Britain's insistence on Spanish abolition as a precondition to a possible British mediation in the colonial question had more influence than Stephen's pamphlet. Webster, *Foreign Policy of Castlereagh*, p. 459.

[70] Joseph Marryat, *Thoughts on the Abolition of the Slave Trade* (London, 1816), pp. 31–46 is a telling attack on the policies of the abolitionists in trying to obtain an international prohibition of the slave trade.

[71] Vaughan to Castlereagh, no. 98, 19 Sept. 1816, and Cevallos to Vaughan, 20 Sept. 1816, encl. in Vaughan to Castlereagh, no. 99, 21 Sept. 1816, F.O. 72/187.

[72] Vaughan to Hamilton, pvt., 27 July 1816, F.O. 72/187.

[73] Castlereagh to Hamilton, 13 Oct. 1816, Londonderry, *Correspondence . . . of Viscount Castlereagh*, 3rd series, vol. 2, p. 303.

[74] *Ibid.*, and Castlereagh to Vaughan, no. 38, draft, 27 Sept. 1816, F.O. 72/184.

[75] Castlereagh to Vaughan, no. 38, draft, 27 Sept. 1816, F.O. 72/184.

[76] Vaughan to Castlereagh, no. 99, 21 Sept. 1816, F.O. 72/187.

[77] Pizarro to Vaughan, 30 Nov. 1816, encl. in Vaughan to Castlereagh, no. 127, 30 Nov. 1816. See also Bécker, *Relaciones exteriores*, vol. 1, p. 428, although his account is incomplete and in places inaccurate.

[78] Pizarro to Vaughan, 30 Nov. 1816, encl. in Vaughan to Castlereagh, no. 128, 30 Nov. 1816, F.O. 72/188.

[79] Pizarro to Vaughan, 30 Nov. 1816, encl. in Vaughan to Castlereagh, no. 128, 30 Nov. 1816, F.O. 72/188. In Spain's financial state no securities she could have offered would have been acceptable to the British money market, so, again, the British government was being asked to underwrite the loan.

[80] Vaughan to Castlereagh, no. 128, 30 Nov. 1816, F.O. 72/188.

[81] Vaughan to Castlereagh, no. 129, secret and confid., 30 Nov. 1816, F.O. 72/188.

[82] Castlereagh to Wellesley, no. 53, draft, 20 Dec. 1816, F.O. 72/184.

[83] Castlereagh to Wellesley, no. 54, draft, 20 Dec. 1816, F.O. 72/184.

[84] Castlereagh to Wellesley, no. 3, draft, 10 Jan. 1817, F.O. 72/196.

[85] Wellesley to Castlereagh, no. 8, 8 Jan. 1817, F.O. 72/197.

[86] Pizarro to Wellesley, 18 Jan. 1817, encl. in Wellesley to Castlereagh, no. 14, 20 Jan. 1817, F.O. 72/197.

[87] Pizarro to Wellesley, 18 Jan. 1817, encl. in Wellesley to Castlereagh, no. 14, 20 Jan. 1817, F.O. 72/197.

[88] Wellesley to Castlereagh, pvt., 15 Jan. 1817, F.O. 72/197. Wellesley's reliability as an observer is attested by the United States historian of the Adams–Onís Treaty of 1819: 'Throughout the study of diplomacy at

Madrid in these years, one receives the impression that the most competent
and cool-headed foreign observer there was the British ambassador,
Henry Wellesley.' P. C. Brooks, *Diplomacy and the Borderlands: the Adams–
Onís Treaty of 1819* (University of California Press, 1939), p. 172.

[89] Wellesley to Castlereagh, pvt., 15 Jan. 1817, F.O. 72/197; Wellesley to
Castlereagh, pvt., 18 March 1817, F.O. 72/198.

[90] Wellesley to Castlereagh, no. 42, 24 March 1817, F.O. 72/198.

[91] Castlereagh to Wellesley, no. 6, draft, 14 Feb. 1817, F.O. 72/196. See also
F.O. 'Confidential Memorandum', 20 Aug. 1817, C. K. Webster, *Britain
and the Independence of Latin America, 1812–1830*, vol. 2 (Cambridge
University Press, 1938), pp. 352–8, esp. p. 355.

[92] Castlereagh to Wellesley, pvt. and confid., draft, 12 Apr. 1817, F.O.
72/196.

[93] Castlereagh to Wellesley, pvt., draft, 27 May 1817, F.O. 72/196.

[94] R. I. and S. Wilberforce, *Life*, vol. 4, p. 320.

[95] For the history of the Spanish–United States negotiations see Brooks,
Diplomacy and the Borderlands, and C. C. Griffin, *The United States and the
Disruption of the Spanish Empire, 1810–1822* (Columbia University Press,
1937).

[96] Wellesley to Castlereagh, no. 80, 15 June 1817, F.O. 72/198.

[97] Wellesley to Castlereagh, no. 77, 15 June 1817, F.O. 72/198, and Brooks,
Diplomacy and the Borderlands, pp. 110–14.

[98] Wellesley to Pizarro, 8 June 1817, encl. in Wellesley to Castlereagh, no. 77,
15 June 1817, F.O. 72/198.

[99] Pizarro to Wellesley, 14 June 1817, encl. in Wellesley to Castlereagh, no.
81, 19 June 1817, F.O. 72/198.

[100] This was an Additional Convention to the treaty signed with Portugal at
the Congress of Vienna, 22 Jan. 1815. The English text can be found in
B.F.S.P. (1823–4), vol. XI, pp. 687–701. For the background see Bethell,
The Abolition of the Brazilian Slave Trade, pp. 18–20.

[101] Castlereagh to Wellesley, no. 33, draft, 24 July 1817, F.O. 72/196.

[102] Wellesley to Pizarro, 8 Aug. 1817, encl. in Wellesley to Castlereagh, no.
106, 12 Aug. 1817, F.O. 72/199.

[103] Minute by Castlereagh on Wellesley to Castlereagh, no. 106, 12 Aug. 1817,
F.O. 72/199. For an English translation of the *cédula* see *B.F.S.P.* (1816–17),
vol. 4, pp. 68–74.

[104] Wellesley to Castlereagh, no. 107, 13 Aug. 1817, F.O. 72/199.

[105] José García de León y Pizarro, *Memorias*, ed. A. Alonso-Castillo, vol. 1,
(Madrid, 1953), p. 226.

[106] Castlereagh to Wellesley, no. 39, draft, 28 Aug. 1817, F.O. 72/196.

[107] Castlereagh to Wellesley, no. 38, draft, 28 Aug. 1817, F.O. 72/196, and
Brooks, *Diplomacy and the Borderlands*, pp. 110–14.

[108] 'Expediente de escuadra rusa', A.H.N., estado, leg. 8.029. This contains
documents relating to the purchase of the Russian ships and a copy of
the treaty of 11 Aug. 1817.

[109] *Ibid.* An account drawn up by Tatistcheff on 27 Sept. 1819 states that

Ferdinand asked him to write to the Russian Tsar in February 1817. For the diplomatic background of the purchase of the Russian ships see Webster, *Foreign Policy of Castlereagh*, pp. 93–95 and 411–12, and Dexter Perkins, 'Russia and the Spanish Colonies, 1817–1818', *American Historical Review*, vol. 28, no. 4 (1923), pp. 656–72, esp. p. 657, n. 4.

[110] Manuel de Saralegui y Medina, *Un negocio escandaloso* (Madrid, 1904).

[111] Wellesley to Castlereagh, pvt., 4 Dec. 1817, F.O. 72/200.

[112] *B.F.S.P.* (1816–17), vol. 4, p. 35. For the complete text see *ibid.*, pp. 33–68.

[113] *English Law Reports*, vol. 165, pp. 1464–82, and J. B. Moore, *Digest of International Law*, vol. 2 (Washington, 1906), p. 916.

[114] Macaulay to Castlereagh, 20 Dec. 1817, F.O. 95/9. This construction of the *Le Louis* judgement was denied by Sir James Mackintosh and Mr C. Grant in the debate on the treaty in the House of Commons, 9 Feb. 1818. Their opinion was that flying a foreign flag would not exempt a Spanish slaver from search and condemnation. *Hansard* (1818), vol. XXXVII, pp. 253–5.

[115] *Hansard* (1818), vol. XXXVII, pp. 232–60.

[116] Wilberforce to Zachary Macaulay, 9 Oct. 1817, R. I. and S. Wilberforce, *Life*, vol. 4, pp. 330–1.

[117] R. Guerra y Sánchez, et al., eds, *Historia de la nación cubana*, vol. 3 (Havana, 1952), p. 80.

[118] Jacobo de la Pezuela y Lobo, *Diccionario geográfico, estadístico, histórico de la Isla de Cuba*, (Madrid, 1863–6) vol. 2, p. 285.

[119] Guerra y Sánchez, *Historia de la nación cubana*, vol. 3, p. 80.

CHAPTER 5
ENFORCEMENT AND RE-ENFORCEMENT

[1] Ramírez to the Minister of Finance, no. 681, 19 May 1818, A.G.I., Audiencia de Santo Domingo, leg. 1707.

[2] Council of the Indies report, 11 May 1819, A.G.I., Ultramar, leg. 3.

[3] Capt.-Gen. Cienfuegos to the Secretary of the Council of the Indies, 20 March 1818, A.G.I., Papeles de Cuba, leg. 1910.

[4] Ramírez to the Minister of Finance, no. 704, 24 Apr. 1818, A.G.I., Audiencia de Santo Domingo, leg. 1707.

[5] Leslie Bethell, *The Abolition of the Brazilian Slave Trade: Britain, Brazil and the Slave Trade Question, 1807–1869* (Cambridge, 1970), p. 18.

[6] Petition of the *Consulado* of Havana, no. 47, 21 Oct. 1818, A.G.I., Audiencia de Santo Domingo, leg. 1706.

[7] Report of the *Contaduría General*, 30 Aug. 1819, and report of the *Fiscal* of New Spain, 14 Sept. 1819, A.G.I., Ultramar, leg. 3.

[8] Council of the Indies report, 25 Oct. 1819, A.G.I., Ultramar, leg. 3.

[9] José Antonio Saco, *Historia de la esclavitud de la raza africana en el Nuevo Mundo y en especial en los países americo-hispanos*, vol. 3 (Havana, 1940), p. 142.

[10] Jabat to Wellesley, 15 May 1820, encl. in Wellesley to Castlereagh, no. 112, 18 May 1820, F.O. 72/235, and Usoz to Castlereagh, 29 May 1820, F.O. 72/239.

[11] Council of State report, 15 May 1822, A.H.N. estado, leg. 8.031.

[12] Kilbee to Hamilton, no. 19, 31 Aug. 1820, F.O. 84/6.

[13] Council of State report, 23 June 1821, A.H.N. estado, leg. 8.031.

[14] Kilbee to Hamilton, pvt. no. 12, 29 June 1820, F.O. 84/6.

[15] Kilbee to Hamilton, 8 March 1820, F.O. 84/6.

[16] Commissioners to Canning, no. 7, 2 Aug. 1822, F.O. 84/18, and Kilbee to Canning, 14 June 1824, F.O. 84/29.

[17] Kilbee to Hamilton, no. 23, 28 Aug. 1821, F.O. 72/261.

[18] For further details on the courts of mixed commission see Leslie Bethell, 'The Mixed Commissions for the Suppression of the Transatlantic Slave Trade in the Nineteenth Century', *Journal of African History*, vol. 7 (1966), pp. 79–93.

[19] Memorandum by Kilbee, 28 May 1819, F.O. 72/230, and Kilbee to Planta, pvt., 17 Aug. 1827, F.O. 72/347. For biographical details about Kilbee see Kilbee to Wm Hamilton, 16 March 1818, F.O. 72/215, and Henry Wellesley to Castlereagh, pvt., 18 Apr. 1819, F.O. 72/224.

[20] Robert Jameson, *Letters from the Havana, during the year 1820* (London, 1821).

[21] Kilbee to Hamilton, 4 March 1822, F.O. 84/18.

[22] Kilbee to Hamilton, no. 22, 28 Aug. 1821, F.O. 84/13.

[23] Jameson to Clanwilliam, 1 Sept. 1821, F.O. 84/13.

[24] Kilbee to Planta, 22 Jan. 1825, F.O. 84/39.

[25] Kilbee to Vaughan, 30 Nov. 1824, Vaughan Papers.

[26] Thomas Randall to Adams, 21 June 1824, State Department, Special Agents, vol. 9.

[27] *16th Report of the Committee of the African Institution* (1822), p. 12.

[28] Jameson to Clanwilliam, 1 Sept. 1821, F.O. 84/13.

[29] Kilbee to Planta, 22 Jan. and 8 Oct. 1825, F.O. 84/39; Kilbee to Planta, 2 Feb. 1825, F.O. 72/304.

[30] José L. Franco, *La batalla por el dominio del Caribe y el golfo de Mexico*; vol. 1: *Política continental americana de España en Cuba*, 2nd ed. (Havana, 1964), p. 114.

[31] Kilbee to Planta, 23 Apr. 1825, F.O. 72/304.

[32] Halsted to Kilbee, 26 Aug. 1825, encl. in Kilbee to Planta, 8 Oct. 1825, F.O. 84/39.

[33] Manuel Moreno Fraginals, *El Ingenio: El complejo económico social cubano del azúcar*, vol. 1 (Havana, 1964), p. 143.

[34] For the yearly totals see Table 1, Chapter 1, p. 18. The figures themselves are taken from José Antonio Saco, *Colección de papeles científicos, históricos, políticos, y de otros ramos sobre la isla de Cuba*, vol. 2 (Havana, 1960), p. 74.

[35] Jameson to Clanwilliam, 1 Sept. 1821, F.O. 84/13.

[36] Hubert H. S. Aimes, *A History of Slavery in Cuba, 1511–1568* (New York, 1907), p. 269.

[37] Kilbee to Canning, no. 2, 1 Jan. 1825, F.O. 84/39.

[38] Commissioners to Canning, no. 3, 1 Jan. 1826, F.O. 84/51.

[39] Commissioners to Canning, no. 3, 1 Jan. 1827, F.O. 84/68.

[40] Commissioners to the Earl of Dudley, no. 3, 1 Jan. 1828, F.O. 84/80.

[41] Macleay to the Earl of Aberdeen, no. 3, 1 Jan. 1829, F.O. 84/91.

[42] Macleay to the Earl of Aberdeen, no. 3, 1 Jan. 1830, F.O. 84/106.

[43] Wilberforce made regular enquiries on the progress of the abolition of the foreign slave trade. Wilberforce to Castlereagh, 7 Feb. and 9 Sept. 1820, F.O. 84/8 and F.O. memorandum, n.d., on Wilberforce's letters, F.O. 84/7. Abolitionists received much shorter shrift from British diplomats in Madrid. The British Minister told one of them, Bowring, 'in the most unequivocal manner' not to interfere. Hervey to Castlereagh, no. 103, 3 Oct. 1821, F.O. 72/248.

[44] Hervey to Castlereagh, *ibid.*

[45] Kilbee to Hamilton, pvt., no. 33, 10 Dec. 1821, F.O. 84/13 and Kilbee to Hamilton, pvt., 4 March 1822, F.O. 84/18.

[46] Capt.-Gen Mahy to the Minister of Foreign Affairs, no. 12, reservado, 12 Nov. 1821, A.G.I., Audiencia de Santo Domingo, leg. 1293.

[47] Council of State report, 15 May 1822, A.H.N. estado, leg. 8.031.

[48] Wellesley to Perez de Castro, 7 Feb. 1821, A.H.N., estado, leg. 8.031, based on Castlereagh to Wellesley, no. 35, draft, 18 Dec. 1820, F.O. 72/233.

[49] Council of State report, 28 July 1821, A.H.N., estado, leg. 8.031.

[50] Nelson to Count Ofalia, 13 May 1824, A.H.N., estado, leg. 8.032.

[51] Marquis of Casa Irujo to Count Ofalia, no. 75, 12 June 1824, A.H.N., estado, leg. 8.032.

[52] Council of the Indies report, 12 July 1824, A.H.N., estado, leg. 8.032.

[53] Wellesley to Castlereagh, no. 44, 7 March 1821, F.O. 72/244.

[54] Wellesley to Castlereagh, no. 50, 26 March 1821, F.O. 72/244; *Diario de las discusiones y actas de las Cortes* (Madrid, 1820–2), vol. 13, no. 11, pp. 31–4. None of the published accounts of this debate reveals that British pressure was responsible for this initiative; e.g. Saco, *Historia de la esclavitud de la raza africana*, vol. 3, p. 143, Aimes, *A History of Slavery in Cuba*, p. 97, and Arthur F. Corwin, *Spain and the Abolition of Slavery in Cuba, 1817–1886* (Austin: University of Texas Press, 1967), pp. 36–7.

[55] Wellesley to Castlereagh, no. 63, 16 Apr. 1821, F.O. 72/244.

[56] Saco, *Historia de la esclavitud de la raza africana*, vol. 3, p. 144; Corwin, *Spain and the Abolition of Slavery*, p. 38.

[57] Saco, *Historia de la esclavitud de la raza africana*, vol. 3, pp. 145–6. For the text of Varela's pamphlet see vol. 4, pp. 1–17.

[58] Hervey to Castlereagh, no. 22, 15 March 1822, F.O. 72/255 and no. 78, 30 June 1822, F.O. 72/256.

[59] Commissioners to Canning, no. 4, 16 Apr. 1823, F.O. 84/23.

[60] For the correspondence on these Articles see Canning to à Court, no. 3, draft, 30 Sept. 1822, F.O. 72/258; à Court to Canning, no. 45, 10 Dec. 1822, F.O. 72/259; Canning to Havana commissioners, no. 1, draft, 16 May 1823, F.O. 84/23; commissioners to Canning, no. 3, 1 Jan. 1826, F.O. 84/51; Duke of Infantado to Lamb, 12 Feb. 1826, encl. in Lamb to Canning, no. 2, 25 Feb. 1826, F.O. 84/54.

[61] Kilbee to Canning, no. 2, 1 Jan. 1825, F.O. 84/39.

[62] Vives to the Minister of Foreign Affairs, no. 1, reservado, 6 Jan. 1825, encl. in Ezpeleta to the Minister of Foreign Affairs, no. 50, 24 Feb. 1839, A.H.N., estado, leg. 8.036.

[63] Tacón to the Ministers of Foreign Affairs and Marine, 27 June 1844, A.H.N., estado, leg. 8.035.

[64] Report of the *Fiscal* to the Council of the Indies, 14 June 1824, cited in his report of 6 Aug. 1826, A.H.N., estado, leg. 8.022(2). For Kilbee's proposal see Kilbee to Canning, no. 2, 12 Jan. 1824, F.O. 84/29; Canning to à Court, no. 3, draft, 5 Apr. 1824, and à Court to Count Ofalia, 18 Apr. 1824, encl. in à Court to Canning, no. 8, 25 Apr. 1824, F.O. 84/31.

[65] L. B. Simpson, *The Encomienda in New Spain*, 2nd ed. (University of California Press, 1966), p. 130.

[66] Canning to Lamb, nos. 1 and 3, drafts, 4 April and 31 May 1825; Lamb to Canning, no. 1, 18 June 1825; Lamb to Cea Bermúdez, 13 July 1825, encl. in Lamb to Canning, no. 2, 8 Aug. 1825, F.O. 84/41.

[67] Canning to Rufus King, 7 Aug. 1825, cited in C. K. Webster, ed., *Britain and the Independence of Latin America, 1812–1830. Select Documents from the Foreign Office Archives*, vol. 2 (London, 1938), p. 521.

[68] Minute, 22 July 1825, on extract of Lamb to Cea Bermúdez, 13 July 1825, A.H.N., estado, leg. 8.032.

[69] Kilbee to Canning, no. 5, 15 Jan. 1825, F.O. 84/39.

[70] José de Heredia to Cea Bermúdez, 18 Aug. 1825, A.H.N., estado, leg. 8.032. For a recent and provocative Marxist interpretation of Arango y Parreño's conversion, see Manuel Moreno Fraginals, *El Ingenio: El complejo económico social cubano del azúcar*, vol. 1 (Havana, 1964), pp. 143–4.

[71] José de Heredia to Cea Bermúdez, 18 Aug. 1825, A.H.N., estado, leg. 8.032.

[72] Council of the Indies report, 14 Oct. 1825, A.H.N., estado, leg. 8.032.

[73] On the immediate background to the royal order see extracts of Council of the Indies reports, 25 Nov. and 1 Dec. 1825 and minute of 1 Jan. 1826, A.H.N., estado, leg. 8.032.

[74] Duke of Infantado to Lamb, 6 Jan. 1826, encl. in Lamb to Canning, no. 1, 9 Jan. 1826, F.O. 84/54; Vives to the British commissioners, 11 Apr. 1826, encl. in commissioners to Canning, no. 11, 15 Apr. 1826, F.O. 84/51.

[75] Commissioners to Canning, no. 10, 19 March 1827, F.O. 84/68.

[76] Commissioners to Canning, no. 3, 1 Jan. 1827, F.O. 84/68.

[77] Capt.-Gen. Ezpeleta to the Minister of Foreign Affairs, no. 50, 24 Feb. 1839, A.H.N., estado, leg. 8.036.

[78] José Verdaguer to Martínez de la Rosa, 15 May 1834, A.H.N., estado, leg. 8.028.

[79] Kilbee to Planta, 21 Feb., commissioners to Canning, no. 5, 22 Feb., and Vives to commissioners, 28 Feb., encl. in commissioners to Canning, no. 9, 16 March 1826, F.O. 84/51. Canning to Lamb, no. 8, draft, 31 May; Lamb to Duke of Infantado, 2 July, encl. in Lamb to Canning, no. 5, 3 July 1826, F.O. 84/54.

[80] Ministry of Foreign Affairs memorandum 14 July 1826, A.H.N., estado, leg. 8.032(2).

[81] Report of the *Fiscal*, 6 Aug. and report of the Council of the Indies, 7 Sept. 1826, A.H.N., estado, leg. 8.022(2).

[82] Extract, 15 May, of Capt.-Gen. Vives to the Ministry of Foreign Affairs, 16 Feb., and minute, 29 May 1827, A.H.N., estado, leg. 8.022(2).

[83] Commissioners to Canning, no. 12, 16 Apr. 1826, F.O. 84/51.

[84] Macleay to Canning, no. 31, 2 Sept. 1826, F.O. 84/52.

[85] Vives to Minister of Foreign Affairs, 29 Aug. 1826, A.H.N., estado, leg. 8.022(1).

[86] Aimes, *History of Slavery in Cuba*, p. 119.

[87] This was the view of the British government. Dudley to Count Alcudia, draft, 30 Apr. 1827, F.O. 84/70.

CHAPTER 6
THE TREATY OF 1835

[1] Lamb to Canning, no. 1, 9 Jan.; Canning to Lamb, no. 4, draft, 31 Jan.; Lamb to Infantado, 19 Feb., encl. in Lamb to Canning, no. 2, 25 Feb. 1826, F.O. 84/54.

[2] Council of the Indies report, 11 Apr., cited in the Council's report, 7 Sept., 1826, A.H.N., estado, leg. 8.022(2).

[3] Ministry of Foreign Affairs memorandum, 12 Sept. 1826, A.H.N., estado, leg. 8.022(2).

[4] Lamb to Infantado, 2 July 1826, encl. in Lamb to Canning, no. 5, 13 July 1826, F.O. 84/54; report of the Council of the Indies, 7 Sept. 1826, A.H.N., estado, leg. 8.022(2).

[5] Ministry of Foreign Affairs memorandum, 12 Sept. 1826, with minutes dated 16 Jan., 29 May and 21 June 1827, A.H.N., estado, leg. 8.022(2).

[6] Bosanquet to Dudley, no. 1, 7 Jan. 1828, F.O. 84/83.

[7] Extract, 12 Sept., of Council of the Indies report, 19 Aug. 1827; minute, 10 Nov., A.H.N., estado, leg. 8.032.

[8] For documents on this case see commissioners to Canning, nos. 24 and 25, 13 and 14 Aug. 1827, F.O. 84/68; Bosanquet to Salmón, 31 Dec. 1827, encl. in Bosanquet to Dudley, no. 1, 7 Jan. 1828, F.O. 84/83; extract, 21 Jan. 1828 of Council of the Indies report, A.H.N., estado, leg. 8.027.

[9] Extract, 19 Feb., of Council of State report, 19 Jan. 1829, A.H.N., estado, leg. 8.022(2).

[10] Ministry of Foreign Affairs memorandum, 25 Aug. 1829, A.H.N., estado, leg. 8.027.

[11] Bosanquet to Salmón, 8 and 21 Apr., encl. in Bosanquet to Aberdeen, no. 8, 22 June 1829, F.O. 84/94.

[12] Ministry of Foreign Affairs memorandum, 19 Feb. 1829 and minute, 26 Sept., A.H.N., estado, leg. 8.032.

[13] The Council of Ministers' decision is summarized in a Ministry of Foreign Affairs memorandum, 23 Dec. 1830, A.H.N. estado, leg. 8.022(2). See also Salmón to Addington, 4 March 1830, encl. in Addington to Aberdeen, no. 1, 8 March 1830, F.O. 84/110.

[14] Addington to Salmón, 8 Dec. 1830, encl. in Addington to Aberdeen, no. 4, 12 Dec. 1830, F.O. 84/110.

[15] Minute, 6 Mar., on Addington to Salmón, 13 Feb. 1831; extract, 25 Apr., of Council of the Indies report, 15 Apr. 1831 and minute, 2 June, A.H.N., estado, leg. 8.022(2).

[16] Macleay to Aberdeen, no. 29, 17 July 1830, F.O. 84/107; Addington to Salmón, 28 Nov. 1831, encl. in Addington to Palmerston, no. 8, 28 Nov. 1831, F.O. 84/121; Capt.-Gen. Vives to the Minister of Foreign Affairs, no. 205, 26 May 1830, A.H.N., estado, leg. 8.033.

[17] Palmerston to Addington, no. 6, draft, 4 June 1832, F.O. 84/130.

[18] Addington to Alcudia, 11 Apr., encl. in Addington to Palmerston, no. 3, 14 Apr. 1832, F.O. 84/130; minute of royal order, 15 Apr., A.H.N., estado, leg. 8.022(2); Capt.-Gen. Ricafort to Minister of Foreign Affairs, no. 11, 30 June 1832, A.H.N., estado, leg. 8.015.

[19] Addington to Bermúdez, 25 Jan., encl. in Addington to Palmerston, no. 1, 18 Feb. 1833, F.O. 84/140.

[20] Memorandum, Ministry of Foreign Affairs, 19 July 1833, A.H.N., estado, leg. 8.022(2).

[21] Report of the commission, 26 Oct. 1833, A.H.N., estado, leg. 8.015.

[22] For these negotiations see Leslie Bethell, *The Abolition of the Brazilian Slave Trade: Britain, Brazil and the Slave Trade Question, 1807–1869* (Cambridge, 1970), pp. 88–121.

[23] Palmerston to Villiers, nos. 2 and 3, drafts, 9 Sept. and 22 Nov. 1833, F.O. 84/140.

[24] Villiers to Palmerston, 8 March and 14 July 1834, Clarendon Mss., c. 451.

[25] Palmerston to Villiers, 15 July 1834, Broadlands Mss., GC/CL/1231/2.

[26] Villiers to Palmerston, 24 Oct. 1834, Clarendon Mss., c. 451.

[27] George Villiers to Edward Villiers, 6 Mar. 1836, in Sir Herbert Maxwell, *The Life and Letters of George William Frederick, Fourth Earl of Clarendon*, vol. 1 (London, 1913), pp. 93–5. The article was subsequently published under the title 'Correspondence relating to the Slave Trade; New Treaty with Spain', *Edinburgh Review*, vol. CXXVIII (July 1836), pp. 388–95.

[28] Villiers to Palmerston, 14 Oct. 1834, Clarendon Mss., c. 451.

[29] Calvo to Martínez de la Rosa, 28 Nov. 1834, A.G.I., estado, leg. 17, fol. 21;

Calvo to Martínez de la Rosa, 22 Apr. 1835, A.H.N., estado, leg. 8.017.

[30] Villiers to Wellington, separate and confidential, 12 Apr. 1835, F.O. 84/177.

[31] The text of the treaty can be found in *B.F.S.P.* (1834–5), vol. 23, pp. 343–74.

[32] Villiers to Palmerston, 8 Nov. 1834, Clarendon Mss., c. 451.

[33] Commissioners to Palmerston, no. 3, 1 Jan. 1836, F.O. 84/196.

[34] Bethell, *The Abolition of the Brazilian Slave Trade*, p. 126; Villiers to Calatrava, 2 June 1837, encl. in Villiers to Palmerston, no. 11, 3 June 1837, F.O. 84/221.

[35] Commissioners to Palmerston, no. 20, 17 March 1836, F.O. 84/196.

[36] For details of the *General Laborde* case see commissioners to Palmerston, no. 7, 11 Jan. 1836, F.O. 84/196 and Palmerston to commissioners, no. 10, draft, 14 Aug. 1837, F.O. 84/217.

[37] For a good description of how these courts operated see Bethell, *The Abolition of the Brazilian Slave Trade*, pp. 128–33, and his article, 'The Mixed Commissions for the Suppression of the Transatlantic Slave Trade in the Nineteenth Century', *Journal of African History*, vol. 7 (1966), pp. 79–93.

[38] Commissioners to Palmerston, no. 8, 26 Jan. 1837, and Schenley to Fox Strangways, 9 Jan. 1837, F.O. 84/216.

[39] This occurred over the *Vencedora*. For the details see Hubert H. S. Aimes, *A History of Slavery in Cuba, 1511–68* (New York, 1907), pp. 132–3, and commissioners to Palmerston, no. 61, 22 Nov. 1837, F.O. 84/217.

[40] Tolmé to Palmerston, no. 5, 15 Oct. 1836, F.O. 84/201.

[41] On the Palmerston Act of 1839 see Bethell, *The Abolition of the Brazilian Slave Trade*, pp. 151–79.

[42] Schenley to Fox Strangways, separate, no. 2, 24 Feb. 1837, F.O. 84/216, and Madden to Palmerston, 10 Aug. 1837, F.O. 84/217.

[43] Warren S. Howard, *American Slavers and the Federal Law, 1837–1862* (University of California Press, 1963), p. 32. For a list of United States vessels in Cuban slave trade, 1837–40, see *ibid.*, appendix F, pp. 241–2.

[44] Kennedy to Palmerston, no. 39, 22 Aug. 1838, F.O. 84/240.

[45] Tolmé to Palmerston, 17 Sept. 1839, F.O. 84/280.

[46] Commissioners to Palmerston, no. 5, 19 Jan. 1839, F.O. 84/274.

[47] *Ibid.* See also David Turnbull, *Travels in the West* (London, 1840), pp. 435–42.

[48] Trist to commissioners, 2 July, encl. in commissioners to Palmerston, no. 35, 27 Oct. 1839; memorandum by Palmerston, 27 Dec. 1839, F.O. 84/274. See also *A Letter to W. E. Channing on the subject of the abuse of the Flag of the United States in the Island of Cuba, and the advantage taken of its protection in promoting the Slave Trade* (Boston, 1839), and *A Letter to W. E. Channing in reply to one addressed to him by R.R.M. on the abuse of the flag of the United States in the Island of Cuba, for promoting the Slave Trade*, By a Calm Observer (Boston, 1840).

[49] R. R. Madden, *The Island of Cuba . . . its Resources, Progress and Prospects con-*

sidered in relation especially to the influence of its prosperity on the interests of the British West India Colonies (London, 1849), pp. 86–7.

[50] Everett to Adams, 30 Nov. 1825; Edward E. Hale, *The Everett Letters on Cuba* (Boston, 1897), pp. 5–14.

[51] Everett to Forsyth, 21 July 1840, Consular Despatches, Havana, U.S. National Archives T 20, vol. 14.

[52] For an assessment of the Trist affair see Howard, *American Slavers and the Federal Law, 1837–62*, pp. 33–6.

[53] The best analysis of Tacón's administration is Juan Pérez de la Riva, *Correspondencia reservada del Capitán General Don Miguel Tacón* (Havana, 1963), pp. 1–96.

[54] *Ibid.*, p. 195.

[55] *Ibid.*, pp. 317–18; see also José A. Fernández de Castro, ed., *Escritos de Domingo del Monte*, vol. 1 (Havana, 1929), 'La Isla de Cuba en 1836', p. 15, and David Turnbull, *Travels in the West*, pp. 156–7.

[56] Tacón to the Ministers of Foreign Affairs and Marine, 27 June 1844, A.H.N., estado, leg. 8.035.

[57] Villiers to Palmerston, nos. 1 and 2, 24 Jan. and 7 Feb. 1836, F.O. 84/201.

[58] Pérez de la Riva, *Correspondencia*, p. 41.

[59] Commissioners to Palmerston, no. 3, 2 Jan. 1837, F.O. 84/216.

[60] Villiers to the Duke of Frias, 14 Nov. 1838, encl. in Villiers to Palmerston, no. 37, 17 Nov. 1838, F.O. 84/246; Ministry of Foreign Affairs memorandum, 29 Nov. 1838, A.H.N., estado, leg. 8.024(1).

[61] Commissioners to Ezpeleta, 31 Jan. 1839, encl. in commissioners to Palmerston, no. 7, 4 Feb. 1839, F.O. 84/274; Ezpeleta to the Minister of Foreign Affairs, no. 50, 24 Feb. 1829 and minute of royal order to Ezpeleta, 15 Apr. 1839, A.H.N., estado, leg. 8.036.

[62] James Bandinel, *Some Account of the Trade in Slaves from Africa . . .* (London, 1842), p. 230; for British reaction to the treaty see *Hansard*, 3rd series (1836), vol. XXXII, pp. 269–73.

[63] [Edward Villiers], 'Correspondence relating to the Slave Trade; New Treaty with Spain', *Edinburgh Review*, vol. CXXVIII (July 1836), p. 393.

[64] David Turnbull, *Travels in the West*, pp. 379–96.

[65] *Hansard*, 3rd series (1837–8), vol. XL, p. 607.

[66] Thomas Fowell Buxton, *The African Slave Trade and its Remedy*, 2nd ed. (London, 1840). See also Howard Temperley, *British antislavery, 1833–70* (University of South Carolina Press, 1972), pp. 42–61, and J. Gallagher, 'Fowell Buxton and the New African Policy, 1838–42', *Cambridge Historical Journal*, vol. X (1950), pp. 36–58.

[67] Buxton, *The African Slave Trade*, p. 184.

[68] *Ibid.*, pp. 29–34.

[69] Turnbull, *Travels in the West*, pp. 361–7; see also MacGregor Laird's review of Buxton's book in the *Westminster Review*, vol. XXXIV (1840), pp. 52–72.

[70] *Proceedings of the General Anti-Slavery Convention called by the Committee of the British and Foreign Anti-Slavery Society and held in London from Friday, 12 June 1840 to Tuesday, 23 June 1840* (London, 1841), p. 242.

[71] Tolmé to Palmerston, no. 18, 17 Sept. 1839, F.O. 84/280. See also commissioners to Palmerston, no. 3, 1 Jan. 1840, F.O. 84/312.

[72] *Ibid.* David Eltis' quantitative analysis of Cuban slave imports for the years 1821–43 yields higher figures than those reported by the British officials. He suggests that the enmity between consul Tolmé and the British commissioners resulted in two rival British reporting systems and his own higher figures come from integrating the two. He has kindly provided me with his yearly totals which are reproduced below.

1830 –	14,299
1831 –	15,026
1832 –	13,450
1833 –	12,093
1834 –	16,410
1835 –	25,032
1836 –	21,014
1837 –	21,461
1838 –	22,703
1839 –	19,951
1840 –	14,688
1841 –	12,498
1842 –	4,317
1843 –	7,128
Total –	220,070

For Eltis' analysis see his doctoral thesis, 'The Transatlantic Slave Trade, 1821–43' (University of Rochester, 1978), and his article, 'The Export of Slaves from Africa, 1821–43', *The Journal of Economic History*, vol. 37, no. 2 (1977), pp. 409–33.

CHAPTER 7
AN ABOLITIONIST ERA

[1] For a description of the revolutionary impact of abolition on Jamaica see Philip D. Curtin, *Two Jamaicas: the Role of Ideas in a Tropical Colony, 1830–65* (Harvard University Press, Cambridge, 1955), esp. pp. 81–98.

[2] Circular, 25 Feb. 1796, A.G.I., estado, leg. 4.

[3] Cited in *Fiscal* to Tacón, 9 Dec., encl. in Tolmé to Palmerston, no. 14, 16 Dec. 1837, F.O. 72/489.

[4] Vives to Minister of Foreign Affairs, 8 Aug. 1831, A.H.N., estado, leg. 8.033.

[5] Council of the Indies report, 11 Apr. 1833, A.H.N., estado, leg. 8.034.

[6] Villanueva to Minister of Finance, no. 5078, 30 Aug. 1833, A.H.N., estado, leg. 8.034.

[7] Tacón to Minister of the Interior, no. 121, 31 Aug. 1835, Pérez de la Riva, *Correspondencia reservada del Capitán General Don Miguel Tacón...*, pp. 177–9.

[8] Exod. 21:16, 'And he that stealeth a man, and selleth him, or if he be found in his hand, he shall surely be put to death.'

[9] Minute of a royal order to Tacón, 25 Oct. 1835, A.H.N., estado, leg. 8.036.

[10] Tacón to Minister of the Interior, nos. 168 and 170, 30 Jan. and 6 Feb. 1836, A.H.N., ultramar, leg. 4603.

[11] Tacón to Minister of Foreign Affairs, no. 3, reservado, 31 March 1836, Pérez de la Riva, *Correspondencia*, pp. 223–7; see also A.H.N., estado, leg. 8.035 and ultramar, leg. 4603 for further documents on Apodaca's mission.

[12] Calderón de la Barca to Minister of Foreign Affairs, no. 86, 8 Dec. 1836, A.H.N., estado, leg. 8.036.

[13] Royal order, 12 March, cited in Tacón to Minister of Marine and Colonies, no. 436, 31 Aug. 1837, A.H.N., estado, leg. 8.036.

[14] Tolmé to Tacón, 25 Oct., encl. in Tolmé to Palmerston, no. 9, 28 Oct. 1837; Tacón to Tolmé, 12 Dec., encl. in Tolmé to Palmerston, no. 14, 16 Dec. 1837; memorandum by Palmerston, 12 Dec. 1837, F.O. 72/489. For British protests against similar United States discriminatory treatment against black sailors from Britain's Caribbean colonies see Philip M. Hamer, 'Great Britain, the United States and the Negro Seamen Acts, 1822–48', and 'British consuls and the Negro Seamen Acts, 1850–60', *Journal of Southern History*, vol. I (1935), pp. 3–28 and 136–68.

[15] Franklin Knight, 'Slavery, Race and Social Structure in Cuba during the Nineteenth Century', R. B. Toplin, ed., *Slavery and Race Relations in Latin America* (Greenwood Press, Westport, Conn., 1974), p. 211. On the repression of free blacks in Cuba see also Franklin Knight, 'Cuba', David W. Cohen and Jack P. Greene, eds., *Neither Slave nor Free, the Freedmen of African Descent in the Slave Societies of the New World* (The Johns Hopkins University Press, Baltimore, 1972), pp. 301–2, and Gwendolyn Hall, *Social Control in Slave Plantation Societies, a Comparison of St. Domingue and Cuba* (The Johns Hopkins University Press, Baltimore, 1971), pp. 129–32.

[16] Tacón to Minister of Marine and Colonies, no. 436, 31 Aug. 1837, A.H.N., estado, leg. 8.036.

[17] Memorandum by Palmerston, 9 March, on Tolmé to Palmerston, no. 3, 2 Feb. 1838, F.O. 72/513.

[18] Tolmé to Palmerston, no. 8, 21 May 1838, F.O. 72/513.

[19] James Thompson to Rev. A. Bandram, no. 163, 16 Aug. 1837, British and Foreign Bible Society, London, Corres. Inwards, vol. III.

[20] Thompson to Bandram, no. 185, 9 Sept. 1837, *ibid.* I am indebted to Mr and Mrs D. A. Barrass of Cambridge, England, for these two references.

[21] Tacón to Minister of Marine and Colonies, no. 450, 3 Oct. 1837, A.H.N., estado, leg. 8.036.

[22] Petition of Havana *Ayuntamiento,* 2 Sept. 1837, A.H.N., estado, leg. 8.036.

[23] Count Ofalia to John Eaton, 22 Feb. 1838, W. R. Manning, *Diplomatic Correspondence of the United States. Inter-American Affairs, 1831–60,* (Washington, 1932–9), vol. XI, pp. 307–9; Ofalia to Villiers, 22 Feb., encl. in Villiers to Palmerston, no. 81, 3 March 1838, F.O. 72/502.

[24] Eaton to Ofalia, 10 March 1838, Manning, *Diplomatic Correspondence,* vol. XI, pp. 310–13; Villiers to Ofalia, 10 Apr. 1838, encl. in Villiers to Palmerston, no. 133, 14 Apr. 1838, F.O. 72/503.

[25] Minute on Minister of Marine and Colonies to Minister of Foreign Affairs, 20 Jan. 1838, A.H.N., estado, leg. 8.036.

[26] Antonio Brosa to Minister of Foreign Affairs, no. 35, 20 Feb. 1838, A.H.N., estado, leg. 8.036.

[27] Brosa to Minister of Foreign Affairs, no. 38, 15 March, and minute of reply, 25 May 1838, A.H.N., estado, leg. 8.036.

[28] For an account of Madden's Caribbean career see D. R. Murray, 'Richard Robert Madden: His Career as a Slavery Abolitionist', *Studies* (Ireland), vol. LXI (Spring 1972), pp. 41–53.

[29] R. R. Madden, *A Twelvemonth's Residence in the West Indies . . . ,* vol. 2 (London, 1835), p. 163.

[30] Buxton to Madden, 23 Oct. 1835, T. M. Madden, ed., *The Memoirs (chiefly autobiographical) from 1798 to 1886 of Richard Robert Madden, M.A., F.R.C.S.* (London, 1891), pp. 203–4.

[31] Villiers to Istúriz, 27 May, and reply 4 June, encl. in Villiers to Palmerston, nos. 6, 29 May and 10, 12 June 1836, F.O. 84/201.

[32] Tacón to Minister of Foreign Affairs, no. 4, reservado, 31 Aug. 1836, Pérez de la Riva, *Correspondencia,* pp. 252–5.

[33] *Ibid.*

[34] Calatrava to Villiers, 21 Nov., encl. in Villiers to Palmerston, no. 17, 26 Nov. 1836, F.O. 84/201.

[35] Minute of Calatrava to Aguilar, 22 Nov. 1836, A.H.N., estado, leg. 8.022(2).

[36] Palmerston to Villiers, no. 14, draft, 15 Dec. 1836, F.O. 84/201.

[37] Aguilar to Tacón, 28 Dec. 1836 and 15 June 1837; Tacón to Aguilar, 9 Mar. and 31 Aug. 1837, all encl. in Tacón to Minister of Foreign Affairs, no. 192, 31 Aug. 1837, A.H.N., estado, leg. 8.022; Palmerston to Aguilar, draft, 15 May 1837, F.O. 84/221.

[38] Commissioners to Tacón, 26 Oct., and reply, 29 Oct., encl. in commissioners to Palmerston, no. 77, 5 Nov. 1836, F.O. 84/197.

[39] Palmerston to Villiers, no. 16, draft, 22 Dec. 1836, F.O. 84/201; Almodóvar to Villiers, 12 March, encl. in Villiers to Palmerston, no. 7, 25 March 1837, F.O. 84/221.

[40] Tacón to British commissioners, 26 Aug., encl. in commissioners to Palmerston, no. 51, 23 Sept. 1837, F.O. 84/217; Tacón to Minister of Foreign Affairs, no. 192, 31 Aug. 1837, A.H.N., estado, leg. 8.022(2).

[41] Capt. John Leith to Schenley, 30 Aug., encl. in commissioners to Palmerston, no. 51, 23 Sept. 1837, F.O. 84/217.

[42] Madden to Schenley, 30 Aug., encl. in *ibid.*

[43] Memorandum by Palmerston, 5 Nov., and Palmerston to Villiers, no. 15, draft, 14 Nov. 1837, F.O. 84/221.

[44] Tacón to Minister of Foreign Affairs, no. 196, 30 Oct. 1837, A.H.N., estado, leg. 8.025(2).

[45] Minute of royal order to Tacón, 25 Feb. 1838, A.H.N., estado, leg. 8.025(1).

[46] Memorandum by Palmerston, 18 Jan., on Villiers to Palmerston, no. 1, 7 Jan. 1838, F.O. 84/244.

[47] Commissioners to Palmerston, no. 13, 20 Apr. 1838, F.O. 84/240.

[48] Commissioners to Ezpeleta, 1 May, and reply, 2 May, both encl. in Kennedy to Palmerston, no. 20, 15 May 1838, F.O. 84/240.

[49] Ezpeleta to Minister of Foreign Affairs, no. 13, 31 May 1838, A.H.N., estado, leg. 8.025(2).

[50] Minute of royal order to Ezpeleta, 12 July 1838, A.H.N., estado, leg. 8.025(2).

[51] Kennedy to Palmerston, no. 35, 10 Aug. 1838, F.O. 84/240.

[52] *Ibid.*, and Palmerston to commissioners, no. 27, draft, 17 Nov. 1838, F.O. 84/239.

[53] Ofalia to Hervey, 31 Aug., encl. in Hervey to Palmerston, no. 15, 1 Sept. 1838; Villiers to the Duke of Frias, 18 Oct., encl. in Villiers to Palmerston, no. 34, 20 Oct. 1838, F.O. 84/246.

[54] Commissioners to Palmerston, no. 51, 24 Dec. 1838, F.O. 84/240.

[55] Minute of royal order to Ezpeleta, 3 Apr. 1839, A.H.N., estado, leg. 8.025(1); Pérez de Castro to Southern, 3 Apr., encl. in Southern to Palmerston, no. 2, 6 Apr. 1839, F.O. 84/279.

[56] Commissioners to Palmerston, no. 30, 30 Sept. 1839, F.O. 84/274.

[57] Minute, 30 Nov., on Kennedy to Palmerston, 27 Sept. 1839, F.O. 84/274.

[58] Anglona to Minister of Foreign Affairs, no. 13, 31 March 1840, A.H.N., estado, leg. 8.025(1).

[59] Fernando Ortiz, *Hampa afro-cubana: los negros esclavos* (Havana, 1916), p. 323.

[60] Richard Kimball, *Cuba and the Cubans* . . . (New York, 1850), p. 71.

[61] D. Justo Zaragoza, *Las insurecciones en Cuba: Apuntes para la historia politica de esta isla en el presente siglo*, vol. 1 (Madrid, 1872), p. 481.

[62] For recent critical assessments of Cuban abolitionists see Raul Cepero Bonilla, *Obras históricas* (Havana, 1963), pp. 1–79, and Manuel Moreno Fraginals, *El Ingenio: El complejo económico social cubano del azúcar*, vol. 1, *1760–1860* (Havana, 1964), pp. 143–5.

[63] J. A. Saco, 'Análisis de una obra sobre el Brasil', *Papeles sobre Cuba*, vol. 2 (Havana, 1960), pp. 30–90.

[64] Macleay to Backhouse, pvt., 11 Aug. 1834, F.O. 84/151.

[65] For these pamphlets see Saco, *Papeles sobre Cuba*, vol. 3, pp. 101–87.

[66] J. A. Saco, 'Mi primera pregunta ...' (Madrid, 1837). This essay was republished in an expanded version in 1845; see Saco, *Papeles sobre Cuba*, vol. 2, pp. 90–154.

[67] For two Cuban analyses of Saco's ideas see Fernando Ortiz, 'José Antonio Saco y sus ideas', *Revista bimestre cubana*, vol. XXIV (1929), pp. 387–409, and Manuel Moreno Fraginals, 'Nación ó plantación (el dilema político cubano visto a través de José Antonio Saco)', *Homenaje a S. Zavala* (México, 1953), pp. 243–72.

[68] The questionnaire can be found in José A. Fernandez de Castro, ed., *Domingo del Monte*, Colección de libros cubanos, XII (Havana, 1929), pp. 133–43. Madden's address was published as *Address on Slavery in Cuba presented to the General Anti-Slavery Convention* (London, 1840) and later included in his book, *The Island of Cuba* (London, 1849), pp. 114–56.

[69] For Madden's own account of this episode, see *The Memoirs (chiefly autobiographical) from 1798 to 1886 of R. R. Madden* (London, 1891), pp. 81–3, and *The Island of Cuba*, appendix 2. Reports of the affair from Havana can be found in F.O. 84/274. See also Betty Fladeland, *Men and Brothers: Anglo-American antislavery co-operation* (Urbana: University of Illinois Press, 1972), pp. 324–29, and Christopher Martin, *The Amistad Affair* (New York, 1970), pp. 142–7.

CHAPTER 8
THE TURNBULL AFFAIR

[1] Howard Temperley, *British antislavery, 1833–70* (University of South Carolina Press, 1972), p. 68.

[2] For assessments of the British and Foreign Anti-Slavery Society see Temperley, *British antislavery*, pp. 62–92, and Betty Fladeland, *Men and Brothers: Anglo-American antislavery co-operation* (Urbana: University of Illinois Press 1972), pp. 257–73.

[3] See above, Chapter 6, pp. 110–11.

[4] For the background and ultimate failure of the Niger expedition see Temperley, *British antislavery*, pp. 51–61, and Philip Curtin, *The Image of Africa, British Ideas and Action, 1780–1850* (London, 1965), pp. 298–305.

[5] Buxton appeared at the 1840 anti-slavery convention to defend his book on the slave trade against Turnbull and to contrast the society he had founded, the Society for the Extinction of the Slave-Trade and the Civilization of Africa, with the British and Foreign Anti-Slavery Society: ' ... your first blow is aimed at slavery, ours at the slave trade; you wish to extinguish the demand, we desire to crush the supply; your operations are in one hemisphere, ours in another'. *Proceedings of the General Anti-Slavery Convention called by the Committee of the British and Foreign Anti-Slavery Society* (London, 1841) [hereafter cited as *Proceedings* (1840)], p. 243.

[6] The biographical information on Turnbull is taken from Turnbull to Palmerston, 22 Jan. 1841, F.O. 72/584.

[7] See, for example, Kilbee to Hamilton, no. 23, 28 Aug. 1821, F.O. 84/13.

[8] David Turnbull, *Travels in the West. Cuba: with Notices of Porto Rico and the Slave Trade* (London, 1840) p. 343.

[9] Turnbull to Palmerston, 28 Feb. 1840, F.O. 84/342.

[10] Minute by Palmerston, 28 Feb. 1840, F.O. 84/342.

[11] Turnbull to Leveson, 9 and 19 Mar. 1840, F.O. 84/342.

[12] Turnbull to Palmerston, 13 Mar. 1840, F.O. 84/342.

[13] Memorandum by Palmerston, 15 Mar. 1840, F.O. 84/342.

[14] Memorandum by Bandinel, 3 Apr., and minute by Palmerston, 18 Apr. 1840, F.O. 84/318.

[15] *Morning Chronicle,* 9 March 1840.

[16] [MacGregor Laird] *Westminster Review*, vol. XXXIV (June 1840), p. 151.

[17] Palmerston to Aston, no. 13, draft, 25 May 1840, F.O. 84/318.

[18] Turnbull, *Travels in the West*, p. viii.

[19] Fladeland, *Men and Brothers*, p. 251. Historians writing about Turnbull have incorrectly assumed he was a member of the British abolitionist movement when he first visited Cuba. See, for example, Arthur F. Corwin, *Spain and the Abolition of Slavery in Cuba, 1817–1886* (Austin: University of Texas Press, 1967), p. 75; P. S. Foner, *A History of Cuba and its Relations with the United States*, vol. 1 (New York, 1962), p. 201; and Mario Hernández y Sánchez-Barba, 'David Turnbull y el problema de la esclavitud en Cuba', *Anuario de estudios americanos*, vol. XIV (1957), p. 266.

[20] British and Foreign Anti-Slavery Minute Books, 10 Apr., 25 June 1840, Br. Emp. Mss. S20 E2/6, Rhodes House, Oxford. See also *Proceedings* (1840), pp. 474–5.

[21] For the debate and resolution see *Proceedings* (1840), pp. 251–62 and 474–6.

[22] Turnbull to Palmerston, 4 July, and Turnbull to Tredgold, 25 July, encl. in Tredgold to Palmerston, 25 July 1840, F.O. 84/342.

[23] British and Foreign Anti-Slavery Society Minute Books, 31 July 1840, Br. Emp. Mss. S20 E2/6. Palmerston later admitted the influence of abolitionist pressure to the Spanish envoy in London. González to the Spanish Minister of Foreign Affairs, no. 1, 4 Mar. 1841, A.H.N., estado, leg. 8.053.

[24] For a general account of the British consular service in the nineteenth century see D.C.M. Platt, *The Cinderella Service, British Consuls since 1825* (London, 1971), pp. 16–67.

[25] Kennedy to Palmerston, 5 Dec. 1838, F.O. 84/239.

[26] Unsigned memorandum, 29 July 1839, F.O. 84/274.

[27] Cuba until the middle 1860s is thus a noteworthy exception to D.C.M. Platt's description of British policy in nineteenth-century Latin America: 'Trade and investment formed the basis of British interest in Latin America, and trade, together with the protection of the lives and pro-

perty of British subjects was the preoccupation of British diplomacy.'
D.C.M. Platt, *Finance, Trade and Politics in British Foreign Policy, 1815–1914*
(Oxford at the Clarendon Press, 1971), p. 312.

[28] Memorandum by Palmerston, 3 Jan. 1840, on James Stephen to Backhouse, 31 Dec. 1839, F.O. 72/538.

[29] Turnbull, *Travels in the West*, pp. 43–4; *Proceedings* (1840), pp. 461–2;
Palmerston to British commissioners, no. 10, draft, 24 Aug. 1840, F.O.
84/312.

[30] Kennedy to Palmerston, 17 Dec. 1840, F.O. 84/312. He was later censured
by Palmerston. Palmerston to Kennedy, draft, 6 May 1841, F.O. 84/347.

[31] Jackson admitted this and received a severe reprimand. Jackson to
Palmerston, 18 Aug., and Leveson to Jackson, draft, 26 Aug. 1841, F.O.
84/347.

[32] The correspondence on the issues of slave-holding and slave-hiring by
British officials in Cuba is voluminous and can be found in F.O. 84/347,
F.O. 84/356 and F.O. 84/357.

[33] Commissioners to Palmerston, 14 Oct. 1841, F.O. 84/347, and same to
same, nos. 54 and 55, 12 and 14 Oct. 1841, F.O. 84/349.

[34] Commissioners to Capt.-Gen. Valdés, 22 May, encl. in commissioners to
Palmerston, no. 29, 25 May 1841, F.O. 84/348; Valdés to Turnbull,
19 June, encl. in Turnbull to Palmerston, no. 61, 23 June 1841, F.O.
84/358.

[35] He continues to be a controversial subject of historical interpretation.
For modern, albeit very differing, views of what he did in Cuba see
Hernández y Sánchez-Barba, 'David Turnbull', pp. 241–99; Eric Williams,
'The Negro Slave Trade in Anglo-Spanish Relations', *Caribbean Historical
Review*, vol. 1 (December 1950), pp. 33–4; P.S. Foner, *A History of Cuba*,
pp. 201–13; Humberto Castañeda, 'El caso de Mr David Turnbull, El
Consul Inglés', *Revista de la Universidad de la Habana*, vols. 168–9 (July–Oct.
1964), pp. 127–53; Corwin, *Spain and the Abolition of Slavery*, pp. 75–81;
R. Guerra y Sánchez, et al., eds., *Historia de la nación cubana*, vol. 4 (Havana,
1952), pp. 66–71.

[36] Capt.-Gen. Anglona to the Minister of Foreign Affairs, no. 50, 1 Nov.
1840, A.H.N., estado, leg. 8.053.

[37] *Junta de Fomento* to Capt.-Gen. Anglona, 18 Nov., encl. in Anglona to the
Minister of Foreign Affairs, no. 53, 30 Nov. 1840, A.H.N., estado, leg.
8.053.

[38] *Junta de Fomento* to Villanueva, 28 Nov., encl. in Villanueva to the Minister
of Marine and Colonies, 28 Nov. 1840, A.H.N., ultramar, leg. 3547.

[39] Anglona to the Minister of Foreign Affairs, no. 51, 17 Nov. 1840, A.H.N.,
estado, leg. 8.053.

[40] Turnbull to Anglona, 28 Dec. 1840, encl. in Anglona to the Minister of
Foreign Affairs, no. 57, 2 Jan. 1841, and no. 58, 10 Jan. 1841, A.H.N.,
estado, leg. 8.053.

[41] Memorandum by Palmerston, 20 July, on Turnbull to Palmerston, no. 49,

8 May 1841, F.O. 84/357, and Aberdeen to Turnbull, no. 22, draft, 18 Oct. 1841, F.O. 84/358.

[42] Turnbull to Aberdeen, no. 86, 23 Dec. 1841, F.O. 84/359.

[43] *Ibid.*, no. 87, 24 Dec. 1841.

[44] Tanco to del Monte, 5 March 1841, *Centón epistolario*, vol. VII, p. 158; Cisneros to del Monte, 30 March, 22 May and 20 June 1841, *ibid.* vol. V, pp. 14, 24, 31.

[45] La Sagra's letter appeared in *El Corresponsal*, 24 Dec. 1840. For the protests of the *Tribunal de Comercio de la Habana*, 30 March, and the *Real Junta de Fomento de Agricultura y Comercio*, 27 Feb. 1841, see A.H.N., ultramar, leg. 3550. The involvement of the British and Foreign Anti-Slavery Society was made public in the 1843 general anti-slavery convention. See *Proceedings* (1843), p. 167.

[46] Details of the proposed convention were given to the Spanish Foreign Minister in June 1840, but owing to the turbulent state of Spanish politics it was not until December that the Minister formally proposed the convention. Aston to Palmerston, no. 9, 13 June 1840, and no. 18, 30 Dec. 1840, with enclosures, Aston to Ferrer, 17 Dec., and reply, 26 Dec. 1840, F.O. 84/318.

[47] It was not an order to the Captain-General to prepare for the emancipation of all slaves illegally brought into the island after 1820 as is alleged by Corwin, following an earlier Spanish interpretation. See Corwin, *Spain and the Abolition of Slavery in Cuba*, pp. 73–4. Nor did the affair amount to a 'near invasion of the island to force the emancipation of all slaves imported since 1820' as Kenneth Kiple states in his *Blacks in Colonial Cuba, 1774–1899* (Gainesville, 1976), p. 14.

[48] Palomino to del Monte, 9 Sept. 1841, *Centón epistolario*, vol. V, pp. 39–41.

[49] Argaiz to Valdés, 12 Oct., encl. in Valdés to the Minister of Foreign Affairs, no. 4, reservado, 4 Nov. 1841, A.H.N., estado, leg. 8.052.

[50] [Anon.] *Biografía del Excmo. Señor D. G. Valdés* (Madrid, 1850). For the Spanish political background see Raymond Carr, *Spain, 1808–1939* (Oxford, 1966), pp. 210–46, and E. Christiansen, *The Origins of Military Power in Spain, 1800–1854* (Oxford, 1967), pp. 67–135.

[51] Valdés to the Minister of Foreign Affairs, no. 57, 3 Nov. 1841, A.H.N., estado, leg. 8.052.

[52] Turnbull to Palmerston, no. 72, 31 Aug. 1841, F.O. 84/358.

[53] Valdés to the Minister of Foreign Affairs, no. 57, 3 Nov. 1841, with enclosures, A.H.N., estado, leg. 8.052; Turnbull to Aberdeen, nos. 76, 77, 83, 6 and 25 Nov. and 17 Dec. 1841, F.O. 84/359; and commissioners to Aberdeen, no. 65, 10 Dec. 1841, with enclosures, F.O. 84/349. Copies of the major reports also were published in José Antonio Saco, *Historia de la esclavitud de la raza africana en el Nuevo Mundo y en especial en los países americo-hispanos*, vol. 4 (Madrid, 1837), pp. 61–173. Corwin analyses them in his *Spain and the Abolition of Slavery in Cuba*, pp. 69–73.

[54] For a discussion of the fate of liberated Africans, both in Africa and in

the British West Indies, see Johnson U. J. Asiegbu, *Slavery and the Politics of Liberation, 1787–1861* (London, 1969).

[55] Turnbull's despatches present a vivid picture of the heated debate in the Royal Economic Society of Havana over the contents of the report to be presented to the Captain-General. Turnbull to Aberdeen, no. 77, 25 Nov. 1841, F.O. 84/359.

[56] [Domingo del Monte] 'Ecsamen de las causas de la continuación actual del tráfico de negros en la isla de Cuba, y medios de conseguir su efectiva abolición', 17 Dec. 1841, encl. in Turnbull to Aberdeen, no. 84, 18 Dec. 1841, and Memorial of the *Hijos del País* to the London Anti-Slavery Society, 3 Oct. 1841, encl. in Turnbull to Aberdeen, no. 76, 6 Nov. 1841, F.O. 84/359.

[57] For biographical details on del Monte's life see Francisco Calcagno, *Diccionario biográfico cubano* (New York, 1878) pp. 232–7, and José A. Fernández Castro, ed., *Domingo del Monte*, Colección de libros cubanos, XII (Havana, 1929).

[58] Minute on Valdés to the Minister of Foreign Affairs, no. 57, 3 Nov. 1841, A.H.N., estado, leg. 8.052; González to Aston, 20 Dec. 1841, encl. in Aston to Aberdeen, no. 57, 22 Dec. 1841, F.O. 84/355; Sancho to Aberdeen, 31 Jan. 1842 and reply, 12 Feb. 1842, F.O. 84/400.

[59] Aston to Aberdeen, pvt., 29 Jan. 1842, B.M. Add. Mss. 43145, fol. 65; Hinton to Aberdeen, 21 Dec. 1843, F.O. 84/501.

[60] For the failure of European colonization projects see D. C. Corbitt, 'Immigration in Cuba', *H.A.H.R.*, vol. XXII (1942), pp. 280–308.

[61] R. R. Madden, *The Island of Cuba* . . . (London, 1849), p. 86.

[62] Ferrer to Aston, 16 Feb., encl. in Aston to Palmerston, no. 5, 23 Feb. 1841, F.O. 84/354; minute of a despatch to the Spanish Ambassador, London, 16 Feb. 1841, A.H.N., estado, leg. 8.053.

[63] Aston to Palmerston, pvt., 23 Feb. 1841, Broadlands Mss., GC/AS/171/3.

[64] *Ibid.* A *real* was worth about 2 1/2 pence.

[65] Alava to the Minister of Foreign Affairs, no. 668, 4 March, and González to the Minister of Foreign Affairs, no. 1, 4 March 1841, A.H.N., estado, leg. 8.053.

[66] Memorandum, 18 March 1841, A.H.N., estado, leg. 8.026.

[67] Flores to the Minister of Foreign Affairs, no. 38, 29 July, and minute of reply, 14 Aug. 1841; Valdés to the Minister of Foreign Affairs, no. 4, 3 Apr., and minute of reply, 28 June 1841, A.H.N., estado, leg. 8.053.

[68] *Anti-Slavery Reporter*, 14 July 1841. The original letter identifying the author can be found in Br. Emp. Mss., S18, G77, Cocking to Tredgold, 1 May 1841.

[69] Minute of a royal order to the Capts.-Gen. of Puerto Rico and Cuba, 3 Aug. 1841, A.H.N., estado, leg. 8.053.

[70] Palmerston to Flores, draft, 17 Aug. 1841, F.O. 84/353; Flores to the Minister of Foreign Affairs, no. 55, 30 Aug. 1841, A.H.N., estado, leg. 8.053; same to same, no. 44, 14 Aug. and no. 66, 30 Sept. with encl.,

Flores to Aberdeen, 22 Sept.; Aberdeen to Flores, 18 Oct., encl. in Flores to the Minister of Foreign Affairs, no. 78, 21 Oct. 1841, A.H.N., estado, leg. 8.054.

71 Valdés to the Minister of Foreign Affairs, no. 29, 31 July 1841, A.H.N., estado, leg. 8.054.

72 Valdés to the Minister of Foreign Affairs, no. 66, 30 Nov., and minute of despatch to the Spanish Ambassador, London, 20 Dec. 1841, A.H.N., estado, leg. 8.054.

73 Petition of 21 shipowners and merchants of London to Aberdeen, 12 Jan., and petition of 16 shipowners and merchants of Havana to Aberdeen, 20 Jan. 1842, F.O. 84/611. Valdés obtained a copy in advance of the Havana petition and sent it to Spain. Encl. in Valdés to the Minister of Foreign Affairs, no. 4, reservado, 6 Dec. 1841, A.H.N., estado, leg. 8.054.

74 Aberdeen to Turnbull, draft, 10 Feb. 1842, F.O. 72/608.

75 Saco to del Monte, 19 March 1843, *Centón epistolario*, vol. v, pp. 91–2.

76 Valdés to the Minister of Foreign Affairs, no. 5, reservado, 10 Feb. 1842, A.H.N., estado, leg. 8.054.

77 Minister of Marine and Colonies to the Minister of Foreign Affairs, 25 May 1842, A.H.N., estado, leg. 8.054.

78 His successor, Crawford, found him there when he arrived. Crawford to Aberdeen, 13 June 1842, F.O. 84/401. Turnbull complained of receiving threatening letters, but it was later established he had written them himself and arranged to have them sent anonymously. Crawford to Bidwell, 1 Oct. 1842, F.O. 72/609.

79 Turnbull to Aberdeen, 14 June 1842, F.O. 84/608.

80 Valdés to the Minister of Foreign Affairs, no. 140, 30 June 1842, A.H.N., estado, leg. 8.054; same to same, no. 120, 18 Apr. 1842, leg. 8.025 (1).

81 For details of this incident see Saco, *Historia de la esclavitud de la raza africana*, vol. 4, pp. 174–94.

82 Crawford to Aberdeen, no. 26, 15 Aug. 1842, F.O. 84/401. Turnbull had previously written to Aberdeen asking for another post or for compensation. He was never at a loss for schemes. He had suggested that he might be made a Lieutenant-Governor of a West Indian island, or, alternatively, sent to Peru as consul with authority to negotiate the cession of the guano islands. Turnbull to Aberdeen, 26 March 1842, F.O. 72/608, and Turnbull to Joseph Sturge, 12 Apr. 1842, Br. Emp. Mss, S18 C110/56 a–c.

83 J. G. Taylor, *The United States and Cuba: Eight Years of Change and Travel* (London, 1851), p. 284.

84 For accounts of Turnbull's arrest and expulsion see Crawford to Bidwell, no. 38, 5 Nov. 1842, F.O. 84/401, and same to same, 7 May 1843, F.O. 72/634; Valdés to the Minister of Foreign Affairs, nos. 181 and 187, 5 and 30 Nov. 1842, A.H.N., estado, leg. 8.054. Turnbull later published his own version. David Turnbull, *The Jamaica Movement for promoting the enforcement of the Slave-Trade Treaties and the suppression of the slave-trade …* (London, 1850), pp. 221–32. He also recounted the episode in testimony

before a Select Committee of the House of Lords, 7 May 1850. *Report from the Select Committee of the House of Lords on the African Slave Trade* (1850), 590, IX, paras. 810–18.

[85] Turnbull to Aberdeen, 13 Feb., F.O. memorandum, 16 Jan., and Aberdeen to Turnbull, draft, 15 March 1843, F.O. 72/635.

[86] Enclosures in Valdés to the Minister of Foreign Affairs, no. 187, 30 Nov. 1842, A.H.N., estado, leg. 8.054.

[87] Enclosure in Valdés to the Minister of Foreign Affairs, no. 201, 31 Dec. 1842, A.H.N., estado, leg. 8.038.

[88] Valdés to the Minister of Foreign Affairs, no. 196, 6 Dec. 1842, A.H.N., estado, leg. 8.054; Crawford to Bidwell, 6 Jan., and no. 20, 5 May 1843, F.O. 72/634.

[89] Valdés to the Minister of Foreign Affairs, no. 196, 6 Dec. 1842, A.H.N., estado, leg. 8.054.

[90] Minister of Marine and Colonies to the Minister of Foreign Affairs, 14 Jan., and reply, 27 Jan. 1843, A.H.N., estado, leg. 8.054.

[91] Spanish Ambassador, London, to the Minister of Foreign Affairs, no. 251, 12 Jan. 1843, A.H.N., estado, leg. 8.054.

[92] Valdés to the Minister of Foreign Affairs, no. 222, 31 March 1843, A.H.N., estado, leg. 8.054.

[93] Eric Williams, 'The Negro Slave Trade in Anglo-Spanish Relations', *Caribbean Historical Review*, vol. 1 (1950), pp. 33–4.

CHAPTER 9
THE ESCALERA CONSPIRACY

[1] Duvon C. Corbitt, 'A Petition for the Continuation of O'Donnell as Captain-General of Cuba', *H.A.H.R.*, vol. XVI (1936), p. 537.

[2] Franklin Knight, *Slave Society in Cuba during the Nineteenth Century* (Madison: University of Wisconsin Press, 1970), p. 81; Arthur F. Corwin, *Spain and the Abolition of Slavery in Cuba, 1817–1886* (Austin: University of Texas Press, 1967), p. 81.

[3] Gwendolyn Hall, *Social Control in Slave Plantation Societies, a Comparison of Saint Domingue and Cuba* (Baltimore: Johns Hopkins Press, 1971), p. 57.

[4] José de Ahumada y Centurión, *Memoria histórico-política de la isla de Cuba* (Havana, 1874), p. 76.

[5] *Ibid.*, pp. 47–254. For a similar interpretation by another peninsular historian see José Ferrer de Couto, *Los negros en sus diversos estados y condiciones: tales como son, como se supone que son, y como deben ser* (New York, 1864), pp. 75–84.

[6] D. Justo Zaragoza, *Las insurrecciones en Cuba: Apuntes para la historia política de esta isla en el presente siglo*, vol. 1 (Madrid, 1872), p. 512. See also pp. 283, 287–8, 480–1, 545–51, 560–5, for his account of British abolitionism and the Escalera conspiracy.

[7] 'Sentencia pronunciada por la Sección de la Comisión Militar establecida en la Ciudad de Matanzas para conocer de la causa de conspiración de la gente de color, 30 June 1844', A.H.N., estado, leg. 8.057.

[8] Mario Hernández y Sánchez-Barba, 'David Turnbull y el problema de la esclavitud en Cuba', *Anuario de estudios americanos*, vol. XIV (1957), pp. 298–9

[9] Humberto Castañeda, 'El caso de Mr David Turnbull, El Consul Inglés', *Revista de la Universidad de la Habana*, vols. 168–9 (July–Oct. 1964), pp. 150–1.

[10] Valdés to the Minister of Foreign Affairs, no. 46, 9 Oct. 1841, A.H.N., estado, leg. 8.015. The uprising is discussed in Vidal Morales y Morales, *Iniciadores y primeros mártires de la revolución cubana*, vol. 1 (Havana, 1963), pp. 251–2.

[11] Turnbull to Palmerston, no. 75, 30 Oct. 1841, F.O. 84/358.

[12] Cocking to Palmerston, 1 Oct. 1846, F.O. 72/709.

[13] Biographical information on Cocking can be found in: unsigned memorandum 23 May 1843, F.O. 72/635; Turnbull to Palmerston, nos. 26, 35 and 42, 7 and 18 March and 2 Apr. 1841, F.O. 72/584, and Turnbull to Palmerston, no. 50, 22 Apr. 1841, F.O. 72/585; Cocking's correspondence with the British and Foreign Anti-Slavery Society is in Br. Emp. Mss., S20, G77, Rhodes House, Oxford.

[14] Turnbull to Crawford, 26 June, and reply, 27 June, encl. in Crawford to Aberdeen, no. 3, 30 June 1842, F.O. 84/401; Crawford to Bidwell, 1 Oct. 1842, F.O. 72/609.

[15] Cocking to Palmerston, 1 Oct. 1846, F.O. 72/709.

[16] Minute 149, meeting of 30 June 1843, Br. Emp. Mss., S20, E2/7.

[17] Cocking to Wilson, 10 Apr., 6 May 1844, 18 Apr. 1845, 7 and 10 July 1846, F.O. 199/20.

[18] Stanley to Cocking, draft, 17 Nov. 1846, F.O. 72/709.

[19] *Boletín del Archivo Nacional de Cuba*, 2nd ed. (Havana, 1904), no. 5, pp. 3–9, and no. 6, pp. 1–9.

[20] Crawford to Bidwell, 1 Aug. 1842, F.O. 72/609.

[21] Crawford to Bidwell, 1 Oct. 1842, F.O. 72/609.

[22] Crawford to Aberdeen, 8 Nov. 1842, F.O. 84/401.

[23] Cocking to Palmerston, 1 Oct. 1846, F.O. 72/709.

[24] Herminio Portell Vilá, *Narciso López y su época*, vol. 1 (Havana, 1930), p. 151.

[25] Crawford to Aberdeen, 6 Dec. 1842, F.O. 72/609, and Crawford to Bidwell, 6 Jan. 1843, F.O. 72/634.

[26] Crawford to Aberdeen, 20 Nov. 1842, F.O. 84/401.

[27] *Ibid.*, 8 Nov. 1842.

[28] Turnbull to Russell, 19 May 1841, F.O. 84/357. For the Turnbull–del Monte correspondence see *Centón epistolario*, vol. V, pp. 26–7 and 53.

[29] Turnbull to Palmerston, with encl., 15 Dec. 1840, F.O. 72/559.

[30] The letter is acknowledged in Everett to del Monte, 6 Jan. 1843, *Centón epistolario*, vol. V, pp. 86–7.

[31] [Dr J. G. F. Wurdemann] *Notes on Cuba* (Boston, 1844), p. 252.

[32] *Ibid.*, p. 265.

[33] Everett to del Monte, 20 May 1843, *Centón epistolario*, vol. V, pp. 101–3.

[34] For some of these rumours see Thompson to Butler, 24 Nov. 1841, Tyler to Webster, 16 Dec. 1841, Calhoun to Webster, 14 Feb., and nos. 37 and 39, 4 and 6 Nov. 1842, Department of State, Consular Despatches, Havana, T. 20, vol 18.

[35] W. R. Manning, ed., *Diplomatic Correspondence of the United States, Inter-American Affairs, 1831–1860,* vol. XI (Washington, 1932–9), Forsyth to Vail, 15 July 1840, p. 23.

[36] *Ibid.*, Webster to Campbell, 14 Jan. 1843, pp. 26–9.

[37] *Ibid.*, Webster to Irving, 17 Jan. 1843, pp. 29–30, and Irving to Webster, 10 March 1843, pp. 331–2. See also Reynolds to Buchanan, 12 Aug. 1847, pp. 414–28, for an indication of the long-lasting suspicions produced by these reports.

[38] Charles Francis Adams, ed., *Memoirs of John Quincy Adams, comprising portions of his Diary from 1795 to 1848,* 12 vols (Philadelphia, 1874–7), vol. XI, pp. 351, 353.

[39] Argaiz to Valdés, 16 Jan. 1843, encl. in Valdés to the Minister of Foreign Affairs, no. 16, 8 Feb. 1843, A.H.N., estado, leg. 8.039.

[40] Valdés to Argaiz, 8 Feb. 1843, encl. in *ibid.*

[41] Turnbull to Russell, 19 May 1841, F.O. 84/357.

[42] Crawford to Aberdeen, 12 Aug. 1842, and unsigned memorandum, n.d., F.O. 72/609.

[43] Turnbull to Hill, 1 July 1842, encl. in Cocking to Palmerston, 1 Oct 1846, F.O. 72/709.

[44] Crawford to Aberdeen, no. 16, 18 Apr. 1843, with encl., Rodríguez to Crawford, 22 March 1843, F.O. 72/634.

[45] Memorandum by Palmerston, 6 Nov. 1846, on Cocking to Palmerston, 1 Oct. 1846, F.O. 72/709.

[46] Memorandum by Bidwell, 11 Nov. 1846, F.O. 72/709.

[47] Palomino to del Monte, 16 Sept. 1844, *Centón epistolario,* vol. VI, pp. 109–12.

[48] Manning, *Diplomatic Correspondence,* vol. XI, Campbell to Upshur, 5 Oct. 1843, p. 333.

[49] Crawford to Aberdeen, no. 15, 18 Apr. 1843, F.O. 72/634.

[50] Cocking to Palmerston, 1 Oct. 1846, F.O. 72/709.

[51] Crawford to Aberdeen, no. 35, 9 Aug. 1843, F.O. 72/634.

[52] Crawford to Aberdeen, nos. 17 and 24, 19 Apr. and 20 May 1843, F.O. 72/634.

[53] Crawford to Aberdeen, no. 22, 6 May 1843, F.O. 72/634; Crawford to Vice-Admiral Adams, 20 and 22 May 1843, encl. in Admiralty to Foreign Office, 19 June 1843.

[54] Crawford to Aberdeen, no. 42, 27 Dec. 1843, F.O. 84/520. For different views of this uprising and the alleged conspiracy it exposed see Vidal Morales y Morales, *Iniciadores y primeros mártires de la revolución cubana,*

vol. 1 (Havana, 1963), pp. 277–304; P.S. Foner, *A History of Cuba and its Relations with the United States*, vol. 1 (New York, 1962), pp. 214–28; and Francisco G. del Valle, 'La Conspiración de la Escalera', *Cuba Contemporánea*, vol. 39 (Nov.–Dec. 1925), pp. 117–45 and 225–54. Pedro Guiteras, in his *Cuba y su gobierno* (London, 1853), pp. 42–55, suggested that the Matanzas slave revolt gave rise to rumours that British abolitionist agents were sending English-speaking Africans on slave ships going to Cuba in order to start a revolution within the island. These rumours spread quickly and, according to Guiteras, were the real reason for the intervention of Military Commissions.

55 The validity of the 1841 census has been questioned both at the time and subsequently, most recently by Kenneth Kiple in his *Blacks in Colonial Cuba*, pp. 47–58. Creoles in the 1840s used it, however, as evidence that the whites were steadily becoming a smaller minority of the island's population.

56 Franklin Knight discusses the measures imposed on the free blacks in his *Slave Society in Cuba*, pp. 96–7, and also analyses the 1842 slave code, pp. 126–32. For a more detailed coverage of the free coloured community in Cuba see his article entitled 'Cuba' in D. W. Cohen and Jack P. Greene, eds., *Neither Slave nor Free*, pp. 278–308.

57 D. B. Davis, *The Slave Power Conspiracy and the Paranoid Style* (Baton Rouge, La., 1969), p. 5.

58 *Ibid.*, p. 6.

59 *Ibid.*, p. 35.

60 Crawford to Aberdeen, no. 1, 17 Jan. 1844, F.O. 84/520.

61 Crawford to Aberdeen, no. 40, 31 Jan. 1844, F.O. 84/520. For eye-witness reports of the torture see Sánchez to Crawford, 8 March 1844, encl. in Crawford to Aberdeen, no. 9, 9 March 1844; José de Castilla to Crawford, 9 Apr. 1844, encl. in Crawford to Aberdeen, 15 Apr.; and Bell to Crawford, 29 July 1844, encl. in Crawford to Aberdeen, no. 26, 7 Aug. 1844. See also Richard Kimball, *Cuba and the Cubans* . . . (New York, 1850), pp. 83–92.

62 Francisco G. del Valle, 'La Conspiración de la Escalera' *Cuba Contemporánea*, vol. 39 (Nov.–Dec. 1925) p. 143. On the numbers involved see Joaquín Llaverías y Martínez, *La comisión militar, ejecutiva y permanente de la isla de Cuba* (Havana, 1929), pp. 92–3.

63 Commissioners to Aberdeen, nos. 20 and 23, 8 Apr. and 8 May 1844, F.O. 84/508.

64 Commissioners to Aberdeen, no. 23, 8 May 1844, F.O. 84/508.

65 *Anti-Slavery Reporter*, vol. V, 24 July 1844. See also, 17 Apr., 29 May and 26 June.

66 Crawford to Palmerston, no. 9, 4 Aug. 1847, F.O. 84/674.

67 O'Donnell to the Minister of Foreign Affairs, no. 30, 28 Feb. 1844, A.H.N., estado, leg. 8.025(1).

68 Kennedy to Aberdeen, no. 35, 31 July 1844, F.O. 84/509.

69 José Gutiérrez de la Concha, *Memorias* . . . (Madrid, 1853), p. 15, cited in Knight, *Slave Society in Cuba*, p. 95.

[70] Crawford to Aberdeen, 7 Dec. 1842, F.O. 72/609.

[71] Hall, *Social Control in Slave Plantation Societies*, p. 61.

[72] Turnbull to Aberdeen, 21 Aug. 1844, F.O. 84/516. Bulwer to Martínez de la Rosa, 24 Oct. 1844, A.H.N., estado, leg. 8.057.

[73] O'Donnell to the Minister of Foreign Affairs, no. 95, 5 Jan. 1845, A.H.N., estado, leg. 8.057; Sotomayor to Aberdeen, 25 June 1845, F.O. 84/576. The British government did not reply to this note.

[74] Manning, *Diplomatic Correspondence*, vol. XI, Campbell to Upshur, 5 Oct. 1843, p. 332.

[75] Aberdeen to Crawford, draft, 1 March 1843, F.O. 72/634. This phrase was not, however, included in the despatch as sent.

[76] *Proceedings* (1843), p. 144.

[77] *Ibid.* pp. 180–3, 190.

[78] [Domingo del Monte] 'The Present State of Cuba', *The United States Magazine and Democratic Review*, vol. XV (1844), p. 478. Everett's behind-the-scenes role in the publication of this article is described in Everett to del Monte, 27 Nov. 1844, *Centón epistolario*, vol. VI, p. 129.

[79] Vicente Vásquez Queipo, *Cuba, ses ressources, son administration, sa population ...* , trans. A. d'Avrainville (Paris, 1851), p. 43. Saco's original pamphlet, 'Carta de un cubano a un amigo suyo', was incorporated into the French translation of Vásquez Queipo's work. For Saco's various exchanges with Vásquez Queipo, see José Antonio Saco, *Colección de papeles científicos, históricos, políticos, y de otros ramos sobre la isla de Cuba*, vol. 3 (Havana, 1960), pp. 192–328.

[80] Knight, *Slave Society in Cuba*, p. 132.

[81] Everett to Calhoun, 17 June 1844, in *Correspondence Addressed to John C. Calhoun 1837–1849*, ed. C. S. Boucher and R. P. Brooks, *American Historical Association Annual Report* (1929), pp. 240 and 216–17.

[82] Basil Rauch, *American Interest in Cuba, 1848–1855* (New York: Columbia University Press, 1948), p. 44.

[83] *The United States Magazine and Democratic Review*, vol. XV (1844), p. 477.

CHAPTER 10

THE PENAL LAW OF 1845

[1] Palmerston to Villiers, no. 1, draft, 22 Feb. 1836, F.O. 84/201.

[2] Minutes of 5 and 20 May on extract, 25 March, of Villiers to Mendizábal, 10 March 1836, A.H.N., estado, leg. 8.035. See also Villiers to Palmerston, no. 4, 12 March 1836, F.O. 84/201.

[3] Palmerston to Villiers, no. 2, draft, 28 Feb, 1837, F.O. 84/221.

[4] Villiers to Calatrava, 2 Apr., encl. in Villiers to Palmerston, no. 8, 8 Apr. 1837; Calatrava to Villiers, 9 June, encl. in Villiers to Palmerston, no. 12, 18 June; Palmerston to Villiers, no. 10, draft, 10 Aug. 1837; Villiers to Bardají, 25 Aug., encl. in Villiers to Palmerston, no. 20, 26 Aug.,

Villiers to Palmerston, no. 28, 3 Dec. 1837, F.O. 84/221. See also Villiers to Palmerston, no. 15, 10 March, and no. 16, 14 Apr. 1838, F.O. 84/244.
⁵ Villiers to Palmerston, no. 30, 7 July 1838, F.O. 84/245. For accounts of General Lorenzo's rebellion and the exclusion of the Cuban deputies see Juan Pérez de la Riva, ed., *Correspondencia reservada del Capitán General Don Miguel Tacón* (Havana, 1963), pp. 56–70, and José Antonio Saco, *Colección de papeles científicos, históricos, políticos, y de otros ramos sobre la isla de Cuba*, vol. 3 (Havana, 1960), pp. 91–159.
⁶ Villiers to Palmerston, no. 30, 7 July 1838, F.O. 84/245.
⁷ Memoranda by Palmerston, 27 Aug. and 23 Sept. 1838, F.O. 84/246.
⁸ Palmerston to Villiers, no. 31, draft, 26 Oct. 1838, F.O. 84/246.
⁹ Aberdeen to Aston, no. 24, draft, 31 Dec. 1842, F.O. 84/400.
¹⁰ *Hansard*, 3rd series (1844), vol. LXXVI, pp. 951–2.
¹¹ Aberdeen to Bulwer, pvt., 30 June 1844, B.M. Add. Mss. 43146, fol. 323.
¹² *The United States Magazine and Democratic Review*, vol. XV (1844), p. 480.
¹³ Turnbull to British commissioners, 26 Apr., encl. in commissioners to Palmerston, no. 28, 22 May 1841, and memorandum by Palmerston, 21 July 1841, F.O. 84/348.
¹⁴ Commissioners to Palmerston, no. 60, 29 Oct., with encl., Valdés to commissioners, 22 Oct.; commissioners to Aberdeen, no. 65, 10 Dec. 1841, F.O. 84/349.
¹⁵ Commissioners to Aberdeen, no. 6, 17 Jan. 1842, with encl., Valdés to commissioners, 10 Jan., F.O. 84/395.
¹⁶ Commissioners to Aberdeen, no. 9, 26 Jan. 1842, F.O. 84/395; Turnbull to Aberdeen, no. 5, 1 March 1842, F.O. 84/401.
¹⁷ Commissioners to Aberdeen, no. 14, 7 March 1842, F.O. 84/395.
¹⁸ Commissioners to Aberdeen, no. 50, 23 Aug. 1842, F.O. 84/396; Crawford to Aberdeen, no. 13, 25 Aug. 1842, F.O. 84/401.
¹⁹ Crawford to Aberdeen, no. 4, 30 June 1842, with encl., Valdés to Crawford, 28 June, F.O. 84/401.
²⁰ Warren S. Howard, *American Slavers and the Federal Law, 1837–1862* (Berkeley: University of California Press, 1963), p. 39.
²¹ *Ibid.*, pp. 30–3, 37–40, 43, and Appendix F, pp. 241–2. On the Webster–Ashburton Treaty see H. G. Soulsby, *The Right of Search and the Slave Trade in Anglo-American Relations, 1814–1862* (Baltimore, 1933), pp. 78–117, and for the participation of American vessels in the Brazilian slave trade see Leslie Bethell, *The Abolition of the Brazilian Slave Trade: Britain, Brazil and the Slave Trade Question, 1807–1869* (Cambridge, 1970), pp. 188–93.
²² Commissioners to Aberdeen, no. 56, 14 Sept. 1842, encl. a translation of the petition, F.O. 84/396; Crawford to Aberdeen, no. 17, 27 Sept. 1842, F.O. 84/401.
²³ Valdés to the Minister of Foreign Affairs, no. 159, 13 Sept. 1842, A.H.N., estado, leg. 8.038.
²⁴ Commissioners to Aberdeen, no. 56, 14 Sept. 1842, F.O. 84/396; Crawford to Aberdeen, no. 17, 27 Sept. 1842, F.O. 84/401.

25 Valdés to the Minister of Foreign Affairs, no. 157, 31 Aug. 1842, A.H.N., estado, leg. 8.038.

26 Commissioners to Aberdeen, no. 5, 2 Jan. 1843, F.O. 84/451.

27 Crawford to Aberdeen, no. 28, 7 Dec. 1842, F.O. 84/401.

28 Valdés to the Minister of Foreign Affairs, no. 224, 21 March 1843, A.H.N., estado, leg. 8.035.

29 Memoranda, Ministry of Foreign Affairs, 4 Apr., and minute 23 Apr. 1843, A.H.N., estado, leg. 8.035.

30 Cited in memorandum, Ministry of Foreign Affairs, 7 Jan. 1844, A.H.N., estado, leg. 8.035.

31 Minute, 30 May, on extract dated 21 May, of Valdés to the Minister of Foreign Affairs, no. 224, 21 March 1843, A.H.N., estado, leg. 8.035.

32 A translation of this royal order is encl. in commissioners to Aberdeen, no. 13, 20 Feb. 1844, F.O. 84/508. Domingo del Monte analysed it in 'The Present State of Cuba', *The United States Magazine and Democratic Review*, vol. xv (1844), pp. 478–83.

33 Crawford to Aberdeen, 12 Apr. 1843, F.O. 84/463.

34 Aberdeen to Aston, no. 6, draft, 7 June 1843, F.O. 84/462; commissioners to Aberdeen, nos. 18 and 24, 18 Apr. and 1 June 1843, F.O. 84/451; Kennedy to Aberdeen, 7 Oct. 1843, F.O. 84/452; Aberdeen to Aston, no. 11, draft, 20 July 1843, F.O. 84/462.

35 For the political background in Spain see Raymond Carr, *Spain, 1808–1939* (Oxford, 1966), pp. 210–46, and E. Christiansen, *The Origins of Military Power in Spain, 1800–1854* (Oxford, 1967), pp. 67–135.

36 Kennedy to Aberdeen, separate, 7 Oct. 1843, F.O. 84/452.

37 Valdés to the Minister of Marine and Colonies, no. 31, reservado, 1 June 1843, A.H.N., estado, leg. 8.039.

38 I have examined these figures in my article, 'Statistics of the Slave Trade to Cuba, 1790–1867', *Journal of Latin American Studies*, vol. 3, no. 2 (1971), pp. 144–5.

39 *Ibid.*

40 Carr, *Spain*, p. 260. For biographical details on O'Donnell see V. Kiernan, *The Revolution of 1854 in Spanish History* (Oxford, 1966), p. 14; Francisco Calcagno, *Diccionario biográfico cubano* (New York, 1878), pp. 457–8; Antonio Rivera, *Reseña sucinta é historia de los hechos mas notables del general don Leopoldo O'Donnell, en la isla de Cuba* (Madrid, 1854); Manuel Alfaro Ibo, *Apuntes para la historia de D. Leopoldo O'Donnell* (Madrid, 1868), pp. 75–209 for his early life and pp. 785–833 for an unconvincing defence of his Cuban career.

41 Commissioners to Aberdeen, nos. 49 and 52, 8 Nov. and 8 Dec. 1843, F.O. 84/452.

42 Commissioners to Aberdeen, no. 5, 1 Jan. 1844, F.O. 84/508; Crawford to Aberdeen, no. 9, 9 March 1844, F.O. 84/520.

43 Crawford to Aberdeen, no. 28, 19 Aug. 1844, F.O. 84/520.

44 O'Donnell to the Minister of Foreign Affairs, no. 2, reservado, 20 March 1844, A.H.N., estado, leg. 8.039.

45 Commissioners to Palmerston, no. 3, 2 Jan. 1837, F.O. 84/216; same to same, no. 4, 1 Jan. 1841, F.O. 84/348; commissioners to Aberdeen, no. 4, 1 Jan. 1842, F.O. 84/395.

46 Petition of Matanzas planters, 30 Nov. 1843, encl. in commissioners to Aberdeen, no. 13, 20 Feb. 1844, F.O. 84/508.

47 Commissioners to Aberdeen, no. 5, 1 Jan. 1844, F.O. 84/508.

48 Commissioners to Aberdeen, no. 13, 20 Feb. 1844, F.O. 84/508; Crawford to Aberdeen, no. 5, 8 Feb. 1844, F.O. 84/520.

49 Reports of Royal Tribunal of Commerce, 29 May, and Royal Patriotic Society, 24 Apr. 1844, A.H.N., ultramar, leg. 3547; see also Kennedy to Aberdeen, no. 36, 3 Aug. 1844, F.O. 84/509, and Crawford to Aberdeen, no. 29, 8 Sept. 1844, F.O. 84/520.

50 Crawford to Aberdeen, no. 29, 8 Sept. 1844, F.O. 84/520.

51 Vásquez Queipo's report was written 13 March 1844 and later published. See V. Vásquez Queipo, *Cuba, ses resources*... trans. A. d'Avrainville (Paris, 1851), pp. 342–50.

52 Extract dated 27 Aug. of Villanueva to the Minister of Foreign Affairs, 20 Apr. 1844, A.H.N., estado, leg. 8.035.

53 Report of the commission on the penal law, 17 Aug. 1844, A.H.N., ultramar, leg. 3547.

54 Commissioners to Aberdeen, nos. 13 and 14, 20 Feb. and 7 March 1844, F.O. 84/508; Bulwer to Aberdeen, no. 7, 2 March 1844, with encl., *El Corresponsal*, 25 Feb., F.O. 84/519.

55 Bulwer to Aberdeen, no. 5, 24 Feb. 1844, with encl., *El Heraldo*, 21 Feb., F.O. 84/519.

56 Aston to Almodóvar, 21 March, encl. in Aston to Aberdeen, no. 3, 31 March; Jerningham to the Duke of Frías, 14 Sept., encl. in Jerningham to Aberdeen, no. 1, 15 Sept.; Jerningham to the Duke of Frías, 2 Nov., encl. in Jerningham to Aberdeen, no. 2, 4 Nov. 1843, F.O. 84/462.

57 Aberdeen to Bulwer, no. 16, draft, 31 Dec. 1843, F.O. 84/462.

58 Bulwer to González Bravo, 5 & 6 Feb., encl. in Bulwer to Aberdeen, no. 3, 9 Feb.; Bulwer to González Bravo, 6 Apr., encl. in Bulwer to Aberdeen, no. 9, 10 Apr.; González Bravo to Bulwer, 26 Apr., encl. in Bulwer to Aberdeen, no. 11, 15 May 1844, F.O. 84/519.

59 Valdés to the Minister of Marine and Colonies, 25 Apr. 1844, encl. the report and the draft penal law, A.H.N., ultramar, leg. 3547. Bulwer enclosed a translation of the draft law in Bulwer to Aberdeen, no. 13, 28 June 1844, F.O. 84/519.

60 Minister of Foreign Affairs to Minister of Marine and Colonies, 11 Apr., and reply, 25 May 1844, A.H.N., ultramar, leg. 3549.

61 Aberdeen to Bulwer. pvt., 9 May 1844, B.M. Add. Mss. 43146, fol. 230.

62 *Ibid.*, pvt., 30 June 1844, fol. 323.

63 Bulwer to Aberdeen, pvt., 15 May and 3 June 1844, B.M. Add. Mss. 43146, fols. 233 and 254.

64 Royal order of 15 June, encl. in Bulwer to Aberdeen, no. 12, 17 June 1844, F.O. 84/519.

[65] Minute of Minister of Foreign Affairs to Ministers of War and Marine and Colonies, 18 June 1844, A.H.N., estado, leg. 8.039; minute of royal order to Capts.-Gen. of Cuba and Puerto Rico, 19 June 1844, A.H.N., ultramar, leg. 3547.

[66] Bulwer to Aberdeen, nos. 13, 14, 18 and 19, 28 and 29 June, 1 and 8 Nov. 1844, F.O. 84/519.

[67] Commissioners to Aberdeen, no. 12, 8 Feb. 1844, F.O. 84/508.

[68] O'Donnell to the Minister of Foreign Affairs, no. 67, 10 Aug. 1844, A.H.N., estado, leg. 8.039. For similar criticisms of the attitudes of the creole planters see Raul Cepero Bonilla, *Azúcar y Abolición* (Havana, 1960), pp. 32 and 36.

[69] O'Donnell to the Minister of Foreign Affairs, no. 70, 30 Aug. 1844, A.H.N., estado, leg. 8.039.

[70] Kennedy to Aberdeen, nos. 39 and 40, 20 and 30 Aug. 1844, F.O. 84/509.

[71] *Anti-Slavery Reporter*, vol. V, no. 11, 29 May 1844.

[72] *Hansard*, 3rd series (1844), vol. LXXVI, pp. 922–74. Dr Eric Williams' pungent comment is really unfair to Palmerston: 'In office he accomplished little. Out of office he goaded the government to greater efforts to accomplish what he had failed to do.' *Capitalism and Slavery*, 2nd ed. (London, 1964), p. 174.

[73] Aberdeen to Bulwer, pvt., 17 July 1844, B.M. Add. Mss. 43146, fol. 343.

[74] *Ibid.*, 15 Oct. 1844, fol. 405.

[75] Bulwer to Canning, pvt. and confid., 1 Nov. 1844, F.O. 84/519.

[76] Martínez de la Rosa to Bulwer, 7 Nov., encl. in Bulwer to Aberdeen, no. 22, 12 Nov. 1844, F.O. 84/519; Aberdeen to Bulwer, pvt., 27 Nov. 1844, B.M. Add. Mss. 43147, fol. 4.

[77] Minute of a royal order to Capt.-Gen. O'Donnell, 20 Dec. 1844, A.H.N., estado, leg. 8.035.

[78] The report was published in *El Heraldo*, 26 Jan. 1845. A copy can be found in A.H.N., estado, leg. 8.035.

[79] *Anti-Slavery Reporter*, vol. VI, no. 2, 22 Jan. 1845.

[80] Bulwer enclosed a copy of the amended law in Bulwer to Aberdeen, no. 9, 11 March 1845, F.O. 84/574.

[81] Bulwer to Martínez de la Rosa, 9 Jan., and reply, 14 Jan., encl. in Bulwer to Aberdeen, no. 2, 25 Jan. 1845; Martínez de la Rosa to Bulwer, confid., 14 Jan., encl. in Bulwer to Aberdeen, no. 3, confid., 25 Jan. 1845; Aberdeen to Bulwer, no. 2, draft, 13 Feb. 1845, F.O. 84/574. See also Bulwer to Aberdeen, pvt., 11 Jan. 1845, B.M. Add. Mss. 43147, fol. 86.

[82] Aberdeen to Bulwer, pvt., 13 Jan. and 1 March 1845, B.M. Add. Mss. 43147, fols. 92 and 109.

[83] *Hansard*, 3rd series (1845), vol. LXXX, pp. 199–223.

[84] *Anti-Slavery Reporter*, vol. VI, no. 11, 28 May 1845.

[85] For accounts of the Aberdeen Act of 1845 see Bethell, *The Abolition of the Brazilian Slave Trade*, pp. 242–66 and W.D. Jones, 'The Origins and

Passage of Lord Aberdeen's Act', *H.A.H.R.*, vol. XLII (1962), pp. 502–20. Britain also was engaged in a heated diplomatic controversy with France in the early 1840s over the most effective means to suppress the foreign slave trade. On this see Lawrence C. Jennings, 'France, Great Britain, and the Repression of the Slave Trade, 1841–1845', *French Historical Studies*, vol. X, no. 1 (Spring 1977), pp. 101–25.

[86] Saco, *Papeles sobre Cuba*, vol. 2, p. 155.

[87] Technically, it was the second law, but the Criminal Code of 1822 was suppressed before the article on the slave trade became effective.

[88] Saco's 1844 pamphlet was entitled 'La Supresión del tráfico de esclavos africanos . . . ' and has been included in his *Papeles sobre Cuba*, vol. 2, pp. 90–154. For del Monte's role in its publication see Domingo del Monte, *Escritos*, ed. José A. Fernández de Castro, *Colección de libros cubanos*, XII (Havana, 1929), pp. 206–10. 'La Supresión' also received a very favourable review in the *Revue des Deux Mondes*. The reviewer, M. X. Durrieu, echoed Saco's fears about the likelihood of race revolution in Cuba if the slave trade was not checked: 'Cuba finds herself in a most perilous situation; Spain's authority, the supremacy of the white race, European civilization, are there endangered more than ever.' M. X. Durrieu, 'La traite à Cuba et le droit de visite', *Revue des Deux Mondes*, new series, vol. 9 (Paris, 1845), pp. 900–1. The whole article, pp. 899–923, is really a commentary on Saco's work and the need for major reforms in Cuba.

[89] Vásquez Queipo, *Cuba, ses ressources*, especially, pp. 11–13, 38–9, 80–1, and 109–21.

[90] D. Ramón de la Sagra, *Estudios coloniales con aplicación a la isla de Cuba* (Madrid, 1845). For an analysis of La Sagra's views see Manuel Núñez de Arenas, 'D. Ramón de la Sagra, reformador social'. *Revue hispanique*, vol. LX, no. 138 (April 1924), pp. 329–531. Professor Corwin, comparing the views of Saco and La Sagra, suggests they were 'in basic agreement' on the question of the slave trade, *Spain and the Abolition of Slavery in Cuba, 1817–1886* (Austin: University of Texas Press, 1967), pp. 83–4, notes 48 and 49. Both men opposed the continuation of the slave trade, but this should not obscure the fact that their opposition was founded on very different reasons and their solutions for Cuba's problems were poles apart. The peninsular, La Sagra, unquestioningly desired the abolition of slavery; the Cuban creole, Saco, refused even to discuss the issue.

[91] Tacón to the Minister of Foreign Affairs, 27 June 1844, A.H.N., estado, leg. 8.035; Valdés commission report, 25 Apr. 1844, A.H.N., ultramar, leg. 3547.

[92] O'Donnell to the Minister of Foreign Affairs, no. 5, reservado, 15 Feb. 1845, A.H.N., estado, leg. 8.035.

[93] Kennedy to Aberdeen, no. 14, 8 March 1845, F.O. 84/561.

CHAPTER 11
FREE TRADE AND ANNEXATIONISM

[1] C. Duncan Rice, '"Humanity Sold for Sugar!" The British Abolitionist Response to Free Trade in Slave-Grown Sugar', *The Historical Journal*, vol. XIII, no. 3 (1970), p. 408. See also Howard Temperley, *British antislavery, 1833–1870* (University of South Carolina Press, 1972), pp. 153–67, for another assessment of the British abolitionists' response to free trade.

[2] Cited in Rice, 'Humanity Sold for Sugar!', p. 410.

[3] Stephen Cave, *A Few Words on the encouragement given to Slavery and the Slave Trade . . .* (London, 1849), pp. 26, 29.

[4] John Taylor, *The United States and Cuba: Eight Years of Change and Travel* (London, 1851), p. 197.

[5] See, for example, Exeter Anti-Slavery Committee to Palmerston, 18 Jan. 1848, and Scoble to Palmerston, 6 Oct. 1848, F.O. 84/739.

[6] Scoble to the Earl of Derby, 10 Aug. 1852, F.O. 84/887.

[7] Memorandum by Ward, 2 May 1854, F.O. 84/921.

[8] Temperley, *British antislavery*, p. 176. See also Scoble to Palmerston, 26 Oct. 1846, F.O. 84/663.

[9] *Hansard*, 3rd Series (1847–8), vol. XCVI, p. 1101. For his earlier attempt see *Hansard*, 3rd Series (1845), vol. LXXXI, pp. 1156–72.

[10] Temperley in his *British antislavery*, pp. 176–9, contrasts Hutt's position and that of the British and Foreign Anti-Slavery Society.

[11] James Richardson, *The Cruisers: being a Letter to the Marquis of Lansdowne, Lord President, etc, in Defence of Armed Coercion for the Extinction of the Slave Trade* (London, 1849), p. 4. See Leslie Bethell, *The Abolition of the Brazilian Slave Trade: Britain, Brazil and the Slave-Trade Question, 1807–1869* (Cambridge, 1970), pp. 296–304, for a recent study of the rival camps.

[12] A Barrister, *Analysis of the Evidence given before the Select Committees upon the Slave Trade* (London, 1850), p. 95.

[13] W. L. Mathieson, *Great Britain and the Slave Trade, 1839–1865* (London, 1929), pp. 85–144.

[14] *A Letter from Lord Denman to Lord Brougham on the Final Extinction of the Slave-Trade* (London, 1848), p. viii. See also *A Second Letter . . .* (London, 1849). For his speeches in the House of Lords in 1848 see *Hansard*, 3rd Series (1848), vol. XCVI, pp. 1051–55, and vol. CI, pp. 365–74.

[15] *A Letter from Lord Denman . . .* , p. 59.

[16] Lieut. Henry Yule, *The African Squadron Vindicated* (London, 1850), p. 36.

[17] *P.P.* (1850), vol. IX, p. 8.

[18] Bethell, *The Abolition of the Brazilian Slave Trade*, p. 301.

[19] This paragraph is based on Bethell's excellent account, *ibid.*, pp. 321–63.

[20] *Hansard*, 3rd Series (1848), vol. XCVI, p. 41. Bentinck previously had advocated the seizure of Cuba to pay Spanish debts owing to British

bondholders. *Hansard*, 3rd Series (1847), vol. XCIII, pp. 1295–6.

[21] *P.P.* (1847–8), vol. XXIII, part 1, p. 5.

[22] F.O. memorandum, 11 Dec. 1851, F.O. 97/430.

[23] *P.P.* (1847–8), vol. XXII, p. 116.

[24] Russell to Palmerston, 1 Apr. 1850, Broadlands Mss., GC/RU/332/1.

[25] West Indian petitions were the instruments used to force debates on the Cuban slave trade in the House of Commons and the House of Lords in 1853, 1855 and 1857. See *Hansard*, 3rd Series (1853), vol. CXVII, pp. 488–92 and 762–76; (1855), vol. CXXXIX, pp. 113–16; (1857), vol. CXLVI, pp. 1492–1501. In 1861, the Chairman of the West India Committee initiated a similar debate, *Hansard*, 3rd Series (1861), vol. CLXI, pp. 950–89.

[26] David Turnbull, *The Jamaica Movement for promoting the enforcement of the Slave-Trade Treaties and the suppression of the slave-trade* (London, 1850), p. 61.

[27] *P.P.* (1850), vol. IX, pp. 84–5; Hall Pringle to Palmerston, 12 July 1850, F.O. 84/819.

[28] *P.P.* (1850), vol. IX, p. 69. For similar views see Edward Derby, *Further Facts connected with the West Indies. A Second Letter to . . . Gladstone* (London, 1851), p. 39.

[29] C. D. Donald, Secretary of the Glasgow West India Assoc. to Clarendon, 22 Apr. 1853, F.O. 84/921.

[30] A. Macgregor to Clarendon, 18 Jan. 1854, F.O. 84/951.

[31] Wodehouse to Macgregor, 14 Feb. 1854, F.O. 84/951.

[32] *P.P.* (1852–3), vol. XXXIX, pp. 131–2.

[33] Spanish consul, Jamaica, to Minister of Foreign Affairs, 20 Feb. 1857, encl. *The Colonial Standard and Jamaica Despatch*, 10 Feb., A.H.N., ultramar, leg. 4650.

[34] For the background to his campaign and the petitions themselves see Turnbull, *The Jamaica Movement* (London, 1850). The British and Foreign Anti-Slavery Society also renewed its support for Turnbull's plan; Scoble to Palmerston, 6 Oct. 1848, F.O. 84/739. See also the Glasgow West India Assoc. to Palmerston, 16 Jan. 1849, F.O. 84/777.

[35] *P.P.* (1849), vol. XIX, p. iv.

[36] Hutt to Lord Eddisbury, 26 May 1849, F.O. 84/777.

[37] *P.P.* (1849), vol. XIX, pp. 1–8.

[38] *P.P.* (1850), vol. IX, pp. 5 and 60–67.

[39] Palmerston to Lord Howden, no. 5, draft, 17 Sept. 1850; Howden to Palmerston, no. 2, 8 Oct. 1850, F.O. 84/796.

[40] Howden to Palmerston, no. 4, 24 Oct. 1850, with encl., Pidal to Howden, 19 Oct. 1850, F.O. 84/796.

[41] Minute by Palmerston, 31 May, on F.O. draft to Mrs Turnbull, 30 May 1851; Mrs Turnbull to Palmerston, 17 May 1851, F.O. 84/860. For Turnbull's instructions see Addington to Turnbull, draft, 17 Oct. 1850, F.O. 84/791.

[42] Turnbull to Palmerston, 16 July 1850, F.O. 84/791.

[43] Robert Baird, *Impressions and Experiences of the West Indies and North America in 1849*, vol. I (Edinburgh, 1849), pp. 179 and 195–6.

[44] Taylor, *The United States and Cuba*, p. 319.

[45] Hon. Amelia M. Murray, *Letters from the United States, Cuba and Canada*, vol. 2 (London, 1856), p. 85.

[46] Anthony Trollope, *The West Indies and the Spanish Main* (London, 1859), p. 155.

[47] A. Gallenga, *The Pearl of the Antilles* (London, 1873), p. 5.

[48] W. H. Hurlbert, *Gan-Eden: or Pictures of Cuba* (Boston, 1854), p. 115.

[49] *Hansard*, 3rd Series (1854), vol. CXXXV, pp. 1485–7.

[50] *P.P.* (1852–3), vol. XXXIX, p. iii.

[51] Hume to Lord John Russell, 15 Aug. 1853. See also Hume to Clarendon, 15 Aug. 1853, F.O. 84/921. Two copies of the report were presented to the Spanish government. Clarendon to Otway, draft, no. 57, 15 Oct. 1853, F.O. 84/904.

[52] Buchanan to Saunders, 17 June 1848, W. R. Manning, ed., *Diplomatic Correspondence of the United States. Inter-American Affairs*, vol. XI, doc. 5065, pp. 54–64.

[53] *La Verdad*, vol. I, no. 7, 9 Apr. 1848, encl. in Roncali to the Minister of the Colonies, no. 80, 9 June 1848, A.H.N., ultramar, leg. 4628.

[54] Kennedy to Palmerston, separate, 22 Apr. 1848, F.O. 84/714.

[55] Basil Rauch, *American Interest in Cuba, 1848–1855* (Columbia University Press, 1948), p. 208. Frederick Merk terms the coming together of annexationism and Manifest Destiny a 'Caribbeanized Manifest Destiny'. Cuba was not the only area of the Caribbean to be affected. Frederick Merk, *Manifest Destiny and Mission in American History* (New York, 1963), esp. pp. 202–14.

[56] Cited in Robert E. May, *The Southern Dream of a Caribbean Empire, 1854–1861* (Louisiana State University Press, Baton Rouge, La., 1973), p. 6. For his analysis of the annexationist background see pp. 3–21.

[57] On the López expeditions see Robert Caldwell, *The López Expeditions to Cuba, 1848–1851* (Princeton University Press, 1915); Herminio Portell Vilá, *Narciso López y su época*, 3 vols. (Havana, 1930–58).

[58] Kennedy to Commodore Bennett, 24 Sept., encl. in Kennedy to Palmerston, no. 10, 26 Sept. 1849, F.O. 72/760. Palmerston was well informed on the progress of the annexationist movement in Cuba. The British consul-general's reports from Havana can be found in F.O.72/748. See also Doyle to Palmerston, confid., no. 94, 15 Nov. 1849, F.O. 50/231.

[59] Chatfield to Palmerston, separate, 30 Apr. 1850, F.O. 15/64.

[60] John Gregory to B. Hawes, M.P., pvt. and confid., 17 June 1850. Hawes sent the letter to the Colonial Office which forwarded it to Palmerston. C.O. to F.O., confid., 29 July 1850, F.O. 72/776. Palmerston, too, stressed strategic reasons as the basis of British opposition to American

possession of Cuba. Palmerston to Howden, 1 Aug. 1850, Broadlands Mss., GC/HO/958.

[61] Adm. to F.O., 5 Aug. & 11 Sept. 1850, F.O. 72/776.

[62] Bulwer to Palmerston, pvt. & confid., 1 July 1850; memorandum by Palmerston, 10 Aug. 1850, F.O. 5/513.

[63] *Hansard*, 3rd Series (1850), vol. CXI, pp. 872–8.

[64] Istúriz to Palmerston, 18 July; Palmerston to Istúriz, draft, 17 Sept. 1850, F.O. 72/774; Howden to Palmerston, no. 4, 3 Aug. 1850, F.O. 72/765; Palmerston to Howden, no. 26, 22 Aug. 1850, F.O. 72/764; Palmerston to Howden, 1 Aug. 1850, Broadlands Mss., GC/HO/958.

[65] Palmerston to Istúriz, draft, 26 Dec. 1850, F.O. 72/774.

[66] A. A. Ettinger, 'The Proposed Anglo-Franco-American Treaty of 1852 to Guarantee Cuba to Spain', *Transactions of the Royal Historical Society*, 4th Series, vol. XIII (1930), p. 151. Ettinger's study, pp. 149–85, is the best examination of the Cuban diplomacy of the period. A revised version appears in his book, *The Mission to Spain of Pierre Soulé, 1853–1855* (Yale University Press, 1932), pp. 34–100.

[67] Minister of Foreign Affairs to the Minister of the Colonies, 31 July 1850; royal order to the Captain-General of Cuba, 2 Aug., and Capt.-Gen. Roncali to the Minister of the Colonies, 13 Sept. 1850, A.H.N., ultramar, leg. 4645.

[68] Instructions for José de la Concha, 30 Sept. 1850, A.H.N., ultramar, leg. 4645.

[69] See, for example, Bulwer to Crawford, 11 March 1851, F.O. 72/793. Crawford's extensive reports on the 1851 insurrection and the López filibuster are also in F.O. 72/793.

[70] Crawford to Palmerston, no. 30, 31 July 1851, F.O. 72/793.

[71] Bulwer to Palmerston, 12 Aug. 1851, Broadlands Mss., GC/BU/472/4.

[72] Palmerston to Crawford, no. 15, confid., draft, 17 Sept. 1851, F.O. 72/793. See also Ettinger, *The Mission to Spain of Pierre Soulé*, p. 48.

[73] Palmerston to Howden, drafts, nos. 37 and 38, 7 Aug. 1851, F.O. 84/836; F.O. to Adm., 4 July, F.O. 84/863, and reply, 5 July, F.O. 84/865.

[74] Palmerston to Howden, no. 43, draft, 11 Sept. 1851. See also nos. 40 and 42, 10 and 11 Sept. 1851, F.O. 84/836.

[75] Palmerston to Howden, no. 45, draft, 11 Sept. 1851, F.O. 84/836.

[76] Palmerston to Howden, no. 50, draft, 20 Oct. 1851, F.O. 84/836. I have found no evidence to support Professor Urban's conclusion that there was a change in British policy, beginning in 1851, to force Spain 'to inaugurate radical changes in the Cuban labor structure'. C. Stanley Urban, 'The Africanization of Cuba Scare, 1853–1855', *H.A.H.R.*, vol. XXXVII, no. 1 (Feb. 1957), p. 31.

[77] Ettinger, *The Mission to Spain of Pierre Soulé*, pp. 58–64.

[78] *Ibid.*, pp. 69–77.

[79] Everett to Sartiges, 1 Dec. 1852. An identical note was presented to Crampton. For the text see W. R. Manning, *Diplomatic Correspondence*,

vol. VI, doc. 2488, pp. 466–75; Ettinger, *The Mission to Spain of Pierre Soulé*, pp. 78–85.

[80] Crampton to Clarendon, pvt., 7 Feb. 1853, cited in R. W. Van Alstyne, 'Anglo-American Relations, 1853–1857', *American Historical Review*, vol. 42, no. 3 (Apr. 1937), pp. 493–4.

[81] Memorandum by Lord Stanley, 17 Nov. 1852, F.O. 84/874.

[82] Memorandum by Lord Malmesbury, 26 Nov. 1852, F.O. 84/874; Malmesbury to Lord Howden, no. 26, draft, 26 Nov. 1852, F.O. 84/873. His criticisms of Palmerston's policy towards Brazil also can be found in Malmesbury's memoirs, *Memoirs of an ex-Minister*, vol. I (London, 1884), p. 358.

[83] Howden to Malmesbury, no. 10, 22 Dec. 1852, F.O. 84/873.

[84] Russell to Howden, no. 8, draft, 31 Jan. 1853, F.O. 84/903.

[85] Memorandum by Lord Stanley, 21 Dec. 1852, F.O. 84/870.

[86] *Anti-Slavery Reporter*, 3rd Series, vol. I, no. 1, pp. 13–14.

[87] *Ibid.*, 3rd Series, vol. I, no. 2, 1 Feb. 1853. The letter was dated 8 Jan. See also Betty Fladeland, *Men and Brothers: Anglo-American antislavery co-operation* (Urbana: University of Illinois Press, 1972), pp. 338–9.

[88] Undated extract of Howden to Clarendon, Mss. Clar. dep. C 9, fols. 33–4, and same to same, 12 May 1853, *ibid.*, fols. 26–7.

[89] Crampton to Clarendon, pvt., 7 Feb. 1853, as cited in R. W. Van Alstyne, 'Anglo-American Relations, 1853–1857', *American Historical Review*, vol. 42 no. 3 (Apr. 1937), p. 494. Contrast these views with Lord Carlisle's statement in the House of Lords at the end of May: 'But Spain ought to be told that if she does not observe her treaties . . . she must, if her possession of Cuba is ever endangered, be at least prepared to find this country neutral in the conflict.' *Hansard*, 3rd Series (1853), vol. CXXVII, p. 771. Similar feelings were expressed a year later in a Commons debate by two M.P.s, Baillie and Cobden, *Hansard*, 3rd Series (1854), vol. CXXXII, pp. 426–31.

[90] Ettinger, *The Mission to Spain of Pierre Soulé*, pp. 221–338.

[91] C. Stanley Urban, 'The Africanization of Cuba Scare, 1853–1855', p. 29.

[92] Otway to Clarendon, pvt., 11 July, and no. 8, confid., 8 Aug. 1853, F.O. 84/904; Otway to Clarendon, pvt., 1 and 8 Aug. 1853, Mss. Clar. dep. C9 fols. 89–92 and 133–6. For the Parliamentary debates see *Hansard*, 3rd Series (1853), vol. CXXVII, pp. 488–92 and 762–76.

[93] Clarendon to Otway, pvt., 23 July 1853, Mss. Clar. dep. C 126.

[94] Mariano Torrente, *Slavery in the Island of Cuba* . . . (London, 1853), p. 19. Cañedo also published his own rebuttal in the Havana *Gazette*. Cañedo to the President of the Council of Ministers, no. 559, 29 June 1853, encl. *Gaceta de la Habana*, no. 133, 28 June 1853, A.H.N., ultramar, leg. 4639.

[95] Basil Rauch, *American Interest in Cuba*, p. 277.

[96] Madan to Pierce, 4 Oct. 1853, cited in Rauch, *ibid.*, pp. 276–7.

[97] Buchanan to Marcy, 7 Oct. 1853, Manning, *Diplomatic Correspondence*, vol. VII, doc. 3009, pp. 508–9. Professor Urban's contention that Clarendon offered 'evasive answers' to Buchanan's questions rests on the faulty

premise that Britain was trying to disguise her attempt to force abolition on Spain. There was no such attempt and Clarendon was quite candid with the American envoy. Urban, 'The Africanization of Cuba Scare, 1853–1855', pp. 32–3.

[98] Clarendon to Graham, pvt., 4 Jan., and Graham to Clarendon, 4 Jan. 1854, Graham Papers, microfilm reel 43, Cambridge University Library. See also J. B. Conacher, 'Lessons in Twisting the Lion's Tail: two sidelights of the Crimean War', Michael Cross and Robert Bothwell, eds., *Policy by Other Means; Essays in Honour of C. P. Stacey* (Toronto, 1972), pp. 77–94.

[99] See Chapter 13, pp. 292–3.

[100] Urban, 'The Africanization of Cuba Scare', p. 34. See also Soulé to Marcy, 23 Dec. 1853, doc. 5498, pp. 729–35; Robertson to Marcy, 14 Feb. and 20 March 1854, docs. 5500 and 5508, pp. 737 and 748–9, Manning, *Diplomatic Correspondence*, vol. XI; Rauch, *American Interest in Cuba*, pp. 278–9. Africanization was not the only point at issue between the United States and Spain. Cuban authorities had seized an American steamer, the *Black Warrior*, at the end of February for failure to comply with Spanish customs regulations, producing a potentially serious incident which eventually was settled through diplomatic channels.

[101] Crampton to Clarendon, 6 March, and reply, 27 March 1854, *P.P.* (1854), vol. LXXIII, Class B, pp. 840–1. Spain also vigorously denied the rumours; Minister of Foreign Affairs to the President of the Council of Ministers, 26 Jan. 1854, A.H.N., ultramar, leg. 4642.

[102] Marcy to Davis, 15 March, doc. 5150, pp. 170–3; Marcy to Soulé, confid., 3 Apr., doc. 5153, pp. 175–8; Marcy to Robertson, 8 Apr. 1854, doc. 5154, pp. 178–9, Manning, *Diplomatic Correspondence*, vol. XI.

[103] C. Stanley Urban, 'The Abortive Quitman Filibustering Expedition, 1853–1855', *Journal of Mississippi History*, vol. 18, no. 3 (1956), p. 193. See also May, *The Southern Dream of a Caribbean Empire*, pp. 46–76; Rauch, *American Interest in Cuba*, pp. 262–75; Arthur F. Corwin, *Spain and the Abolition of Slavery in Cuba, 1817–1886* (Austin: University of Texas Press), 1967), pp. 113–25. Quitman was not the only American to contemplate a filibustering expedition against Cuba in these years. For another abortive attempt see W. O. Scroggs, 'William Walker's Designs on Cuba', *Mississippi Valley Historical Review*, vol. I (1914), pp. 198–211.

[104] Crampton to Clarendon, pvt., 26 March 1854, Mss. Clar. dep. C 24, fols. 208–11.

[105] Clarendon to Cowley, pvt., 18 Apr. 1854, F.O. 519/70, cited in K. Bourne, *Britain and the Balance of Power in North America, 1815–1908* (London, 1967), p. 180.

[106] Graham to Clarendon, 11 May 1854, Graham Papers, Microfilm Reel 44, Cambridge University Library.

[107] For the British demand see Clarendon to Otway, no, 56, 15 Oct. 1853, F.O. 84/904; Pezuela to the Minister of Foreign Affairs, no. 8, 7 Feb.

1854; Calderón de la Barca to the President of the Council of Ministers, 13 March 1854, A.H.N., ultramar, leg. 4642.

[108] Roberston to Marcy, 7 May, doc. 5523, p. 772; same to same, 10 May, doc. 5526, p. 782, Manning, *Diplomatic Correspondence*, vol. XI. Crawford's despatches, which can be found in F.O. 84/936 and 937, give a very different picture of Pezuela and his measures. Clarendon and his officials at Madrid and Havana openly supported Pezuela and wanted him to remain at Havana because of his unbending determination to suppress the slave trade. See Howden to Clarendon, no. 91, confid., 24 March 1854, F.O. 84/934; Clarendon to Crawford, draft, no. 10, confid., 8 Apr. 1854, F.O. 84/935; and Crawford to Clarendon, nos. 62, 26 July, 66, 3 Aug., and 69, 25 Aug. 1854, F.O. 84/937.

[109] Davis to Marcy, 22 May 1854, doc. 5532, p. 790, Manning, *Diplomatic Correspondence*, vol. XI.

[110] Crampton to Clarendon, pvt., 7 May 1854, Mss. Clar. dep. C 24, fols. 291–301. Crawford had sent Pezuela's decree to Crampton and the British envoy did his best in Washington to dispel the Africanization rumours, Crampton to Clarendon, pvt., 29 May 1854, *ibid.*, fols. 331–9.

[111] Crampton to Clarendon, 29 May 1854, encl. Washington *Globe*, 23 May, *P.P.* (1854–5), vol. LVI, Class B, pp. 642–54.

[112] May, *The Southern Dream of a Caribbean Empire*, pp. 60–7; R. F. Nichols, *Franklin Pierce* (University of Pennsylvania Press, 1932), pp. 339–47, 357–9 and 366–71.

[113] For the attack on Pezuela's policy by Spain's Minister to Washington and the Captain-General's defence see Leopoldo A. de Cueto to the Minister of Foreign Affairs, no. 10, reservado, 13 June, and Pezuela to de Cueto, 10 July 1854, A.H.N., ultramar, leg. 4648. Crawford saw the exchange of letters and reported the contents to London. Crawford to Clarendon, pvt., 14 July 1854, Mss. Clar. dep. C 20, fols. 233–4. See also D. M. Estorch, *Apuntes sobre la administración del marqués de la Pezuela . . .* (Madrid, 1856). There was no love lost between Pezuela and his successor, José de la Concha. See Howden to Clarendon, no. 18, 7 Aug. 1854, F.O. 84/934.

[114] *Hansard*, 3rd Series (1854), vol. CXXXV, p. 1534.

[115] Buchanan to Marcy, 31 Oct. 1854, doc. 3028, p. 586, W. R. Manning, *Diplomatic Correspondence*, vol. VII. The text of the Ostend Manifesto can be found in the same volume, doc. 3026, pp. 579–85. Spain adroitly used the Africanization scare to reject recommendations made both by Pezuela and by the British government that she declare the slave trade piracy. Pacheco to Howden, 27 Oct., encl. in Howden to Clarendon, no. 26, 29 Oct. 1854, and Howden to Clarendon, no. 24, 11 Oct. 1854, F.O. 84/934. See also Crawford to Clarendon, no. 71, pvt. and confid., 28 Aug. 1854, F.O. 84/937.

[116] Crampton to Marcy, 8 Jan., encl. in Crampton to Clarendon, 15 Jan. 1855. *P.P.* (1854–5), vol. LVI, Class B, p. 681. For the background to this see Howden to Clarendon, no. 29, 13 Dec. 1854, reporting Pierre Soulé's

belief that a treaty existed between Spain and Britain to Africanize Cuba. Clarendon minuted 'there is not the shadow of a foundation' for this rumour, F.O. 84/934. See also Clarendon to Howard de Walden, draft, 11 Nov. 1854, cited in Gavin B. Henderson, 'Southern Designs on Cuba, 1854–1857, and some European Opinions', *The Journal of Southern History*, vol. V (1939), p. 379.

[117] Memoranda by Wodehouse, 18 Feb. and 25 Feb.; minute by Clarendon, 22 Feb. 1856, on Chamerovzow to Clarendon, 18 Feb. 1856, F.O. 84/1004. The pamphlet subsequently was published as *The Slave Trade to Cuba . . .* (London, 1861).

[118] Crawford to Clarendon, pvt., 29 June 1854, Mss. Clar. dep. C 20, fols. 186–9.

[119] Russell to Clarendon, 9 Dec. 1854, as cited in Henderson, 'Southern Designs on Cuba', pp. 378–9, n. 15.

[120] Minute by Palmerston, 18 June; Palmerston to Clarendon, 4 July 1857; Napier to Clarendon, no. 80, 26 May 1857, as cited in Henderson, 'Southern Designs on Cuba'. See also Palmerston to Clarendon, 31 Dec. 1857, as cited in Van Alstyne, 'Anglo-American Relations', p. 500. On this question see also K. Bourne, *Britain and the Balance of Power in North America, 1815–1908*, pp. 178–9 and 204–5; and his article, 'The Clayton–Bulwer Treaty and the Decline of British Opposition to the Territorial Expansion of the United States, 1857–1860', *Journal of Modern History*, vol. XXXIII (1961), pp. 287–91.

Palmerston was by no means the only British politician to believe in the inevitability of American Manifest Destiny. Edward Derby, Lord Stanley, who had been Malmesbury's Parliamentary Under-Secretary in 1852 and was later to serve as Foreign Secretary himself, wrote in 1850 that 'throughout a great part of the southern continent, especially along its western coast, the dominant race will be ultimately composed of United States emigrants, I for one do not entertain a doubt'. *Six Weeks in South America* (London, 1850), p. 2.

CHAPTER 12
THE FAILURE OF THE PENAL LAW

[1] O'Donnell to the President of the Council of Ministers, no. 3, 15 Feb. 1845, and no. 550 to the Minister of Foreign Affairs, 4 July 1846, A.H.N., ultramar, leg. 3550. In December 1846, he enclosed a petition of the *Junta de Fomento de Agricultura y Comercio*, wanting the Spanish Government to negotiate revisions in the slave trade treaties with Britain because of the depression prevailing in Cuba. The Spanish government decided not to risk British hostility by proposing such a renegotiation of her slave trade obligations. O'Donnell to the Minister of the Navy, Commerce and Colonies, no. 137, 18 Dec. 1846, A.H.N., ultramar, leg. 3552.

[2] Report of the *Consejo de Ultramar del Consejo Real*, 22 Dec. 1846, A.H.N.,

ultramar, leg. 4655. See also the confidential royal order to O'Donnell, 6 July 1847, A.H.N., ultramar, leg. 3552.

[3] Commissioners to Clarendon, no. 4, 14 Jan.; no. 50, 30 Oct. 1856, and Lousada to Clarendon, separate, 8 May 1856, F.O. 84/984.

[4] As cited in Hugh Thomas, *Cuba or The Pursuit of Freedom* (London, 1971), pp. 126–7. See also Roland T. Ely, *Cuando reinaba su majestad el azúcar: estudio histórico–sociológico de una tragedia latinoamericana* (Buenos Aires, 1963), pp. 428–30.

[5] Kennedy to Palmerston, no. 3, 1 Jan. 1849, F.O. 84/753.

[6] Professor Curtin has incorporated these figures into his overall statistics on the Cuban slave trade. See his *The Atlantic Slave Trade: A Census* (Madison: University of Wisconsin Press, 1969), p. 39. He took his figures directly from the estimate prepared for the Parliamentary Committee on West Africa and he reproduces a Parliamentary misprint for 1853. The estimate for that year should be 12,500 instead of 2,500. These figures, with the exception of the one for 1853, are the same as those which appear within brackets in my Table 9, p. 244. The table presented to the Parliamentary Committee on West Africa in 1865 is printed in full as an appendix to Archibald Hamilton, 'On the Trade with the Coloured Races of Africa', *Journal of the Statistical Society of London*, vol. XXXI (1868), pp. 25–48. I have gone into the problem of these statistics in my article, 'Statistics of the Slave Trade to Cuba, 1790–1867', *Journal of Latin American Studies*, vol. 3, no. 2 (1971), pp. 146–9.

[7] Memorandum by Ward, 20 Jan. 1855, on Backhouse to Clarendon, no. 5, 1 Jan. 1855, F.O. 84/959.

[8] Memorandum by Wylde, 6 Feb. 1860, F.O. 84/1130.

[9] For one such attack see Warren S. Howard, *American Slavers and the Federal Law, 1837–1862* (Berkeley: University of California Press, 1963), pp. 56–7. Nor should their accuracy be tested against Spanish figures. Professor Corwin cites a Spanish figure for 1862 when it is really the British estimate for 1861. The Spanish government refused to accept its accuracy. Arthur F. Corwin, *Spain and the Abolition of Slavery in Cuba, 1817–1886* (Austin: University of Texas Press, 1967), p. 143. The figures cited by Aimes, and reproduced by Ely, are even less reliable. Hubert H. S. Aimes, *A History of Slavery in Cuba 1511–1568* (New York, 1907), Appendix II, p. 269; Roland T. Ely, *Cuando reinaba su majestad el azúcar: estudio histórico–sociológico de una tragedia latinoamericano* (Buenos Aires, 1963), p. 616.

[10] Backhouse to Clarendon, no. 5, 2 Jan. 1854, F.O. 84/929.

[11] By the end of June 1855, over 7,700 Chinese labourers had arrived and over 400 Indians from Yucatan were brought in during the first six months of 1855. Crawford to Clarendon, nos. 50, 53 and 55, 7, 16 and 27 Aug. 1855, F.O. 84/965. See Thomas, *Cuba*, Appendix IX, pp. 1541–2, for a table of Chinese coolies brought to Cuba between 1847 and 1873, a total of 121,810.

[12] Backhouse to Clarendon, no. 5, 1 Jan. 1855, F.o. 84/959.

[13] Crawford to Clarendon, no. 54, 4 July 1853, F.O. 84/906.

[14] Crawford to Clarendon, no. 106, 26 Nov. 1853, F.O. 84/906.

[15] Backhouse to Clarendon, no. 72, 9 Dec. 1854, F.O. 84/930.

[16] Crawford to Clarendon, no. 97, 27 Nov. 1854; same to same, no. 80, 29 Sept., and no. 67, 24 Aug. 1854, F.O. 84/937. The American authorities prosecuted another well-known Cuban slave-trading captain the following year, a naturalized American named Darnaud, who had been responsible for taking a cargo of slaves to Cuba aboard the *Grey Eagle* in the summer of 1854, but he was acquitted. For the trial of James Smith see Howard, *American Slavers and the Federal Law*, pp. 192–6. Howard has an excellent account of the very poor American record in prosecuting slave trade offenders, pp. 155–205.

[17] Crawford to Clarendon, no. 70, 29 Aug. 1853, F.O. 84/906; same to same, no. 28, 28 March 1854, F.O. 84/936.

[18] Crawford to Clarendon, no. 69, 29 Aug. 1853, F.O. 84/906.

[19] Crawford to Clarendon, no. 6, 18 Jan., no. 8, 28 Jan., and no. 12, 8 Feb. 1854, F.O. 84/936; Clarendon to Crawford, nos. 33 and 35, 22 and 27 Sept. 1853, and no. 49, 22 Nov.; Crawford to Clarendon, no. 60, 2 Aug. 1853, F.O. 84/906.

[20] Cited in Robert Ralph Davis, Jr, 'James Buchanan and the Suppression of the Slave Trade, 1858–1861', *Pennsylvania History*, vol. XXXIII, no. 4 (October 1966), pp. 447–8.

[21] Clarendon to Backhouse, no. 9, draft, 24 Nov. 1854, F.O. 84/930; Backhouse described the slave traders' system in no. 65, to Clarendon, 10 Oct. 1854, F.O. 84/930.

[22] Cañedo to the President of the Council of Ministers, no. 459, 7 Apr. 1853. A.H.N., ultramar, leg. 3547. See also Howden to Clarendon, no. 19, 12 May, no. 21, confid., 23 May, and Otway to Clarendon, no. 2, 20 June 1853, F.O. 84/903.

[23] Cañedo to the President of the Council of Ministers, 21 June 1853, A.H.N., ultramar, leg. 3548; Crawford to Clarendon, no. 41, 21 June, and no. 65, 9 Aug. 1853, F.O. 84/906.

[24] Clarendon to Otway, no. 56, draft, 15 Oct. 1853; same to same, no. 45, 3 Sept.; Clarendon to Howden, no. 65, draft, 15 Dec. 1853, F.O. 84/904. See also Crawford to Clarendon, no. 65, 9 Aug., no. 72, 31 Aug., no. 74, 1 Sept., no. 90, 28 Oct. 1853, F.O. 84/906.

[25] Concha to the President of the Council of Ministers, no. 79, 28 Feb. 1852; Cañedo to the President of the Council of Ministers, no. 144, 2 Sept. 1852, A.H.N., ultramar, leg. 4639.

[26] Cañedo to the President of the Council of Ministers, no. 459, 7 Apr. 1853, A.H.N., ultramar, leg. 3547.

[27] Concha to the President of the Council of Ministers, 7 Nov. 1851. The case dragged on in Madrid for two more years before a decision was reached. Royal order to the Captain-General of Cuba, 5 May 1853, A.H.N., ultramar, leg. 3548.

[28] Howden to Clarendon, no. 1, 10 Jan. 1854, F.O. 84/934.

[29] Pezuela to the Minister of Foreign Affairs, no. 8, 7 Feb. 1854, A.H.N., ultramar, leg. 4642.

[30] Howden enclosed the original decree in no. 13, Howden to Clarendon, 13 Apr. 1854, F.O. 84/934. The decrees were printed and presented to Parliament. *P.P.* (1854), vol. LXXII, pp. 245–86.

[31] Clarendon to Howden, no. 16, 28 Apr. 1854, F.O. 84/933; Crawford to Clarendon, no. 38, 4 May; separate, no. 39, 5 May, and no. 40, 11 May 1854, F.O. 84/936. In Parliament, the government used the decrees to head off criticism of the lack of success of British suppression policies against the Cuban slave trade. *Hansard*, 3rd series (1854), vol. CXXXII, p. 1223; (1854–5), vol. CXXXI, p. 793.

[32] Crawford to Clarendon, no. 42, 22 May 1854, F.O. 84/936.

[33] Howden to Clarendon, pvt., 29 July; Otway to Clarendon, pvt. 30 July and 2 Aug. 1854, Clarendon Mss., dep. C 20, fols. 291–3, 294–6 and 1303–4.

[34] Howden to Clarendon, no. 18, 7 Aug., no. 19, 20 Aug., and no. 21, 19 Sept. 1854, F.O. 84/934; Clarendon to Howden, draft, no. 30, 13 Sept. 1854, F.O. 84/933.

[35] Crawford to Clarendon, pvt. and confid., 28 Aug. 1854, F.O. 84/937; Howden to Clarendon, no. 24, 11 Oct. 1854, F.O. 84/934; Clarendon to Howden drafts, no. 35, 27 Sept. and no. 37, 5 Oct. 1854, F.O. 84/933.

[36] Howden to Clarendon, no. 26, 29 Oct. 1854, encl. Pacheco to Howden, 27 Oct., F.O. 84/934.

[37] Crawford to Clarendon, no. 81, 31 Oct. 1854, F.O. 84/937.

[38] Memorandum by Ward, 20 Dec.; Crawford to Clarendon, no. 93, 22 Nov. 1854, F.O. 84/937; Backhouse to Clarendon, no. 71, 9 Dec. 1854, F.O. 84/930; Concha to the Minister of Foreign Affairs, no. 57, 12 Dec. 1854, A.H.N., ultramar, leg. 3548.

[39] Crawford to Clarendon, no. 92, 7 Nov. 1854, F.O. 84/937.

[40] Howden to Clarendon, confid. and separate, 18 Dec., confid. no. 30, 28 Dec. 1854, F.O. 84/934; Clarendon to Howden, draft, no. 44, 5 Dec., 1845, F.O. 84/933.

[41] Howden to Clarendon, no. 31, confid., 31 Dec. 1854, F.O. 84/934; no. 1, confid., 8 Jan. 1855, F.O. 84/963.

[42] Royal order, *reservado*, to Concha, 8 Jan. 1855, A.H.N., ultramar, leg. 3552.

[43] Concha to the Minister of Colonies, no. 211, 12 May 1855, A.H.N., ultramar, leg. 3552.

[44] Crawford to Clarendon, no. 13, 28 Feb. 1855, F.O. 84/965.

[45] Luzuriaga's speech in the Cortes on 8 March 1855 was encl. in Howden to Clarendon, no. 5, 23 March 1855, F.O. 84/936.

[46] Colonial Ministry to Ministry of Foreign Affairs, 30 Apr., and reply 17 May 1855, A.H.N., ultramar, leg. 3550.

[47] Royal order to Capt.-Gen. Concha, 5 June 1855, A.H.N., ultramar, leg. 3550.

[48] Concha published the decree in the Havana *Gazette*, 19 Dec. 1854. It is

encl. in Crawford to Clarendon, no. 100, 21 Dec. 1854, F.O. 84/937. See also Concha to the Minister of the Colonies, no. 137, 12 Feb. 1855, A.H.N., ultramar, leg. 3551.

⁴⁹ Crawford to Clarendon, no. 25, 31 Dec. 1855. For other comments on the *cédula* system see Backhouse to Clarendon, nos. 36 and 39, 9 and 21 July 1855, F.O. 84/959; Crawford to Clarendon, no. 45, 21 July 1855, F.O. 84/965.

⁵⁰ Commissioners to Clarendon, no. 32, 5 July 1856, F.O. 84/984.

⁵¹ Franklin Knight, in his *Slave Society in Cuba during the Nineteenth Century* (Madison: University of Wisconsin Press, 1970), uses them for some of his analysis of Cuba's slave population, e.g. Table 7, p. 79, Table 9, p. 108, and Table 10, pp. 134–5. He discusses the problems of the *cédula* system on p. 144. Kiple also uses the figures in his *Blacks in Colonial Cuba, 1774–1899* (Gainesville: University Presses of Florida, 1976), pp. 60–1.

⁵² Clarendon to Otway, draft, no. 13, 17 Oct. 1855. For earlier British protests see Clarendon to Otway, draft, no. 7, confid., 11 Aug., and draft, no. 10, confid., 15 Sept. 1855, F.O. 84/962.

⁵³ Howden to Clarendon, no. 11, 28 Oct. 1855, F.O. 84/963.

⁵⁴ Memorandum by Palmerston, 6 Nov. 1855, F.O. 84/963.

⁵⁵ Howden to Clarendon, most confid., 12 Nov.; no. 12, 16 Oct., and no. 16, 10 Nov. 1855, F.O. 84/963; same to same, no. 3, 10 Jan. 1856, F.O. 84/987.

⁵⁶ Crawford to Clarendon, no. 70, 6 Oct., and no. 92, 24 Dec. 1855, F.O. 84/965.

⁵⁷ Howden to Clarendon, 13 Nov. 1855, F.O. 84/963.

⁵⁸ Lousada to Clarendon, separate, 8 May 1856, F.O. 84/984.

⁵⁹ Commissioners to Clarendon, no. 50, 30 Oct. 1856, and no. 54, 5 Dec. 1856, F.O. 84/984.

⁶⁰ F.O. to Adm., 13 Dec. 1856, F.O. 84/1008.

⁶¹ Adm. to F.O. 10 Jan. and 15 June 1857, F.O. 84/1038; F.O. to Adm., 7 and 10 Jan.; 4 Apr.; 23 May; 11 and 20 June 1857, F.O. 84/1037.

⁶² Crawford to Commodore Kellett, 26 Jan., and to Rear. Adm. Fanshawe, 2 Feb., both encl. in Crawford to Clarendon, no. 4, 6 Feb. 1857, F.O. 84/1016.

⁶³ Crawford to Clarendon, no. 19, 6 Apr. 1857, F.O. 84/1016.

⁶⁴ Howden to Clarendon, no. 8, confid., 5 June; no. 9, 7 June and no. 10, 8 June 1857; Clarendon to Howden, drafts, no. 15, 21 Apr., no. 16, 18 May, no. 18, 19 May, no. 19, 20 May, nos. 20 & 21, 20 May and no. 23, 13 June 1857, F.O. 84/1015.

⁶⁵ *The Times*, 25 May 1857.

⁶⁶ *Hansard*, 3rd series (1857), vol. CXLVI, pp. 1492–1501.

⁶⁷ Royal order to Concha, *muy reservado*, 6 Jan. 1856, and reply, 20 Feb.; A.H.N. ultramar, leg. 3552. See also Concha to the Minister of the Colonies, no. 452, 12 Sept. 1857, leg. 3551, and same to same, no. 414, 12 Aug. 1857, leg. 3552.

⁶⁸ Otway to Clarendon, no. 3, 20 Dec. 1857, F.O. 84/1015.

[69] Concha to the Minister of the Colonies, no. 414, 12 Aug. 1857, A.H.N., ultramar, leg. 3552.

[70] Commissioners to Clarendon, no. 15, 4 Aug. 1857; no. 13, 1 July 1857, F.O. 84/1017.

[71] Memoranda by Clarendon, 4 Sept., & by Palmerston, 6 Sept. 1857, F.O. 84/1037.

[72] Clarendon to Crawford, draft, 29 Sept. 1857, F.O. 84/1016. The decision to send the boats was announced in Parliament in August. *Hansard*, 3rd series (1857), vol. CXLVII, p. 1974.

[73] F.O. to Adm., 30 June 1857, F.O. 84/1037.

[74] Crawford to Clarendon, no. 43, 21 Sept.; Lousada to Clarendon, nos. 51 and 53, 6 and 7 Nov. 1857, F.O. 84/1016.

[75] F.O. to Adm. 12 and 17 March and 14 May 1858, F.O. 84/1067.

[76] Commander Vesey to Commodore Kellett, 29 May, encl. in Adm. to F.O., 3 July; Vice-Adm. Sir Houston Stewart to the Secretary of the Admiralty, no. 128, 21 June, encl. in Adm. to F.O., 13 July 1858. See also Adm. to F.O., 13 July, 26 July and 2 Aug. for the British naval reports on the American accusations, F.O. 84/1069.

[77] *Hansard*, 3rd series (1857–8), vol. CL, p. 2208.

[78] Crawford to Malmesbury, no. 18, 9 May; Malmesbury to Crawford, draft, no. 3, 11 June 1858, F.O. 84/1046.

[79] H. G. Soulsby, *The Right of Search and the Slave Trade in Anglo-American Relations, 1814–1862* (Johns Hopkins Press, Baltimore, 1933), pp. 157–68. Mathieson rightly criticizes Malmesbury for giving way too easily and too quickly, without obtaining anything in return, although no one else in Britain was prepared to uphold the legality of British actions, W. L. Mathieson, *Great Britain and the Slave Trade, 1839–1865* (London, 1929), pp. 155–8. The crisis also raised again the thorny question of the rights of visit and search in international maritime law. On this see R. W. Van Alstyne, 'The British Right of Search and the African Slave Trade', *Journal of Modern History*, vol. II (1930), pp. 37–47.

[80] Crawford to Malmesbury, no. 26, 1 July 1858, F.O. 84/1046.

[81] Crawford to Malmesbury, no. 29, 8 July 1858, F.O. 84/1046.

[82] Robert Ralph Davis Jr, 'James Buchanan and the Suppression of the Slave Trade, 1858–1861', *Pennsylvania History*, vol. XXXIII, no. 4 (Oct. 1966), pp. 446–59; Howard, *American Slavers and the Federal Law*, p. 59.

[83] *Hansard*, 3rd series (1857–8), vol. CL, pp. 1286–1345.

[84] Crawford to Russell, no. 33, 19 Nov. 1859, F.O. 84/1080; same to same, separate, 11 Sept. 1860, F.O. 84/1109.

[85] Crawford to Russell, no. 37, 20 July, and no. 41, 4 Aug. 1860, F.O. 84/1109.

[86] Memorandum by Wylde, 28 Aug. 1860, F.o. 84/1109; Crawford to Russell, no. 24, 3 Oct. 1859, F.O. 84/1080.

[87] Malmesbury to Buchanan, draft, no. 1, 23 June 1858; memorandum by J. Murray, 22 June, F.O. 84/1045.

[88] *Hansard*, 3rd series (1857–8), vol. CL, p. 2205.

[89] Malmesbury to Buchanan, draft, no. 1, 23 June 1858, F.O. 84/1045.

[90] Malmesbury to Buchanan, draft, no. 7, 13 May 1859, F.O. 84/1079.

[91] Russell to Edwardes, draft, no. 9, 29 Sept. 1860, F.O. 84/1108.

[92] Crawford to Russell, no. 27, 27 Oct. 1859, encl. Concha's decree of 26 Oct., F.O. 84/1080; Buchanan to Russell, no. 1, 7 Jan. 1860, F.O. 84/1108

[93] Buchanan to Russell, no. 7, confid., 10 May 1860, F.O. 84/1108.

[94] Grey to the Secretary of the Admiralty, 11 Feb. 1858, *P.P.* (1859), Sess. 2, vol. XXXIV, pp. 194–8. See also same to same, 12 Nov. 1858, *ibid.*, pp. 211–12.

[95] Duke of Somerset to Palmerston, 11 Jan. 1860, encl. 'Memorandum on the Slave Trade, 1859', Broadlands Mss. GC/50/22/1 and 2.

[96] Russell to Palmerston, 16 Jan. 1860, Broadlands Mss., GC/RU/574/1.

CHAPTER 13
A NEW CLASS OF SLAVES

[1] For the treatment of the Africans liberated in Sierra Leone see Johnson Asiegbu, *Slavery and the Politics of Liberation, 1787–1861* (London, 1969), *passim*; for Brazil see Leslie Bethell, *The Abolition of the Brazilian Slave Trade: Britain, Brazil and the Slave Trade Question, 1807–1869* (Cambridge, 1970), pp. 380–3, and Robert Conrad, 'Neither Slave nor Free: The *Emancipados* of Brazil, 1818–1868', *H.A.H.R.*, vol. LIII, no. 1 (Feb. 1973), pp. 50–70.

[2] Kilbee to Hamilton, 8 March 1820, F.O. 84/6.

[3] Kilbee to Canning, nos. 11 and 17, 31 July and 20 Sept. 1824 with encls., secret decree of the Court of Admiralty, and Kilbee to Vives, 12 Sept., F.O. 84/29.

[4] Kilbee to Canning, no. 31, 31 Dec. 1824, with encl., 'Conditions for Emancipated Negroes', F.O. 84/29.

[5] Kilbee to Canning, pvt., 30 Dec. 1824, F.O. 84/29.

[6] Canning had forwarded Kilbee's proposals to Spain, Canning to Bosanquet, no. 1, draft, 24 Jan., and Bosanquet to Cea Bermúdez, 10 Feb. encl. in Bosanquet to Canning, no. 3, 17 Feb. 1825, F.O. 84/41. Pinillos to the Council of the Indies, 15 March, cited in the Council's report, 14 Apr. 1825, A.H.N., ultramar, leg. 3549.

[7] *Fiscal* to the Council of the Indies, 18 March, cited in Council's report, 14 Apr. 1825, A.H.N., ultramar, leg. 3549.

[8] This was recognized later in a report on the *emancipado* problem for Francisco de Cea Bermúdez, 26 Oct. 1833, A.H.N., estado, leg. 8.017.

[9] Vives to the Minister of Foreign Affairs, no. 1, reservado, 6 Jan. 1825, A.H.N., ultramar, leg. 3549.

[10] Spanish commissioners to the Minister of Foreign Affairs, 28 Apr. 1825, A.H.N., ultramar, leg. 3549.

11 Reports of the Council of the Indies, 18 May and 17 Nov. 1825, A.H.N., ultramar, leg. 3549.

12 *Ibid.*

13 Commissioners to Canning, no. 25, 30 June 1826, F.O. 84/51, and same to same, no. 46, 31 Dec. 1826, F.O. 84/52.

14 Petition of the *Ayuntamiento* of Havana, 13 Oct. 1826, A.H.N., ultramar, leg. 3549.

15 Report of the Council of State, 4 Feb. 1828, A.H.N., ultramar, leg. 3549.

16 Minute by Ferdinand, 21 Apr., on report of the Council of State, 4 Feb. 1828, A.H.N., ultramar, leg. 3549.

17 Minute of 29 Apr. on same report.

18 Macleay to the Earl of Dudley, no. 23, 27 June 1828, with encl., Vives to British commissioners, 19 June, F.O. 84/80.

19 Aberdeen to Bosanquet, no. 5, draft, 17 Apr. 1829, F.O. 84/94; Report of King's Advocate, 3 Apr. 1829, F.O. 83/2345.

20 Vives to the Minister of Foreign Affairs, no. 277, 18 March 1831, A.H.N., estado, leg. 8.033.

21 Capt.-Gen. Ricafort to the Minister of Foreign Affairs, no. 6, 29 May 1832, A.H.N., estado, leg. 8.032.

22 Vives to the Minister of Foreign Affairs, no. 277, 18 March 1831, A.H.N., estado, leg. 8.033.

23 Petition of the *Ayuntamiento* of Havana, 4 Nov. 1829, A.H.N., estado, leg. 8.033.

24 Petition of the *Junta de Fomento* of Havana, 24 Sept. 1832, A.H.N., estado, leg. 8.034.

25 Memorandum of the Ministry of Foreign Affairs, 4 May, minute of 15 May, and minute of a royal order to Capt.-Gen. Ricafort, 28 May 1833, A.H.N., estado, leg. 8.019. The statistics on the distribution of *emancipados* in 1831 are contained in Vives to the Minister of Foreign Affairs, no. 277, A.H.N., estado, leg. 8.033.

26 Macleay to Palmerston, no. 26, 19 June 1832, F.O. 84/128.

27 Same to same, no. 27, 20 June 1832, F.O. 84/128.

28 Same to same, no. 26, 19 June 1832, F.O. 84/128.

29 Capt.-Gen. Ricafort to the Minister of Foreign Affairs, no. 13, 30 June 1832, with encl., 'Acta de una Junta estraordinaria', 13 June, A.H.N., estado, leg. 8.015.

30 Minute of 29 Jan. on Minister of the Indies to Minister of Foreign Affairs, 25 Jan. 1833, A.H.N., estado, leg. 8.015.

31 Memorandum of the Ministry of Foreign Affairs, 19 July 1833, A.H.N., estado. leg. 8.019.

32 Report prepared for Cea Bermúdez, 26 Oct. 1833, A.H.N., estado, leg. 8.017.

33 F.O. to C.O., draft, 17 Aug.; C.O. to F.O., 22 Aug. and 5 Oct. 1832, F.O. 84/133. The Foreign Office asked originally if the Colonial Office had any objection to the liberated Africans being sent to Sierra Leone at the

expense of the Spanish government. The Colony Secretary found this 'in every respect objectionable' and, as an alternative, he suggested conditions for the reception of the Africans in Trinidad. They were communicated to the Cuban government early in 1833. British commissioners to Intendant Villanueva, 16 Jan., encl. in commissioners to Palmerston, no. 10, 21 Jan. 1833, F.O. 84/136.

34 Villanueva to commissioners, 23 Jan., encl. in commissioners to Palmerston, no. 12, 31 Jan. 1833, F.O. 84/136.

35 Commissioners to Palmerston, no. 18, 16 Apr. 1833, F.O. 84/136.

36 Capt.-Gen. Ricafort to the commissioners, 11 Apr., encl. in commissioners to Palmerston, no. 19, 23 Apr. 1833, F.O. 84/136.

37 Cea Bermúdez to Ricafort, 20 Aug.; Ricafort to commissioners, 20 Nov.; both encl. in commissioners to Palmerston, no. 44, 26 Nov. 1833, F.O. 84/136.

38 Commissioners to Palmerston, no. 49, 24 Dec. 1833, F.O. 84/136; same to same, nos. 7 and 12, 25 Jan. and 22 March 1834, F.O. 84/150.

39 Hill to commissioners, 27 Feb., encl. in commissioners to Palmerston, no. 13, 25 March 1834; Ricafort to Macleay, 13 May, encl. in Macleay to Palmerston, no. 22, 14 May 1834, F.O. 84/150.

40 Commissioners to Palmerston, no. 11, 3 March, F.O. 84/150; Macleay to Wellington, no. 22, 24 Feb., F.O. 84/171; commissioners to Palmerston, no. 60, 6 Aug. 1835, F.O. 84/172.

41 Commissioners to Palmerston, no. 92, 31 Dec. 1835, F.O. 84/172; commissioners to Wellington, no. 43, 22 May 1835, F.O. 84/171; K. O. Laurence, 'Immigration into Trinidad and British Guiana, 1834–1871', Ph.D. dissertation (University of Cambridge, 1958), fol. 5.

42 Macleay to Wellington, no. 20, 18 Feb. 1835, F.O. 84/171; Hill to Macleay, 23 Sept., encl. in commissioners to Palmerston, no. 78, 3 Nov. 1835, F.O. 84/172.

43 Schenley to Palmerston, no. 32, 2 May 1836, F.O. 84/196.

44 Cockburn to Macleay, 21 Jan., encl. in Macleay to Palmerston, 31 Jan.; Macleay to Wellington, no. 20, 18 Feb. 1835, F.O. 84/171; Schenley to Palmerston, no. 32, 2 May 1836, F.O. 84/196.

45 Laurence, 'Immigration into Trinidad and British Guiana', fol. 8.

46 *Ibid.* For Turnbull's testimony see *P.P.* (1850), vol. IX, p. 74.

47 Wellington to commissioners, no. 3, draft, 1 Jan. 1835, F.O. 84/170.

48 Macleay to Cockburn, 21 Aug., encl. in commissioners to Palmerston, no. 75, 12 Oct. 1835, F.O. 84/172; Schenley to Palmerston, no. 32, 2 May 1836, F.O. 84/196. The original instructions from the Colonial Office, Gladstone to Mahon, 6 Apr. 1835, are in F.O. 84/184.

49 Palmerston to commissioners, no. 6, draft, 31 Dec. 1831, F.O. 84/119; commissioners to Palmerston, no. 13, 29 March 1832, F.O. 84/128.

50 Report prepared for Cea Bermúdez, 26 Oct. 1833, A.H.N., estado, leg. 8.019.

51 Memorandum by José Maria Calvo, 22 Apr. 1835, A.H.N., estado, leg. 8.017.

52 José Verdaguer to Martínez de la Rosa, 18 May 1834, A.H.N., estado, leg. 8.028.
53 Palmerston to commissioners, no. 11, draft, 26 June 1835, F.O. 84/170.
54 Kilbee to Shee, 16 Nov. 1833, F.O. 84/136.
55 Palmerston to commissioners, no. 11, draft, 26 June 1835, F.O. 84/170; Villiers to Palmerston, 3 Nov. 1834, Clarendon Mss. C451.
56 Macleay to Tacón, 8 Dec., and reply, 11 Dec., both encl. in Macleay to Palmerston, no. 43, 26 Dec. 1834, F.O. 84/151; Tacón to the Minister of Foreign Affairs, *reservado*, 31 Dec. 1834, and minute, 1 March 1835, A.H.N., estado, leg. 8.034.
57 Commissioners to Palmerston, no. 15, 17 Feb. 1836, F.O. 84/176. Their findings were forwarded to the Spanish government, Villiers to Istúriz, 27 May, encl. in Villiers to Palmerston, no. 5, 29 May 1836, F.O. 84/201.
58 Tacón to the Minister of Foreign Affairs, no. 148, 31 Aug. 1836, A.H.N., estado, leg. 8.035.
59 Ezpeleta to the Minister of Foreign Affairs, no. 12, 31 May 1838, A.H.N., estado, leg. 8.035. For the proposal itself see Villiers to Bardají, 25 Aug., encl. in Villiers to Palmerston, no. 19, 26 Aug. 1837, F.O. 84/221.
60 Commissioners to Palmerston, no. 31, 20 Sept. 1839, F.O. 84/274.
61 Commissioners to Palmerston, no. 4, 15 Jan., and memorandum by Palmerston, 14 March 1840, F.O. 84/312; Palmerston to Aston, nos. 8 and 9, drafts, 30 March 1840, F.O. 84/318; Anglona to the Minister of Foreign Affairs, no. 34, 31 July 1840, A.H.N., estado, leg. 8.023.
62 David Turnbull, *Travels in the West. Cuba: with Notices of Porto Rico and the Slave Trade* (London, 1840), pp. 73 and 161–3.
63 Turnbull to Anglona, 21 and 28 Dec. 1840, encl. in Anglona to the Minister of Foreign Affairs, no. 57, 2 Jan. 1841, A.H.N., estado, leg. 8.053; Turnbull to Palmerston, no. 3, 30 Dec. 1840, F.O. 84/319.
64 Turnbull to commissioners, 4 Jan., encl. in commissioners to Palmerston, no. 6, 22 Jan. 1841, F.O. 84/348; commissioners to Palmerston, 31 Dec. 1840, F.O. 84/312.
65 Commissioners to Palmerston, no. 6, 22 Jan. 1841, F.O. 84/348.
66 Turnbull to commissioners, 13 Jan., encl. in commissioners to Palmerston, no. 6, 22 Jan. 1841, F.O. 84/348.
67 Commissioners to Turnbull, 13 Jan., encl. *ibid.*; Turnbull to Palmerston, nos. 8 and 15, 4 and 26 Jan. 1841, F.O. 84/356.
68 Palmerston to Aston, no. 5, draft, 4 March 1841, F.O. 84/353.
69 Palmerston to Turnbull, no. 1, draft, 4 March 1841, F.O. 84/356; Palmerston to commissioners, no. 6, draft, 15 March 1841, F.O. 84/347.
70 Commissioners to Valdés, 7 May, and reply, 7 May, encl. in commissioners to Palmerston, no. 27, 15 May 1841; Valdés to the Minister of Foreign Affairs, no. 14, 31 May 1841, A.H.N., estado, leg. 8.035.
71 Valdés to the Minister of Foreign Affairs, no. 20, 30 June 1841, with encl. statistics on liberated Africans, A.H.N., estado, leg. 8.035.

⁷²Valdés to the Minister of Foreign Affairs, no. 26, 31 July 1841, A.H.N., estado, leg. 8.035.

⁷³Sancho to Aberdeen, 15 July & reply 2 Aug. 1842, F.O. 84/400; Valdés to the Minister of Foreign Affairs, no. 176, 31 Oct. 1842, A.H.N., estado, leg. 8.037.

⁷⁴Commissioners to Aberdeen, no. 4, 1 Jan. 1844, F.O. 84/508; same to same, no. 8, 25 Jan. 1842, F.O. 84/395.

⁷⁵Commissioners to Aberdeen, no. 34, 13 June 1842, F.O. 84/395.

⁷⁶*P.P.* (1850), vol. IX, p. 73.

⁷⁷O'Donnell to the Minister of Foreign Affairs, no. 55, 15 June 1844, A.H.N., estado, leg. 8.039.

⁷⁸Alcoy to the President of the Council of Ministers, 9 Feb. 1853, A.H.N., ultramar, leg. 4666.

⁷⁹Crawford to Clarendon, no. 13, 30 Sept. 1869, F.O. 84/1315.

⁸⁰Franklin Knight, *Slave Society in Cuba during the Nineteenth Century* (Madison: University of Wisconsin Press, 1970), pp. 130–1; H.H.S. Aimes, 'Coartación: a Spanish Institution for the Advancement of Slaves into Freedmen', *Yale Review*, vol. XVII (1909), pp. 412–31.

⁸¹Commissioners to Palmerston, no. 43, 8 Oct. 1846, F.O. 84/621.

⁸²Statistical account of *emancipados*, 6 Feb. 1854, A.H.N., estado, leg. 8.046; Hubert H. S. Aimes, *A History of Slavery in Cuba, 1511–1568* (New York, 1907), p. 236. Compare this with the report of the British commissioners, 10 Oct. 1854, F.O. 84/930.

⁸³Commissioners to Palmerston, nos. 39 and 44, 30 Sept. and 30 Oct. 1846; memoranda by Palmerston, 8 Nov. and 9 Dec. 1846, F.O. 84/621.

⁸⁴Memorandum by Palmerston, 10 July 1846 on Crawford to Palmerston, no. 10, 10 June 1846, F.O. 84/629.

⁸⁵Crawford to Palmerston, no. 8, 8 Oct. 1847, F.O. 84/668. See also Palmerston to commissioners, no. 3, draft, 2 March, and reply, no. 21, 8 May 1847, F.O. 84/667. For British protests see Palmerston to Istúriz, draft, 22 June; Bulwer to Palmerston, no. 7, 11 Oct. 1847, with encls., F.O. 84/673.

⁸⁶Royal order to Capt.-Gen. Alcoy, 27 Oct. 1848, A.H.N., estado, leg. 8.042; Alcoy to the Minister of Foreign Affairs, 5 Apr. 1848, A.H.N., estado, leg. 8.040.

⁸⁷Instructions, 30 Sept. 1850, A.H.N., ultramar, leg. 4645; Concha to the Minister of Foreign Affairs, no. 11, 27 Jan. 1851, A.H.N., estado, leg. 8.044.

⁸⁸Kennedy to Palmerston, no. 53, 21 Dec. 1850, F.O. 84/789. See also Crawford to Palmerston, no. 5, 24 Dec. 1850, F.O. 84/797; Palmerston to Howden, no. 8, draft, 27 March, and Palmerston to Istúriz, draft, 27 March 1851, F.O. 84/836.

⁸⁹Concha to the Minister of Foreign Affairs, 9 June 1851, A.H.N., ultramar, leg. 4666. For Concha's defence of his handling of the *emancipados* see

José de la Concha, *Memorias sobre el estado político, gobierno y administración de la isla de Cuba* (Madrid, 1853), pp. 161–6.

[90] Crawford to Palmerston, no. 4, 1 Jan. 1852, F.O. 84/870.

[91] Crawford to Malmesbury, no. 9, 15 Apr. 1852, F.O. 84/874.

[92] Crawford to Malmesbury, nos. 14, 15, 16 and 21, 22 May, 17 June, 21 June and 15 July 1852; memorandum by Stanley, 20 July, minute by Malmesbury, 21 July 1852, F.O. 84/874.

[93] Foreign Office memorandum, 22 July 1852, F.O. 84/874.

[94] Malmesbury to Otway, nos. 15 and 16, drafts, 29 July 1852, no. 23, 8 Oct.; Otway to Malmesbury, nos. 2 and 3, 17 Sept., with encl. de Lis to Otway, 9 Sept.; no. 9, 11 Oct., with encl. de Lis to Otway, 7 Oct.; Malmesbury to Howden, no. 26, draft, 26 Nov. 1852; Howden to Malmesbury, no. 10, 22 Dec. 1852; Crawford to Malmesbury, no. 43, 2 Dec., with encl. Cañedo to Crawford, 30 Nov. 1852, F.O. 84/874. De Lis to Cañedo, 14 Oct., and reply, 8 Nov. 1852, A.H.N., estado, leg. 8.046.

[95] Alcoy to the President of the Council of Ministers, 9 Feb. 1853, A.H.N., ultramar, leg. 4666; report of the *Consejo de Ultramar*, 5 March, A.H.N., estado, leg. 8.046, Alcoy to Colonial Minister, 14 March, A.H.N., ultramar, leg. 4666. Royal order to Capt.-Gen. of Cuba, 31 March, *ibid.* British pressure had been continuous. See Russell to Howden, no. 4, draft, 18 Jan., and Clarendon to Howden, no. 12, draft, 12 March 1853, F.O. 84/903.

[96] Howden to Clarendon, no. 10, 16 March 1853, F.O. 84/903.

[97] Memorandum by Clarendon, 23 March. Clarendon to Howden, no. 15, draft, 26 March 1853, F.O. 84/903; minute of meeting with the Secretary of the British and Foreign Anti-Slavery Society, 24 March 1853, F.O. 84/921; *Hansard*, 3rd series (1853), vol. CXXVII, pp. 771–4.

[98] Cañedo to the President of the Council of Ministers, no. 552, 7 June 1853; royal order to Capt.-Gen. of Cuba, 18 Oct. 1853, A.H.N., ultramar, leg. 4666. British protests were also responsible for this royal order. Clarendon to Howden, draft, no. 42, 27 Aug. 1853, F.O. 84/904.

[99] Memorandum by Lord Wodehouse, 17 Jan. 1854, F.O. 84/906. On Pezuela see A. Urbina, *Cheste, o todo un siglo (1809–1906), el Isabelino tradicionalista* (Madrid, 1935), and for his treatment of the *emancipados*, pp. 178–9. D. M. Estorch, *Apuntes sobre la administración del marqués de la Pezuela* (Madrid, 1856), pp. 10–11 and 133–6. His ordinance on the *emancipados* was enclosed in Pezuela to the President of the Council of Ministers, no. 49, 6 Jan. 1854, A.H.N., ultramar, leg. 4666. See also Crawford to Clarendon, nos. 118 and 119, 20 Dec. and 28 Dec. 1853, F.O. 84/906; Backhouse to Clarendon, no. 5, 2 Jan. 1854, F.O. 84/929; Crawford to Clarendon, nos. 1 and 4, 2 and 6 Jan. 1854, F.O. 84/936.

[100] Clarendon to Howden, nos. 5 and 7, drafts, 27 Jan. and 13 Feb. 1854, F.O. 84/933.

[101] Concha to the Minister of the Colonies, nos. 84 and 121, 12 Jan. and 12 Feb. 1855, A.H.N., ultramar, leg. 4666; Crawford to Clarendon, no.

103, 30 Dec. 1854, memorandum by Clarendon, 18 Jan., and by Ward, 19 Feb. 1855, F.O. 84/937. Backhouse to Clarendon, no. 5, 1 Jan. 1855, F.O. 84/959.

[102] Concha to the Minister of the Colonies, nos. 201 and 209, ? Apr. and 12 May 1855, A.H.N., ultramar, leg. 4666. Clarendon to Crawford, no. 8, 24 Feb.; Crawford to Clarendon, nos. 8, 24 and 33, 1 Feb., 10 Apr. and 1 June 1855, F.O. 84/965; Crawford to Clarendon, no. 5, 26 Feb. 1856, F.O. 84/988.

[103] Serrano to the Minister of War and Colonies, no. 1185, 26 May 1861; Minister of Foreign Affairs to Minister of War and Colonies, 11 Sept. 1861; report of the colonial section of the Council of State, 14 Nov. 1862; royal order to Capt.-Gen. of Cuba, 21 Dec. 1862, A.H.N., ultramar, leg. 4666.

[104] John Crawford to Russell, no. 22, 28 Aug. 1863, F.O. 84/1203.

[105] Russell to Crampton, no. 9, draft, 27 Oct., and reply, no. 10, 13 Nov. 1863, F.O. 84/1163; Minister of Foreign Affairs to Minister of War and Colonies, 7 Nov. 1863, A.H.N., ultramar, leg. 4666.

[106] Royal order to Capt.-Gen. of Cuba, 27 Jan. 1864, A.H.N., ultramar, leg. 4666.

[107] Report of the Council of State, 28 June 1865, A.H.N., ultramar, leg. 4666.

[108] For the freeing of Brazilian *emancipados* see Leslie Bethell, *The Abolition of the Brazilian Slave Trade: Britain, Brazil and the Slave Trade Question, 1807–1869* (Cambridge, 1970), pp. 381–3.

[109] Dulce to the Minister of the Colonies, no. 188, 26 Sept. 1865, A.H.N., ultramar, leg. 4666.

[110] Royal order, *reservado*, to the Capt.-Gen. of Cuba, 28 Oct. 1865, A.H.N., ultramar, leg. 4666.

[111] Royal decree, 28 Oct. 1865, A.H.N., ultramar, leg. 4666.

[112] Dulce to the Minister of the Colonies, 29 Dec. 1865; Minister of Foreign Affairs to Minister of the Colonies, 27 Dec. 1865, A.H.N., ultramar, leg. 4666.

[113] Dulce to Minister of the Colonies, no. 35, 28 Feb. 1866; Manzano y Manzano to Minister of the Colonies, no. 39, 15 Feb. 1867; royal order to Capt.-Gen. of Cuba, 28 Jan. 1866, A.H.N., ultramar, leg. 4666.

[114] Royal order to Capt.-Gen. of Cuba, 6 Apr. 1867; Manzano y Manzano to the Minister of the Colonies, no. 201, 15 Aug. 1867, A.H.N., ultramar, leg. 4666.

[115] Crawford to Clarendon, no. 13, 30 Sept. 1869, F.O. 84/1315.

[116] For the Moret Law see Arthur F. Corwin, *Spain and the Abolition of Slavery in Cuba 1817–1886* (Austin: University of Texas Press, 1967), pp. 239–54 and 277–9.

[117] Dunlop to Granville, no. 16, 19 Nov. 1870, F.O. 84/1321.

[118] Layard to Granville, no. 16, 23 Dec. 1870, F.O. 84/1320; Granville to Layard, no. 5, draft, 31 March, no. 6, 10 Apr., no. 10, 12 May, no. 11, 30 May, no. 20, 5 Oct., no. 22, 24 Nov. 1871, F.O. 84/1340. Granville to

Layard, no. 3, draft, 1 Feb. 1872; Layard to Granville, no. 9, 25 March, 1872, F.O. 84/1353; *Hansard*, 3rd series (1872), vol. CCX, pp. 7550–73 for the account of the debate held on 19 Apr. 1872.

[119] Crawford to Derby, nos. 4 and 10, 4 March and 22 May 1876; Layard to Derby, nos. 1 and 5, confid., 7 Feb. and 8 March 1876, F.O. 84/1446.

CHAPTER 14

THE ABOLITION OF THE CUBAN SLAVE TRADE

[1] This figure is taken from the published British estimates. I have analysed the slave trade statistics for these years in my article, 'Statistics of the Slave Trade to Cuba, 1790–1867', *Journal of Latin American Studies*, vol. 3, no. 2 (1971), pp. 146–8.

[2] *Ibid.*

[3] Ramiro Guerra y Sánchez, *Sugar and Society in the Caribbean: an Economic History of Cuban Agriculture*, trans. Marjorie M. Urquidi (New Haven: Yale University Press, 1964), pp. 31–67.

[4] Franklin Knight, *Slave Society in Cuba during the Nineteenth Century* (Madison: University of Wisconsin Press, 1970), pp. 32–40.

[5] Roland T. Ely, *Cuando reinaba su majestad el azúcar: estudio histórico-sociológico de una tragedia latinoamericana* (Buenos Aires, 1963), pp. 582–3; Knight, *Slave Society in Cuba*, p. 29; Hubert H. S. Aimes, *A History of Slavery in Cuba 1511–1568* Appendix 1, pp. 267–8. E. Phillip Leveen suggests there is a direct causal relationship between British policies and the rise in price of Cuban slaves in his quantitative study, 'A Quantitative Analysis of the Impact of British Suppression Policies on the Volume of the Nineteenth Century Atlantic Slave Trade', Stanley L. Engerman and Eugene D. Genovese, *Race and Slavery in the Western Hemisphere: Quantitative Studies* (Princeton University Press, 1975), pp. 51–81.

[6] Crawford to Russell, no. 2, 5 Feb. 1861, F.O. 84/1135.

[7] *Hansard*, 3rd series (1861), vol. CLXI, pp. 984–5. The debate was initiated by Stephen Cave, the chairman of the West Indian Committee, who also bitterly condemned the Spanish slave trade. For the whole debate see *ibid.*, pp. 950–89. The West Indian interest criticized Britain's failure to stop the Cuban slave trade and blamed it on the futile effort to check the supply of slaves instead of concentrating on demand. Their real purpose, however, lay in promoting schemes for bringing Chinese labourers to the British West Indies to make British plantations more competitive. Stephen Cave, *Papers relating to Free Labour and the Slave Trade . . .* (London, 1861).

[8] F.O. memorandum, 26 March, and memorandum by Palmerston, 2 Apr. 1861, F.O. 84/1159.

[9] Thomas Wilson to Russell, 12 Sept. 1860, F.O. 84/1130.

[10] 'Remarks and Conclusions of the Council of the African Aid Society

upon the Resolutions proposed to be submitted by the Committee of the Anti-Slavery Society . . . ' 14 June 1861, F.O. 84/1139.

[11] Paper and Resolutions of the Slave-Trade Conference, 15 June 1861, F.O. 84/1139. For earlier indications of the gròwing militancy of the abolitionists see the *Anti-Slavery Reporter*, new series, vol. VIII, no. 10 (1 Oct. 1860), pp. 261–3; vol. VIII, no. 11 (1 Nov. 1860), pp. 282–3; and for a report of the conference see vol. IX, no. 7 (1 July 1861), pp. 148–64.

[12] Executive Committee of the British and Foreign Anti-Slavery Society to Russell, 2 July, and Chamerovzow to Russell, 14 Oct. 1861, F.O. 84/1160; *Anti-Slavery Reporter*, new series, vol. IX, no. 8 (1 Aug. 1861), pp. 182–92.

[13] *Anti-Slavery Reporter*, new series, vol. IX, no. 11 (1 Nov. 1861), pp. 249–51; vol. X, no. 7 (1 July 1862), pp. 145–56; vol. X, no. 8 (1 Aug. 1862), pp. 183–8; vol. XI, no. 12 (1 Dec. 1863), pp. 266–7. The Society also took advantage of the industrial exhibition held in London in 1862 to publish a special appeal to Spaniards: *Spain and the African Slave Trade: An Address to Spaniards from the Committee of the British and Foreign Anti-Slavery Society* (London, 1862).

[14] Spanish consul, Newcastle, to the Minister of Foreign Affairs, no. 7, 14 March 1862, encl. *Northern Daily Express*, 14 March 1862, A.H.N., estado, leg. 8.049. For a report of this and another public meeting held in Edinburgh on 3 March 1862 see the *Anti-Slavery Reporter*, new series, vol. X, no. 4 (1 Apr. 1862), pp. 90–1.

[15] Vice-Adm. Milne to Secretary to the Admiralty, no. 162, 20 Jan. 1864, with encl. petition from a meeting held in Kingston, Jamaica, 22 Dec. 1863, *P.P.* (1865), vol. LVI, Class A, p. 181.

[16] Wilmot to Russell, 30 July 1861, with encl., 'Notes on the African Slave Trade', F.O. 84/1160.

[17] Adm. to F.O., 31 Aug. 1861, F.O. 84/1149; F.O. to Adm., drafts, 5 and 11 Oct. 1861, F.O. 84/1150.

[18] Memorandum by Wylde, 7 Aug. 1861, F.O. 84/1160.

[19] Memorandum by Palmerston, 9 Aug. 1861; memoranda by Wodehouse and Russell, 7 and 8 Aug. 1861, F.O. 84/1160. Support for an attack on Whydah had been expressed in the House of Commons by the abolitionist, Charles Buxton, *Hansard*, 3rd series (1861), vol. CLXIV, pp. 1641–4.

[20] For British policy on the West African coast in this period see K. O. Dike, *Trade and Politics in the Niger Delta, 1830–1885* (Oxford, 1956), and John Hargreaves, *Prelude to the Partition of West Africa* (London, 1963).

[21] 'Despatches from Commodore Wilmot respecting his visit to the King of Dahomey in December, 1862, and January, 1863', F.O. Confidential Print, F.O. 84/1203; Sir Richard Burton, *A Mission to Gelele, King of Dahomey*, ed. and with an introduction by C. W. Newbury (London, 1966), pp. 15–26.

[22] F.O. to Adm., draft, 27 Aug. and 20 Sept. 1861, F.O. 84/1149; Adm. to F.O., 15 Feb. 1861, F.O. 84/1148.

[23] For an analysis of the campaign in the southern states to reopen the African slave trade see Ronald T. Takaki, *A Pro-Slavery Crusade: the Agitation to Reopen the African Slave Trade* (New York, 1971).

[24] A. T. Milne, 'The Lyons–Seward Treaty of 1862', *American Historical Review*, vol. 38 (1932–3), pp. 511–25; H. G. Soulsby, *The Right of Search and the Slave Trade in Anglo-American Relations, 1814–1862*, pp. 173–6; Warren S. Howard, *American Slavers and the Federal Law, 1837–1862* (Berkeley: University of California Press, 1963), pp. 59–65; Robert Wm Love, Jr, 'The End of the Atlantic Slave Trade to Cuba', *Caribbean Quarterly*, vol. 22, nos. 2 and 3 (June–Sept. 1976), pp. 51–8.

[25] W. L. Mathieson, *Great Britain and the Slave Trade, 1839–1865* (London, 1929), pp. 175–6.

[26] British commissioners, New York, to Russell, no. 24, 31 Dec. 1863, F.O. 84/1197.

[27] Frederick C. Drake, ed., 'Secret History of the Slave Trade to Cuba Written by an American Naval Officer, 1861', *The Journal of Negro History*, vol. LV, no. 3 (1970), p. 229.

[28] Russell to Palmerston, 23 July 1862, Broadlands Mss., GC/RU/717.

[29] Russell to Palmerston, 2 Aug. 1863, *ibid.*, GC/RU/797.

[30] F.O. to Adm., draft, 3 Sept. 1862, F.O. 84/1162.

[31] Adm. to F.O., 4 Aug. 1862, F.O. 84/1185; Adm. to F.O., 13 Oct. 1862, F.O. 84/1186.

[32] F.O. to Adm., draft, 31 July, and memorandum by Murray, 18 July 1863, F.O. 84/1206; Edwardes to Russell, no. 6, 25 June, and Russell to Edwardes, draft, no. 10, 31 July 1863, F.O. 84/1196.

[33] Report of the Council of State, 26 March 1863; Serrano to the Minister of the Colonies, no. 3,353, 30 Oct. 1862, A.H.N., ultramar, leg. 4685.

[34] F.O. to Adm., draft, 16 Sept. 1863, F.O. 84/1206.

[35] Adm. to F.O., 17 Apr. 1863, F.O. 84/1208.

[36] Adm. to F.O., 3 March 1863, F.O. 84/1207.

[37] Adm. to F.O., 13 March 1863, F.O. 84/1207.

[38] Serrano to the Minister of the Colonies, no. 499, 12 Sept. 1860, A.H.N., ultramar, leg. 4697.

[39] Minister of the Colonies to Minister of the Navy, 10 Aug. 1860, A.H.N., ultramar, leg. 4697.

[40] Serrano to the Minister of the Colonies, no. 2619, 15 July 1862, A.H.N., ultramar, leg. 4697.

[41] Minister of the Colonies to the Ministers of Foreign Affairs and the Navy, 6 Apr., and reply, 22 Apr. 1865, A.H.N., ultramar, leg. 4697.

[42] Serrano to the Minister of the Colonies, no. 1379, 25 July 1861; same to same, 6 Sept. 1861, A.H.N., ultramar, leg. 3552.

[43] Royal order to the Captain-General of Cuba, *reservado*, 25 Oct. 1861, A.H.N., ultramar, leg. 3552.

[44] Serrano to the Minister of the Colonies, no. 1932, 4 Jan., and no. 4,

reservado, 15 Apr. 1862, A.H.N., ultramar, leg. 3552.

[45] Dulce to the President of the Council of Ministers, 28 Feb., and no. 1021, 28 July 1863, A.H.N., ultramar, leg. 4692.

[46] Royal order to the Captain-General of Cuba, 12 Apr. 1863, *reservado*, A.H.N., ultramar, leg. 3550.

[47] Dulce to the President of the Council of Ministers, 14 May 1863, A.H.N., ultramar, leg. 3550.

[48] Russell to Edwardes, draft, no. 8, 9 July 1863, F.O. 84/1196; Crawford to Russell, no. 10, confidential, 23 May, and 17 June 1863, F.O. 84/1203.

[49] Dulce to the Minister of the Colonies, 28 June 1863, A.H.N., ultramar, leg. 4648.

[50] John Crawford to Russell, no. 15, 7 June, and Joseph Crawford to Russell, 19 Aug. 1863, F.O. 84/1203.

[51] Minister of the Colonies to Dulce, no. 44, 11 July 1863, A.H.N., ultramar, leg. 3547; Secretary-General, Council of State, to the Minister of the Colonies, 30 Nov. 1863, A.H.N., ultramar, leg. 3552.

[52] José Agustín Arguelles, *El General Dulce y Los Negreros* (New York, 1864). He also wrote letters to the *Herald* and to the *New York Times*. The most complete account of the affair can be found in Crawford's despatches in F.O. 84/1218, some of which were printed for the Cabinet before being published in an edited version, the following year, in *P.P.* (1865) vol. LVI, Class B, pp. 230–56. Crampton's despatches from Madrid detail the reaction in Spain. See especially Crampton to Russell, no. 18, 14 June, and no. 26, confidential, 3 Aug. 1864, F.O. 84/1217.

[53] Crawford to Russell, separate and reserved, 10 May 1864, F.O. 84/1218.

[54] Crampton to Russell, no. 26, confidential, 3 Aug. 1864, F.O. 84/1217.

[55] Crawford to Russell, confidential, no. 13, 16 June 1864, F.O. 84/1218.

[56] Memorandum by Wylde, 8 July 1864, and minute by Russell, n.d., F.O. 84/1218.

[57] *Hansard*, 3rd series (1865), vol. CLXXX, pp. 333–4 and 431.

[58] *Ibid.* (1865), vol. CLXXVII, p. 558. A last attempt to force the withdrawal of the African Squadron occurred in 1867, but the government remained its firm defender. *Hansard*, 3rd series (1867), vol. CLXXXVIII, pp. 2074–82; Mathieson, *Great Britain and the Slave Trade*, p. 186.

[59] The best account of the growth of a reforming colonial spirit and the expansion of abolitionist feeling within Spain can be found in Arthur F. Corwin, *Spain and the Abolition of Slavery in Cuba, 1817–1886* (Austin: University of Texas Press, 1967), pp. 129–71.

[60] *Revista Hispano-Americana*, vol. 1 (1865), pp. 6–11. On Vizcarrondo see Corwin, *Spain and the Abolition of Slavery in Cuba*, pp. 154–60.

[61] José Ferrer de Couto, *Enough of War* . . . (New York, 1864), p. 298. The book originally was published in Spanish as *Los negros en sus diversos estados y condiciones* . . . See also Corwin, *Spain and the Abolition of Slavery in Cuba*, pp. 164–5.

[62] The Senate debates of 20 and 21 Jan. 1865 are reproduced in the *Revista Hispano-Americana* (27 Jan. 1865), pp. 32–3.

[63] Crampton to Russell, no. 5, 18 Feb. 1865, F.O. 84/1239.

[64] The petition is reproduced in *Revista Hispano-Americana*, 12 June 1865, pp. 100–2, and applauded in an editorial, pp. 99–100; Corwin, *Spain and the Abolition of Slavery in Cuba*, pp. 150–1; see also *Apuntes sobre la cuestión de reforma política y de la introducción de africanos en las islas de Cuba y Puerto Rico* (Madrid, 1866), pp. 18–116.

[65] Crampton to Russell, no. 10, 9 July 1865, F.O. 84/1239.

[66] Calixto Bernal, 'El Gobierno y la trata de esclavos en las Antillas', *Revista Hispano-Americana* (12 Nov. 1865), pp. 504–6.

[67] Dulce to the Minister of the Colonies, no. 226, 14 Nov. 1865, with encl. petition, 1 Nov. 1865; royal order to the Captain-General of Cuba, 16 March 1866, A.H.N., ultramar, leg. 4701; Bunch to Russell, no. 19, 31 Oct. 1865, F.O. 84/1241.

[68] Crampton to Russell, no. 5, 18 Feb. 1865, with encl. *Gaceta de Madrid*, 18 Feb., F.O. 84/1239.

[69] Julio Vizcarrondo, 'El proyecto de ley de 19 de febrero para la represión y castigo del tráfico negrero', *Revista Hispano-Americana* (12 March 1866), pp. 351–5.

[70] The debates are reproduced in their entirety in the *Revista Hispano-Americana*. For the Senate debates of 18–20 Apr. 1866 see the issue of 27 Apr. 1866, pp. 492–506, and for the Congress debates of 6 and 11 July see the issue of 12 July 1866, pp. 673–90. Corwin also analyses the debates in his *Spain and the Abolition of Slavery in Cuba*, pp. 177–81.

[71] It is reproduced in full in the *Revista Hispano-Americana* (12 Apr. 1866), pp. 446–8.

[72] Crampton to Clarendon, no. 2, 21 Feb. 1866, F.O. 84/1262.

[73] Memorandum by Wylde, 28 Feb. 1866, F.O. 84/1262.

[74] Clarendon to Crampton, draft, no. 6, 6 March 1866, F.O. 84/1262.

[75] Crampton to Clarendon, 23 Apr. 1866, F.O. 84/1262.

[76] Graham-Dunlop to Clarendon, no. 2, 11 May, and memorandum by Wylde, 16 May 1866, F.O. 84/1263.

[77] Follett Synge to Clarendon, no. 3, 4 Apr. 1866, F.O. 84/1272.

[78] Memorandum by Wylde, 10 May 1866, F.O. 84/1272; Clarendon to Crampton, draft, no. 16, 15 May 1866, F.O. 84/1262.

[79] Crampton to Clarendon, no. 11, 5 July 1866, F.O. 84/1262.

[80] Crampton to Stanley, nos. 14 and 15, 18 July and 1 Oct. 1866, F.O. 84/1262.

[81] Memorial of the British and Foreign Anti-Slavery Society, 16 Nov. 1866, F.O. 84/1270.

[82] Memorandum by Wylde, 27 Nov., and Stanley to the Secretary, British and Foreign Anti-Slavery Society, draft, 30 Nov. 1866, F.O. 84/1270.

[83] General Dulce's report to the Spanish Colonial Ministry, encl. in Follett Synge to Stanley, confidential, 9 May 1867, F.O. 84/1287.

[84] Corwin, *Spain and the Abolition of Slavery in Cuba*, pp. 189–214. His analysis of the actual abolition of slavery in Cuba appears on pp. 215–313; Knight, *Slave Society in Cuba*, pp. 150–78.

[85] Manzano to the Minister of the Colonies, no. 140, 15 June 1867, with encl. regulations, 6 June; royal order to the Captain-General of Cuba, 11 July 1867, A.H.N., ultramar, leg. 4711.

[86] Crawford to Stanley, no. 4, 30 Apr. 1868, F.O. 84/1288; Stanley to Crampton, draft, no. 4, 6 March 1868, with encl., Adm. to F.O., 2 March, F.O. 84/1268.

[87] Crawford to Stanley, nos. 5, 7, 8 and 11, 6 July, 3 Aug., 4 and 5 Oct. 1867, F.O. 84/1274.

[88] Graham-Dunlop to Wylde, 18 June 1867, pvt., F.O. 84/1274.

[89] Stanley to Crawford, draft, no. 2, 30 Aug., with encl., Adm. to F.O., 20 Aug. 1867, F.O. 84/1274.

[90] Follett Synge to Clarendon, no. 1, 5 Apr. 1866, F.O. 84/1263.

[91] Memorandum by Wylde, 20 July 1866, F.O. 84/1270. He had testified in a similar vein to the House of Commons Select Committee on West Africa in 1865. *P.P.* (1865), vol. V, pp. 108–11.

[92] Leslie Bethell, *The Abolition of the Brazilian Slave Trade: Britain, Brazil and the Slave Trade Question, 1807–1869* (Cambridge, 1970), pp. 386–7.

[93] Granville to Graham-Dunlop, draft, no. 5, 6 Apr. 1871, F.O. 84/1340.

[94] Memorandum by Wylde, 7 Oct. 1872; Graham-Dunlop to Granville, no. 13, 16 Sept. 1872, F.O. 84/1353; Granville to Graham-Dunlop, drafts, nos. 2 and 6, 13 Jan. and 30 Aug. 1873, with encls., F.O. 82/1408.

BIBLIOGRAPHY

MANUSCRIPTS

I. PUBLIC RECORD OFFICE (LONDON)

Foreign Office records:

1. F.O. 72 (Spain): vols. 60, 75, 93, 103–5, 108, 110, 112, 114, 117, 119–23, 127–8, 134, 137–9, 142, 150, 153, 158, 160–1, 163, 172–6, 179–80, 182, 184–203, 205, 207–12, 215, 218, 220, 224–6, 230, 233, 235–6, 239, 241, 244–8, 252, 255–6, 258–9, 561, 588, 611, 635, 709, 764, 770, 776, 774.
2. F.O. 72 (Cuba): vols. 261, 275, 304, 347, 355–6, 402, 415, 431, 449, 468, 489, 513, 538, 559, 584–6, 608–9, 611, 634–5, 662, 664, 682–3, 705, 731, 748, 760, 771, 793, 811, 830, 852, 878, 902, 926, 943–4, 966, 989.
3. F.O. 84 (Spain): vols. 24, 31, 41, 54, 70, 83, 94, 110, 121, 130, 140, 155, 177, 201, 221, 244–6, 279–80, 318, 353–5, 400, 462, 519, 574–8, 628–9, 673–4, 721–2, 760–1, 796–7, 836–8, 873–4, 903–7, 962–5, 987–8, 1015–16, 1045–6, 1079–80, 1108–9, 1139–40, 1173–4, 1196–7, 1203, 1217–18, 1239–41, 1262–3, 1274, 1288, 1303, 1320–1, 1340, 1353, 1368, 1396, 1408, 1410, 1446, 1481.
4. F.O. 84 (Cuba): vols. 6, 13, 18, 23, 29, 39, 51–2, 68, 80–1, 91–2, 106–7, 119, 128, 136, 150–1, 170–2, 195–7, 216–17, 239–40, 274, 312, 319, 347–9, 356–9, 394–6, 401, 451–2, 463, 508–9, 520, 561–2, 578, 620–1, 629, 667–8, 674, 714–16, 722, 753–4, 760, 789, 791, 797, 832, 838, 870, 874, 898–900, 905–6, 929–30, 936–7, 959, 965, 984, 988, 1012, 1016, 1042, 1046, 1073, 1080, 1106, 1109, 1135, 1140, 1174, 1197, 1203, 1215, 1218, 1236, 1241, 1272, 1287, 1300, 1315, 1334.
5. F.O. 84 (Various): vols. 6–8, 124, 133, 185, 208, 342, 500–1, 615–16, 663, 709–10, 739, 749, 777, 818–19, 860, 887, 921, 924, 951, 953, 977–8, 980, 1004, 1008, 1034, 1037–8, 1067, 1069–70, 1100, 1122–3, 1130, 1148–50, 1159–60, 1182–5, 1206–9, 1213, 1233, 1257, 1270.

II. BRITISH MUSEUM

1. Egerton Mss., vol. 520.
2. Add. Mss. 34427 (Auckland Papers), 51820 (Holland House Papers), 37 309 (Wellesley Papers), 43 145–6 (Aberdeen Papers).

III. NATIONAL LIBRARY OF SCOTLAND

Ms. 5559 (Liston Papers).

IV. CAMBRIDGE UNIVERSITY LIBRARY

Sir James Graham Papers.

V. BODLEIAN LIBRARY (OXFORD)

Clarendon Papers.

VI. ALL SOULS COLLEGE (OXFORD)

Vaughan Papers.

VII. RHODES HOUSE LIBRARY (OXFORD)

British Empire Mss. (British and Foreign Anti-Slavery Society Papers).

VIII. NATIONAL REGISTER OF ARCHIVES (LONDON)

Broadlands Mss. (Palmerston Papers).

IX. ARCHIVO GENERAL DE INDIAS (SEVILLE)

1. Estado, legajos 4, 12, 17.
2. Audiencia de Santo Domingo, legajos 1292–5, 1705–7, 2207.
3. Indiferente General, legajos 2826–7, 2770.
4. Ultramar, legajos 3–6.
5. Papeles de Cuba, legajos 1908–10.

X. ARCHIVO GENERAL DE SIMANCAS

1. Secretaria de Hacienda, legajo 3542.
2. Estado, legajos 8.194, 8.266, 8.277, 8.298, 8.310.

XI. ARCHIVO HISTÓRICO NACIONAL (MADRID)

1. Sección de Estado, subsección de esclavitud, legajos 8.015–8.061.
2. Sección de Ultramar, papeles de ultramar:
   a. Esclavitud, legajos 3547–55.
   b. Gobierno, legajos 4462, 4603–4, 4606, 4608, 4610, 4613, 4626, 4627–9, 4638–9, 4641–3, 4645–6, 4648–50, 4652, 4655–6, 4658, 4660, 4665–6, 4668, 4672, 4676, 4681, 4685–6, 4691–2, 4697, 4700–1, 4707, 4711, 4713, 4716, 4862.

XII. BIBLIOTECA NACIONAL (MADRID)

Sección de manuscritos, colección de Justo Zaragoza, legajo 752.

PRINTED SOURCES

British and Foreign State Papers, 1812– . London, 1841– .
The British and Foreign Anti-Slavery Reporter, 1840–67.
Centón epistolario de Domingo del Monte, ed. Domingo Figarola–Cañeda and Joaquín Llaverías y Martínez. 5 vols., Havana, 1923–38.

402 *Bibliography*

Correspondence, Despatches and Other Papers of Viscount Castlereagh, ed. Marquess of Londonderry. 12 vols., London, 1848–53.

Correspondencia reservada del Capitán General Don Miguel Tacón con el gobierno de Madrid, 1834–1836, ed. Juan Pérez de la Riva. Havana, 1963.

Diario de las actas y discusiones de las Cortes. 23 vols., Cadiz, 1811–13.

Diario de las discusiones y actas de las Cortes. 34 vols., Madrid, 1820–2.

Documentos inéditos sobre la toma de la Habana por los Ingleses en 1762, ed. Juan Pérez de la Riva. Havana, 1963.

Dodson, J. *Reports of cases argued and determined in the High Court of Admiralty*, 2 vols., London, 1815–28.

Donnan, Elizabeth, *Documents Illustrative of the History of the Slave Trade to America*. 4 vols., Washington, 1930–5.

Edinburgh Review.

Hansard's Parliamentary Debates, 3rd series.

Manning, W. R., ed. *Diplomatic Correspondence of the United States. Inter-American Affairs, 1831–1860*. 12 vols., Washington, 1932–9.

P.P., 1847–8; XXII (272), (366), (536). Four Reports of the House of Commons Select Committee on the Suppression of the Slave Trade.

P.P., 1849, XIX (309), (410). Two further Reports of the House of Commons Select Committee on the Suppression of the Slave Trade.

P.P. (Lords), 1849, XVIII (32). Report of the House of Lords Select Committee on the Slave Trade.

P.P. (Lords), 1850, XXIV (35). Second Report of the House of Lords Select Committee on the Slave Trade.

P.P. 1852–3, XXXIX (920). Report of the House of Comm   Select Committee on the Slave Trade Treaties.

Proceedings of the General Anti-Slavery Conventions called by the British and Foreign Anti-Slavery Society, London, 1841, 1843.

Reports of the Committee of the African Institution. vols. 1–21, London, 1807–27.

Revista Hispano-Americana, 1865–6.

Stapleton, Edward J., ed. *Some Official Correspondence of George Canning*. 2 vols., London, 1887.

Supplementary Despatches, Correspondence and Memoranda of Arthur Wellesley, 1st Duke of Wellington, ed. by his son. 15 vols., London, 1858–72.

The Times.

Webster, C. K., ed. *Britain and the Independence of Latin America, 1812–1830. Select Documents from the Foreign Office Archives*. 2 vols., London, 1938.

Wilberforce, A. M., ed. *Private Papers of William Wilberforce*. London, 1897.

Wilberforce, R.I. and S. *The Life of William Wilberforce*. 5 vols., London, 1838.

SELECT LIST OF BOOKS AND ARTICLES

Adams, Charles Francis, ed. *Memoirs of John Quincy Adams, comprising portions of his Diary from 1795 to 1848*, 12 vols., Philadelphia, 1874–7.

Ahumada y Centurión, José de. *Memoria histórico-política de la isla de Cuba.* Havana, 1874.

Aimes, Hubert H. S. *A History of Slavery in Cuba, 1511–1868.* New York, 1907, reprinted 1967.

'Coartación: A Spanish Institution for the Advancement of Slaves into Freedmen', *Yale Review,* vol. XVII (1909), pp. 412–31.

[Anon.] *Biografía del Excmo. Señor D. G. Valdés.* Madrid, ?1850.

Anstey, Roger. 'A Re-interpretation of the Abolition of the British Slave Trade, 1806–1807', *English Historical Review,* vol. 87 (1972), pp. 304–32.

'The Volume of the North American Slave-Carrying Trade from Africa, 1761–1810', *Revue française d'histoire d'Outre-Mer,* vol. LXII (1975), pp. 47–66.

The Atlantic Slave Trade and British Abolition, 1760–1810. London, 1975 and Hair, P. E. H. *Liverpool, the African Slave Trade, and Abolition.* Historic Society of Lancashire and Cheshire, Occasional Series, vol. 2, 1976.

'The Slave Trade of the Continental Powers, 1760–1810', *Economic History Review,* 2nd series, vol. 30 (1977), pp. 259–68.

Antillón y Marzo, Isidoro de. *Disertación sobre el origen de la esclavitud de los Negros, motivos que la han perpetuada . . . publicada en 1811 con notas.* Valencia, 1820.

Apuntes sobre la cuestión de la reforma política y de la introducción de africanos en las islas de Cuba y Puerto Rico. Madrid, 1866.

Ashley, A. E. M. *The Life of H. J. Temple, Viscount Palmerston, 1846–1865.* 2 vols., London, 1876.

Asiegbu, Johnson U. J. *Slavery and the Politics of Liberation, 1787–1861.* London, 1969.

Baird, Robert. *Impressions and Experiences of the West Indies and North America in 1849.* 2 vols., Edinburgh, 1849.

Bandinel, James. *Some Account of the Trade in Slaves from Africa . . .* London, 1842, reprinted 1968.

A Barrister, *Analysis of the Evidence given before the Select Committees upon the Slave Trade.* London, 1850.

Bartlett, C. J. *Great Britain and Sea Power, 1815–1853.* Oxford, 1963.

Bécker y González, Jerónimo. *Historia de las relaciones exteriores de España durante el Siglo XIX.* 3 vols., Madrid, 1924–6.

Bernstein, Harry. *Origins of Inter-American Interest, 1700–1812.* University of Pennsylvania Press, 1945.

Bethell, Leslie. 'The Mixed Commissions for the Suppression of the Transatlantic Slave Trade in the Nineteenth Century', *Journal of African History,* vol. 7 (1966), pp. 79–93.

'Britain, Portugal and the suppression of the Brazilian Slave Trade: the origins of Lord Palmerston's Act of 1839', *English Historical Review,* vol. 80 (1965), pp. 761–84.

404 *Bibliography*

The Abolition of the Brazilian Slave Trade: Britain, Brazil and the Slave Trade Question, 1807–1869. Cambridge, 1970.

Blanco White, Joseph. *Bosquexo del Comercio en Esclavos: y reflexiones sobre este tráfico considerado moral, política y cristianamente.* London, 1814.

Bourne, K. 'The Clayton–Bulwer Treaty and the Decline of British Opposition to the Territorial Expansion of the United States, 1857–1860', *Journal of Modern History,* vol. XXXIII (1961), pp. 287–91.

Britain and the Balance of Power in North America, 1815–1908. London: Longman, 1967.

Bowser, Frederic P. *The African Slave in Colonial Peru, 1524–1650.* Stanford: Stanford University Press, 1974.

Breve contestación de Don Juan de la Pezuela, Capitán General que ha sido de la isla de Cuba . . . Madrid, 1855.

Brooks, P. C. *Diplomacy and the Borderlands: the Adams–Onís Treaty of 1819.* Berkeley: University of California Press, 1939.

Brougham, H. *An Inquiry into the Colonial Policy of the European Powers.* 2 vols., Edinburgh, 1803.

Burton, Richard. *A Mission to Gelele, King of Dahomey,* ed. and with introduction by C. W. Newbury. London, 1966.

Buxó de Abaigar, Joaquín. *Domingo Dulce, General Isabelino, vida y época.* Barcelona, 1962.

Buxton, Thomas Fowell. *The African Slave Trade and its Remedy.* 2nd ed., London, 1840.

Calcagno, Francisco. *Diccionario biográfico cubano.* New York, 1878.

Caldwell, Robert Glanville. *The López Expeditions to Cuba, 1848–1851.* Princeton: Princeton University Press, 1915.

Callahan, James Morton. *Cuba and International Relations: a historical study in American diplomacy.* Baltimore: Johns Hopkins Press, 1899.

Carillo y Arango, A., ed. *Obras del excmo. Señor D. Francisco de Arango y Parreño.* 2 vols., Havana, 1888.

Carr, Raymond. *Spain, 1808–1939.* Oxford, 1966.

Castañeda, Humberto. 'El caso de Mr. David Turnbull, El Consul Inglés', *Revista de la Universidad de la Habana,* vols. 168–9 (July–Oct. 1964), pp. 127–53.

Cave, S. *A Few Words on the encouragement given to Slavery and the Slave Trade by recent measures and chiefly by the Sugar Bill of 1846.* London, 1849.

Papers relating to Free Labour and the Slave Trade . . . London, 1861.

Cepero Bonilla, Raul. *Obras históricas.* Havana, 1963.

Christelow, Allan. 'Contraband Trade between Jamaica and the Spanish Main, and the Free Port Act of 1766', *H.A.H.R.,* vol. XXII (1942), pp. 309–43.

Christiansen, E. *The Origins of Military Power in Spain, 1800–1854.* Oxford, 1967.

Clarkson, Thomas. *The History of the Rise, Progress and Accomplishment of the*

Bibliography 405

Abolition of the African Slave Trade by the British Parliament. 2 vols., London, 1808.

Cohen, David W. and Greene, Jack P., eds *Neither Slave nor Free, the Freedmen of African Descent in the Slave Societies of the New World.* Baltimore: The Johns Hopkins University Press, 1972.

Conacher, J. B. *The Aberdeen Coalition 1852–1855.* Cambridge, 1968.

'Lessons in Twisting the Lion's Tail: two sidelights of the Crimean War', Michael Cross and Robert Bothwell, eds. *Policy by Other Means; Essays in Honour of C. P. Stacey.* Toronto: University of Toronto Press, 1972, pp. 77–94.

Conrad, Robert. *The Destruction of Brazilian Slavery 1850–1888.* Berkeley: University of California Press, 1972.

'Neither Slave nor Free: The *Emancipados* of Brazil, 1818–1868', *H.A.H.R.*, vol. LIII (1973), pp. 50–70.

Corbitt, Duvon C. 'A Petition for the Continuation of O'Donnell as Captain-General of Cuba', *H.A.H.R.*, vol. XVI (1936), pp. 537–43.

'Immigration in Cuba', *H.A.H.R.*, vol. XXII (1942), pp. 280–308.

'Saco's History of Negro Slavery', *H.A.H.R.*, vol. XXIV (1944), pp. 452–57.

Corwin, Arthur F. *Spain and the Abolition of Slavery in Cuba, 1817–1886.* Austin: University of Texas Press, 1967.

Coupland, Reginald. *The British Anti-Slavery Movement.* 2nd ed., London, 1964.

Cuba desde 1850 á 1873, colección de informes, memorias, etc. Madrid, 1873.

Curtin, Philip D. *Two Jamaicas: the Role of Ideas in a Tropical Colony, 1830–1865.* Cambridge: Harvard University Press, 1955.

The Image of Africa: British Ideas and Action, 1780–1850. London, 1969.

The Atlantic Slave Trade: A Census. Madison: University of Wisconsin Press, 1969.

Daget, Serge. 'L'abolition de la traite des Noirs en France de 1814 à 1831', *Cahiers d'Études africaines,* vol. II (1971), pp. 14–58.

'Long cours et négriers nantais du trafic illégal (1814–1833)', *Revue française d'histoire d'Outre-Mer,* vol. LXII (1975), pp. 90–134.

Dana, Richard H. Jr. *To Cuba and Back: A vacation voyage.* Boston, 1859.

Davis, David Brion. *The Problem of Slavery in Western Culture.* Ithaca: Cornell University Press, 1966.

The Slave Power Conspiracy and the Paranoid Style. Baton Rouge: Louisiana State University Press, 1969.

The Problem of Slavery in the Age of Revolution, 1770–1823. Ithaca: Cornell University Press, 1975.

Davis, Robert Ralph Jr. 'James Buchanan and the Suppression of the Slave Trade, 1858–1861', *Pennsylvania History,* vol. XXXIII (1966), pp. 446–59.

Deerr, Noel. *The History of Sugar.* 2 vols., London, 1949–50.

Denman, Capt. Joseph. *The Slave Trade, the African Squadron and Mr. Hutt's Committee*. London, 1850.

Denman, Lord (Thomas). *A Letter from Lord Denman to Lord Brougham, on the Final Extinction of the Slave Trade*. London, 1848.

A Second Letter from Lord Denman to Lord Brougham on the Final Extinction of the Slave Trade. London, 1849.

Derby, E. H. S. *Six Weeks in South America*. London, 1850.

Further Facts connected with the West Indies. A Second Letter to the Rt. Hon. W. E. Gladstone, M.P. London, 1851.

Díaz Soler, Luis M. *Historia de la esclavitud negra en Puerto Rico 1493–1890*. Madrid, 1953.

Dike, K. Onwuka. *Trade and Politics in the Niger Delta, 1830–1885*. Oxford, 1956.

Drake, Frederick C., ed. 'Secret History of the Slave Trade to Cuba Written by an American Naval Officer, 1861', *The Journal of Negro History*, vol. LV (1970), pp. 218–35.

Drescher, Seymour. *Econocide: British Slavery in the era of Abolition*. Pittsburgh: University of Pittsburgh Press, 1977.

Du Bois, W. E. *The Suppression of the African Slave-Trade to the United States of America, 1638–1870*. Cambridge: Harvard University Press, 1896.

Eltis, David. 'The Export of Slaves from Africa, 1821–1843', *The Journal of Economic History*, vol. 37 (1977), pp. 409–33.

Ely, Roland T. *Cuando reinaba su majestad el azúcar: estudio histórico-sociológico de una tragedia latinoamericana*. Buenos Aires, 1963.

Engerman, Stanley and Genovese, Eugene D., eds. *Race and Slavery in the Western Hemisphere: Quantitative Studies*. Princeton: Princeton University Press, 1975.

Entralgo, Elías. 'Los fenómenos raciales en la emancipación de Cuba', *El Movimiento Emancipador de Hispanoamericana, actas y ponencias*. 4 vols., Caracas, 1961, vol. 3, pp. 325–49.

Estorch, D. M. *Apuntes sobre la administración del marqués de la Pezuela en la isla de Cuba* ... Madrid, 1856.

Ettinger, Amos A. 'The Proposed Anglo-Franco-American Treaty of 1852 to Guarantee Cuba to Spain', *Transactions of the Royal Historical Society*, 4th series, vol. 13 (1930), pp. 149–85.

The Mission to Spain of Pierre Soulé, 1853–1855. New Haven: Yale University Press, 1932.

Fernández de Castro, José A. *Medio siglo de historia colonial de Cuba. Cartas a J. A. Saco*. Havana, 1923.

ed. *Escritos de Domingo del Monte*. Havana, 1929.

Ferrer de Couto, José. *Enough of War* ... Originally published as *Los negros en sus diversos estados y condiciones: tales como son, como se supone que son, y como deben ser*. New York, 1864.

Fladeland, Betty. 'Abolitionist Pressures on the Concert of Europe, 1814–1822', *Journal of Modern History*, vol. XXXVIII (1966), pp. 355–73.

Men and Brothers: Anglo-American antislavery co-operation. Urbana: University of Illinois Press, 1972.

Foner, Philip S. *A History of Cuba and its Relations with the United States.* 2 vols., New York, 1962–3.

Frias y Jacott, Francisco de, conde de Pozos Dulce. *La Question de Cuba.* Paris, 1859.

Gallagher, John. 'Fowell Buxton and the New African Policy, 1838–1842', *Cambridge Historical Journal*, vol. X (1950), pp. 36–58.

Gallenga, Antonio C. *The Pearl of the Antilles.* London, 1873.

Green-Pedersen, Sv. E. 'The Scope and Structure of the Danish Slave Trade', *The Scandinavian Economic History Review*, vol. XIX (1971), pp. 149–97.

'The History of the Danish Negro Slave Trade, 1733–1807', *Revue française d'histoire d'Outre-Mer*, vol. LXII (1975), pp. 196–220.

Griffin, C. C. *The United States and the Disruption of the Spanish Empire, 1810–1822: a study of the relations of the United States with Spain and with the rebel Spanish colonies.* New York: Columbia University Press, 1937.

Guerra y Sánchez, Ramiro. *En el camino de la independencia; estudio histórico sobre la rivalidad de los Estados Unidos y la Gran Bretaña en sus relaciones con la independencia de Cuba, con un apéndice titulado de Monroe a Platt.* Havana, 1930.

et al., eds. *Historia de la nación cubana.* 10 vols., Havana, 1952.

Sugar and Society in the Caribbean: an Economic History of Cuban Agriculture, trans. Marjorie M. Urquidi. New Haven: Yale University Press, 1964.

Guiteras, Pedro J. *Historia de la isla de Cuba.* 2nd ed., 3 vols., Havana, 1927–8.

Gutiérrez de la Concha y de Irigoyen, José, marqués de la Habana. *Memorias sobre el estado político, gobierno y administración de la isla de Cuba.* Madrid, 1853.

Hale, Edward E. *The Everett Letters on Cuba.* Boston, 1897.

Hall, Gwendolyn. *Social Control in Slave Plantation Societies, a Comparison of Saint Domingue and Cuba.* Baltimore: Johns Hopkins Press, 1971.

Hargreaves, John. *Prelude to the Partition of West Africa.* London, 1963.

Haring, C. H. *The Spanish Empire in America.* New York, 1947.

Henderson, Gavin B. 'Southern Designs on Cuba, 1854–1857, and some European Opinions', *The Journal of Southern History*, vol. V (1939), pp. 371–85.

Hernández y Sánchez-Barba, Mario. 'David Turnbull y el problema de la esclavitud en Cuba', *Anuario de estudios americanos*, vol. XIV (1957), pp. 241–99.

Hertslet, Edward. *Recollections of the old Foreign Office.* London, 1901.

Houghton, Walter E., ed. *The Wellesley Index to Victorian Periodicals, 1824–1900.* Toronto: University of Toronto Press, 1966.

Howard, Warren S. *American Slavers and the Federal Law, 1837–1862.* Berkeley: University of California Press, 1963.

Humboldt, Alexander von. *Ensayo político sobre la isla de Cuba.* Havana, 1960.

Tableau statistique de l'île de Cuba pour les années 1825–1829. Paris, 1831.

Huntley, H. V. *Free Trade, the Sugar Act of 1846 and the Slave Trade.* London, 1849.

[Hurlbert, W. H.] *Gan-Eden: or, Pictures of Cuba.* Boston, 1854.

Ibo, Manuel Alfaro. *Apuntes para la historia de D. Leopoldo O'Donnell.* Madrid, 1868.

Información sobre reformas en Cuba y Puerto Rico. 2 vols., New York, 1867.

Jameson, Robert. *Letters from the Havana, during the year 1820.* London, 1821.

Jenks, L.H. *Our Cuban Colony: a Study in Sugar.* New York, 1928.

Jennings, Lawrence C. 'France, Great Britain, and the Repression of the Slave Trade, 1841–45', *French Historical Studies*, vol. X (1977), pp. 101–25.

Johnson, W. F. *The History of Cuba.* 5 vols., New York, 1920.

Jones, W. D. *Lord Aberdeen and the Americas.* Athens: University of Georgia Press, 1958.

'The Origins and Passage of Lord Aberdeen's Act', *H.A.H.R.*, vol. XLII (1962), pp. 502–20.

Kaufmann, W. W. *British Policy and the Independence of Latin America, 1804–28.* New Haven: Yale University Press, 1926.

Kiernan, V. *The Revolution of 1854 in Spanish History.* Oxford, 1966.

Kimball, Richard. *Cuba and the Cubans . . .* New York, 1850.

King, James Ferguson. 'The Evolution of the Free Slave Trade Principle in Spanish Colonial Administration', *H.A.H.R.*, vol. XXII (1942), pp. 34–56.

'The Latin-American Republics and the Suppression of the Slave Trade', *H.A.H.R.*, vol. XXIV (1944), pp. 387–411.

Kiple, Kenneth. *Blacks in Colonial Cuba, 1774–1899.* Gainesville: University Presses of Florida, 1976.

Klein, Herbert S. *Slavery in the Americas: A Comparative Study of Virginia and Cuba.* Chicago: University of Chicago Press, 1967.

'The Trade in African Slaves to Rio de Janeiro, 1795–1811: Estimates of Mortality and Patterns of Voyages', *Journal of African History*, vol. 10 (1969), pp. 533–49.

'North American Competition and the Characteristics of the African Slave Trade to Cuba, 1790 to 1794', *The William and Mary Quarterly*, 3rd series, vol. XXVIII (1971), pp. 86–102.

'The Portuguese Slave Trade from Angola in the Eighteenth Century', *The Journal of Economic History*, vol. 32 (1972), pp. 894–918.

'The Cuban Slave Trade in a Period of Transition, 1790–1843', *Revue française d'histoire d'Outre-Mer*, vol. LXII, nᵒˢ 226–7 (1975), pp. 67–89.

The Middle Passage. Comparative Studies in the Atlantic Slave Trade. Princeton: Princeton University Press, 1978.

Klingberg, F. J. *The Anti-Slavery Movement in England: a Study in English Humanitarianism.* New Haven: Yale University Press, 1926, reprinted 1968.

Knight, Franklin. *Slave Society in Cuba during the Nineteenth Century.* Madison: University of Wisconsin Press, 1970.

Le Riverend Brusone, Julio. 'La economía cubana durante las guerras de la revolución y del imperio franceses, 1790–1808', *Revista de Historia de America*, vol. 16 (1943), pp. 25–64.

A Letter to W. E. Channing on the subject of the abuse of the Flag of the United States in the Island of Cuba, and the advantage taken of its protection in promoting the Slave Trade. Boston, 1839.

A Letter to W. E. Channing in reply to one addressed to him by R.R.M. on the abuse of the flag of the United States in the Island of Cuba, for promoting the Slave Trade, By a Calm Observer. Boston, 1840.

Llaverías y Martínez, Joaquín. *La comisión militar, ejecutiva y permanente de la isla de Cuba.* Havana, 1929.

Lloyd, Christopher. *The Navy and the Slave Trade: the Suppression of the African Slave Trade in the Nineteenth Century.* London, 1949.

Love, Robert Wm Jr. 'The End of the Atlantic Slave Trade to Cuba', *Caribbean Quarterly*, vol. 22 (1976), pp. 51–8.

Lynch, John. *Spanish Colonial Administration, 1782–1810: the Intendant System in the Viceroyalty of the Río de la Plata.* London, 1958.

MacPherson, David. *Annals of Commerce, Manufactures, Fisheries and Navigation.* 4 vols., London, 1805.

Madden, R. R. *A Twelvemonth's Residence in the West Indies during the Transition from Slavery to Apprenticeship.* 2 vols., London, 1835.

Poems by a slave in the island of Cuba . . . London, 1840.

The Island of Cuba . . . *its Resources, Progress and Prospects considered in relation especially to the influence of its prosperity on the interests of the British West India Colonies.* London, 1849.

Madden, T. M., ed. *The Memoirs (chiefly autobiographical) from 1798 to 1886 of Richard Robert Madden, M.A., F.R.C.S.* London, 1891.

Manchester, Alan K. *British Preeminence in Brazil: its rise and decline: a study in European expansion.* Chapel Hill: University of North Carolina Press, 1933.

Manning, W. R. *Early Diplomatic Relations between the United States and Mexico.* Baltimore: The Johns Hopkins University Press, 1916.

Marryat, Joseph. *Thoughts on the Abolition of the Slave Trade and the Civilization of Africa, with remarks on the African Institution and an examination of the report of their Committee* . . . 3rd ed., London, 1816.

More Thoughts still on the . . . *West India Colonies, and the Proceedings of the African Institution.* London, 1818.

Mathieson, W. L. *British Slavery and its Abolition, 1823–38.* London, 1926.

Great Britain and the Slave Trade, 1839–65. London, 1929.

Matson, H. J. *Remarks on the Slave Trade and the African Squadron.* London, 1848.

Maxwell, Herbert. *The Life and Letters of George William Frederick, Fourth Earl of Clarendon.* 2 vols., London, 1913.

May, Robert E. *The Southern Dream of a Caribbean Empire, 1854–61.* Baton Rouge: Louisiana State University Press, 1973.

Mellafe, Rolando. *Negro Slavery in Latin America.* Berkeley: University of California Press, 1975.

Merk, Frederick. *Manifest Destiny and Mission in American History; a reinterpretation.* New York, 1963.

Mettas, Jean. 'Honfleur et la traite des Noirs au XVIIIe siècle', *Revue française d'histoire d'Outre-Mer*, vol. LX (1973), pp. 5–26.

'Pour une histoire de la traite des Noirs française: sources et problémes', *Revue française d'histoire d'Outre-Mer*, vol. LXII (1975), pp. 19–46.

Meyer, J. 'Le commerce négrier nantais (1774–92)', *Annales: économies, sociétés, civilisations*, vol. XV (1960), pp. 120–29.

L'armement nantais dans la Deuxième Moitié du XVIIIe siècle. Paris, 1969.

Milne, A. T. 'The Lyons – Seward Treaty of 1862', *American Historical Review*, vol. 38 (1932–3), pp. 511–25.

Morales y Morales, Vidal. *Iniciadores y primeros mártires de la revolución cubana.* New ed., 3 vols., Havana, 1963.

Moreno Fraginals, Manuel. 'Nación o plantación (el dilema político cubano visto a través de José Antonio Saco)', Julio Le Riverend Brusone, et al., eds. *Homenaje a Silvio Zavala: estudios históricos americanos*, México, 1953, pp. 241–72.

El Ingenio: El complejo económico social cubano del azúcar. vol. I: *1760–1860.* Havana, 1964.

Murray, Amelia M. *Letters from the United States, Cuba and Canada.* London, 1856.

Murray, David R. 'Statistics of the Slave Trade to Cuba, 1790–1867', *Journal of Latin American Studies*, vol. 3 (1971), pp. 131–49.

'Richard Robert Madden: His Career as a Slavery Abolitionist', *Studies* (Ireland), vol. LXI (1972), pp. 41–53.

'British Abolitionists in Cuba, 1833–1845', *Historical Papers* (1976), pp. 105–21.

Nelson, Lowry. *Rural Cuba.* Minneapolis: University of Minnesota Press, 1950.

Nichols, Roy F. 'Trade Relations and the Establishment of the United States Consulates in Spanish America, 1779–1809', *H.A.H.R.*, vol. XIII (1933), pp. 289–313.

Advance Agents of American Destiny. University of Pennsylvania Press, 1956.

Ortiz, Fernando. *Hampa afro-cubana: los negros esclavos.* Havana, 1916.

'José Antonio Saco y sus ideas', *Revista bimestre cubana*, vol. XXIV (1929), pp. 387–409.

Cuban Counterpoint: Tobacco and Sugar, trans. Harriet de Onís. New York, 1947.

Parry, J. H. and Sherlock, P. M. *A Short History of the West Indies.* London, 1963.

Perez Cabrera, José M. *Historiografía de Cuba.* México, 1962.

Bibliography 411

Perkins, Bradford. *Prologue to War: England and the United States, 1805–1812.* Berkeley: University of California Press, 1961.

Castlereagh and Adams: England and the United States, 1812–1823. Berkeley: University of California Press, 1964.

Perkins, Dexter. 'Russia and the Spanish Colonies, 1817–18', *American Historical Review,* vol. 28 (1923), pp. 656–72.

The Monroe Doctrine, 1823–26. Cambridge: Harvard University Press, 1927.

The Monroe Doctrine, 1826–67. Baltimore: The Johns Hopkins University Press, 1933.

A History of the Monroe Doctrine. New ed., London, 1960.

Pezuela y Lobo, Jacobo de la. *Ensayo histórico de la Isla de Cuba.* New York, 1842.

Diccionario geográfico, estadístico, histórico de la Isla de Cuba. 4 vols., Madrid, 1863–6.

Pierson, W. W. 'The Establishment and Early Functioning of the *Intendencia* of Cuba', *The James Sprunt Historical Studies,* vol. 19. University of North Carolina Press, 1927, pp. 74–133.

'Francisco de Arango y Parreño', *H.A.H.R.,* vol. XVI (1936), pp. 451–78.

Platt, D.C.M. *The Cinderella Service, British Consuls since 1825.* London, 1971.

Finance, Trade and Politics in British Foreign Policy, 1815–1914. Oxford, 1971.

Portell Vilá, Herminio. *Historia de Cuba en sus relaciones con los Estados Unidos y España.* 4 vols., Havana, 1938–41, reprinted Miami, 1969.

Narciso López y su época 1848–50. 3 vols., Havana, 1930–58.

Postma, Johannes. 'The Dimensions of the Dutch Slave Trade from Western Africa', *Journal of African History,* vol. 13 (1972), pp. 237–48.

'The Dutch Slave Trade. A Quantitative Assessment', *Revue française d' histoire d'Outre-Mer,* vol. LXII (1975), pp. 232–44.

Ragatz, L. J. *The Fall of the Planter Class in the British Caribbean, 1763–1833.* New York, 1928.

Rauch, Basil. *American Interest in Cuba, 1848–55.* New York: Columbia University Press, 1948.

Rice, C. Duncan. '"Humanity-Sold for Sugar!" The British Abolitionist Response to Free Trade in Slave-Grown Sugar', *The Historical Journal,* vol. XIII (1970), pp. 402–18.

Richardson, James. *The Cruisers: being a Letter to Marquis of Lansdowne, Lord President, etc. in Defence of Armed Coercion for the Extinction of the Slave Trade.* London, 1849.

Rippy, J. Fred. *Rivalry of the United States and Great Britain over Latin America, 1808–30.* Baltimore: The Johns Hopkins University Press, 1929.

Rivera, Antonio. *Reseña sucinta é historia de los hechos mas notables del general don Leopoldo O'Donnell, en la isla de Cuba.* Madrid, 1854.

Rodríguez Vicente, Maria Encarnación. 'El comercio cubano y la guerra de emancipación norteamericana', *Anuario de Estudios Americanos,* vol. XI (1954), pp. 61–106.

Rose, J. Holland. *William Pitt and National Revival.* London, 1911.

Rout, Leslie B. Jr. *The African Experience in Spanish America.* Cambridge, 1976.

412 *Bibliography*

Russell, N. V. 'The Reaction in England and America to the Capture of Havana, 1762', *H.A.H.R.*, vol. IX (1929), pp. 303–16.

Saco, José Antonio. 'Mi primera pregunta.¿ La abolición del comercio de esclavos africanos arruinará ó atrasará la agricultura cubana?' Madrid, 1837.

Historia de la esclavitud de la raza africana en el Nuevo Mundo y en especial en los países américo-hispanos. New ed., 4 vols., Havana, 1938–40.

Colección de papeles científicos, históricos, políticos, y de otros ramos sobre la isla de Cuba. New ed., 3 vols., Havana, 1960.

Contra la anexión. 2 vols., Havana, 1928.

Sagra, Ramón de la. *Historia económico-política y estadística de la Isla de Cuba, ó sea de sus progresos en la población, la agricultura, el comercio, y las rentas.* Havana, 1831.

Estudios coloniales con aplicación a la isla de Cuba: de los efectos de la supresión en el tráfico negrero. Madrid, 1845.

Historia física, política y natural de la isla de Cuba. 13 vols., Paris, 1842–61.

Saralegui y Medina, M. de. *Un negocio escandaloso en tiempos de Fernando VII.* Madrid, 1904.

Scelle, Georges. *La traite négrière aux Indes de Castille.* 2 vols., Paris, 1906.

'The Slave Trade in the Spanish Colonies', *American Journal of International Law*, vol. IV (1910), pp. 612–61.

Scroggs, W. O. 'William Walker's Designs on Cuba', *Mississippi Valley Historical Review,* vol. I (1914), pp. 198–211.

Shafer, Robert J. *The Economic Societies in the Spanish World (1763–1821).* New York: Syracuse University Press, 1958.

The Slave-Trade and its Remedy. London, 1848.

The Slave-Trade to Cuba ... London, 1861.

Soulsby, H. G. *The Right of Search and the Slave Trade in Anglo-American Relations, 1814–62.* Baltimore: The Johns Hopkins University Press, 1933.

Spain and the African Slave Trade ... London, 1862.

Stephen, James. *The Opportunity: or Reasons for an Immediate Alliance with St. Domingo.* London, 1804.

War in Disguise, or the Frauds of Neutral Flags. London, 1805.

The Dangers of the Country ... London, 1807.

Slave Trade of Spain in Northern Africa. London, 1816.

Takaki, Ronald. *A Pro-Slavery Crusade: the Agitation to Reopen the African Slave Trade.* New York, 1971.

Taylor, John Glanville. *The United States and Cuba: Eight Years of Change and Travel.* London, 1851.

Temperley, H.W.V. *The Foreign Policy of Canning, 1822–27.* New ed., London, 1966.

and Penson, L. M. *A Century of Diplomatic Blue Books, 1814–1914.* London, 1966.

Temperley, Howard. *British antislavery, 1833–70.* University of South Carolina Press, 1972.

Thomas, Hugh. *Cuba or the Pursuit of Freedom.* London, 1971.

Toplin, R. B., ed. *Slavery and Race Relations in Latin America.* Westport, Conn., 1974.

Torrente, Mariano. *Memoria sobre la esclavitud en la isla de Cuba, con observaciones sobre los asertos de la prensa inglesa relativos al tráfico de esclavos.* London, 1853.

Trollope, Anthony. *The West Indies and the Spanish Main.* London, 1859.

Turnbull, David. *Travels in the West. Cuba: with Notices of Porto Rico and the Slave Trade.* London, 1840.

The Jamaica Movement for promoting the enforcement of the Slave-Trade Treaties and the suppression of the slave-trade ... London, 1850.

Urban, C. Stanley. 'The Abortive Quitman Filibustering Expedition, 1853–55', *Journal of Mississippi History,* vol. 18 (1956), pp. 175–96.

'The Africanization of Cuba Scare, 1853–55', *H.A.H.R.,* vol. XXXVII (1957), pp. 29–45.

Urbina, A. *Cheste, o todo un siglo (1809–1906), el Isabelino tradicionalista.* Madrid, 1935.

Valle, Francisco G. del 'La Conspiración de la Escalera', *Cuba Contemporánea,* vol. 39 (Nov.–Dec. 1925), pp. 117–45, 225–54.

Van Alstyne, R. W. 'The British Right of Search and the African Slave Trade', *Journal of Modern History,* vol. II (1930), pp. 37–47.

'Anglo-American Relations, 1853–57', *American Historical Review,* vol. 42 (1937), pp. 491–500.

Vásquez Queipo, Vicente. *Cuba, ses ressources, son administration, sa population* ..., trans. Arthur d'Avrainville. Paris, 1851.

Vidalenc, Jean. 'La traite des nègres en France au début de la Révolution (1789–93)', *Annales historiques de la Révolution française,* vol. 29 (1957), pp. 56–69.

Viles, Perry. 'The Slaving Interest in the Atlantic Ports, 1763–92', *French Historical Studies,* vol. 8 (1972), pp. 529–43.

Ward, A. W. and Gooch, G. P., eds. *The Cambridge History of British Foreign Policy, 1783–1919.* 3 vols., Cambridge, 1922–23.

Webster, C. K. *The Foreign Policy of Castlereagh, 1815–22.* 2nd ed., London, 1934.

The Foreign Policy of Palmerston, 1830–41. 2 vols., London, 1951.

Williams, Eric. 'The Negro Slave Trade in Anglo-Spanish Relations', *Caribbean Historical Review,* vol. 1 (1950), pp. 22–38.

Capitalism and Slavery. New ed., London, 1964.

Wright, Irene A. *The Early History of Cuba, 1492–1586.* Reprint ed., New York, 1970.

[Wurdemann, J.G.F.] *Notes on Cuba.* Boston, 1844.

Yule, Sir H. *The African Squadron Vindicated.* London, 1850.

Zaragoza, Justo. *Las insurrecciones en Cuba: Apuntes para la historia política de esta isla en el presente siglo.* 2 vols., Madrid, 1872–73.

INDEX

CAMBRIDGE LATIN AMERICAN STUDIES

Printed in the United Kingdom
by Lightning Source UK Ltd.
1756